THE BIOGRAPHICAL DICTIONARY OF POPULAR MUSIC

ALSO BY DYLAN JONES

When Ziggy Played Guitar:
David Bowie and Four Minutes That Shook the World

Heroes

Cameron on Cameron: Conversations with Dylan Jones

Mr. Jones' Rules for the Modern Man

iPod, Therefore I Am

Meaty, Beaty, Big & Bouncy!

Sex, Power and Travel

Paul Smith: True Brit

Jim Morrison: Dark Star

THE BIOGRAPHICAL DICTIONARY OF POPULAR MUSIC

FROM ADELE TO ZIGGY, THE REAL A TO Z OF ROCK AND POP

DYLAN JONES

PICADOR

NEW YORK

For Ed Victor

Introduction

Everything You Know Is Wrong

"As through this world I've wandered,
I've seen lots of funny men;
Some will rob you with a six-gun,
And some with a fountain pen."*
Woody Guthrie, "Pretty Boy Floyd"

* Or indeed a Mont Blanc ballpoint, a BlackBerry, an iMac,
or a pencil...

Many blue moons ago, back in the mid-Nineties, during that peculiar, heightened time when Swinging London seemed important again – a period when "Brit" very quickly became the only acceptable prefix for cultural insurrection – an acquaintance in the music press tried to get a new publication off the ground. I was working in a managerial capacity for a publishing company at the time, and he came to see me one day with his proposition.

The premise was simple: he wanted to produce a regular music magazine (I can't remember the proposed frequency, not that it matters) that roughly mirrored the *London Review of Books* – it may even have been called the *London Review of Records*.

The proposed dummy was going to look very elegant, I was told, and very smart in a sub-*Modern Review*-type way. It was going to be printed on heavy-stock newsprint, with the type of over-designed borders, rules and curlicues used in certain old-school newspapers. It was going to look scholarly, refined, almost arch (a bit like *Rolling Stone* did when it launched). It was going to look lovely, with fine writers writing fine words about the likes of RADIOHEAD, BECK, BLUR, and every heritage act worth their salt-and-pepper goatees. This would be the place to go for a proper soup-to-nuts 3,000-word review of the latest BOB DYLAN or PETER GABRIEL album, the sort of magazine (or was it a newspaper? A newspaper sounded even fancier!) where the editor might throw caution – and budgetary restrictions – to the wind and ask two writers to review the same record. Jeez, didn't the *NME* used to do that back in the early Seventies? What the hell. A 6,000-word treatise on the FLAMING LIPS? Coming up!

It was going to be the sort of magazine – I imagined – that might contain a 5,000-word piece explaining why DAVID BOWIE's *Young Americans* really *was* his best album of the Seventies.

My acquaintance's magazine was a lovely idea, and one that I would have looked forward to reading. But I didn't like it so much that I wanted to publish it. No one bought the idea, and TLROR faded into the past, yet another great idea without a benefactor.

When I told friends about the pitch, they scoffed. "He may as well have called it 'Music I Like'," said one. "'Music I think is good because I am so much smarter than you, and a person with much better taste'."

Music magazines were already on the wane, and the advertising base was diminishing to such an extent that even established periodicals were finding it increasingly difficult to hit their like-for-likes. Even in the mid-Nineties, the business was shrinking. Back in the Seventies, record companies couldn't afford not to advertise in the *NME*, *Sounds*, or *Rolling Stone*, but in the Nineties you advertised music like you would soap or a new Hollywood hopeful – everywhere and anywhere. Who needed to advertise in a magazine or newspaper that you knew was going to treat your new release like a joke with no punchline? What the industry wanted for its product was exposure, not criticism. It needed viral hits, social media, a commercial.

Commercially unpromising it may have been, but I liked the idea of something so prescriptive, something so judgmental (while also thinking that Judge Mental might be quite a good name for an imaginary support band), so authoritative, yet so subjective. It chimed with an idea I'd had myself.

Every couple of years, whenever I ended up having a conversation with my agent about what book I should do next, we would discuss the things that were currently interesting me – technology, politics, music, my inability to make my children to do anything I asked them to, even when bribed with pantechnicons full of chocolate and DVDs. And the conversation would always end the same way: Ed would tell me to write a novel, and I would say that what I'd love to read – and possibly write – was a "biographical dictionary of music, the sort of book that treats subjectivity with respect...", a book not too dissimilar to DAVID THOMSON's *Biographical Dictionary of Film.*

Ed would say, "Yeah, yeah, yeah, OK, that's all very well, but that's not the kind of book you want to write. Firstly, it would take you years, and secondly it would drive you insane. That's a job for someone else."

Which is why Ed is such a good agent – carefully trying to protect me from myself. But I pig-headedly persevered, and, many years later, here we are.

There are dozens of music encyclopedias, and many of them are very cleverly written, full of career minutiae and critical acuity. They're also obsessively objective and pathologically comprehensive.

In his tremendously entertaining treatise on Seventies cinema, *Blockbuster*, TOM SHONE says that a book is a series of conversations passing themselves off as a monologue. I suppose that is an apt description of this book. This is a book that springs from personal prejudice, contrary predilections, and non-cognitive taste. This book is idiosyncratic and highly opinionated, although I hope it has a sense of logic (tempered with a bit of objectivity and the chorus of reason). Yes, it did take me some time to do, and while it didn't make me mad, it certainly forced me to confront all the reasons I had for forming the opinions about everyone I've written about in this book. Many of the pieces here are rewritten versions of pieces I've written before – edited, updated, and hopefully with some (though probably not all) of the grammar improved. Some of the longer profiles are based on actual interviews. It's obviously not necessary to meet a person in order to have an opinion on their records, and in some cases it's probably best not to. There are artists whose music I love but whom I don't especially want to meet in case I don't like them, but there are some people you'd fall over yourself to meet, at least I have: Tony Bennett, Shirley MacLaine, Paul McCartney, Stevie Wonder, the Sex Pistols, Quincy Jones, Bono, John Barry, Jarvis Cocker, Burt Bacharach, the Clash. It's rarely the waifs and strays you want to talk to, it's the bona fide legends, along with anyone who is "hot". Why wouldn't you want to meet Lady Gaga, Prince, Tinie Tempah, Adele, or Mark Ronson? And you want the experience to produce two things: selfishly you want it to give you a greater understanding of their work and personality (and, a great failing in a journalist, I know, privately you want to like them, too), and professionally you want to walk away with sufficient secrets to build on the established understanding of them. I've never set out to uncover human folly, although it's a blessing when it happens.

I have interviewed enough celebrities to know that, from the moment we meet, there is often a kind of war of attrition between us. Because they are famous they have usually created a self – a self that is not completely them, but curiously it is not *not* them either. Which is what the journalist and profile writer Thomas B. Morgan said back in the mid-Sixties, "Most better-known people tend toward an elegant solution of what they, or their advisors, call 'the image problem'," he said. "Over time, deliberately, they create a public self for the likes of me to interview, observe, and double-check. This self is a tested consumer item of proven value, a sophisticated invention, refined, polished, distilled, and certified OK in scores, perhaps hundreds of engagements with journalists, audiences, friends, family, and lovers. It is the commingling of an image and a personality, or what I've decided to call an Impersonality."

These days, impersonalities have become so successful that it's nigh impossible to tell the difference between what is real and what is mediated. Often, because they are always "on", some celebrities treat their impersonality as their real identity, their real character. And, as a lot of famous people long ago decided that fame was the only way to diminish, if not completely banish, their past, they are completely happy with this.

And, oddly, often we are, too.

Many of the people here have been included because I've found them fascinating, others because I've found them intriguing, and many more because it would have been perverse not to have included them. Others are here for different reasons. We all know that JULIAN LENNON will never have as much cultural resonance as his father, but as the child of one of the most influential entertainers of the 20th Century, his story is no less fascinating. And LLOYD COLE might not have built a career as sturdy as LEONARD COHEN's, yet as a tale of unfilled promise, his CV is second to none. As for the Motown snare sound? Well, I'm interested in the Motown snare sound.

I'm also interested in the parameters of "authenticity". We all understand quality control – or the lack of it: *The West Wing* after AARON SORKIN left (when nuance left the White House, slipping out a side door), the CLASH's last LP, *Cut The Crap* (all attitude and bad haircuts, but no decent tunes) – but I've rarely liked the sort of militant absolutism that refuses to acknowledge music that isn't the result of particular counter-cultural forces. When PAUL SIMON wrote and recorded "Bridge Over Troubled Water", he didn't know it would become a supper-club classic, destined to be covered by any MOR singer wanting some of the SIMON & GARFUNKEL magic; but as soon as he ceased to take ownership of it, so critics ceased wanting ownership of him. "I consider his soft sound a cop-out," wrote the *New Yorker* music critic, ELLEN WILLIS at the time. "And I hate most of his lyrics; his alienation, like the word itself, is an old-fashioned, sentimental, West-Side-liberal bore."

Well, maybe, maybe not. But if so, then so what?

Some of what follows is exhaustive (some might say exhausting), some of it dismissive. Some of it macro, a lot of it micro. But on the whole, I hope it's sympathetic to its subject.

As a critic, the music you like completely informs any objectivity you might attempt about a particular artist, or indeed about anything, really – if you're seeking communion with something, how can you not have an opinion about it? When music moves you, it makes you dizzy, and you've got every right to dismiss music that leaves you cold and unmoved. Yes, you might trust the judgment of those whose opinion you respect – I know enough people who like PJ HARVEY to understand that she must be good, even though I don't much care for her myself, and so many friends told me that ELBOW stole the show at Glastonbury in 2011, it made me wonder why their music refuses to move me – but in the end, personal prejudice has to win out.

So go with it. Don't worry if you don't like DAVID BOWIE's *Young Americans*. You can't be right about everything.

Subject Index

A

B

C

Subject Index

D

E

F

Subject Index

I

J

K

Subject Index

L

M

N

O

P

Q

R

S

T

Subject Index

A

A Tribe Called Quest

As the foundation of Lou Reed's "Walk On The Wild Side" glides across the stereo, a loop that immediately sounds as though it should come with its very own Lava Lamp, we hear Q-Tip and Phife Dawg shuffle into the picture, gibbering away as though they were in *The Goon Show*. And suddenly – as if from nowhere – "Can I Kick It?" is in full view. A Tribe Called Quest's jazz-rap fusions can still play all night, moving from hotel lobby to shebeen to the iPad with ease, and you can dip in and out of their tunes without any great shock to the system. With laid back loops involving Cannonball Adderley, Roy Ayres, the Average White Band, and the Rotary Connection, unperturbing dynamics and the kind of restrained vocals usually associated with the coffee house, ATCQ invented a new kind of hip-hop, a decade after the first kind.

"Nothing was touching Tribe, nothing," said Pharell Williams of these exponents of jazz-hop fusion, and for a while he was right. There was no boasting with Tribe, and as one critic succinctly put it, they "heralded the advent of a generation of intellectual, philosophical, sociological rappers that investigated the condition of the African-American soul rather than the street epics of gangsters." Didn't they just.

Hip-hop had embarked on a lexical inflation game in which each particular sub-genre of gangster rap had to be bigger, badder and more aggressive than the one before, whereas ATCQ were content to roll everything back, turn down the volume and allow things to take their natural course. Perhaps assuming there were many who thought rap was morally and culturally non-nutrient, Tribe created a bouillabaisse that was rich in content, rich in diversity, and diverse in delivery.

Out of Queens they came, all goatees and whispers, a central part of the Native Tongues Posse (a collective that also included DE LA SOUL), surfing a wave of fresh alt hip-hop, determined to mix it up, elegantly fusing rap with jazz and getting justly rich in the process. Q-TIP, PHIFE DAWG, ALI SHAHEED MUHAMMAD, and JAROBI WHITE launched themselves in 1985, and in their first incarnation lasted until 1998. Their first album, *People's Instinctive Travels & The Paths Of Rhythm*, was similar to DE LA SOUL's *Three Feet High And Rising* in that it celebrated its own eclecticism, not just musically, but lyrically, too, referencing safe sex and vegetarianism, and appearing unembarrassed about having a sense of humour – not something you find often with gangster rap. One reviewer said that record was, "So sweet and lyrical, so user-friendly, you could play it in the background when you're reading PROUST." This was hip-hop moving from the foreground to the background, from upstage to downstage, from the dancehall to the gallery. With *People's Instinctive Travels & The Paths Of Rhythm*, hip-hop crossed the Rubicon of enforced recognition – you no longer had to pay attention to it, you could just listen to it passively. Hip-hop had left the classroom.

As you can see in the award-winning documentary *Beats Rhymes & Life: The Travels Of A Tribe Called Quest* (which kick-started its critical victory lap by winning the Audience Award for Best Documentary Feature at the Los Angeles Film Festival), ATCQ fell apart acrimoniously, rather unnecessarily soiling their reputation as one of the most important founding fathers of modern hip-hop.

The iTunes algorithms seem to have produced the right rankings here, and they click with my personal choices: "Can You Kick It?" (obviously, predictably), "Bonita Applebum" from *People's Instinctive Travels & The Paths Of Rhythm*, and "Electric Relaxation" from *Midnight Marauders*.

They have their detractors, too. "ATCQ?" said a friend of mine, when asked. "Like yoga, Starbucks, BANKSY, camping, political prisoners, hummus, and Facebook – they're just more stuff white people like."

ABBA

Anyone who has been dragged kicking, screaming, and quite possibly frothing at the gills to see the musical *Mamma Mia!* will know – even against their so-called better judgement – how disarmingly engaging the experience is (the musical, that is, not the kicking, screaming, or frothing). I saw it in London in the middle of the Noughties, and as I sat there with kith and kin, nodding along to "Does Your Mother Know", "SOS", "Take A Chance On Me", and all the rest, far from being stultified by the sheer tedium of it all, I was transported. Instantly. To a pink fluffy place called Abbaville. I loved it, every single minute of it, even the interval.

Mamma Mia! is the Ronseal theatrical experience: it does exactly what it says on the posters, which is make you feel happy, happier than you thought you could be at an ABBA musical. For many people the show, like *The Sound Of Music*, is restorative, resulting in many repeat visits. And it works because, unlike many things in life, it is actually a lot better than you think it's going to be. My expectations were minimal, so low, actually, that even the world's greatest limbo dancer wouldn't have been able to squeeze underneath. But *Mamma Mia!* was like musical manna from heaven. Only with better tunes.

And oh my word it's successful. At any given time, the show is being performed in over 200 countries. Professionally. When I started telling people how much I'd enjoyed the show, everyone and their mother admitted – rather reluctantly, obviously – they'd seen it, too. And they all seemed to have loved it. LOVED it. Turns out practically everyone I know has seen it. Which, given that it's currently playing in over 200 countries, is perhaps not so surprising.

ABBA obviously weren't meant to be hip – two over-made-up barmaids and a couple of chaps who looked like musical hall comedians – and in the years since they first became famous they have become as British as chicken tikka masala, chicken chow mein, or BILL BRYSON.

But I always knew that ABBA were cool. I knew that ELVIS COSTELLO had based "Oliver's Army" on "Dancing Queen" ("There's a real melancholy in [Abba's] songs... all the flourishes, like big double octaves on the piano. We stole them like crazy," said Costello), knew that "Knowing Me Knowing You" was revered as one of those perfect pop records by those in the know. Yes, there was the Partridge problem ("Knowing me ALAN PARTRIDGE, knowing you..."), but since MADONNA sampled "Gimme Gimme Gimme (A Man After Midnight)" for her single "Hung Up", I think it's fair to say that Sweden's finest have been on an upswing.

While the average *Mamma Mia!* audience member probably isn't au fait with the work of DAVID HARE or TOM STOPPARD, at my performance they were a very long way from the tracksuit-wearing, full-fat Coke-swigging, knuckle-draggers I had feared. The audience didn't breathe through their mouths, they simply sang with them. Yes, there were a fair share of hen-nighters in micro shorts, boob tubes, and hastily applied lipstick, but no more than you'd find in your local pub come closing time. I saw more than a few slightly too-tipsy secretaries out for a midweek knees-up, an extended family that appeared to take up two entire rows, and a Japanese couple sitting next to us who were weighed down with *Mamma Mia!* programmes, posters, CDs, DVDs, and what looked like a couple of bejewelled sarongs and a pair of leatherette carriage clocks, too. If the concession stand had been selling *Mamma Mia!* polyester pillowcases, these two would have bought enough for the entire population of Sapporo.

Not that I cared a fig about the audience, as they seemed totally benign. How refreshing to sit in a theatre full of people determined to have a good time regardless of what's put in front of them, rather than be surrounded by a bunch of been-there, done-that, already accessorised the T-shirt, know-it-alls.

There's only one real drawback to going to see *Mamma Mia!,* and that happens about a week later, when you're in the gym, sprinting along the treadmill, and all of a sudden, out of nowhere, you start singing "Dancing Queen" at the top of your voice, as everyone turns round to gawp. (Oh, and the film? Strangely appalling, the first film I've walked out of since KEN RUSSELL's *Altered States* in 1980.)

ABC

MARTIN FRY's group pre-empted the entire Eighties New Pop Deal, creating a thoroughly convincing pop property with a light sense of irony – earnest backing vocals, gold lamé suits, and snarky lyrics. The only problem was, their first album, *The Lexicon Of Love* (1982), said it all, and every release that came in its wake was either reductive or arch (although much of their inactivity during the Eighties was in part due to Fry's ill-health). On "The Look Of Love", when Fry sings "Sisters and brothers, should help each other", you just know his tongue is firmly in his cheek. Once he'd done it, he'd done it.

"It was like disco, but in a BOB DYLAN way," said the record's producer, TREVOR HORN, although it was actually much better than that. With "The Look Of Love", "Poison Arrow", "Tears Are Not Enough", and "All Of My Heart", ABC managed to create totally modern-sounding records that celebrated the very idea of pop itself. If the BUZZCOCKS' PETE SHELLEY had written songs for Motown they may have sounded like this. In a way, ABC were doing what ROXY MUSIC did ten years previously, which was create a shiny pop environment, slightly at odds with the times. In ABC's world, men wore suits and women were grateful. The defining quality of their music is its intelligence, driven by a desire to elevate the pop genre, rather than simply turn it into a commodity.

Former BUGGLES member Horn had only recently produced a series of clever singles for the slightly naff pop duo DOLLAR, yet the collaboration with ABC worked wonderfully well. Fry introduced him to New York records by DEFUNKT and JAMES CHANCE AND THE CONTORTIONS, while Horn introduced Fry to

A

the wonders of the recording studio. "He gave us the keys to the candy store," said Fry. "Trevor would say to us, 'If you want pizza, I'll get you pizza; if you want a string section, I'll get you a string section.'" Demos were made using a Minimoog, a sequencer, and a drum machine, with the band recording over the top. "It was like tracing," said Horn. "Which meant that we got it really spot on and snappy and in your face."

On their follow-up album, *Beauty Stab* (1983), Fry included the single "That Was Then But This Is Now", which contains one of the worst rhymes of all time, coupling "mustn't grumble" with "apple crumble".

AC/DC's BACK IN BLACK

Recorded just weeks after vocalist BON SCOTT was found dead (and drunk) in a parked car in London, aged thirty-three, AC/DC's *Back In Black* is now universally acknowledged as the greatest Heavy Metal album of all time – their masterpiece – with the sombre bell of the opener, "Hell's Bells", heralding possibly their finest song. At the time (July 1980) anyone with a fashionable bone in their body was probably listening to KILLING JOKE and JOY DIVISION, but if you ever feel like reliving the past you never had, this is the CD to upload on to the iPod. The album has sold an estimated 49 million copies worldwide to date, making it the second highest selling album of all time (behind *Thriller*). As the band said themselves, "Fucking hell, this is a monster!"

DAVID ACKLES

How could we have forgotten? Born on February 27, 1937, in Rock Island, Illinois, in the very heart of the American Midwest ("Not a bad place for an incipient songwriter to get a start," he once said), David Ackles died of lung cancer on

March 2, 1999, at the age of sixty-two, in Tujunga, California. A singer-songwriter in his adult years, he recorded four albums between 1968 and 1973, but in terms of recognition he has been stepped over time and time again. ELTON JOHN, PHIL COLLINS, and ELVIS COSTELLO have tried to champion his cause (after Ackles' death Costello said, "It's a mystery to me why his wonderful songs are not better known"), but it seems as though we're just not interested.

As his mother's side of the family had already been involved in music hall, and his father was something of an accomplished amateur musician, show business was in Ackles' blood. As a child he formed a vaudeville duet with his sister and he later acted in a series of sub-Lassie B-movies about Rusty the dog. Having been a child star, perhaps he expected success, although as his film career ended abruptly when he hit puberty, perhaps he expected failure, too.

He made seriously great records. Describing Ackles' style in 2003, the critic COLIN McELLIGATT wrote, "An unlikely clash of anachronistic show business and modern-day lyricism... deeply informs his recorded output. Alternately calling to mind HOAGY CARMICHAEL, IRVING BERLIN, ROBBIE ROBERTSON, TIM HARDIN, and SCOTT WALKER, Ackles forged an utterly unique sound out of stray parts that comprise a whole that is as uncompromising as it is unrivalled."

Yup, he wasn't really so bad.

Ackles began his recording career as a staff songwriter for JAC HOLZMAN at Elektra Records. None of the songs he wrote worked for any of Elektra's artists, so Holzman suggested Ackles record them himself. His first album, *David Ackles* (1968), didn't make a mark, even when reissued in 1971 as *The Road to Cairo*, but it was influential among many, many singer-songwriters, who were blown away by his casual and honest delivery (you can hear his voice in work by SCOTT WALKER, RANDY NEWMAN, VAN DYKE PARKS, NICK CAVE, and even in material by Elton himself). The album's highlight was "Down River", which is actually Ackles' best-known song. The song's narrative sees Ackles taking the role of a man recently released from prison who runs into an old girlfriend, Rosie, only to find that the reason she didn't write to him was that she had married his best friend. "It sounds like a corny country song," Costello told *Q* in 1995. "But the way he tells it, the way it unfolds in the course of the song is actually very dramatic." It was a record that changed Costello's life, "It was kind of my teenage angst record," he said. Elvis and Elton chose "Down River" to perform as their first-ever duet together for the finale of the premier episode of Costello's TV series *Spectacle: Elvis Costello with...* in 2008. "Down River" was also covered by SPOOKY TOOTH, "Road to Cairo" by JULIE DRISCOLL & THE BRIAN AUGER TRINITY.

The stentorian *Subway to the Country*, from 1969, with its strong theatrical influences, again failed to ignite. Strike two. *American Gothic*, released in 1972, was produced by BERNIE TAUPIN, and was called by one critic, "The *Sergeant Pepper* of folk." Taupin and Ackles became friends when Ackles opened for Elton at his 1970 Troubadour gigs in Los Angeles. Taupin said of Ackles' style, "There was nothing quite like it. His stuff was sort of Brecht and Weill, and theatrical. It was very different than what the other singer-songwriters of the time were doing. There was also a darkness to it, which I really loved, because that was the kind of material I was drawn to."

After three albums for Elektra, Ackles abruptly left the label. He was signed to Columbia by CLIVE DAVIS, then president of the company and a long-time Ackles admirer. As he tried to create his first album for Columbia he felt the pressure of expectations engendered by *American Gothic's* glowing reviews. All too aware that his last album had been called "a milestone in pop and a study in excellence", and "a new direction in pop music", and himself "an important artist whose work eludes categorisation", Ackles began to second-guess himself.

In 1981 his car was hit by a drunk-driver. Ackles' left arm was nearly severed and his left thighbone "virtually pushed out through his back". He remembered his wife "standing outside the operating theatre, shouting, 'Don't cut off his arm!

He's a piano player!'" He spent six months in a wheelchair, receiving a steel hip. Ackles fought cancer for many years before finally succumbing in 1992.

Many admirers bemoan his lack of success, but one wonders why he actually wanted it. The untalented can often make a habit of being overly ambitious, so it's always nice to come across genuinely talented people who actually aren't that bothered. I've often thought that if you really want to get on, then you don't let anything get in your way, and in this case I'm not sure Ackles was really that hungry.

ADAM ANT

During punk, to me, the 100 Club in London's Oxford Street always felt like a malevolent student bar, as every time I went there a fight broke out. The place was cursed. I saw ADAM & THE ANTS play there in 1977 and as guest vocalist Jordan (was she a singer? Well, she had an ability to stand in front of a microphone, shrieking, and looking vaguely intimidating) walked by me on her way to the front, a pint glass went spinning across my face, landing somewhere near a speaker stack to the right of the stage. The Ants weren't what you would call accomplished – in 1977 no one was, and you would have been suspicious had they been – but they knew what to do on stage: namely create a din that spoke of every transgressive act one could imagine, be it sexual, political or cultural. Before "Adam" successfully reinvented himself as a dandy highwayman and short-term pin-up, he actually made some interesting records, most memorably "Young Parisians" and "Dirk Wears White Socks". None of them are the type of thing you're ever going to hear at a wedding, yet they're still capable of instantly evoking a particularly incendiary period of British pop culture.

ADELE

The only way to properly bridge the generation gap is by having cultural ubiquity, by having the sort of demographic spread and cross-generational traction that wins elections and appeals to critics, aficionados, and those who simply need something to stick in the CD player when they're driving to and from work. Oh, and children. Look at the history of any truly mass pop act and they will more than likely have been hugely popular with the under tens. The BEATLES. TAKE THAT. JUSTIN BIEBER. Adele.

In April 2011, Adele Laurie Blue Adkins (as it says on her passport) overtook MADONNA as the female star with the highest consecutive number of weeks at the top of the UK album charts, breaking a record set twenty-one years previously by *Immaculate Collection*. Which is ironic when you consider that at the time Adele was often referred to as the anti-LADY GAGA (who is often referred to as the 21st Century MADONNA).

She was also the first living artist to have two top five hits in both the Official Singles Chart and the Official Albums Chart simultaneously since the BEATLES back in 1964.

And she did it the old fashioned way, by making a strikingly direct record that didn't rely on gimmicks, trends, or tie-ups with annoyingly fashionable hip-hop stars. And by having a great big walloping voice.

In the Noughties, the accepted wisdom concerning pop ingénues was that anyone could be moulded into something approaching a star. TV talent shows didn't just facilitate this, they demanded it. With Auto-Tune, Pro Tools, and all the other software that modern pop stars had been persuaded were more important than amps, guitars, talent, and a bit of old-fashioned heads-down-I'll-see-you-at-the-end enthusiasm, it was now possible for almost anyone to convincingly pass themselves off as an entertainer; sort of like professional karaoke for the social media age.

Again ironically, Adele was no stranger to hot-housing, being a graduate of the Brit School in Croydon, which is partially funded by the music business and focuses on the performing arts – the same school that produced AMY WINEHOUSE, JESSIE J, LEONA LEWIS, KATIE MELUA, and KATE NASH. "It's quite interesting to be around 700 kids who want to be something, rather than 700 kids who just want to get pregnant so they get their own flat," Adele said. Her first choice had been the SYLVIA YOUNG theatrical school, but her mother couldn't afford the tuition fees. She was a proper, fully-formed Argos barmaid, a gobby, bawdy livewire brought up in the parts of London that don't get celebrated in the in-flight magazines of foreign airlines. Properly beautiful, she says she wasn't bothered by not being tuning fork thin, "I don't believe I need to look like that. I'm very confident. Until I start not liking my body, until it gets in the way of my health then I don't care."

An ALISON MOYET for her time, she's a big girl who sings "heartbroken soul" (her own words) in a big, big voice, the sort of voice you want to be there when you're going into battle (or at least when you're overtaking someone on the dual carriageway section of the M3, the section just passed the first turn-off to the A303). She released her debut album *19* in 2008, the follow-up *21* just over two years later, and following her performance on the Brits in February 2011 – where she sang her song "Someone Like You" as though the future of mankind on this planet, and possibly on every other, somehow depended on her reducing everyone who heard it to tears (like all of her songs, it would have passed a polygraph test with flying colours) – overnight became as famous as KATE MIDDLETON. Within an hour of her performance the song was sitting right at the top of the download charts.

My own kids love her records, in spite of the fact she doesn't look or sound like RIHANNA, BEYONCÉ, LISSIE, or any of the other female singers they tended to like previously.

Although my ten-year-old daughter has some reservations about the subject matter of her songs.

"They're all about love," she said to me at breakfast one morning. "Why can't she write some songs about what it's like to wake up in the morning or going to the supermarket…"

AEROSMITH

Like FLEETWOOD MAC, LEONARD COHEN, TAKE THAT, and dozens of other unsuspecting luminaries who have fallen (or been pushed) down crevices when they were least expecting it – usually because they have reached such depths of physical, financial or creative turpitude that they find themselves unable to do anything but acknowledge this – Aerosmith have had two careers. Their first involved being a Seventies Stones copycat bar band, with a suspicious penchant for Lowry-thin leather trousers and long, flowing silk scarves. They were phenomenally successful, until – with a predictability that could almost have been written into their contracts – drug addiction and internal rivalries took their toll (with band members JOE PERRY and BRAD WHITFORD even being kicked out for four years, in 1980).

The band got clean, sobered up, got a new deal with Geffen Records and started having hits again, giving the Aerosmith sound the business class treatment. In 1986 they appeared on RUN D.M.C.'s version of their own "Walk This Way", having a worldwide smash and introducing them to a whole new generation in the process. Even bigger hits followed, and they became adept at the BON JOVI-style power ballad (notably "Crying", "Amazing", "Crazy", "I Don't Want To Miss A Thing", "Jaded", repeat till fade).

AIR SNARE

In my time I have seen politicians do many things. I have seen them attempt to dance (badly). I have seen them attempt to tell jokes (poorly). I have seen them dodge fruit and vegetables thrown by disgruntled members of their constituencies (always unsuccessfully). I have seen them talk with their mouths full (disgustingly), with food falling all over the table. And, on one occasion, I even saw one play air guitar – although to be honest with you, it was actually a politician's wife (her husband was too busy having his chest hair shaved in full view of thirty, frankly astonished, members of a magazine team).

This in itself was odd, as air guitar has usually been the domain of the adolescent boy, or at least any man who's an adolescent boy at heart (i.e. most of us). I have been as guilty as anyone else, and although I haven't done it since my twenties, during my youth I was up there with the very best, noodling for Britain, the Commonwealth, and the Empire. The first record I can remember pretending to play the guitar to was the BEATLES' "Revolution" (I was eight, and already apparently hard-wired into the spirit of counter-cultural agitprop), and started to seriously get into it around the time of DAVID BOWIE's ZIGGY STARDUST records, pretending to bend a pool cue in the style of MICK RONSON (not that I ever managed to find a six-stringed pool cue). To this day I can think of very few things from my adolescence that gave me as much fun as bouncing around the bedroom playing air guitar to "Jean Jeanie", "Five Years", or "Starman".

I never used the family cricket bat – heaven forbid – although there were various secondhand badminton and tennis rackets that came in very useful when trying to get to grips with the intricacies of the convoluted guitar solos in STEELY DAN's "Reelin' In The Years", the ALLMAN BROTHERS' "Jessica", or "Bell Bottom Blues" by DEREK AND THE DOMINOES.

In true life – as my youngest daughter still says – I was actually rather better at the "air snare", and would happily while away the hours drumming along to the fills in the WHO's "Baba O'Riley". And let me tell you this came in very handy when it was determined by the gods that I was going to be a drummer, rather than a guitarist. When the BUZZCOCKS' STEVE DIGGLE formed his spin-off band, FLAG OF CONVENIENCE, in 1981, he actually asked me if I'd like to join him; but although the idea obviously appealed to my ego, I wasn't about to follow in the footsteps of JOHN MAHER, the BUZZCOCKS' original drummer, and probably one of the best of all time. Oh yes, and I'd just sold my drum kit for rent money.

And that's the problem, air guitar is not the sort of thing you should ever talk about in public; and as for actually doing it, well, these days that's as socially acceptable as admitting that you're sexually attracted to sheep. Which is why I was shocked when CHRISTINE HAMILTON jumped up on a table during the *GQ* Christmas lunch a few years ago to expertly strum along to ROD STEWART's "Maggie May".

If it had been TONY BLAIR I would have obviously been less surprised – when he was in UGLY RUMOURS he was a dab hand at the Stratocaster swipe – but he hadn't accepted our invitation that year (I think he was with CLIFF RICHARD or SILVIO BERLUSCONI). Our celebrity politicos that year were the disgraced Tory MP NEIL HAMILTON and his bubbly wife Christine – principally because we'd just photographed them naked for the magazine, posing as Adam and Eve (a joy to organise, let me tell you, although not necessarily to behold), and we thought it would be a wheeze to ask them along. We couldn't have wished for better sports, and while Neil stripped down to his boxers in order for one of our girls to shave his chest hair (having failed to get him to shave his head), Christine, perhaps emboldened by seven or eight glasses of vintage champagne, leapt onto the boardroom table and played some of the most enthusiastic air guitar I've ever seen, belting out Townshend-esque windmill chords to "Maggie May" without a care.

When I woke up the next day, I couldn't quite believe it, but I suppose that's the point of office parties. You never know what's going to happen, and considering what can and what does it's probably best this way.

As for myself, I didn't join in that day, although in the privacy of my own home, if the conditions were right, I think I could be persuaded. Yes, it might take an awful lot of good Bordeaux, and yes, the blinds would have to be drawn, and yes, cameras would have to be handed in at the door, along with mobile phones. But I could do it. I would cue the iPod to play "Goodbye To Love" by the CARPENTERS, fall on my knees, adopt the white man's overbite, and then attempt a few deft power chords before working my way up and down my imaginary fretboard.

ALAN ALDRIDGE

I was onstage at Central St Martin's Cochrane Theatre, as part of an extended series of interviews with various notable designers, and the illustrator Alan Aldridge was being engagingly indiscreet. Having told us all about working with LORD SNOWDON ("I was working alone in his house once and the phone rang. 'Hello,' I said, 'Can I help?', 'Yes, is Margaret there?' 'No love, she's out. Who wants to know?' 'Her sister…'"), his frustrations with the BEATLES ("At Apple it was very difficult to get paid"), the saga of the cover and aborted film of ELTON JOHN's *Captain Fantastic And The Brown Dirt Cowboy* (with Hollywood showing its homophobic side), he told us the story of creating the sleeve for CREAM's final album, *Goodbye*, in 1969.

Aldridge has always been something of an enigma, and even when he was riding high as the rock'n'roll graphic designer du jour in the Sixties, always tended to let his work do the talking. He designed the cover of *A Quick One* by the WHO (1966), *The Beatles Illustrated Lyrics* (1969), *The*

Penguin Book Of Comics (1971), and *The Butterfly Ball And The Grasshopper Feast* (1973). But in the Noughties he began to talk himself, and with great self-deprecation.

CREAM had already broken up when they came to release *Goodbye*, and couldn't stand the sight of each other, so he had to tell ERIC CLAPTON, JACK BRUCE, and GINGER BAKER that they'd be photographed separately and the pictures glued together afterwards. When they arrived at the studio, they discovered that Aldridge was pulling a fast one, and that the only way the picture would work was if they were in the same frame together. Cue the sound of toys, drumsticks, Fenders, and plectrums being thrown out of prams, and three of the world's biggest rock stars screaming like children. Frustrated beyond belief, Aldridge went outside for a cigarette, only to see the dancer and choreographer LIONEL BLAIR about to board a bus. As a last resort, the designer coerced Blair into coming into the studio to try to convince the band to sit for the session. Remarkably, Blair did just that, and soon had the band running around, posing and laughing as though they were in the first flush of youth.

MARC ALMOND

Towards the end of ALLISON PEARSON's *I Think I Love You*, her more than marvellous evocation of female teenage obsession, she describes a DAVID CASSIDY concert in Las Vegas in the late Nineties, when his teenage fans had all but turned into middle-aged mums.

"Up onstage, David was apologising. He knew they wanted the songs from before, but, just once, he wanted to try something newer, you know, a little more up to date; a little number that explained how he was feeling NOW..." Pearson describes how the crowd then shifts in their seats, brimming with goodwill ("Couldn't blame the guy, could you, for wanting to break free of the past; give him a chance, right?"), and reluctantly willing to indulge him a little...

before he starts singing the opening words from "How Can I Be Sure", his biggest hit, and the whole place erupts.

With performance, expectation is all. Expectation and a little surprise. And Marc Almond certainly surprised me.

Now, Almond is no DAVID CASSIDY, and his success in the early Eighties with SOFT CELL owed more to the band's quirky electro-pop image than his innate good looks and well-groomed hair. But he was a pin-up just the same, whose image was festooned across bedroom walls all over the country.

There has always been a tendency to describe Almond as having a "ghostly pallor", a gothic screenwash that has helped prolong a career that by rights should have wandered off into oblivion – or at least an Eastern European leather bar – thirty years ago. When JANE AUSTEN wrote, "You have delighted us long enough", I, for one, have always imagined that if she had written those words in 1983 she might easily have been referring to Almond, a man I always assumed had a finite amount of talent.

For years afterwards Almond appeared to want to channel Beelzebub, or at least give the impression he was capable of doing so. His shtick became camp decadence, his trope a pop deviancy. He was a cabaret darling, a former pop idol recalibrated as a cocktail queen, trussed-up in black tie and patents, with Satan's pitchfork in one hand and a silver cigarette case in the other. Sure, he could carry a tune, but he seemed to stagger under the load.

I've always considered him to be in the minor league, but in the autumn of 2011 I was forced to change my mind. This was annoying, as it meant I had to recalibrate everything I felt about him, but there's now nothing I can do about it.

That week I went to the thirtieth anniversary of Le Caprice, the London restaurant that was opened (or reopened rather) with great success by JEREMY KING and CHRIS CORBIN in 1981. During dinner the Scottish R&B singer EMELI SANDÉ sat at the upright piano, playing an impassioned version of her debut single "Heaven" (which was always going to be so much better than the machine gun dance version that reached No.2 at the time), before handing over the microphone to... Marc Almond. Now, if I had known that the shrink-wrapped munchkin was going to be singing, I may have made my excuses ("I don't like Marc Almond" and er, "I don't like Marc Almond") and left. But there I was, trapped, sitting exactly four feet away, and with no escape route in sight. Sure, I could have skipped passed him on the way to the loo and perhaps squeezed myself out of the lavatory window, but then my guests would have been left at the table, forced to endure the chipmunk-like warbling of the neo-gothic elf, self-consciously twirling their wine around and staring at their shoes.

How glad am I that I didn't. Almond had been chosen to celebrate the anniversary as SOFT CELL had been number one with "Tainted Love" when the restaurant opened, and after the meekest of introductions got up to sing it. And it was fairly extraordinary. Just a voice – a pretty good voice, still – and a piano, and enough self-contained charisma, and well-honed stagecraft to carry the room with him. I instantly regretted, and felt embarrassed about all the withering thoughts I'd had about him for the previous three decades. Redemption in one performance, a comeback at the flick of a lash, for me at least. In a restaurant, or indeed any room this size, there is literally nowhere to hide. You either work, or you stink like a three-day-old fish.

Marc Almond worked, and reinforced the fact that you can't beat old-fashioned theatricality. Yes, he reminded me of EARTHA KITT or a camp SCOTT WALKER, but never in a bad way. He finished off with another SOFT CELL song, "Say Hello, Wave Goodbye", and the heat in the room climbed even higher.

Props. Not only is Marc Almond better than he sounds, he doesn't stink like a three-day-old fish.

HERB ALPERT

If history can be caught in a single breath, then there are few better ways of explaining the Populuxe aspirations of American suburbia during the late Fifties and early Sixties (when the advertising industry began to believe its own publicity) than by listening to the piercing yet sweet 'Ameriachi' sound of Herb Alpert and his TIJUANA BRASS.

As the Fifties gave way to the Sixties, the suburban soundtrack of Mai Tai melodies and Space-age bachelor pad music (a kind of homely filter-tipped sonic wallpaper) was displaced by the brash, urban sophistication of men like BURT BACHARACH, SERGIO MENDES, and Herb Alpert. And as teen idols replaced the gruff rock'n'roll greaseballs, so smart young bandleaders replaced the quirkier exponents of 'Exotica'. Alpert in particular credits the delirious, happy sound of the TIJUANA BRASS with ushering in a new era of American pop. "It's not a protest and not a put-down," he said. "I think people were bugged with hearing music which had an undercurrent of unhappiness and anger, even sadism."

In the beginning, it was all serendipity. Born in Los Angeles in 1935 into a musical family (his father played the mandolin, his mother the violin, his sister the piano and his brother the drums), Alpert took up the trumpet at the tender age of eight, later studying with jazz and classical tutors at Fairfax High School. After two years in the army as a trumpeter-bugler at San Francisco's Presidio garrison, he worked in LA as an A&R man, record producer, composer (writing "Wonderful World", amongst others, for SAM COOKE), and session musician. He was a Herb of all trades.

One day in 1962, messing about in his ad hoc studio in the garage next to his house, he began experimenting with a song called "Twinkle Star" which had been written by a friend of his, SOL LAKE. Exploiting the tune's Spanish flavour, Alpert came up with a version that had some of the intonations of Mexican mariachi music; and so "The Lonely Bull", the TIJUANA BRASS and A&M Records (hastily organised with another friend, record promotion man JERRY MOSS) were born. Herb Alpert's TIJUANA BRASS became the South of the Border soundtrack of the Swinging Sixties, flashpointed in "Casino Royale", "Tijuana Taxi", "Spanish Flea", and "A Taste of Honey"; while by 1968 A&M annual turnover was in excess of $50 million, helped by the success of the SANDPIPERS and SERGIO MENDES. During the Seventies and Eighties Alpert concentrated on running his record company, occasionally popping up with funk and dance tracks such as "Rise", "Rotation" (both 1979), and "Keep Your Eye on Me" (1987).

For all his talk of giddy pop, Alpert is a master of moodsong, and his haunting trumpet sound has an innate maudlin quality. To wit: "There are some things which have definitely sad overtones, like the tune we wrote in memory of the matador, CARLOS ARRUZA, who was such a big influence upon my whole idea for the Brass sound. He was fighting in Tijuana on the day I got the inspiration for the sound. Thinking of how tragically he died, in a head-on automobile collision, after fighting bulls for twenty-five years, that music didn't come out too happy."

AMOEBA

A trip to Los Angeles always had a sense of tradition about it. You would arrive, drowsy yet excited, eager not just to explore the city, but also keen not to fall asleep. Yet before the exploring – and this was strictly indoor exploration, as this would inadvertently involve a new hotel bar, cocktail lounge, or restaurant – there would be the obligatory trip to Sunset Strip, and explicitly, the corner of Sunset Boulevard and Palm Avenue. You would park the car in the Tower Records car park – "Patrons only; all other cars will be towed!" – and then stroll across the road to Book Soup, where you would spend a stolen hour picking up the latest magazines and recently published indie busters.

Then, your bag overflowing with art, film, photography, and music books, you'd dart back over the road, dump your load in the boot of the hire car, and wander into Tower like a cowboy, your wallet bulging in the back pocket of your blue jeans, ready to stock up on some prime polycarbonate plastic.

Aaah, the subterranean joys of the record shop.

But those days have gone. Forever. Today the record shop is scarcer than an eel pie and mash house, rarer than a phone box, the last vestige of an analogue, vinyl kingdom, a kingdom where album sleeves had more cultural equity than motorway billboards. While there may be more tattoo parlours in North America than bookstores, record stores have almost disappeared completely. In our world of exponential choice, where the assumption is that everything can be found online if you look hard and long enough, the idea of walking up and down aisles in the vain hope that the longhairs who stocked the shop have exactly the same taste as you might seem stupidly quaint, but for me the record shop – and in particular the independent record shop – has always been the supermarket of the soul.

These days, any LA visit involves an obligatory trip to another part of Sunset Boulevard, many miles from where Tower once stood, to Amoeba, the greatest record store in North America. Here, in Hollywood, the world's largest independently owned record store, you'll find both new and secondhand CDs, new and secondhand vinyl, posters, DVDs, figurines, magazines, and books. This is the dustbin of esoterica, a compendium the size of a warehouse, where you should be able to find just about anything. And even if you can't, this is one of the few places left on earth where you can experience the soothing sensation of traipsing the rows and rows of vinyl, just waiting to be surprised. Here, the flipping of plastic-covered cardboard and the clatter of CD boxes create a chorus of possibility, a symphony of opportunity.

Understandably, the people who used to treat going to a record shop as a leisure activity are now all talking to each other online, via chat rooms, blogs, and social networking. Much of the chat is simply nostalgic, wallowing in those moments of adolescence when an hour in a record shop seemed to easily last a week. There is a lot of kvetching, too, a backwash of bitching about those poor unfortunates (squares, they were called back then) who tended to treat the record shop as a refuelling exercise rather than a conventicle or reference library.

One former owner recalled a phone call he took shortly after opening his shop in 1990.

"I'm looking for a song called 'Kokomo'. Do you know who recorded it?"

"The BEACH BOYS."

"No, this is a new song called 'Kokomo'. Do you know who recorded it?"

"Yes, it is a BEACH BOYS song from a few years ago."

"No, this song is called 'Kokomo'. I just heard it on the radio."

"Bermuda Bahama, Come on pretty Mama?"

"That's it! Do you know who recorded it?"

"The BEACH BOYS."

"No, this is a new song. Is there another store that would know?"

Another store owner, this one sounding not a little unlike the curmudgeonly JACK BLACK character in *High Fidelity* (the one who refuses to sell a copy of STEVIE WONDER's "I Just Called To Say I Love You" to a customer even though they have one in stock), couldn't wait to comment with his own version.

"Yes! This is my favourite! I can't tell you how many times customers would ask a question, only to not believe me when I gave them the answer... To wit:

'I heard this song, sounded just like the BEATLES, I wonder if you know who it was.'

'How did it go?'

'Like, "Tell me that you got everything you want, and your bird can sing".'

'Yeah, that is the BEATLES.'

'...mmm... no, I don't think so...'

'Oh, yes, it is – it's on *Yesterday & Today* but we don't have one right now.'

'No, no, I think you're confused – it just sounds like the BEATLES.'

'NO. It's the BEATLES. Written and sung by Lennon. *Yesterday & Today*. Side two, track one.'

'Mmmm... I think you may be mistaken on this one...'

'So, are you going to buy anything?"'

AQUACRUNK

Anyone hearing for the first time the aquacrunk remix of LADY GAGA's "Paparazzi" – where the disparity between the djembe-like beats of the 0.2 version and the orthodoxy of the original couldn't have been writ any larger – might have wondered just how fractured dance music might eventually become.

Back in the early Eighties, the British weekly music magazine *Record Mirror* had a regular column by a man called JAMES HAMILTON, a journalist who looked like a local councillor, a vet, or perhaps the sort of man who – when you had finally decided to junk it in exchange for some form of digital replica, loaded it up on the Sonos – might come and make an offer for your eight feet of old vinyl (he was once memorably described as a cross between COLONEL SANDERS and JAMES ROBERTSON JUSTICE). He seemed like an odd, almost arcane cove, yet he was responsible for one of the most important parts of the paper: it was his job to tell the DJs who read his column what the exact BPM were of the various twelve inchers released that week. Beats per minute. It was all that mattered to those whose job it was to seamlessly keep the evenings alive in youth clubs, nightclubs, and discos across the country. Hamilton's column made sure you didn't follow a frantic Hi-Energy release with something glacial or postcoital by the SOS BAND, didn't try and dovetail BRONSKI BEAT with SHANNON. He had been exposed to beat-synced mixing in New York's Paradise Garage in the late Seventies, and never looked back.

BPMs have defined dance music since before the delivery of the first mirror ball. From R&B to soul to funk to disco to hip-hop to house to drum'n'bass to grime to aquacrunk and all points between and beyond, the synchronicity of the bass drum and the snare (computerised or not) have defined the nightclub as much as the strobe light, the illuminated checker-board dance floor, or the red velvet rope. But unlike guitar-driven rock music – which, after 1976, took an almost infantile delight in speeding itself up, to the point where acceleration became the raison d'etre of so much punk and thrash metal – dance music was defined by, as well as constrained by, its ability to make people move. Hence the bandwidth of BPMs rarely altered, until the likes of jungle, drum and bass appeared, that is, in the mid-Nineties, taking the BPMs way up to 150-180, rather than the 120+ orthodoxy of House, say.

Speedcore, the hardcore techno that came later, used BPMs between 250 and 300, sometimes going up to an almost Spinal Tapesque 1000 (up there, where the air was thin, the splinter-tags were manifold: hardcore gabber, breakcore, speedcore, splittercore, cyber-grind, step-up, extratone, blah). Beats also wandered downstream, sometimes – in the case of aquacrunk (that weird underwater dubstep) – sinking completely. Here, the beats were no less frantic, they just sounded slightly wonky (which the genre was also sometimes, usually inaccurately, called). And with unquantised beats – where literally anything can happen, often at the expense of rhythm, melody or anything resembling pop as we know it – abstraction almost seemed like a formula. And now it's become so easy to find software to calculate BPM, determine BPM, and mix songs with the same BPM, that it makes JAMES HAMILTON seem almost quaint.

Arcade Fire

If the critics ever decide to kill these particular darlings then Arcade Fire won't know what to do with themselves. Rarely has a band been so applauded, so feted, so universally celebrated from rooftops and pulpits. Ever since they started it's been win, win, win. They came along at a time when it wasn't known whether it was possible to "believe" in rock groups any more, wasn't known if it were possible for anyone or anything to be Zeitgeisty with any dignity or real sense of purpose. Musically speaking we've been living in a post-modern world since 1976, and as post-modernism is subject to the very worst laws of diminishing trends, who knew someone could come along and make earnestness seen fashionable and important again?

Arcade Fire belong to a world that acknowledges that it's easier to sell records if you look like Laura Cantrell rather than Ron Sexsmith, although they don't like it much. And so they hunker down, dig deep, and come up with their own version of the world, with gnarly vocals, watery melodies and abstract accompaniment. It's all about "authenticity", and feeling good about being different. The *Guardian* – which the band has enjoyed the patronage of – has said they are "driven by a fierce desire to punch through layers of cynicism and reserve to make a visceral emotional connection with their audience." They are North America's conscience. And they want to Tell It Like It Is.

They are the sound of quiet desperation (sample lyric: "These days, my life, I feel it has no purpose/ But late at night the feelings swim to the surface"). Best songs: "Wake Up", "Intervention", "The Suburbs".

ARCTIC MONKEYS

It was Salford poet JOHN COOPER CLARKE who gave ALEX TURNER the confidence to call his band Arctic Monkeys. Turner once worked as a barman in a bar in Sheffield, and gradually got to know Cooper Clarke, who first came into the pub when supporting the FALL. "He was the first person who ever said he liked the name," said Turner. "Because it's a bad name, we all know that. [But] if he thought it were a good name, then we were definitely going to keep it."

The link with the Bard of Salford is important, as it underscores the way in which the Monkeys used their locale, their provenance, and their sense of self to define who, and what, they are. One senses that affectation is a sackable offence, up there with indistinct political views, an unhealthy interest in cocktail bars, Maldivian holidays, or sushi. That's not to say the Monkeys are reductive; not at all – they're particular, protective, and completely uninterested in any sort of unnecessary compromise.

LOUIS ARMSTRONG

The most important influence on classic jazz, formative in a completely fundamental way, and "blessed" with the traditional early 20th Century New Orleans upbringing – spending fatherless years in slums, brothels, and the Home for Colored Waifs – Armstrong is a quintessential jazz archetype. He was also one of the half-a-dozen most extraordinary musicians of the century, so important, so influential, that almost everything in jazz can be traced back to his trumpet (Armstrong was to black music what BOB DYLAN was to white rock). "West End Blues", recorded in 1923, is as good a piece of recorded music as anything that came in its wake. He found notes more easily than any of his peers, was the first real improvisatory genius, and worked his way around his horn in such a way that his style was copied for decades afterwards – his authority with the instrument is simply unchallanged. He later had a film career, and to white suburban America became an acceptable member of the emerging black middle class. The mawkish "What A Wonderful World", a hit for Armstrong late in his career, was for a while as popular as "My Way".

"ASTEROID"

The sound of the future has been imagined many times, so many times in fact that it always tends to sound the same. Through attrition, repetition, and – one suspects – laziness, the future always sounds accelerated, robotic, metallic, and otherworldly. And not a little computer-generated. Which is obviously how we like it. WALTER CARLOS has imagined it (he wrote much of the incidental music for *A Clockwork Orange*), as have GIORGIO MORODER and TONTO'S EXPANDING HEAD BAND. NEU did it, JOHN BARRY did it, and KRAFTWERK have been at it for forty years.

But no one imagined the future quite like the British composer and arranger PETE MOORE, the man who wrote "Asteroid", or, as most of us will know it, the Pearl & Dean theme. The cinema advertising business was ignominiously sold off in 2010 for £1, offloaded by the Scottish broadcaster STV Group to the Irish businessman who runs the Empire cinema chain, THOMAS ANDERSON. It wasn't exactly clear what he intended doing with the company, but he would be a lunatic if he decided to ditch its rather wonderful signature tune.

"One of the most reliable methods for writers to make a fool of themselves in print is to try and spell a tune," wrote JONATHAN MARGOLIS. "'Bum bum ti bum booo bah,' we prattle, when trying to describe some well-known theme without the benefit if being able to hum it. If I hit you with this one, however – go on, just one more try, please – you might just get it: 'Pa-paa pa-paa pa-paa pa-paa pa-pa-pa, Pa-paa pa-paa pa-paa pa-paaa pa,' it starts. Got it?"

Pearl & Dean has been around for over sixty years, and for many the theme tune which announced generic ads for Indian restaurants, carpet cleaners, and soft drinks became an ironic institution decades before irony became properly commodified. We somehow knew that it was trying to punch way above its weight, and that its portentousness was almost its saving grace.

Pearl & Dean's addictive advertising jingle has become something of a ritualistic mantra for British cinema-goers since it was first introduced in 1968, and was once so well-known that the company believe their logo was known for its sound rather than its image. People sing it on entering the cinema, sing along with it when they eventually hear it, and even leave singing it. So cherished is this blistering space-age ident that one Welsh cinema manager once arranged to have it played at his own cremation, as his coffin slid behind the curtains. A rather ignominious end, perhaps, but one that suggests that "Asteroid" can elicit the same emotions as Proust's Madeleine.

"When I wrote 'Asteroid', many people in the profession accused me of writing music for the future, and ahead of its time" said PETE MOORE in 2003. "With the longevity of this music I thoroughly agree."

SAINT ETIENNE's BOB STANLEY wrote recently that he initially thought the song was a sample from a HUGO MONTENEGRO version of JIMMY WEBB's "Macarthur Park" (or at least this is what he had been told), and he wasn't able to be sure until it was officially released for the first time in the mid-Nineties, when the easy listening "boom" was in full swing. It was finally released on a compilation called *Nice'n'Easy*, although true aficionados had had recordings of the twenty-second mini-masterpiece for years. Perhaps predictably, the song first appeared in 1968, the same year as *2001: A Space Odyssey*, something the Pearl & Dean graphics still pay homage to.

A few years ago it was covered by a Wolverhampton pop group, GOLDBUG, who welded it on to a version of LED ZEPPELIN's "Whole Lotta Love", creating a huge hit in the process. "We went to see *Terminator 2* and realised we were all looking forward to the Pearl & Dean music," said GOLDBUG member, RICHARD WALMSLEY. "But it didn't happen. It was just not there. And that got us thinking: 'Asteroid' is music that speaks to your darkest regions."

VIRGINIA ASTLEY

In the summer of 1990 I was in Carmel in California, about to have dinner at CLINT EASTWOOD's restaurant, the Hog's Head Inn (at the time he was the town's mayor). As I walked through the centre of town, I passed one of those generic new-age shops, the ones that sell everything from joss sticks and expensively framed GRATEFUL DEAD posters, to designer Lava Lamps and spa creams. It also sold various CDs of ocean sounds, California ocean sounds to boot, and as I had been in love with the idea of the California ocean from the age of about ten, I had to buy one.

And I bought it with one thing in mind. Almost as soon as I got home to London I put it into the CD player, and then played one of my bespoke BEACH BOYS cassettes over the top, so I could listen to "Surf's Up", "Till I Die", and "California Saga", with the sound of the Big Sur waves crashing against the rocks in the background. I had almost completely replicated my Californian experience – which was designed primarily so I could listen to a surf soundtrack ad nauseum as I drove along the Pacific Coast Highway in a rented Mustang – which meant that whenever I wanted to, I could take myself back to Route 1 and "Cabinessence" without leaving the confines of west London.

VIRGINIA ASTLEY's 1983 mini-masterpiece *From Gardens Where We Feel Secure* comes complete with its own natural soundtrack, in the shape of field recordings of birdsong and sheep. There is a little light piano, some woodwind, and some ambient vocals, but mainly this is the sound of the countryside, an instrumental accompaniment to a typical British summer's day. It always reminds me of one of my favourite paintings, "The Badminton Game" by DAVID INSHAW (finished in 1973), which was influenced by the landscape of Wiltshire, and in particular the houses and gardens of Devizes.

Like the painting, the album is a moment in time. This is mood music at its very best. So if you fancy a day in the country, and can't be bothered to fire-up the old MG and drive down the A303, go on to iTunes and download "Morning: Hiding In The Ha-Ha". The day will take on another dimension completely.

All you'll need then is a large glass of rosé and a plate of cucumber sandwiches. Oh, and maybe a small game of badminton.

B

Burt Bacharach

As he padded and pattered around the den in his Pacific Palisades dream home, dressed in his monogrammed burgundy tracksuit, Burt Bacharach looked like a man with a busy day ahead of him. It was 2006 and he was seventy-seven years young, but still moved with the agility of a man thirty years his junior. His skin was thin and his voice was quiet, yet he spoke with an assuredness that sometimes seemed to take even him by surprise.

Burt Bacharach has never really been known for his outspokenness, and his interviews have been as commonplace as his music has been extraordinary. But when we met, as he prepared himself to enter his ninth decade, he was about to embrace the spirit of BOB DYLAN and release his first overtly political record, *At This Time*.

"I hate what's going on in America," he said, with barely concealed contempt, "and I want to say something about it."

The composer of "Trains And Boats And Planes", "Walk On By", "I'll Never Fall In Love Again", "Are You There With Another Girl", "What The World Needs Now Is Love", "I Say A Little Prayer", "Raindrops Keep Falling On My Head", and hundreds more loungecore classics, lives just a few miles from the Pacific Coast Highway, an evocative stretch of tarmac that once lent its name to one of Bacharach's great instrumentals, and one of those parts of California that so inspired the extravagantly landscaped architecture of his songs.

His den was exactly as one would want it: sitting on a ground-floor corner overlooking the hissing of summer lawns, he tinkled at his piano, the charts of a yet-to-be-finished song scrawled over the property section of the *LA Times*. A small cassette player on which he still records all his demos sat on top of the piano, as he closed his eyes and played. A framed cover of *Newsweek* from 1970 picturing Bacharach with the cover line "The Music Man" hung behind him, as did a poster for the B-movie classic *The Blob*, for which, inexplicably,

B

Bacharach wrote the score, as well as dozens of photographs of him with the likes of STEVIE WONDER, ELVIS PRESLEY, DIONNE WARWICK, ELIZABETH TAYLOR, and former writing partner HAL DAVID. There were also pictures of him with his beloved racehorses (he has bred for years) and glass awards for winning just about everything.

He had just come back from playing at the opening of STEVE WYNN's eponymous Las Vegas hotel in front of RUPERT MURDOCH, STEVEN SPIELBERG, BARRY DILLER, and the first PRESIDENT BUSH. He was meeting me this lunchtime to celebrate being handed *GQ*'s Inspiration Award and to tell me about his new CD, the first release from his new deal with Sony UK.

Bacharach had spent the past few months putting the finishing touches to his first new collection of songs in years. Recorded with hip-hop super-producer DR. DRE and featuring drum loops a-go-go, *At This Time* contained elaborate, seven-minute mini-operas, abrasive orchestrations and fairly forthright political sideswipes. One song, "Go Ask Shakespeare", featured RUFUS WAINWRIGHT. Another, "Can't Give It Up", was classic Bacharach bossa nova, while another, the unapologetic "Who Are These People?" was sung by ELVIS COSTELLO. (When I interviewed Bacharach the summer before, he was still at the demo stage of this song and asked me who I thought should sing on it. Having at first suggested NICK CAVE, I then told Bacharach he should really ask Costello to do it, seeing that they had worked together on the *Painted From Memory* album. Which is obviously what he did.)

Bizarrely, at times the record even sounded a bit like DAVID BOWIE's *Low* (with vocals coming in when you least expected them to), which, it has to be said, is not the sort of thing that usually gets said about a new Burt Bacharach record. "This is a new kind of record for me," he said, as he hunkered down over his electric piano. "There's no point in me competing with my past, so I'm now going to compete with everyone else. ROB STRINGER [who ran Sony UK and who signed him to the label, and who now runs the American label] asked me to make an album where I would be taking some risks. He said, 'I don't want you to come up with an album full of songs they're playing on the radio. Even if they're good, you're still gonna get knocked because people are just gonna say you're not as good as you used to be.' So this is a very different album."

The unlikely allegiance with DR. DRE was formed when Bacharach bumped into him in New York. "He was trying to finish an album and when I mentioned working together, the idea kind of appealed to him," Bacharach said. "So he gave me four or five drum loops, I went into the studio with a computer and then began layering things on top of them. Keyboards. An orchestra. A Greek chorus..."

And RUFUS WAINWRIGHT, who he also worked with on the record? "Rufus is such a great guy. When he comes in and cuts a vocal there's such a surprise element to his voice. He sang on this record beautifully, even if the lyrics are quite jagged. Because it still comes down to the same thing when you peel it all back: is there a melody? I was even thinking of asking DAVID BOWIE. Like ELVIS, he has anger in his voice. Rufus has that too."

As I got up to leave, Bacharach saw me notice a small photograph of him taken with CHERIE BLAIR and LAUREN BUSH.

"Oh," he said, embarrassed. "I've been meaning to get rid of that."

CHET BAKER

Chet Baker, as they say, blew it. On Friday May 13, 1988, the celebrated jazz trumpeter and vocalist fell to his death from a second-floor window in the Prins Hendrik Hotel in Amsterdam. He was fifty-eight years old and a long-time heroin user – a small amount of the drug was found in his hotel room, though the autopsy showed, none was found in his blood. The Dutch police initially ruled his death a suicide, though his family and friends said this was unlikely. In the months immediately after his death many conspiracy theories

B

arose, several involving the drug dealers known to have hung around Baker just before he died.

It is a sad irony that Chet Baker, the former heart-throb of the horn who'd spent the last thirty years of his life playing down his extraordinary good looks whilst playing up to the image of a hard-living muso, had just completed a film which, when it was released in 1989, pushed him into the limelight once again. Only this time he wasn't around to enjoy it.

The film in question was photographer BRUCE WEBER's second movie, *Let's Get Lost*, a beautifully shot documentary about the life and career of Baker. A film about love and obsession, it gave more than a glimpse into the sad, often mad world of one of the most accomplished jazz musicians. Using all the techniques he successfully employs in his often magnificent fashion photography, BRUCE WEBER took us all on a long day's journey into the night – 119 minutes in the company of Chet Baker.

Like many people, Weber first became interested in Baker because of the way he looked. At sixteen he stumbled across a copy of *Chet Baker Sings and Plays with Bud Shank and Russ Freeman* (on the World Pacific label), featuring on its back cover a picture of Baker in a short-sleeved white sweater, holding his trumpet like a cigarette. When he got around to playing it, Weber soon realised the young JIMMY DEAN of modernism had a whirlwind of talent as well as alabaster cheekbones. "I just couldn't believe the sounds he came out with – it was like nothing I had ever heard before."

In 1986 Weber directed his first feature, *Broken Noses*, a documentary based on the life of a young pro lightweight boxer called ANDY MINSKER. Included in the film was music by GERRY MULLIGAN, JULIE LONDON, ROBERT MITCHUM, and Chet Baker, which is where the story really begins. "Most of the boxing films which had been made before *Broken Noses*, had either used hard driving rock or some kind of heroic classical music," said Baker. "But I thought jazz had the right soulfulness for the subject – I thought the two genres should meet. Boxers and jazzmen both have the same kind

of sensibilities, experience the same kind of struggle – or at
least they used to. I'd always loved Chet's music, and seeing
that ANDY MINSKER reminded me a lot of the early pictures of
Chet, I decided to use his music in the movie."

B

Weber later met the great trumpet player, and eventually
decided to make a film about his life. He became obsessed
with Baker's lyrical trumpet and melancholy voice, and
also his mythical status within the jazz community. "All the
craziness in Chet's life was in his music – that's why I had to
make this movie. There's also a whole new audience out there
who aren't aware of his music. Well, they deserve his music ...

"We started the movie in a strange way. We knew we didn't
have a lot of money [*Let's Get Lost* eventually cost a little over
one million dollars, all of it Weber's] so it had to be done on
the tightest of budgets. We also had to shoot when Chet was
around, which certainly wasn't all the time. So we could never
have made a structured movie, even if we had wanted to. Chet
would never have got to grips with the shooting schedule. The
initial idea was a three-minute movie. It was my money so I
could basically make the film any length I wanted – then it
started growing and we just went with it. If I'd have gone to a
studio and said I wanted to make a movie about Chet Baker,
they would have said, 'Well why don't you use TOM CRUISE?'
Also, there's no way Chet would have been able to handle the
pressure of outside money – he would have split in the first
week. A lot of people said that Chet would never be on time.
But during filming he wasn't late once."

Chesney Henry "Chet" Baker, Jr., was born on December
23, 1929, in the middle of the Jazz Age, although he was
destined to become one of the true pioneers of the West
Coast Cool School of Jazz. Playing briefly with CHARLIE
PARKER in the early Fifties, he was to become renowned for
his part in GERRY MULLIGAN's legendary piano-less quartet.
Though his style would always be compared to the earlier
work of BIX BEIDERBECKE, Baker established himself as a solo
player, forming his own quartet with RUSS FREEMAN in 1953,
aged twenty-four. Due to his youth, his good looks and his

B

unquestionable talent, Baker rapidly became a West Coast force, and ultimately an icon for hipsters the world over. But in 1956 Chet Baker became too hip. He discovered heroin, and began an affair that would last until his death. In three years he was busted seven times, and in the next three decades would forget how many nights he'd spent in jail. Chet Baker became his very own cliché.

Throughout the Sixties, Baker wandered the less salubrious nightclubs of Western Europe. Shunned by his critics and public alike, his only solace was his music, and, perhaps, his drugs. It's fair to say that Chet Baker paid his dues. "What I loved about him most was the way he looked at the world," said Weber. "He made a lot of the wrong choices in life, but a lot of the right ones too." For Baker this was no adventure of poverty, it was his life.

In *Let's Get Lost* the trumpeter still retained the striking features of his prime, and although Chet Baker in 1987 was a man with a face like the Los Angeles freeway system, time could not entirely erase those classic looks. In his last smack-driven months he looked more like JACK PALANCE than JIMMY DEAN, a hard man with cloudy eyes and a nervous stare, a haunted man, "a broken man too tough to cry". He always looked tough, but never strong.

At just under two hours, *Let's Get Lost* is a real slice of life, an often brutal film which manages to glamorise Chet Baker's world as well as bear witness to his squalid and unnecessary decline. Never wallowing in melodrama or self-pity, Weber was able to bring to life a man who looked like he'd been dead for many years. In trademark Weber black and white, the highs and the lows of Baker's career are charted, leaving numerous images etched on the memory long after the plaintive soundtrack or the interviews with friends and lovers have been forgotten.

Weber's film is no throwaway exercise in style. This is first and foremost a documentary, one that works on many different levels. Moving swiftly from *cinéma vérité* to Po-Mo pop promo, the film's only narrative is the heroin-ravaged trumpet player himself. As well as following Baker from California to Oklahoma to Cannes and back, the movie includes interviews with his family, his girlfriends and various musicians who worked with him through the years. It also uses ANDY MINKSER (the boxing star of *Broken Noses*), CHRIS ISAAK, CHERRY VANILLA, FLEA of THE RED HOT CHILI PEPPERS, and other minor celebrities, models and hangers-on, as accessories to the Chet Baker life.

"When I first started to film," said Weber, "I thought about including a lot of very famous musicians, getting them to sit around and talk about Chet. But Chet was always really on the fringe – I mean he played with some great musicians, but he never hung out with those guys. I was also real tired of seeing films about personalities with a bunch of famous people telling you how wonderful they were. I liked the idea that Chet was the real star, the only star of the movie."

Perhaps in homage to the *Elvis '56* documentary based on the stunning black and white reportage pictures of ALFRED WERTHEIMER, there are scenes in *Let's Get Lost* where Baker is captured as the archetypal young soul rebel – with early footage and photographs (many by WILLIAM CLAXTON) spliced together capturing the Jesus of Cool at work in the studio. The tortured talent, blessed with generic haircut and a breathtaking profile, is a story tailor made for celluloid. (ANDY MINSKER is so physically similar to the man, he looks like the ghost of Chet Baker past.)

Also included are several archive TV appearances, including one from *The Steve Allen Show*, and clips from the movies he appeared in; things like *Hell's Horizon* and *Love at First Sight*. The 1962 movie, *All The Fine Young Cannibals*, told the story of a horny young horn player, and was originally meant for Baker, but when he got himself busted the storyline was changed and the part went instead to the singularly unhip ROBERT WAGNER. A clip is included in *Let's Get Lost* showing Wagner blowing trumpet kisses at NATALIE WOOD while a distraught GEORGE HAMILTON looks on. It is from these vintage pictures that the myth of the romantic horn player

B

stems, though watching his former lovers talking in other parts of the movie convinces you that the only relationships Chet Baker was capable of maintaining were those with his drugs and his music. In many ways he was still a child, but he could also be a nasty, manipulative, two-faced womaniser.

"Even though he could be an astonishingly manipulative person – being a drug addict you have to be like that, to get hold of money – he basically loved his music," said Weber. "All the other stuff just got in the way. Probably my greatest memory of being with him during the making of the film was being in a hotel with him in California and walking down the hall and hearing him practice through the wall. He really captured the world of solitude that so many people know – his music really kept him alive. People say the heroin did, but really it was his music. And music kept him sane."

ALL THAT JAZZ, ALL THOSE GIRLS, ALL THAT DOPE, CHET BAKER TELLS HIS STORY... THE MOST FRIGHTENING JAZZ STORY OF ALL TIME.

This was a front-page headline from one of the many tabloid stories concerning Baker that appeared during the Fifties and Sixties, He was busted countless times, and served time in Italy (in Lucca Prison), in the States (on Riker's Island), and in Britain, a country that also deported him, as did Germany. Towards the end of the Sixties he was brutally beaten up (the film recounts three different versions of the story, Baker's own being the least plausible), and with his mouth and fingers mauled (how else do you incapacitate a trumpeter?) ended up on welfare. During the Seventies and Eighties he made frequent semi-successful comebacks, his most notable achievements being an appearance on the ELVIS COSTELLO version of "Shipbuilding", and a cameo in BERTRAND TAVERNIER's *Round Midnight*. He was a man who had spent his last thirty-seven years in hotels rooms, sometimes with less than a quarter in his pocket, but his music, and his drugs, managed to keep him just afloat. And then he met BRUCE WEBER.

How had Baker first reacted to the idea of someone making a movie about his life – a movie directed by, of all things, a *fashion* photographer? Was he pleased, wary, nonplussed, angry? Did he care at all?

"Chet was always feeling people out. He'd gone through so many years of being ripped off by almost every major record company, and by managers of one shape or another, so he was checking us out for a bit, eventually, after the first section of filming, I think he knew we were really there for him, that we cared. The guy had never really held onto anything in his life. So he didn't have a lot to lose – but he wanted to hold on to what little he had. The whole crew on this film were there from the beginning right till the end – for not a lot of money – and a lot of them did it out of love and out of respect for Chet.

"Apart from anything else, for me it is a record of that generation of musicians from the West Coast – a bunch of white guys trying to be cool like the black bebop boys from back East. And these were really square guys, you know. They had cars – most of the guys in New York didn't have cars. They had real pretty blonde girlfriends. They went to the beach instead of hanging out on the streets of Harlem... real normal guys in a strange way. And all of a sudden they got caught up in this world they were interpreting as the world of jazz."

By this time Baker was no bop Adonis.

"When we started this film we wanted to save him, we wanted him to get a house, a car, a bank account, all those normal things which make life easier. We felt that would really help him, and that he'd stop taking drugs. We were naive. The more we got to know him the more we would realise that he never wanted that – and those things would never happen."

It would have been easy for Weber to exploit Baker's sudden death. A perfect ending to the movie; it would have tied up any loose ends and answered those unanswerable questions. A death is irrefutable. But Chet Baker's death isn't included in the movie, even though his family wanted Weber to shoot his funeral. "I couldn't do that, it just wouldn't have

B

been right. Chet wouldn't have like it – it's sick and stupid." No part of that film was tampered with or re-edited after Baker's death, and none of the music changed.

Let's Get Lost might explain the life of Chet Baker, but it doesn't tackle the issue of what happened on the night of May 13. That's another film altogether. According to the Amsterdam city coroner, he officially died of brain damage. RICHARD LINNETT, writing in the *Village Voice* said, "Police spokesman LEO DETERING, insisting that it was a suicide, said investigators found no evidence of a struggle and concluded that he leaped from a second floor window, about thirty feet above the ground." There are still no explanations, only conjecture, as to exactly what happened that night. One of the only certain things is that Chet Baker didn't leave a will.

Did Weber think that Chet's death was at all sinister?

"There is definitely something which wasn't right. I was in the editing room one night and got a call, from Chet. I was surprised to hear from him because I hadn't spoken to him for about a month, since we had stopped shooting in fact. He sounded really down – he said, 'I just want you to know that if something happens to me, you know, that there are these guys who have been after me. So if I die, then you'll know something's up.' But Chet hallucinated a lot at this point, and he had real paranoid delusions, so I really didn't take him seriously. He told me that his girlfriend Diane was living with this guy out in Carmel in California, which was completely untrue. I sent a girl out to Carmel to see her, and there she was, living totally alone, broke, with nothing to her name. Chet always had these weird things going on in his head. But a week after that phone call he was dead.

"I must say, though, that it was very strange that the police didn't carry out a more thorough investigation into his death – it was all handled very shabbily. All of us over here, the film crew in California and his family in Oklahoma, were given very little information. We just assumed that there would be some kind of investigation, and then an explanation. But there was nothing. I wish I could have done more, but I'm not family...and it's difficult. His wife Carol said it wasn't Chet's style to fall out of a window, and I have to agree with her. He'd get into a motorcycle accident or something, but he'd never fall out of a window."

DANNY BAKER

DAVID FROST once said that television is an invention that permits you to be entertained in your living room by people you wouldn't normally have in your home. The appeal of radio is based on an opposing principal, and when you hear someone you like on the wireless (which is what my father still insists on calling it), you start to wish they were there all the time.

So it is with Danny Baker.

Baker is the only person I've ever stopped my car for, in order to hear the end of his programme. It was about twenty years ago, and I was off to see a fashion show on a Sunday morning in London. I'd been listening to Danny's show for the whole drive, quietly nodding in awe at his ability to spin a candyfloss-like concoction from arcane pieces of pop-cultural tidbits that included the superfluous lyrics contained in a THIN LIZZY song ("Tonight there's gonna be a jailbreak, somewhere in this town..."), the evergreen appeal of LIONEL JEFFRIES, footballers spotted wearing their away strip on holiday (IAN RUSH was one guilty party), and the (totally spurious) mention of a new STEELY DAN album (the "Dan" being one of the defining obsessions of Baker's army of followers: in order to earn his respect you had to genuinely enjoy STEELY DAN's second and – in his eyes at least - greatest record, *Countdown To Ecstasy*). And because I was so transfixed by this torrent, so bewitched by this whirlwind, having arrived at my destination I circled in the Citroen for a while, and then parked in a side street until the end of his show. I felt as though I'd bunked off school to spend an hour with the Mad Hatter, curled up in the bucket-seat with a packet of Fruit & Nut and a cigarillo.

B I've always imagined Danny as a cockney version of LEONARD SACHS, the loquacious compere of *The Good Old Days,* and a man who used language as ammunition. When he was a music critic for the *NME* in the late Seventies, Danny always talked about the music he liked rather than the music he was supposed to like, and even took to extolling the virtues of CHIC when it was socially unacceptable to do so. He wasn't being contrary, he just didn't see what all the fuss was about. If someone liked a record by TODD RUNDGREN, so what? He once even devoted an entire review to the coda on a PAUL MCCARTNEY single, "Take It Away", and for that alone he deserves some sort of award. Many years ago I edited a book of music journalism – it was called *Meaty Beaty Big & Bouncy!,* a title that still makes my daughters giggle behind their Cheerios – and one of my favourite choices was a piece called "The Great Greenland Mystery", which Danny wrote about a trip to Los Angeles in 1981 to interview the JACKSONS, in which he fails to put names to faces ("Let's see. There's Michael and Tito and Marlon and... and... oh sure, Randy the little one and uh... er... Dopey, Happy and Doc. No this is serious...").

Danny has already had a stellar career, and as well as presenting television quizzes, news programmes and chat shows, writing scripts for CHRIS EVANS, and penning the occasional football-related tome, he has presented more radio shows than God has had hot dinners (actually, did they have hot dinners back then?), for GLR, Radio 1, Radio 5 Live, BBC London and Virgin Radio. When JONATHAN ROSS was suspended from Radio 2, Danny and ZOE BALL stood in for him, and there was an immediate campaign to bring Baker to the station for good. Outspoken, idiosyncratic and occasionally volatile, Danny is not exactly a safe pair of hands. Yet he remains probably the best radio presenter in Britain.

"BALTIMORE"

B

One wonders how big a city has to be, or how small a town, to have a song written about it. By now most state capitals must have had a song written about them (with the exception of Juneau and Annapolis, obviously), and even the most inconsequential conurbations have popped up in songs by the kings and queens of Americana and been celebrated by the finest minds in alt.country.

RANDY NEWMAN's "Baltimore" appeared first on his 1977 album *Little Criminals*, with the narrator of the song being a disaffected citizen of the city bemoaning the hard times that had resulted in a sharp decline in the quality of life there. It's vague social commentary, a hastily written post-mortem, but it's beautiful. No, not everyone in Baltimore liked it – online message boards are full of withering insults still, my favourite being, "Go sodomise yourself with a chainsaw, RANDY NEWMAN" – yet it very quickly started to be regarded as one of Newman's very best songs. Melancholy lyrics, a hypnotic piano riff, and a plaintive vocal make for one extraordinarily maudlin travelogue, one that could easily be called "Chicago", "New Orleans", or "The Bronx". Or indeed these days, even neighbourhoods in San Francisco or Santa Barbara. *Time* magazine got it right when they said that Newman the lyricist is a refreshing irritant. "And Newman the composer is a sweet seducer. His music is a lush amalgam of Americana." Or chalk and cheese in the same bun.

"Baltimore" was famously covered by NINA SIMONE, on her 1978 album of the same name. She recorded it when she was living in Paris, for CREED TAYLOR's CTI label (Taylor was famous for bringing bossa nova to the US, and inventing ASTRUD GILBERTO), not that she ever much cared for it. The high priestess of soul found nothing about the record to shout about, let alone eulogise – she thought she had been gentrified, tarted-up and given a "jazz" finish. "Jazz is a white term to define black people," she once said. "My music is black classical music." She complained that she didn't enjoy recording it, as she didn't have any creative control over the song selection, the arrangements, or even the cover (where – shock! – she was actually smiling). Ironically it was one of her strongest albums ever, and her version of Newman's song is seen as definitive (the songs sound autobiographical, yet all were written by other people).

On YouTube you can now find a video of Simone's version of "Baltimore", set to various scenes from *The Wire*. You can also find an Ex-Friendly "refix", a dissonant remix complete with glockenspiel and flute. Not that Nina would have liked it, as she was a purist at heart. "I do not believe in mixing of the races," she said once. "And you can quote me. I don't believe in it, and I never have. I've never changed. I've never changed my hair. I've never changed my colour, I have always been proud of myself, and my fans are proud of me for remaining the way I've always been. I married a white man one time, but he was a creep."

Afrika Bambaataa & the Soul Sonic Force

Along with Kool Herc and Grandmaster Flash, Afrika Bambaataa Aasim – named after a 19th Century Zulu chief, obviously – was one of the most influential New York DJs in the mid-Seventies, responsible in part for the birth of hip-hop (he even helped come up with the name). Brought up in the Bronx, he eventually became a gang leader, but started a community-spirited social network, which gave him access to the crowds he would soon seduce with his entrepreneurial skills. He was also one of the first to swap his record decks for the recording studio, helping to create electro by mixing Kraftwerk-inspired beats with breakbeats, rap and funk.

"Planet Rock" came out in 1982, and was one of the most influential records of the year. Four years later he released

Planet Rock - The Album, a cornerstone of the genre that includes "Lookin' For The Perfect Beat" and "Renegades Of Funk". And so electro-funk was born.

B

I met Block Party Bam once, when he was involved in the SHANGO project, and was visiting London, to play at the Camden Palace in the summer of 1984. He was a great bear of a man, and he looked like GEORGE CLINTON might have done if he'd swallowed a large fridge. Softly spoken, direct, and quite mad-looking in his octagonal sunglasses, big old hoodie, and "tennises" the size of small boats, all Bambaataa really needed to assume the disposition, if not the mantle of an African potentate was a throne. He had a sub-Mohican haircut and the word FUNK razored into the fade. The glasses gave it away, though; he wasn't so much a brother from outer space as a crazy Buddha from the stars. A Buddha or one of the BANANA SPLITS.

BAND NAMES

Every man, at some time I would imagine, has been in a pop group of one kind or another. Whether it's a loose-knit group of spotty friends at school (using jumpers for snare drums rather than goalposts), or a slightly-more-than-half-hearted attempt at forming something with a slightly longer shelf life after college or university ("No, instead of being an unemployed chemistry graduate, I thought I'd be an unemployed rock star"), many are called, but few are chosen. And while almost all of these experiments are doomed to failure, they all share one defining characteristic: every band will have a completely awful name. The FROSTIES. HERMAN AND THE TERMITES. The BAND WAGON. TONGUE AND GROOVE. And on they trot, ad nauseum (who, incidentally, I think I once supported at the Rock Garden, in London's Covent Garden, in 1979).

And while I was in at least four bands between the ages of fourteen and twenty-one, my pop career was limited to a brief

B appearance on JOHN PEEL's radio show, and a self-financed 7" ("It's Magic b/w No Consolation") which managed to be bought by approximately 360 people (well, OK, exactly 360 people, 85 of whom I knew personally). But I was certainly responsible for my fair share of terrible band names. More, maybe.

Ironically my first group didn't have a name at all, although I was so egocentric that, like PHIL COLLINS or the EAGLES' DON HENLEY, I insisted on singing even though I had to play the drums at the same time. Our signature tune was a cover of HOT CHOCOLATE's "Brother Louie" and, until MADONNA released her version of "American Pie", was the worst cover I'd ever heard. But then I was only fourteen at the time, while MADONNA was about sixty-three when she did hers.

Then, thinking I might be better off behind the scenes rather than mucking about onstage, I roadied for a while, first for a local group called HIGHWAY, and then, in 1976, for one of High Wycombe's first punk bands, DEATHWISH. We supported GENERATION X at the infamous punk venue, the Nag's Head (it was owned by RON WATTS, who also owned the 100 Club in London), and the excitement convinced me to take to the stage again. And having experimented with various (awful) punk groups (the UN, for instance, and a white reggae motorcycle band called – I kid you not – BOB HARLEY), I finally joined a British version of the B-52s, eighteen months before the B-52s actually existed, who played Motown covers, primeval ska and a selection of "original" material (most of which sounded like punked-up Motown B-sides).

The worst thing about us wasn't the music, it was our name, the DADS, a moniker apparently rejected by both the MEMBERS and SQUEEZE, as well as MADNESS. Perhaps unsurprisingly –given the time – our songs dealt with urban isolation, social paranoia and the rhythm guitarist's inability to get any woman to sleep with him, although our worst song was undoubtedly the one written by the bass player. It was called "Red Bus" and contained the immortal line, "Oh look, a red bus, I think it's coming towards us." Our first gig was in early 1978, supporting the THUNDERBIRDS in the main hall at St Martins School of Art, the same band that two and a half years previously (in an earlier incarnation as BAZOOKA JOE) had been blown off stage by the SEX PISTOLS at the same venue. Unfortunately the only thing we blew offstage that night was an over-excited student who tried to set fire to the singer's plastic dress.

So after eighteen months of this nonsense, myself and said lead singer – CORINNE DREWERY, who would later go on to form SWING OUT SISTER – split, to form another group with an equally stupid name, the TIMING ASSOCIATION. And while this event didn't exactly make the news pages of the *NME*, perhaps because of that we paid a lot more attention to our image (black), our songs (black), and our rehearsals (blacker than black). (We could tell that the mood of the nation was changing, and we wanted to try and exploit it as efficiently as possible.) We used to rehearse in a disgusting bunker under some railways arches in Leyton, in north east London, a room we shared with an equally dodgy band called – I kid you not, part two – the ARMITAGE SHANKS BAND. Which, I like to think, is the worst name for a pop group. Ever.

The thing is, even successful groups have terrible names, and I offer up the following as empirical evidence: ARCTIC MONKEYS, PHISH, LET'S GET OUT OF THIS TERRIBLE SANDWICH SHOP, MATCHBOX 20, HALF MAN HALF BISCUIT, STRAWBERRY WHIPLASH, ESTONIAN TARTAR, MR. MISTER, DEF LEPPARD, KAJAGOOGOO, CHUMBAWAMBA, LIMP BIZKIT, HOOTIE AND THE BLOWFISH, et al (OK, not all of these have been successful). And it's perhaps interesting to note that most awful band names involve either food or animals, or, in the case of FUDGE GIRAFFE, both.

JOHN BARRY

Milan fashion week June 2006. There is something of a disturbance in the bookshop in 10 Corso Como, CARLA SOZZANI's perennially hip emporium. A sort of a modern-day Biba merchandised like an Oriental bazaar, Sozzani's

B 13,000sqft boutique was still, after fifteen years, the place to go for MARIMEKKO bags, ANDY WARHOL vases, limited-edition HELMUT NEWTON prints, or impossible-to-find (and often difficult to enjoy) jazz CDs. But today the carefully considered calm is broken by a tremendous wash of strings, erupting as if from nowhere, music that shimmers with class and significance, pouring out of the speakers as if through the apertures of lactiferous ducts.

The song playing through the sound system is "007 And Counting" by John Barry, originally from the *Diamonds Are Forever* soundtrack, and as it fills the room, you are immediately transported back to a retro-future world of girls, guns and inflammable clothing. The CD playing isn't *Diamonds Are Forever*, rather the latest installment of *The Trip*, the ten-year series of trendy compilations "navigated" by celebrated DJ JOEY NEGRO. It's proof, if any were needed, that John Barry is still impossibly, ridiculously hip. This much we know: without Barry there would be no DAVID ARNOLD, no GO! TEAM, no PORTISHEAD, no "Millennium", and you can hear his influences on records by 4HERO, AIR, GOLDFRAPP, LEMON JELLY, KOOP, GROOVE ARMADA, MYLO, and MOLOKO. All are valiant citizens and direct beneficiaries of the John Barry world.

Barry was the first man to make film soundtracks sexy, the first to treat them not just as part of the movie experience, but as particular pieces of music in their own right. Music that swaggered with purpose. Back in the Sixties, when Britain's greatest film composer – with more than 120 scores for film and TV – was in his pomp, his themes epitomised glamour when glamour wasn't yet a career option, evoking a sophisticated world full of mystery, travel and sex. He did everything on a grand scale, making music both delirious and maudlin, great orchestral sweeps that made you feel as though you were gliding through space, careering down a ravine, or driving at speed along an Italian motorway.

Take away the music from any JAMES BOND film (and Barry scored eleven and worked on twelve of them), and you're left with a slightly arch caper movie. Barry gave the Bond films their edge, he made them populist and sinister at the same time. Barry's Bond themes were dark, haunting and full of foreboding. As evocations of unbound sexuality, there was nothing to touch them.

B

All the great Bond movies were scored by him: *From Russia With Love, Goldfinger, Thunderball, You Only Live Twice, On Her Majesty's Secret Service, Diamonds Are Forever, The Man With The Golden Gun, Moonraker, Octopussy, A View To A Kill,* and *The Living Daylights.* SEAN CONNERY, GEORGE LAZENBY, ROGER MOORE, and TIMOTHY DALTON may have driven the hairy-chested sports cars, but it was Barry who made them accelerate. JOHN GLEN, director of five Bond films, said, "There is a timeless quality to John's scores. He's one of the chief architects of the Bond film-making style."

Barry's music gleams with menace, and back in the Sixties and Seventies, a time before irony and self-referential art, when prefixes like ultra-, neo-, über-, super-, demi-, and mega-, were not yet necessary, Barry's soundtracks encapsulated pop's ability to transform popular culture by mere association.

Barry's music was the movie song as bachelor pad. When MICHAEL CAINE, as HARRY PALMER, makes himself coffee during the opening credits of *The Ipcress File*, you cannot now imagine it without Barry's theme. His themes were tools of seduction, too, and what better way to worm yourself into his/her affections than by sticking on the haunting overtures of *Séance On A Wet Afternoon, The Knack, Vendetta, King Rat, The Quiller Memorandum,* or *The Lion In Winter*? Think of his big, expansive scores for *Born Free* and *Dances With Wolves,* evoking majestic savannahs and prairies respectively. Think of the claustrophobic themes for *Midnight Cowboy* and *The Ipcress File.* Think *The Persuaders, Body Heat, Zulu.*

Barry fans are everywhere. JONATHAN ROSS – who was once rather obsessed with him – calls him "God", and he is revered by JARVIS COCKER, IGGY POP, CHRISSIE HYNDE, DAVID BOWIE, RADIOHEAD, and COLDPLAY. Fellini once said that *Goldfinger* was his favourite film score, while the previous Pope told

B anyone who was interested that *Dances With Wolves* was his favourite piece of music ever. In the mid-Nineties he was also the inspiration for trip-hop, seemingly a genre based on taking old John Barry records and playing them at whatever the digital equivalent of 16rpm is. When the young composer DAVID ARNOLD, who in the Nineties began his own relationship with Bond (scoring *Tomorrow Never Dies*, *The World Is Not Enough* and *Die Another Day*), came to meet Barry, he was talking to him about things Barry had no knowledge of. He was such a mine of information that he was more *au fait* with Barry's career than Barry was. "He created a whole genre that hadn't existed before," said Arnold. "'Spy Music' is the sound of John Barry." DURAN DURAN's John Taylor was the same. "He knows more about stuff that I've done than I know myself," said Barry.

It is also Barry who is largely responsible for two of the UK's biggest hits of recent years. ROBBIE WILLIAMS famously sampled "You Only Live Twice" for "Millennium", and while Barry enjoyed the money – "I made a lot" – he was still rather irritated that after Williams asked if he could "use a little something", the refrain forms the body of the song. "He said it would be a snippet!"

And then, just a few years later, KANYE WEST plundered Barry's "Diamonds Are Forever" for his blinged-up global hit, "Diamonds". It's a great record, with precision beats and a gorgeous loop, but take away Barry's production and you're left with a lot of shouting.

Barry was sanguine about all of this. "Occasionally you get a nice surprise, when someone covers your song in an extraordinary way," he said. "FRANK SINATRA did 'Born Free', TONY BENNETT did 'Walkabout', but you have no control over who does what, really. So you just hold yourself responsible for the stuff you do, and then get filthy rich on all this stuff that other people have done."

From 1980 until his death from a heart attack in January 2011, Barry lived on Centre Island, a secluded, sylvan community attached to Oyster Bay by a thin peninsula, where neighbours included BILLY JOEL and RUPERT MURDOCH. Oyster Bay is a private community policed by guards, just an hour from New York by car, and one of the most expensive and idyllic parts of Long Island. Barry's house sat in four acres on the water's edge. "It's like being in America," he said. "But not quite."

A meticulous, well-mannered and extraordinarily unassuming man, Barry talked like a mid-Atlantic MICHAEL PARKINSON, his Yorkshire drawl peppered with little Americanisms. Interviewed five years before he died, he carried not an ounce of fat, and still had echoes of the gaunt good looks of his youth. As he sat in his study, surrounded by his Oscars, his Grammys and his BAFTAs (including the BAFTA Fellowship Award he received in 2005 at the age of 71), his charming, sprightly, fourth wife Laurie darted around him, making tea and adjusting the air-con. She was twenty-two years his junior, mother of their son Jonpatrick, who was born on Barry's sixtieth birthday, and who looks a lot like his father.

In a way Barry was predestined to be a film composer, since his mother was a classical pianist and his father owned a string of cinemas. Born in 1933 in Yorkshire, he was smitten from an early age, and developed a fascination for film music from sitting in on dark matinée afternoons. One of his earliest memories is of being carried into his first film, featuring MICKEY MOUSE. Barry remembers thinking, "My father shows huge black and white mice for a living."

The innocence of his childhood ended when the Luftwaffe bombed his school, killing forty people including his headmistress, and the news that his elder brother's best friend had been shot down over Germany. There are many from his generation, like SPIKE MILLIGAN for instance, who used comedy as a way of coping with the war, but Barry's sadness manifested itself in his haunting scores. The abiding motif in all of Barry's greatest themes is melancholy. Even if the piece is up-tempo, there will still be something brooding about it. To paraphrase one critic, his music is "undercut by

B

a languorous sensuality which, in turn, is undercut by an inexorable sadness, a sense of something ominous, the pain of loss." The Sixties may have meant liberation, but most people who lived through them had already lived through the war.

Barry began his first studies of jazz composition and orchestration with BILL RUSSO of the STAN KENTON ORCHESTRA. Russo was living in Chicago and Barry was doing his National Service in Cyprus. He saw an advertisement for his correspondence course in *Downbeat* magazine, obtained some US dollars from a junk shop in Larnaca and took lessons from him for nearly a year and a half. Barry also played trumpet in the local army band, and it's this that paved the way for the brass-based James Bond sound.

On leaving the army he jettisoned his original surname, Prendergast, formed his own band, the JOHN BARRY SEVEN – specialising in instrumental music – and moved to London. It was 1958. It was then that he met ADAM FAITH, and Barry ended up producing a number of hits for him. By the end of 1959 he had a No.1 single with Faith singing "What Do You Want?". The relationship was to continue when Faith began acting in movies, when he asked Barry to score them (for the first one, *Beat Girl*, Barry was paid £250, "all in").

Then, having been asked to arrange MONTY NORMAN's theme for *Dr No*, the first James Bond film, Barry established the unique soundscape of the series, became the resident Bond composer, and the rest is history.

"When I was approached about Bond, well, they'd got this gentleman called MONTY NORMAN to write the music. They said, 'He's a songwriter, and not a very good one. They're not happy with what they've got.' So I did the JAMES BOND theme. All I knew about Bond was the cartoon strip in the *Daily Express*. Then we did *From Russia With Love*, then *Goldfinger*, and the whole thing went mad. It made it much easier for me to get good work then. If you have a successful run, everything comes to you. Nothing succeeds like success."

But while Barry acknowledged his debt to Bond, he was far fonder of the first HARRY PALMER film, *The Ipcress File*, lamenting the fact that the immediate sequels, *Funeral In Berlin* and *Billion Dollar Brain*, failed to live up to expectations. Palmer, played on screen by MICHAEL CAINE, was the anti-Bond. Bond without the frills. A kitchen-sink Bond. No less stylish, but rather more prosaic. "There was a real antihero, a real character," said Barry. "Mike Caine was great in the role and the movies should have been bigger and better than Bond. They had this enormous potential, and I think actually were a truer reflection of the times. The Bond people were smart; they made the same movie twelve times. They should have done something similar with *The Ipcress File*." Barry's score was massively influential though, and every other commission after the Palmer film involved a request for something similar (the most obvious example being MICHAEL ANDERSON's *The Quiller Memorandum*).

Predating the pop video by at least fifteen years, Barry's work is forever associated with the glamour and transcendence of international travel, which, in the early Sixties, was still something of a novelty. Listen to "You Only Live Twice" or "Thunderball" and, if you don't simply think "ROBBIE WILLIAMS" or, "that song that TOM JONES wishes he doesn't have to sing any more", your head will be filled with perfectly calibrated split-screen montages of drip-dry blondes, exploding sports cars and deftly delivered put-downs. In the Savile Row dreamworld of Swinging London, Barry didn't worry about dressing to the left or the right, he dressed on both sides. He was a bachelor king, his swordsmanship was legendary. He shared a flat in Knightsbridge with MICHAEL CAINE and TERENCE STAMP, and there was a procession of eager young fillies regularly traipsing up the stairs. "Barry was a big ladies' man," said Caine, famously.

When Barry married the actress JANE BIRKIN in 1965, *Newsweek* reported that he "drove off in his E-Type Jag with his E-Type wife".

B

Barry liked to tell an anecdote about a meal he had with "Mike" Caine, JEAN SHRIMPTON and TERENCE STAMP that culminated in the unexpected appearance of the Bond film producer HARRY SALTZMAN, who Barry had never much cared for. Saltzman didn't much care for Barry either, and had stated publicly how much he loathed Barry's theme for *Goldfinger*, a song that subsequently became a gigantic hit in more than thirty countries. At that lunch, to make amends, Stamp stood up, and in front of the whole restaurant, called Saltzman, then one of the most powerful men in Hollywood, and I quote, "a c**t".

The partying never got in the way of the work, and vice versa. Back in the Sixties he would get up at eight o'clock and work until one, walk to the King's Road, have a long lunch, maybe a siesta, and then get back in front of the piano before the round of evening parties started. He loved Italian restaurants and wine – in those days trattorias were the only restaurants that stayed open late – and made a point of keeping away from drugs. He was quick then, too. He wrote "Born Free" in twelve minutes and "Midnight Cowboy" in twenty. Sometimes it took a little longer: in Caine's biography the actor recalls being kept awake till dawn one night by Barry putting the finishing touches to "Goldfinger".

During the Seventies his lifestyle was replaced by a studiously maintained career, and in the next fifteen years he worked on nearly as many films as Caine himself (from *The Cotton Club* and *Jagged Edge* to *King Kong* and *The Deep*). Go onto Amazon and you'll find dozens of yet-to-be-deified soundtrack albums bearing his name.

In 1988, after a quarter of a century of success and good living, his oesophagus suddenly ruptured, very nearly killing him. He had been taking a specially prepared health drink made from about sixty types of berry that turned out to be dangerously toxic. A lawsuit followed, but that petered out when the company that made the drink went bankrupt. He couldn't eat solids for a year, and certainly couldn't compose. After having to turn down film after film, by the time he was

offered *Dances With Wolves* in 1990 he was back to his old
self. The score won him his fifth Oscar (the others were for
1967's *Born Free* [Best Score and Best Song], 1968's *The Lion
In Winter*, and 1986's *Out Of Africa*), although it was scant
reward for his enforced leave of absence. He began to respect
mortality though, and on the back of the soundtrack CD he
thanked more doctors than engineers or producers.

By rights, you should hear every new Barry record in the
middle of the stalls, surrounded by darkness. Whether it's the
twangy VICK FLICK guitar riff of"The James Bond Theme", the
sumptuous swells of "The Lion In Winter", or the baroque
tones of the TEN TENORS, Barry's music is most effective when
you're sitting in the middle of it, letting it swirl around you
like smoke.

Barry's music was some of the first I'd heard that had
the ability to take me – a twelve-year-old boy – to a faraway
space, letting me imagine I was in places I'd never been too,
places I probably couldn't even spell, exotic wonderlands
where I imagined they played Barry's music all day long.

There was "Space March", "Mr Kiss Kiss Bang Bang",
"Bond Below Disco Volante", and – how could we forget? –
his theme for *The Persuaders*, the 1971 Bond-on-TV irony-
fest. For many men of my generation, the title sequence was a
formative experience right up there with our first cigarette or
first kiss. TONY CURTIS. ROGER MOORE. An Aston Martin DBS.
A Ferrari Dino. Girls. What more could we want? A decade
before *Miami Vice* or *Moonlighting*, this was a show that had
a gun in its pocket and a tongue in its cheek, while Barry's
haunting theme remains attached to the period like the
broken zip on a pair of purple slacks.

Every one of Barry's Bond scores has hidden gems, lyrical
interludes or variations on a theme, delicious secrets nestling
in the middle of the second side of the soundtrack LP. Maybe
the best Bond abstraction of them all is the string-driven
"Into Vienna", from *The Living Daylights*, the great forgotten
Bond movie, and the great forgotten Bond score.

B

59

B

For Barry, strings were like water, there is a lucidity about them that makes them ideal for expression. When he wrote, he basically wrote for strings and then took it from there. Strings moved the story, he said, and strings propel you. Yet most of his music propels you, envelopes you, regardless of what form it takes. When MICHAEL CAINE makes coffee in the opening sequence of *The Ipcress File*, he uses a coffee-grinder – a novelty in Britain at the time – and it weaves in and out of Barry's theme in beautifully choreographed fashion. The coffee-grinder rubber-stamps Caine's HARRY PALMER as a cultured Francophile, yet it's Barry's music that gives him the cult-figure halo. The main refrain is played on a Hungarian cimbalom, an homage to the zither used on the main theme from *The Third Man*, – Barry's favourite film – an original poster of which hangs in his home. A type of dulcimer, a triangular box with strings that you hit with sticks – like an open piano without the keyboard – the cimbalom's melancholy sound was the Sixties incarnate.

"The most important thing about movie scoring is the atmosphere, the spirit, the uplift. Being accurate to a scene, hitting that scene's feelings accurately and giving it the sense of tragedy, joy, whatever it is. For me that's the fun of it." One scene in *Body Heat*, in which WILLIAM HURT seduces KATHLEEN TURNER, is entirely carried by Barry's music ("I'm Weak"), and must rank as one of his most successful. There is only one word of dialogue, when Turner eventually says, "Yes."

Barry said a great score is one that is able to nail the dramatic thrust of the movie, to answer the question, "What's this film about?" A composer has to be able to go about the actual writing of the music in a way that really penetrates. Music can penetrate an audience like no other aspect of the film; it can really take care of their emotions. Barry says it's how profound you make those movies that matters.

When he was scoring *Out Of Africa* the director SYDNEY POLLACK asked him to "cheer up the scenery". And that's exactly what Barry did.

"It's all down to the theme, and I won't proceed with any of the rest of it until I get that," he said. "And that theme, has to, in a certain way, touch upon the emotional nerve endings of the movie. There's no way you can listen to the theme from *Out Of Africa* and not know where that theme's from. Once you've nailed it you can do all kinds of variants on it. There's a zillion things you can do with it."

When we met, his Bond days were long past, but he wouldn't have gone back even if he had been asked to. As for the remake of *Casino Royale*, he was almost benevolent. "DANIEL CRAIG is a very good actor, probably one of the best. But that's never been a necessity for Bond. This could be the death of him! It's a fine line, that Bondian thing. SEAN [CONNERY] made it work better than anybody else. I hope he doesn't take it too seriously."

Britain's most successful film composer put his success down to consistently being able to pick the right films. The only self-aggrandising thing Barry said all afternoon was his appraisal of his ability to weed out the chaff. "Look at what I've done. Sure, I did *Howard The Duck* and a few other turkeys, but most films I chose were the right ones. I'm happy with my choices.

"Having been in the cinema with my dad, and running a family business, I've always had a good idea of what works and what doesn't. Why people laugh, why they cry. Cinema was my father's Bible and it became mine. So to me, it was the fortune of my background, and seeing movies over and over again, and loving them. I just developed this innate feeling for film music, which I'm eternally grateful for, and which has never let me down."

COUNT BASIE

A true leader of men – he led his jazz orchestra almost continuously for nearly fifty years – a great accumulator of talent, and a man who developed a highly idiosyncratic way

B with a piano – light, sparse, elegant – William "Count" Basie (jazz royalty, basically) is remembered as one of the finest exponents of swing. His sound was identified by its "jumping" beat and the contrapuntal accents of his own piano. His early Decca recordings (including "Pennies From Heaven" and "Honeysuckle Rose") are some of the most compelling blues-based swing tunes of the period. Basie would later add touches of bebop to his sound, "so long as it made sense", but he said, "it all had to have feeling". At this point he was sharing Birdland with bebop greats like CHARLIE PARKER, DIZZY GILLESPIE, and MILES DAVIS, although Basie always kept his rhythmic pulse, strict to the last,"so it doesn't matter what they do up front; the audience gets the beat". Classic Basie songs include "One O'Clock Jump" and "April In Paris" – as dull as rain this stuff ain't.

LES BAXTER

The archetypal virtual tourist, this Texan composer offered baby-boomer suburbanites the chance to explore hitherto taboo regions of illicit sex and exotic ritual, "a sonic conjurer of vicarious experience," according to DAVID TOOP, author of *Ocean of Sound*. Originally a saxophonist who performed in Californian clubs in the Forties, he went on to work as an arranger and musical director for MEL TORMÉ, NAT KING COLE, BOB HOPE, and ABBOT & COSTELLO. In 1953 he scored his first movie, a sailboat travelogue called *Tanga Tika*. He never looked back. Over the next thirty-five years he created soundtracks for dozens and dozens of films, including the *Raven, House of Usher, The Man with X-Ray Eyes, Beach Blanket Bingo, How to Stuff a Wild Bikini*, and *Wild in the Streets*. It was his own, highly personal work that made him notable, however, along with MARTIN DENNY and ARTHUR LYMAN, inventing the hyper-world of exotica.

JOSEPH LANZA notes that Baxter, along with his fellow exoticists, represented "a celebration of America's power to mould the unknown in the image of reconstructed psychosexual fantasies of GIs who had been stationed in the island during World War II". Baxter excelled at space-age bachelor pad music, creating enchanting little symphonies that conjured up exotic images of the Gold Coast, the South Pacific, the Andes, even other planets. "What I like about Baxter is his overkill orchestration in the fine tradition of CARL ORFF, BUSBY BERKELEY, and MAGMA," says former Dead Kennedy JELLO BIAFRA in *Incredibly Strange Music Volume II* (Re/Search 1994). A quiet five-piece cocktail number by [MARTIN] DENNY will, in Baxter's hands, becomes a full orchestra with dozens of deep baritone voices singing *ooh* and *aah* choruses to create the mood of the jungle. If Les Baxter decides to do a folk album, he won't use one person with a guitar – no, he'll use eight guitars and a banjo player *plus* his orchestra!Move over, KINGSTON TRIO – here comes the Kingston family.

Toward the end of Baxter's career, the soundtrack business dried up, so he wrote a considerable amount of music for theme parks and seaworlds. As DAVID TOOP suggests, "Surely the ultimate PoMo job." He died in 1996, aged seventy-three.

THE BEASTIE BOYS

The formidable, downwardly mobile, New York hip-hop trio are standard-bearers of rap reinvention, their success proof that it sometimes pays to overestimate your audience. Politically indulgent and socially minded, back in the Eighties they were once just wigga wannabes, baseball-capped monkeys with ear-to-ear grins. CHARLIE PORTER wrote the following blog for *GQ* in 2011, highlighting the furore that surrounded the band when they first came to the UK:

"Strange how quickly a musical message is diluted. In the recording studio, at gigs, fire is felt. But squish that power down into a cassette, and sell it in Woolworth's in Lyme Regis, and the same music becomes impotent. In 1987, thanks to an on-stage inflatable penis and jokes about leukaemia, Beastie

B

Boys were supposed to be the hardest band in the world. Yet the inadequacy of my cassette – scratched case, easily creased inlay card, chewed tape after a couple of plays – belied what we now know: the Beasties are actually the softest men ever born.

"*Licensed To Ill* was released in late 1986 when I was thirteen, a time of teenage spurts. My musical tastes had already been formed by a lucky early discovery of PRINCE and GRACE JONES. Yet instinct suggested there must be something more, so on a summer family holiday of fossil hunting and National Trust gardens, I tried to acclimatise myself to songs with alien titles: 'Rhymin' And Stealin'', 'She's Crafty', 'Slow And Low'. The fit was always going to be wrong: as a middle-class boy who knew his lot, I had little gel with these nice men trying to be nasty.

"The disconnect became more apparent when the abuse of Volkswagens began. This was a rite-of-passage crime – the theft of the circular VW logo to wear as a pendant in emulation of Beastie Boy, MIKE D. Of course, few in Britain actually had them around their necks, but committing the actual damage itself seemed to prolong this pretence that posh white boys could be thugs. I'm anti-stealth by nature, a klutz who could never perform discreet and swift acts of vehicular terrorism. If I was to crouch in front of someone's bonnet, I'd get caught. So when Volkswagen attempted to stem the damage being done to their cars, I was their sucker. You filled in the form on the advert, sent it off, and in return a genuine VW medallion could be yours. Beastie Boys toughness via the Post Office!

"Except when the package arrived, it felt like the entrails of a scene I had no right to follow. Rather than sending out genuine badges, Volkswagen distributed a tiny, flat key-ring, the perfect circle of MIKE D's medallion corrupted by a notch through which you could only thread a thin chain. To wear it would be to admit that you had only ever liked this band in a desperate attempt to be something you are not. Lesson learnt: don't ever emulate."

THE BEATLES' A HARD DAY'S NIGHT

The rock heritage industry is in danger of eating its own tail, swallowing its cash cow, and over-cooking the various geese that laid the golden eggs. It has exploited its back catalogue so much that speaking as someone who has enthusiastically consumed pop music for forty years, I'm not sure what there is left to eat. Why? Because you and I have eaten it all, that's why, every last morsel – every last alternative version, every last outtake, extended remix, bootleg mash-up and unnecessary re-recording. Rock's back catalogue is, in effect, moribund.

The heritage rock press looks rather weary too, forced into an almost constant celebration of glories from the past; how many more times can you stomach a re-evaluation of LEONARD COHEN, JAPAN, or TOM WAITS? How often have you read an in-depth, blow-by-blow account of the making of the "White Album", how many times have you read a feature about the best live double albums ever made?

Talking of the "White Album", this is currently the Beatles LP it's OK to like. Twenty years ago the received wisdom was that *Sergeant Pepper* was the jewel in the crown, the highlight of the cannon, and then around fifteen years ago the critics started to say that *Revolver* was the real pinnacle of the band's creativity (the formative flushes of psychedelia, a proper spread of styles, etc), but in the last decade it is the "White Album" – a double album that hitherto had been considered a mediocre curate's egg – that has been the subject of the most re-evaluation. According to the powers that be – rock critics over the age of thirty-five – *The Beatles* is not only the best Beatles album ever made, it is also, bar the odd BOB DYLAN LP, the greatest album ever made by anyone.

Which is obviously not the case. Oh no. Right now the best Beatles album is actually *A Hard Day's Night*, the soundtrack album to the Fab Four's second film, recorded in

B

July 1964. It was not only the first Beatles album to feature entirely original compositions, but – while PAUL MCCARTNEY was (is) undoubtedly the stronger songwriter – was the high water mark of JOHN LENNON's Sixties songwriting; never again would he scale these heights, never again would he match McCartney for sheer volume and variety. The second side contains the best selection of Lennon songs on any Beatles LP: songs which actually suggest he could have gone in many other directions had the drugs, the apathy and the cynicism not devoured him. McCartney would go on to write better, more iconic songs, but this album shows the band at their cohesive best.

And as for next year? Well, by then it will probably be the turn of *With the Beatles*.

THE BEATLES' *EVEREST*

In my book *iPod, Therefore I Am*, I (fancifully) wrote at length about the album the Beatles might have made had they not disintegrated. It's 1970, and with their friendships stretched to breaking point, John, Paul, George and Ringo come together at Abbey Road to record one last album. The result was *Everest*. Side One: "My Sweet Lord", "Maybe I'm Amazed", "Cold Turkey", "Come And Get It", "It Don't Come Easy", "The Long And Winding Road". Side Two: "Instant Karma", "Love", "What Is Life", "Teddy Boy", "Let It Be", "Working Class Hero". EP Side One: "Wah-Wah", "Across The Universe". EP Side Two: "All Things Must Pass", "Singalong Junk".

BECK

Having made his slacker anthem "Loser" in 1994, Beck appeared saddled with it (much like RADIOHEAD were with "Creep"), and felt he needed to tell everyone how clever he is.

Which he's been doing ever since. A recording studio maverick with an apparently insatiable appetite for the "wacky" juxtaposition, BECK HANSEN makes funkified bouillabaisse with determination and panache – rim shots sounding out around the world. There are many entry points into Beck's world (and for many it's 2002's *Sea Change*); mine is "Devils Haircut" from 1996's *Odelay*, a song I wished ELVIS had been around to cover.

BELLE AND SEBASTIAN

For a while they were a cottage industry of whimsy, a wry foray, and a winsome bleat. *The Boy With The Arab Strap* (1998) is probably their best work, but I lost my copy soon after I bought it (I think one of my children hid it somewhere, not that they'd ever heard it – at least I don't think so), and have never replaced it.

TONY BENNETT

Tony Bennett is the man FRANK SINATRA once acknowledged as the king, the "real" best singer of his generation. "The high point for me in my career was when Sinatra called me his favourite performer in the Fifties," said Bennett famously. "And I've been sold out ever since." In a 1965 *Life* magazine interview, Sinatra said that, "For my money, Tony Bennett is the best singer in the business. He excites me when I watch him. He moves me. He's the singer who gets across what the composer has in mind, and probably a little more."

Sinatra kept saying it until he died. "I remember he was interviewed late in life by *New York* magazine," said Bennett when I met him in 2007 in New York. "And the interviewer said, 'Everyone listens to you. Who do you listen to?' And he just said, 'Benedetto'."

B

At the age of eighty-five Bennett appeared to have lost little of his edge, and the first thing you noticed about him when you watched him sing in concert was how technically remarkable he was. His voice was completely undiminished by age and at a stage when a lot of singers would be attempting to disguise their failings, or bend the songs to suit their range, Bennett picked up every song and put it in his pocket. That's mine, he appeared to be saying, I own that. And he did. Bennett was a better singer at eighty-five than MICK JAGGER will be, or ELVIS COSTELLO, or BRUCE SPRINGSTEEN, or PETE DOHERTY probably will be come to that. He's already a better singer than either BOB DYLAN or JONI MITCHELL, two performers who are twenty years younger than him.

Seeing Tony Bennett in concert now is probably not that different from what it was like thirty or forty years ago. Listening to him sing "The Way You Look Tonight" or "The Shadow Of Your Smile" in the Albert Hall in 2006 was as intimate an experience as you can have with another grown man with his clothes on. Even when he scats – incidentally these days underground slang for an especially gross sexual practice – it feels as though he's doing it in your front room (singing, that is). Bathed in blue light, swaying in front of his jazz quartet in his midnight blue DOUG HAYWARD suit, his white Brioni shirt and his semi-detached pewter thatch, he seemed personally thrilled to have made it to the end of each song, occasionally even applauding himself.

Many of the songs from his classic period – including "I Left My Heart In San Francisco", "This Is All I Ask" and "Tender Is The Night" – were recorded with a character-defining echo, and Bennett finds it easy to replicate this on stage, giving them even more of an authentic feel, and drawing the audience stealthily back to the past. His manner is easy too – when Bennett talks it's almost as if he's accompanied by a lugubrious drummer quietly brushing a crash cymbal in the background, a metronomic measure of the singer's importance and worth.

He has released over 105 albums (he once made three albums a year for twenty-three years straight), the most recent of which won a Grammy. Whereas most duet albums between fading or ageing stars and young pretenders, or those with slightly more commercial clout, are usually uneven affairs. Bennett's most recent collaborations – collated on *Duets: An American Classic*, released to honour his eightieth birthday, and including contributions from JOHN LEGEND, BONO, DIANA KRALL, ELTON JOHN and the DIXIE CHICKS among others – are little short of a triumph. This is largely because Bennett can still sing, and has enough of a range left to convincingly attempt many classic songs from his past. He always sang in a straight line, which has meant that he hasn't had to adapt the way his sings as much as other crooners his age (not that there are any comparable ones left).

He also has acres and acres of class to go with the acres and acres of silk suits in his wardrobe. When once roused from his hotel bed by an earthquake, he famously changed into a three-piece suit before joining the evacuation. "That is from getting on-stage; you learn how to dress fast if you have to. But actually I don't have that many clothes, just essentials. If you go to an expensive tailor, they last a long time, and if you need to change them they fix them for you. It's better that way."

And Tony should know. Truly, Bennett is the godfather of smooth, the perennial role model of white cool. Having had such a lengthy career, Bennett hasn't been restricted – or restricted himself – by genre. He's crooned, he's done pop, and in the Sixties he traded in his torch songs for lifestyle ballads as soon as it became expedient to do so. And while the phrase "jazz singer" might defy definition, there is more than the jazz singer about him. He was heavily influenced by jazz from an early age – he loved LOUIS ARMSTRONG and BILLIE HOLIDAY – and over time he worked with COUNT BASIE, HERBIE MANN, CANNONBALL ADDERLEY, STAN GETZ, BILL EVANS and many, many more. He also had a renaissance of sorts, and having been out of favour for much of the Seventies and Eighties, in the early Nineties – due principally to the *Unplugged* album, featuring ELVIS COSTELLO and K.D. LANG – he was reintroduced to a completely new generation of fans. In short, he has become

B

classic American popular music's most powerful ambassador to the generations raised on rock.

He appears to be as popular in London as he is in New York, and in both cities he is greeted like a benevolent uncle whenever he takes to the streets. And when you meet him – big smile, leather skin, Roman profile – benevolence is one of the key words that spring to mind. Another is statesmanlike, another is warm, and yet another is cool. But above all else, Bennett is friendly. Keen to interact. Still enjoying the benefits of long-term acclaim, and still wanting to talk about it. Also – and this is something particular to his generation of performers – he is genuinely effusive about performers he likes and admires. *GQ*'s ROBERT CHALMERS interviewed Bennett in 1994, and he said that when praising other singers, Bennett lapsed into the extravagantly sentimental vernacular that afflicts light entertainers of his generation. A friend of Chalmers had offered him a bet on the time of Bennett's first use of the adjective "wonderful". The singer delivered slightly later than expected, in one minute twenty seconds.

But there's a level of sincerity with Bennett that it is impossible to be cynical about. Recently he said about Sinatra, "The first time I met him was after I was established as a successful recording artist in my own right. I was given the summer replacement spot for PERRY COMO on his Kraft Music Hall television show. Since I was still new at show business, I was nervous as heck. I thought I'd take a big chance and seek Sinatra's advice. Sinatra was over at the Paramount, and I decided to visit him backstage. A friend of mine warned me not to go because Sinatra had a reputation for being tough. But I took a deep breath and showed up at his dressing room. The Sinatra I met was quite different from the one I had expected. Sinatra was wonderful to me. I asked him, 'How do you handle being nervous onstage?' He said, 'It's good to be nervous. People like it when you're nervous. It shows you care. If you don't care, why should they?' And then he told me to stay away from the cheap songs. It was great advice. I've followed it since."

Anthony Benedetto was born in Astoria, Queens, New York City on August 3, 1926, the son of an Italian-American seamstress and a grocer who had emigrated, with thirty-five dollars in his pocket, from Podàrgoni, a rural eastern district of the southern Italian city of Reggio Calabria. (Bennett likes to say that Astoria is a lot like Acton, in London, which he visited a lot when he lived here, albeit in Mayfair, in the late Sixties.) With two siblings and a father who was ailing and unable to work, the family grew up in poverty. His father died when Tony was just ten years old. With an uncle as a tap dancer in vaudeville, he had an early window into show business, and by the time his father died he was already singing and performing. Leaving school at sixteen to support his family, he set his sights on a professional singing career, becoming a singing waiter in several Queens Italian restaurants. His singing career was interrupted when he was drafted into the US Army in November 1944 during the final stages of World War II, seeing active duty in France and Germany (in 1945 Bennett's platoon was involved in the liberation of a Nazi concentration camp near Landsberg in Germany). In March 1945 he joined the front line, an experience he describes as a, "Front-row seat in hell. Anybody who thinks that war is romantic obviously hasn't gone through one."

Back in Civvy Street, he returned to waiting tables, singing when he could, often using his voice to imitate STAN GETZ's saxophone and ART TATUM's piano. In 1950, having been championed by the likes of PEARL BAILEY and BOB HOPE, he started making serious inroads, and in 1951 had his first hit with "Because of You", swiftly followed by "Cold Cold Heart" and "Blue Velvet". He became so famous so quickly that when he got married in 1952, to an Ohio art student and jazz fan, PATRICIA BEECH, two thousand female fans dressed in black gathered outside the ceremony at New York's St Patrick's Cathedral in mock mourning.

There followed ten years of solid success, a decade in which he became something of an American institution, successful both in suburbia and the urban world of jazz. In

B

1962, Bennett released "I Left My Heart in San Francisco," and although it only reached No.19 on the Billboard Hot 100, it spent close to a year on various other charts, and created a swirl of media attention. Ironically, it was initially only a B-side, and not one that Bennett much cared for. The album of the same title was a top five hit, and both the single and album achieved gold record status. The song won Grammy Awards for Record of the Year and Best Male Solo Vocal Performance, and quite quickly became known as Bennett's signature song. In 2001, it was ranked 23rd on an RIAA/NEA list of the most historically significant songs of the 20th Century. (When Bennett was the guest star of *The Muppet Show*, there was the following exchange between the two grouchy old men on the balcony, Statler: "What's the name of that famous song Tony Bennett sings?" Waldorf: "'I Left My Heart in San Francisco'." Statler: "Big deal. I left my teeth in Minneapolis.")

The first law of American politics is, "Define your opponent before he gets the chance to define himself." If you were to trace Tony Bennett's career back to his heyday, he wasn't defined by anyone, because he wasn't deemed to be a threat. In fact he wasn't even defined by himself. That's not to say he was anodyne, only that he didn't make as much noise as his contemporaries, didn't court the same sort of publicity. But after a while, Bennett would begin to ask himself: who needs personal publicity when everyone in the world knows who you are? During the Sixties he had such huge success – big records, big gigs, lots of awards – and even though the world was fawning at the feet of the electric guitar and the counter-cultural scream, Bennett became a torch-bearer of the classic American song. Along with Sinatra, he was the old-school crooner it was hip to like.

These days Bennett is very much the technician, a master craftsman, an old-fashioned singer who doesn't let his back-story get in the way of his performance. If you look at the NICK CAVES, or the KEITH RICHARDS, or the LOU REEDS of this world, they are all keen on allowing their experience to show on their face, eager to let the world know that they have supped from the cup of human unkindness, and come out the other side – not unscathed, but ultimately as better men. Bennett doesn't wear his wounds on his face at all, and doesn't appear to need the extravagances of his long life – and extravagances there certainly have been – for him to feel validated and happy in his skin. He is simply pleased to still be able to do the one thing that continually makes him happy, which is sing in front of an audience. He lived through the Depression, through WWII, and his conversation is based on the premise that you should accentuate the positive at all times.

"I'm happy because I'm doing what I love," he told me. "My son Danny did such a good job sorting out my finances that I could have retired ten years ago quite comfortably, but I like doing it. I like entertaining people. Also, I'm still learning. I just try and get better and better and I try and learn something every time I sing. It's true. You learn more control the older you get, you learn where to place your voice for the best effect, you learn how to get the most out of it."

He has lived on Central Park South for the last fifteen years, in a beautiful and specious fifteenth floor apartment that looks right over the park. He has his own painting studio here, full of gifts, mementos, and at its entrance a photographic portrait of the singer by DAVID HOCKNEY. The living room is nearly the size of a five-a-side football pitch, is carefully decorated, and is full of flowers and framed paintings (many his own). On the window sill is an enormous leather-bound book the size of a paving slab, full of birthday greetings celebrating his seventy-fifth. It's an astonishing collection, with notes from them all: MOHAMMED ALI, BILL CLINTON, BARBRA STREISAND, DAVID HOCKNEY, JOHN TRAVOLTA, LIZA MINNELLI, MADONNA, DONALD TRUMP, BARBARA SINATRA, ROBERT DeNIRO and AL PACINO (same page), PAUL McCARTNEY, BETTE MIDLER, HARRY BELAFONTE, HARRY CONNICK JR., JULIE ANDREWS, and pretty much everyone you've ever heard of. A few doors along he has another studio, this one full of easels, paintbrushes and semi-completed canvasses. As we walk to

B one of his favourite restaurants – Michael's – he is stopped every ten yards or so; people point, smile, whisper or shout his name, and generally treat him like the properly loved person he is. At Michael's he orders the scallops, some still water and then a decaffeinated black coffee, which still seems to me to be exactly what you imagine Tony Bennett might eat – what Tony Bennett ought to eat.

It was DEAN MARTIN who told him to always order half the amount you want to eat, and he talks about Martin nearly as often as he mentions Sinatra – you don't get the impression he's name-dropping as such, just talking about old friends who aren't around anymore. His conversation is rich with names from the past. Want to hear a story about STEVIE WONDER, MADONNA, or JUDY GARLAND, or about how ELLA FITZGERALD turned down a meeting with PICASSO because she had some dry cleaning to pick up? Just ask Tony. DEAN MARTIN once took Bennett to an Italian restaurant in Manhattan, back in the late Fifties. As soon as they sat down to order, Martin noticed something odd about the menu – on it were pictures and eulogies to Sinatra, SAMMY DAVIS JR. and himself, but nothing about Bennett. He promptly called for the owner, and proceeded to give him a hard time, getting him to promise to put something on the menu about his friend, or even to name a dish after him. "I've even got the name for you right here," deadpanned Martin, "Rigatoni Bennett."

Sinatra has stayed with him in so many ways throughout his career. As the Seventies turned into the Eighties, Bennett was asked to do a show at Radio City in New York called, "The Night Of One Hundred Stars". The singer was meant to be brought out on stage in a horse-drawn Central Park carriage, and Bennett was worried that the animal might get spooked by the lights or the crowd and throw him into the orchestra pit. ORSON WELLES was backstage that night, smoking a large cigar and watching Bennett start to crumble with anxiety. With perfect grace he went up to Bennett and started telling him what a great, great singer he was. "I go to every party at Sinatra's house, and he plays nothing but Tony Bennett records," he said, beaming at Bennett. After than, Bennett was pulled out onto the stage and gave a sterling performance.

B

"I still get a little nervous before performing," he said. "If you're nervous, and the audience can see it, they know you care," he continued, echoing Sinatra. "You don't want to forget a lyric, you don't want to make a mistake. I still get butterflies. You can try and judge an audience but you can only really judge things by the applause."

Bennett is the last link that any of us has to that bygone age of supper-clubs, silver cigarette cases, snap-brim hats, and old-school ratpackery – even if he wasn't a member of Sinatra's notorious gang himself. In a special issue of *Life* magazine, published to celebrate the tenth anniversary of Sinatra's death, Bennett is quoted as saying, "I wasn't in the Rat Pack. I was in New York, they were out there. I had my singing and my painting, and with the hours they kept – whoa! – it's just as well I wasn't in that scene."

He could tell Sinatra stories all day, "Sinatra invited me once to his birthday party in LA. I was young and I felt great about it. But when I got there, the Rat Pack were all in the kitchen laughing their heads off. And in the living room were all these great actors – GREGORY PECK, SIDNEY POITIER, SEAN CONNERY, and all these elegant actors and actresses, and I ended up in the card room. Why was I in the card room? I didn't want to play cards, I wanted to talk to the actors! But he'd actually seated me next to the head of the Bank of America. He thought that was funny. We never spent that much time together, but he helped me so much, got me engagements, got me work in the hotels for years. He was good to me. He was my master. He even said he made love listening to my music."

Today, Tony Bennett is the master – the custodian, almost – of the great American songbook, those timeless classics written mostly in the Thirties, Forties, and Fifties by COLE PORTER, IRVING BERLIN, GEORGE and IRA GERSHWIN, JOHNNY MERCER, RICHARD RODGERS, and the like. Presidents might come and go, but Tony Bennett is Hollywood royalty. He is

B simply the most famous singer of his kind still performing. You hear him in the airport when you land in New York. You hear him in taxi cabs. You even hear him in hotel lobbies. In fact by the time you check in you can feel as though Tony Bennett is the soundtrack of Manhattan. And there is a sense that when Bennett goes, those days will be gone forever.

"Fifty years from now all that music, all those songs, they'll be our classical music," he said. "Nothing will ever match it. Nothing. There were never more beautiful popular songs ever. There's an intelligence there that you just don't get with modern music. And as for rap, it's just talking. Rap isn't music, it's just speaking. It's one note, there is no harmony. Good songs are like good clothes. They last, and they never go out of style."

"Everything he sings is utterly confidential, completely distinctive," said ELVIS COSTELLO a few years ago. "He's always done the songs he loves, and by becoming available again he is introducing those songs to a generation who've never heard them before."

The man with the basking-shark smile is all solicitation and easy charm, and speaks softly because he doesn't need to talk any louder. And although he has a reputation as a stylish man who takes great care with the way he looks and conducts himself, he isn't ostentatious, he doesn't have a property portfolio, and doesn't even drive a car, "If I'm playing Carnegie Hall and it's not raining, I'll walk." He nearly went bankrupt in the Seventies but is remarkably anti-acquisitive for someone of his vintage. He has a simple work ethic. "The studio isn't a clubhouse," he once said. "We're here to work. Singing intimately is almost like thinking into a microphone, so it helps to have the song buried inside you." Bennett practises a song for days, weeks, before he records it, and never goes into the studio unprepared. He admires professionalism, too. The fact that ELTON JOHN took just thirty-one minutes to exit his limo, record "Rags To Riches" for Bennett's *Duets* album, and return to his limo, as one critic said, is mentioned around Bennett's studio as if it were a historic sexual conquest.

Since his brush with cocaine in the Seventies – a period he understandably has little interest in retrawling – he has kept the darkness at arm's length, and has been steadfast about living the good life rather than the high life. "When you achieve celebrity," he said a few years ago, "it takes a long time to live with that helium in the brain. You need lead weights to hold you down." He admits to, "Moderate drug use," back at some point in the past, "but then the whole country did. You have to remember that this was a time of MARTIN LUTHER KING being assassinated, BOBBY KENNEDY and JACK KENNEDY too, and it really smashed America. The whole country went out and did things. We were devastated about what was happening to our people, and so we... we tried drugs. But I never had a habit. I was never hung up on it."

When I mentioned that AMY WINEHOUSE was a huge fan of his, he looked warily across the table, and put down his fork. "You know, this encouragement of drug-induced music is so bad. I've seen so many friends, so many great artists who have died as a result of drugs, it shouldn't be glamorised by anyone. Life is short enough as it is, believe me. I'm trying to make it longer, not shorter."

He has political opinions too, and every now and then shares them. You never know whether entertainers will talk about their political beliefs, even if they've expressed them in the past, and I felt slightly nervous about bringing them up with Bennett, but he answered in much the same leisurely way as he had when I asked him if he wanted to try some of my Cobb Salad (now why on earth did I do that? What idiot would think that Tony Bennett would want to eat a forkful of his salad?).

He has endorsed Obama, and when we met was organising to sing at the Democratic Convention. He's always been a liberal democrat, and talks about corporate greed as though it were a Republican policy. "Ownership used to be controlled in the United States, but when Reagan came along, you could buy as much of anything as you wanted if you had enough money. I love America, and we're the only country where the

B

constitution states that the country is owned by the public. But it doesn't much feel like that these days. These days if you say you're a liberal, people think you're a communist. People are so ignorant."

He was not afraid to criticise Bush either, and having been a pacifist since he came back from WWII, hated the fact that his country is in Iraq. "These guys are crazy. We've had Cambodia, Vietnam, Iraq, and it's a terrible thing for America to be hated around the world. It's never been like this before. Which is why we need a change, which is why we need Obama."

Having spent an afternoon with Tony Bennett, I got a very strong sense that he is a moralist of sorts, at least a traditionalist, a man who believes in standing up for what he thinks is good and honourable and sensible and decent and particular. He is rich but not ostentatious. After a sixty-year career he is still hip but couldn't be less full of himself. And to look at him, in his pale blue linen jacket, white shirt, club tie and navy slacks, you see a man who's going to get dressed up no matter what day of the week it is. Because he wants to do the right thing.

Bennett's longevity has been the result of many things, not least his decision to dump the saccharine songs he started out performing early in his career, moving on to classic ballads and torch songs as well as immersing himself in the world of jazz, working with STAN GETZ, COUNT BASIE, BILL EVANS, and other icons of pop's discordant flipside. He still feels jazz is not taken seriously enough by either record companies or radio stations, and – irrationally perhaps – thinks the industry's attitude towards it is borderline racist. "People are scared of jazz in the same way they are scared of blacks moving into their neighbourhood," he said. "The big corporations think white, they don't think black."

When his career hit a brick wall, it was kick-started again in the Eighties by his son Danny (from his first marriage), who became his manager and brilliantly plotted his father's resurrection, transforming him from a nostalgia act to an icon of the golden age of cool, the elder statesman of smooth. He re-signed him to Columbia Records, got him on the *David Letterman Show*, and began issuing edicts about quality control. The album that really sealed his comeback was the MTV *Unplugged* album in 1995, on which Bennett duetted with ELVIS COSTELLO and KD LANG; while the event that did the same trick was the Glastonbury festival in 1998, when he appeared alongside BOB DYLAN and PULP (on the way to the stage he walked over bales of hay as if they were a red carpet, solely to save his suit from the mud). He was also the first real-life character on *The Simpsons*.

Life is still full for Bennett. He has been married three times, and finally married his long-term girlfriend SUSAN CROW in 2006. He recorded a cameo in the Hollywood series *Entourage* ("It's silly," he said), was a guest on ELVIS COSTELLO's Sundance/Channel 4 Show *Spectacle* (produced by DAVID FURNISH), recorded a jazz album with STEVIE WONDER, and released his second Christmas album soon after we met ("It's happy," he says, "not religious").

When he isn't singing, he's painting. He paints under his real name, Anthony Benedetto, selling pictures for up to $50,000. "His paintings cleave determinedly to his philosophy of optimism and beauty," said a critic a few years ago, and while you sense this wasn't a ringing endorsement, it's a fair enough approximation of his work. "I learnt from DUKE ELLINGTON. He said, do two things, don't do one. And it was so wonderful, because when I sing, after a while, I get burnt out. So I paint. Painting is total therapy for me. I sing, and then I paint to slow down. It's a different tempo, and it gives me space."

The singer still practises every day, "Because you have to. Whenever an old singer wobbles it means he's not trying hard enough, and you've got to care. You've got to take care of yourself, too. Singing is athletic, so I make sure I run and walk regularly and practice my breathing. If you don't, then it's all gonna fall apart. If you don't do your scales, on the first day you can hear it. On the second day the band will hear it, and on the third day the public will hear it."

B

When I asked him what he thinks it is about the Tony Bennett he knows that has kept people coming back to see him all these years, he smiles and says, in the softest of his voices, "You know what? I'm anti-demographic, and I appeal to all ages, which good music ought to. I can only go by the applause. And I'm still getting it... You know all those entertainers who say they don't read their reviews, well they're lying. But the most important critics are always the public. Richard Rodgers once said to me, if the audience like it, go to sleep on it. And I do. I can't analyse it. It's the applause."

BEYONCÉ

"Oui, c'est mois, Miss Polyvalent! Xx"

JAMES BLAKE

One of the most experimental artists of the 21st Century so far, Blake is a suburban twenty-something intent on doing everything his own way. His version of LESLIE FEIST'S 2007 album track "Limit To Your Love" was a baby hit in October 2010, but it in no way prepared anyone for his eponymous 2011 album. Full of distorted dub, incomprehensible vocal loops, fractured sub-bass, and general electronic wizardry. When I first put it into the car CD player, I thought it might be broken, as it sounded a little like those CDs that skip so much they appear to be eating the songs they're playing. Basically James Blake makes polite gonzo dubstep. In a good way.

BLONDIE

B

Though DEBORAH HARRY, with her metaphorical and literal appropriation of platinum blonde hair, spray-on micro-skirts and melodic monosyllabic pop, became the most acceptable – and ultimately the most successful – of all the punk pin-ups, she never tried to hide the fact that her iconographic hair was dyed; she was a punk, after all, and on the cover of the first Blondie LP you can clearly see her brown roots. Blondie's tongue was firmly in its collective cheek. Even their name was a giveaway – a band called Blondie fronted by a girl who obviously wasn't. DEBBIE HARRY may have been a sex kitten, but she was certainly no bimbo, and set about exploiting her sexuality before anyone else got a chance.

From the beginnings of the group, Harry was always toying with the ambiguity of pop iconography and the implications of sexual role-playing. The endless Monroe comparisons were taken with liberal pinches of salt by both Harry and her boyfriend, band member CHRIS STEIN. The irony was eclipsed when Blondie went on to become one of the most commercially viable pop bands of the late Seventies – the supreme global wet dream (they were also one of the first groups to successfully fuse disco and punk).

THE BLUES

Found on the Internet, and subsequently published by *GQ*, *The Word* and possibly others.

Writing and singing the blues: some guidelines.

1. Most Blues begin, "Woke up this morning..."

B

2.   "I got a good woman" is a bad way to begin The Blues, unless you stick something nasty in the next line like, "I got a good woman, with the meanest face in town."

3.   The Blues is simple. After you get the first line right, repeat it. Then find something that rhymes – sort of. "Got a woman with the meanest face in town. Yes, I got a woman with the meanest face in town. Got teeth like MARGARET THATCHER, and she weigh 500 pound."

4.   The Blues is not about choice. You stuck in a ditch, you stuck in a ditch. Ain't no way out.

5.   Blues cars: Chevys, Fords, Cadillacs, and broken-down trucks. Blues don't travel in Volvos, BMWs, or Sport Utility Vehicles. Most Blues transportation is a Greyhound bus or a southbound train. Walkin' plays a major part in the Blues lifestyle. So does fixin' – to die.

6.   Teenagers can't sing The Blues. They ain't fixin' to die yet. Adults sing The Blues. In Blues, "adulthood" means being old enough to get the electric chair if you shoot a man in Memphis.

7.   Blues can take place in New York City but not in Hawaii or any place in Canada. Hard times in Minneapolis or Seattle is probably just clinical depression. Chicago, St Louis and Kansas City are still the best places to have The Blues. You cannot have The Blues in any place that don't get rain.

8.   A man with male pattern baldness ain't The Blues. A woman with male pattern baldness is. Breaking your leg 'cos you were skiing is not The Blues. Breaking your leg 'cos a alligator be chompin' on it is.

9. You can't have no Blues in an office or a shopping mall. The lighting is wrong. Go outside to the parking lot or sit by the dumpster.

10. Good places for The Blues: a) The highway, b) The jailhouse, c) An empty bed, d) At the bottom of a whiskey glass.

11. Bad places for The Blues: a) Nordstrom's, b) Gallery openings, c) Ivy League institutions, d) Golf courses.

12. No one will believe it's The Blues if you wear a suit, 'less you happen to be an old ethnic person, and you slept in it.

13. You have the right to sing The Blues if: a) You older than dirt, b) You blind, c) You shot a man in Memphis, d) You can't be satisfied.

14. You don't have the right to sing The Blues if: a) You have all your teeth, b) You were once blind but now can see, c) The man in Memphis lived, d) You have a pension fund.

15. Blues is not a matter of colour. It's a matter of bad luck. TIGER WOODS cannot sing The Blues. SONNY LISTON could.

16. If you ask for water and your darlin' give you gasoline it's The Blues.

17. Other acceptable Blues beverages are: a) Cheap wine, b) Whiskey or bourbon, c) Muddy water, d) Nasty black coffee.

18. The following are *not* Blues beverages: a) Perrier, b) Chardonnay, c) Snapple, d) Slim-Fast.

B

19. If death occurs in a cheap motel or a shotgun shack, it's a Blues death. Stabbed in the back by a jealous lover is another Blues way to die. So is the electric chair, substance abuse and dying lonely on a broke-down cot. You can't have a Blues death if you die during a tennis match or while getting liposuction.

20. Some Blues names for women: a) Sadie, b) Big Mama, c) Bessie, d) Fat River Dumpling.

21. Some Blues names for men: a) Joe, b) Willie, c) Little Willie, d) Big Willie.

22. Persons with names like Michelle, Amber, Debbie and Heather can't sing The Blues no matter how many men they shoot in Memphis.

23. It don't matter how tragic your life: if you own even one computer, you cannot sing The Blues.

BLUR

Parklife, the 1994 album that infused Britpop with a real sense of self, could easily have swayed into the arch; it was originally going to be called *Soft Porn*, with a photograph of Buckingham Palace on the cover (which is still a good idea for someone like... GORILLAZ!). But *Parklife* was Britpop and Britpop was *Parklife*. Lovingly described as owing as much to the cynicism of the KINKS' Sixties as it did to the emerging New Lad culture of the Nineties (staffed by those untuckables with an alcopop in one hand, a copy of *Trouser Snake* in the other), the songs were as British as tea towels. Blur delivered many wonderful things in their time, not least ALEX JAMES who vies with U2's ADAM CLAYTON, DURAN DURAN's JOHN TAYLOR, and the CLASH's PAUL SIMONON, for being the nicest bass player in the business.

THE SOUND OF BOLLYWOOD B

If you ask me the real sound of India is not the wailing and the shouting that you hear every day in the dusty streets, it is not the tortuous Muslim prayers that can keep you up all night as you lie in anticipation 800 yards from the Taj Mahal, it is not even the traditional north Indian folk music that still seems to be piped into every open space (the constant drone produced by the four-stringed tambura.).

I'm not even sure that the real soundtrack is the sound of Bollywood pop you hear blaring out of overloaded Tata trucks, tuk-tuk taxis, shops, roadside barbers and hotel lobbies. A few years ago I spent two weeks listening to Bollywood pop, as I travelled around the Golden Triangle between Delhi, Agra and Jaipur, and I'd forgotten how powerful it can be. When I was young, I commandeered a soundtrack LP of an Indian film that belonged to my father; I'm not sure he ever saw the film, although the music was extraordinary in itself. This was back in the early Seventies – Lord knows where he got it – and at the time it sounded like nothing I'd ever heard before. The record consisted of a woman who sounded as though the love of her life had just absconded with her heart, juxtaposed over a difficult time signature that seemed to make no sense to my callow Western ears.

Little did I know that most Bollywood pop sounded like this, and, judging by what I heard when I was in Rajasthan, still does. But I loved that record, probably because I played it until I liked it (how many other records did I do that with? Hundreds probably), loved it so much that I remember being irrationally upset when it went missing.

And, although the form doesn't seem to have changed much, at least judging by the material I heard the other day, nothing I've ever heard comes close. Obviously I will never be able to find my record, as I never took a note of what it was called. Phonetically it went something like, SAJEENAY,

B COOLY SAJEENAY, and had some sort of spoken intro, like an old soul song. Which I suppose it was, in its own way.

But it is gone, just another one of those things I can remember lying around the house as the Sixties turned into the Seventies, along with the NEVILLE SHUTE novels, the NINA AND FREDERICK EPs, coffee-flavoured Angel Delight, and various blue metallic soda siphons (which at the time were a symbol of sophistication like no other).

Oh, and the real soundtrack of India? That's easy: the horn.

MICHAEL BOLTON

Whenever I think of Michael Bolton I'm reminded of something the film critic TOM SHONE once wrote, about high-concept movies: "...films that had been shorn of peripherals, strip-mined for their pockets of triumph, their character arcs reduced to telegraphic shorthand, and strung out along a gleaming bead of hit songs – that's what high concept was or felt like to cinemagoers: like being told about another, greater movie by a highly excitable intermediary." That's Michael Bolton.

BOMBAY BICYCLE CLUB

"That difficult second album" (or sophomore slump) is a syndrome that many have been affected by (the JAM, ABC, TERENCE TRENT D'ARBY, the STONE ROSES, GUNS N' ROSES, JEFF BUCKLEY, the STROKES, the FEELING, etc), yet towards the end of the Noughties many bands simply decided to make their second albums so different from their debuts, that they neatly avoided the problem. The MACCABEES did it, as did the HORRORS, as did Bombay Bicycle Club. With their 2010 album, *Flaws*, BBC went "Nu-Folk", kick-started by their very brilliant single "Ivy & Gold", a song which is probably still their best.

B

BON IVER

What did BARNEY HOSKYNS say? The sound of ecstatic aloneness. "Heavily-garlanded backwoods-cabin DIY... sung in that richly soulful whiteboy falsetto over deep blue acoustic chords."

BON JOVI'S "IT'S MY LIFE"

When I was in my formative years – fourteen-fifteen – the record that made me want to be a man was "Behind Blue Eyes" by the WHO. Later, when I was seventeen, the record that I thought summed up being a man was "Complete Control" by the CLASH. But since I've actually been a man, dozens of records have made me feel like putting on my boots, picking up my gun and walking through the valley of death. Often, that record is "It's My Life" by Bon Jovi. Written by JON BON JOVI, RICHIE SAMBORA, and MAX MARTIN, it is just about the most generic Jovi record of them all. A line in the second verse, "For Tommy and Gina, who never backed down", refers to Tommy and Gina, the fictional working class couple that Bon Jovi and Sambora first wrote about in the 1986 classic "Livin' on a Prayer." When JBJ sings, "Like Frankie said, I did it my way," the hairs on the back of my neck start facing Hoboken.

DAVID BOWIE

B

The first time I met David Bowie, he asked me for a light. We were standing in the downstairs pool room in a nightclub called Heaven, down by the arches underneath Charing Cross Station in central London. This was back in 1981. He was filming the uber-vampire film *The Hunger*, and I was an extra, three months out of college, employed to wear a goatee beard, a silver zoot suit and a ridiculously long key-chain, and to walk down a metal flight of stairs as Bowie and his co-star CATHERINE DENEUVE walked up them, nodding along to "Bela Lugosi's Dead" by BAUHAUS as I went. It was a fairly dismal film – in fact it was a shocker – but I was only twenty-one, and couldn't quite believe that I was in the same room as the most influential pop star there had ever been.

Brushing past my hero would have been enough for me to brag about for months afterwards, although my anecdote moved up a gear around two o'clock that afternoon when everyone's favourite space-bloke marched up to me and promptly asked me for a light for his Marlboro Red. Now, this may not be up there with watching JOHN TRAVOLTA rehearse the dance scene in *Pulp Fiction,* may not be up there with ROBERT DE NIRO asking you to help him with the mirror scene in *Taxi Driver* ("You talkin' to me?"), but for someone from my generation, for whom David Bowie had been as revelatory as ELVIS and the BEATLES had been to the previous generation, it was a bit like sharing a beer with God. Not only that, we smoked the same cigarettes!

Since then, since I became a "professional", I have met him dozens of times, and have interviewed him in London, Switzerland, New York, LA, all over the place. But I never fail to get goose bumps, never fail to get nervous, and have never taken him for granted. Yes, it's nice when he remembers your name (he's one of the most professional pop stars you'll ever meet, and has spent forty years dealing with the press), and yes it's cool to have the occasional shared experience, but I never forget that he's the star, and I'm the fan; I never forget that he is the man responsible for my adolescence, never forget that he was the man I pretended to be as I danced around my bedroom at the age of twelve, singing along to "Life On Mars", using an HB pencil as a substitute microphone and wishing I had a shock of flame-red hair.

The last time we formally spoke, he told me, "I've made over twenty-five studio albums, and I think probably I've made two real stinkers in my time, and some not-bad albums, and some really good albums. I'm proud of what I've done. In fact it's been a good ride."

David Bowie was the first pop star to refuse to have anything to do with the past. To him, the past wasn't necessary, wasn't particularly interesting, wasn't what he was about. His first proper hit, "Space Oddity", was testament to his way of looking at the world. From space.

Not only did Bowie invent glam rock, not only did he invent space-age rock, but in the last forty years or so he's pretty much invented it all. He was a soul boy. He went ambient just as everyone else was going punk (after all, he'd already produced several seminal proto-punk albums for LOU REED and IGGY POP), and in the Eighties he went global – "Let's Dance" – when everyone else was still copying the esoteric stuff he did back in the Seventies.

Today he is a lifetime away from the androgynous android of the Seventies, when Bowie could be found lolling about in the back of large American limousines, a crumpled heap of black kamikaze silk drinking Tequila Gold from a brown paper bag. This was when his ambition and ego were most blind. "I get so much fan mail it has to be handled by a computer," he said in 1975. Computers? What were they? "I'm an instant star. Just add water and stir." Any one of Bowie's Seventies personae might have been apocryphal, yet they were all excessive.

In the four decades that Bowie has been a star, he has recorded some of the most important music of the post-BEATLES era, and although he is still largely known for the raft

B

of ground-breaking albums he released in the Seventies, his work since then has been equally fascinating, and almost as prescient. If you were to compile Bowie's alternative greatest hits, many of them would be from the last twenty-five years, little known songs that are equally as good as anything he recorded before: "Loving The Alien" (one of the few good tracks from 1985's *Tonight*, and equally as good as any space-age stuff from the early Seventies), "Dancing In The Street" (the much-maligned cover version with MICK JAGGER, organised to coincide with Live Aid in 1985), "Absolute Beginners" (the intricate long version, 1986), "Shades" (the song he wrote for IGGY POP's 1986 album *Blah Blah Blah*), "Amazing" (yes, a TIN MACHINE song, from the first album in 1989, and a great one), "Pretty Pink Rose" (a song he gave to guitarist ADRIAN BELEW in 1990), "Real Cool World" (from the 1992 film *Cool World*), "Sound And Vision Vs. 808 State" (1991), "Looking For Lester" (from 1993's *Black Tie White Noise*), "Buddha Of Suburbia" (1993), "Strangers When We Meet" (1995's single version), "Hallo Spaceboy" (PET SHOP BOYS remix, 1995), "I'm Afraid Of Americans" (from 1997's *Earthling*), "Seven" (from 1999's *hours...*), "Thursday's Child" (ditto), "This Is Not America" (*Bowie At The Beeb*, 2000), "I Would Be Your Slave", "5.15 The Angels Have Gone", "Slow Burn", "Everyone Says 'Hi'" (all four from 2002's *Heathen*), "New Killer Star", "Fall Dog Bombs The Moon" (both from 2003's *Reality*), "Changes" (with Butterfly from 2004's *Shrek 2*), and "Rebel Never Gets Old" (yet another "Rebel Rebel" remix, a mash-up from 2004, and a great record from gun to tape).

And my favourite album of his? If ALAN YENTOB, MELVYN BRAGG or KIRSTY YOUNG ever held a gun to my head I'd have to admit that *Young Americans*, his infamous "plastic soul" record, is my favourite ever Bowie album, a slab of heartbreaking sophisti-soul that might just be the best seduction record ever made. Although he was criticised at the time for turning his back on Britain and embracing the insincere world of Seventies soul, this record proved that he could be as romantic as MARVIN GAYE.

B

These days Bowie lives in New York, tending to his daughter Lexi, his website, his wife and his back catalogue. At the moment he doesn't feel compelled to jump up on stage, and tends to turn down most invitations to croon away with the great and the good. He is asked to participate in most global pop events – Live 8, the PRINCESS DIANA tribute, Glastonbury – but would rather spend his time analysing the future rather than exploiting the past. He is also rather dismissive of his fan base's obsession with his other-worldliness. A few years ago I asked him what people most misunderstood about him.

"What's to misunderstand?" he said. "I mean, honestly, I'm just a bloke doing his job, and it's not terribly complicated. What I do is I write mainly about very personal and rather lonely feelings, and I explore them in a different way each time. You know, what I do is not terribly intellectual. I'm a pop star for Christ's sake. As a person, I'm fairly uncomplicated. I don't need very much – I'm not needy in that way. I'm not as driven as I once was."

When you consider that Bowie has probably been the most inventive, most influential, most commercially daring singer of the last forty years, it would be churlish to deny him some reflection, or even a semi-retirement, although each new record brings with it a whole host of new opportunities for hero-worship, a whole host of musical touchstones that inadvertently contribute to one of the greatest bodies of work in the industry.

In the last twenty years or so, Bowie has embraced most forms of multi-media, and was one of the first pop stars to seriously understand the possibilities of the Internet. But although being a renaissance man can be a full-time occupation, it is the music that still fires Bowie's soul, music that still brings out the best in him. Like his hero SCOTT WALKER, Bowie has a way of walking around a song instead of addressing it head-on. "I know my strengths and one of them is creating atmosphere," he told me once. "JOHN LENNON was good at telling people off, but not me. Whenever I do didactic stuff it always seems ham-fisted. I often pull myself

B back if I feel something is becoming too melodic. But then melody comes in many forms. He'll hate me for saying it but the person who is better at hooks than almost anyone is BRIAN ENO, and the solo on 'Virginia Plain' is probably one of the greatest three-note hooks in the history of pop. Some people call me pretentious for working like this, but I don't think there's anything wrong with thinking of pop as an art form, you've just got to think of it without a capital A. Lower case art is always best. And anyway, a lot of what was considered art in 1978 is now just part of our vocabulary."

And so say all of us.

The fourth time I met David Bowie, was just before his Serious Moonlight gig at the Milton Keynes Bowl on July 1, 1983. I was backstage, wolfing down the free drinks and exotic canapés, standing with a friend on the elevated walkway that stretched from Bowie's dressing room all the way to the stage. He had perfect "Let's Dance" hair, a beautifully tailored baggy pale blue suit, a white shirt, braces and a PAUL SMITH old-school tie (I know about stuff like this), and he looked as though he'd just arrived from some sort of virtual reality, fully formed, and aesthetically indestructible. And as he walked up to the stage, he stopped, turned to Cynthia and me, and said, apropos of nothing, "You know, at times like this, it's great to be surrounded by your friends." We weren't his friends. We were acquaintances, hardly knew the man, and if we'd have known him better it would have been unbearably presumptuous for us to call him a friend. But in those few seconds – seconds before he was due to give one of the defining concerts of his career – he made us feel like the most important people on earth. It wasn't us who were special, it was him.

He is, when all is said and done, a proper star. Yes, he's a musician, and at times an actor (although never a properly convincing one), and he's been responsible for so many pop-cultural zeitgeist shifts it can make you dizzy just thinking about them, but above all of this he is a star. And recognised as one. When Bowie was recording *Young Americans*, LUTHER

VANDROSS was one of his backing singers, and Bowie wanted to work on one of Vandross's songs, which eventually became "Fascination". In the studio, Bowie asked Vandross if he minded if he rewrote some of the lyrics. Vandross's response, "You're David Bowie, I live at home with my mother, you can do what you like."

He did, and he has.

"I'm an instant star," Bowie had said, back when God was a boy. "Just add water and stir."

He not only meant it, he was good at it too, and in his forty-five-year career Bowie has reinvented himself more times than LADY GAGA probably ever will. Back in the Sixties, when he was just starting out, he was a convincing London dandy before morphing into an effete singer-songwriter with stars in his eyes. Five minutes later he invented glam rock with Ziggy Stardust, and then kept reinventing himself throughout the Seventies with each subsequent record. With TIN MACHINE he even reinvented the yuppie, dressing like a banker who had decided to form a rock band.

For two generations he has been something to everyone, from Aladdin Sane, the Young American Plastic Soul Boy and the Thin White Duke through to the man who graced the covers of *Earthling, The Buddha of Suburbia* and *Heathen*. He is the quintessential rock chameleon, the archetypal pop changeling, everyone's favourite space face.

But he's never been fat. Which is what I think he ought to do next, if he ever decides to present himself to the public again.

Since his heart attack in 2004. Bowie has been in semi-retirement, and hasn't released an album since *Reality* in 2003, but there will undoubtedly come a time when he decides to reconnect with his audience, when he decides he must throw caution to the wind and step out once again into the spotlight.

And when he does I think he ought to be fat. Really fat.

Bowie has been thin, and he's been skeletal. He's been blonde, and he's been flame-haired. He's wrapped himself in

Bacofoil, worn the sort of thigh-high boots that would have shamed MADONNA, and, in *Labyrinth* he even looked like something out of *Fraggle Rock*. He's done it all.

But he's never been fat. Which is why I think this should be his next career move.

When Ziggy eventually crawls out from his lair I want to see the Fat White Duke, I want to see Bowie waddle up onto stage looking like ALFRED HITCHCOCK or PETER USTINOV. I want Bowie to look properly fat. ORSON WELLES fat. FALSTAFF fat. Epically fat. So fat he has his own postcode fat. I don't want to demean him, and wouldn't want him to appear unnecessarily overweight or sweaty. I'm not for one minute suggesting that he reappear as a tragic and bloated version of his former self, not suggesting he parade around as a 21st Century Vegas-period ELVIS, popping out of his rhinestone jump-suit as he hurries his way through "Life On Mars", "Absolute Beginners", or "Let's Dance."

No, I want Bowie to descend on us looking grand, groomed and incredibly well-manicured, like ORSON WELLES promenading in Paris – an unlit cigar in his mouth, his hands pushed deep into his suit pockets, and his belly stretching all the way from here to over there. He would be wearing a bespoke suit (obviously – how else was it going to fit?), bench-made shoes, and possibly a purple suede fedora. Yup, he should supersize himself.

The only problem, as far as I can see, is that Bowie is banned from enjoying all the good stuff that could make him look this way. Orson used to consume four or five large portions of caviar every day, along with at least twenty cups of coffee, and many more tumblers of 100 percent proof vodka. And that was just the snacks between meals. A typical lunch might start with a bottle of champagne (for himself, mind), followed by Boudin Noir aux Pommes (blood sausages with apples), then a bottle of hearty red to ease down a Terrine de Canard, followed by something sickly and sweet along with a treble calvados. Bowie rarely eats anything that isn't organic these days, and hasn't drunk (or smoked) in years. If he attempted to "do an Orson" he'd probably explode.

So maybe he'll have to come back as a hologram, or a 3D viral, bouncing around our laptops and our iPads as though he were MAX HEADROOM reinvented as a cyber cipher. No matter. I'm sure Bowie would look cool, even if he were eighteen stone.

Of course such a radical departure would warrant – nay, would demand – a serious marketing campaign, along with some well-placed TV interviews, a couple of concerts, as well as the product itself (a selection of overwrought torch songs, obviously). There hasn't been a new Bowie album for a decade, so the title would have to be catchy as well as fitting. And after considering various options, I think I've got it. His new record is simply going to be called this:

"David Bowie: *Chubby*."

OWEN BRADY

Just when you thought it was no longer safe to go down to the beach, Owen Brady reinvented Chill Out. Just when you thought you couldn't bear to be serenaded by yet another Birkenstock balladeer knocking off JACK JOHNSON or JAMES BLUNT, along came a young singer-songwriter with a genuinely modern slant on a classic genre. Owen Brady evoked the spirit of such sweet Seventies soundmakers as HALL & OATES, the STEVE MILLER BAND, 10CC, and BOZ SCAGGS, writing unashamedly commercial pop songs with great holiday hooks. Brady made blue-eyed soul for the Noughties. Chill out music for the Radio 2 set. Modern-day exotica for the Guilty Pleasures crew.

This young, Dublin-based former soprano has the brooding – and it has to be said, irritating – good looks of a long-haired COLIN FARRELL, although his music displays an unusual and appealing vulnerability

And you can't get his songs out of your head. Brady occupies an open-topped world where late-Seventies ISLEY BROTHERS meets SADE meets ALESSI. With knobs on. Brady sounds like the HIGH LLAMAS – if they wanted to be successful, that is. He also sounds like JACK JOHNSON, but in a much less cloying way. He also reminds you of a European MICHAEL FRANKS, with Franks' telltale laconic vocal delivery, lyrical landscapes and subtle beats. And for those who remember them, there are even echoes of EG & ALICE, the early Nineties duo who made the sort of music you wanted to listen to as the sun goes down (or, if you're that way inclined, as the sun goes up).

There are eleven songs on Brady's first CD, 2008's *Prepare To Be Happy*, the two most immediate of which are "Angry" and "Waiting For The Sun", two songs that defy you not to start humming them immediately you hear them. There are hits everywhere: "Been A Lot Better", "Sun Shining Down", and the Shuggie Otis-like "One Cool Child." There are beats, there are strings, unplugged ballads, and even a bit of blues. To top it all, Brady offers a refreshing take on BOZ SCAGGS' classic late-night lounge disco classic, "Lowdown", a cover that sounds like it was made to be played at The Jockey Club on Salinas Beach in Ibiza as you sip your café con leche and nibble your ensamadas.

In fact, if they've got any sense, they're playing it right now.

CLIFFORD BROWN

Imagine the opening of a French movie, as the camera pans across Parisian rooftops at dusk, and then drops several storeys below before entering a small basement window. There we see curls of cigarette smoke climb towards a vaulted ceiling, and saxophones glinting like polished weapons. Well, that pretty much sums up what Clifford Brown sounds like. He was a sentimental horn player, some say the best of his generation, but he was killed in a car crash a year after this was recorded, so never fulfilled his potential. *Clifford Brown With Strings* (Verve), from 1955, is his legacy.

JAMES BROWN

You still see James Brown everywhere. You see him in PRINCE videos on MTV; you see him in reruns walking through the halls of *The West Wing* in the shape of Josh Lyman, moving his weight from one shoulder to another, you see him in the stage craft of BONO and JAY-Z. Everywhere.

The influence of The Hardest Working Man In Show Business can be seen in a generation of entertainers for whom braggadocio and "moves" are a quintessential part of performance. And performance was what he did best. By 1962, Brown was doing more than three hundred gigs a year – working himself up, shivering himself down, and generally trying to evoke the devil – and so decided to record a concert at the Apollo in Harlem, subsequently releasing it with great success: it reached No.2 on the Billboard charts and continues to be on the list of the best records made by anyone ever.

His reach is exponential, his influence almost unquantifiable. He is the king, the master of the dance, the creator of all things good and funky, the manipulator of the groove, the custodian of the funk.

He was also a keen disciplinarian, demanding precision and his own sort of perfection from his band and crew. MACEO PARKER, who played saxophone in Brown's band for much of his career, offered this description of what it was like being in his master's band: "You gotta be on time. You gotta have your uniform. Your stuff's got to be intact. You gotta have the bow tie. You got to have it! You can't come up without the bow tie. You cannot come up without a cummerbund. [The] patent leather shoes we were wearing at the time gotta be greased. You just gotta have this stuff. This is what [Brown expected]..."

I saw Brown and his immaculately turned-out band at the Hammersmith Odeon in London in 1986, and the experience

B

was a bit like a glory-romp: Brown knew he had to get through a selection of crowd-pleasers and so had obviously briefed the musicians to churn out the hits accordingly. The Godfather Of Soul played everything at 78 rpm, whizzing through his catalogue – "Night Train", "Papa's Got A Brand New Bag", "Get Up Offa That Thing", "Get Up (I Feel Like Being A) Sex Machine", and his then current hit "Living In America" – as though legally obliged to. It felt a bit like watching a speeded-up VHS copy of his career, participating in it, almost. But even at chipmunk speed, Brown was funky. He was always funky.

THE BRILL BUILDING

Located at the corner of Broadway and 49th Street, the Brill Building was, during the Fifties and early Sixties, the Pentagon of Pop. 'Teen Pan Alley' was an eleven-storey address that housed every jobbing songwriter on the block, including LIEBER & STOLLER, BARRY & GREENWICH, and GOFFIN & KING. In dark and invariably smoke filled cubby holes, with perhaps only a piano, a bench and maybe a chair for the lyricist, hundreds of young and established songwriters would bash away at their three-minute masterpieces, and then try and place them with the dozens of publishing companies which occupied the rest of the building. Once the home of the great American standard, after the emergence of rock'n'roll the Brill Building became the breeding ground of every aspiring PHIL SPECTOR, with baby-faced songwriters falling over themselves to pen the latest hit for the SHIRELLES or the DRIFTERS. "Two of its most gifted graduates were BURT BACHARACH and HAL DAVID," wrote PAUL DU NOYER, "who escaped the teenage ghetto sophisticated songs of an adult romance. Like the Brill itself, they were a link to the older world of American popular song. And perhaps the wordsmith, HAL DAVID, gets overlooked: his scenarios ('Trains to San Jose', etc.) were vivid and essential."

Years earlier, when somebody remarked that JEROME KERN had written "Ol' Man River", the wife of Kern's lyricist OSCAR HAMMERSTEIN interrupted sharply. "Indeed not," she scolded. JEROME KERN wrote 'dum dum dum-dum.' My husband wrote "Ol' Man River."'

B

BARNEY BUBBLES

Barney Bubbles drew my youth, carved it out of coloured paper, counterintuitive typography, bald modernist graphics, old bits of cardboard and photographs of ELVIS COSTELLO, NICK LOWE, GENERATION X and IAN DURY. Unwittingly I had bought into his world via a HAWKWIND album that he designed and I bought it in 1974, when I was thirteen and he was thirty-two, but it was the punk explosion two years later that really brought him into my life, like it did for thousands of others.

Bubbles was one of the most important designers of the punk and post-punk era – working with all the artists above and many more – a rarely celebrated creature who was always far more interested in achievement than acclaim. The iconography of punk would have been a lot more reductive were it not for Bubbles' inclusive mix of modernist graphics and Sixties playfulness. With Bubbles you always felt that whatever he was working on was treated as a genuine artefact rather than simple decoration. At heart, he was an artist, which led to the creative strain he put himself under. After all, he was responsible for the cover of ELVIS COSTELLO's 1979 album *Armed Forces*, one of the few visual masterpieces of the post-punk era.

There has been remarkably little written about Bubbles, although he was the subject of a book by PAUL GORMAN, *Reasons to Be Cheerful: The life and work of Barney Bubbles*. A lovingly researched biography, it is also an alternative history of the post-punk scene, from Stiff to Radar to F-Beat to 2-Tone to Go! Discs to – gulp! – Red Wedge and beyond.

B

It's easy to forget the wealth of talent that managed to seep up from under the floorboards during that time, and while the received wisdom is that there was a line drawn in the sand between Old Wave and New Wave, many of the creatives involved in punk had been at it for years.

Gormon pays scant attention to Bubbles' suicide in 1983 at the age of forty-two, and while this slightly undermines the picture of the designer that he spends two hundred pages building, in some ways it keeps the enigma alive. In the book's foreword, graphic guru PETER SAVILLE says, "The publication of *Reasons to Be Cheerful* is … missionary work; Barney Bubbles should be canonised." He couldn't have put it better had he used Stencil Bold Letraset and a 0.5 Rotring Rapidograph.

BUENA VISTA SOCIAL CLUB

This is a studio album by Cuban bandleader JUAN DE MARCOS GONZÁLEZ and guitarist RY COODER with traditional Cuban musicians, recorded in 1996, and released a year later. It was hugely popular. Played with double bass and brushes, these are songs about flowers and girls, doleful tunes that, like the people who inspired them, seem trapped. RY COODER's romance with Cuban music is understandable: here, like time, music has stood still, its branches unadorned by modern baubles. WIM WENDERS' low-gear documentary let some light in on the magic.

JOHNNY BURNETTE

A pioneer of wildman rockabilly, Johnny Burnette and his ROCK'N'ROLL TRIO made records so fiery, so sparse, they sounded almost elemental, as though nothing could have possibly come before them. This is field music, bashing out a rhythm with two big sticks, a fuzzy guitar and a raucous yell. Collars up, lip curled, grease in hand: "Lonesome Train", "Honey Hush", "Drinkin' Wine Spo-De-O-De" – oh Lawdy!

THE BYRDS

ROGER MCGUINN: "I was interested in getting an electric 12-string, so I took a pick-up and put it in my acoustic 12-string, but it didn't quite have the sound that I was looking for... and around 1964/1965 the BEATLES came out, and I was really interested in the sound they were getting, so I went to see GEORGE HARRISON playing a Rickenbacker in *A Hard Day's Night* and that gave me the idea of the Rickenbacker 12. At the time I heard the BEATLES I was working as a songwriter at the Brill Building in New York. And my job was to listen to the radio and emulate the songs that I heard. And when the BEATLES came out I was doing that, so naturally I jumped right into that kind of music and started mixing folk songs that I'd known before, with the BEATLES' beat. [In] things like "Turn Turn Turn" I used a lot of my banjo technique on the guitar. I started doing a rolling thing. And that would be the sub-structure of the song. And then I'd put lead lines over it, which were influenced by JOHN COLTRANE's saxophone work." And folk-rock was born.

THE B-52S

The B-52s took their name from Sixties slang for the beehive sported by the band's non-male members - CINDY WILSON and KATE PIERSON - so called because of its resemblance to the vast, phallic B-52 bomber. Their kitsch blend of post-punk dynamics and Sixties memorabilia was first heard on their

B

"Rock Lobster" single in 1978, and all their songs had titles as silly as the girls' hair: "Quiche Lorraine", "53 Miles West of Venus", "There's A Moon In The Sky (Called The Moon)", "Wig", etc. The B-52s were symptomatic of the Seventies re-use and re-appraisal of Sixties pop and its associated styles. Suddenly *Batman, Top Cat,* beach parties, B-movies, the checkerboard twist, paper op-art, mini-skirts, pillbox hats, pantsuits, turtleneck sweaters and Nehru jackets, Corvette Sting Rays and Barracudas, Mary Quant, flecked mohair, the MONKEES and all the other peripherals of Sixties US/UK kitsch-culture were hip again. Their debut London concert at the Electric Ballroom in the summer of 1979 (supported by the rockabilly band WHIRLWIND) was one of the most anticipated gigs of the year; they lived up to expectations, and it went down as one of the most fondly-remembered concerts of the whole post-punk period.

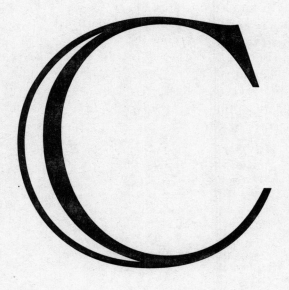

THE CAMBRIDGE

The Cambridge is still there, but it isn't the same. How could it be? The Cambridge pub sits on the north west corner of Cambridge Circus in London's West End – in1977 it was just a hundred yards from the Marquee, a hundred yards from the 100 Club, and only fifty yards from Saint Martins School of Art. From 1976 to 1980, The Cambridge was the most important pub in Soho, and every band who wanted to leave an impression in the neighbouring venues usually ended up there, pumping money into the jukebox, drinking green and yellow bottles of Pils, and throwing shapes in their leather jackets.

The downstairs bar often felt like a Parisienne brasserie – long, busy, everyone giddy with expectation – but the upstairs bar was where you went if you knew what was going on. It was always full of demanding people – punks, art students, pop stars and fashion designers – and so you had to be on your guard. MALCOLM MCLAREN had his own stool, the SEX PISTOLS seemed to be there every Friday night, and SIOUXSIE AND THE BANSHEES took up residency by the jukebox. The Pistols' designer JAMIE REID was the coolest man there. He always wore a tight, thigh-length black leather suit jacket, his hair was always fashioned into this greasy, truck-driver quiff, and he had a bottle of Pils seemingly grafted to his left hand. Pils was the only thing that anyone drank, making it seem as though it was the only thing they sold.

Everything happened at the Cambridge: a girl was decapitated by a lorry after she bet her friend she could crawl underneath it before it pulled away; a St Martin's painter called Alan was beaten senseless because he persisted in dressing like Hitler (floppy fringe, jackboots, leather trenchcoat and tell-tale moustache). The first time we saw him we immediately took bets on how long it would take before someone kicked the living daylights out of him. And just two weeks later he stumbled into the Cambridge covered

C

in the most fearsome bruises. Alan had, to quote an old NICK LOWE song, been nutted by reality, and soon left the college.

Most people congregated at the Cambridge before moving off into the night, to the latest tranche of nightclubs sprouting up all over the city. With the fancy-dress parade at its height, a generation of young entrepreneurs were taking over nightclubs for one night a week, installing their own DJs and creating a phenomenon out of nothing.

GLEN CAMPBELL

For years I thought I was the only person who liked GLEN CAMPBELL's "Wichita Lineman" (Capitol Records, 1968); in truth I thought I was the only person who had actually heard of it. The song was as much a part of my childhood as the other records my parents filled the house with, and along with DEAN MARTIN, FRANK SINATRA, MATT MONRO, NINA AND FREDERICK, and JOHN BARRY (whose "Vendetta" was my co-favourite song as a boy), the work of Glen Campbell saturated my life.

As I developed a taste for the loungecore torch song (although in those days they were known by the rather more prosaic moniker "middle of the road"), I discovered that "Wichita Lineman", like most of Campbell's great songs, had been written by JIMMY WEBB – "By The Time I Get to Phoenix", "Where's The Playground Susie", "Galveston", etc – and that "Lineman" had become known as the first existential country song. I discovered Campbell played guitar on the BEACH BOYS' *Pet Sounds*, recorded the little-known BRIAN WILSON classic "Guess I'm Dumb", and that he played the bass himself on "Lineman" on a Danelectro six-string. I became obsessed with "Lineman", sought out JIMMY WEBB concerts (including his 1994 Café Royal gig in London), and even wrote a piece about the provenance of the song for the *Independent*.

"Wichita Lineman" is the first existential country song. As 1968 is often celebrated as the high-water mark of post-

WWII cultural insurrection, it might seem perverse to lionise a middle-of-the-road ballad that harks back to a more innocent era, but JIMMY WEBB's heartbreaking torch song was as evergreen then as it is now, and still seems to exist in a world of its own.

A dribble of bass, searing strings, tremolo guitar and one of the most plaintive vocals ever heard on record courtesy of Glen Campbell, Webb's paean to the American West describes the longing that a lonely telephone lineman feels for an absent lover who he imagines he can hear "singing in the wire" he's working on. Like all good love songs it's an SOS from the heart; there are even snatches of synthesizer-generated Morse Code heard after the lyric, "And the Wichita Lineman, is still on the line."

Webb was asked by producer AL DE LORY in October 1968 for a follow-up to "Phoenix..." that was in a similar vein; and so he set to work, crafting another song based around a geographical reference. "Some time earlier," said Webb, "I had been driving around northern Oklahoma, an area that's real flat and remote — almost surreal in its boundless horizons and infinite distances. I'd seen a lineman up on a telephone pole, talking on the phone. It was such a curiosity to see a human being perched up there."

Putting himself up his pole, Webb spent two hours on his green baby grand in his apartment in the former Philippine embassy in Hollywood and wrote what he thought was three-quarters of a song. "It wasn't finished," he said. "There was a whole section in the middle that I didn't have words for, which eventually became the instrumental part."

What Webb didn't know was that De Lory's uncle was a lineman in Kern County, California. "So as soon as I heard that opening line," said De Lory, "I could visualise my uncle up a pole in the middle of nowhere. I loved the song right away." Overruling Webb's insistence that "Lineman" wasn't finished, De Lory laid synthesiser lines over the instrumental passage, one of the most evocative instrumental breaks ever recorded, the coda as travelogue.

C

The following year Campbell and Webb were determined to make lightning strike thrice. Their next collaboration? "Galveston."

CAPTAIN BEEFHEART

As a painter, DON "VAN" GLEN VLIET was a tad more orthodox than he was as a singer and musician. His work has been described as "progressive", "free", and "directional", even when it was patently just wayward, fractured, or just the result of taking a lot of drugs. As a teenager he devoured jazz and blues, alternating between a penchant for esoterica, and an instinctive love of R&B (copying his vocal style from HOWLIN' WOLF). He also found time to build myths around himself: apparently he once worked as a door-to-door salesman, and sold one to ALDOUS HUXLEY. His sales pitch? "Well, I assure you sir, this thing sucks."

By being autocratic in the recording studio – he screamed, punched, discharged, and all this after giving his band members silly new names – Beefheart controlled his ever-changing posse of musicians by trying to capture a sound only he could hear (or at least pretend to hear). He couldn't play a musical instrument, and would demand his musicians play particular colours. By all accounts he was a hard man to love.

Trout Mask Replica (1969), long estimated to be his finest work, was an avalanche of disjointed rhythms, reckless slide guitar, wailing and shouting – and was influential in its disregard for traditionally recognised forms of music rather than any of its actual songs.

After the years of heroic experimentation came the fitful Seventies, when being formerly influential wasn't the same as having a career, and when it became expedient to at least attempt a more commercial attitude. A friend suggested to me some time ago that one of the sexiest records in his collection (at least in terms of its usefulness as a seduction tool) was

Beefheart's 1972 album *Clear Spot,* a record I only knew because one of its tracks, the willfully obtuse "Big Eyed Beans From Venus", was played on *The Old Grey Whistle Test* in the early Seventies and helped convince me that I should stop buying *Popswap* and start buying the *NME* immediately. My friend reckoned it was one of the most romantic records ever made, and played me some of it over the phone. The three salient tracks are "Too Much Time", "My Head Is My Only House Unless It Rains", and "Her Eyes Are A Blue Million Miles", where the Captain sounds like OTIS REDDING on acid, which is sort of how Beefheart sounded at the best of times I suppose. He was infamous for corrupting the blues, although his unhinged "anti-music sound sculptures" were never commercially viable, hence DOOBIE BROTHERS producer TED TEMPLEMAN, was brought in to add some radio sheen to *Clear Spot* (and went on record saying his client was physically intimidating). It didn't trouble the charts of course, but the record was six-out-of-ten astonishing.

THE CARDIGANS

Rather unfairly referred to as the Swedish PIZZICATO FIVE, or else the true heirs to the ABBA legacy, this co-ed Stockholm quartet were actually the finest exponents of lounge pop in all Scandinavia. Their almost-remarkable album *Life* (Minty Fresh Records, 1995), contains thirteen original songs (including "Daddy's Car", which is begging to be covered by DIONNE WARWICK) as well as a bizarre and not totally successful version of BLACK SABBATH's "Sabbath Bloody Sabbath".

CATWALK MUSIC

While it's often disconcerting to be stirred by language that resists comprehension, the ambiguity of a song's words can often be its prime attraction. How many songs do you love, that you can sing along to on a regular basis, which contain great swathes of unintelligible phrases, songs where the vocals appear to almost randomly skirt across the surface of the tune?

Of course, the vogue for the past fifteen years or so has been for deliberate obscuration, with producers, remixers and DJs taking great pride in weaving the most unlikely samples together (the CARPENTERS with SONIC YOUTH, for instance, or RADIOHEAD with MICHAEL JACKSON). You hear a lot of this still at fashion shows, where the DJs like to experiment with their aural bouillabaisse.

One season in Milan I heard everything from JOHN BARRY and the ROLLING STONES, to BJORK, PRINCE, and FLORENCE & THE MACHINE, all mashed up, bootleg-style, curdled and frothy: OASIS folded into DEPECHE MODE folded into LED ZEPPELIN folded into "Rise from the Shadows" by the mighty ALBERTA CROSS. A fashion show wouldn't be a fashion show without a bit of DAVID BOWIE, and that season the song I kept hearing was "Cat People", which in turn had been tweaked and bleeped so much it sounded as though it had been recorded the week before.

Sometimes the music at a show can swamp the whole experience. At one show in Milan many, many seasons ago, the producer had decided to play the famous calypso version of "Over The Rainbow" (by ROB MEHL), a track with limited appeal at the best of times. However this wasn't played as part of a sequence: it was the entire soundtrack. After about twenty-five minutes of this, when we were listening to the song for the fourth time (it rather unnecessarily mixes in "Wonderful World" and lasts for over seven minutes), some in the audience were biting their hands in order to try to stop themselves collapsing in fits of giggles. It was almost as though someone had put the song on a permanent loop and then left the building, bound for Mexico, in an effort to see just how much we could take. It made me wonder how long we would have stayed – although there are some in the industry who are so sycophantic, I'm sure they would have still been on their seats an hour later, worried that any attempt at escape might have offended the designer.

Me, I would have been way above the chimney tops.

RAY CHARLES

He played the blues so slow, you could shave between the beats. Few homages work better than DONALD FAGEN's "What I Do".

NENEH CHERRY

She has made more popular records, and – all told – has had something of a respectable career (working with GROOVE ARMADA, MASSIVE ATTACK, MICHAEL STIPE, YOUSSOU N'DOUR, and TRICKY). Yet it is 1988's "Buffalo Stance" for which she will be remembered, probably the best single released that year in the UK. Produced by BOMB THE BASS's TIM SIMENON, her debut single managed to blend the colloquial strains of West London rap and the bottom-heavy groove of a thousand Bronx basslines with the soaring melodic guitar of every Mancunian indie-darling – if you were to imagine SHANNON mixed with JOY DIVISION in a Notting Hill dancehall then you would have got the picture.

Her muse was raw but never crude. At the time, hip-hop-hamburger culture had become so boorish that a lot of British rap came across like phallic press releases. Cherry was twenty-four at the time, writing songs about sexual survival as though she were a sex-wars veteran.

CHIC

C

NILE RODGERS and BERNARD EDWARDS' late Seventies disco band made the greatest dance records ever. Their anthem, "Le Freak" (1978), was inspired by a failed attempt to get into Studio 54 on New Year's Eve in 1977. Invited by GRACE JONES to come to her gig at the club, when Rodgers and Edwards turned up they were refused entry. So incensed were they, on returning to their apartment they came up with this famous riff, and the words, "Aaaaaahhhh, fuck off!"

They wrote the disco rule book, pumping out dancefloor templates so regularly they became known as their own hit factory, and were so hyper-active they produced other people's records as well as their own (SISTER SLEDGE, SHEILA & B. DEVOTION, DEBORAH HARRY, DAVID BOWIE, CARLY SIMON, etc). Some said they changed styles so often it was as though they were going out of fashion. But at the time the fashion was all determined by Rodgers and Edwards anyway, upwardly mobile disco anthems that would turn out to be the apotheosis as well as the termination of the Motown dream. Soon rap, DJ culture and hip-hop in general would amp-up the militancy in black dance music, ironically using the riff from Chic's "Good Times" as its initial bedrock (it was sampled to great effect on "The Adventures Of Grandmaster Flash On The Wheels Of Steel").

In the imaginary box containing the greatest dance records in the world, Chic contributions include "Everybody Dance", "My Feet Keep Dancing", "I Want Your Love", "Dance, Dance, Dance (Yowsah, Yowsah, Yowsah)". Their SISTER SLEDGE records are pretty awesome too, along with the very best thing they produced, "Spacer" by SHEILA AND B. DEVOTION. (Chic songs, which are now a hen party staple, can easily lend themselves to reappropriation; a few years ago my goddaughter Mimi liked to sing – while staring at me pointedly in the face – "We are family, even though you're fatter than me...")

CHICAGO

C

Never has a pop logo acted as a better marketing device, a swooping Coca Cola-like script created by former CBS designer NICK FASCIANO that over the years has covered a multitude of sins (its various iterations have included brushed silver, wood, chocolate and leather). Difficult to dislike: "Saturday In The Park", "Wishin' You Were Here", "Beginnings", "Feelin' Stronger Every Day".

CHILL OUT

You've got the expensive wooden decking, a group of sunken rattan sofas, a row of Canary Island date palms, some pale green up-lighters, candles the size of cheese wheels, and a Sonos music system. All you need now is the following: "Adiemus" by ADIEMUS, "Crossing" by AGARTHA, "La Femme d'Argent" by AIR, "Enchant Me" by the AMALGAMATION, "Any Other Name" by ANDREW BERNSTEIN, "Out Of The Rain" by Aora, "Moments In Love" by the ART OF NOISE, "Since I Left You" by the AVALANCHES, "Disillusion" by BADLY DRAWN BOY, "Signs (Bonobo Mix)" by BADMARCH & SHRI, "Romeo (Acoustic Version)" by BASEMENT JAXX, "Swollen" by BENT, "California Dreamin'" by BOBBY WOMACK, "The Sicilian" by BONOBO, "The Plug" by BONOBO, "Deep Blue Day" by BRIAN ENO, "In Time" by CARL VEGA, "No Ordinary Morning" by CHICANE, "State Of Grace" by CHILLED BY NATURE, "Drifting" by CHRIS WHITLEY, "Bakerloo" by THE CINEMATIC ORCHESTRA, "Jupiter" by CRAIG PRUESS, "City Outrage" by CROSS BLEND, "Angi" by DAVEY GRAHAM, "On An Island" by DAVID GILMOUR, "Deepest Blue" by DEEPEST BLUE, "Silence" by DELERIUM, "Reveries" by DIMITRI FROM PARIS, "Keep On Steppin'" by DJ FIDELITY, "Heaven" by DJ SAMMY & YANOU, "Café De Flore" by DOCTOR ROCKIT, "Spread Love" by DOUG WILLIS, "Café Del Mar" by ENERGY 52, "Hayling"

C

by FC Kahuna, "Pavane" by Gabriel Fauré, "Symphony To Innerself" by George Bartram, "Open Your Mind" by Gerardo Frisina, "Black Cherry" by Goldfrapp, "At The River" by Groove Armada, "My Friend" by Groove Armada, "Satellite" by Guster, "The English Garden" by Henry Preece, "Daydream In Blue" by I-Monster, "The Independent Colors/Fly-Way" by The Independent Colors, "Soul Vibration" by J-WALK, "Try Me" by J. Boogie's, "American Dream" by Jakatta, "It's Too Late" by James Morrison, "High And Dry" by Jamie Cullum, "Joyful Caravan" by Jango, "Half Forgotten Daydreams" by John Cameron, "Sunshine's Better" by John Martyn, "Golden Lady" by José Feliciano, "Heartbeats" by José Gonzalez, "Gates Of Triumph" by Julius Affleck, "Magical Arif" by Karuan, "While My Guitar Gently Weeps" by Kenny Rankin, "Slip Into Something More Comfortable" by Kinobe, "Waltz For Koop" by Koop, "Bright Lights" by Koop, "High Noon" by Kruder & Dorfmeister, "Everything" by Lustral, "Lay Lady Lay" by Magnet, "Love Forgotten" by A Man Called Adam, "Written On The Sky" by Max Richter, "Sun" by Megablast, "If I Lost You" by Michelle Shaprow, "Tubular Bells Part 1" by Mike Oldfield, "Light My Fire" by Minnie Ripperton, "Life In Mono" by Mono, "Spiritual High" by Moodfood, "Sunworshipper" by Mylo, "Are You Ready For Love" by Nancy Wallace, "What I'm Feeling" by Nightmares On Wax, "Sinnerman" by Nina Simone, "Angry" by Owen Brady, "Cymbaline" by Pink Floyd, "The Return" by Rithma, "Stairway To Heaven" by Rodrigo Y Gabriela, "Another Chance (afterlife Mix)" by Roger Sanchez, "I Am The Black Gold Of The Sun" by Rotary Connection, "Hurry To Me" by Roy Budd, "Eple" by Royksopp, "Smokebelch II" by the Sabres Of Paradise, "Samba Pa Ti" by Santana, "Das Glockenspiel" by Schiller, "Waters Of March" by Sergio Mendes, "6 Underground" by Sneaker Pimps, "Lifesize" by Soulstance, "(Who?) Keeps Changing Your Mind" by South Street Player, "Beautiful Crazy" by Space Raiders, "Rose Rouge" by St Germain, "Street Tattoo" by Stan Getz, "Remember" by Stereo, "In The Mood For Love" by Stone-Inc, "Waltzinblack" by The Stranglers,

"Sueno Latino" by Sueno Latino, "Alpine Crossing" by Swing Out Sister, "Lebanese Blonde" by Thievery Corporation, "Never" by Tiefschwarz, "Love Theme (From Bladerunner)" by Vangelis, "Diamond Day" by Vashti Bunyan, "Promenade Sentimentale" by Vladimir Cosma, "Summertime" by Wass Featuring Earl T, "Adagio" by William Orbit, "Home" by Zero 7, "It's Automatic" by Zoot Woman, "Les Fleur" by 4Hero, "Living Out Loud" by 912 Players.

Eric Clapton

Whenever I find myself listening to Eric Clapton, I always feel as though I ought to be in a car commercial. Not an ad for one of those little city runabouts, not a Skoda Fabia, not a Chevrolet Matiz, or a Renault Laguna or one of those miniature Citroens that look as though they were designed – like *Glamour* magazine – to fit into your handbag as well as your life. No, I mean the sort of ads for proper German behemoths, the gas-guzzling, road-hogging monsters like a Mercedes S-Class, a serious BMW, or any of the new Audis.

A few years ago I went to see Clapton play the Hampton Court Palace Festival, principally because I'd never seen him perform a non-blues show before, and secondly because of the venue. Stately home rock is everywhere these days (everywhere they have stately homes, that is), with everyone from Bryan Ferry, Jools Holland, and Van Morrison, to Texas, Elton John, and the Pretenders playing the sort of lovingly-tendered, manicured lawns that are usually reserved solely for croquet. Catering for a demographic that no longer wants to queue up outside overcrowded venues in inhospitable, dangerous parts of town, these concerts offer Arcadian surroundings, the type of service you'll find at the opera, and – most importantly – car parks the size of Wales. Also, this was the only gig I've ever been to where they gave you a blanket to cover your knees in case it got cold.

Clapton came on stage looking like MIKE SKINNER's father – black, untucked shirt, baggy jeans and decidedly non-boxfresh trainers. There once was a time when Clapton would have been wearing what we were wearing in the cheap seats – a pale blue shirt and a khaki suit – but these days he's adopted the rock dad look. And although MIKE SKINNER's clothes presumably have a more pronounced provenance, as far as Clapton is concerned, it suits him.

We were not a tough crowd (newspaper proprietor, celebrity chef, design critic, Morgan Stanley troubleshooters, and lots of middle-aged men and women who were going to have a good time regardless), and we lapped it up – the old stuff, the new stuff, the classic stuff and the CREAM stuff. The money shot was a perfectly reconstructed "Layla", which every person should see Clapton play at least once in their lives. And instead of disguising his most famous tune, like some artists might do – acknowledging its existence, but subverting it so as to appear modern and cool – he played it straight, and had everyone swaying.

THE CLASH

Was there ever a hipper band? Was there ever a group who enjoyed dressing up as rebels as much as they did? Was there ever a band that produced such a strident, insurgent noise? Will there ever be a group who make a better rock single than "London Calling" or "Complete Control"?

Well over a quarter of a century since they met in a west London dole office, and over twenty years since they last played live, the Clash are still revered as one of the best rock'n'roll bands ever. The princes of punk, the kings of cool. There was MICK JONES, an unabashed guitar hero who looked like KEITH RICHARDS' uppity younger brother; JOE STRUMMER, a manic, pompadoured public school troubadour with sloganeering Tourette's (and a man who disguised his voice so much he was actually difficult to understand – Strummer wrapped himself in an accent as thick as a pair of seditionary's bondage strides – "I sound like someone speaking Arabic through silt at the bottom of the Nile," he said); PAUL SIMONON, not only the best-looking bass player in the world (sorry Macca), but possibly the best-looking rock star since ELVIS; and a couple of drummers, first TERRY CHIMES – aka TORY CRIMES, who played on their first album, and then TOPPER HEADON, who ended up writing the band's biggest American hit, "Rock The Casbah". And they all played with Bensons dangling from their lips, JIMMY DEAN-style.

And still they are honoured: in an eighteen-month period in the early Noughties they won a godlike Genius award at the *NME* Awards, won a Grammy for their *Westway To The World* video (with BRUCE SPRINGSTEEN, STEVE VAN ZANDT, ELVIS COSTELLO, and DAVE GROHL, playing a supergroup version of "London Calling"), won a Lifetime Achievement Award from British *GQ* and were inducted into the Rock'n'Roll Hall of Fame. Soon after, *The Essential Clash*, a CD and DVD compilation, reminded us all how good they were. On top of this, PIERCE BROSNAN's JAMES BOND garnered some rude boy cool when "London Calling" was heard in *Die Another Day* (one of the rare times the band have agreed to license one of their songs). Tragically, this was all overshadowed by the death from a heart attack, in December 2002, of JOE STRUMMER. He was fifty, and a hero to a generation of young men for whom "White Riot" wasn't a song, but a call to arms.

In honour of Strummer's passing, over that Christmas period the radio was full of the Clash, while on the night in question, the band's studded leather anthems could be heard pouring out of flats, mansions and pub doorways all over west London: "Garageland", "(White Man) In Hammersmith Palais", "Clash City Rockers", "The Guns Of Brixton", "London's Burning", "Safe European Home", "Train In Vain", the lot. They remain the quintessential punk group, more vital, more influential than the SEX PISTOLS, the DAMNED, the JAM, the STRANGLERS, the FALL, the BUZZCOCKS, all of them. And

C not only were they the group who truly defined what punk should sound like (it is an undisputed fact that the opening chords of "Complete Control", their third single, epitomise the punk ethos both in noise and attitude), they were the first to move away and successfully experiment with other types of music (one can't really imagine the Jam making *London Calling* – well, you can, but it would have been called *Woking Calling* and all the songs would have been about marginal mod characters in mohair sweaters and pointy shoes). There were plenty of punk groups for the punters who weren't fast enough for the Clash, but who wanted to follow the UK Subs or 999 when you could have the real thing?

They were massively politicised, too, initially at the behest of their manager Bernie Rhodes, and later because of Strummer's own passionate beliefs. In *The People's Music*, Ian MacDonald's collection of essays, the author of the seminal Beatles book *Revolution In The Head* described John Lennon's propensity for climbing up on his soapbox, "Even at its most sloganeering, his political output was driven by a fidelity to the truth as he saw it – and to him the true and the personal were indivisible." This could so easily apply to Joe Strummer, and to the Clash in general. They had high ambitions, the Clash, and usually had the talent to see them through.

In short, there are few groups who have embodied the communally energising spirit of rock'n'roll as much as they did. Ironically, the Clash arrived at a time when the rock'n'roll rulebook was about to be rewritten, although in reality what they did was draft a new blueprint. Just look at the facts. Their first album, *The Clash*, released in April 1977, was the definitive punk album, not just a statement of intent, but the punk rock experience in essence. Every song is now a classic, not just of the genre, but of rock music in general (they even created a punk-reggae hybrid with their Gary Glitter version of Junior Murvin's "Police & Thieves", a song they only recorded because the album was deemed to be too short – it added an extra six minutes, which in punk terms was almost the length of a rock opera, and introduced a whole generation to Jamaican music).

Give 'Em Enough Rope, the self-aggrandising follow-up released in November 1978, was full of pomp and bluster and given an American sheen (i.e. it sounded commercial) by producer SANDY PEARLMAN in an effort to break the USA. Their third album, *London Calling*, released thirteen months later, was a compendium of cool, featuring rockabilly, soul, reggae, rock, in fact almost anything but punk, and has since been called one of the best rock albums ever, by everyone from *Rolling Stone* and the *NME* to the *Sunday Times* and *GQ*; as double albums go, it is more consistent than the "White Album", and almost as good as *Blonde On Blonde*. The band's fourth album, the unwieldy three-disc *Sandinista!* (December 1980), was almost a BOB DYLAN-like exercise in image-destruction, confusing the fan base that had bought into *London Calling*, and alienating the critics (at the time the band thought that by releasing a triple album they would be working their way through their somewhat onerous record contract, whereas CBS naturally only counted the album as a single release). It did, however, introduce hip-hop to their audience. Their fifth album, *Combat Rock*, unleashed in 1982, was a consolidated return to form, full of panache and hit singles ("Rock The Casbah," "Should I Stay Or Should I Go"), and was the record that finally granted them a global audience.

But then the story gets messy: 1) Strummer and Simonon oust Jones from the band for being too much of a rock star. 2) Jones forms BIG AUDIO DYNAMITE and gets kudos and hits in equal measure. 3) Strummer asks him to come back, and on being rebuffed records the less-than-successful *Cut The Crap* (1985), an album largely driven by BERNIE RHODES' ego. And then they split up.

In a way the band's history is the ultimate rock'n'roll soap opera, a saga that ended with the unfortunate denouement of Strummer's untimely death. And unlike the SEX PISTOLS, whose standing has been diminished by the endless compilations,

C

their constant reforming and karaoke-like tours, and the erratic behaviour of JOHN LYDON, the Clash continue to rise in our estimations. Their compilations are few, far between, and always tastefully done; the remaining members have never tried to cash in on their legacy (something which is almost unheard of in this business); and the original band have never reformed. They haven't toured since MICK JONES left the group in 1983.

Unless you are one of those who thought that the band compromised themselves when they signed to CBS back in 1977, the Clash are one of the few bands to have never sold out. Above all else, the Clash have dignity, which is one of the reasons they are so well loved. After a generation and a half, the Clash continue to appeal to the rebel in all of us.

Which is why we still like pretending to be rebels.

In the mid-Noughties, as MICK JONES was trying to interest us all in his new band CARBON/SILICON, I spent an afternoon with him.

"You're not going to plug it in, are you?" said Jones, with a decidedly odd look on his face.

My first guitar lesson with MICK JONES was not going well. He was teaching me to play "Complete Control" – the Clash's finest hour and simply one of the best songs ever written – and he could tell that my six-stringed skills were not exactly what they should be. And I hadn't even turned my guitar on yet.

"You start with your fingers here, making an E, then you go here, and then end with an open A, before going into the chorus," he said, as he helped me move my fingers along the fretboard.

"Like this?" I asked, eagerly.

"Well, sort of," replied the ex-punk guitar hero. "Only, not really."

We were in his dilapidated west London studio, with ex-GENERATION X founder TONY JAMES – Jones' partner in CARBON/SILICON – and he was teaching me the rudiments of being a nascent guitar god. His initial reservations were tempered when I began to successfully pick out the chords. But then I blew it by admitting I used to be a drummer.

"I used to hang around with musicians," I said, echoing the oldest rehearsal joke in history.

Seeing that I spent a rather large part of my youth playing air guitar to "Complete Control" in front of my bedroom mirror, to actually be in the same room as the man who wrote it, the man who played it, having him teach me how to play it was, I have to admit, something of a fantasy come true. The Clash were for me, like they were for many boys of my generation, simply the most exciting, most visceral pop experience there had ever been.

Aged seventeen, a fully fledged musical butterfly, already well-versed in the musings of everyone from DAVID BOWIE, the MONKEES, and GRAM PARSONS, to OTIS REDDING, CAN, and JONI MITCHELL, nothing – and I mean nothing, not even MC5, the WHO, the STOOGES, or the RAMONES – had prepared me for the sonic amphetamine that was "Complete Control". Punk had thrown up many guitar-based calls to arms – "Anarchy In The UK" by the SEX PISTOLS, "Boredom" by the BUZZCOCKS, and "In The City" by the JAM, to name only the first three that spring to mind – but even the Clash's first LP had nothing that compared to their third single, an extraordinary barrage of buzzsaw guitar produced by reggae superstar LEE "SCRATCH" PERRY.

Many of the band's fans thought they had "sold out" by signing to CBS, and when the record company decided to release "Remote Control", a third-division track from their debut album, without consulting the band, they felt vindicated. The Clash, meanwhile, went berserk. This was the chief lyrical inspiration for "Complete Control", a song largely composed by MICK JONES, even though it's credited to both him and JOE STRUMMER. It had such a sense of defiance, in both a micro and macro way, it not only quickly became the benchmark by which other Clash records would be judged, but all other punk records full stop. Released on September 23, 1977, it was the apotheosis of punk, and not a better record would be released under its generic umbrella. Everything on "Complete Control" had been amped-up: the dials on the mixing desk, the furious vocals, the anger and especially the guitar.

But could I learn to play it? Ironically, MICK JONES had actually taught TONY JAMES to play guitar when he joined CARBON/SILICON, and if he'd taught him, then why not me? James had spent twenty-five years playing bass, and it was only when the two schoolboy friends began playing together again in the early Noughties that James switched toys. "I'd been a guitar hero for most of my life," said MICK JONES, "so I thought it was someone else's turn."

As TONY JAMES looked on, MICK JONES took me through my paces once more, singing along at the top of his voice, his Westway whine taking me all the way back to the 100 Club, the Roxy and the Hammersmith Palais.

JARVIS COCKER

It is not often that I go to auctions, but this one was too good to miss, far too good. It was 1997, and Bonhams in Knightsbridge was holding one of its irregular design sales. Lot 114 was something I had lusted after for years: a complete bound set of *Nova* magazine, from 1965 to 1975, this collection including the dummy edition, as well as – bizarrely – a book of promotional matches. *Nova,* not only the perfect manifestation of the Swinging Sixties, but one of the most influential women's magazines of its time, a kaleidoscopic amalgam of provocative fashion, hard-edged journalism and gender politics. The estimated sale price was £500-£800, something of a bargain, so I thought I was in with a serious chance.

As I waited for my lot to come up I could hear the room slowly filling up, and feel the cold sweat begin to form a shallow pool in the middle of my back. And when we finally got to Lot 114, my heart felt and sounded like KEITH MOON's kick drum, only louder. The opening bid was small, in the hundreds, but as it quickly climbed, way up passed one thousand, and then two, there were only two people left bidding – me, stupidly sitting in the front row, and someone right at the back. As it reached £2,400 I shook my head and bowed out. And as I wiped the sweat from my brow, my wife leant over and whispered, "It's Jarvis Cocker."

"Him?!" I whispered back. "What the hell does he want those for? I hope he's going to steal the ideas and use them as well as I was!" In a way he already had. The cover of PULP's 1995 LP, *Different Class*, was based on an old *Nova* layout, while the band's designers continued to plunder the magazine's typography throughout their career. In a way Cocker has always been very *Nova* himself: quintessentially arch, decidedly irreverent, and studiedly cool. And someone who likes to wear his social conscience on his sleeve. Next to the braiding.

Afterwards, we found ourselves in the same coffee bar. While I queued up for some conciliatory cappuccinos, my wife went up to Cocker and asked him how high he would have gone, though on this occasion Cocker's legendary wit deserted him and he just shrugged and stared at the floor. So much for my second brush with one of Britain's most iconoclastic pop stars.

Nine months later, a brightly dressed Lowry stick man loomed into the basement that once housed Bunjies Coffee House and Folk Cellar, a bunker just off Charing Cross Road that probably hadn't changed since it opened over forty years previously (it closed in 1999); Cocker first discovered the place when he was studying at Central Saint Martins College of Art round the corner. That day he was wearing a black and white gingham overcoat, an ill-fitting black suit, a brown jersey, and a pair of brownish pointy boots. He looked as though he bought his clothes in a place called the Dandy Fashion Charity Shop (a sort of blend between JAKE THACKERAY and SERGE GAINSBOURG), and his middle-aged student ensemble

C

– Cocker was thirty-four when we met then – was amplified by the carrier bag full of books he held with both hands. He seemed distant, but quite personable. He did, however, look incredibly miserable. Both in person and on record, Cocker has always had the requisite dour sensibility of a northern post-punk bard, which was perfectly reasonable seeing that his songs with PULP were like MIKE LEIGH plays set to music – little kitsch'n'sink dramas about urban deprivation and strange sex. Cocker's lyrics, which were always the group's mainstay, were perfect examples of lo-fi realism, full of dirty fingernails and soiled undergarments, damp council flats and indiscriminate muggings. His songs back then concerned misfits, inadequacy (he once went on stage in a wheelchair), drugs and, most pertinently, class. At the time he also liked to make a virtue out of celebrating the commonplace. Cocker was a man who liked fish and chips ("not fries"), PG Tips, Marmite (with the pre-1983 metal lids), red post boxes and Routemaster buses, smokestack skylines, the World Service and good old-fashioned right-wing politicians he could despise (he admitted TONY BLAIR totally confused him, not really understanding that this was the point of Blair all along). And I very much got the feeling that he would prefer things to stay the same so he could remain in opposition.

Cocker has always had genuine outsider status, and while the rock and roll blueprint has for some years been an acceptable and expected lifestyle option, he remains genuinely bohemian, and consequently totally believable. He doesn't appear to be a bohemian for the sake of it; it's not a lifestyle choice. As someone once said of BRUCE SPRINGSTEEN, he understands that great art is something that happens because of everyday life, not in place of it. ALAN SAMSON, a man who published one of my books a few years ago, has a perfect story about Cocker. Returning one year from the book fair in Frankfurt, Samson had come across Cocker going round and round the luggage carousel at Heathrow. "He wasn't doing anything, he didn't look drunk. He was just being a suitcase. It was real carry-on Cocker."

It is over ten years since the end of Cocker's first proper flush of fame, and not only has he successfully distanced himself from the "weed in tweed"/Britpop poet laureate label, he has reinvented himself as some sort of laissez-faire renaissance man. Still, like other miserabilists before him, Cocker is paradoxically vain. Speak to people who know him and they'll tell you that his biggest crime – probably his only crime, to be fair – is being too self-obsessed. It's hardly surprising that a pop star should be self-conscious, particularly one who has wanted to be famous from an early age, but some are better at it than others. "He knows exactly how his shirt's behaving when you photograph him," said someone who has shot him several times over the past few years. "He composes his whole body in front of the camera as though he were a mannequin. It's like there's this ordinary man transforming himself into this weird-looking nerdy guy. But a weird-looking nerdy guy who knows exactly how he should be photographed, and from which side." Of course this may just be the result of what he calls "an absurd level of self-consciousness," one that he says makes any sort of social encounter an ordeal for him.

The thing is, Cocker led such a bold, mediated life in the Nineties that much of the apocrypha surrounding him is true. The women. The drugs. The confrontation. It would be easy to imagine Cocker as a Britpop constant, an arch northerner determined to bring a little MORRISSEY-esque patois to the lady environment created by OASIS and BLUR, but his archness was largely a result of his diffidence. If he imagined himself as PEE-WEE HERMAN diffused by INGMAR BERGMAN, in truth he was more like an ALBERT FINNEY character accessorised and scripted by MALCOLM MCLAREN. There is a preening importance about Cocker, but not an importance that's unwarranted. Yes, he can be slightly tricky in restaurants, but he's never going to lord it over people – although he would be too embarrassed to fully embrace JACK NICHOLSON's chicken salad sandwich routine in BOB RAFELSON's 1970 film *Five Easy Pieces*, one can easily imagine him doing it in a slightly chippy northern way.

C He is such a traditional English eccentric that by rights he ought to be gay, but he is anything but. While he looks more like an elongated, first-year biochemistry student than a pop star, he has become something of a heterosexual rock god. When I first interviewed him – for the *Sunday Times Magazine* – back in 1993, he was just on the cusp of fame, and found this notion ridiculous. "If I do become a sex symbol I'll be overcoming my natural disabilities," he said. "I look more like a game-show contestant – I'm lanky, with bad eyesight. In reality I look more like an ugly girl."

By 2009 – perhaps slightly disingenuously – he said he still hadn't come to terms with it, and in 1997, when he was probably at the height of his fame, it was the same. "I think I've passed my sell-by date on that score. You might be sexy but you can't have sex with people, because it ends up in the papers. You've probably got more opportunities than you've ever had at any other period in your life, but you can't really take advantage of them. Plus I think there's something deeply unsound about sleeping with someone who thinks you're great. Why spoil their beautiful dream by actually doing it to them? There's a friend of mine who used to say that he wanted to become famous and then have sex with people really badly, to puncture their illusions. He never became famous but I believe he did the second part quite a lot."

So, did he have a moral code?

"Well, I'm not an angel, but your life loses its shape if you don't impose some discipline on it. Maybe I just keep saying it to try and keep myself out of trouble."

He was approaching fifty, and while there were flecks of silver in his hair, he was still wearing stack-heeled leather shoes, making him look like a gangly polytechnic lecturer from the very early Seventies. "It's like, what are you going to gain from wearing flat shoes," he told me in 2009. "You're still tall, so why not just go for it? I admire that about BETH DITTO – she just goes, 'Here you are, that's it.' I think it's great. By not being ashamed of it, and accentuating it even, you turn it into something quite positive rather than something you're ashamed of."

Since folding PULP after their last album *We Love Life* in 2001, Cocker has found the time to write songs for MARIANNE FAITHFULL, CHARLOTTE GAINSBOURG, and NANCY SINATRA, curate the Meltdown festival on London's South Bank, direct pop videos, contribute songs to both *Harry Potter and the Goblet of Fire* and *Children of Men*, guest edit Radio 4's *Today* programme (quizzing JONNY WILKINSON about quantum physics), write and record his own solo work – his 2006 album *Jarvis* was awarded four stars by practically every magazine and newspaper – tour sporadically, and give a series of lectures on lyric-writing. "Most of the great riffs, chord sequences and basslines have already been written," he said in a lecture at Manchester's In The City conference in 2008. "But lyrics can breathe fresh life into rock music... [although] they're not essential. Take the KINGSMEN's 'Louie Louie'. You can't tell a word the singer's singing but it's the definitive version of that song. Lyrics are an optional extra, like a patio or a sunroof. You can live without them, but they do improve the quality of life."

At the end of 2008, the professional malcontent joined the likes of LAURIE ANDERSON, KT TUNSTALL, and MARTHA WAINWRIGHT on a voyage to the aptly named Disko Bay in the Arctic Circle to investigate climate change. They were among an eclectic band of musicians, artists and scientists aboard the Russian research ship, Grigory Mikheev, in the Cape Farewell project partly funded by the Arts Council. The two-week voyage to the remote west coast of Greenland was aimed at highlighting the potentially cataclysmic threat of global warming which is causing the Polar Regions to melt.

It was a laudable exercise, but not very Jarvis. Why did he go? "Well, it was obvious," said Jarvis, sitting in the considered mess of his Paris apartment. "I was saving the world..."

In many ways his second solo album, *Further Complications* (2009), was a far more confident attempt at

C

self-justification than his first. This one was more aggressive, more straightforward, and much less arch. The Cocker you meet on this record is like a far more hetero MORRISSEY, a sophisticate acrobat rifling through a bunch of old MOTT THE HOOPLE and FACES records. The CD sampler came with room on the back for reviewers' notes, and some of mine included "glam" (for the song "Angela"), "the FALL" (for "Pilchard"), "the FACES, overwrought, classic, awesome, loser, 'Mandolin Wind'" ("Leftovers", the standout track on the album), "maudlin disco" ("You're In My Eyes (Discosong)").

Cocker was born in Sheffield, and went to school in a downtrodden suburb called Intake. By the time he had reached his teens, most of the city's industry had gone, and it was a bleak and depressing landscape for any adolescent to grow up in, let alone one as introverted as Cocker. His father had left home when Jarvis was only seven. An acquaintance of the singer JOE COCKER, his father would often pretend to be his brother, a pose he kept up when he moved to Australia. Jarvis's mother – who would, much to her son's irritation, later work as a Conservative councillor – was so hard up after he left that she took a job emptying fruit machines. Two years ago Cocker was reunited with his father when he flew to Australia with his sister Saskia to meet him. At the time Cocker admitted the reunion was far from a happy occasion. "If this happened on a TV show we'd all have been in floods of tears and declaring how much we loved each other. But although we are biologically related it was like meeting someone I didn't know. We didn't have a parent-child relationship."

Forced to wear glasses after he contracted meningitisaged five, Jarvis's demeanour wasn't helped by the fact that his mother sent him to school wearing lederhosen, a present from some German relatives that she thought might look cute. He was not exactly an outgoing child. When he was fourteen he was kidnapped by two middle-aged men in an Escort van, reluctantly agreeing to a lift after his mother had told him to be more sociable. The men then tried to sexually assault him, though Cocker says – undoubtedly with the gift of hindsight

– he outwitted them with sarcasm. There was a strong duality to his teenage years, with half of him lusting after an imagined Martini lifestyle ("I took far too much notice of magazines and TV"), and the other half firmly rooted in the housing estates of Intake. He had ambition, but wasn't sure what to do with it, and after narrowly failing to get into Oxford to read English, he went on the dole. For six long years.

"I was always on the fringes of things at school, but when I left it became even worse. You can't help but feel marginalised when you're unemployed. We were a demographic group that absolutely no advertising was aimed at – basically we were the doley scumbags. And then after a while people become adrift, and without a structure you can quite easily end up sitting in your kitchen smoking all day, which obviously isn't a good way to spend your life."

On a whim, he formed PULP with a bunch of friends in 1980, but during the next six years they experienced such a spectacular lack of success that not once did he come off Social Security. Such was his disillusionment with the group that he interrupted their rickety climb to stardom by enrolling at Central Saint Martins in 1988 to study film-making. This obviously necessitated a move to London, which helped the nascent rock god become acclimatised to a world that up until then he had only fantasised about. He was both excited and repelled by what he found, as never before had he been exposed to so many people from so many different backgrounds. Saint Martins was also where he met the "posh" girl from Greece for whom dirty East End bedsits and "common" working-class guttersnipes such as Jarvis seemed perversely exotic. It was she who would inspire the class-war anthem, "Common People", that would later turn PULP from an interesting bunch of second-raters into world-beating pop iconoclasts.

"Back home I was very anti-London, very anti the fact that everything was based down here," said Cocker. "I'm glad I was brought up in Sheffield because although there wasn't anything going on, if there's no culture then you have to invent it. When I moved to London I was quite resentful. But I got over that. I didn't want to end up like one of those people with a chip on their shoulder who'll only go to pubs if they serve northern ale.

"The thing I had to get used to is that in Sheffield everything happens in the centre of town, it's like a village. When we came to London we used to do the same thing, we'd come into the centre of town on a Saturday night and stand in Piccadilly Circus and think, what the f*** are we supposed to do now?"

While at college, Cocker kept his band going, albeit on a part-time basis. Then, in 1993, having left Saint Martins, the world suddenly seemed to catch up with him and things stared going right. All of a sudden PULP were fashionable. Their single "Babies" (the narrative of which concerns a boy hiding in a wardrobe to watch his girlfriend's sister having sex) was picked up by a major record label, Island, and became a hit with the leather-jacketed inkslingers from the weekly music press. This was followed in 1994 by genuinely popular singles such as "Lip Gloss" and "Do You Remember the First Time?" (loosely based on Cocker's own loss of virginity, at the age of nineteen) and a hit album, *His'n'Hers*. Critical mass was soon achieved with the monumentally successful singles "Common People" (a classic class song), "Sorted for Es & Wizz" (a classic drugs song), and "Disco 2000" (a classic teenage song) a year later, along with their critically applauded breakthrough album, *Different Class*. Suddenly Jarvis Cocker was a household name.

And then no sooner had Cocker become famous than he did something so out of character that his world was changed forever. On February 19, 1996, he invaded the stage at the Brit awards when MICHAEL JACKSON was halfway through one of his messianic hymns. It was a long time ago but still it defines him. Overnight, Cocker became a tabloid star, splashed all over the *Mirror,* the *Sun*, and the *News of the World*, the lanky northerner who dared to attack the King of Pop. The attention still rankles. "It was like suddenly turning into MICKEY MOUSE," says Cocker. Rather ridiculously, this display cast him as some kind of rock'n'roll animal. "Lots of people still expect me to be a NOEL EDMONDS type who's always doing a Gotcha, planting whoopee cushions under people's seats. It was only an expression of moral indignation, and I hate the fact that I'm still known for it.

"In Sheffield I had a lot of time to build up a picture of what fame might be like. But when you become famous you begin to wonder what defect in your personality made you want to be famous in the first place. It was a very strange experience for us, having been so out of step with what was going on for years and years, to suddenly realise that we were producing something that was right for the time. Everything about the group happened in the wrong way, because by the age of thirty-one most people would have knocked it on the head."

His ambivalence to fame was later manifested in PULP's somewhat transgressive single, "This Is Hardcore", which was famously inspired by the lonely nights in hotel rooms where Jarvis's only friend was in-house pornography. Having gone out in a major way in the mid-Nineties - "You can snort as much cocaine as you want and have as many beautiful women as you want," he famously said, "but it doesn't make you happy" – he decided to stay in, in a major way, too. "There's always an adult channel in the hotels where we stay, and each night I'd usually end up watching them," Cocker said at the time. "It's safer to stay in and watch a porno video than to go out on the town, and it made me think about the people watching." Perhaps predictably the song was also about coming a bit too close to the object of your desires. Perhaps the most pertinent lyrics on the record were these: "I am not Jesus though I have the same initials, I stay at home and do the dishes."

These days the ninth arrondissement of Paris is his home. He lives with his wife, a French stylist called CAMILLA BIDAULT-WADDINGTON, and their young son, Albert (a name that Jarvis thinks makes his boy sound like a trade union leader). There is an air of gentrification in his Paris flat, and it is a

C long way from the elegant Maida Vale tip he used to live in back in London. With piles of uneaten food in the kitchen, dirty cocktail glasses in the bathroom, and rows and rows of Cocker's oddball LPs pushed up against the living-room walls, it had all the trappings of student accommodation. It was also very Seventies, and was full of tan leather sofas, smoked-glass tables and chrome-fronted mirrors. "The estate agent said, don't worry about the décor, it can be changed," said Cocker. "I went to look at it and it was perfect, it was somebody's Seventies bachelor pad and looked like the kind of place where you could make a porn movie. In a way it was good because I didn't have to take it seriously as a place to live." In contrast, the Paris flat could be described as having the sort of bohemian chic you might find in a film: huge Sixties lamps, extravagant paper flowers, framed Pop Art prints, carefully thrown throws.

Those who have never met Cocker assume he takes himself so seriously that he has no real sense of humour. This isn't so, although his SOH is very particular, to wit: "I met a friend the other day who said, 'You'll never guess who I just saw filling up his car at the petrol station.' I said, 'No, who was it?' He said, 'RON JEREMY.' I said, 'How did you know it was RON JEREMY?' He said, 'Well, halfway through, he took the nozzle out of his car and sprayed the rest all over the windscreen.'"

Irony has always been the big thing in Cocker's world, something he used with ease when working his way through the mid-Nineties, digital version of Swinging London. "It would be great to walk into a club like JOHN TRAVOLTA does in *Saturday Night Fever* and have everyone give you a high five and yelp hello, but the reality is having some drunk going, 'How's MICHAEL JACKSON, eh?' Having said that, I've been lucky. I've not had too many people wanting to kick my face in. At first I shied away from public places because I was embarrassed. I became a bit of a social liability." So for a while he did the private members' club in Soho where a paranoid pop star is always welcome, and where it's easier to indulge in the kind of behaviour that can get you thrown out of places where real people go. He was courteous, too, to the Imogens, Camillas and Jaspers he bumped into along the way, the very people he privately professed to despise. He stopped going out, he says, when he read that he'd attended the tenth anniversary party of *Starlight Express*.

Cocker still enjoys making records, still enjoys performing, although you get the feeling that he knows that being a pop star isn't a dignified profession for a man of his age, even if he does still occasionally talk like an eighteen-year-old punk. Maybe he really wants to be DAVID BOWIE but feels vaguely embarrassed about the fact (although if truth be known there are probably hundreds of thousands of men in their thirties, forties and fifties who still, rather stupidly, dream about being DAVID BOWIE back in the Seventies). Whatever, he certainly cares about his place in the grand scheme of things.

When I spell-checked his quotes after transcribing the 1997 interview, I was surprised to see the number of times Cocker had used the word "cliché", as though it were the devils own mantra. The thought of softening at the edges obviously caused him great anguish, as it does now. At the time he was worried, too, that he was beginning to tolerate many of the things he used to despise. Having lived with failure for fifteen years, having been the victim of cultural biorhythms, he was finding it hard to throw off his convictions. It's been said that Cocker's epitaph should be, "Be careful what you wish for, lest it come true," and it seems perfectly fitting. In the last fifteen years he appears to have found a way to loosen up without abandoning what he believes in, although you're never going to see him in a Ferrari, or hobnobbing with the Politerati in Corfu. Yes, he should probably be a little less hard on himself, but then that's not a very Jarvis Cocker thing to do, is it?

A few months after his successful bid for the *Nova* set at Bonhams, and several weeks after I had stopped putting pins in a small Jarvis-like Action Man doll, he was asked why he bought them. He said he wanted the magazines "for the look and the graphic style" which he happily admitted to having plundered for the artwork on *Different Class*. When I spoke

C

to him a few weeks ago he said he was taking good care of the magazines, and that if he ever tired of them, he'd let me have them. "But I doubt I will," he said. Asked by his interrogator back in 1997 if he had to go through an ugly bidding war to get them, he replied, "I did actually. My rival was a man I vaguely recognised, and it became a really macho thing in the end. Whoever didn't get the women's magazines was going to leave that room never able to get an erection again."

LEONARD COHEN

Leonard Cohen makes the sort of music you send to people who are gravely ill, perhaps because the texture and sonorous nature of his voice can give the listener the sense that their illness has a kind of gravitas (and perhaps that they themselves might be too important to die). OK, we mutter to ourselves, here is a guy who has lived. Been around. Even worked with PHIL SPECTOR, which can't have been easy. He lived for five years as a Buddhist monk, and had experienced huge swathes of depression. And he liked the ladies, too.

Maybe he's not had the most distinguished of careers, and yes there is the distinct feeling that he has been so celebrated in the last few years because we have finished celebrating every other pop icon of the Sixties, and there is simply no one left. But heigh ho – we feel quite benevolent towards him. He's an underdog, right? Quite like his records, every now and then, actually. Yes, it's not that hard to buy into him.

The Canadian BOB DYLAN, the SAMUEL BECKETT of pop, Cohen is a Boomer artist who wasn't properly acknowledged until he was in his dotage. And then it was only by accident. In 2006, he won a lawsuit against a former manager, after millions of dollars went missing from his retirement fund, leaving Cohen virtually penniless (rumour has it that even his cashpoint card wouldn't work, so potless was he). Hence a hastily arranged world tour, with Cohen donning the grey fedora and the *Guys And Dolls* double-barrelled suit (he couldn't have looked more like JOSEPH BEUYS if he'd tried), traversing the globe on a valedictory mission, to speak to his people one last time. A well-read, bass-baritone crooner with a great bedside manner, Cohen's comeback was surprisingly dignified, and he really had got better with age (he hadn't performed live for fifteen years). The songs sound better from a distance, too: "Suzanne", "Bird On A Wire", "Who By Fire", "Hallelujah", and the great mid-period material, "First We Take Manhattan", "Everybody Knows", and "I'm Your Man".

NIK COHN

"Most of the people I knew from the Sixties are dead," said Nik Cohn, forty-seven, in 1992. "I feel very lucky that I've survived. In those days it was complete Russian roulette – why is JIMI HENDRIX dead and ERIC CLAPTON alive, when it should be the other way round? It's completely a spin of the wheel.

"I should be dead. If I had died when I was thirty-three, which I suppose was the age when I was attempting to die, I would have missed out on by far the most interesting part of my life."

It is half a lifetime since Nik Cohn's name first appeared in print, yet he remains one of the most widely imitated writers on popular culture. A pop prodigy, he produced his first novel, *Market*, when he was eighteen ("Nobody dared turn down an eighteen-year-old in 1964," Cohn said, "just in case he might turn out to be the literary equivalent to the BEATLES"), and his second, *I Am Still The Greatest Says Johnny Angelo* (in which he perfected the fictionalised pop biography), at twenty. Two years later he bashed out, in four weeks, the classic thesis on pop. *Awopbopaloobop Alopbamboom,* a paean to the glory days of "teendream" and the three-minute single, and dedicated to JET POWERS, JOHNNY ACE and DEAN ANGEL. These

C

were followed by two more novels, *Arfur: Teenage Pinball Queen*, which inspired the Who's PETE TOWNSHEND to write the rock opera *Tommy*, and later, *King Death*.

Cohn's high-octane, Cuban-heeled, Day-Glo, bobby-dazzler prose turned pop writing on its head. He loved the brash, hated the pretentious; loved ELVIS, hated Dylan. Like TOM WOLFE before him and PETER YORK after him, Cohn was a pulp man, someone who understood the implicit elitism of the popular. He appreciated the simplicity, intelligence and wit.

Cohn was as obsessed with fashion as he was with pop, and in 1971 wrote *Today There Are No Gentlemen*, which contained portraits of every style and subculture from Mod to Hippy, from Carnaby Street to Mayfair. Ten years before PETER YORK reinvented style journalism with *Style Wars*, Cohn devoted thousands of carefully manicured words to the art and meaning of the trouser. Then in 1973 came *Rock Dreams*, the illustrated history of rock'n'roll by Belgian artist GUY PEELLAERT, to which Cohn contributed the pithiest of captions. For surface smarts, waspish wit and sartorial exposition, Cohn was the man.

Upstairs in London's Groucho Club, Cohn was lunching on calves' liver and Chardonnay, having walked in from Soho clutching a plastic carrier bag full of sports books. He was in London to receive the Thomas Cook Travel Book Award for his book about Broadway, *The Heart of the World*. Rather more portly than he had been in his prime, Cohn had literally grown into himself, yet beneath the beard you could still see the smug, agreeable face which careered around London in the Sixties, poking fun at pop stars, fashion plates and socialites.

During the giddy times Cohn wrote like a man possessed. Finding himself at the centre of a youthquake whirlpool of fashion, pop and media, he used his pen like a gun, shooting everything in sight; though he was never one for rose-tinted spectacles. "Nik is no obituarist," Kit Lambert, the former co-manager of the WHO, wrote in his introduction to

Awopbopaloobop, "but if he did write your obituary you'd be better off dead." He wasn't lying.

Always a dandy, Cohn in his forties was a little less fastidious, and dressed like an off-duty GEORGE MELLY (though he was still partial to fedoras). He had a soft manner, and only became demonstrative when presented with a "fact" that was only fiction.

"Some people much prefer me as someone who writes mythology," he said, a little disingenuously, "and they build stories around me, as though I were a tree. I always hated icons, and certainly don't want to become one."

There is no need to exaggerate the Nik Cohn myth (even if he has done so himself at times), as he has lived an extraordinary life. If he doesn't quite read like one of his own characters, it is only because he's not dead.

He was born in London in 1946, and grew up in Northern Ireland. His father, the academic NORMAN COHN, wrote *The Pursuit of the Millennium*, and various other books about mass lunacy. It was in Derry, at the age of eleven, that the young Nik Cohn fell in love with rock'n'roll America, and himself. Wandering into a café in the Catholic part of town, he heard LITTLE RICHARD on the jukebox and found a reason to be young: "I had no idea anything could be that good or exciting." As for America, "I would have moved then and there if someone had given me money for the passage."

Instead, the family Cohn moved to Newcastle. And as they did, Cohn made a promise to move to London. Two years later he was there, living in Islington, working for the *Observer* sports desk – "There was appalling, ritualistic drinking in those days. Journalists, literally, were poured into taxi cabs" – attempting freelance journalism and writing fiction.

Having written *Market* and *Johnny Angelo*, Cohn became part of a scene which he then proceeded to disembowel. He hit Swinging London with a vengeance, and didn't look back. The extravagance of pop, the significance of fashion, the brutality of fame. A moralist at heart, he was both fascinated and appalled by what he saw, never failing to mention this in his copy. Cohn was always too big for his Cuban heels, and when his subjects began to bore him, moved himself centre stage.

Though Cohn strenuously denies it, it was often assumed that he embellished his encounters. He even said as much in an interview with GORDON BURN in *The Face* in 1987, "Not having been to a place never stopped me from describing it. Any more than not meeting someone stopped me talking about my interview with them." One apocryphal story has him on a press trip to the Caribbean, then fabricating a mugging in order to jazz up his copy. Stories like these are legion. The reason for many people's distrust of Cohn's sources dates back to a feature he wrote for *New York* magazine in 1976 entitled "Tribal Rites Of The New Saturday Night", a journalistic essay which was subsequently turned into the phenomenally successful *Saturday Night Fever*, the film which brought disco and JOHN TRAVOLTA to the world stage.

Cohn had moved to New York as the Seventies began, abandoning London and his pop icon status, and began writing a column for *New York* called Low Outside. In one of his first pieces he focused on a nightclub in the New York suburb of Bay Ridge, called Odyssey 2001, where disco had firmly taken root. It was such an evocative piece that it was immediately optioned by film producer ROBERT STIGWOOD, who, along with Paramount Pictures, turned it into an urban safari of immense proportions. But the remarkable thing was that Cohn had made the whole thing up. Unable to infiltrate Odyssey's tightly-knit groups of disco disciples, and believing that "nasty pieces of work aged nineteen are the same in any country, any generation", he decided to base his characters on the mods he had known in London's Shepherd's Bush ten years previously. Astonishingly, no one noticed.

Nevertheless, Cohn claims not to have made a habit of it, "In *The Heart of the World* there are two people whose names have been changed because of the law. But none of it's made up, it's all incredibly, ploddingly real. Apart from *Fever*, *King Death* is the one really spurious thing I wrote. It wasn't written with anger or lunacy, it was manufactured."

Fever made Cohn a dollar millionaire, and the logical step seemed to be in the direction of Hollywood. With a friend from the music business called PETER RUDGE, Cohn signed a production deal with Paramount, and committed himself to making movies. Paramount wanted hits, but not the kind of hits Cohn wanted to produce.

"I was Mr Big," said Cohn, the noise from the rapidly filling restaurant adding unnecessary poignancy to the remark. "We had these huge four-page ads in *Variety* saying Mr Big says come on boys, jump on board! And then, like everyone else who's ever gone there, I found out that all the clichés about Hollywood are true, and a week later I was back. I've got a lot of faults, but I've never been overwhelmed by the idea of more money, and that seemed to be the only reason to go to Hollywood. When I had money, I couldn't wait to give it away. If I got rich now, what would I do? Probably get back into drugs again."

And it was drugs which occupied him for much of the next five years, drugs helped him Hoover up most of those cool million bucks. During this period Cohn was using cocaine heavily, and the drug became an obsession, almost to the exclusion of everything else. Like many of his contemporaries – young, talented upstarts who had gained entry to the good life on the coat tails of the Swinging Sixties – Cohn ignored work, and, instead, coasted. "My excessive behaviour was always the symptom, not the cause. I didn't fuck up because I was using drugs, I was fucked up so I used drugs. And a very nasty piece of work I was too. For me, excess was very much a denial of being human. Drugs aren't that bad for you – yes, of course, they might kill you – but they make it absolute hell for those around you who aren't on drugs.

"If I had died when I was thirty-three in a drug haze, I would never have experienced what it's like to love another human being, which is after all the most interesting thing about being alive. Suddenly I woke up one day and didn't want to do it anymore. I saw what damage I was causing, and I was horrified. So I stopped."

C Even so, Cohn's lost years weren't over yet. In 1983, when he was thirty-seven, in the course of an FBI investigation into an alleged drug smuggling ring, he was arrested at his townhouse in New York, and charged with conspiring to distribute drugs. Cohn faced ten years mandatory, and spent two desperate nights in jail before being released on bail.

"That first night was the worst of my life. If you get thrown into a jail in New York, it really changes your ideas about what you want to do with the rest of your life if you ever do get out, because at that point you're convinced you won't. It's not the fear that gets to you, it's the unbelievable corruption, and how hopeless the individual is. Even my lawyer couldn't believe I wasn't guilty of something."

Immediately after release they brought back the charges, "I knew they'd bought someone in jail. So in the end I pleaded guilty to something I hadn't done, possession. Because if I hadn't done, I can guarantee that I wouldn't be talking to you today."

After two weeks of freedom he met his third wife, Michaela, with whom he moved to the serenity of Shelter Island, New York. (His first wife was an East End mod called Jill, whom he married when he was nineteen; while his second – a pragmatic arrangement, to grant her a work permit – was apparently a Canadian pinball champion called Arfur, whom he managed for a while and later mythologised in his third novel). It was here that Cohn began the long, slow climb back. Not through therapy, not through medication, but through reading.

For the next few years Cohn spent more time in libraries than he had once spent in bars, devouring thousands of classic texts, including one – ROBERT BURTON's *The Anatomy Of Melancholy* – which he claims to have read ten times.

Soon, it was time to get back to work. Having purged himself of his past, Cohn set off on another journey, along Broadway, New York's Great White Way. He spent the best part of two years sitting in bars, on benches, and in taxis, mixing with the local stars, hearing their stories, and turning them into parables. *The Heart Of The World*, as the book was subsequently called, was part travelogue, part odyssey. In a flurry of Runyonesque pathos he described his encounters with boxers and magicians, artists and dealers, strippers and con-men, prophets and fools. He was accompanied, on occasions, by a Puerto Rican transvestite called Lush Life, one of the many reasons this book couldn't have been written about London. "A walk along Oxford Street doesn't have quite the same resonance," Cohn said. "It's impossible to imagine Whitehall running into Brick Lane, which is what happens on Broadway; you go past City Hall, then you're in the art world, then you're in Chinatown, all in a matter of four or five blocks. In England everything's in a box."

And everybody's in a tribe, be they banker, baker, or new-age traveller. During the Eighties, people-spotting was almost as popular as money, and the style press – quickly followed by Fleet Street – fell over themselves to create suitably scathing subcultural acronyms. For all that, without Cohn, without his social anthropology, little of this would have happened. He might not have liked the fact that he helped spawn a decade of narcissistic endeavour – "this obsession with pop and style is terribly overdone, here" – but Cohn was saddled with it.

Had he ever been tempted to climb back on the horse, and tackle some of the contemporary pop icons? "I like dirty bastards and dirty bitches, always have done, but the only person I like is PRINCE. Rock and roll for me has always been simply a matter of being full of it, and this boy is stuffed to the very gills with it, he oozes it. The idea of this little hybrid, mulatto wimp from Minneapolis turning into Prince? Forget it. Which is why I like him so much.

"But I'm an old geezer, it's somebody else's turn. To take my opinions seriously would be mad. Journalism is about opinions, and one of the penalties of spending a lifetime in bars is that you realise that there's no such thing as an interesting opinion. When I don't write I become even more unpleasant than usual, and everything in my life fucks up. From the age of sixteen on, it's been as simple as that. If I don't write every day, I've got nothing to do."

C When we met, Nik Cohn didn't feel he had left much of a legacy – "A good writer is someone who's died and left five good books. I've got four and a half to go" – and felt obliged to correct this. "It's always a shock for me when I come to England, because suddenly I become my past. Where I live, years go by without anyone mentioning *Today There Are No Gentlemen*. Then I come here and see people actually carrying these books, which I don't even own. It's very flattering at one level, yet the least interesting aspect of my life is that I once wrote *Awopbopaloobop*. The people who hold that stuff in high esteem miss the whole point of it, which was always, if it's wrong, who gives a fuck? It was ephemera. My pieces were like pop songs, and if you can still hum them, then fine.

"We all made a promise in our twenties, to give it up when we reached twenty-five. I kept it, but MICK JAGGER and PETE TOWNSHEND lied. I felt like I was charging forward on a battlefield, only to look around and find nobody had moved! In this business you're either young or old, and I'm an old dog. I like it; I don't even mind being fat, although I'd like to be a little less fat."

The wine glass was set down, and he ordered a vodka and tonic (he was under doctor's orders not to drink whisky), as his daughter (a psychiatric nurse, then in her early twenties) arrived to take him to another appointment. Lunch was technically over (Cohn barely touched his), but you got the impression that it could have gone on all afternoon, and merged seamlessly into dinner. But then this was an all too readily painted portrait. For Cohn was not sad. And Cohn was not bitter. He might have relinquished his throne, but it was one he didn't particularly want in the first place.

"I write about totally unimportant, irrelevant things," he said in an interview in 1967, "but I fill a demand and as a result I've never had it so good. I've made a wonderful thing out of the young cult, which I despise. I've done very well out of Swinging London and I despise that too. It's churlish of me I know, because I wouldn't be making so much money if these things didn't exist, but I really do loathe the falsity an the intellectual campness of these worlds.

"I'm terribly overpaid. But I think the excitement of money will wear off and I hope to be able to manoeuvre from having made money to do the thing I want to do, which means write really good books."

Cohn would go on to write more books, the best being *Triksta*, a terrifically unsentimental account of his engagement with hip hop.

COLDPLAY

They are the revenge of nice. And they do it very well. Coldplay were probably the UK's biggest success story of the Noughties, a truly epic band who have been able to get most of the world to light their lighters in appreciation. Their songs are big, expansive and laden with hooks, the kind never achieved by all those who are meant to have influenced them (RADIOHEAD, TRAVIS, ECHO & THE BUNNYMEN, etc). They are a proper, no-nonsense rock group (frontman CHRIS MARTIN once said they were closer to "limestone rock" than "hard rock"), with more of a sense of humour than they are given credit for.

And yet they're called nice, too nice for their own good ("GWYNETH PALTROW angered Americans by calling them dull. Before you get upset, consider that she's married to the guy from Coldplay – she knows dull"). Which is a shame, as all their records are enormously good: who doesn't want to sing along to "Yellow", "Trouble", "Clocks", "Fix You", or "Speed of Sound"? With their fourth album, *Viva La Vida Or Death And All His Friends,* they succumbed to the inevitable by wielding an unwieldy album title and getting BRIAN ENO to produce it. Many years ago DANNY BAKER had a section on his Sunday morning radio show in which he played songs with superfluous lyrics. Highlights included MINK DEVILLE ("Brother Johnny, he caught a plane, and he got on it..."),

C

to which can now be added Coldplay's *Viva La Vida* single "Violet Hill": "From the rooftops I remember there was snow, white snow..."

LLOYD COLE

How difficult the life of unfulfilled promise. When Lloyd Cole And The Commotions released their album *Rattlesnakes* in 1984, great things were expected of him. The record was wonderful undergraduate stuff full of literary allusions, linguistic jokes and intricate melodies played by a band who had obviously spent many months devouring the BYRDS songbook, and who were probably well versed in the recorded works of TELEVISION, too. Cole's songs were magnificent (he was twenty-three at the time): "Perfect Skin", "Forest Fire", "Are You Ready To Be Heartbroken", etc. There were two more albums, then he went solo, and then, well, a career spent largely in obscurity.

I went to New York to interview him in 1989, to help publicise his first solo album, and I found the same troubled soul I'd interviewed five years previously, a man who was expecting great things from himself. There was an arrogance about him that had been missing the first time around, though. However when I first met him, I thought he was going to be a huge star, a transformative star. By the time I met him a second time I figured this was not going to happen.

We were in a bar, somewhere in Greenwich Village, where Cole had recently moved. It was late in the morning, and we were playing pool and drinking beer. And Cole was drinking a *lot* of beer.

"I would argue against a word like contrived," he said, looking up from his early lunch. "All I'm interested in is being remembered as someone who wrote good songs, I guess. I'm never going to be the world's best singer or guitarist or

anything like that. I think I'd have problems getting anyone
else to sing my songs.

"When I started I'd just come out of studying literature at
Glasgow and I was really interested in what you could do with
words. I'd recently discovered vintage BOB DYLAN so I should
imagine one naturally imitates one's heroes, and I suppose
that's the way I got started. I don't think it's a bad thing,
but having evolved a way of writing now which is my own, it
doesn't sound like anyone else, not to me."

It wasn't that easy to engage Cole in conversation – he
deliberately looked perplexed, even a bit bored, as he gave
me that expression that says: "I've been asked this question a
hundred times, and I know what you're driving at, but I've got
a bloody good answer for it." Consequently I found it easier
than expected to accuse him of everything from mediocrity
on a small scale to pomposity on a grand one.

In his own way he *encouraged* criticism; you could say what
you liked about Cole, call him contrived, mannered, precious,
earnest, every niggling adjective under the sun, and he'd take
it in, pause, look you in the eye and bounce back with, "Look,
I've had to come to terms with what kind of writer I am, to
accept it and not worry about it. As for being contrived there
would be a lot more contrivance if I tried to make myself
into something else. With the Commotions we tried to turn
ourselves into different groups on numerous occasions, and
they were all very unsuccessful – most of which no one's
heard. We tried to be the ROLLING STONES once, and couldn't
do that, too self-conscious; tried to be TALKING HEADS for a
while, couldn't do that, thank God. Lots of things."

While Cole encouraged criticism, he deflected it too; he had
had some savage attacks in the press, and appeared to know
all the angles. On the other hand he was initially hailed as the
best songwriter Britain had produced since, well, RAY DAVIES,
ELVIS COSTELLO, MORRISSEY, etc. But the thing that wound critics
up the most was the fact that they simply didn't believe him.
Though they knew he often wrote in the third person, this
didn't stop them from labelling him the bourgeois bohemian;

that quiet kid who wrote the jangly soporific sophomoric pop. You know, the slumming singer-songwriter.

"I've always said that I'm totally entrenched in the bourgeoisie, I always have been. These guys are always middle-class, you know? Jagger and Richards, Dylan, Lennon... I'm not bohemian, I'm comfortable. The only two things I feel any affinity with – regarding the Beats – is their dress sense and their sensitivity. Insensitivity is not something to champion. It gets championed a lot in rock'n'roll, and that's one of the reasons people don't like me – because I champion sensitivity, education, at the same time as admitting I like a drink. There's *this* and there's *this*, and then there's this jerk who won't fit in."

It was mid-summer. Later, in a cheapish SoHo restaurant (inexplicably called Elephant & Castle), Lloyd Cole ordered his fourth beer of the day, and we sat down to lunch. He didn't eat much, and seemed distracted by the noise from the street. He smoked Lucky Strikes constantly, and talked in an annoying mid-Atlantic accent.

He moved to New York at the end of 1988 after the Commotions split up. After *Rattlesnakes*, *Easy Pieces* (1985) and *Mainstream* (1987), seemingly endless tours and more than a modicum of success, Cole thought his future looked brighter without the others.

"I was tired and unhappy," he said. "Unhappy with the decision-making process – unhappy that money was becoming more relevant in the way decisions were being made. Before we made the first record I told the other guys that we might only make one record. I didn't know if I could keep doing it. There's quite a lot of stress involved in being in a band. It just got to the point where the grief factor was too much. We'd taken the group as far as we could, and I didn't want to make a record which sounded just like one of the other ones."

The first time I met Cole was in the supposed haven of rock'n'roll debauchery, The Columbia Hotel, opposite Hyde Park in London. From his first record and his publicity pictures I had been expecting an angry ball of confusion, but instead was greeted by an opinionated shy bookworm, obviously confused by the fact that the mythical rock'n'roll lifestyle glamorised in his Brit-crit music wasn't reflected in this London hostelry. He'd recently left college and enrolled in the University of Life, and he looked worried, anxious, and dreadfully homesick – hardly the man sat opposite me in this SoHo café.

In New York Cole was far surer of himself, if a little less bothered by the success or the influence of his work. Of course he still cared, was still assured he was "one of the best songwriters in the world", but maybe less urgent, less interested in forcing himself upon the world. By going solo, he was not only making a determined effort to gain a slightly higher profile, but he had also slowed down. He thought if he made grand enough statements then the world would surely come to *him*.

In the five years since he'd been with the band he had written some good songs – "My Bag" was a particular favourite of mine – and his fair share of mediocre ones. Like every good songwriter, he was at his best (which, it has to be said, wasn't as often as he'd like) when he combined T-shirt slogans with clever, nagging melodies, songs that lingered. None of the songs on his first solo LP, *Lloyd Cole*, could be considered classic, but there were some very good ones, and in general he appeared to have stepped up a gear, relying less on the clever-clever wordplay of previous years, becoming more "adult" in the process.

"When someone writes fiction they make up composite characters, usually using real people as the basis. And so it goes with pop songs. This is the first time I've written obvious love songs – you've got to get out of it to be able to write about it. When I started out I made a conscious decision to write in the third person. I was more interested in prose, journalistic prose. But I look back and realise those songs were about me anyway. You never really know why you're writing a song.

"I've never tried to make overstatements in my songs. I've always despised dogma in lyrics. The Clash's politics were

C awful – I remember JOE STRUMMER saying once that they were more interested in their sunglasses than their politics. They were a great rock'n'roll band. But their politics sucked. I don't really like picking individuals and tearing their work apart, but PAUL WELLER knows that I think 'Walls Come Tumbling Down' is one of the worst lyrics ever written. In terms of that area of music I'm just totally detached from it."

Nevertheless, he was still immersing himself in the mythology of America, and in particular New York. Did he simply move to the source of his muse? Or was he trying to exorcise his obsession?

"It was either here or Barcelona, basically, I just wanted to get out of London. I liked the idea of coming to the place which is the home of what got me interested in music in the first place – home of TELEVISION, the VOIDOIDS, etc. That was one of the reasons New York was romantic to me before I ever set foot in it. Since I was about sixteen I've never really had a permanent home. I've lived in Derbyshire, Lancashire, Glasgow, London – so I've never really written about things close to home. Abstract notions have always made more sense. I've got no fondness for Britain any more, and now I realise that New York is the only place I've ever wanted to make my home."

Cole also showed a reactionary side to him when we met in New York. At the time, black music had temporarily ceased to be fashionable with some of the white faces who had grown up with guitar-based pop, and the garage/house/swingbeat re-mix had come to be regarded with the same disdain as the disco remix a decade previously. Cole was particularly uninterested, "After 'The Message' I saw no reason for any more rap music. I like TONE LOC, he's funny, but I haven't really been affected by any black music since CHIC and FUNKADELIC. Having listened to YO! MTV every afternoon for six months in the studio, I'm sick of it. My favourite records of all time are pretty traditional; I've got no funk in me at all. Zero. But I've got a fair bit of rock'n'roll, and that's what I'm best at."

I asked Lloyd Cole how good he thought he was and he told me in no uncertain terms. "I've got to think I'm good. I can write songs better than a lot of people. MORRISSEY has two songs, just like BRYAN FERRY said he used to have; he's got his angry one and he's got his maudlin one. Ferry used to have his melancholy one and his up-tempo one." But Lloyd Cole made no secret of the fact that he thinks he's got more than two.

"People hardly ever understand that some of my songs are funny. This business is just light entertainment. I'm not interested in people writing critical essays about them. I just want them to like them. Some people just can't understand that I'm capable of putting my tongue in my cheek. It's not high art, you know. 'Perfect Skin' is probably one of my funniest songs. Here is this ridiculous bohemian character who's using as many long words as he possibly can, to create this image with which he's trying to attract women. And then in the chorus he collapses, realising how stupid he is... because when she smiles he just falls apart, and he's a jerk like everybody else, I guess."

After the interview he took me to a little bar – his favourite in New York – in Prince Street, in the middle of SoHo. We shot some more pool, drank some more beer and waited for the photographer. Slowly Cole began to merge with the blue-collar regulars of the bar. Even with his JIM MORRISON-style clothes, his spectacles and his sullen, puffy cheeks he blended in with the biceps, the braggadocio and the beer swilling. Like Morrison, Cole knew that alcohol is a great leveller.

"I can disappear here, he said, buying me another beer. "I can merge, and I can relax."

He did. He merged. He relaxed. And the like of *Rattlesnakes* was never heard again.

NAT KING COLE

C

With his distinctive timbre, distinctive enunciation, it was hardly a surprise that Nat King Cole would "abandon" jazz piano for a highly lucrative career as a singer. He was not one for improvising, either, preferring to stick to melody, even if those melodies were often sometimes quite anodyne. Lyrically, he was even more circumspect, careful not to imply he had any sexual vanity, or improper designs. Slowly, he would become a balladeer, one of the first romantic black males to have a career in "the white time".

And it all happened by accident. Playing piano one night in a small bar in Los Angeles, a drunk demanded he sang. And Cole, being a gentleman, and not one for causing a fight, acquiesced. "It was lucky that I could sing a little," he said. "So I did, for variety."

His success was enormous, and swift, yet he was still a black man in a white man's world. When he took up residence in Los Angeles' Hancock Park in August 1948, with his new wife, someone had posted a sign on their lawn: "Nigger Heaven." In GENE LEES' book *You Can't Steal A Gift*, he recalls the following story: "Cole was playing the Fountainebleu. A little white girl got away from her parents and toddled on to the stage. A kind of hush seized the audience. This was Miami, and Miami was one of the most racist cities in America. She drew closer to him. Nat had someone bring him a chair. He sat down, took the little girl on his lap, and sang her to sleep."

JOHN COLTRANE

There are four great Coltrane albums – OK, maybe five or six, but these are the very best.

1. *Blue Train* (Blue Note), 1957: Cool bop, essentially. This is one of Coltrane's easiest records. "The most convenient and tolerable example of the first period of a difficult musician," according to RICHARD COOK, author of *Blue Note Records: The Biography*. Recorded with a classic line-up – pianist KENNY DREW, bassist PAUL CHAMBERS, trumpeter LEE MORGAN, trombonist CURTIS FULLER and drummer PHILLY JOE JONES – the album consists of four very distinct pieces, each one representing a stage of spiritual development. Hard to believe now, but its popularity was helped enormously by the cover: Coltrane in close-up, his eyes looking down, deep in thought, his right hand raised to his lips. It is perfectly enigmatic, while the album's title suggests cool, mellow, dinner party pop. Essential track: "Locomotion".

2. *Giant Steps* (Atlantic), 1960: This was a breakthrough album for Coltrane, in particular its title track, and in the words of one critic, "was thick with constant chord changes (moving the rate of a new chord every other beat) and with a melody whose endlessly unfolding odd intervals – giant steps – appeared to be designed to make life difficult for its soloist." Coltrane also experimented with modal jazz on this album, which isn't so surprising: at the time he was working with MILES DAVIS on *Kind Of Blue*. Essential track: "Spiral".

3. *My Favourite Things* (Atlantic), 1961: Here Coltrane played a soprano sax, a horn that produced a sound that was almost like some eastern-Indian instrument. The public loved it, and this soon became one of the bestselling jazz albums of the time. In 1962, Coltrane explained how he adapted the *Sound Of Music* waltz to a

C

model jazz riff, "This piece is built on two chords, but we prolonged the two chords for the whole piece." An impressed, if rather irritated, MILES DAVIS said, "Only he could do that and make it work." And he was right. Essential track: "Summertime".

4.   *A Love Supreme* (Impulse!), 1964: One of the most popular jazz records of all time, a collection of songs that highlight jazz at the very highest level of achievement. Coltrane was a genius, but he's also tagged with encouraging everyone who came in his wake to think a saxophone solo could last several weeks. When Coltrane died, aged forty, PHILIP LARKIN wrote that the only compliment that one could pay him was one of stature, "If he was boring, he was enormously boring. If he was ugly, he was massively ugly." Nevertheless, this is extraordinary. (On no account buy ALICE COLTRANE's version of her husband's classic; it will disturb the neighbours, give you a piercing headache and quite possibly damage your laptop.) Essential track: "Acknowledgement".

THE CONGOS

It's 1977, and reggae is considered to be the only true radical path to follow, or at least listen to. Music not made so much by mavericks, but by people (well, almost exclusively) men who have no truck with anything else (past, present or future). Forget rock, forget funk, forget pretty much anything else. Reggae existed in a hermetically sealed environment, encouraged by an island mentality, religious militancy, and dress codes.

It was also extraordinarily varied, and if you delved deeply would come up with everything from Rastafarian vocal groups in the WAILERS' tradition, toasting, lovers' rock, leftover bluebeat and ska, and, of course, the subterranean sounds of dub.

The Congos' beautiful *Heart Of The Congos* was released in January 1977, at a time when dub was starting to take precedence. Consequently it sounded even sweeter than it might have done eighteen months earlier, which is why it became so popular with those who were interested/could find it. The standout track on this album is "Fisherman", one of the greatest reggae records ever made. CEDRIC MYRON's falsetto describes poor Jamaicans toiling on the waves, in an almost Biblical setting, with an unusually profound sense of purpose.

ALICE COOPER

Many years ago, before reinventing himself as a golf-monster and the granddaddy of goth (OZZY OSBOURNE with khol eyes), Vince Furnier was a Route One IGGY POP-style Detroit rocker looking for a gimmick to get into the music business. First, he took a girl's name (this was in 1968, and was inspired even back then), and then stole his look from the film *Barbarella*: "When I saw ANITA PALLENBERG playing the Great Tyrant in that movie in 1968, wearing long black leather gloves with switchblades coming out of them, I thought, 'That's what Alice should look like.' That, and a little bit of Emma Peel from *The Avengers*."

He had a huge hit with "School's Out" in 1972, and was swept up in the British glam scene, for a while being more famous than DAVID BOWIE, T.REX, ROXY MUSIC, or GARY GLITTER. He was helped in this by the Welsh Labour MP LEO ABSE, who took exception to Cooper, and tried to get him banned in the UK. He claimed Cooper was, "peddling the culture of the concentration camp. Pop is one thing, anthems of necrophilia are quite another." Alice reaped the rewards of the added

C

publicity while keeping quiet about the fact that the band had absolutely no plans to tour the UK anyway.

DAVID BAILEY shot Alice and his band for the cover of his 1973 album *Billion Dollar Babies* (a wonderful theatrical cavalcade from gun to tape), the result of a relationship that was forged in Bailey's north London studio in early 1973, on a shoot for American *Vogue*. This was a very excessive time for Cooper, and for Bailey too. The photographer's house was party central at the time, and Alice fitted in perfectly. "It was almost normal to have a naked man covered in make-up and scars with a boa constrictor around his neck," said Bailey. "The first picture we did of Alice, the naked picture, happened after he drank an entire bottle of Seagram's. People made a big deal of the snake around his neck, although I always thought his scars were more interesting. The snake was just a necklace. Alice always told people that the scar was a shark bite, but I know it was actually because of appendicitis."

Cooper liked the experience so much he asked Bailey to shoot the cover of *Billion Dollar Babies*. And for the shoot they obviously needed a baby. And a million dollars in cash (even as a wheeze the record company balked at a billion). "Alice really got on well with babies, and he put the mascara on the kid himself," said Bailey. "The baby was laughing and giggling and didn't appear to be too concerned by the whole thing. Surprisingly no one was that bothered by a heavily made-up baby, it was the money that caused the fuss. Alice insisted on having real money in the pictures, so we had a million dollars in the studio surrounded by two security guards from the bank with sub-machine guns. Once we were in the studio these two guys locked the door and no one was allowed to go in or out. Alice and I thought the whole thing was hilarious, so we started kicking the money around and playing with it and driving these two guys mad. So we did the shoot, and then right at the end I said, 'Hold on, I just want to try one more picture.' And I picked up as much money as I could carry and threw it into the air. The security guys went ballistic, started screaming and told everybody to stop what they were doing and not to move. And they got down on their hands and knees and started frantically picking the stuff up. They went crazy. It backfired on us as we had to be there for an extra hour as the money was counted and weighed and put back in its containers. When they finished counting it they were twenty dollars short. We looked for it everywhere and then found it burning on top of one of the studio lights. The bank got all its money back, but the US Customs got involved. They found out we'd photographed a million of their dollars and were very unhappy about it. There were counterfeiting issues, apparently."

Cooper become renowned for his stage shows, which featured guillotines, the gallows, the electric chairs, fake blood, boa constrictors and baby dolls.

ELVIS COSTELLO

Punk's scarecrow singer-songwriter became a televisual pop star, a conceptual band-leader (the ATTRACTIONS, the CONFEDERATES, the IMPOSTERS, etc), and apparently innately turned his short stories –lacerating tales of romantic frustrations, political expediency, hapless social climbing and all the rest – into any form he wanted to. His first half-a-dozen records are almost concept albums, with Costello moving through genres as though they were time zones. Confident of his instincts and virtuosity, he has continued in this vein for thirty-five years, happy to dip in and out of styles, and collaborate at will (notably with BURT BACHARACH on 1998's *Painted From Memory*, and ALLEN TOUSSAINT on 2006's *The River In Reverse*). Note: *Blood & Chocolate* from 1986 is one of my very favourite records, and the concerts that Costello did to promote it, rank as some of the best I've ever seen – his performance of "I Want You" being one of the most chilling things I've ever seen or heard.

C COVER VERSIONS: 75 OF THE BEST

They are often redundant, frequently pointless, and rarely remembered. Some are little more than cheap photocopies, with someone hitherto unknown (or, increasingly, far too well known) colouring in the original and trying not to go outside the lines. Some can be transformative, but often they are nothing but corruptions of your favourite memories (I feel ambiguous towards it, but I would imagine if you had formative experiences with, or fond memories of, NEW ORDER's "True Faith", you would probably think GEORGE MICHAEL's cover is rather redundant; ditto ROBBIE WILLIAMS' live version of BLUR's "Song 2", or SIMPLE MINDS' frankly confusing version of PRINCE's "Sign O' The Times"). Others are just plain perverse: does anyone really want to hear WILLIAM SHATNER cover PULP's "Common People"? Maybe Shatner's agent and JARVIS COCKER's publishers, but anyone else? The cover version has become such a cheap, reductive shot, a contrary "interpretation" that appeals to a no-brow sensibility, it's now a risky strategy. Which makes the best ones even better:

1. "Hallelujah" (original by LEONARD COHEN) by RUFUS WAINWRIGHT.

2. "I'm Only Sleeping" (the BEATLES) by the VINES.

3. "Windmills Of Your Mind" (NOEL HARRISON) by DUSTY SPRINGFIELD.

4. "Ol 55" (TOM WAITS) by the EAGLES.

5. "Jersey Girl" (TOM WAITS) by BRUCE SPRINGSTEEN.

6. "Got To Get You Into My Life" (the BEATLES) by EARTH WIND AND FIRE.

7. "Ride Like The Wind" (CHRISTOPHER CROSS) by EAST SIDE BEAT.

8. "Tomorrow's Just Another Day" (MADNESS) by ELVIS COSTELLO.

9. "Do Ya" (the MOVE) by UTOPIA.

10. "Dancing In The Moonlight" (KING HARVEST) by TOPLOADER.

11. "Nothing Compares To You" (the FAMILY) by SINEAD O'CONNOR.

12. "Little Wing" (the JIMI HENDRIX EXPERIENCE) by DEREK AND THE DOMINOES.

13. "Macarthur Park" (RICHARD HARRIS) by DONNA SUMMER.

14. "Songbird" (FLEETWOOD MAC) by EVA CASSIDY.

15. "The Only Living Boy In New York" (SIMON & GARFUNKEL) by EVERYTHING BUT THE GIRL.

16. "Someone To Watch Over Me" (GERTRUDE LAWRENCE) by FRANK SINATRA.

17. "Killing Me Softly With His Song" (LORI LIEBERMAN), by the FUGEES.

18. "I'm Not In Love" (10CC) by the FUN LOVIN' CRIMINALS.

19. "Whiskey In The Jar" (trad.) by THIN LIZZY.

20. "Largo" (HANDEL) by the SWINGLE SINGERS.

21. "Walk On By" (DIONNE WARWICK) by the STRANGLERS.

C

22. "Goin' Back" (DUSTY SPRINGFIELD) by NILS LOFGREN.

23. "Satisfaction (I Can't Get No)" (the ROLLING STONES) by DEVO.

24. "Let 'Em In" (PAUL McCARTNEY & WINGS) by STARBELLY.

25. "Manha De Carnaval" (LUIZ BONFA) by STAN GETZ.

26. "As" (STEVIE WONDER) by GEORGE MICHAEL.

27. "La Vie En Rose" (EDITH PIAF) by GRACE JONES.

28. "We've Only Just Begun" (the CARPENTERS) by GRANT LEE BUFFALO.

29. "Knockin' On Heaven's Door" (BOB DYLAN) by GUNS N' ROSES.

30. "Louie Louie" (the KINGSMEN) by IGGY POP.

31. "The Look Of Love" (DUSTY SPRINGFIELD) by ISAAC HAYES.

32. "Up On The Roof" (the DRIFTERS) by JAMES TAYLOR.

33. "Wind Cries Mary" (JIMI HENDRIX) by JAMIE CULLUM.

34. "So What?" (MILES DAVIS) by RONNY JORDAN.

35. "Reason To Believe" (TIM HARDIN) by ROD STEWART.

36. "California Sun" (JOE JONES) by the RAMONES.

37. "They Shoot Horses Don't They" (RACING CARS) by BECK.

38. "A Whiter Shade Of Pale" (PROCOL HAREM) by ANNIE LENNOX.

39. "Stop Your Sobbing" (the KINKS) by the PRETENDERS.

40. "Dancing In The Dark" (BRUCE SPRINGSTEEN) by PETE YORN.

41. "Where The Streets Have No Name" (U2) by the PET SHOP BOYS.

42. "My Favourite Things" (JULIE ANDREWS) by OUTKAST.

43. "A Forest" (the CURE) by NOUVELLE VAGUE.

44. "Only With You" (the BEACH BOYS) by NORMAN BLAKE.

45. "Baltimore" (RANDY NEWMAN) by NINA SIMONE.

46. "Handbags And Gladrags (CHRIS FARLOWE) by the STEREOPHONICS.

47. "I Want To Know What Love Is" (FOREIGNER) by the NEW JERSEY MASS CHOIR.

48. "Dear Friend" (WINGS) by the MINUS 5.

49. "Summertime" (BILLIE HOLIDAY) by MILES DAVIS.

50. "My Little Red Book" (MEL TORMÉ) by LOVE.

51. "Hallelujah" (LEONARD COHEN) by JOHN CALE.

52. "At Last I Am Free" (CHIC) by ROBERT WYATT.

53. "Back On My Feet" (PAUL MCCARTNEY) by COCKEYED GHOST.

54. "Dear Prudence" (the BEATLES) by SIOUXSIE & THE BANSHEES.

C

55. "Sweet Jane" (the Velvet Underground) by the Cowboy Junkies.

56. "Martha" (Tom Waits) by Tim Buckley.

57. "I'm A Believer" (the Monkees) by Robert Wyatt.

58. "I Heard It Through The Grapevine" (Marvin Gaye) by the Slits.

59. "The Promised Land" (Chuck Berry) by Johnnie Allan.

60. "A Message To You Rudy" (Dandy Livingstone) by the Specials.

61. "Mr Tambourine Man" (Bob Dylan) by the Byrds.

62. "Comfortably Numb" (Pink Floyd) by Scissor Sisters.

63. "Hurt" (Nine Inch Nails) by Johnny Cash.

64. "Tears Of A Clown" (Smokey Robinson & The Miracles) by the Beat.

65. "Police And Thieves" (Junior Murvin) by the Clash.

66. "I Will Always Love You" (Dolly Parton) by Whitney Houston.

67. "Wild Horses" (the Rolling Stones) by the Flying Burrito Brothers.

68. "Everything I Own" (Bread) by Ken Boothe.

69. "Just" (Radiohead) by Mark Ronson.

70. "Gloria" (Them) by Patti Smith.

71. "I Fought The Law" (BOBBY FULLER) by the CLASH.

72. "I Just Don't Know What To Do With Myself" (DUSTY SPRINGFIELD) by the WHITE STRIPES.

73. "Rocket Man" (ELTON JOHN) by KATE BUSH.

74. "Is That All There Is" (PEGGY LEE) by CRISTINA.

75. "All Along The Watchtower" (BOB DYLAN) by the JIMI HENDRIX EXPERIENCE.

THE CRAMPS

LUX INTERIOR's band was a dark, gothic interpretation of the LINK WRAY legacy, and at their height (probably around 1979-1980) made some fearsome records – I remember "Human Fly" and "Garbageman" being especially good. He was a twisted ELVIS, an outrageous frontman who lived for performance. But according to PRIMAL SCREAM's BOBBY GILLESPIE he was some sort of messiah figure. Following Interior's death in 2009, Gillespie wrote, "Lux was one of the great rock'n'roll showmen/shaman, right up there with IGGY [POP], JERRY LEE LEWIS, and JIM MORRISON. Like them he seemed to want to burst free from his body and explode outta this world and transport himself to other planes, taking his audience with him. The Cramps, alongside the BIRTHDAY PARTY, GUN CLUB, and the JESUS AND MARY CHAIN kept the beautiful, feral, ecstatic, raging, diseased spirit of rock'n'roll alive at the end of the Seventies and through the early Eighties... a time of nothingness... when punk had prostituted itself and turned into new wave, which then begat DURAN DURAN, DIRE STRAITS, and the legions of Reagan/Thatcher-pleasing cocksuckers who shared the stage at Live Aid." Calm down dear, calm down!

C Even when I was much younger I never understood why the most fervent people, consumers and entertainers alike, wanted everyone to be the same. The mods shared this sensibility, and I didn't understand that either. Why on earth would you want everyone to look the same, wear the same clothes, and listen to *exactly* the same records? Having achieved that, what would we do then? In this world, everyone buys the latest scarlet ARNE JACOBSEN edition at exactly the same time on exactly the same day, and then calls their friends to tell them all about it. The only problem being, all their friends are in the same shop.

Who knows – maybe a world where every band operated in a domain dominated by punk bands with rockabilly trash aesthetics would be rather fun. For an hour. (And by the way, is BOB DYLAN really a "cocksucker"?)

CROSBY, STILLS & NASH

A varnished log cabin.

CROSBY, STILLS, NASH & YOUNG

A varnished log cabin with an unvarnished door.

CROWDED HOUSE

I remember putting on a Crowded House CD (possibly their greatest hits) during a dinner party at my house in the mid-Nineties, and two people at the table actually started laughing. Apparently I had committed a terrible cliché, and although I was actually in the mood to hear "Weather With You", "Four Seasons In One Day", "Don't Dream It's Over", "Fall At Your Feet", "Into Temptation", and all the rest, the mood of the room (v. male, three hours in and, I thought, oblivious to what music might be playing in the background) told me otherwise. Their derision was instant and total (I may as well have referred to them by their Australian nickname, the "Crowdies"). This was a sin tantamount to playing DIRE STRAITS' *Brothers In Arms* in the mid-Eighties (not guilty), or indeed anything by BILLY JOEL (guilty, though not in company) or FLEETWOOD MAC (ditto). I was intimidated, cowed, and never did it again. Not in company, anyway.

JULEE CRUISE

It is not difficult to see why DAVID LYNCH's *Twin Peaks* was – for a while – the largest selling television soundtrack album in history. There was ANGELO BADALAMENTI's haunting, evocative sound sculptures, Lynch's ethereal and often banal lyrics, and the extraordinary voice of the extraordinarily striking Julee Cruise (best heard on the closing song, "Falling"). Much of the music had first appeared on Cruise's widely acclaimed debut album, *Floating Into The Night*, released earlier in 1990, though the trio first worked together on Lynch's 1986 cult classic, *Blue Velvet*. They had also performed a full-length symphony at the Brooklyn Academy of Music, worked on the rather lacklustre *Twin Peaks* prequel, *Fire Walk With Me*, and then recorded Cruise's second album, *The Voice Of Love*. Her voice on this record was, if anything, even more chilling than it was before; it was a whole octave higher due to the surgery she underwent to bevel her nasal passages.

Cruise's *Twin Peaks* persona was as much of a Lynch creation as the Log Lady or Laura Palmer; and for someone with such an otherworldly image, in person she was rather a blithe spirit and quite bluff about her work with Lynch and

Badalamenti. She started her career as an actress, and for years tried to balance both pursuits – appearing in *Return To The Forbidden Planet* while touring with the B-52s. Perversely, her ambitions didn't involve Lynch, Badalamenti or even her own voice. "Pop music is a short-lived business," she said. "I want to become one of those character actresses that people point to in airports without quite knowing who they are. That's me, that's completely me." She got her way.

JAMIE CULLUM

One of the most engaging things about Jamie Cullum is his complete lack of self-consciousness (on his website he's even wearing a Santa hat, in a way that only GYLES BRANDRETH or ALAN TITCHMARSH could convincingly carry off). Whereas other stars of his magnitude would think twice about leaping about the stage, slapping his thighs in time to the beat (air snare!), Cullum embraces the opportunity like a child. He is an old-fashioned entertainer in that sense, keen as mustard and full of vim. You could never imagine Cullum, for instance, sloping on stage and staring at his shoes, apologetically introducing his art. You won't find anyone who cares more about their work, although you'd be unlikely to find anyone more self-deprecating, either. I once saw him jump onto a piano in a small club in Amsterdam, and he spent half an hour bopping around the stage like a Duracell-powered ELTON JOHN, BEN FOLDS, or JERRY LEE LEWIS. As well as entertaining, it was extraordinarily refreshing.

However the thing I find fascinating about Cullum is not just his innate self-confidence – "I come from a good, strong, normal, supportive family – what can I say?" – but the fact he appears impervious to criticism. Tell him his new album sucks and he'd probably nod, offer a wry smile, and carry on talking. "You can occasionally read something quite hideous, even from writers you admire, and they can be quite hurtful.

But then I look at my blissful life and it helps temper any ill feeling you might have! To be on a tour bus, in the heartland of America, drinking a cold beer and driving to a town where people have paid to hear your music? That's not a bad life, really, is it?"

He also appears to go out of his way to Ac-Cent-Tchu-Ate the Positive, and eliminate the negative, as the great lyricist JOHNNY MERCER once put it. Cullum doesn't wear his heart on his sleeve, and doesn't have his own cross to bear. At least not a very big one. "I don't think I'm any less torturous than anyone else, it's just that I choose not to share that with my audience or in my songs. Choosing not to share is a cardinal sin in this business. Not sharing your heartache or your bowel movements is frowned upon these days. But even though I don't share in that way, I hope there's enough in my music to move people."

Well, there obviously has been so far. One of the things that resonates with his audience is the fact that he does actually know what he's talking about, and is something of a scholar where jazz is concerned. He'll say that he doesn't know as much as he should, and that his technique is only four percent of what he'd like it to be, but he knows his stuff, and compared to old-school jazz bores doesn't inflict his personal obsessions on you. He is inclusive in that respect, and when we met spent a good five minutes eulogising about a particular album of lush ballads JOHN COLTRANE recorded with JOHNNY HARTMAN in 1963 (it was re-released in 2005, in case you're interested – and you ought to be – on the Verve label. When I said I didn't know it, he didn't sneer and look superior, he took me through it, blow by blow. Like me, when he started investigating jazz he turned the world upside down only to discover another – very noisy one, full of odd time signatures – underneath.

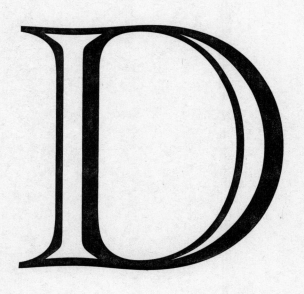

Dr. Alimantado

In 1976, the good doctor was big down the Roxy, and when DJ DON LETTS needed records to play when the bands weren't on stage in the legendary London punk club, would turn to imported reggae rather than New York urchin rock or old garage bands. One of his favourites was Alimantado's "Best Dressed Chicken In Town", originally recorded in 1975. Known principally as a toaster, WINSTON JAMES THOMPSON (born between 1950 and 1952, no one appears to know exactly when) boasted over singers such as JOHN HOLT, GREGORY ISAACS, and HORACE ANDY. JOHN LYDON was a fan, and he was mentioned in the CLASH song "Rudie Can't Fail" ("Like a doctor who was born for a purpose..."). Some said he came across like BIG YOUTH, others that he resembled CAPTAIN BEEFHEART.

The Damned

A conundrum: what to do when the punk bubble bursts, after all the bashing and thrashing has become distinctly old hat? What befits a punk legend most? For the Damned, it meant imploding, going on a bit of a psychedelic bender, helping invent goth, going BROAD. Famously the first punk band to release a record ("New Rose", October, 1976), their first singles were more in the spirit of thrash garage rock than anything frightening or genuinely incendiary. Oddly, they got better the longer they went on. For a while, anyway. Best songs: "I Just Can't Be Happy Today", "Smash It Up", "Eloise".

D TERENCE TRENT D'ARBY

Oh Lord. Terence Trent D'Arby was sitting in a reclining wooden chair on the balcony of his studiedly ramshackle retreat high up in the Hollywood Hills, reciting WALT WHITMAN's "Leaves of Grass" instead of telling me about his long-awaited new LP. He was using the poem to punctuate a story about his own particular spiritual rite of passage, which he had been laboriously explaining all afternoon. Whitman's mystical transformation happened around 1850, when he suddenly changed from a simple jobbing journalist into America's foremost poet of the new age. "Leaves of Grass" was Whitman's declaration; it was also D'Arby's favourite book, his "bible".

"Whitman is the man, the only man. His experiences seem so close to mine. There are times when I have had experiences —which, for the record, have not been the result of artificial inducement; one in particular lasted ten days, round the time of my last birthday. Ten days of complete acceptance and euphoria. I had such a feeling of complete peace in my heart. It was ineffable, or at least in my ability to articulate it."

Articulation was never Terry D'Arby's problem. Egocentric, arrogant, imperious, in his time he caused more than one journalist to describe him as the most self-assured performer in pop. If everyone ate according to the size of their ego, then D'Arby should have resembled Texas.

He was the pop sensation of 1987. At a time when "designer" soul (cf SIMPLY RED) was becoming increasingly popular in Britain, D'Arby slipped into a music scene that was suggesting it might want the "genuine" article. His sophisticated and often cerebral mixture of rock and funk was lapped up, and he had huge hits with "Wishing Well", "If You Let Me Stay", and "Sign Your Name", while his debut LP *Introducing The Hardline According To Terence Trent D'Arby* eventually sold eight million copies. He subsequently had hits all over Europe, and a number one in the US.

He wasn't just a successful singer, though, and it was his outspoken views (telling journalists that he considered himself to be at least the equal of MICHAEL JACKSON and PRINCE) and his self-aggrandisement ("I think I'm a genius, point fucking blank") that made him noteworthy. His pre-discovery years made for good copy, too; raised in a strict Pentecostal church family in New York, the son of a preacher and a gospel-singing mother, he moved from Manhattan to New Jersey via Florida and Chicago, before joining the army and boxing in the Golden Gloves. Posted to Germany (supposedly with ELVIS PRESLEY's old regiment, although I'm not sure it was ever substantiated), he went AWOL, joining various local groups, quit the forces, and moved to London. In his own head he became the London rock scene's favourite adopted black American son since JIMI HENDRIX. Young (he was twenty-five in 1987), handsome, bright and outspoken, here was a marketing man's dream; razor thin, with big piscine eyes and fusilli-like dreadlocks, D'Arby was a sex symbol who moved like JAMES BROWN and sang like SMOKEY ROBINSON.

D'Arby's follow-up LP, *Neither Fish Nor Flesh* (1989), was not so marketable. A collection of self-absorbed soliloquies, it contained no hit singles, was a critical and commercial disaster, and was quickly deleted by the record company. Self-regulation went out of the window as D'Arby indulged his passions for sex and spirituality (the soul man's staples), and gave the impression that he had to be himself or he'd just burst. It was cosmic plasma of the worst kind, and hardly the kind of product that CBS had anticipated (three good songs does not an album make, not even in 1989). But then D'Arby never wanted to be a male WHITNEY HOUSTON, being more interested in becoming the kind of celebrity archetype that LENNY KRAVITZ and SEAL had been trying to emulate: a styled-up, freaky-deaky space cadet, a cosmic marionette complete with blood-curdling singing voice.

With *Neither Fish Nor Flesh* he had taken things too far, and it was this humbling experience that brought him, eventually (there was a brief, mystical sojourn to Massachusetts), to

D

California. Here in Los Angeles D'Arby found "more space, less scrutiny, less negativity".

This was 1993, and Terence Trent D'Arby's rented Hollywood Hills home was a low-rise, wooden, ranch-style bungalow, a palatial shack that stood at the top of a particularly steep incline. His neighbours on Astral Drive included JULIA ROBERTS, FRANK ZAPPA, RICHARD GERE and CINDY CRAWFORD, TODD RUNDGREN, and DEPECHE MODE'S DAVE GAHAN. A gigantic totem pole on the edge of a basketball-court-cum-garage stared out into the valley as the early mist gave way to the hard California sun. A punch-bag hung like a pendulum from the garage roof, D'Arby's polished burgundy Jaguar lying immobile under a canvas wrap.

All mod cons were here: the house had a multi-gym, recording studio, swimming pool, music room (how Seventies!), en suite bathroom (containing more oils and balms than you'd hope to find in any spa) and a resident Hispanic maid, Gladys, who called daily, to clean, field visitors and prepare D'Arby's vegetable-based meals and health drinks.

His considerable library was full of philosophical tomes, books about healing, and biographies and videos of great men (ALI, MICHAEL JORDAN, DON CORLEONE). There were two magazine piles on the floor, a straight 50:50 mix of fashion mags and recent copies of *Playboy*. This was where D'Arby spent his mornings, reading poetry, flicking through centrefolds, and singing (while I was there he made various attempts at the old music hall standard "I'm Henery the Eighth I Am"). It was the consummate LA dream home, a hammock gently swinging on the balcony, bulbous hummingbirds buzzing around the bird feeders. "This is sanctuary," said D'Arby, or "T", as he liked to be called. "I'm reclusive by nature – not out of any eccentricity – and LA offers me that."

Few celebrities these days consider journalists to be within their comfort zone. Publicists are increasingly protective of their clients, and it's not unusual for one-on-one celebrity interviews to be limited to sixty, sometimes thirty minutes' duration. In the golden days of Hollywood only the biggest stars commanded such treatment, but these days even daytime quiz show hosts play hard to get. In direct contrast, even twenty years ago, D'Arby was a generous – and prepossessing – interviewee, actually talking too much, rambling at times, working things out in his head as he spoke. Perhaps he shouldn't have told me about his messiah complex, his religious experiences, or his rather nebulous personal philosophies; but when he was famous, there was little that D'Arby liked more than talking about himself.

"Any rock star worth a damn has always had a pretty decent messiah complex," said the singer, gazing out into the valley below. "It's to be expected. I was raised in the church, and my father always wanted me to be a preacher. But he has no idea how closely my work parallels his. He has his message. I've got mine. He has his way of preaching, I've got mine. He's got his congregation, and maybe I've still got mine." He barked something at Gladys, then turned back to me.

"Artists have a tremendous privilege, because we get to interpret God's voice. I don't care how that sounds, because I truly believe it. As I look back through my life I realise there's a lot of things that I didn't do, things that were beyond my control."

This, you soon realised, was D'Arby's Big Thing: he believed himself to be a conduit. During promotion for his disastrous second LP he made great play of the fact that MARVIN GAYE appeared to him in a dream and offered him a song ("To Know Someone Deeply Is To Know Someone Softly"). He still didn't understand the reaction this caused, "People thought I was nuts, but if I said that last night I had this really weird dream that I was flying through the air, then turned into this great big blue elephant, and then I started blowing my nose and it turned into a trumpet – people wouldn't think that was abnormal. But if I say that I dreamt MARVIN GAYE came up to me and said, 'Here, take this song,' then suddenly I'm a crazy person. Maybe I should have said I'd taken a shit load of acid."

D Gladys, having finished her chores, brought D'Arby's specially prepared fruit and vegetable drink out on to the balcony. He sipped and stared into space. It wasn't just MARVIN GAYE who was preying on his mind today, as D'Arby had known for some time that *other* people talked through him, too. "What's the difference between me and a guy in any Baptist church in any large city in America? Is it that I'm better? I don't really think so. There's something else that propels me to do this. I have a power, and I intend to use it... I think I can be of some kind of service. I don't feel like the gods give you the type of potential that I think I have without a responsibility, and it would be remiss of me to think that they aren't going to ask for something in return. I have to satisfy myself, but I have to answer to them. Nothing pisses the gods off more than a reluctant messiah, you know. I am not a craftsman, I can't sit down and write a song, I have to wait for the muse. And if it doesn't come then there's no song."

Well, the gods had been busy. Three-and-a-half years after *Flesh* ("I've got a weird, fluctuating, molecular relationship with time," he said, no irony forthcoming) came D'Arby's third LP, *Symphony Or Damn*. A dark, brooding record, it was nevertheless highly commercial and was musically as varied as any latter-day BEATLES LP. Bluntly speaking it was a mixture of the dynamic pop of his first LP (one song, the ballad "Delicate", being a dead ringer for "Sign Your Name") and the more free-form stuff on his second (proving, at least, that *Flesh* was a turning point, not an aberration). Throughout, D'Arby's voice was extraordinary: he sang soft (sighing like MARVIN GAYE), he sang loud (like WHOOPI GOLDBERG, invoking the devil). An autocrat to the last, D'Arby wrote, recorded, and produced the record largely by himself, here in his personal studio on Astral Drive. However, wary of giving D'Arby complete control, Sony insisted it be mixed with the help of a professional producer, and then asked for parts to be remixed.

"My vanity is such that I'm not disappointed in what I do," said the singer. "Not ever. But I'm not building the Taj Mahal here, it's only a fucking pop record. I know that it's good, though." He's right. It was.

D'Arby had been reading Whitman for the past forty minutes. Exhausted, he leant back in his chair and gazed out into the valley. The recitation had apparently inspired him, "All I'm saying is, if you're marked to do a certain thing, it's not because of you, it's in spite of you. Jesus had a dark side too; he certainly doesn't appear to have had much patience or time for his mother. Here was a nice Jewish boy who ignored his mother! He wasn't perfect. Neither am I."

This was good to know. "The most precious, most lyrical poetry comes from guys who are most probably shits. If the gods only depended on good, sound men to do their work, much wouldn't get done. So why not use shits like us?"

Six hours after my arrival it was time to leave. As the sun began setting over Los Angeles, D'Arby took me inside the house to watch some videotaped castings of girls auditioning for the promo for his next single. In front of a static camera, one by one a series of extraordinarily scantily clad girls walked on to the sound stage and began gyrating to the strains of "Do You Love Me Like You Say?", D'Arby's first record for three years. Bump. Grind. Bump. Vertical expressions of a horizontal activity, these girls danced as though their libidos depended on it. D'Arby pressed the pause button for a moment, then let it go. "Shit, she's a major babe. Do you know what it feels like, on a rudimentary level, to watch a girl dance like that to a record you've made? Fuck world peace, man." Then, to the girl dancing on the screen, "You should never trust a mystic without a dick. Never."

And with that, I left Astral Drive.

In 1994 D'Arby replaced MICHAEL HUTCHENCE for INXS's performance at the Sydney Olympics. He changed his name to SANANDA MAITREYA, moved to Italy and occasionally still makes records.

BOBBY DARIN

D

"Beyond The Sea" was the "Stairway To Heaven" of its day, beginning quietly, almost casually, and then building into something of a euphoric crescendo. Bobby Darin's swinging version was definitive – honestly, there really isn't another version you need to own – is one of the greatest singles of its year – 1959 – a record that sounds as wistful today as it probably did when it was released. The song "La Mer" was originally written by CHARLES TRENET just after the end of the Second World War, although the English lyrics weren't written until a few years later (by JACK LAWRENCE). Trenet's French version was an ode to the changing moods of the sea; all Lawrence had to do to turn it into a torch song ("Somewhere waiting for me, my lover stands on golden sands...") was add the word "Beyond".

By rights, the arrangement should have been a lot slower to reflect the maudlin nature of the words, but Darin's version is a jaunt, a visual journey that more than hints at the possibilities of redemption.

For his sins, Darin was born Walden Robert Perciville Cassotto, in 1936, in the middle of the Bronx ("My crib was a cardboard box"). A sickly child, rheumatic fever left him with a weak heart, a condition that coloured pretty much everything he did (in his thirties, when he was often on stage in Las Vegas, he was administered oxygen during his performances). Driven by ambition, he worked his way through the Catskill resort hotels, borrowed his new name from a Chinese restaurant (Mandarin Duck), and eventually broke into the music business. He had hits with "Splish Splash", "Dream Lover", and lots of other examples of anodyne pop, but it will be for his version of KURT WEILL's "Mack The Knife" and "Beyond The Sea" that he will be remembered.

Darin experimented with folk, but was dragged back into light entertainment in 1972, starring in his own TV variety show, *The Bobby Darin Amusement Company* (an enthusiastic chess player, the show included an occasional segment in which he would explain a particular move).

On December 11, 1973, Darin entered Cedars-Sinai Medical Center in Los Angeles for surgery to repair two artificial heart valves he had received in a previous operation. Eight days later, a five-man surgical team worked for over six hours to repair Darin's damaged heart. He died minutes afterward in the recovery room without regaining consciousness. He was thirty-seven.

RAY DAVIES

In pop terms it's a career arc to die for, although in Ray Davies' case, death very nearly happened.

The four decades of Davies' extraordinary career can be roughly broken down into the following: in the early Sixties, with his younger brother Dave, he formed the KINKS, probably the quintessential British beat group of them all. (And like any self-respecting pop group, the KINKS were so-called because of the way they dressed, i.e. kinky.) During the Seventies, using the band as his vehicle, he became something of a music-hall impresario, creating a bunch of concept albums with wildly varying success. At the start of the Eighties, the band became a monstrously successful stadium act, relentlessly touring America to huge acclaim. Finally, in the Nineties, Davies was crowned the grand old man of Britpop, lauded by everyone from DAMON ALBARN to JARVIS COCKER, and fêted by critics for writing the sort of three-minute kitchen sink dramas that are now considered to be the cornerstone of Great British Pop. Oh, and in 2004 in New Orleans, he was shot, and seriously wounded.

While it might be easy to imagine that one of Britain's most successful singer-songwriters has been all but invisible recently, this is not the case. His music is still everywhere: 2007 saw the release of two CD EPs, "The Tourist" and

D

D "Thanksgiving Day", which were swiftly followed by the release of Davies' first-ever solo album, *Other People's Lives*. It was the Ray Davies of old, curmudgeonly, acerbic but with a newfound vigour, a metaphorical spring in his step. Songs such as "Next Door Neighbour", and "Stand Up Comic" prove that, in Davies' case, talent isn't necessarily finite.

We, like the man himself, can never escape his music. The Sixties hits are forever on the radio, he is name checked in every interview by every aspiring Britpop arriviste (stand up KAISER CHIEFS, stand up ARCTIC MONKEYS), and "Waterloo Sunset" regularly tops lists of all-time favourite pop songs. Just a few seasons ago, Burberry's creative director CHRISTOPHER BAILEY sent his models down the catwalk to the strains of Davies' demo version of his classic "I Go To Sleep", and "Living On A Thin Line" featured heavily in *The Sopranos*. When Sky Sports ran a compilation of video clips to mark the passing of GEORGE BEST before the game between West Ham and Manchester United, it was accompanied by one of the KINKS' most poignant singles, "Days".

You can't escape Davies' voice either, and his trademark north London whine, with its nasal, secondary modern lilt, has been copied by everyone from DAMON ALBARN to, bizarrely, LIAM GALLAGHER. A recent model was PETE DOHERTY, whose vocal style seems to get closer to Davies' the older he gets. It's also difficult to imagine many LIBERTINES or BABYSHAMBLES songs without first acknowledging Davies in his pomp. Even Doherty's description of his green and unpleasant Albion sounds like it came from Davies' pen: "Gin in teacups and leaves on the lawn, violence in bus stops and the pale thin girl with eyes forlorn."

Ray Davies once listened to a radio documentary about the KINKS and he came across, so he said, as a semi-neurotic, psychotic person. "If that's the way people want to remember me, so be it," he said. "I had my moments, but I don't see it that way."

Speak to people in the record industry about Davies and they'll raise an eyebrow. One television producer I know said to me, "He used to be the most difficult man in the music business." Say you're off to meet him and they'll advise you to be "careful". According to legend he is "difficult" and "contrary". Awkward and prickly, he has ploughed his own furrow, distancing himself from popular culture.

So much for reputations. Maybe Ray Davies had his moments – maybe he still does – but the man I met in Konk Studios in north London's Muswell Hill in 2006 was a shy, self-deprecating and extremely sharp sixty-one-year-old. He appeared to have mellowed somewhat, helped no doubt by the substantial royalties he must still be earning. Three other journalists I know who met him at the time said the same. "What a nice, funny man," said one. And like his contemporary, PAUL MCCARTNEY, Davies easily looked fifteen years younger than he was. Uncannily, he looked like he did on so many Eighties album covers, with flowing locks, bright quizzical eyes, good skin and the trademark gap in his teeth (the result of a childhood fight with his brother). Still, he did once describe himself as "innocent, conniving and gentle – and dangerous". And let us not forget that his younger brother Dave has described Ray as "cruel and creatively draining", adding that he was "spiteful and completely self-absorbed".

Konk is the place where the Kinks recorded many of their most famous songs, deep in one of those parts of north London that still looks like it probably did forty years ago. There's an outpost of Starbucks, a couple of tapas bars, and a proliferation of minicab offices and charity shops, but other than that it doesn't look much different than it did when the band were recording 1971's *Muswell Hillbillies*. In one of the studios here, the one in which I talked to Davies, there is a framed photograph of Morecambe and Wise with the inscription: "To Ray, from the ERIC MORECAMBE Fan Club. Wishing you every success with 'Come Dancing'. Elizabeth." That's very Ray Davies, quintessential Ray Davies in fact. No telegrams from presidents or congratulatory letters from fellow celebs, but a photo of Eric and Ernie.

D

Many songs on *Other People's Lives* cast him as a grumpy old man, something he's probably been since the age of twenty. "I'm a grumpy suburbanite, and I think I've always been a grumpy old man," he said, smiling. "A lot of my early songs were written for an older generation, because I wrote those when I was twenty, twenty-one, twenty-two. My sensibility has always been a bit old and grumpy. But a lot of people who know me really well say I'm very juvenile! I think one of the great characteristics about London is its grumpiness; rising above adversity, everything's such a terrible struggle but we get there. It's part of our siege mentality, bulldog spirit."

Davies last made the news on the evening of January 5, 2004, when he was shot in the leg by a mugger while he was having dinner with a girlfriend in New Orleans. A professional thief snatched her handbag and Davies bravely gave chase, running after him until the mugger turned around and shot him, got into a car and drove off. The next day, the *Sun* ran the headline, "You Really Shot Me".

"It was brave and stupid," said Davies. "The police were a bit critical. They said to the local press, 'Tourists shouldn't chase people when they're being robbed.' I'd had a bad day. It's the old thing, fight or flight? It's odd because I'm a relaxed person in normal circumstances, I think."

Davies had been living in the city on and off for two years, and was in the middle of a concentrated period of recording. One song, "The Tourist", ironically about the divisive nature of New Orleans, was almost finished. But as it was, Davies spent the next six months in hospital and the record, and a proposed tour, had to wait.

"Mentally, physically, it was difficult," he said, clutching his leg. "The recording stopped, and I had some dates scheduled for April, but I was still on crutches when we were doing the rehearsals, and I couldn't face it, couldn't do it. I couldn't even sing that song."

He remains remarkably sanguine about being attacked, "It's still playing over and over, but with all the recent thing with Katrina, it's difficult to keep a grip on the court case, but they arrested a couple of guys." The driver hailed from New Orleans, while the attacker was a professional criminal from Atlanta, and both have now been indicted. Davies has since been in contact with many of the friends he had made in New Orleans, and having written about the time he spent there for the *Times*, is still in negotiation to write a book in the form of a diary.

"It was always on the cards, this sort of disaster, and in a bizarre way I feel the attack on me was kind of ominous. And, interestingly enough, some of the sound effects on 'The Tourist' are kids on the street in New Orleans. I recorded the kids from my bedroom window on Barrack Street, in the 'hood, the mansion where my friend lived, a place called 'Esplanade'. I was staying in the back of the house, the coach house, which was right by the 'hood. There's a lot of anger on the streets there. I would record it on my cassette player. And I put a lot of those sound effects on the track."

Like many, Davies was appalled by GEORGE BUSH's bungled clean-up campaign, although not altogether surprised. "When you spend time in New Orleans, you understand the divisive nature of the city. I think anyone does who lives or stays down there. People say, 'If the lights are red, drive straight through.' Because it's a dangerous place, and people get robbed, there are car hijackings. I think what amazed me and prompted me to write the piece in the *Times* was the shock not just of foreign journalists, but of network journalists who went down there and said, 'There are poor people here!' I mean, there are poor people in America, there have been poor people everywhere for years, but I think because America's been fighting this war, leading the so-called 'civilised world' for so long, they've forgotten. How can this country look after the whole world when it can't look after its own?"

Davies' recovery took a lot longer than normal because his doctors didn't want him to travel due to the risk of infection and blood clotting. He also had a difficult break in his leg that they didn't see straight away.

"My leg broke while I was trying to go to the bathroom. It was broken, but it hadn't snapped until then. But they've done a wonderful job. My orthopaedic guy said that in the circumstances they did brilliantly. Because it was like the Third World down there."

Unsurprisingly, Davies' attack, his convalescence, the fallout from the hurricane and his ambivalent feelings about the city and its people helped put many of his creative anxieties in context.

"In my case it was like a watershed, in the respect that life is really important. Yeah, I'm making a record, so? Nothing's that important any more. The big deal was getting up and going to the bathroom every day on crutches, and suffering a lot with the emotional afterburn."

That record marked the first time in an age that Davies had been involved in a project without his younger brother Dave. The latter has also had his fair share of problems recently, and in 2005 suffered a debilitating stroke, one that left him in the care of his brother in north London.

"He stays with me now," said Davies. "There's still some tension, but he's easier to get along with. Having said that, I'm sure if we sat down with guitars and started writing songs, all the anger would come back. He's doing OK. He stayed with me a lot, but now he's going up north, as he's got a relationship going on up there. I think he tried to rush back too quickly. Hopefully, it's gradually improving. He did an interview on telly recently, and his speech was really bad. It's not a good situation."

Over the years there has been little love lost between the brothers. In their day, the Davies brothers were more spiteful, more attritional and more violent towards each other than LIAM and NOEL GALLAGHER in their heyday. In fact, compared to these two, Liam and Noel look like the CHUCKLE BROTHERS. During the first two decades of the Davies' career, journalists lost count of the number of times they threw guitars at each other on stage. Dave once co-wrote a song called "Hatred (A Duet)" featuring the line, "Hatred is the only thing that keeps us together". One night while dining in a Manhattan restaurant, Davies junior made the mistake of trying to steal one of his brother's chips. Ray's response? He apparently stabbed his brother in the chest with his fork.

"Dave bit my cheek," Ray recalled of another altercation. "So I kneed him in the groin." On their first American tour in 1965, the band fought so much and missed so many gigs that they were banned by the American Federation of Musicians from playing in America for four years. DAVE DAVIES' 1996 autobiography, *Kink,* contains liberal use of the C, F and A words, almost always in connection with his elder brother. *Kink* is a lurid and excruciatingly self-revelatory history laced with bitterness about the way the band's affairs were handled.

It's worth bearing in mind that Davies junior's only real solo hit was forty years ago, in the shape of "Death Of A Clown", while his brother has written more than 1,000 songs.

Although not for other people. Davies' lack of success with songs for other people is even stranger because of his innate ability to write in character, something that has almost defined him as a songwriter.

"When MICK JAGGER goes on stage he's always Jumpin' Jack Flash. In my show, I'm four or five different characters during the course of an evening. It's like doing a play. Not because I can't reveal the real me, it's just that I'm part of all these characters. I'm a character writer.

"It's got us into trouble in the past, when I was with the KINKS. I remember one tired and weary record executive said, 'I'm looking forward to the next album, but please can it be the same as the last one, so we can have some continuity.' Because I went from writing a musical soap opera to writing something about, I don't know, teenage pregnancy. I think I did that to keep my interest going."

Ray Davies will probably never again have the definitive cultural authority he had between 1964 and 1971, when the KINKS produced over twenty of the greatest singles ever released. These were picture-perfect musical postcards that summed up lower middle-class life in post-war Britain, songs

D

such as "Dead End Street", "Where Have All The Good Times Gone", "Tired Of Waiting For You", "Everybody's Gonna Be Happy", "Set Me Free", "Sunny Afternoon", "Dedicated Follower Of Fashion", "All Day And All Of The Night", "Days" and "Lola" – the "Angels" of its day.

Concentrating on tragicomic observation, Davies' songs revolved around predominantly male lower middle -class aspirations, expressing his ambivalence towards wealth, fame and class, and examining the strange mixture of predetermination and hazard to which human relationships are subject. The ordinary and the obvious were spelled out in his lyrics, but, contrastingly, never in a manner that was either. For years he has written about what SAUL BELLOW calls the melancholy of affluence, and suggested that Modern Life Is Rubbish when DAMON ALBARN was still in the playground trying to affect a cockney accent.

Davies also, lest we forget, absent-mindedly invented the heavy-metal guitar riff when the KINKS recorded "You Really Got Me" in 1964. When he heard one sniffy record company executive comparing the guitar sound to a barking dog, he replied, "Yes, but what a dog, and what a bark!" As if this weren't enough, he wrote what is widely considered to be the best British single ever, 1967's "Waterloo Sunset", a deathlessly beautiful record that single-handedly made existentialism a viable subject for pop music. Like PAUL MCCARTNEY and "Yesterday", Davies woke up singing it, albeit in a swing arrangement à la FRANK SINATRA and NELSON RIDDLE. "I wanted to write a song about a Liverpool sunset because of the death of Merseybeat and all that. Then I thought, 'I'm a Londoner, why all the tributes to Liverpool?' There's no memory of that song that isn't a pleasure."

He says he never tires of it, although he would like to remix it.

"There are so many compressors and things now that you can get to make it sound more subby, more dynamic. But it's a piece for its time. It wouldn't be the same piece of 'art' because it was made to evoke an image. When I was an art student, Monday was always the day we went outdoors to get our source material for sketching. I'd always go to stations and cafeterias, watching people in places where they've forgotten about the rest of the world and they're not aware that they're being watched. And if it was sonically different, people wouldn't close their eyes and think, 'That's the image.'

"It sets the scene. It's kind of perfect in a way. I had a dream of a record I wanted to make, I heard it as a record. So it was one of the first records I produced wholly by myself. I wouldn't say it's my favourite KINKS record, though."

Which is? "'All Day And All Of The Night'. I don't know why. It was the first single we put out that hadn't been rehearsed in front of an audience. I presented the song at a sound check in Birmingham. Went down that night to London, went in the studio at ten o'clock the following morning and recorded it. It was over in three hours. Did another gig up north in the evening."

In the Seventies, post-"Lola", Davies concentrated on rock opera as opposed to soap opera, and the band moved, metaphorically at least, from the village hall to the stadium. And perhaps no pop star has pursued the unstable marriage between drama and music with such dedication as Davies. In the late Sixties, having tired of turning out perfect pop single after perfect pop single (giving himself a nervous breakdown in the process), he turned to the rock opera and the concept album, churning out, in quick succession, and with rather diminishing returns, *The Kinks Are The Village Green Preservation Society* (1968); *Arthur Or The Decline And Fall Of The British Empire* (1969); *Lola Versus Powerman And The Moneygoround* (1970); *Percy* (1971, the soundtrack to a film about a penis transplant); *Muswell Hillbillies* (1971); *Everybody's In Showbiz* (1972); *Preservation Act 1 And 2* (1973 and 74), and *Soap Opera* (1975). It would be an overstatement to say that they were even moderately successful. "If there was ever a period of my life when I should not have been allowed to make records, that was it," said Davies later.

D The first of those records, *The Village Green Preservation Society,* is the thinking man's *Sergeant Pepper,* a continuous music-hall evocation of the passing of time, a sepia snapshot of Old England. It's an undisputed classic, a lovely if slightly over-fetishised record that is ethereal as well as psychedelic. Listening to *The Village Green*... reminds me why I started liking music in the first place, because it has the capacity to immediately transport you to somewhere you've never been before, in this case somewhere quite nice. In *X-Ray,* Davies' autobiography (written partly – irritatingly – in the third person), he says, *"Village Green* suddenly unleashed inside me memories of events that I had not yet experienced." Like PAUL MCCARTNEY and the BEACH BOYS' BRIAN WILSON, Davies sang the praises of childhood, and his personal Arcadia was always the past, always behind him.

"The Village Green Preservation Society is a classic example of a record that took time to get recognition," says Davies. "At the time I wrote it, we were banned from the US, and never thought we'd go back there again, so I wrote an album about English dreams and lost innocence. And we didn't give a shit about not being at Woodstock. I think if we hadn't have been banned, I wouldn't have made that album. The album was an enormous disappointment to the record company. But, down the line, it's one of the most loved albums of anyone who follows music."

Perhaps Davies experimented with theatrical productions because as a working-class boy from north London, he had always felt excluded by it. He says he dislikes aspects of the theatre, especially some of the people it attracts. "They're what used to be called 'the leisure class'," he says. *"Come Dancing* is basically a working-class musical. I don't see the point in someone who basically writes middle-class music, or music for the theatre-going classes. I haven't seen *Cats* or *Evita.* I've only seen *Phantom Of The Opera,* and I have to say I was thrown out of the theatre."

For making too much noise?

"It was after a Christmas party. I was thrown out of *The Mousetrap* for laughing as well. I was thrown out before it even started! I have a problem going to the theatre when I've had a drink. I was thrown out of a GLENDA JACKSON play once. It was five hours long. So I went to the pub for the first two, and thought I'd go along for the last half. I'd been given a box seat. As I walked in with my friend, someone recognised me, and I just did a wave from the balcony, just as Glenda made her entrance!"

And if the band seemed to disappear somewhat during the Seventies and Eighties, that's primarily because they were so successful in the States. The KINKS became a stadium band, playing the same-sized venues as AEROSMITH, the ROLLING STONES, and BRUCE SPRINGSTEEN.

So, how to listen to the KINKS? The early years are easy, and because they have been victim to the most unscrupulous compilations, it's possible to pick up the cream of their Sixties work for just a few pounds (*The Ultimate Collection* was released in 2002 by Sanctuary and includes most of the early stuff, plus some later songs). For me, the KINKS' Sixties records were an alternative soundtrack to punk and, back in 1977, as I got ready to go out to the Roxy, the 100 Club, or the Marquee, *Golden Hour Of The Kinks* was the record I posed in front of the mirror to. It was a cheapo Pye compilation, one I still have, covered with the same yellow Rotring ink that I managed to spill over my copy of *The Clash*. As I got onto the No.19 bus to take me up the West End, my ears would be ringing with "Tired Of Waiting For You", "See My Friends", or "All Day And All Of The Night", records that set you up for anything.

The KINKS soon became part of the Zeitgeist, and in the late Seventies and early Eighties, the PRETENDERS ("Stop Your Sobbing", "I Go To Sleep") and the JAM ("David Watts") had hits with Davies' songs. The KINKS heavily influenced the JAM, MADNESS, SUPERGRASS, and BLUR, all exponents of maudlin London pop. No KINKS, no SQUEEZE. No KINKS, no XTC. Davies became the godfather of Britpop, not once, but twice, being rediscovered by the likes of DAMON ALBARN more than a decade later. The JAM's *Sound Affects* and BLUR's *Parklife* owe a lot to the KINKS' 1967 LP *Something Else*, while BLUR's

D "Country House" could have easily appeared on *Face To Face*, the 1966 KINKS album.

"I don't think JOHNNY ROTTEN was trying to sound like me," said Davies, "but there was something in the imagery the music conjured up. There was that comic anger. I always thought the Seventies punks were humorous, like 'Dedicated Follower Of Fashion'. That was an angry song, but with humour. It was written in a fit of anger. Trendy people in the Sixties came up to my flat to a party, in a suburb of north London, and it was an argument over trousers. Someone said, 'Oh, are you wearing those?' I said, 'Yes, I like these pants.' He said, 'But you should be wearing these.' It was someone from a trendy newspaper or some sort of shop. We had a terrible argument, throwing things and everything. So I went back and locked myself in my room, typed it all out, and didn't change a word. It comes over as humorous, but there's a lot of anger in that song.

"I guess that was my first experience of political writing, in the sense that you get the best results through fun and comedy, rather than anger. And I think the punks had that. I think Britpop celebrated the style, it was more to do with sensibility, Englishness, like 'Parklife', 'Country House', and things like that. They've all touched on different aspects of me. Certainly with the vocal style. I admire their ability to take conceptual ideas and turn them into something that's theirs. It's not theft, in that respect, it's an inspirational thing."

The early Seventies are distilled on *Celluloid Heroes: The Kinks' Greatest Hits* (1976), while the heavier years can be heard in all their glory on *Come Dancing With The Kinks, The Best Of The Kinks 1977-1986*. You should also check out *Phobia* (1993), primarily because of "Scattered", a song inspired by the death of Davies' mother, and as good as anything he has ever written. It's also fascinating to hear other people's interpretations of his songs. It is heartily recommended that anyone interested in Davies' oeuvre should invest in two CDs of cover versions: SUB POP's *Give The People What We Want*, and the recent *This Is Where I Belong*. Both are an absolute revelation, not least because they focus on some of the more obscure work ("Who Will Be The Next In Line", "Wicked Annabella", "No Return", and "Fancy", for instance). Also vital is *To The Bone*, a 1994 unplugged session recorded in front of a small audience at the KINKS' own headquarters in London's Crouch End, and containing semi-acoustic versions of some of Davies' finest songs (the highlights of which are "See My Friends", "I'm Not Like Everybody Else", and a mad, unplugged Tex-Mex version of "Apeman"). This was to be one of the group's last concerts. Since then, Davies has largely performed solo.

MILES DAVIS

Few other jazz musicians have been mythologised so obsessively as Miles Davis, few other jazz musicians have been so closely associated with cool. And cool was certainly something he cultivated. "For me, music and life are all about style," he said.

Davis was unpredictable, vain, cryptic, and contemptuous of friends, musicians, lovers and critics. He was full of existential self-examination, and his persona – distant, solitary, and apparently uninterested in any meaningful relationship with his audience – helped create the post-war idea of "cool" as much as his music did. He dressed cool, too. In his pomp, as he liked the style of CARY GRANT and FRED ASTAIRE, so he created a kind of hip, quasi-black English look: Brooks Brothers suits, high top trousers, and tab-collar shirts that were so stiff he could hardly move his neck. He was determined to be hip. Hipper than all those other motherfuckers. "I really was into clothes – I was clean as a motherfucker, or like they used to say back in St Louis, cleaner than a broke-dick dog."

The man in the green shirt on the cover of *Milestones* was almost beyond cool. Photographed at the behest of the record

D company by DENNIS STOCK, the Magnum photographer who had taken so many of the iconic-building pictures of JAMES DEAN, Davis appeared typically insouciant. "...the trumpeter sits on an elegantly plain Fifties-moderne chair," wrote one critic, "his right hand lies on the thigh of his dark slacks, his left hand supports his trumpet, whose bell rests lightly on the plain curved disc of the seat. He looks at the camera with a calm, level gaze. His face is strong and beautiful, like MUHAMMAD ALI's before things went fuzzy. And the shirt tells you almost as much as the music inside." Cool.

Davis had no poor background to live down – his father was a staunch member of the emerging black middle-class in East St Louis, a dentist who also owned a substantial ranch in northern Arkansas – and spent most of his life in affluence. He loved European sports cars, and owned a Mercedes, a Lamborghini and a canary yellow 308 GTSI Ferrari coupé with a targa top.

"Miles Davis is my definition of cool," BOB DYLAN said. "I loved to see him in the small clubs playing his solo, turn his back on the crowd, put down his horn and walk off stage, let the band keep playing, and then come back and play a few notes at the end." He did this all the time, wandering off the stage to go and make a phone call, or see a woman, or score drugs, or just hang out backstage, letting others do the work. He was the first real insouciant jazz star, a man who hated the idea of pleasing people. He obviously didn't care, went out of his way to show that he didn't care. This is such a cliché that it's pretty much embarrassing these days, but in the Forties it was almost revolutionary.

He didn't forget to tell people what he thought of white society, either, and adopted an anti-white pose for most of his life. He espoused the back-to-Africa theories of MARCUS GARVEY, and could be aggressive towards white band members (when the white pianist BILL EVANS first started rehearsing with Miles, the trumpeter told him that in order to join the band he had to sleep with them all). In the spring of 1962 Miles was the subject of the first *Playboy* interview. An unknown

ALEX HALEY returned from an assignment to interview Davis, and emptied a briefcase of tapes at the magazine's editorial offices in Chicago. The transcribed conversations were stitched together to form the first proper interview in *Playboy*, establishing an institution. And it wasn't the music talk that was so gripping, it was the barely concealed rage about being a black man in white America. The meeting had begun by Davis forcing Haley to spar with him, and the resulting interview was no less combative. "Look man, all I am is a trumpet player," he told Haley, referring to his so-called disdain for the audience. "I only can do one thing – play my horn – and that's what's at the bottom of the whole mess. I ain't no entertainer, and ain't trying to be one. I am one thing, a musician."

He was often a difficult man to be around. "Miles tells it exactly like it is," said the drummer ART BLAKEY once. "Guys come up to Miles, hugging him. 'Hey Miles – hey baby, gonna give me a gig?' And Miles says, 'Doin' what?'"

The guitarist JOHN McLAUGHLIN, who often worked with him, recalled a recording session: "I said, 'Do you want all the chords?' He said, 'Yeah.' I said, 'That's gonna take some time.' He said, 'Is that a fact?'"

In the Fifties Miles underwent surgery to remove some polyps from his throat, and, having been told not to speak after the operation, got involved in a fiery argument with someone from his record company, which severely damaged his vocal cords. Forever after, his speaking voice would sound as though some half-human were whispering and shouting at the same time. This made him appear even more sinister.

Davis appeared to speak in Morse code, and was deliberately contrary. One of his road managers said he worked with him for two years and never got to understand his hand signals.

"If you understood everything I said, you'd be me," Miles would say.

Davis was born in Alton, Illinois in 1926, but his parents moved to East St Louis almost immediately, the city that was so beautifully evoked by DUKE ELLINGTON in "East St Louis

D Toodle-Oo", recorded in the year of Miles's birth. "The very first thing I remember in my early childhood is a flame, a blue flame jumping off a gas stove somebody lit," wrote Miles in 1989. "It might have been me playing around with the stove. I don't remember who it was. Anyway, I remember being shocked by the whoosh of the blue flame jumping off the burner, the suddenness of it. That's as far back as I remember; any further back than this is just fog, you know, just mystery. But that stove flame is as clear as music is in my mind. I was three years old."

He would listen to a radio show called "Harlem Rhythms", he'd hear music in the fields, in the streets, in church, and it all started to make sense to him. "That blues, church, back-road funk kind of thing, that Southern, Midwestern, rural sound and rhythm." By the time he was twelve, music had become the most important thing in his life, and a year later he was having trumpet lessons. Jazz soon started taking over his life, and if you blew trumpet, then there was only one place you needed to be, and that place was New York. So in the autumn of 1944, barely eighteen, following graduation from high school, Davis moved to Manhattan, ostensibly to study at the Juilliard School of Music. But Davis and Juilliard didn't get along. "The shit they was talking about was too white for me," he said, even though he picked up techniques and ideas by the likes of STRAVINSKY and PROKOFIEV that he would later use in his career. And so, having asked his father for permission, dropped out of college, and began hawking his wares along the jazz clubs of Harlem and 52nd Street. He played with CHARLIE PARKER, with DIZZY GILLESPIE, embroiling himself in bebop, the anti-swing, punk jazz that was sweeping America. Miles could play bebop, but it was an older man's blues. He wanted something else. A different sound.

In his autobiography, the word his co-writer QUINCY TROUPE had to type more than any other was "motherfucker", and if you deleted it the book would probably be fifty pages shorter. The dominant theme of the book – if one ignores the sex, the drugs, the pimping, the fights, etc – is Miles' constant search for players, as though he was trying to build the perfect football team. Davis was always trying to put together the Justice League of jazz, and he worked with everyone from CHARLIE PARKER, JOHN COLTRANE, and CANNONBALL ADDERLEY, to GERRY MULLIGAN, WAYNE SHORTER, and HORACE SILVER, from THELONIOUS MONK, CHICK COREA, and KEITH JARRETT, to DAVE HOLLAND, HERBIE HANCOCK, and GEORGE BENSON.

D

He wanted to build the perfect beast, but just when he thought he'd achieved it, it either fell apart, or he broke it in pieces. Davis loved risk, hated compromise. "The music... changed every fucking night," he said. "Even we didn't know where it was all going to. But we did know it was going somewhere." The Picasso of jazz, Miles was at the forefront of most of the major developments in jazz, including bebop, cool jazz, hard bop, modal jazz, and jazz fusion. "I have to change, it's like a curse," he said. Like BOB DYLAN, Davis hated the way in which critics would try and label him, and often moved off into a different thing altogether just to escape the tag, annoyed by the press trying to take ownership of his music. He adored LOUIS ARMSTRONG – "You can't play nothing on the trumpet that doesn't come from [LOUIS ARMSTRONG], not even modern shit" – but he had no interest in trying to please his audiences like Armstrong did, no interest in playing the fool, or even pretending to enjoy himself. "That sonofabitch is bad for jazz," said one booking agent. "He doesn't give a damn for audiences, and he lets them know it by paying no attention to them. I mean you don't have to wave a handkerchief or show your teeth like LOUIS ARMSTRONG to let the audience feel you care what they think about your music. But not him."

Davis gained a reputation for being distant, cold, and withdrawn, and for having a quick temper. The "nocturnal" quality of Davis' playing and his sombre reputation, along with his whispering voice, earned him the lasting moniker of "prince of darkness", adding a patina of mystery to his public persona.

He not only formalised the idea of "cool" as a persona, he soon formalised it as a type of jazz, too, initially as a reaction against the hectic complexity and cacophony of bebop. He wanted an urbane sound, a jazz style that verged on the glacial, with notes hanging in the air like clouds.

A contract with Capitol Records granted Davis several recording sessions between January 1949 and April 1950. The material they recorded was released in 1956 on an album whose title, *Birth Of The Cool*, gave its name to the "cool jazz" movement that developed at the same time and partly shared the musical direction begun by Davis' group. For Miles, bebop was simply turning into a screaming match, and, unable to emulate Dizzy Gillespie's quick-fire playing, the man in the green shirt moved on.

In the late Fifties and early Sixties, Davis recorded a series of albums with Gil Evans, whose orchestral touch added lustre to his sound, often playing flugelhorn as well as trumpet. The first, *Miles Ahead* (1957), showcased his playing with a jazz big band and a horn section arranged by Evans. It's strange to think that Miles was recording this masterpiece at exactly the same time Elvis was recording "All Shook Up", but then it's also bizarre to think that the Bee Gees were recording "Staying Alive" at the same time as the Clash were completing their first album. The port and velvet quality of *Miles Ahead* appealed to a larger audience than Miles had ever experienced, an audience that "responded instinctively to its prevailing air of modernity". There was a new generation of suburban hipsters who wanted modern furniture in their ranch-style homes, modern art prints on their clutter-free walls, and well-packaged cool jazz on their turntables (*Miles Ahead* originally came in a cover featuring a white woman on the deck of a sailing boat, appealing to a white consumer and infuriating Davis in the process).

At this point in his career, Miles seemed to bang out another classic album every few months, including in 1958 alone, *Milestones*, *Porgy And Bess*, and *Ascenseur Pour L'Echafaud*. Then, in 1959, Miles made the record that would define him, whether he liked it or not, *Kind Of Blue*. With its soft muted trumpet sound (dry as a martini), this has become synonymous with "cool" jazz, and there is no better example of the genre, or of his art, than this album. *Kind Of Blue* is the bestselling recording in his catalogue and the bestselling classic jazz album ever – the jazz album for people who don't like jazz. The album's durability has been described as invincible. It regularly tops All Time Favourite lists, and has become a template for what a jazz record is meant to be. It is perhaps also the most influential jazz record ever released. Musically, it's where modal jazz really hit paydirt, and where linear improvisation came to the fore (Davis playing Beckett to JOHN COLTRANE's Joyce), and its tunes have been covered by everyone from LARRY CARLTON to RONNY JORDAN. Its influence is far-reaching: "Breathe" from PINK FLOYD's *Dark Side Of The Moon* was based on a chord sequence from this album. From its vapory piano-and-bass introduction to the full-flight sophistication of "Flamenco Sketches", *Kind Of Blue* is the very personification of modern cool. Once described as "that haunting kind of sitting alone in Alaska sound", it wasn't bebop, and it wasn't good-time music. He minimised his trumpet sound, wanting something much smaller. For the moment, Miles wanted to junk all the bells, whistles and armies of percussionists and concentrate instead on simplicity, clear thought and calm.

"Before *Kind Of Blue* there had been slow jazz, mournful jazz, romantic jazz, astringent jazz," writes RICHARD WILLIAMS in *The Blue Moment*, his book about Miles' greatest record. "But there had never been anything that so carefully and single-mindedly cultivated an atmosphere of reflection and introspection, to such a degree that the mood itself became an art object. *Kind Of Blue* seemed to have taken place in a sealed environment." Miles achieved a mournful sound that sometimes feels like it's being played in space. He slowed everything down, wanting the instruments to sound like voices, like melancholy velvet. Recorded in a converted church in midtown Manhattan in just nine hours, the sleeve notes compared the record's creation to those Japanese artists who spend a day preparing their brushes before starting work.

The record wasn't considered black enough by some – "the hippest easy-listening album of them all" said one critic – which was ironic given Miles' legendary distaste for the way in which jazz was marketed to whites.

The Miles you heard on the records and the Miles you might meet in person were two different people completely. The music was cool, refined, elegant. Yet the man himself was a ball of neuroses, usually fuelled by drink and drugs. He was addicted to cocaine, to heroin, and to the inevitable mixture of both – speedballs. This made his relationships with women all the more haphazard. He fought with his girlfriends, took pornographic Polaroids of them, and, during more than one period of his life, pimped them out to feed his drug habit. "I had a whole stable of bitches out on the street for me," he said once, unable, or unwilling to admit that he knew better. When asked in 1985 if he had any intention of writing an autobiography, he said, "The trouble is, I'd have to think about all of those bitches..."

But if his sense of cool had turned him into a malevolent misogynist, his music remained largely sublime. Perhaps his most important record of the Sixties was *Sketches Of Spain*, released at the start of the decade, the soundtrack to a movie that's yet to be made. Miles's foray into the Spanish interior includes stunning versions of classical composers RODRIGO's "Concierto De Aranjuez" and GIL EVANS' "Solea"; the former is arguably the most successful jazz treatment of any European classical work, while the latter is simply one of the most beautiful things Miles ever recorded. As the original liner notes suggest, the music is so natural, so innate, it is as if Miles had been born of Andalusian gypsies.

Towards the end of the Sixties, sensing that jazz was becoming the music of the museum, he changed styles again, moving into an extreme version of jazz rock. Influenced by the likes of JIMI HENDRIX, SLY STONE, and JAMES BROWN, he started to use more electronic instruments. *In A Silent Way*, from 1969, was the first proper jazz-rock album. "There are no wrong notes in jazz," Davis once said, and with this album he proved it. The trumpeter had first flirted with rock the year before, on *Filles De Kilimanjaro* (his collaborator GIL EVANS shaping the title tune from the chords of Hendrix's 'The Wind Cries Mary'); this, though, was something quite different, a full-length "album" album, an electronic masterpiece that feels like the jazz buff's answer to VAN MORRISON's *Astral Weeks*. A few years later with *On The Corner*, Miles would combine JAMES BROWN with STOCKHAUSEN and the world would hate him for it. With good reason. Miles would describe this jazz-rock phase of his life thus: "Like trying to make conversation never using any words you ever used before." Six months later he recorded *Bitches Brew* – another album of jams that ended when the tapes ran out – which became a huge seller. He moved onto the rock circuit, too, and acted as the support act for the GRATEFUL DEAD, NEIL YOUNG, the STEVE MILLER BAND, and SANTANA. Who were these white motherfuckers?

He was determined to make music for the young African-American audience. *On The Corner* (1972) blended funk elements with the traditional jazz styles he had played his entire career. This new music demanded a new uniform, too, and Davis was soon to be seen wearing huge hexagonal sunglasses, kaftans, silk shirts and ridiculously baggy trousers. This was the time of African dashikis and laced-up denim, when Davis looked like a bug-eyed bad boy from Planet Blow.

From 1975 to 1980 he didn't pick up his horn once. "Mostly during those four or five years I was out of music, I just took a lot of cocaine [about $500 a day at one point] and fucked all the women I could get in my house." He had a hair weave, was forced to wear a truss, and had a hip replacement. He suffered from sickle-cell anaemia, chronic depression, bursitis, ulcers, and a renewed dependence on alcohol and drugs (primarily cocaine). And in 1982 he had a stroke that paralysed his right hand. He recorded with both PRINCE and JOHN LYDON's PUBLIC IMAGE, but neither collaboration was released, although he did successfully make a record with GREEN GARTSIDE's SCRITTI POLITTI. His last important record was *Tutu* (named after

D Archbishop Desmond), released in 1986. A haunting record, if rather decorative, its only downside is the (now) very obvious 1980s production. Some said the tunes on *Tutu* were no better than the sort of soundtrack music heard on *Miami Vice*; he answered his critics by appearing on the show in 1986, playing a dope-dealing pimp.

Miles Davis died in Santa Monica on September 28, 1991, from the combined effects of a stroke, pneumonia and respiratory failure. He was sixty-five, and broken. And cool would never be the same again.

SAMMY DAVIS JR.

Go on, close your left eye. Close it tight. Real tight. Keep it shut, the eyelid pushed right down, shutting out half the world, and focus on the rest of it with just the one, like Sammy did the day they took off his bandages. The day was November 24, 1954, and Sammy Davis Jr. was lying in his room at the Community Hospital in San Bernardino, having had his left eye removed. Five days earlier, on November 19, Sammy had almost died when his car was involved in a horrific crash on a railway bridge on Highway 66 just outside Victorville in California. He was on a return trip from Las Vegas, on his way to a recording studio in LA. Although he was a star before this, the incident proved to be somewhat pivotal, and almost as soon as he left San Bernardino, on November 27, Sammy was suddenly more famous than he'd ever been. Friends worried what the effect of the accident would have on Sammy's psyche – "Sammy never started out as handsome," said TONY CURTIS. "It was frightening for him" – but although he couldn't pass a polished surface without taking sneak peeks at himself, his increased celebrity only made him bigger. Cooler. More attractive to the white girls he'd hounded all his life. The one-eyed black man, born in Harlem Hospital Center twenty-nine years earlier, was now as famous as his buddy, FRANK SINATRA. Who would have thought it!

Many years later, in a different time and place, when he was still a budding novelist, JAY MCINERNEY made a trip out to Hollywood. Not knowing the name of a single hotel in Los Angeles, he phoned ahead and asked a studio executive where he should stay.

"How about the Chateau Marmont?" was the reply.

"Is that good?" asked McInerney. "Is that good?" the executive repeated, a little shocked. "Well, JOHN BELUSHI died there."

Fifty years ago, the spot where Sammy lost his eye was no less famous, no less talked-about, and no less legendary. It would become as famous as the desolate, windblown Highway 46 just outside Paso Robles where JAMES DEAN was to crash his Porsche Spyder a year later. When MONTGOMERY CLIFT emerged from his own horrific car crash, eighteen months after Davis, in May 1956, he was a broken man, his looks shattered (Clift needed extensive reconstructive surgery on his face, although his broken nose was never repaired), his confidence shaken. With Sammy it somehow just increased the pathos, gave him more definition.

While recovering in hospital, Sammy's friend EDDIE CANTOR told him about the similarities between Jewish and black cultures. So during his stay, immersing himself in Jewish history, soaking it up through his one good eye, Davis converted to Judaism. One paragraph about the ultimate endurance of the Jewish people intrigued him in particular: "The Jews would not die. Three millennia of prophetic teaching had given them an unwavering spirit of resignation and had created in them a will to live which no disaster could crush." Wasn't that what Sammy was all about? (As soon as he converted he would always refer to God as "the cat upstairs".) When Sinatra came to visit him in hospital, he said, "We all hit bottom sometime, Smokey. It passes." And it did. Self-conscious about his looks, he would tend after the crash to close his eyes when he sang, but in all other respects the accident propelled Sammy Davis Jr. to even greater stardom.

D   Weirdly, the most defining thing about Sammy – the eye, the accident, the one fact that anyone who knows anything about the rambunctious days of the entertainment business in mid-century America will know – is called into question by QUENTIN TARANTINO. At a fashion auction in September 2009, at the Victoria and Albert Museum in London, as the likes of PRINCE, KATE MOSS, and BRYAN FERRY worked their way around the tables, Tarantino smacked his hands up in the air when asked about Sammy (RAZORLIGHT'S JOHNNY BORRELL, who was sitting on Tarantino's other side, had already disappeared into the garden for a cigarette). For Tarantino, like anyone of a similar age in the movie industry, Davis is one of those guys you can't not have an opinion about.

"He was great with kids, and was something of a hero to children growing up in the Fifties and Sixties. He was on TV all the time back then, and he was a stand-up guy. How could anyone not love Sammy?

"But man, he had a dark side. The legend is that a wayward mob guy actually took out Sammy's eye, acting alone, and then faked the car accident. He did it because of the white girls, all the white girls he was fucking, and he didn't like him fucking around with them. And if you believe the legend, the mob weren't too happy about this, and got FRANK SINATRA to smooth things over with Sammy, and to keep his mouth shut. The payoff? That Sinatra and Sammy would play Vegas for the rest of their careers."

And while he might be a fan of Sammy, Tarantino is no fan of the idea of a Sammy Davis Jr. biopic, and can't see how anyone could do justice to Sammy's extraordinary life. "I would never go and see a movie like *Walk The Line*, no matter how good it's meant to be. Those movies are just about actors trying to win awards. I mean, who wants to see TOM HANKS play DEAN MARTIN? [He was meant to play him when MARTIN SCORSESE optioned the rights to NICK TOSCHES' *Dino* biography.] What's that all about? If I was going to make a movie about ELVIS, say, the whole film would be about the day he walked into Sun Studios."

Sammy Davis Jr. had it all, from suits to nuts. He was the epitome of an old-fashioned song and dance man, the stereotype ROBBIE WILLIAMS would emulate all those years later, a little man in a big tuxedo, a little man with truck-drivers' hair, a cartoon underbite, and one all-seeing eye (Sammy that is, not Robbie). Born in 1925 to a tap-dancing father and foot-stomping mother from Puerto Rico (with Cuban heritage), Sammy never went to school and never read a book until he became famous. His mother ran off when he was still a dote, so from the age of five he accompanied his father and his father's partner, WILL MASTIN, touring the clubs of North America with their vaudeville act. By the time he'd been on the road for three years he had equal billing, while three decades later he would turn into one of the highest-paid entertainers in the land.

In the late Forties, Davis (still with the WILL MASTIN TRIO) opened for FRANK SINATRA at the Capitol Theatre in New York, igniting a friendship that would last a lifetime. It was Sinatra who encouraged the Hollywood, New York, and Vegas establishments to start booking Sammy, and Sinatra who made sure Sammy got paid properly. "All the great things happened after that," said Sammy. "Sammy might never have made it if it wasn't for him," said MARILYN SINATRA, a cousin whose father worked as a gofer for Frank on the West Coast.

And Davis' time is coming again. The iconic Rat Pack entertainer died from throat cancer two decades ago – a lifetime in Hollywood terms – and yet suddenly he seems to be sort of everywhere. He's there in DANNY KLEINMAN's "Evolution" commercial for Guinness (telling the story of mankind's three-billion year wait for the perfect pint, accompanied by "Rhythm Of Life", one of Sammy's classics); he's referenced in AMY WINEHOUSE's extraordinary "Me And Mr Jones" ("What kind of fuckery are you? 'Side from Sammy you're my best black Jew..."); he's the subject of WIL HAYGOOD's above-weight biography, *In Black And White: The Life Of Sammy Davis Jr.;* and he's there, in person, in the gargantuan coffee-table book of his actually-quite-good celebrity photographs, published at the end of last year.

D And Sammy's life has it all: sex (lots, in fact, with white girls), booze (like all the guys in the Clan he liked a drop, so much so that in 1983 he was diagnosed with a dangerously enlarged liver), drugs (during the Seventies he was a cocaine hound like no other), tragedy (the 1954 car crash), violence (the mob threatening to make him blind in the other eye if he continued mucking about with white girls, specifically KIM NOVAK), and, saliently, race, and Sammy's lifelong struggle not just to be accepted in a white world, but also to try to escape his black past (there were times when Sammy Davis Jr. didn't just act white, he actually thought he was white). But unlike COLEMAN SILK in PHILIP ROTH's *The Human Stain,* Sammy couldn't disguise the fact that he wasn't white. And never would be, not even in death.

His story is the story of America, a tale of being black in a white world and wishing he wasn't. No matter that when he enlisted in the army his fellow infantrymen wrote "coon" and "I'm a nigger" across his forehead, Sammy just didn't think they were talking about him. After all, he may have been born black, but that didn't mean he had to stay black, did it? Did it? "He did so want to be white," said his first love, HELEN GALLAGHER, an Irish-American Catholic. "I think he thought he would be accepted more." Of that there is no doubt. "Being a star made it possible for me to get insulted in places where the average Negro could never hope to go and get insulted," said Sammy, with a smile.

Unlike Sinatra, or even Dino, Sammy's life has yet to be subjected to the kind of surgical scrutiny now popular with 21st-Century media, but if DENZEL WASHINGTON's film is a tenth as good as the book it's based on, then it might just be enough.

It was MARLON BRANDO who once called the 5'3" Harlem-born entertainer an "audience junkie", and he couldn't have been more pin-sharp. Sammy Davis Jr. loved the stage not just because it gave him love but because it gave him a career (as opposed to a life sweeping up after white folk), and because it gave him acclaim ("I am somebody!") but also because his success when running about on it gave him the arrogance to hope that it might put him on the same level as his Caucasian peers. Sammy wanted success not just for success' sake, but because Sammy wanted to be white. Famously insecure about his place in the world, the stage would offer him sanctuary, respite, peace.

There is no clearer picture of its sanctity than the one painted in PETER KAY's autobiography *The Sound Of Laughter*. Describing one of his nascent performances, Kay writes, "What a wonderful feeling it was to step on stage and listen to the sound, the sound of laughter. I felt happy, I felt safe." Kay's book is seriously, almost obsessively unpretentious, yet in these short sentences he pretty much distils the quintessential successful theatrical experience.

Like many entertainers, particularly entertainers from the early 20th Century, Sammy needed the stage, became addicted to it, like he became addicted to everything in his life: white women, booze, cocaine, dope, pornography, the whole kit-and-caboodle. Although JAMES BROWN would claim the title of the "Hardest-Working Man in Show Business", you could easily say that Sammy deserved it more. For instance, in 1964 he was starring in Golden Boy at night and shooting his own New York-based afternoon talk show during the day. When he could get a day off from the theatre, he would either be in the studio recording new songs or else performing live, often at charity benefits as far away as Miami, Chicago and Vegas, or doing TV variety specials in Los Angeles. Even at the time, he knew he was cheating his family of his company, but he couldn't help himself; as he later said, he was incapable of standing still.

And "Mr Charisma" – like JAMES BROWN, he had a multitude of nicknames – spent so much time up there under the lights that his performances became faultless. When he sang one of the songs from his small, if perfectly-formed collection of hits – "The Candy Man" (From *Willy Wonka & The Chocolate Factory*), "Mr Bojangles" (which could have been written about him), "The Rhythm Of Life", "A Lot Of Livin' To Do",

D "Eee-O-Eleven (from *Ocean's 11*), "Gonna Build A Mountain", "Too Close For Comfort" (perhaps his masterpiece), and "Me And My Shadow", the hardy perennial he always performed with Sinatra, the classic they can be heard singing together on any number of budget Rat Pack CD collections – you always knew they would be pitch perfect. He was a great dancer and he was a great mimic, a great comedian and a great singer, but he was very much a performer. And while some marvelled at his range (one critic said his voice always sounded too epic for such a small body), listening to it now, his emotions sound premeditated. Someone such as Sinatra or TONY BENNETT sang from their core, whereas Sammy was essentially a song and dance man at heart, so his singing was textbook rather than heartfelt. But what a textbook.

His place of identity was the road. He flew across the country, free as a bird, with his Gucci and Louis Vuitton luggage, his Tiffany jewellery, his custom-made suits and bench-made shoes, like a gentrified vaudevillian, unable to slow down and certainly unable to stop. This tiny giant forever in motion. And he took a sweet shop of accoutrements with him: a pair of six-shooters, a cape, a sword, half a dozen tape recorders, three record players, four transistor radios, cases of Scotch, cartons and cartons of cigarettes (he always had cigarettes), a set of barbells that no one ever saw him use, a silver shoehorn, a trumpet, a brace of tambourines, a four-season wardrobe, a prop case full of old vaudevillian trinkets, trunks and trunks of gaudy jewellery and, obviously, a box containing an assortment of glass eyes.

On the road, Mr Peripatetic was answerable to no one – as long as he stayed away from the South, and the potential embarrassment of being refused entry to restaurants and hotels. As he described it in his first autobiography, 1965's *Yes I Can*, Sammy combed his audiences for "haters," and as soon as he spotted one, he gave his performance "an extra burst of strength and energy", in order to "get those guys", to "neutralise them and make them acknowledge" him. Thus Sammy turned potential liabilities into sources of strength

and inspiration, trying to surmount racial prejudice. And
he partied, too. "He was on the road fifty weeks a year," said
Sammy's former agent from William Morris, SY MARSH. "He
was fucking everything he could get his hands on."

When he came to London in the early Sixties, Sammy
Davis Jr. fell in love. He fell in love with the people, with
traditions and artifice he'd never seen before, and with the
sartorial fervour he saw all around. He loved the old men
smoking pipes, swinging walking sticks, wearing bowler hats
and bespoke suits from Savile Row. He hung out with PETER
O'TOOLE, ANTHONY NEWLEY, and LESLIE BRICUSSE, mimicking
their accents and making them his own. He was happy – he
even got to meet the BEATLES – because by then he was a star.

Having spent most of his life with his face pressed up
against the white world, not being allowed to sleep in many
of the hotels he performed in, sometimes not even being
allowed a dressing room, in 1959, when he joined the Rat
Pack, everything changed. Now he was a star. Black, but a
star. In among Sinatra, DEAN MARTIN, PETER LAWFORD, and
JOEY BISHOP, he was the black mascot, and if it bothered
him, it bothered him in private. Sammy wasn't going to let
it show. When Dean Martin asked, rhetorically, on stage
one night, "How does it feel to sit at the back of the bus?"
to hoots of laughter from the audience, Sammy just smiled.
Once, Martin picked up Sammy from the stage and presented
him to Sinatra: "Here, this award just came for you from
the National Association for the Advancement of Colored
People." And if he ever overran at the Copacabana in New
York, the manager, JULES PODELL – who was not known for his
delicacy of manner – would yell, "Get off my stage, nigger!"
And Sammy would get off the stage.

Sinatra could do anything to Sammy, because if Sammy
complained, he'd be out in the cold. KATHY MCKEE, a Vegas
showgirl who was also Sammy's lover, recalls her first
encounter with Sinatra and Martin. She was backstage at the
Sands. "When the two of us walked into Sammy's dressing
room, FRANK SINATRA was there. Sammy had to leave for a

few minutes, and when we were alone, Sinatra told me DEAN MARTIN was due at any moment. He suggested that, as a gag, I should strip down to my underwear to greet him. I was hesitant at first, but thought I was being put to the test to see if I could play in the big league. So I slipped out of my black and white polka-dot jumpsuit and greeted DEAN MARTIN wearing my black bra, matching bikini panties, and white go-go boots. 'Wonderful, charming,' said Martin, who then told me to get dressed again, 'because Frank is an asshole'."

But Sinatra was Davis' great benefactor; the man who helped him become a star, the man who lifted him out of vaudeville and into the white clubs. In all the dozens of books about Sinatra, Martin and Sammy, there is a familiar refrain: Frank wouldn't go into any place if Sammy wasn't accepted in exactly the same way he was, and if Sammy ran into problems with hotels in Vegas because of his colour, he never had any problem when he was with Sinatra, because Frank wouldn't stand for it. The only thing you really need to know about their relationship is the fact that when Sammy died, Sinatra gave Sammy's widow, Altovise, a million dollars. In cash. And when he was quizzed by the Feds about the comings-and-the-goings, about the boys in dark suits with strong jaws who always seemed to be hanging around backstage at the Rat Pack's – or, more accurately, the Clan's – parties, Sammy took the Fifth. "Baby, let me say this," he once told an FBI man who was quizzing him about Sinatra's mob connections. "I got one eye, and that one eye sees a lot of things that my brain tells me I shouldn't talk about. Because my brain says if I do, my one eye might not be seeing anything for a while."

Of all the Clan, Sammy was the most easily drawn, the most easily recognised, what with his ebony anvil head, itsy-bitsy goatee, his pronounced JIMMY HILL chin, and his dancing skeleton stage presence. He was a black inch-high private eye, all three-button suit, patent winkle-pickers, and silver tie clips. In his Brooks Brothers suit he looked like an elfin Negro banker or a funeral director, with his thick horn-rimmed spectacles and slicked-back "do". He wore specially made pewter baby alligator boots that made him look five inches taller. A two-inch heel was fastened on the outside, while a platform was placed inside the boot.

The Clan gave him his best movie roles too: in *Ocean's 11* (1960), *Sergeants 3* (1962), and *Robin And The 7 Hoods* (1964). He appeared in more than thirty films, including *Porgy And Bess* (1959), *Nightmare In The Sun* (1965), *A Man Called Adam* (1966), and *Sweet Charity* (1969). He also appeared in his fair share of trash – he would make the mistake, like Frank and Dino, of appearing in the *Cannonball Run* films – while a lot of his performances were simply squandered (his cameo was eventually cut from *Diamonds Are Forever*, although you can catch it on the latest DVD). Trawling through the racks and racks of budget Rat Pack DVDs you find in HMV today, the films that give the best indication of what Sammy really meant are the recordings of old TV shows and stage performances. It was here – there, right there! – on stage, in front of an audience, where he shone, where he felt safe, where he did things that no other entertainer of his generation could really do, hoofing it up, goofing about, and running around like a headless chicken. In a tuxedo.

But there was one thing that Davis liked more than the stage – and that was women, particularly white women. So obsessed was he that he bought black silk sheets for his bed, so the contrast of a white girl lying on them was more extreme. White women – especially blondes – gave Sammy parity with all the white boys, took some of the blackness out of him, and made him feel like more of an American. Even though America hated him for it. When he hooked up with Hollywood starlet KIM NOVAK in 1957, everyone told him to cease and desist – his friends, his enemies, the studios (Columbia boss HARRY COHN told him he'd never work again unless he dumped her), the media, and eventually even the Mafia, who threatened to take out his other eye unless he chose someone his own colour ("You're a one-eyed nigger Jew," he was told. "You ever see this blonde again, you're gonna be a blind nigger Jew. You're

D

getting married this weekend – go figure out who you're marrying"). He listened, and in 1958 consented to a phoney marriage to a barely-known black Vegas singer called Loray White. The marriage didn't last, unsurprisingly, and in 1960 he threw caution to the Nevada wind by marrying a twenty-six-year-old Swedish actress, MAY BRITT.

Britt wasn't just white, she was the whitest girl anyone had ever seen.

Not only was he obsessed with white women, they were obsessed with him. Agent SY MARSH said, "The women used to say to me, 'Sy, when he walks out on stage, you realise how unattractive he is, but one and a half hours later he's six foot tall and handsome.'"

Black women say he reminded them of a trained mosquito in a tux. "The black girls wouldn't pay him any mind," says dancer MAURICE HINES. "The white girls looked at the money – not colour. The white girls were aggressive." And after a while it became the norm. Big publicity for Sammy was if he dated a black woman. "White womanhood is what he wanted," says WIL HAYGOOD. "It thrilled him so. But it rattled bones in the American psyche, and those bones made loud noises."

The actress JANET LEIGH visited him once in New York. "I remember we were walking down the street to his place. We were talking about this movie idea – about a black man and a white woman – and Sammy said, 'You have no idea how hard it is with me and May. You see this?' He showed me the umbrella he was carrying. You pressed it and the tip became a knife. He said, 'This is how hard it sometimes gets.'"

He would photograph his girls, too, as if to prove to himself that he'd actually conquered them. In the downstairs office of his Beverly Hills home on Summit Drive, there was a waist-high cabinet that ran the length of the 25ft wall. It had two shelves filled with the latest cameras, with lenses and filters for all of them. Sammy never stopped taking photographs, worried he might lose forever what his one good eye had just seen flash by. Get it on film, get it on paper, to prove to the world it had happened. One girlfriend said she wasn't allowed to show up anywhere dressed casually. "I wasn't allowed to show up some place and look like I wasn't ready for a photograph. Sammy thought if you were gonna climb a mountain, then every move should be a picture."

In the recently published book, *Photo by Sammy Davis Jr.,* in among the obligatory social realism and the old shots of the WILL MASTIN TRIO and the west side of Las Vegas where he stayed when he first performed there, in among all that are dozens of photos of the great and the good – if Sammy had anything, he had access – and the underlying feeling you get from flicking through is that the photographer was simply happy to be in the places he found himself. Who wouldn't want to take a picture of KIM NOVAK, or CHARLOTTE RAMPLING, or MARILYN MONROE, or SHIRLEY MACLAINE, or CELESTE HOLM, or MIA FARROW, or ELIZABETH TAYLOR, or DEBBIE REYNOLDS, or JANE RUSSELL, or CHER, or JUDY GARLAND, or JACKIE O?

But not even that great libertarian and arbiter of social change, President Kennedy, could cope with the idea of Sammy with a white girl. At a White House reception in 1962 designed to ingratiate him with Negro leaders, Kennedy spent the evening pumping flesh and slapping backs, but when he saw Sammy with Britt he whispered to an aide, "What's he doing here? Get them out of here!" He told his aides to tell his wife to usher MAY BRITT out of the room before the photographers arrived. The couple left the White House that evening deeply aware of the awkward treatment they had received. And Sammy would never forget it.

The marriage to Britt lasted until 1968, when Sammy moved onto a dancer, ALTOVISE GORE (a black girl), who he stayed with until his death in 1990. Although he never allowed his vows to stand in the way of a good time. After every show there would be parties, sex parties, orgies where dozens of (white) girls would be invited up to Sammy's suite in order to get down. Dancer SALLY NEAL heard about the sex parties, but she stayed away: "They were wild, bizarre, sick." After his show "Golden Boy" moved from New York to London, during the run Sammy carried on three affairs at once, with both black and white girls. "Mr Davis loves confusion," said one of them.

D

During the Seventies he also became addicted to porn, and would get the small Hollywood studios that specialised in the genre to send over prints so he could run them in his home. His valet, Rudy, would set up the projector, and then Sammy, Altovise, and their friends would sit around and gawp. And Sammy couldn't get enough. It was during this time that he struck up a relationship with the star of *Deep Throat,* LINDA LOVELACE. "He had his own code of marital fidelity," she said. "He explained to me that he could do anything except have normal intercourse because that, the act of making love, would be cheating on his wife. What he wanted me to do, then, was to deep-throat him. Because that would not be an act of infidelity." Sammy subscribed to the maxim that "eating ain't cheating".

Sex for Sammy was all-consuming. Famously less well-endowed than Sinatra, he wasn't shy about offering himself to any woman who appeared interested. Predictably, the sex and the booze would eventually begin to pall, and having seemingly exhausted the possibilities of both, in the Seventies Sammy started to use cocaine heavily. The Candy Man wanted white candy, and there were lots of people around to supply it. Everyone was doing drugs at the time, just as they were all into rediscovering the Beats, dropping out, listening to songs that lasted four hours as opposed to four minutes, wearing kaftans, demonstrating against any form of punitive legislation, and, with a force and a fanfare that was felt around the world, the fight for civil rights.

Sammy's commercial decline in the late Sixties coincided with the popularisation of the civil rights movement, a movement he was reluctant to embrace. Sammy wasn't interested in black causes because he didn't want to be black; he wanted to be white. And white only. When he was interviewed by *Playboy* in 1966, the first question he was asked was, "Have you ever wished that you weren't a Negro?" Sammy wasn't interested in the cause of his brothers, he was only interested in his own. One day in the Seventies, asked about his golf handicap, he said, "My handicap?! Man, I am a one-eyed black Jew! That's my handicap!" In 1965 he released five albums: *When The Feeling Hits You! Sammy Davis Jr. Meets Sam Butera & The Witnesses*; *Sammy Davis & Count Basie – Our Shining Hour*; *If I Ruled The World; The Nat King Cole Songbook*; and *Sammy's Back On Broadway*, and there wasn't a political lyric on any of them.

Sammy caught up with the civil rights movement late in the day, finally realising that Black Power meant him, too. In May 1970, Motown released its first Sammy Davis Jr. album. Called *Something For Everyone*, it boasted nine singles, all of which bombed. It was an odd, beguiling record, both in terms of its content and its sleeve design. Sammy covered white bread songs such as "Spinning Wheel", "You've Made Me So Very Happy", and "In The Ghetto", while dressed like a fancy-dress born-again pimp on the cover, wearing an Afro, a long robe and tinted glasses, holding a drink and a cigarette, surrounded by more than two dozen – mostly white – women. It smacked of an old timer trying to keep up with the kids and getting it terribly wrong. "What's Going On" it wasn't.

Sammy compounded his gauche embrace of his own kind by offering very public support for President Nixon in the run-up to the 1972 election. At a Republican youth rally, the night Nixon was nominated for re-election, Sammy embraced the president in a way he probably had never been embraced before, not even by his wife, giving him a huge I-love-you hug in front of thousands of adoring delegates. And Sammy was vilified for it – for failing to understand blacks' distrust of Nixon's ultraconservative views. He didn't seem to care, or perhaps know, that one of Nixon's campaign vows was to keep up his attack on busing – to stop the effort being made to get black children into decent school districts. Until his death he would face accusations of being an Uncle Tom.

Not that Sammy was unduly concerned. After all, he didn't want to be seen as an outcast because he had been cast out himself, in the cruelest, most fundamental way possible. Sammy's Rosebud was always his mother, a mother who more or less abandoned him when he could barely walk. She was a

D dancer, and in those days dancers went where the money was: on the road. Mother and son spent decades leading peripatetic lives, occasionally bumping into each other in far-flung towns, neither one able to offer a big enough olive branch for reconciliation.

In TONY PARSONS' novel, *My Favourite Wife*, about a young British couple who move to Shanghai to experience the Klondike spirit of the first city of the 21st Century, one of the characters uses an old Shanghai saying, "Everything is fake except your mother." Sammy Davis Jr. appears to have spent most of his life secretly hoping exactly the opposite was true. "ELVERA DAVIS chased after her own future," writes WIL HAYGOOD. "She left home and family; the fires she started, she let rage. In pursuing her dream, she was possessed of a wilful purpose. Her belief in herself was supreme. She packed her bags and climbed aboard train after train. A vision of her children crying out in the night did not slow her forward motion. She was all about execution."

Of Elvera's two children (Sammy's sister Ramona was born in 1927), the one most like her – wilful, determined, and with a messianic belief in self – was Sammy. "In drifting apart, there was also something that fused them together. It is quite possible that a child dropped on to an ever-widening path of seeking constant approval never stops hearing a kind of hum, an echo from beyond. And that echo becomes the maternal knock against the conscience. Can't you see me? Can't you hear me? It becomes a sound that constantly escapes the width of the path, and the knock keeps echoing and echoing." But so what. His mother was not one to stage reconnaissance missions of the mind: she didn't look back.

In 1989, after a lifetime of smoking, Sammy was diagnosed with throat cancer, and although he took it stoically, physically he soon became diminished, shrinking into his tuxedos, his features becoming hollow and accentuated, his body seemingly weightless. Soon the tiny entertainer was becoming smaller than ever.When he was told he could be saved by surgery, Sammy said he'd rather keep his voice than have a part of his throat removed, although a few weeks prior to his death his entire larynx had to be taken out anyway.

At his funeral, on May 18, 1990, two days after he died, the sun was so bright that almost everyone wore sunglasses, making it look like the whole thing had been heavily – overly – art-directed. Sunglasses meant glamour, meant Hollywood, meant distance, coolness, duplicity, insincerity, style, glitz, exotica, disguise – all of which had been salient components of Sammy Davis Jr.'s life.

In 1978, when Sammy was trying to revive his faltering Broadway career, a critic for *Time* wrote that the fifty-something entertainer projected "the image of an over-age child parched for affection, aggressively demanding approval". Which is what he'd been doing all his life. The sad thing is, and this is one of the few areas of his life where Sammy actually possessed self-awareness, that when success eventually came, it didn't make any difference.

BLOSSOM DEARIE

It's never been especially fashionable to say so, but Blossom Dearie had one of the greatest voices in jazz. She died in 2010, aged eighty-two, one of the forgotten archetypes of the American post-war era, an idiosyncratic singer who brought some levity to the otherwise often self-regarding world of jazz.

She looked a little like a petite SHELLEY WINTERS, and with her blonde curls, SWIFTY LAZAR specs, and buttoned-up shirts, often gave the impression that she'd be much happier poking around a public library than singing scat in Greenwich Village, knocking out "Lullaby Of Birdland", "Old Devil Moon", and "Unpack Your Adjectives". Actually born with the name Blossom Dearie in the Catskills, she began playing piano at an early age and studied classical music before making the switch to jazz while in high school – a switch that always seemed to define her as a performer.

D

JOHN LENNON was a huge fan, and when he took the stage for a live British television show on which Dearie was also scheduled to appear, he said, "I'm going to do my Blossom voice" and moved right up into his high register. Dearie, predictably flattered by the experience and by the admiration of a Beatle, wrote the song "Dear John", in which JIM COUNCIL's lyrics celebrate Dearie "digging you digging me" (she also wrote tribute songs for GEORGIE FAME and DUSTY SPRINGFIELD).

She had a small voice but a big personality, one that could be seen in every line of her formidably detailed performance contracts: no smoking in the audience, no photography, no talking, no background music, no waitress service while she was on stage. Find her on YouTube and you'll see her castigate a member of the audience for daring to take out his camera. What you can also find on YouTube are various versions of one of her signature songs, "I'm Hip", a slap in the face for anyone who says that jazz can't be funny ("I'm hip. I'm no square. I'm alert, I'm awake, I'm aware. I am always on the scene. Makin' the rounds, diggin' the sounds... I even call my girlfriend 'man', 'cuz I'm hip..."). The song has also been covered by GEORGE SHEARING, ROSEMARY CLOONEY, BARRY MANILOW, TONY BENNETT, and BETTE MIDLER, and has been performed over so many decades that when the singer grapples with the stanza beginning, "I read *Playboy* magazine, 'cuz I'm hip...." the magazine title switches between *People, GQ* and *Rolling Stone*.

THE DELLS

For me, my pets are my records, when I can find them that is. I have spent a good deal of my life sifting through rows and rows of old LPs, boxes of secondhand singles, and racks of rare CDs in search of those records that continue to elude me. Even though Amazon and iTunes have made it easier to source deleted and difficult-to-find records, there is still little to rival the involuntary yelp you make when you stumble across something on your list while idly looking through another dusty, dilapidated record store.

It happened to me once in 2009, while I was cruising the aisles of Amoeba – not only the best record shop in Los Angeles, but, the way things are going, soon to be the only one. With a scrappy piece of paper in my hand I was scouring the D section of the soul section, looking for a copy of the impossible-to-find 1972 album *The Dells Sing Dionne Warwick's Greatest Hits*, when suddenly I was holding one. There it was, brand new, for $9.99.

When something like this happens I usually do a double take, and look for the flaw: is it a live version, is that the real price, am I dreaming, etc? But on this occasion it was the real deal, one of the greatest baroque soul albums ever made.

Why? Well, its architect was the great CHARLES STEPNEY, a man who had already gone baroque with MINNIE RIPPERTON, ROTARY CONNECTION, and even RAMSEY LEWIS. Stepney was a PHIL SPECTOR character in terms of his sonic ambitions, and his approach to recording sessions always involved a full string section, a funky backbeat, and some soaring vocals. In this instance he also had one of the foremost singing groups of the era, a band who had already had many hits of their own on Chess Records.

The title of the album is a slight misnomer, perhaps designed to appeal to their core fan base, as it's actually a collection of BURT BACHARACH covers. The record includes "Walk On By", "A House Is Not A Home", "I Say A Little Prayer", and eight others, although the standout track is Stepney's extraordinary version of "Wives And Lovers", one of Bacharach's most complex pop songs. Stepney's version is layered with so many washes of sound that it feels and sounds like a small symphony.

So not only did I find one of the scarcities on my list, but also – and this isn't always the case – it totally exceeded expectations.

See you at Amoeba, maybe.

DEPECHE MODE

D

The Basildon boys formed what was to become "the most popular electronic band the world has ever known" in 1980, and soon started having hits with inconsequential stuff such as "New Life", "Just Can't Get Enough", and "Get The Balance Right". They had geometric haircuts, clothes that could have come from GERRY ANDERSON's costume department, and always looked terribly serious about what they did whenever they were on television. They appeared to be quite small whenever you saw them in a London club (although, bizarrely I saw them once at a party on Canvey Island, not long after they'd become famous, and they looked a lot bigger), and never really appeared to have the power of their convictions.

Their work ethic was never in dispute, though, and they bashed out the hits as if they were working in one of the local car factories: "Everything Counts", "People Are People", "Blasphemous Rumours", etc – most of which were fairly inane. As the Eighties wore on, the darker they got, seduced by the allure of sex, drugs, and a career that didn't look like ending any time soon. In 1989 they started recording *Violator*, a wonderfully rich record, epic in scale, and strong on melody ("Personal Jesus", "Policy Of Truth", "Enjoy The Silence", "World In My Eyes", etc). They filled stadiums, cavorting about in leather and lace, magnified by ANTON CORBIJN's austere black and white photographs, which had turned the Essex Thunderbird puppets into coarse-grained electro rock stars.

DEVO

ANDY WARHOL said, "They always say time changes things, but you actually have to change them for yourself." To wit: Devo's re-imagining of the ROLLING STONES' "Satisfaction".

NEIL DIAMOND

D

You shouldn't feel guilty about guilty pleasures. A few years ago, on holiday in Barbados, I became obsessed with a record I kept hearing on the radio. From hotel to beach bar to rental car, I heard it everywhere I went. Rather irritatingly, it got to me, a piece of expertly manufactured pop that kept swimming round my mind like a trapped fish. Did anyone know what it was? Did they hell. The legendary jazz pianist OSCAR PETERSON was also staying at the hotel and it was all I could do to stop myself from asking him (thankfully dignity got the better of me).

Back in London I began my search; on a bum steer, not only did I invest in a couple of CORRS CDs (something I'm still obviously trying to come to terms with), I even started singing what I thought was the song to shop assistants in HMV (I am no longer allowed in the Oxford Street branch). Eventually, more through luck than judgement, I found it: "You're Still The One" by SHANIA TWAIN, from, I discovered, her thirty-five million-selling album, *Come On Over*.

At first I thought that Shania would be a guilty pleasure, down there with the likes of SIMPLY RED, MICHAEL CRICHTON, and the early work of CHRIS FARLEY, but soon the album became a fixture on the car CD, where it stayed for nearly two months. As all guilty pleasures should.

A few years later I came across another, a record by an "artist" I've spent many years avoiding (he's my mother-in-law's favourite singer, for one thing). As I was searching iTunes for KATE BUSH's version of ELTON JOHN's "Rocket Man" (which, I'd read, was pretty damn spectacular, and is), I found another version, a live one no less, by that sultan of schmaltz, Neil Diamond. And I have to say that for a few weeks it became the record I played more than any other. I've always loved the song (who doesn't love it?), but to find such an extraordinary version by such an underwhelming singer – a recording so good it should be pavilioned in splendour and girded with praise – was strange indeed. A happy accident.

D

But then I remembered that MARTIN SCORSESE had insisted that Diamond perform at the BAND's "Last Waltz" (to represent Tin Pan Alley), that he had written "I'm A Believer" for the MONKEES, that I'd always turned the radio up when "Sweet Caroline", or "Beautiful Noise" came on, and that I actually quite liked my mother-in-law.

THE DIVINE COMEDY

If nostalgia really is homesickness, then who wouldn't want to go home to the Divine Comedy? Rarely has a band been so arch yet so strangely accessible. Call them baroque pop, call them a chamber pop band (others have been far ruder about them), NEIL HANNON's fabulous creation make the type of disturbingly polite music that is so obviously out of sync with pretty much everything that surrounds it that it seems perverse. So perverse they ought to be painted by JOHN CURRIN.

They had a whole bunch of hits in the Nineties ("National Express" included), although their more recent material has been better, stuff such as "Absent Friends" and "Assume The Perpendicular". Even so, you can have too much of a good thing, and there is only so much Divine Comedy you can take (you can't have high tea all day). Hannon has such a distinctive, mannered voice that – maybe like RUFUS WAINWRIGHT, or even RYAN ADAMS – after twenty minutes or so, at which point RANDY NEWMAN turns into GILBERT O'SULLIVAN, you want to move on.

DOO-WOP

One of the only genres to define itself through onomatopoeia, doo-wop was the alternative sound of the US in the Fifties, the sound of Young America, the street-corner barbershop gear-change that ratified the likes of the FIVE SATINS, the CROWS, the CLOVERS, the CHORDS, the MOONGLOWS, the PLATTERS, and all the others. It had its roots in the early recordings of the INK SPOTS and the MILLS BROTHERS, and became a nationwide craze. While rock'n'roll was scaring parents, confusing broadcasters, and perverting teenagers, doo-wop was simply accessorising adolescence with an innocence and a style that alienated no one (black and Hispanic included). The CRESTS, the FIVE DISCS, the DEL-VIKINGS, FRANKIE LYMON & THE TEENAGERS, the DIAMONDS, the SKYLINERS – all of them had voices like birds.

There were probably over 15,000 doo-wop groups performing professionally during the late Fifties, and of the few who had hits, most were one-hit wonders. There were so many because the music could be performed a capella, just kids on a corner practising harmonies, the rappers of their day. Low-budget, sparse, no frills. Predictably this meant it was relatively easy for record labels to cover songs originally recorded by African-American groups, using white singers instead. For instance, the CHORDS' "Sh-Boom" was covered by the CREW-CUTS and the MOONGLOWS', "Sincerely" by the McGUIRE SISTERS.

There are many claims on its origins. The syllables first appeared on wax, in 1954, on a song called "Never" by the Los Angeles group CARLYLE DUNDEE & THE DUNDEES, when the backing singers (who later became the CALVANES) sang "doo-wop" in the chorus. However, CLYDE McPHATTER & THE DRIFTERS' 1953 recording of "Let The Boogie Woogie Roll" featured the phrase, though it wasn't released until 1960.

The British invasion killed doo-wop overnight.

NICK DRAKE

Think back to a time before tower blocks and bondage trousers, before geometric haircuts and multi-pleated shirts, before logo-intensive training shoes and baseball caps worn back to front. Think back to a time before grunge, before drum and bass, to a time – roughly from the mid-Sixties to the mid-Seventies – of tea cakes, cricket and big country houses, when all was well in the English country garden, when young rich men with acoustic guitars, flutes and ever-so-whimsical keyboards made pastoral music that more than contemplated their surroundings.

This was the period when rock stars began moving to the stockbroker belt, hanging out in country houses, or squatting in Welsh cottages – assuming aristocratic airs and graces, buying vintage sports cars and often sporting garish candy-stripe blazers or burgundy crushed velvet jackets. Escaping the suburbs of South East London and Liverpool, and then the penthouses of Mayfair, JOHN LENNON moved to Weybridge, CHARLIE WATTS bought Lord Shawcross's 13th Century moated farmhouse in Lewes, and BILL WYMAN became lord of the manor after buying the enormous Gedding Hall in Suffolk. Soon every self-respecting rock god was moving to the country, dressing like KEVIN AYERS (whose *Joy Of A Toy*, from 1969, is English Country Garden Rock at its most freshly mown and herbaceously bordered) and penning lullabies to dewy-eyed debutantes.

Of course, a lot of this stuff was rubbish (CLIFFORD T. WARD come on down!), and only a few artists ever managed to capture it – English Country Garden Rock, that is – without drowning in self-parody. The genre is best represented by "Pinball" by BRIAN PROTHEROE, "Song For Insane Times" by KEVIN AYERS, "One Of Those Days In England" by ROY HARPER, and "River Man" by NICK DRAKE, while other records simply discuss the genre: "House In The Country" and "Sunny Afternoon" by the KINKS, "Time Of The Season" by the ZOMBIES, and "Country House" by BLUR. It was a style that didn't really survive punk, and though people such as DREAM ACADEMY, EVERYTHING BUT THE GIRL, and PAUL WELLER made various records which might warrant inclusion, the very idea would probably be anathema to them. And as for the Americans, well, they obviously don't get a look in (consequently you can't really count Neil Young's magnificent "Country Home" or CSNY's "Our House").

So be it. To get in the mood, one should ponder the liner notes from TRAFFIC's 1991 retrospective, *Smiling Phases*: "There is a land where crickets chirrup in sunlit meadows and bright red poppies wave a greeting across the hedgerows. And in that land, across the valley, nestling on the side of a hill is a white painted cottage, with roses round the door. The deep silence of the English countryside is gently interrupted by the rhythmic sound of breathing from four young musicians, slumbering inside..."

Nick Drake's music was always rather more solemn than those who operated in similar territory, and by his nature he tended to be more morose. He suffered from depression and insomnia, and his reluctance to perform live or be interviewed further contributed to his lack of commercial success. However his wistful style was as influential in this country as GRAM PARSONS' was in America. Drake was the original pastoral neurotic boy outsider, a fragile singer-songwriter whose records are some of the least urban ever made ("River Man" is entry level Drake, a melancholy paean that is one of his most beautiful). As he died young – onNovember 25, 1974, at the age of twenty-six, Drake died from an overdose of amitriptyline, a prescribed antidepressant – there is a finite body of work, and one it is difficult to tire of. He was the pale male prototype, a thin, reedy, velvet-jacketed auteur whose records are some of the most maudlin ever made.

DURAN DURAN

Once, many, many moons ago, for two weeks, I was a model. OK, I wasn't a model as such, not a proper model (not even a hand model), but rather someone who had been photographed in a nightclub (White Trash in London's Piccadilly, a place where for nine months every Saturday in 1983, the likes of GEORGE MICHAEL, BOY GEORGE, VAUGHAN

TOULOUSE, and JERRY DAMMERS would gossip and carouse) by two small Japanese people, who wanted to know if I'd like to go to Tokyo for two weeks to appear in a fashion shoot for a designer called TAKEO KIKUCHI.

Did I want to go? Well, I was twenty-two, unemployed, and all I had to look forward to most days was getting up at midday, trying to keep warm until it was time to go to a nightclub, and hoping that one day a cross-party coalition wouldn't come alone and whisk away my dole money.

So I said, yes. A two-week holiday in Tokyo? Yes please.

The trip was wonderful, as it largely consisted of turning up at nightclubs and being given free drinks. So it was actually a lot like being in London, only I was being paid to do it.

One of the clubs we went to was at the top of one of Tokyo's most glamorous skyscrapers, one that looked over the Shinjuku district. There were eight of us and we went everywhere together, eight single young men with silly haircuts from London wearing VIVIENNE WESTWOOD clothes and permanent "we can't believe our luck" expressions. This particular night, as we stepped out of the lift on the 23rd floor, we stepped straight onto a dancefloor and into heaven. The club appeared to be full of Japanese girls in their twenties, all of whom were dressed up as BOY GEORGE, and most of whom appeared to be quite keen to talk to eight single young men with silly haircuts from London wearing VIVIENNE WESTWOOD clothes and smug expressions.

So. We sat down, people brought us drinks, and one particularly attractive Japanese girl turned to me and asked, "Do you know Duran Duran?"

"Know them? Do I know them? Why, we're practically related!"

Of course this wasn't strictly true, but I didn't think it was appropriate to share this information, and seeing that there was no one around to contradict me, found myself suddenly being on first name terms with every British pop star from ADAM ANT ("Close personal friend of mine", etc) and NICK HEYWARD ("Nick? We were in the same class at school..."), to

DAVID BOWIE ("Yup, we used to share a flat together...") and the THOMPSON TWINS ("You like the THOMPSON TWINS? Sure, if you like them, then so do I...").

Duran Duran have been dear to my heart ever since then, and whenever anyone has dismissed them as little but pastel-suited fops with no standing in the pop firmament, I have staunchly defended them, not simply because they were responsible for one particularly enjoyable night in Tokyo in 1983, but also because they have, in their time, created some truly great pop.

They have never been particularly fashionable – even when they were meant to be fashionable themselves, ironically – yet they made classic pop that defied (and annoyed) the critics. Even if you hated what they stood for – and many did, quite vociferously – it was difficult to objectively say that they didn't write extremely good songs: "Is There Something I Should Know", "Rio", "Save A Prayer", "Skin Trade", etc. They've continued in this vein over the years, without any great success, but have continued to write the occasional song worthy of their prime: "Ordinary Day", "Come Undone", "What Happens Tomorrow", and "Box Full O' Honey". Yes, admittedly Duran were responsible for *Thank You*, an album of cover versions that included a misguided attempt at Public Enemy's "911 is A Joke", but their cover of LED ZEPPELIN's title track is actually a lot better than it ought to be, and Duran almost make it sound like an original.

In 2010, MARK RONSON, the T-BONE BURNETT of the digital age, produced *All You Need Is Now*, a Duran album which he envisaged as the follow-up to *Rio*, and which sounded like it, too. It contained a song called "Girl Panic" which was so good it appeared to suggest an ability to be immediately transported back to 1983.

It certainly worked for me, as soon after hearing it I was standing on the 23rd floor of an apartment building in Tokyo, dressed head-to-toe in VIVIENNE WESTWOOD, telling a rather bewitching Japanese girl that NICK RHODES was my best friend...

D   BOB DYLAN

When he was hanging around the New York Clubs in the early Sixties, trying to get a break, Dylan spent a lot of time with CHIP MONCK, the rock'n'roll FORREST GUMP-like character who had an apartment adjacent to the Village Gate, on the corner of Bleecker and Thompson Streets in Greenwich Village. Essentially a lighting designer, Monck would be involved in the Monterey International Pop Festival in 1967, GEORGE HARRISON's Concert For Bangladesh, many ROLLING STONES tours of the Seventies, the original New York run of *The Rocky Horror Show*, and Woodstock, where he was the Master of Ceremonies.

Having met Dylan a fair few times, Monck bumped into him in the Village one afternoon.

"Dylan said, 'You got a typewriter, don't you?'

"'Yes, I do...'

"'I want to use it.'

"'OK, here are the keys. I'll show you where I live. And by the way, it's right next door to the Village Gate. So if there is anything you want to listen to or want to eat or have something to drink you can just walk through the door with this key and you are in the Gate.'

"Every now and then I'd come back into the apartment after my two shows at the Gate and he'd be there plucking away.

"'Can I see it?'

"'Yeah.'

"'Don't you think it would be better if it was phrased like...'

"'I don't need a fuckin' co-writer! Nor do I need to pay royalties to your typewriter. You can read it but just keep your fuckin' mouth shut.'"

Dylan wrote many songs there, including "A Hard Rain's A-Gonna Fall".

Bob Dylan's "Blind Willie D McTell"

Bob Dylan has always been a master of the perverse, and the man they call Alias has often paid scant regard to the treasures his obsessive fans hold dear. Live versions of his songs often bear no resemblance to the original recordings, largely because Dylan doesn't regard the original recordings as gospel, just the way it all went down in the studio when he did them. However if Dylan has a particular idea of how a song should sound, he'll bash away at it for years until he gets it right. Or simply leaves it to rot. This was the fate of one of his best songs, one he thought he would never finish.

The Bootleg Series Volume 1-3 (Rare & Unreleased) 1961-1991 (Columbia) is a synopsis of a parallel Dylan career, a shadow career spanning thirty years and fifty-eight performances. "Blind Willie McTell" is generally regarded as the best song from this shadow career – and from this record – a piano-led performance that is now considered to be a classic, a landmark song of the decade, dark and deep and all-consuming. It was an outtake from the 1983 album *Infidels*, a country blues protest song, a song of the South, and the failure of humanity writ large (driven by a melody borrowed rather too easily from the blues standard, "St James Infirmary"). "The singer finds not evil in the world but that the world is evil," wrote GREIL MARCUS. "The whole world is an auction block; all are bidders, all are for sale." There is no redemption here, and while Dylan played McTell's songs when he was young (McTell's style was called a cross between Mississippi Delta blues and East Coast blues), like pretty much everything he did, this is masterpiece metaphor all the way.

From the window of a New Orleans hotel room, the narrator contemplates the history of slavery, and the murder among the magnolias. He sings of damaged, condemned

D lands, "All the way from New Orleans to Jerusalem," traversing "appalling sights and sounds" (according to SEAN WILENTZ, author of *Bob Dylan In America*). And what does the singer know from these sights and travels? That "no one can sing the blues like BLIND WILLIE MCTELL", the images conjured up by Dylan here have more resonance than usual. "The song is exquisitely concrete from start to finish," said PAUL WILLIAMS. "You can see, hear and smell everything – but it is also, and in a truer sense, the window of memory, of awareness, of feeling, where everything one has heard and seen in relation to one particular subject is suddenly conjured up in a moment of pure feeling, like Proust's sweet cake epiphany."

MARK KNOPFLER played guitar on *Infidels*, and when he lobbied too hard to have it included on the album after Dylan junked it (like many of the songs he left behind, he couldn't realise what he had in his head), Dylan finished the record without him. The writer LARRY SLOMAN recalls Dylan saying, "Aw Ratso, don't get so excited. It's just an album. I've made thirty of them."

BOB DYLAN'S "POSITIVELY 4ᵀᴴ STREET" IN THREE ACTS

1. "You got a lotta nerve to say you are my friend...

2. "...when you know as well as me, you'd rather see me paralysed...

3. "...you'd know what a drag it is to see you" - STEVEN PRESSFIELD.

E

THE EAGLES

For many of my generation, the band that we loved to hate more than anyone else was the Eagles. When I was at art school in the late Seventies (when I would regularly frequent the 100 Club, the Roxy, and the Vortex), admitting you liked the Eagles was tantamount to admitting that you not only knew nothing about music, but also that you probably harboured a secret desire to light joss sticks and cover yourself in patchouli oil. Worse, it hinted that you may have been slightly more interested in cruising down Ventura Highway in an open-top Mustang rather than slumming it at the back of some dirty nightclub above a pub on the outskirts of Basildon.

I've received some pretty angry letters in my time, but even I was surprised by the negative attention I got after writing what I thought was a rather innocuous piece recently in praise of the Eagles. I'd simply said that while it was fashionable in the late Seventies to listen to *Never Mind The Bollocks Here's The Sex Pistols* rather than any album by the Eagles, these days I almost never listen to any punk albums, but play *One Of These Nights* and *On The Border* at least every six months. I've still got a Sex Pistols poster I ripped off the reception wall at the Roxy, but I honestly can't remember the last time I played "Bodies".

While the punk canon is one of the most important in the sixty-year history of pop, the screeching, guitar wielding, bass-bin busting likes of the Pistols and the Ramones do not a modern soundtrack make. In 1976, I was obsessive about the Ramones – I dressed like them, spoke like them, and covered my bedroom walls with pictures of Johnny, Joey, Tommy, and Dee Dee torn from the pages of the *NME* (and, ever keen on punk paraphernalia, still have a miniature GABBA GABBA HEY! banner given away at a Ramones gig at the Rainbow on New Year's Eve in 1977), but apart from "I Remember You" – one of the great forgotten punk singles – I almost never play them.

I'm sure there are still some of you who would rather have lighted matches slipped slowly under your fingernails than admit to buying *Their Greatest Hits*, yet how many of you can honestly say you turn the dial down when "New Kid In Town" comes on the car radio? And while the band's singing drummer, DON HENLEY, still has the ability to come out with the most asinine nonsense, as though he were still trying to get into the head of a thirteen-year-old ("A man with a briefcase can steal millions more than any man with a gun," is one of my favourites), they still have their grip on the hair-trigger of collective consciousness.

ECHO AND THE BUNNYMEN

If LIAM GALLAGHER had his origins anywhere it's in the lippy demeanour and media swagger of the Bunnymen's IAN McCULLOCH, who was forever telling anyone who would listen that not only were his band the best in the world but they would soon be the biggest. Neither claim turned out to be true, though they did produce three B+ albums, *Crocodiles* (1980), *Heaven Up Here* (1981), and *Ocean Rain* (1984).

EEL PIE ISLAND

If you take a train to Twickenham, in west London, and then walk down to the edge of the Thames, you will discover a magical place that feels as though it's from another era. People like to say that the Isle of White feels like Britain did in the Fifties, while Eel Pie Island feels like London probably did back in the early Sixties, when jazz and R&B were still the pulse-beat of the city.

This is where the grand Eel Pie Island Hotel once stood, a place that CHARLES DICKENS described as a "place to dance to the music of the locomotive band". A bridge to the island was proposed in 1889, but it was not until 1957 that one was actually completed (before that you got to the island by boat, pulling yourself slowly across on a rope), which is when Londoners first began making the pilgrimage in serious numbers. The hotel was already a Mecca for jazz fans, but it was soon to play host to the likes of LONG JOHN BALDRY'S HOOCHIE COOCHIE MEN (including a young ROD STEWART), the ROLLING STONES, the WHO, the YARDBIRDS, PINK FLOYD, and JOHN MAYALL'S BLUESBREAKERS (featuring an even younger ERIC CLAPTON). For a period the island became so popular it even began issuing its own passports.

Demolished in a mysterious fire in 1971 (in 1969 it had become occupied by a small group of local anarchists), the hotel's history is still preserved in the stories, poems and songs of the old islanders and the musicians who played there. Today, the island has about fifty houses with a hundred and twenty inhabitants and some small businesses. It has nature reserves at either end, and is also home to Twickenham Rowing Club, one of the oldest rowing clubs on the Thames, and Richmond Yacht Club.

A book celebrating the place, *Eel Pie Island* by DAN VAN DER VAT and MICHELLE WHITBY, was published a few years ago, proving that there is no pop cultural minutiae too miniscule to catalogue. It contained some wonderful photographs, not least the ones of the dancing girls at the Eel Pie Island Hotel. GEORGE MELLY, who appeared at the hotel regularly, described the rundown premises, with its ornate columns and arches, as being like "something from a TENNESSEE WILLIAMS novel". More saliently, he also said, "You could see sex rising from it like steam from a kettle – it was very difficult not to get laid on Eel Pie Island."

E

ELBOW

Oh my goodness, aren't they lugubrious? They always look so mournful in photographs, and on the surface it's a wonder they wanted to enter the industry in the first place. Their most famous song is probably "One Day Like This", from 2008's *The Seldom Seen Kid*, and it's the only one I really like. It's a wonderful song, and makes you think they could pull rabbits out of hats if they put their minds to it. So many people I know like Elbow, and it worries me; not because I necessarily think they're wrong, but because Elbow's music fails to affect me in the way it affects them. But I'm sure Elbow will live, as will I.

DUKE ELLINGTON

What to pick? Since he is still regarded as America's greatest composer in any genre, it's difficult to choose individual albums to sum Ellington up, but *Money Jungle* (Blue Note), from 1962, is his best Sixties album, being quirky, but cool (especially "Wig Wise").

Anatomy Of A Murder (Columbia), released in 1959, is another good place to start. Ellington's first soundtrack (to OTTO PREMINGER's classic courtroom drama) is one of the best examples of "crime jazz", the sort of melodramatic cloak and dagger, big band stuff heard in movies like *The Wild One*, *Sweet Smell Of Success*, and *The Man With The Golden Arm*. Underappreciated at the time, this has now been afforded classic status. The Ellington band never sounded so good, and they were especially gifted in the way they managed to articulate sex. "Flirtbird", written about the female lead, LEE REMICK, appears to have been inspired by her derrière.

In his fifty-year career, Ellington composed over 2,000 pieces of "Negro music" (he preferred the term to "jazz"), including sprawling orchestral suites, pop, dance tunes, and everything in between. He also kept an orchestra on the road his whole professional life, and in that respect resembled BOB DYLAN (and his never-ending "never-ending tour"), a wandering journeyman. Being on the road enabled Ellington to indulge in his other great passion, sex (he was a self-confessed "sexual intercourse freak"). It was this lust for travel that caused him to visit the Middle East and Japan in 1963 and 1964, a tour that resulted in *Far East Suite* (RCA Bluebird), recorded in 1967, which ranks among his very greatest achievements.

EMINEM

Marshall Bruce Mathers III is proof that white trash can do hip-hop just as well as black trash. With DR. DRE along for the ride, and some credibility, Eminem proved that a white boy from Detroit could get under the skin of the American public just as easily as PUBLIC ENEMY, N.W.A., or SNOOP DOGG. And unlike most of his predecessors, he did it with irony. Did his best work on *The Slim Shady* LP (1999) and *The Marshall Mathers* LP (2000).

BRIAN ENO

If KEITH RICHARDS has been a "global avatar of wish fulfillment", so Brian Eno has been the go-to guy-rope for those in the industry for whom wish fulfillment is a constant struggle. Responsible for recalibrating everyone from DAVID BOWIE, the TALKING HEADS, and U2, to DEVO, COLDPLAY, and even GRACE JONES, Eno is where you might naturally go, if you needed a quick blood change. Eno is actually a small-time (and unsuccessful) pop maestro, whose mid-Seventies records display a keen commercial sensibility; listening

E to his work on *Taking Tiger Mountain (By Strategy)* will convince you that, for a while at least, Eno was a buttoned-up British TODD RUNDGREN.

ERIC B. & RAKIM

Hip-hop's Golden Age was still going strong in 1987, as ERIC BARRIER and WILLIAM GRIFFIN's 4th And Broadway album *Paid In Full* proved, mixing elements of soul, funk and rock into their sound. They influenced SOUL II SOUL, EMINEM, and a generation of lesser talents who would also "hold the microphone like a grudge".

ESG

Mixing disco and punk was a familiar beat in New York at the very end of the Seventies, and if you wanted to be taken seriously in the downtown nightclubs (and if you wanted legendary Manhattan doorman HAOUI MONTAUG to let you in), you needed to prove your polyglot credentials. ESG had more than most, noticeably on the slouching towards punk-funk classic, "You're No Good".

BILL EVANS

As JAMES PEARSON, the house pianist at Ronnie Scott's, once said: "Bill Evans invented the piano trio as we know it today. You think it's been around forever, but that first trio set the blueprint."

Having left MILES DAVIS' group because he couldn't cope with the hostility at gigs (he was white and played in a more subtle way than his colleagues),* Evans formed a trio and, having released two good albums, 1959's *Portrait In Jazz*, and 1961's *Explorations*, spent one Sunday in June 1961 recording what would be the most fitting testament. *Sunday At The Village Vanguard by the Bill Evans Trio* (Riverside/ Original Jazz Classics) is one of the most important recordings in all jazz; this is the best example of Evans' ability to encourage successful interplay between his band. According to his producer ORRIN KEEPNEWS (great name, Orrin), it was "a relatively painless way to extract an album from the usually foot-dragging pianist."

I once commissioned ROBERT RYAN to write an appreciation of Evans for *GQ*, and he included this lovely passage: "... still his name is treated with respect and awe by musicians. KEITH JARRETT was once asked a question about technique and he replied: 'Are you talking about Bill Evans or the rest of us?'"

* When asked why he hired this gangly white boy, Miles said, "Bill had this quiet fire that I loved on piano. He had a sound that was like crystal notes or sparkling water cascading down from some clear waterfall."

F

FAIRPORT CONVENTION

F

"The Fairports" are one of those bands that are so treasured by their supporters that it's impossible to spend any time in their company without them getting out their pens and papers or BlackBerrys or whatever and reconfiguring exhaustive lists of their greatest songs. Their fans are obsessive to the point of mania. They care. For a novice – me, someone who quite likes their music but who finds it difficult to get worked up about them – there is one song that soars above all others. When I was much younger the Fairport songs I liked the most were the seemingly inconsequential "Portfolio" from their first album (eponymous!), and "Meet On The Ledge" (first heard on the 1969 Island Records sampler, *You Can All Join In*, which also contained "Rainbow Chaser" by NIRVANA, and "Dusty" by JOHN MARTYN), but after a while I also fell in love with "Eastern Rain", "I'll Keep It With Mine", "White Dress", "Fotheringay", and "Chelsea Morning." However, they were all replaced later by the best song on their third album, *Unhalfbricking*, released in 1969: "Who Knows Where the Time Goes".

Listening to the song is almost transfigurative, as you immediately sense you're walking along a deserted British beach in the middle of winter, surrounded by little but cloud. The song was written and beautifully sung by SANDY DENNY – who actually recorded it with the STRAWBS two years earlier – and became a classic almost immediately. In 2007 the song was voted "Favourite Folk Track Of All Time" by listeners in the Radio 2 Folk Awards. The album itself was partly inspired by the band listening to bootleg recordings of BOB DYLAN's *Basement Tapes*, which ironically caused the band to become more English. The *Observer*'s JOHN HARRIS described Denny as possessing a voice "both peerless and gloriously English". Note: the cover features a photograph of Denny's parents, Neil and Edna, standing outside their house in Wimbledon, in South London, with the group visible through the "unhalfbricked" garden trellis wall.

F

THE FALL

MARK E. SMITH: aggressive, eccentric, and full of brio, a working class hero with little but contempt for the world around him. The Fall were what happened if you had taken acid in an outside loo, and then hired someone like Smith to go and tell everyone about it. Their early work is the most transgressive – "Bingo-Master's Break-Out", "It's The New Thing", "Repetition", etc – completely contrary rock music that wallowed in its bitterness. Smith's success as a counter-cultural figure exacerbated his belief that his skewed world-view was incontrovertible. Which made quality a problem.

THE FEELING

As the redoubtable MAT SNOW once suggested, copping licks and textures from old WINGS and SUPERTRAMP blockbusters is regarded, oddly enough, as outré in the extreme when you could be doing the same to low-selling CAN albums from the same period. Heigh ho: the Feeling were a product of a fame academy, so had less qualms about this than most of their peers – and made great, breezy pop in the process.

BRYAN FERRY

Bryan Ferry has been something of a style icon for forty years, since his band ROXY MUSIC formed back in 1971. So cool was he when Roxy were in their first flush of success – "Virginia Plain", "Pyjamarama", "Do The Strand" – that he became, almost overnight, a unique arbiter of style, so influential that fans would copy every little detail of his dress, whether he was trussed-up like a Fifties retro-future crooner, an American

GI, or a tuxedo-clad lounge lizard. MARCO PERRONI, the former guitarist of ADAM AND THE ANTS was such a fan of Ferry when he was young that he once used a magnifying glass to study a photo of Ferry just to see what cigarettes he was smoking. "Even the cigarettes were really good, because they were all white. It was an important statement," he said.

Ferry has made many statements since, and in recent years has become something of an idiosyncratic English gent, dressing in bespoke clothing from the likes of Mayfair tailors, Anderson and Sheppard. First and foremost Ferry is a musician, and as he has said himself, "Dressing well is not exactly rocket science, and in my case it's always been secondary. I have, however, always been a keen student." Ferry's own style icon is the designer ANTONY PRICE, who was responsible for many of Ferry's best looks. "Antony was the real architect of the Roxy look, and he made these amazing sculpted clothes. Whether he's designing for men or for women, he really understands the bodies, understands what looks good, what looks sexy. He was doing HEDI SLIMANE before Hedi was born."

He is also a huge fan of Savile Row, both old and new, and though he still frequents Anderson and Sheppard, also likes the way in which the Row has undergone its recent overhaul, helped by the likes of RICHARD JAMES, OZWALD BOATENG, and (for a time) CARLO BRANDELLI.

His fastidiousness has played against him, however, and critics mistake his fondness for archness for phoniness. Which is a shame as it isn't true.

THE FESTIVAL

My quintessential rock festival experience happened in 1975, when I was just fifteen, at Reading, the small Berkshire town that for three days each August turned into a wretched, swirling mud bath full of long-haired layabouts in patchwork denim jeans, patchwork denim jackets, and patchwork denim

F waistcoats, every one of them smelling of Brut, Bacardi or patchouli, or some combination thereof. Every year it would rain, every year we would be surprised, and every year we would spend three days wallowing around like spaced-out Gloucester Old Spots in knee-high mud, experiencing our very own suburban lifestyle version of the Somme. I went to a lot of festivals in the mid-Seventies, and the weekends were always exactly the same; oh, how I wish I'd known then what I know now, namely that, "There's no such thing as bad weather, only inappropriate clothing." But there was nothing we could do. There was such an orthodoxy surrounding denim at the time that if you saw someone dressed in anything else, you didn't think they were being different, didn't think they were being in any way idiosyncratic or fashion forward – you simply thought they'd made a mistake.

Ostensibly people have always gone to festivals to conjure up a sense of community (however bogus it might be), although along the way you will, at some point in the proceedings, be forced to actually listen to some music. In 1975 this was supplied by the likes of WISHBONE ASH, YES, HAWKWIND, the CLIMAX BLUES BAND, DR FEELGOOD, UFO, CARAVAN, and ALBERTO Y LOS TRIOS PARANOIAS.

And all were equal in the eyes of the audience. If we liked someone they received a barrage of empty beer cans; if we loathed someone they received a barrage of empty beer cans; and if we simply found someone mediocre (this I remember being largely the case whenever I went to Reading), to be on the safe side they received a barrage of empty beer cans. JOHN PEEL would occasionally get pelted too, for simply having the temerity to walk across the stage in an attempt to play some records. There was a strange kind of democracy at work here, one based on fairly egalitarian if not exactly utopian principles.

When I first started going to them, the pop festival was basically rock'n'roll camping, and the only survival kit you needed – or at least the only one you were expected to bring

– consisted of a Great Coat, a sleeping bag, an industrial-sized pouch of Old Holborn, a packet of economy-sized Rizla and a substantial amount of clear plastic sheeting. Oh, and a tent. You needed a tent so that, at four o'clock in the morning, some drunk, loon-panted idiot could come falling onto it, singing "Smoke On The Water", "Stairway To Heaven", or "Free Bird" at the top of his voice while brandishing a Party Seven (which, for the uninitiated, was essentially a tin the size of a punch bag containing seven pints of what tasted like decidedly flat light ale). You see, if we hadn't had a tent, there would have been nothing to break his fall.

These days, though, festivals are a cornerstone of the Alternative Season, along with the Monaco Grand Prix, the Cannes Film Festival, and the August bank holiday weekend in Ibiza. A few years ago I sent AA GILL to Glastonbury for a magazine feature and he only agreed to do it if we organised a Winnebago for him. Unsurprisingly, he wasn't alone in this, and take a peak backstage at Glastonbury and you'll think you've walked into Celebrity Trailer Trash. A few years ago the Isle of White festival was so civilised, so subdued, it was almost like being at the Chelsea Flower Show, the only difference being the fact that the men wore hoodies, military-style knee-length khaki shorts, and cagoules rather than blazers, chinos, and Panamas.

The apotheosis of the modern festival is Cornbury. It takes place in the Cotswolds, in the grounds of Cornbury House, and – because a healthy percentage of the audience hails from Notting Hill and Kensington – it has already been nicknamed Poshstock. And when you see a CATH KIDSTON stall next to the more traditional vegeburger stand, you realise that when people call this the middle-class Glasto, they're not being ironic. When I went I spent the afternoon drinking Pimms and watching the UKELELE ORCHESTRA OF GREAT BRITAIN, a dinner-jacketed supper-club band that at the time had won acclaim everywhere from Tokyo to Chicago, via Sadler's Wells and the Festival Hall,

F playing pleasantly extraordinary versions of "Life On Mars" and "Miss Dynamite". As an afternoon's entertainment they sure beat HAWKWIND, WISHBONE ASH, or ALBERTO Y LOS TRIOS PARANOIAS.

But apart from the fact that a large proportion of modern festival-goers might normally drive 4x4s ("My other car's another Chelsea Tractor"), sport imported white Birkenstocks, and hold down unbelievably serious jobs in the City, not that much has changed. Kudos is still determined by your haircut (when in doubt: shave), by your clothes (if you're over thirty then never, ever, try to dress younger) and by your ability to convincingly claim to know someone who knows someone who knows someone else who might be able to conjure up a little something For Personal Use Only.

Oh, and most importantly, having the number of someone who can give you a lift home.

50 CENT

RONALD REAGAN: "I was brave but in a kind of low budget fashion."

ELLA FITZGERALD

Ella Fitzgerald's "Baby, It's Cold Outside" is a great seduction tool. Or at least an alternative to three or four pints of Wife Beater, half-a-dozen flaming sambucas, a rented kebab (let's face it, they're not often kept for long), and a night in the cells. I was reacquainted with it because of a YouTube clip of a breathtaking performance of the song by Ella and DINAH SHORE, from Shore's own TV show in 1959. It's regarded by many aficionados as one of the greatest jazz performances ever, and the duo's vocal dexterity is something to behold.

The song is a double hander written by FRANK LOESSER (think "Luck Be A Lady", "Two Sleepy People", and "[I'd Like To Get You On A] Slow Boat To China") in 1944, starring a dinner-jacketed chap ("the wolf") smitten with a gal ("the mouse") who's got to get home by curfew (real or imagined). It's a classic case of insincere pleading and indecisive protests and is consequently extremely sexy.

Most seduction songs either envelope you in swirls of maudlin or libidinous instrumentation, or tug at your heart strings with melodramatic lyrics (and if we're honest, the best do both), but few simply plonk you down in the middle of a cocktail party, stick a martini glass in your hand and let you fend for yourself. This is what gives Loesser's song such depth and, like a lot of other COLE PORTER-style-white-tie-and-tails-cigarette-holder-type tunes from that era, it reinforces the fact that frivolity can be so moving. To wit:

"The neighbours might think…"

"Baby, it's bad out there…"

"Say, what's in this drink…"

"No cab's to be had out there…"

"I wish I knew how…"

"Your eyes are like starlight now…" etc, etc.

In 1948, after years of informally performing the song at parties (the writer had premiered the song at a housewarming party, singing it with his wife), Loesser sold the rights to MGM, which inserted it into the 1949 film, *Neptune's Daughter*, earning Loesser an Oscar in the process. Due to the wintertime lyrics, when the song was most popular (and in the Fifties it was covered as often as "Angels" is now sung by drunk secretaries on karaoke evenings) the song was usually only played during the Christmas season, although as popular culture increasingly thrives on incongruity, I'm lobbying for it to become an ironic summer standard.

Take care out there: wear a coat.

FLEET FOXES

Back to the land, they whisper, running ahead of you in their chambray shirts, lumberjack coats, and grizzly facial hair. When they emerged at the tail end of the Noughties, Fleet Foxes espoused a liberal, peppermint tea, log cabin lifestyle, one that dissed "The Man", eulogised filesharing – "It's not good or bad, it's just the way it is," said the band's ROBIN PECKNOLD. "MP3s just happen to be a very downloadable size" – and went out of its way to put the modern world at arm's length. Their records were great – earthy, a bit earnest, but toe-tappers just the same.

FLEETWOOD MAC

In 1975, Fleetwood Mac 0.2 – loaded up with STEVIE NICKS and LINDSEY BUCKINGHAM – achieved something quite rare, conquering a country and seemingly able to define it, too. In the late Seventies, their only rivals in this – bottling the musical essence of Los Angeles and Southern California – were the EAGLES, and they had spent the best part of the decade working up to it; with Fleetwood Mac it sort of happened by accident. Before Nicks and Buckingham joined, the group were a middle-ranking British blues band that had recorded half-a-dozen already classic songs ("Black Magic Woman", "Albatross", "Man Of The World", "Oh Well", etc, all composed by the band's guitarist, PETER GREEN).

0.2 were a different proposition altogether, able to fuse the singer-songwriter pretensions of the early Seventies with a slick pop sensibility (and a great drum sound) that sounded just fine on FM radio, especially in your first car, with the top down, and four or five friends in the back, passing beers and smokes between them. Their records – when they choose to make them – largely sound the same as those they made in the mid-Seventies (*Fleetwood Mac, Rumours*). Visually, they play it safe too, their image synonymous with the leather and lace of STEVIE NICKS – a look that originally consisted of a chiffon dress, a leotard, a small jacket, a pair of suede platforms and a top hat. All black.

F

BEN FOLDS

Folds has called his music "punk rock for sissies", although I've always thought of him more as a new wave ELTON JOHN. I first came across him in a Kings Cross pub in London in the mid-Nineties. He was playing in a small back room and was making the noise of twenty men. There were only three members of the BEN FOLDS FIVE (piano, bass and drums) but I swear the racket they were producing could be heard several postcodes away. They were fairly extraordinary. An American on tour, Folds looked as though he'd come straight from the campus, although you weren't quite sure if he were a mature student or a recently appointed lecturer. Didn't matter, they were great, banging out a piano-driven noise full of vim, va-va-voom, and great zinging melodies. He's been solo for some time, but still writes great songs and makes wonderful records. Try these for size: "Philosophy", "Heist", "Rockin' The Suburbs", "Brick", "Alice Childress", "Landed", "Jesusland" and his covers of "Tiny Dancer", "Golden Slumbers", and "Raindrops Keep Fallin' On My Head".

FOO FIGHTERS

On cursory terms, you could be forgiven for thinking that DAVE GROHL's band had some perverse remit to only write and record songs good enough for B-sides, and just good enough to get themselves booked onto an apparently endless stream of summer festivals, thrashing about in front of 50,000 numb

F

nuts. Then you hear "Times Like These", "Big Me", "Wheels", and "Breakout", and you want to be a numb 'nut too, down in the moshpit, casually wondering why Grohl wasted so much time playing with NIRVANA. And then you hear "Learn To Play" and "Long Road To Ruin" and you begin to think you can cheat death.

FOUNTAINS OF WAYNE

If you've heard "Halley's Waitress", "Hackensack", "I-95", or their CARS homage "Stacy's Mom", then you won't need any further reason to love the power pop band that always punches above its weight. But if you need a kicker, then just consider that they took their name from a lawn ornament store in Wayne, New Jersey. In a nutshell, funny-sad-funny-sad.

MICHAEL FRANKS

One of my least successful book ideas – when I told my agent about it he told me to go and have a long lie down – was a music and travel book, identifying the best soundtracks to listen to in various places around the world. I thought this was a brilliant wheeze, an encyclopedia of great road songs, awesome beach ballads, soaring urban anthems (lots of CLASH, U2 and yes, BILLY IDOL), and the exact KRAFTWERK tunes you'd need for a ten day skiing holiday in the Alps.

My book would tell you the right places to play DONALD FAGEN, ARCADE FIRE, and BURT BACHARACH, the correct Ibizan islands to listen to HED KANDI, chillwave, and the best Californian beaches to whack on some difficult-to-find DENNIS WILSON.

And as I drew up a tentative list of records, one man's name kept cropping up. Whether I was making a list of songs to be played when flying over a Scandinavian lake in a biplane, driving down the coast to San Diego, or cycling along the Cote d'Azur, there were certain songs that kept nagging away at me, and they were all recorded by one man.

Of course Michael Franks makes the sort of music that works best when it's played quietly at dusk, as you're sipping a sundowner, watching the sun sink into the Indian Ocean. You actually need to be able to imagine that he's playing live in the cocktail bar up near the restaurant. And while he's something of a musical travel agent – he's written songs about Brazil, Hawaii, Japan, and Tahiti to name only a few – to me his songs always sound best in the Maldives, where the stillness of the islands offers the perfect background noise: absolutely none at all.

Some find the Maldives antiseptic and anodyne, and they're probably the same sort of people who think similar thoughts about Franks' music. Some call it supperclub jazz, elevator jazz, or Quiet Storm jazz, and they're not being kind when they say it. Personally, I love it, probably because it's some of the most polite music ever made. It is not raw, it is not earthy, and in no way does it feel "authentic". So it's sort of like staying in a seven star hotel.

Listening to Franks' music is like leisurely flicking through a travel magazine, as it takes you to far-flung places without you having to make any effort at all.

FUNERAL MUSIC

It is not possible to be prescriptive with funeral music, ever, as it will be the most personal record selection you'll ever make, the playlist from hell, if you like. Rather morbidly, like many people I would imagine, I have been refining this list since I was about thirty, when mortality usually tends to make itself felt. Having experimented with the BEATLES, VAN MORRISON, and various other random selections (for a while

F I was obsessed with the PET SHOP BOYS' "Being Boring"), I decided to focus all my energies in one particular area: the BEACH BOYS.

As a pub discussion this has always been a successful diversion (I remember doing this once with *The Word*'s MARK ELLEN, and I think we got so engrossed, we were still arguing when they turned the lights on), and can encourage people to show off a bit. And the topic comes around with such regularity you really ought to have put some thought into it (my old pal Adrian certainly has: he still maintains he wants to leave this mortal coil to the strains of JOY DIVISION's "Atmosphere", which then segues into RUSS ABBOTT's "Atmosphere" – if you don't know who RUSS ABBOTT is, there is no reason for you to find out).

On the third page of my will there is a clause detailing my funeral arrangements. It states I want to be cremated and to have my ashes scattered in the churchyard at Alvediston, in Wiltshire, where I was married, although I now want them scattered on the mountain behind our house in Wales. It also lists the songs I want played at the ceremony. These remain the same four songs by the BEACH BOYS:

1. "In My Room", the classic single that most people in the church will know.

2. "The Warmth Of The Sun", another maudlin song that BRIAN WILSON wrote the morning after JFK's assassination.

3. The killer blow, so to speak, which starts just as the casket is conveyed into the furnace – "Till I Die", the original version from the 1971 *Surf's Up* LP. Hopefully everyone will by now be in floods of tears. Cathartic, eh?

4. The coffin is now gone, handkerchiefs have been returned to handbags and trouser pockets, and people begin filing out of the crematorium,

accompanied by "All Summer Long", the exhilarating song you hear at the end of GEORGE LUCAS's *American Graffiti*. This sends the mourners out on a giddy note, hopefully into the sunshine, and into the sight-line of a man holding a large tray of drinks.

G

Peter Gabriel

Starting life as the tallest poppy in Britain's uncoolest band (a totally unfair soubriquet – they were simply doing things their own way, without worrying about the market), when Gabriel left GENESIS after their double (and coincidentally cool) album *The Lamb Lies Down On Broadway* in 1975, he quickly developed a highly successful anti-persona, one that would see him through pretty much everything he tried to do in the two decades that unfolded (deliberately genre-swapping, promoting world music, inventing WOMAD, comprehensively conquering MTV, becoming a serious heritage act). He is something of a pioneer, and appears to have spent most of his career doing things on his own terms, usually with great success. Gabriel has written dozens of songs in a wide variety of styles, and for my money, his best (though not necessarily his most representative) is "Oh Father". His determination to go off-piste helped baste the small turkey that was *Scratch My Back* (orchestral versions of important songs, without a snare drum or click-track in sight), though he can still fill large halls. By all accounts a very nice man, which has to account for a lot.

Marvin Gaye

The soul song as seduction tool is such a seasoned cliché it's sometimes difficult to escape. TEDDY PENDERGRASS. Cliché! BARRY WHITE (the Round Mound of Sound). Not Safe In Taxis! SMOKEY ROBINSON. Here it comes again! The problem is usually familiarity, not the content. Which is why MARVIN GAYE's *I Want You* is still considered to be an acceptable album to play in these circumstances: very few people have heard it. Gaye was obsessed with joyous celebrations of sex; his social commentary was more widely appreciated, more

G readily praised, not least because he was such a surprising exponent – but he was truly a master of the candlelit lunge. "Is this me?" he asked, disingenuously. "Be serious! How in the name of a just God did I ever turn myself into a sex god? And why?"

GENESIS

"The Carpet Crawlers" and "Los Endos" are officially the two Genesis songs you're allowed to like.

THE GENTLE PEOPLE

DOUGEE DIMENSIONAL, HONEYMINK, LAURIE LEMANS, and VALENTINE CARNELIAN sure gave good pressure release. "They have travelled from the outer reaches of the galaxy to the inner sanctum of your heart. They call this music easy core: utilising the digital technology of today and the lost sounds of yesterday to create the music for the millennium generation." Though back in the Nineties they were part and parcel of Britain's burgeoning Cocktail Nation, the Gentle People produced easy listening for the techno brigade, a unique ambient sound – fromage collage, easy hard core? – that is genuinely extraordinary. As *Wired* said, "It's as if BRIGITTE BARDOT, the APHEX TWIN, and JASON KING have all put on multicoloured fun-furs and jetted on to your patio for a fondue party." Alternatively you could say they sounded like a head-on collision between BRIAN ENO and SERGE GAINSBOURG, between *Barbarella* and *The Jetsons*.

ASTRUD GILBERTO

G

For more than forty years Astrud Gilberto has been singing the gentle, lyrical samba ballads of Brazil, a career that was kick-started by a happy accident in a New York recording studio in 1963. Earlier that year STAN GETZ called up the celebrated Brazilian pianist ANTONI CARLOS JOBIM, asking him to bring along some of his new material. Getz was looking to record the follow-up to *Jazz Samba* and *Jazz Samba Encore* – his two breakthrough LPs that had resulted in the hits "Desafinado" (Slightly Out Of Tune) and "Samba De Una Nota So" (One Note Samba). The sensual sun-kissed samba Jobim brought to the studio that day was "The Girl From Ipanema"; he also brought along a friend, the guitarist JOAO GILBERTO. The song vividly showcased Getz's pure-toned tenor sax and the intimate, burry voice of Gilberto, though as the recording progressed it became all-too evident that Gilberto could only sing in Portuguese, and was therefore unable to interpret the English Lyrics written by NORMAN GIMBEL. And so Getz asked Gilberto's twenty-four-year-old Bahia-born wife to sing it for him.

"I just happened to be in that studio that day," said Astrud. "I had never sung professionally before, but everything seemed to click." Initially her contribution was considered so slight that she was not even credited on the resulting album, STAN GETZ/JOAO GILBERTO, though stardom beckoned when an edited single version of the song went to number five on the US charts, staying on the nation's Hot 100 for three months.

"I lived in Ipanema for twenty years," she said. "So I guess I was a *girl* from Ipanema, but not *the* girl from Ipanema – that girl could have been anyone, and it probably was. I love the song and I really don't mind if people associate it with me because it has become a standard. The bossa nova ["new wave"] has come to signify all the happy things in life: at the movies, whenever you hear a bossa nova start to play, you know that the boy and girl are going to kiss. It's *so* sexy."

G Gilberto has since become synonymous with all that is filigree and sensual, and has covered every classic tune from "Fly Me To The Moon" and "Trains And Boats And Planes", through to "It Might As Well Be Spring" and "I Haven't Got Anything Better To Do". The liner notes to her 1965 LP *The Shadow Of Your Smile* say it all: "Astrud Gilberto ... the sound of innocence remembered. A clear voice, light and graceful, weighed only with the soft haze of autumn moonlight. A voice that shares with you a sense of things *felt* rather than things *seen*. A voice filled with shadows and memory."

DIZZY GILLESPIE

One of the kings of bebop, Diz always dressed the part: in an act of supreme self-parody he would wear a large, flowing tie à la boheme, with a beret, goatee and extravagant horn-rimmed glasses (always with plain glass inside them), and then speak in beat vocab. For the sake of publicity and self-preservation he turned himself into something of a fashion plate as well as a musical icon (and let's not have any fuss over whether or not this is the appropriate word to use – Gillespie was a proper cultural icon), and his style became so closely associated with jazz that whenever cartoonists try to represent a jazz motif, they simply copy Diz, even now. And the music? Well, it rocked, obviously. "Dizzy Atmosphere" from *Groovin' High* is one of his greatest achievements, and one of the great moments in jazz.

GO-GO

Dance music, not almost defunct. Washington DC's percussive double-funk began loping through the arteries of European club culture during 1983. Two years later it was the hippest groove on the globe. The origins of Chocolate City Go-Go lay in the Seventies, when all-night parties rocked to its Neanderthal rhythms – a blend of funk, rhythm and blues, and early hip-hop, with a focus on lo-fi percussion and funk-style jamming, featuring live audience call and response. The big bands were TROUBLE FUNK, CHUCK BROWN & THE SOUL SEARCHERS, REDDS & THE BOYS, and EU. Go-Go proved more popular in Britain than anywhere else outside DC, TROUBLE FUNK's "Good To Go" and CHUCK BROWN's "We Need Some Money" becoming mini-anthems. With their 1986 European tour, TROUBLE FUNK provided some of the year's finest shows, and some of those who saw them say they were the best gigs of the decade (while I'd say their Town & Country Club gig on that tour was one of the best concerts I've ever seen). Things cooled off quickly, and the movement suffered through negligent radio, a disastrous blaxploitation movie (1986's *Good To Go*, starring, of all people, ART GARFUNKEL), and the musicians' growing dissatisfaction with their lack of worldwide success. In the Chocolate City itself, happy feet are still dancing, albeit quietly, and not very often.

THE GO-GO'S

They were briefly America's jukebox sweethearts, and wrote and recorded a classic radio knockabout, "Our Lips Are Sealed" (also recorded by the FUN BOY THREE, who were more like jukebox vandals).

GONZALEZ

No sombre moment can possibly be complete without Gonzalez's extraordinary *Solo Piano*. I've heard it played at memorial services, in galleries, at fashion shows (sombre fashion shows, you understand, the sort where models wear black just in case) at dinner parties, and I'm seriously considering taking a copy to play during my next appointment with my accountant. Maybe several, in fact.

Honestly, this music is sad.

I've always had a penchant for maudlin music, something that was probably kick-started by watching hours and hours of silent movies on TV when I was young, when any scene involving pathos (and even the slapstick episodes were imbued with pathos) was accompanied by an extravagant and rather florid version of "So Deep Is The Night", a heartbreaking ballad based on an old tune by CHOPIN.

And since then I've devoured every classic weepathon I've been able to lay my hands on, from the soundtracks to *Once Upon A Time In America* and *Diva*, to default elegiac masterpieces like ARVO PART's "Tabula Rasa", *The Koln Concert* by KEITH JARRETT, ALBINONI's "Adagio In G minor", or something (anything!) plaintive by GLENN GOULD.

Gonzalez – who is actually a Canadian called JASON CHARLES BECK – released *Solo Piano* in 2004, and he immediately enjoyed favourable comparisons with ERIK SATIE. The record does what it says on the tin, being nothing more complicated than a very long portmanteau piano recital, albeit one that can move people to tears. If you're feeling particularly sad, that is.

Alternatively, if there are currently no tragedies in your life, simply stick it on when you've got a hangover. The world won't make any more sense to you, but you'll feel slightly less awful about your inability to decipher it all.

GORILLAZ

The Po-Mo MONKEES operate in the middle of such a very particular Venn diagram, one that includes so many disparate strands of skittled-out pop culture – some old, others new, and many way over yonder – that there is really no one like them.

A virtual band in a fictional universe they may be, but the music transcends all that. And, contrivance or not (and come on, what does it really matter anyway?), rarely have a band so convincingly captured the zeitgeist. It's all the exquisite creation of JAMIE HEWLETT and DAMON ALBARN, the frankly often far-too-talented leader of the Gorillaz' lo-fi orchestra. With BLUR, Albarn's mockneyisms would occasionally grate – here, they are one of the things you willingly grab on to as you're being flung around the room in a dozen different directions by half-a-dozen different people at once (all of whom appear to be manically grinning). The music is so inventive, so multi-layered, so complex and so funny (just listening to SNOOP sing "Welcome to the world of the plastic beach" puts a smile on my face), it deserves some sort of critical amnesty.

I love the description of their show by the U2 set designer and multi-media guru WILLIE WILLIAMS in his marvellous tour blog:

"Thursday, December 16, 2010. Sydney. Day off. Had a bit of a busman's holiday in the evening and went to see Gorillaz at the Entertainment Centre. I've wanted to see this show for ages so was delighted that our tours finally crossed paths. It was quite the spectacle, with so many people on stage that I can only begin to imagine what sound checks must be like; large band, half-a-dozen string players, a Syrian orchestra (why not?), rappers and singers for days including, amazingly, the actual BOBBY WOMACK. Oh, and half of the CLASH. All this in an hour and a half – I felt like I'd been to a festival. The films are brilliant – a fascinating and pleasantly unsettling look into an obsessed mind. Manga meets ROGER DEAN."

AL GREEN

It was once said that Al Green's voice was an instrument capable of leaping, with no advance notice, from a scratching growl to an aching falsetto. It was most definitely a tool of

G seduction, a slippery and sexy thing that always sounds better if heard after 10pm. Green abandoned a traditional secular pop path for the pulpit, but not before making some classic records, the best of which remains *Let's Stay Together* (1972).

GREEN DAY

The biggest cartoon punk band in the world. And why not?

GRIZZLY BEAR

I first heard Grizzly Bear's "Two Weeks" blasting out of the PA system, in the interval before a U2 gig in Montreal during the summer, as the light was finally giving way. I'd never heard it before, and my ignorance of the song was underscored when great swathes of the crowd started singing along. It made those precious moments before the band came on even more joyous, as the sense of anticipation was somehow exacerbated by this mass karaoke moment. The *New Yorker* called it "a big, fat ice-cream cone of a song", a song that sounds like a junk-shop, choir-boy summer (assemble words at will). Ranked No.162 in *Pitchfork Media*'s Top 500 Tracks of the 2000s, "Two Weeks" is cloudy, orchestral, and full of BEACH BOYS dreams. Much like the band themselves. (When I made a last.fm playlist, the tags on the songs that followed looked as though someone had plucked them from Roget's Thesaurus, and made me long for the days of rock, pop, R&B, blues and soul: dream pop, bedroom pop, tweegaze, bridge underwater, tropical, drone, chillwave, noise pop, indie love, weak folk, etc.)

EMMETT GROGAN

G

There are so many apocryphal stories surrounding Emmett Grogan's short life that it would be easy to think of him as an imaginary hero. After all, he is all but forgotten now. The British-bulldog-style street game that inspired the title of Grogan's notorious autobiography, *Ringolevio*, might have survived, and his name may be mentioned in passing in the rapidly expanding library of memoirs concerning the US counterculture of the Sixties, but in reality, Grogan has all but disappeared. He was once "America's most famous invisible man". Today he's just invisible, at best a peripheral figure in a roll call of flower-power icons.

According to the nostalgia industry, the major players of the American hippie revolution were KEN KESEY, HUNTER S. THOMPSON, ABBIE HOFFMAN, JERRY GARCIA, TIMOTHY LEARY, and BILL GRAHAM. Apparently even TINY ("Tiptoe Thru The Tulips") TIM and SCOTT ("If you're going to San Francisco...") MCKENZIE are more deserving than ZELIG-like Grogan.

But it was Grogan who was largely responsible for the birth of the hippie movement in San Francisco: he was the first rebel leader to try to change Californian society; he wrote songs with the BAND; had an affair with JANIS JOPLIN; became a part-time Hells Angel; and, perhaps more than anything, was a galvanising storyteller, both on and off the page. The *Times Literary Supplement* once called him "the superman of the underground". He was a sybarite, but also something of a devout idealist, an avenging angel. He was a militant beatnik, the world's first proper freak. A man who wore black leather and a snake-tooth necklace. A hippie who hated hippies. A lothario who thought only of himself. A misanthrope who thought only of other people.

Emmett Grogan was one big loud charge of vitality. He is also something of a legend. To read his autobiography is to believe he was a fighter, a dreamer, a renegade, a visionary. And a shameless liar. Then there are the stories that weave themselves around his myth, tales that weren't even in the book. Stories concerning the year he spent the entire summer in New York's Chelsea Hotel, moving from room to room, picking the flimsy locks and amassing huge bills on the way. Or the one about him passing through the city and making a public performance of burning thousands of dollar bills (the next day the dollar dropped six points on the New York stock exchange). And this was years before the KLF. According to some, he even brokered a truce between Puerto Rican gang leaders from the Lower East Side and the NYPD.

If you believe JERRY GARCIA, late leader of the GRATEFUL DEAD – another bunch that were in part responsible for the blossoming of the cultural revolution in San Francisco in 1966 – Grogan also had incredible powers of foresight. When the ROLLING STONES were lining up a free concert in 1969 – the gig that eventually materialised at the Altamont Speedway, where a young black man was beaten to death by a Hells Angel, hired by the band to act as security – Grogan, cynical to the max, called the forthcoming event, "The first annual Charlie Manson Death Festival". This was "before it happened", said Garcia in 1988.

"He was a mature street person at a time when there were so many novices," said the late concert promoter BILL GRAHAM. "In that era, puppies were being born by the truckload." According to WILLIAM PHILLIPS, Grogan's editor at Little, Brown, the book's original publisher, "He showed intense loyalty to his friends. He was straight with them up and down, once they passed the test of friendship." In his introduction to the 1990 reissue of *Ringolevio*, Grogan's friend, the actor PETER COYOTE wrote, "There is no way that I can tell you who Emmett was, neither will this book."

In a way Grogan was a man who willed himself to be a hero. While it is true that he is the forgotten point man of the Haight-Ashbury revolution, the years leading up to it are a mystery. Perversely, it was *Ringolevio*, originally published in 1972, which originally made him a star, yet most of its contents could be built on sand.

A spellbinding, quasi-autobiographical romp, *Ringolevio* is a self-aggrandising mix of Spartan ideologies, homespun philosophy, sexual conquests, drugs and the odd bit of violence – to quote one reviewer, "an infuriating alloy of blarney and fact". It's written like one of those first-person adventure books of the late Sixties and early Seventies that mix JAMES BOND-style heroics with soft pornography.

But though it reads like a collection of fables, what great fables they are. The book is the literary equivalent of a rock'n'roll rush, a headlong push through the crowd, a visceral shock to the system. Think of the first time you heard "Complete Control", "Born To Run", or "Smells Like Teen Spirit", *Ringolevio* (subtitled, with good reason, "A Life Played For Keeps") is like that. And more. *Ringolevio* is one short life squeezed into one fat book. And if you needed proof that the original hippies were far more radical than the punks who replaced them ten years later, here it is. For anyone who thinks that those were days only of peace, love and flower power, the book will be a revelation, as it evokes the gritty urban sensibility that supplied the backbone to the San Francisco community's free flights of fancy.

As for the book's veracity, it is as uncertain as it was when it was published. Whether he actually did everything he claimed, in exactly the way he claimed, is immaterial. As Grogan himself said in his Author's Note, "This book is true," although that doesn't mean that it all happened.

By his own account, the teenage Grogan had been the best ringolevio player in Fifties Brooklyn, when he started shooting heroin and pulling outrageous robberies to support his habit. He scammed himself into an ultra establishment prep school in Manhattan and "brought off a string of daring jewel robberies". When things got too hot in New York he took off for Europe, where he "scaled the Matterhorn", met Fellini, slept with untold women, went pub-crawling with ANTHONY QUINN and –somewhat implausibly – became a terrorist. He ended up in San Francisco at the height of the Haight-Ashbury hippie explosion, where he took up

G the lifestyle that helped turn him into a legend. In his own mind, anyway.

Perhaps he wrote *Ringolevio* because he knew his myth was not going to last, because he knew he could get away with it; if he couldn't live the life of the legend then maybe he should create one. Which is what he did. The book has the same hyperbolic charge as *On The Road,* or *Fear And Loathing In Las Vegas*; the same sense of urgency as *The Electric Kool-Aid Acid Test,* only without the same burden of rational perspective.

A lot of *Ringolevio* sounds as if it were made up. The parts which chronicle the heady days of flower power in northern California in the mid- to late Sixties, though, are definitely true.

San Francisco in 1966 was the lodestar of the new bohemia. If Los Angeles was, in JOHN UPDIKE's words, "the capital of organised unreality", then San Francisco at that time was exactly the opposite. During a period when the world was still divided into hip and square, in the mid-Sixties San Francisco quickly became the hippest place on the planet – a primal soup of musicians, actors, self-promoters, writers, journalists and psychedelic wannabes descending on Haight-Ashbury, the funkiest part of the city, as though it were the church of regeneration. San Francisco's summer of 1966 was extraordinary, and as the heat waves solidified in the air like the waves in a child's marble, tolerance, bonhomie, and sexual benignity filled the streets. This was the birth of hippie, when LSD and sunshine forged a generational shift. In San Francisco in 1966, bourgeois behaviour was not merely unwelcome, it was impermissible.

But before Haight-Ashbury, the summer of '66, the love generation and all that came after it turned it into a doll's house of teenage hedonism, before the hippies turned into a mediated target group, before psychedelic became an adjective, the San Francisco counterculture was a definable if elusive and therefore dangerous movement, complete with ideologies all its own. And Grogan was at its helm.

The forebears of the hippies were a group of disaffected reprobates who went loosely by the name of Diggers, a group of cultural revolutionaries, pranksters, or what PETER COYOTE still likes to call "a radical anarchist group". It sounds silly now, naive, far from unusual. But not in 1966. The Diggers were to Sixties San Francisco what the Situationists were to Paris and the Provos were to Amsterdam.

Coyote, who would become a successful actor, starring in *ET* and ROMAN POLANSKI's *Bitter Moon* among many other mainstream films, was a left-wing intellectual who arrived in San Francisco just as Grogan had been discharged from San Francisco's Letterman General Hospital (he had been committed there after attacking an officer in an effort not to be indicted into the army). One day in 1965, Coyote was rehearsing a play at the San Francisco Mime Troupe's studio when a "lithe, freckled man with flinty, Irish features walked in to observe." Actually, Grogan had come to audition.

"He carried with him the spotlit absorption of an actor," continues Coyote. "Men and women attended when he entered and moved through the room with the detached concentration of a shark, because he had a developed sense of drama in his posture, his cupped cigarette, his smoky, hooded eyes. His being declared him a man on the wrong side of the law; a man with a past; a man who would not be deterred. This was Emmett Grogan, the self created by young Eugene Grogan in a life sentence of hard labour with his soul."

"His face was as thin as the spine of a book and sprayed with freckles, eyes sharp as knifepoints," says the writer JAMES KOCH. "He strutted, his head in the lead, chest expanded, a wiry-Giacometti figure in wheat-coloured Levi's showing a lot of ankle and wearing cheap flip-flops."

Grogan liked to think of himself as an old-fashioned criminal poet, and while he was always more middle-class than he liked to let on, he had a genuine air of Brooklyn menace, which made him a great leader.

He soon got bored of the mime troupe, and persuaded Coyote and several others to take their art to the street. Grogan decided to start the Diggers after watching the beginnings of a race riot in the Fillmore district, describing them as a "large, informal group of people dedicated to non-violent anarchy". In a way they were also a response to the swelling ranks of collar-hair kids flooding the Haight.

He named them after one of the17th Century religious dissident communities the hippies were beginning to resemble (the original Diggers had farmed wasteland, only to be violently dispersed by local landowners). Guided by these techniques of self-sufficiency, Grogan's Diggers started a farming community from which fresh vegetables were, for a while anyway, driven every day into the city's Golden Gate Park and given away at 4pm sharp. The Digger's free clothing shop, meanwhile, was run on a kind of jumble-sale principal, providing the raw material for the extravagant hippie tribal dress. For a short time at least, Grogan became Robin Hood.

The Diggers combined street theatre, anarcho-direct action, and art happenings in their social agenda of creating a Free City. They were also responsible for coining various slogans – "Do Your Own Thing", "Today Is The First Day Of The Rest Of Your Life" – that worked their way into the fabric of the Sixties as well as inventing tie-dye clothing (something that Grogan grew to dislike intensely), and reintroducing communal celebrations of natural planetary events, such as the solstices and equinoxes.

Like the Hells Angels, the Diggers liked to call themselves "One Percenters". The American Motorcycle Association used to claim that "Ninety-nine percent of all motorcyclists are decent, law abiding citizens." So the Angels wore shoulder patches proclaiming their one per cent status as bike riders. The Diggers borrowed the slogan, wearing T-shirts proclaiming themselves to be "One Percent Free". In short, they believed themselves to be the one per cent of Americans prepared to do anything to help change society.

KEN KESEY and his Merry Pranksters may have been the standard-bearers of the psychedelic experience, but Grogan was the man who tried to turn it into a religion. It may have

been Kesey who initiated the Acid Tests, the first multi-media "love-ins" where the like of the GRATEFUL DEAD played
to a couple of hundred spaced-out proto-hippies, but it was
Grogan who tried to mobilise the troops. While Kesey's
Merry Pranksters were off tripping the light fantastic, the
Diggers were transforming the Haight from a seedy district
of abandoned Victorian houses into an evanescent paradise
on earth.

As much as anything the Diggers were a spontaneous
experiment in social and cultural change, and they contributed
much to the mystique that was so much a part of Haight-Ashbury. They would wander the streets carrying mirrors
and then holding them up to tourists: "Know thyself!" they'd
exclaim, before dissolving into hysterics. Essentially the
Diggers were guerrilla street theatre. They'd hand out strips
of paper with the word "Now" silk screened onto them in six-inch-high red letters, or parade down Haight Street with a
coffin of money to represent the "Death Of Money, Now".
One prank involved their Frame of Reference, a huge wooden
frame that they set up in the street and asked people to walk
through, "So we'll all be in the same frame of reference."

Grogan began to hate hippies even more than he hated
the establishment, and was fond of breaking up keynote
"alternative" speeches and student conferences by challenging
the organisers' motives. "You're going to start a revolution?"
he would ask. "You'll piss in your pants when the violence
erupts!" "You haven't the balls to go mad!" he screamed at
one 1967 Michigan student sit-in.

On October 6 that year, Grogan, the Diggers, and hundreds
of Haight-Ashbury residents celebrated the last important
event of The Summer Of Love, "The Death Of Hippie", a parade
that weaved its not so merry way through San Francisco. Its
leaders handed out press releases which read: "The media
cast nets, create bags for the identity-hungry to climb in."

Coyote could feel that Grogan's philanthropy was gradually
giving way to his ego. "His notion of anonymity was to give
his name away, so that countless people would claim it for

G

countless purposes." (Eventually, some reporters asserted there was no Emmett Grogan, that the name was a fiction created by the Diggers to confound the straight world.) While it was a way of demonstrating lack of attachment, it also made him ubiquitous, an instant legend.

"Life with Grogan was a daily refinement of one's understanding of 'truth'," Coyote says. "One could never be sure exactly where the hair had been split and how. If, for instance, he came into a room late for a meeting, he might apologise with a story about being attacked by street toughs taking revenge on him for some earlier intervention in their affairs."

You never knew.

As hundreds of thousands of bug-eyed teenagers continued to descend upon the city looking for love, peace, and maybe a little sex and drugs and rock'n'roll on the side, so the movement's so called leaders moved on: KEN KESEY went back up to his family's ancestral home in Oregon; the GRATEFUL DEAD and the JEFFERSON AIRPLANE signed record contracts; and Emmett Grogan sat down to write his own legend, the myth that would eventually become *Ringolevio*.

Published at the beginning of the Seventies, the book briefly made Grogan something of a star, and as a raconteur he was fêted for a good couple of years by Manhattan's literary slummers. He married a beautiful French-Canadian actress, and doted on his new son, Max, whom he swore weighed 26lbs at birth. To the end, exaggeration and invention were in his lifeblood.

A child of his age, Grogan was the Sixties incarnate. A social guerrilla with a tendency to charm and an appetite for drugs. He was never going to grow old and respectable, was never going to turn into an executive beatnik with bongos in his briefcase and a gig on VH-1. For Emmett Grogan there was never going to be a "deadhead" sticker on his Cadillac. His face was never going to adorn a packet of Stars And Stripes cigarette papers.

"All artists desire an audience, and much as we would criticise and change our culture we want, at the same time, to be accepted and rewarded by it," says Coyote. "Emmett was no different, and it is this contradiction – of simultaneously spurning and yearning [for an] audience – which became the crucifix on which he finally impaled himself. It does not require too much of a stretch of the imagination to see in a crucifix the outline of a syringe."

He had begun using heroin early, in the summer of 1957, though he had kicked the habit by the time he moved to California, so it was only natural that it would be the cause of his downfall. He soon took it up again. The man was an edge-dweller after all, so transcendence came in many forms. Towards the end of the Sixties Grogan began looking like the countryside after a long and fierce war. Battle-weary, exhausted, trapped by the glamour of his persona, and fantastically disillusioned with the peace movement, he drifted across America, ending up back in New York where he wrote a mediocre nuclear thriller called *Final Score* (published in 1976), while continuing to take huge amounts of heroin and methadone. His drug use eventually put an end to his relationship with PETER COYOTE, who would write many years later that, "Though time and observation have *modified* my early perception [of Grogan], they have never totally obliterated it."

Although you can no more pin down the details of his death than you can those of his life, some facts are indisputable. Grogan died from a massive methadone overdose on April Fools Day, 1978, at the suitably young age of thirty-five. He was found on a New York subway train to Coney Island, on Brooklyn's south coast, not far from where he'd grown up. He had been dead for three days. A detective attached to the medical examiner's office, who saw Grogan's dead body soon after, said, "I've seen a lot of DOAs. I looked at this one and I said, 'I don't know who this guy is, but he was a Somebody.'"

And he was. Considering the way in which minutiae of pop culture has become victim to over-zealous media studies, students and retro-centric TV programmers, it can't be long before Grogan's life is exposed for what it most certainly was

G

– a lie in search of a good ending. But perhaps we should forgive him his trespasses.

Because he was, if only for a short time, a Somebody.

DAVID GUETTA

Remember: be careful what you wish for. Back in the early Eighties, back when the British and US charts were full of synthesised "like-punk-never-happened" pop, I remember lobbying hard for more dance music to be played on the radio. Oh, what a fuss I made. I would write long, rambling essays about why the national pop curriculum was failing "black" music, and how the world would be a much better place if it were somehow turned into one giant disco. These were the urgent mutterings of a dance-obsessed journalist barely out of his teens, and I have to say that these "essays" don't warrant much rereading.

There were a few of us doing this – writing in *The Face, i-D*, the *NME*, etc – and we were all so very earnest. The radio is full of pap, we'd complain, thinking we were the first generation to do so. Why couldn't the underground be overground? Why couldn't everyone have the same taste as us? Why couldn't everyone be as insufferably trendy and as up-to-the-minute as we were? Why didn't the world see everything through our eyes? Why, indeed.

Then, all of a sudden, probably while we were out on the dancefloor, grinding and weaving along to BROTHER D & COLLECTIVE EFFORT ("How We Gonna Make The Black Nation Rise?"* they sang, somehow managing to seduce a generation of spoilt nightclub parasites), it all came true.

Almost overnight, it seemed, as club culture became the dominant force in British youth culture – as nightclubs metaphorically, psychologically and (yes) actually morphed from being aggressively exclusive to passively inclusive – DJs were suddenly not just cool, they were ubiquitous. Nobody wanted to be on the dancefloor anymore, they wanted to be in the DJ booth. Ten-year-old boys no longer wanted to be astronauts or footballers, they wanted a ten o'clock session at Manumission (with a decent rider and at least twelve names on the door). Teenagers no longer dreamed of going on tour with their rock group of choice, and instead fantasised about carrying PETE TONG or DANNY RAMPLING's record box.

In 1980, being a DJ was a hobby, something you did in spite of your day job. By 1990 it was a fully-fledged profession, the career of choice for anyone mad enough to be interested in entering the music industry.

These days, DJs don't even have to lug their twelve inches around the globe, as all they need is their iPad, a memory stick or a portable hard drive. It is something of an easy job, too. Hired for their taste, their pre-releases and remixes, and their ability to "build" a room, all they have is their reputation. Build enough equity in your brand and you can command a bigger fee than almost any B+ touring band. Cut to 2011 and all they needed was a plane ticket (first class), a good accountant, and the best suite in the new W. The music? Well, it's all up in the Cloud, somewhere, isn't it? Don't worry – I'll download it before I go on. Promise!

And today they all make records, too, at least the sharper ones, the ones who know how best to exploit their brand, the ones who understand that the only people truly responsible for their equity is themselves.

David Guetta has been doing this for years, and since 2001, when he started making records as well as simply choosing them, he's had over a dozen hits, worked with dozens of achingly cool performers – KELLY ROWLAND, FLO RIDA, RIHANNA, AKON, etc – been celebrated by various DJ institutions, won Grammys, and remixed everyone from MADONNA to the BLACK EYED PEAS.

He is not infallible, though, and there is an extraordinarily silly sequence in the video for his single "When Love Takes Over" (featuring KELLY ROWLAND), in which he's filmed walking

G around Venice Beach pushing his DJ equipment, looking not unlike RHYS IFANS might do if he had spent all night on the beach (and I think it's very churlish to suggest that RHYS IFANS looks like he spends every night on the beach). On closer inspection, Guetta (who's French) actually looks like MARK RONSON might if he wanted to emulate HARRY ENFIELD and PAUL WHITEHOUSE's SMASHIE & NICEY, and one can imagine the apotheosis of DJ culture getting to grips with BACHMAN-TURNER OVERDRIVE's "You Ain't Seen Nothing Yet" (SMASHIE & NICEY's "favourid" barnstormer) – maxing out the Jomox XBASE 999 as FERGIE and KID CUDI wail in near-harmony over the top.

*Using a sampled backdrop of CHERYL LYNN's "Got to Be Real" as a sampled backdrop.

GUILTY PLEASURES

The journalist DAVID HEPWORTH once described the fundamental difference between men's and women's appreciation of music. If you're in a crowded office – say – and something comes on the radio, or someone starts playing a CD or a song on their iPod, a woman will say, "I like this". Whereas a man's immediate response will be, "What is this?" Because men have to temper their enthusiasm in case said record is made by someone unbelievably naff. Whereas women are not only far more honest, but don't actually care who made it.

So there I was, in the second floor breakfast bar in the fantastically swanky Ritz-Carlton overlooking New York's Central Park, idly watching my young children try to force as many mini croissants into their mouths as inhumanly possible. One of the joys of watching small children eat is the way in which they have absolutely no concept of over-indulgence or gluttony, and will simply eat and eat and eat until they either throw up or explode. But as devouring the entire contents of the pastry basket was keeping them quiet (their mouths were so full I couldn't have heard them even if they had started screaming), I wisely let them get on with it.

And as they hoovered up the brioche, the pain au chocolat, the doughnuts, and the blueberry and chocolate-chip muffins, I caught myself enjoying the piped supper club jazz (well, breakfast club jazz actually). Not enjoying it in an ironic, "inverted comma"-type way, but seriously, diligently enjoying it. My head nodded, my foot tapped, my fingers drummed the laminated table as though it were stuck in the dimly-lit corner of a subterranean, downtown, spats-and-cigars supperclub. I was a living, breathing metronome, and loving every minute of it. The particular song I was chair-dancing to sounded a lot like MILES DAVIS if his records had, by some weird fluke of circumstance, been arranged by RICHARD CARPENTER, which I realise is most people's idea of transgressive hell but is actually my idea of musical nirvana.

Guilty Pleasure? You bet. However I don't feel the least bit guilty and I've never tried to keep it a secret. Never have, never will.

These days there is something of an Astroturf cottage industry in Guilty Pleasures. Newspapers and magazines regularly ask celebrities, non-celebrities, and media-whores what naff records or cheesy TV programmes they like to watch; there are club nights devoted to playing those forgotten Sixties and Seventies songs that are too unfashionable even for karaoke ("Up, Up And Away" by RAY DAVIES & THE BUTTON-DOWN BRASS, anyone?); while some enterprising record companies even started collecting those very same songs on compilation CDs. But both the producers and the consumers of these so-called "Guilty Pleasures" do so with collective tongue firmly in collective cheek, always keen to flag-up the fact that they know what they're celebrating is rubbish.

I got called by one of these newspapers once, asking me to give them a list of my own personal guilty pleasures, but in the end I couldn't do it. I mean, how could I, when most of my lifestyle choices over the last thirty years have been tainted by what many would deem "poor taste"? I like the novels of NIGEL WILLIAMS, the records of HALL & OATES (is "Out of Touch" the best 12" single of the Eighties?), the songs of NEIL SEDAKA, and the films of CHEVY CHASE (even the pretty awful ones). TERRY WOGAN makes me laugh (regularly), *Love Actually* made me cry (twice), and I didn't miss a single episode of the last series of *The X-Factor*, not one.

As far as music is concerned, I'm the biggest fan of what record companies now call lounge, but in my day was simply called middle of the road or easy listening. I don't just like the trendy stuff, like JOHN BARRY, BURT BACHARACH, SERGIO MENDES, and FRANK SINATRA, I like it all: HELMUT ZACHARIUS, BERT KAEMPFERT, CHRIS MONTEZ, and NEAL HEFTI. Yes, I'm fully aware that the likes of HERB ALPERT, MICHAEL FRANKS, and XAVIER CUGAT are now considered by top-drawer critics to be noble artisans and idiosyncratic soothsayers, but what about bog-standard journeymen like GLEN CAMPBELL, RAY CONNIFF, or TONY HATCH? Spend any time in my house and you'll hear little else.

Probably my greatest guilty pleasure, or at least the one that would be judged my greatest by the taste police, is *Lovejoy*, the old IAN MCSHANE TV series about a lovable rogue antique dealer. I loved this programme nearly as much as I loved my immediate family, and would regularly cancel social engagements in order to stay in (alone) and watch it on Sunday evenings. So disciplined was I, that when I rushed back to my flat, Cinderella-like, late on a Sunday afternoon, my girlfriend at the time starting thinking I had another woman. Her suspicions were compounded when she persisted in calling me at home when it was on, while I would just sit there, beer in hand, ignoring her increasingly overwrought phone messages.

The thing is, while "good" taste, and the things you actually like are often mutually exclusive, few people own up to their guilty pleasures – scared, perhaps, that admitting what they really like will pigeonhole them as a No-Mark. But so what if it does? Like a lot of people, I know what constitutes good taste, and I'd be guilty of false humility if I admitted otherwise, but I hardly see how that precludes me from liking GEORGE MACDONALD FRASER, the EAGLES, or mediocre DANNY DEVITO films (what do you mean, all DANNY DEVITO films are mediocre?).

Frankly, the only people who can criticise me are my children, and they're usually too busy with the bread basket to notice.

GUNS N' ROSES

For a while AXL ROSE was a wonderful rock'n'roll archetype, and always looked as if a spotlight and wind machine were constantly trained on him. Few could wield or straddle a microphone stand like him, fewer still could wear a bandana or such corny gypsy fancy dress with so much conviction. In those few short years either side of *Appetite For Destruction*, there was no one to match him, or his band – the gristle of "Sweet Child Of Mine", "Paradise City", and all the rest making them for a period the most exciting rock group in the world. But there was no cookie-cutter consistency ("November Rain" was pretty good, but then what?), and Rose turned into a temperamentalist.

H

Daryl Hall & John Oates H

Hall & Oates were never cool. Not ever. Not at the start of their career (when DAVID BOWIE was cool), not at the height of their success (when MADONNA was about as cool as cool can be), nor indeed now (when most people are cool).

The problem was a simple one. Even though they made – and occasionally continue to make – some of the best blue-eyed soul ever recorded, they had an image problem, with DARYL HALL looking like a market town hairdresser, and JOHN OATES looking like SUPER MARIO's smaller, uglier brother.

They were a duo, but although it was more than plain what Hall did (sing, a lot, very well), it was never apparent what his partner did. In that respect they were like an American WHAM! Not only that, but whereas some people are born with a sense of how to clothe themselves, and others acquire it, JOHN OATES always looked as if his clothes had been thrust upon him. And whenever he wore something expensive it looked stolen. In essence Hall was the tall, blonde good-looking one who sang all the songs, while Oates was rather short, had a small unnecessary moustache, and hair like badly turned broccoli. Hall looked like the one who had all the fun, whereas Oates had the melancholy appearance of a man who has spent too much time searching for the leak in life's gas-pipe, with a lighted candle.

More importantly, though, they are still around. In the music business, a partnership is considered a success if it outlasts milk, but theirs has turned out to be one of the most enduring partnerships in the business, and they're still together after forty years.

Hall & Oates have a permanent home in the global jukebox hall of fame, and you could fill an iPod Nano with their greatest hits: "She's Gone", "Sara Smile", "I Can't Go For That", "Rich Girl", "Every Time You Go Away", "Wait For Me", "Back Together Again", "Private Eyes", "Method Of

H

Modern Love" – songs that have become as ubiquitous on the radio as Motown standards or *X-Factor* cover versions. They are the most successful duo in the history of pop. Not that you're allowed to admit it, though. When I first worked at *The Face* in the mid-Eighties I remember one junior editor almost going into shock when I recommended one of their records. In her eyes the only thing worse than admitting to liking a Hall & Oates record would have been to actually BE Hall or Oates. But their records sounded great, especially in the nightclubs of Manhattan. On my first trip to New York, in 1984, Danceteria, Area, Limelight, and all the other downtown hotspots reverberated to the thumping sounds of AFRIKA BAMBAATAA, NUANCE, the SOS BAND... and Hall & Oates' "Out of Touch", one of the great forgotten dance anthems of the decade.

I first saw them perform in the same year, in a place called Cedar Rapids, which is in the wilds of Nowhere – which if you closely study a map of Iowa, is in the upper reaches of the state, right near the border. They were playing a sports arena, to around 5,000 screaming hermaphrodites – at least that's how I remember them. These people were all aged between eighteen and twenty-five, and all had identical honey-coloured mullets (the sort that BONO successfully sported at the time), seemingly spray-on stone-washed denim, tiny white leather pixie boots and burgundy satin tour jackets. Everyone looked like a member of, or a roadie for, VAN HALEN, or one of those LA "Hair Metal" bands that were all the rage back then. Cedar Rapids was the sort of place where you didn't dare chat anyone up because you weren't exactly sure what sex they were.

The band themselves were simply marvellous, and got the crowd jumping up and down and hollering in the way that only hermaphrodites can truly jump and holler. My enjoyment was only tempered by the fact I was seriously bereft in both the honey-coloured mullet and the burgundy satin tour jacket departments.

After becoming the most successful double act in American entertainment history, the duo went surprisingly quiet. One day they looked like two of the most famous men in the world, and the next they looked like a hairdresser from Weybridge and his dodgy looking pal. After that, DARYL HALL released a couple of so-so solo albums, and JOHN OATES appeared with HARRY ENFIELD in his legendary scousers sketch on television (what do you mean, it wasn't him?).

They never went away in my car, though, and on any given weekday, as I carefully weave my way through the London traffic, silently cursing the partially-sighted cab drivers and overly-caffeined cyclists who endeavour to interrupt my journey to work, I push the pedal to the metal and sing along to "Maneater", "Private Eyes", or "She's Gone", drifting back to that balmy Saturday night in 1984 in Cedar Rapids.

I wonder if she/he still thinks about me?

HERBIE HANCOCK

Hancock's career has mirrored QUINCY JONES's, as he's had success as a pianist, arranger, composer, bandleader, producer, and solo artist (remember "Rockit"?), and there is just so much good stuff to recommend.

1. *Takin' Off*(Blue Note), from 1962, is probably the best jazz debut ever, and it includes the massive hit single "Watermelon Man".

2. *Maiden Voyage*, from 1964, is one of Hancock's best early Blue Note albums (it includes the wonderful "Dolphin Dance") – this is basically the MILES DAVIS band of the time, with the trumpeter replaced by the young FREDDIE HUBBARD.

3. *Gershwin's World* (Verve), from 1988, is the sound of one 20th Century maverick reinvented by another (download/upload "Overture (Fascinating Rhythm)").

4. *Empyrean Isles* (Blue Note), from 1964, includes "Cantaloupe Island", which became a jazz standard almost as soon as it was released. The piano riff was famously incorporated into a song – "Cantaloop" by Us3 on their Blue Note, *Hand On The Torch*, album in 1993, produced by GEOFF WILKINSON and MEL SIMPSON (worried that Blue Note would sue, they were shocked when the company instead gave them access to its entire back catalogue).

5. *Headhunters* (CBS), from 1973, was the world's first proper fusion record, and was Hancock's reaction to funk, rock and everything else that was storming the charts in the early Seventies. It was funky and rocky and owed not a little to SLY STONE ("Thank You Falettinme Be Mice Elf Agin" in particular), but essentially it was without boundaries, which made it all the more exciting. There was a huge African influence, too. "The roots of music came from there," said Hancock at the time, before everyone else started saying it.

GEORGE HARRISON

Having seen the BEATLES *Love* show in Las Vegas – it is unremittingly FABULOUS – the release of a DVD documentary about its creation was always going to find a permanent home in the Jones household. And, perhaps surprisingly, the DVD, *Altogether Now*, is as enjoyable and as uplifting as the show itself. There is also a twenty-minute additional feature that charts the reworking and splicing together of the songs for the tapestry-like soundtrack (a soundtrack on which RINGO STARR appears to redeem himself, and for once actually sounds like he knows his way round a drum kit), that for some of us is tantamount to cutting up the holy grail and then sticking it back together again.

Love was George Harrison's brainchild, and it was Harrison's music I delved into as soon as I came back from Vegas; not his BEATLES work, but some of the more obscure stuff he wrote back then that wasn't recorded until after he left. I'd found Harrison's original version of "Not Guilty" on a bootleg in Tokyo in 1994 (a record which, because I'd buggered-up the exchange rate, cost me £120), and only caught up with the rerecording a few years later – it's on the 1978 album *George Harrison*, along with the sequel "Here Comes The Moon", and is excellent. Similarly his rerecording of the unreleased BEATLES song "Circles" (on 1982's *Gone Troppo*) employs Harrison's traditional detached melancholia and self-effacement – and, like many things he recorded in his lifetime, sounds as though it was recorded on the same front lawn where RAY DAVIES imagined "Sitting In The Midday Sun".

There is a world of re-evaluation to be conjured with, as the more you listen to George's solo work the more you hear the through-line back to the Sixties. Harrison's post-BEATLES work is generally considered to be susceptible to the law of diminishing returns, but on closer inspection deserves even closer inspection, and there are many songs he recorded in the twenty years after *All Things Must Pass* that would warrant inclusion in their own Las Vegas-style extravaganza.

Call it *George!*, give it to Cirque du Soleil, get GILES MARTIN to splice-up "Wah-Wah", "When We Was Fab", and "Give Me Love (Give Me Peace On Earth)", and let the good times roll. They could even weave in the McCartney/Clapton/Starr version of "While My Guitar Gently Weeps" played at Beatle George's memorial concert.

Let's have the show right here!

RICHARD HAWLEY

H

Richard Hawley is the ROY ORBISON of the Noughties. With his dour demeanour, large-frame spectacles, BILL HALEY-standard quiff (grease, I think, not gel), and his velvet-collared jacket, Hawley is a genuine oddity, an entertainer who has made it his business to walk the walk of the singular and the aloof. He is anachronistic to a T.

He is genuinely gifted, though.

Born in Sheffield in 1967, in the Nineties Hawley bumped around on the fringes of Britpop as a member of the LONGPIGS and a confidante of JARVIS COCKER, yet it is as a semi-studied PoMo crooner that he has achieved notoriety. A late developer? Well, you could say so. But his success could only have happened because of his earlier failure. It's almost as though it were a business plan. Hawley has a deep baritone, a voice so rich it sounds almost ironic (did someone in the cheap seats mention JIM REEVES?). He isn't averse to using sweeping strings or old-fashioned showbiz arrangements, and you could be forgiven for thinking – on initial hearing – that Hawley is simply rather orthodox (by default rather than design). Study the work and it all becomes clear. He wants to be epic, but on his terms. Just listen to the echo, the vibrato, the longueurs, the wistful nature of the chord changes. SCOTT WALKER, one of pop's most extreme examples of the tortured crooner, says that Hawley is right up there with the best. Which we have to assume is a compliment. "All I set out to do was make the music that I wanted to hear," he has said. "Music that was gentle without being pedestrian. This job is pretty selfish in that respect."

His classic song remains "Open Up Your Door" (a ballad that positively reeks of melancholia, and which was used to great success in a television advertisement for ice cream), while his quasi-Springsteen tune "Tonight The Streets Are Ours" (which featured in the 2010 BANKSY documentary *Exit Through The Gift Shop*), sounds as though it ought to have been covered by U2, or GREEN DAY. Maybe it eventually will, irony or no irony.

Hawley likes to say he was born opposite a graveyard, and next to a butchers, and a taxidermist – a more than perfect metaphor for his creative microclimate. Gruff, rough round the edges, and terse when it suits him (he has been successfully nicknamed "Leatherface", and there is something of the weather-beaten about him), he has made the noir lullaby something of a speciality. "I'm a soft fucker," he says.

H

ISAAC HAYES

By deliberately fusing soap opera and ghetto chic in the late Sixties and early Seventies, Isaac Hayes created his own, highly rhythmic, symphonic environment, and in his way was as influential as SLY STONE. Both men moved away from R&B and into traditionally white areas: Stone into rock, Hayes into the orchestral world of BURT BACHARACH, JIMMY WEBB, and CAROLE KING. The son of a Memphis sharecropper, Hayes joined Stax Records in 1964, aged twenty-two, eventually writing, arranging and producing dozens of hits for SAM AND DAVE, CARLA THOMAS, and JOHNNIE TAYLOR ("Hold On I'm Coming", "Soul Man", "B-A-B-Y", etc).

It was his 1969 solo LP *Hot Buttered Soul*, however, which really brought him personal acclaim and at the time it was cited as the most important black album since *James Brown Live At The Apollo* (1962). *Hot* included an eighteen-minute version of JIMMY WEBB's "By The Time I Get To Phoenix" and an elaborate reworking of BACHARACH's "Walk On By", Hayes draping white bread orchestral arrangements around his seemingly interminable monologues, as though experimenting with various convoluted seduction techniques. With his lush raps and funeral beats, Hayes gave you the impression he could turn a thirty-second hairspray commercial into a three-hour symphony complete with several different movements and at least a dozen costume changes.

He had a dark brown coroner's voice which perfectly suited the type of rich ballads which became his forte: "It's Too Late", "Windows Of The World", "The Look Of Love", "Ain't No Sunshine", etc. He was a remarkable arranger, and the bulk of his 1971 LP *Shaft* – in which he reached critical mass while winning two Grammy's and an Oscar – is almost worthy of BERNARD HERRMANN. But self-abortion was only just around the corner, hovering like a stalker in the rain. The records became more bombastic – check out his bizarre 1977 duet with DIONNE WARWICK (*A Man And A Woman*) and the kitsch-in-sink extravaganza that is 1973's *Live At The Sahara Tahoe* – as Hayes's personal life became more extreme.

Die-hard libidinist, funky renaissance man, Hayes preferred the Black Moses moniker: he delivered. Talking about *Hot Buttered Soul*, he said once, "Like rock groups, I always wanted to present songs as dramas – it was something white artists did so well but black folks hadn't got into it. Which was why I picked those, if you like, white songs for that set, because they have the dramatic content."Of "Phoenix..." he said, "To preserve the vibe we cut it live, with no retakes – if you listen hard on the CD you can hear how my vocal mike picked up my fingernails clicking on the organ keys as I played those big swirls. When I played the whole album back to company bigwigs they sat there in shock. I got worried and said, 'Well?' After a while the promotions manager said, 'That motherfucker is awesome. Won't nobody give it airplay, but that ain't even gonna matter.'" He was right, as within three months the album had outsold every LP the company had on release, reaching the top of the soul, jazz and pop charts. By the end of 1970 the album was platinum.

LEE HAZELWOOD

H

"My Autumn's Done Come" by Lee Hazelwood is quite possibly the best retirement song ever written. The maverick singer-songwriter was only thirty-seven when he wrote and recorded it in 1966, yet it's one of the most evocative autumnal songs ever attempted, an unflinching look at the bath chair period. "Let those 'I-don't-care-days' begin," he sings, "I'm tired of holding my stomach in... Bring me water short and scotch tall, A big long black cigar that ain't all, Hang me a hammock between two big trees, Leave me alone, damned! Let me do as I please..."

A sometime mentor to DUANE EDDY, ANN MARGRET, and PHIL SPECTOR, he became a sort of Svengali figure during the Sixties, and when recording his song "These Boots Are Made For Walking", instructed NANCY SINATRA to sing it, "like a sixteen-year-old girl who fucks truck drivers". In the Seventies he released a bunch of wilfully eccentric solo albums; all were commercial failures, and his 1973 album *Poet, Fool Or Bum* received a one-word review in the *NME* – "bum". Having been rediscovered in the Nineties he was also championed by JARVIS COCKER, and covered by PRIMAL SCREAM (who recorded a version of his "Some Velvet Morning" with KATE MOSS).

Crucially, "My Autumn's Done Come" has more than an air of humility about it, and paints a picture of domestic minutiae that is far from luxurious (he discusses both his faulty blood pressure and his indolence). Most retirement songs are either expressions of repeated frustration or wistful ballads of regret, songs that betray an unrequited passion of one sort or another. The other type is the exotic validation, the exaggerated autobiography that adds a colourful – and usually completely inappropriate – wash to your life. The quintessential retirement song is obviously PAUL ANKA's "My Way", written for FRANK SINATRA, but obviously more than suitable for anyone wishing to frame their incomplete and far-from-successful time on Earth – especially if they happen to be performing in a glorified men's room on the fringes of a

H provincial industrial estate (subtext: I chose to be here, you understand, for reasons I probably don't need to explain to you right now).

The thing is, who is ever honest enough to acknowledge that their own particular race is over? Singing in the third person is one thing; admitting the game is up is another altogether.

Lee Hazelwood died of renal cancer in Henderson, Nevada, on August 4, 2007.

HED KANDI

The Ministry of Sound's JAMES PALUMBO might not be the world's greatest novelist, but his purchase of Hed Kandi in 2007 will probably turn out to be a very shrewd investment. Astonishingly successful, they are probably the best dance compilations on the market, appealing equally to excitable teenage monster and equable fifty-something creative.

These days the Hed Kandi brand can be found in bars, clubs (over fifty events now taking place every month in every continent), on fragrance bottles, branded clothing, even chartered Boeing 757s. But it's the compilations albums that people hold dear, the compilations albums you remember to rescue from the hire car when you're handing it back. And the enduring chill out series is the most popular of all. Wander into a house party on Ibiza, Sardinia, or Majorca, in the middle of the afternoon and the music you'll hear will probably be some sort of Hed Kandi compilation, the default soundtrack choice for every lazy, hungover, over-dressed host – seamless island beats that encourage you to kick the Birkenstocks off and open another beer. Even if you've only just finished breakfast. Chill out is the broadest church in pop, a cathedral of bizarre juxtaposition, where camp ballads meet hard house on the dancefloor of subversity – and Hed Kandi are usually there to capture it.

One of the reasons for the brand's enormous success is the choice of illustrator used for the CD covers, which nearly always feature a cartoon beach babe, drawn slightly ironically, inferring glamour, sex and travel. The illustrator is JASON BROOKS, a man whose career I like to think I was partially responsible for. I hired him twenty years ago to be the illustrator – the only illustrator, as it happened – for the magazine I was editing. The illos were mainly of girls, and they didn't look too dissimilar to the plastic bootilicious Hed Kandi girls of today.

JIMI HENDRIX

In the Sixties, the science of rock changed on an hourly basis, as technology, ambition, experimentation and drugs made parameters elliptical. Add talent to this mix – real, innate, intuitive talent – and you make history. Jimi Hendrix did, and while it is easy to take him for granted, nodding in his direction as you acknowledge the pantheon of iconic Sixties rock stars, you only need to spend an afternoon with *Electric Ladyland* to remind yourself what all the fuss was about.

JOE HENRY

The Go To Guy for any melancholy roots sheen, Henry is the producer's producer. He has worked with SOLOMON BURKE, AIMEE MANN, ELVIS COSTELLO, LOUDON WAINWRIGHT III, and TEDDY THOMPSON, and might also be the only person to have worked in any meaningful way with both MADONNA and MOSE ALLISON. Saliently, he was responsible for crafting the ALLEN TOUSSAINT near-masterpiece, *The Bright Mississippi*. He has become so associated with the producer's chair that it sounds patronising to say that he is a performer in his own right, but he is, with a potent voice (what the *New York Times* called

H

an "embattled growl") and a bandleader's authority. You only need to watch him play his song "God Only Knows" on YouTube to see how proficient he is.

THE HIGH LLAMAS

Nowadays the work of BRIAN WILSON can be heard in the most unlikely places, from R.E.M. to BRUCE SPRINGSTEEN, and back again, via everyone from STEREOLAB and PORTISHEAD, to the GORILLAZ and the FOUNTAINS OF WAYNE. Even Wilson rips himself off these days, perfectly re-imagining his Sixties highlights. Of all the people who have tried to lose themselves in the warmth of the sun, those who perhaps came closest were the High Llamas. Their album *Gideon Gaye* (Alpaca Records, 1994) is the sound of SEAN O'HAGAN, chief High Llama, painstakingly trying to finish Wilson's previously lost masterpiece, *Smile*, using vibes, Vox organs, banjos, muted horns, violins and flutes (on one song, "Track Goes By", flautist MARCEL CORIENTES plays a solo for fifteen minutes). "With a little STEELY DAN thrown in for good measure (notably the single "Checking In, Checking Out"), it was Brianhead's wet dream," wrote BARNEY HOSKYNS in *Mojo*. "Slow arrangements full of shakers and flutes and vibraphones: sugary baa-baa-baa harmonies, startlingly lovely chord changes; strings sliding around in a manner that suggested mild chemical imbalance. Nothing quite like 'The Fire Section' of 'The Elements Suite', I grant you, but a sound close to the strange rustic-baroque world of 'Cabinessence'." And it only cost £2,500 to record.

Their 1996 follow-up, *Hawaii*, took the vibrato-less organs, Moog interludes and even the sub-VAN DYKE PARKS Americana a few steps nearer the ocean with songs such as "Snapshot Pioneer", "The Hokey Curator", and "Rustic Vespa". "Imagine classic Bacharach writing, but with Mingus brass and a MIKE NESMITH feel," said ex-MICRODISNEY leader O'Hagan. "Listening to this swooning seventy-seven minutes is like having a marshmallow explode on your tongue," wrote

The Idler on the album's release. O'Hagan's blush-tinted view of the world is summed up by the words to the gorgeous title track of *Gideon Gaye*: "In the harbour town, perfect sunsets, People keep their yachts close at hand, The car parks are full of the giddy and gay as the band slips away..." There have been eight further records since then, all intriguing in their own way, while 2011's *Talahomi Way* is really rather wonderful.

BILLIE HOLIDAY

For many, Lady Day was the finest singer who ever lived (and for those who think differently, all they need do is listen to her voice as it eventually appears on "Strange Fruit"), yet she died in typically ignominious circumstances, and her life has been diminished because of it. Long before JANIS JOPLIN, Holiday died the classic clichéd entertainer's death. In 1959, having been a drunk and a junkie for much of her life, she was still apparently begging for heroin on her deathbed, in a guarded ward at the run-down Harlem Metropolitan Hospital. A lifelong fan, FRANK SINATRA came to visit her on the night she died (at the age of forty-four). Holiday pleaded with him to get her a "bag". Hours later the dope arrived but the dealer couldn't get past the guards. Billie died minutes later of liver failure. A starter for ten: *The Voice Of Jazz: The Complete Recordings 1933-40* (Affinity, 1999).

EDDIE "SON" HOUSE

The Delta bluesman's Delta bluesman, House's abrasive guitar style (often using a bottleneck) influenced ROBERT JOHNSON, CANNED HEAT'S ALAN WILSON, and many blues guitarists of the early Seventies. He said the blues possessed him like "a lowdown shaking chill", and YouTube clips show

H

this to be true. To JACK WHITE, he is little short of a legend: "By the time I was about eighteen somebody played me Son House. That was it for me. This spoke to me in a thousand different ways. I didn't know that you could do that, just singing and clapping. And it meant everything. It meant everything about rock'n'roll, everything about expression and creativity and art. One man against the world. And one song, 'Grinnin' In Your Face' is my favourite song. It still is. It became my favourite song the first time I heard it, and it still is. I heard everything disappearing. It didn't matter that he was clapping off time, it didn't matter that there were no instruments being played. All that mattered was the attitude of the song."

THE HUMAN LEAGUE

They made some marvellous electro-pop dance records in the early Eighties, while *Dare* remains a classic of its time ("Don't You Want Me?", "Open Your Heart", "The Sound Of The Crowd", "Love Action (I Believe In Love)", etc); in the years since they've been afforded the kind of attention usually reserved for soul singers who were big in the Sixties. Singer PHIL OAKEY was such a keen evangelist of their craft that he was looked on fondly by those who had long stopped disliking them instinctively, yet he will forever be the punchline to a *New Yorker* cartoon: "Great stupid haircut."

MICHAEL HUTCHENCE

HELENA CHRISTENSEN was in Michael Hutchence's kitchen, unpacking her shopping, which mainly consisted of expensive crockery she'd brought from a nearby village. The live-in housekeeper fussed around her as Hutchence sipped a cold Carlsberg, the first of many that day. The sun was slowly setting behind the tiny olive grove and all was well with the world. At least with Michael and Helena's world.

This was a celebrity interview, 1993 style: a weekend spent with a rock star and his supermodel girlfriend in his whitewashed villa near a little town called Valbonne on the French Riviera. It was the typical rock star retreat, furnished with Conran Shop sofas, scented candles, and third world bits and pieces from DAVID WAINWRIGHT on Portobello Road. A satellite dish jutted out of the lavender, opposite the covered breakfast terrace and the lip-sided swimming pool. A gardener glided across the lawn on one of those mowing machines that look like a small tank. The place – which Hutchence bought in 1989 – was not opulent or ostentatious. Various friends and gofers milled about – one was painting a mural on a bedroom wall; another was harassing a travel agent on his (very) mobile phone; while Helena's friend and fellow model GAIL ELLIOT sunbathed by the pool.

Oh, and it was called Venus.

In person, the thirty-four-year-old Hutchence looked bigger than he had ever done on video, without any of the boy-girl SANDRA BERNHARD looks he affected in pictures and on film. His face bore traces of a pockmarked youth, his stubble was anything but designer, and like your humble journalist, he spoke with a lisp (Hutchence did a mean KARL LAGERFELD impression). His hair was tousled, like MICK JAGGER's, though unlike Jagger he didn't have that huge labial smile. He was courteous and personable, without much of the disingenuous familiarity practised by so many rock stars. Like INXS's music, he appeared bright but uncomplicated, with no obvious side to him. Although he did like his booze.

Hutchence bore all the hallmarks of a bona fide Nineties rock star: he smoked and drank, admitted to taking drugs – for him, getting "fucked up" wasn't a political or strategic decision, it was part of his job – and was engaged to his supermodel (*and,* conceivably more importantly, at least at the time, he wore a black leather waistcoat, like BONO, DEPECHE MODE's DAVE GAHAN, and the man he was most often

H

physically compared to, JIM MORRISON). Oh, and despite the fact that he was the focal point of INXS, he wasn't a supreme egotist; an egotist, yes, but not an unbearable one (a few years before we met the band had turned down a *Rolling Stone* cover because the magazine would only put Hutchence on the front). "In this band it's all for one, and one for all," he said to me, leaning over his distressed oak dining-room table. "So it's out of friendship, I suppose, that I have played down the sex-symbol thing. It's nothing more than a tongue-in-cheek distraction. I have never been the leader as such, and I suppose ANDREW [FARRISS, who co-wrote most of the songs] is a sort of phantom leader. So I guess we kind of share that. I'm a team player."

INXS were always a first division rock band, not premiere league, like, say U2, in whose shadow they occasionally squatted. The band reached this position through sheer hard work, by spending fifteen years touring, playing everywhere from Adelaide to Iowa (in 1981 they played three hundred dates in Australia alone). They started life as the FARRISS BROTHERS in Sydney in 1977 (apart from Hutchence the band comprised TIM, ANDY and JOHN FARRISS, KIRK PENGILLY, and bass player GARRY "GARY" BEERS), before changing their name to INXS IN 1979 ("When I started in this group I was a dip-shit from Fuckoff, Nowhere, sitting in the back of the room shaking," Hutchence once said). Enormous success in their homeland was followed by international fame when they finally cracked the US in 1984, having dropped their sub-new romantic blousy style for a more orthodox rock'n'roll look. ("I must be one of the most effeminate singers in Australia, and it caused us problems in the early days – *Well, I dunno mate, it's what they do overseas, innit?* But Australian culture is so odd that people got intrigued.")

The extensive touring promoted a succession of increasingly effective LP's, including *Listen Like Thieves* (1985), *Kick* (1987), *X* (1990), and *Welcome To Wherever You Are* from 1992. The band also had their share of hit singles: "Need You Tonight", "Heaven Sent", "Suicide Blonde". Never extraordinary, INXS were always reliable, struck the requisite rock poses, and, as one journalist noted, could "carry a tune powerfully and dependently much in the way that a brickie carries a hod".

With success, though, came languor, and INXS found it necessary to dabble in a bit of reinvention, pouring old wine into new bottles. Earlier in the year they had embarked on a no-frills tour of small venues instead of the arenas and stadia they were used to playing (the band mingled freely with hacks, hangers-on and fans in unpretentious warm-larger-and-crisps après-gig scenarios – and appeared to enjoy it. Very Nineties). Live, INXS really made sense. As tight as they should have been after sixteen years together, the tour also highlighted Hutchence's easy bond with his audience. He combined charisma and a brand of avuncular charm with statutory rock god poses, removing his shorts and orchestrating some very rock and roll stage diving antics. You spent a lot of time smiling at an INXS gig. It was an irony-free zone.

Irony apart, comparisons with U2 were easily made, although INXS always looked as though they were copying BONO and co. And whereas BONO's lyrics appeared to be cathartic, INXS's often seemed pedestrian. It would be unfair to call Michael Hutchence BONO-lite, but he was certainly aware of the comparisons. "I was [even] worried about using ENO because of his association with U2," he said, "But fuck it, he's a free party, and he liked the song. We send our songs to lots of different people with views to remixes. We went shopping."

Most musicians will refer to their own back catalogue if asked who they're competing against, but not Hutchence. "Our peers," he blurted out before I'd even finished the question. "Our peers and everyone who came before us. Everyone. It's ego, it's healthy. It's a game of poker – they play their cards and we play ours. This is not something we talk about. We're all very friendly people generally, when we meet each other, but behind their backs it's different. In Australia you learn

H to take success from numbers, it's all about bums on seats. It's always been a people thing, so we've tended to measure success by how many people come to see us. Who cares if we're not as good as the next guy? Everyone always played the same pubs – us, MIDNIGHT OIL, CROWDED HOUSE, HUNTERS & COLLECTORS, NICK CAVE – so you always knew who was drawing the bigger crowd.

"Twenty years ago you just didn't buy records by Australian artists. In those days most people copied overseas artists, and there was very little homegrown creativity. Up until recently very few overseas people toured Australia. The BEATLES came, of course, and that was a big deal, but hardly anyone came in the mid-Seventies – DEEP PURPLE, ARETHA FRANKLIN. When they came it was front page news."

With so few national idols, so few home-grown role-models, Hutchence and co looked abroad for their inspiration, became pop-cultural sponges, soaking up the remnants of punk (Australian punk band the SAINTS were local heroes) and the burgeoning disco wave, and mixing it with traditional Australian pop-rock.

"The pub scene consisted of COLD CHISEL, MIDNIGHT OIL, ANGELS, all those macho, guitar-based bands," Hutchence said. "We were one of those at first, because if you didn't play in a pub in those days you were nowhere. They were sweaty, violent places, and pub culture was very nationalistic, still is, in fact. What made us different was that we tried to acclimatise Australians to our love of soul and funk, mixing it with rock music. We tried to mix all three things together. It wasn't altruistic, just fun.

"Australian people, or at least those in Sydney and Melbourne, are a lot less naive about music than in a lot of major cities I've been to. It's the eternal hunger for what's new. It's constant inferiority. 'Am I OK? Do I look alright?' In fact when I finally came to London I was incredibly disappointed at the quality of the music scene. Because everything is filtered before it gets to Australia, so it's like manna from heaven. Everyone's perfect because *they're from overseas, mate.* Or at least the crap's been cut out along the way because it doesn't make it. So we get the best, we get the best version of the best."

It was perhaps this cultural vacuum, and their understanding of it, which made Hutchence and INXS so tenacious, something borne out by their long-standing manager at the time, CHRIS MURPHY: "I used to compare INXS work patterns to a sportsman's. A sportsman doesn't walk out at Wembley and suddenly win the match. He's trained and trained to get himself into that position. With INXS we took exactly the same approach. If we weren't working one night, we'd be rehearsing, if we weren't rehearsing, we're recording, if we weren't recording, we're playing."

"We became known because we worked bloody hard," said Hutchence. "In the studio from midnight to dawn, then rehearsing, and then playing. We never stopped. Practically as soon as we left school we all moved into a house together and totally went for it. It was the band or nothing. There was amazing perseverance. PETER GARRETT from MIDNIGHT OIL once asked me how we achieved what we did, and the answer is simply hard work. We've worked harder than most people. It's the pub ethic that keeps us going – getting better than anyone else."

Hutchence worked hard elsewhere, too, partying as though it had just been made legal. Not that there was anything very legal about the partying. As a friend of mine who spent a lot of time with him said, he drank and took drugs in a robustly Australian way: never take a half when half a dozen were available. Heroin, cocaine, ecstasy, and all points in between and beyond. During the acid house craze he had a strobe light and a smoke machine in his dressing room. "I was an idiot, but a lovable idiot." Cigarettes would regularly fall from his mouth as he failed to grip them with his lips, and when he walked into a room, drinks would fall over like skittles. He was doing what all nascent rock stars do: paaarty. Hard, with conviction, and with no thought as to what tomorrow might bring.

H

In spite of this, INXS became the embodiment of a new pop culture, one which has been turned into an art form by MTV: be everywhere at once!

After the global success of *Kick* in 1988, Hutch cut his hair and donned expensive designer suits and started wearing glasses in public (he was *appallingly* short-sighted). He said this was to try and diffuse some of the "sex symbol stuff" that was surrounding him at the time (no, nobody believed him), but he then exacerbated the situation by dating KYLIE MINOGUE. "No ambitious rock star would have gone out with Kylie, because at the time I met her she wasn't considered to have any credibility at all," said Hutchence. "She was an enormous star but nothing else. How about that for integrity! Going out with Kylie and not giving a fuck!" It was the fucking that got them through, too. It was "great sex," he said. "Just great sex."

And then he traded her in for a supermodel. *So* rock'n'roll. "We treat it with amusement, sure," he told me, with a thin smile, in 1993, "but a lot of the time it's gallows laughter. Helena is Danish, and their sensibility is quite Australian, so you're not allowed to wallow in your own success. It's not like it is in America, where you're allowed to rise above yourself. It's difficult for her because there's only five million in her country and she's the only big star they've got. But we still walk the streets together, we still *hang*. The strangest reaction is from famous people; they're the ultimate star fuckers, which is endearing in a way as it makes them human. Fame is indiscriminate, as some people are famous because they have been unsuccessful, some because they were abused as children, some because they have money. But once you're in the club it doesn't matter why or how you got there. A nod and wink's all you need."

One journalist once told Hutchence he'd have a much easier time with the British press if he was more of an arsehole. However Hutchence had been extremely open in the press about his sybaritic ways – the drinking, the indiscriminate sex (which Hutchence always called his "dick" period), and

the drugs. Towards the end of the Eighties he threw himself
into the British acid house scene with a passion and fervour
not usually associated with rock stars worth close to £10
million. ("When I first got into ecstasy I had a guy on the road
with me with a big jar of it. It was almost the break-up of the
band.") "I've got into trouble with that in the past," he said to
me, untroubled by the mention of his narcotic indiscretions,
"but fuck it. I've done lots of things which I have owned up
to. Why should I bullshit about it? I've recently tried to take
things a bit more seriously than I used to. I've come across a
bit of a... it's my sense of humour I guess. But I have never
been totally misrepresented in the press. I've never hit a
journalist, although I have hit a photographer, *but hey mate,
everyone does that, sport*. Really, though, I'm surprised that
anyone bothers to ask anyone under thirty anything. By the
time you're old enough to answer some questions, nobody
really wants to know the answers. However if you're a young
rock star..."

And with that he opened another beer, and wandered off
to the bathroom.

INXS were never taken as seriously as they would have
liked to have been, but if Hutchence was a bitter man, he
kept it well hidden. He seemed content to be the leader of
Australia's foremost rock group, the biggest Antipodean band
in the world. And if INXS were only a first division rock band,
then, if only in his own eyes, surely Hutchence was a premier
league rock star.

He didn't appear to be an overtly greedy person, though
he was already inordinately wealthy. He had invested well
– property, recording studios, the usual things – and had
put tax-efficient money into the Australian film industry.
(In a move that was worthy of the scam attempted in *The
Producers*, Hutchence and the rest of the band invested in
Crocodile Dundee – as a tax loss only. "We soon had twenty
times the tax problem," he said.) He also tried his hand at
the renaissance man business, forming an offshoot group
called Max Q, and appearing in two low-budget movies, *Dogs*

H

In Space, directed by long-term friend and video director RICHARD LOWENSTEIN in 1986, and *Frankenstein Unbound,* a typical ROGER CORMAN B-movie from 1990. When the world and his wife (particularly the wife) are watching your every move, it becomes dangerous to experiment too much in public, but Hutchence said that he wanted to direct, produce, and star in his own movie before too long. But he didn't say this the way I imagine STING or PETER GABRIEL would have; he said it in italics: *Yeah, sure mate, wanna direct movies, know what I mean!* You could take Michael Hutchence out of Australia, but you could never take the Oz out of Michael Hutchence.

"It's weird going back now because in a lot of ways nothing changes. The same bullshit, the same people in the same bars saying the same things – you know, *I really gotta get to New York mate; no-one understands me here.* Musically things have changed for the worse, because during the Eighties the combination of house music and yuppies killed off live music. The yuppies would sit in the same places we used to play, and instead of watching a live band they'd sip their cocktails watching videos. And the parochial sensibility is still really strong, a sensibility that doesn't work in New York, London, or Los Angeles. Recently there was this event called The Wizards of Oz, which was a night of Australian bands in a club in LA, and then New York, I think. But that's a mentality that will never make it for Australian music – you know, let's have a couple of Aboriginals and roos on stage. We could have stayed in Sydney pubs with people shooting bullets at our feet saying, *Dance, boy, dance. Whaddya gonna do next, we saw you last week.* But we decided to get out.

"I think we came across as international, much more so than someone like U2, although they've done their darndest to be the biggest American band in the world. We don't play that kind of anthemic music anyway, we play a hybrid, and I think we've done a lot to break down certain barriers. We're not AC/DC [pronounced Acker-Dacker]."

Later that night we went for dinner at a nearby restaurant, eight of us, having darted through the hills in Hutchence's Mercedes jeep and Christensen's little Peugeot. After dessert someone said something that confused Helena. When she finally grasped the full meaning of the remark she said, "That's no cow on the ice," a Danish expression meaning, it's no big deal. For Hutchence – the sexy boho from down under, the guileless ocker who became a rocker – global domination was probably only a wish, or a world tour away. No cow on the ice.

But then it all went horribly wrong.

Hutchence would soon move on from Christensen, getting disastrously involved with BOB GELDOF's wife, PAULA YATES. If anything she had an even bigger personality than he did, and when they met was in the middle of a profound personality crisis. Perhaps predictably, they both descended into a co-dependent drug spiral. Hutchence collapsed in full view of the world media. "Whereas before he would glide into a room as if on celestial castors," wrote GQ's ADRIAN DEEVOY, "he now hobbled bow-legged like a cowboy who had been abruptly estranged from his horse." And Hutchence couldn't handle it, hanging himself in a Sydney hotel room in November 1997. With his own belt. At the age of thirty-seven.

The cow was on the ice.

I

IGGY POP

By any indices of assessment, James Newell Osterberg is the coolest man in the entire business. Probably always will be (regardless of which insurance company he endorses). He is certainly the sexiest, and there are few rock stars of his age (he was sixty-four in 2011) who can take their shirt off with such confidence. When the STOOGES were starting out in Ann Arbor, Michigan, in the late Sixties, they were a spectacle, an oddity, and yet girls and boys both came to see the band as they were not only weirdly mesmeric, but they were also unlike anything anyone from that generation had ever seen before. They came to stare and they came to dance. But mainly they came to stare (snickering to fend off the fear).

Everything Iggy has recorded has some merit, even the rubbish, all the way from "1969" to "Shades" (his best, most unrecognised composition, written with DAVID BOWIE), via "TV Eye", 1993's awesome *American Caesar* (containing a cute version of "Louie Louie"), and of course the seminal punk soundtrack albums, *The Idiot* (urban decadence) and *Lust For Life* (exuberant non-conformity) – both from 1977, and simply two of the best records made by anyone ever. My personal favourites include the proper blitzkrieg version of "I Got A Right", and the *Kill City* album, released in 1977 but recorded in 1975. Like Iggy, it is a very strange beast, but sounds as detached and disjointed as Iggy probably was when he made it (at the time he was in a mental institution as he was being treated for heroin addiction; he recorded his vocals for the album at weekends). Favourite Iggy quote: "She looked at me penetratingly. So I suppose you can figure out what happened next."

I

INTERPOL

The ugly FRANZ FERDINAND. Oh, and with absolutely no A+ hits. Or tunes. Or indeed anything. Great apart from that.

THE INTERVIEW

How do you go about interviewing famous rock stars? What's the best way to prise open a celebrity? The celebrity interview has been so devalued, so diminished by the extraordinary number of people who are now famous that it's often difficult to think of them as anything other than glorified press releases.

Years ago, in the golden days of long-form journalism – when any new journalist worth his ink would spend the best part of six months with his subject before finally filing his copy – the celebrity interview was "a very important thing". But now, in a world in which TV's *Big Brother* has made celebrities out of nobodies, where fame is so homogenised, is conducting an interview still a skill?

Time and restrictions are hugely important to the success rate of the celebrity interview, and if you've only been allotted ten minutes or so, then it's best to go armed simply with twenty quick-fire questions that you can turn into a breezy Q&A (Q: You're trapped with BILLIE JOE ARMSTRONG, KYLIE MINOGUE, and JAKE SHEARS. With a gun to your head, which one do you have sex with? Q: What colour is Tuesday?). Conversely, if you can convince your rock star to spend a few days with you, driving through the Hollywood Hills and hanging out at the private views, exclusive concerts and film premieres, then so be it. This is obviously the best way to get to know your subject and, who knows, they might even become your new best friend. It's totally possible to build up a relationship with a celebrity over a period of time, and though they will expect you to treat them with slightly more decorum than they do your bog-standard hack, the access afforded will, on occasion, counteract any sycophancy.

Any decent interview needs a certain amount of compromise; there needs to be a modicum of give and take. Ideally it should be an "I win, you win" situation, with both parties coming away feeling as though their lives have been enriched – if only in a small way. Both parties need to give, while the interviewee needs to be generous with their time and anecdotes.

I once interviewed GWYNETH PALTROW on the set of *Shakespeare in Love* for the *Sunday Times Magazine* and she couldn't have been less interested. She gave nothing but monosyllabic answers, and a good impression of someone who'd rather be picking skewers out of her eyeballs than talking to me. For me, it was an enervating experience so, having not got what I needed, I proceeded to interview everyone else on the set: the carpenters, the caterers, the sound guys, her chauffeur, the studio concierge, the make-up girls, the hairdressers – anyone I could find who had anything to do with her. I wasn't looking for a particularly negative story but, given Paltrow's unwillingness to talk to me, I had to get a story somehow. The feedback I got from those around her was not exactly positive. So, in the end she got what she deserved, which is a shame – for her. I'm an easy person to charm, and if she had spent half an hour working her magic on me, no doubt I would have come away thinking GWYNETH PALTROW was a born-again AUDREY HEPBURN. But she didn't, so I didn't.

Journalists' techniques are fascinating. When AA GILL was interviewed by LYNN BARBER a few years ago, he said it was like being interrogated by Columbo. "Oh, Adrian. Just one thing: you said you were wearing a cummerbund fashioned from yak gut and corduroy on the day in question. Where exactly did you say you bought it?"

As for myself, I don't think I've ever been particularly good at it, even though I've interviewed hundreds of famous people in the past three decades. For years, I made the cardinal error of trying to impress the people in front of me; I wanted them to like me, wanted them to understand how bright I was, and how well-versed I was in their work. I wanted PAUL MCCARTNEY to think I was the only person who really understood why he was the most talented Beatle, and wanted KEITH RICHARDS to think of me as a made man, a groovy young guy who never went to bed and had taken nearly as many drugs as he had. When I met GEORGE BUSH in Dubai a few years ago, I tried, in the space of two minutes, to impress upon him that my view of the Gulf War was more incisive than anyone else's. I even once tried to contradict SHIRLEY MACLAINE's anecdotes about FRANK SINATRA.

Fool. Just SHUT UP AND LET THEM TALK. That's what you've got to do. Ask a question, let the famous person start rambling, and then occasionally steer them in the direction of the place you want to end up. My biggest sin has probably been interrupting. You know, just as SIOUXSIE SIOUX was about to tell me who she had been taking crack with last night (that's a joke, by the way; I know that SIOUXSIE SIOUX doesn't take crack), I'd butt in with: "That's great Siouxsie, but tell me about that bit in 'Hong Kong Garden' where..."

My worst ever interview, or at least the one I was least involved with (so it may actually have been my best), was in the mid-Nineties, with WOODY ALLEN in the Dorchester in London. As soon as I shook his hand I started thinking about FRANK SINATRA's cock. Why? Well, Woody used to sleep with MIA FARROW, who, years before, used to sleep with Sinatra. So I instantly realised that I was only one female sex organ away from Frank's johnson. This thought preoccupied me all through my chat with Woody. It may, as I say, have been a good thing (at least I didn't keep interrupting him...).

In general, my problem was I couldn't bear for there to be any gaps in the conversation, and in that respect I'm probably like a lot of journalists. But the trick is to let the celebrity fill that space because, in reality, they're just as embarrassed by the silence as you. I know one music journo who is a master at this: a man who thinks nothing of keeping silent for two, three, four minutes after his subject has temporarily stopped talking, thus forcing said rock star to start burbling about nothing in particular. Or, more pertinently, everything in particular.

Sometimes, with celebrities, you are told to adhere to ridiculous restrictions, so you're forced to resort to nonsensical methods. When DAVID BOWIE was involved with TIN MACHINE, he initially refused to do interviews unless the rest of his band were present. This put a lot of people off, but when TONY PARSONS interviewed them (at my behest, we were at *Arena* at the time), he turned the situation to his advantage in the most obvious way: he ignored Bowie – for forty-five minutes. In that time he quizzed Bowie's backing band (which is essentially what they were) about stage dynamics, recording techniques and group compositions, until the Thin White Duchess could take it no more. Bowie almost exploded into the conversation, falling over himself to tell Tony the reason for his solo volte-face, and his frustrations with the music industry. By ignoring him, Tony got an extraordinary interview.

Another way to avoid the dark tunnel of product-specific-questions is to confront the interviewee with "the problem".

"Hi, Mick. Your PR says that I can only ask questions about the record, but you don't mind talking about your sex life, do you? I mean, how does being gay affect your faith?"

"My PR said that? I don't mind at all. I've got some pictures on my phone of me having sex in church, if you'd like to see them."

Of course, this won't always work but, as a journalist, you must assume that the PR's restrictions are rarely imposed by the stars themselves. And even if they are, you can usually cajole your rock star into talking about the subject – if only in a defensive way.

With most rock stars, there will be this one question that is forever off limits: one question that history has taught you to avoid. With HUGH GRANT, it's his experience with DIVINE

BROWN; with MADONNA, *Swept Away* (the shocking film directed by her ex-husband, GUY RITCHIE); and as for MICHAEL JACKSON... Well, you could take your pick.

But you have to ask it. You just have to. MARK ELLEN, the very brilliant former editor of *Smash Hits*, *Q*, and now *The Word*, has a fail-safe way of asking the "difficult question". Throughout the interview he will say things like, "Look, I know you won't want to talk about the thing, but I'm going to bring it up later," or "That's all very well, but I must warn you that we're going to have a little bit of a fight later!" Mark said, "It softens them up – lets them know you're going to ask them something they don't especially want to answer. So by the time you get around to it, they're almost relieved."

Once, many years ago, when I worked on the *Observer*, we were offered an interview with EDDIE MURPHY who, at the time, was enjoying a second flush of fame. However, the product Eddie was pushing was a fairly useless rap record, and his Hollywood publicist told us that he would only answer questions relating to this particular project. Not only that, but we were only to be given forty minutes and it was to be in Los Angeles – not a cheap place to get to at the best of times. Oh, and the PR had to sit in on the interview. Great! Just about the only thing they didn't demand was copy approval, but it was still a tall order. We ummed and aahed about it, but decided that it was too good an opportunity to miss; we'd have to find someone good enough to exploit the situation. That person, we decided, was HUGH McILVANNEY, the greatest sports writer the world has ever known (Scottish, gruff, then already in his sixties, known to enjoy a drink).

Now, we could have picked someone whose job it was to interview celebrities. Or we could have chosen someone famous themselves (LENNY HENRY? STEPHEN FRY?). We thought about a flirty female who could flutter her eyelashes and cross/recross her legs; we even considered the likes of MARTIN AMIS (who was then writing for us). But we decided we needed someone with some specific attributes: who wasn't going to be intimidated (by anyone), who knew nothing about hip-hop (thus eliminating the need for any protracted discussions about inspirations, motivations, choice of producers, etc), who was smart enough to side-step the PR's restrictions, and clever enough to run rings around Eddie himself. And that person was obviously Hugh.

Boy, did we choose the right person. The interview Hugh came back with was remarkable, covering all aspects of the celeb's life: his movies, girlfriends, ambitions, race, politics, sex – the lot. Oh, and there was even stuff about the record (the awful, pitiful record). So how had Hugh done it? The tape of the interview did the rounds in the office for weeks afterwards, and it was almost a masterclass in the art of interviewing difficult, protected and protective celebs. Stupidly, pathetically, I have since lost the tape, but I still remember Hugh's opening question as though he asked it only yesterday.

"So, Eddie. I must say this new record of yours is quite a remarkable thing. I'm not an aficionado of this sort of music at all, but the way in which you paint yourself as the catalyst for this furore around you – the instigator – it strikes me that you are a man totally in charge of your own destiny, if indeed that's what we can call it. How did the making of this record, of all the things you've done, affect the way you see yourself? How does this latest project redefine what you are as a man?"

In fact, thinking about it now, the actual question was probably four times as long as that, but the convoluted way in which Hugh approached his subject – and the meandering way in which he asked his question – opened EDDIE MURPHY up like an oyster. And, for the next two hours, the comedian talked, and talked, and talked, and talked. Which, after all, was the object of the exercise.

And the record? The pathetic rap record Eddie was so keen to puff? It wasn't a hit.

THE ISLEY BROTHERS

I

If you were to look quickly at their CV you could easily think that the Isleys had three main periods of activity in their career – the Sixties period of "Shout", "This Old Heart of Mine (Is Weak for You)", "Twist And Shout", and "Behind A Painted Smile" (their best song from this time); the *3+3* period of the early Seventies ("Summer Breeze", "That Lady", etc) and then the Indian Summer of *Between The Sheets* in 1983 (a sound liberally appropriated by PAUL WELLER).

But there is so much more to them. Every album between these last two periods of their career contains some insanely good music, a lot of which can easily be classified as "bedroom-friendly" (music to solve any marital dispute). Take "Hello It's Me" from *Live It Up* (1974), "For The Love of You" from *The Heat Is On* (1975), "Let Me Down Easy" from *Harvest For The World* (1976), "Voyage to Atlantic" on *Go for Your Guns* (1977), and "Inside You" from *Inside You* (1981).

With vocals bathed in echo, high-flying freaky guitar solos wafting out of the bedroom window like Disney fairies (they had once employed JIMI HENDRIX as a session guitarist and he left an indelible mark), bass notes reverberating as if off a mattress, the Isleys knew how to sing about sex. Lurve was their bag, so much so they made BARRY WHITE sound like a supermarket MARVIN GAYE – Jesus, they even made MARVIN GAYE sound like a supermarket MARVIN GAYE. They dressed the part, too, galumphing on stage in rhinestone and spandex, medallions swinging from pec to pec. They flirted with message songs – "Fight the Power!" – but were always far happier in the boudoir than the streets.

MICHAEL JACKSON

"The merry-go-round stands rusting and lifeless. An elaborate floral display that used to stand proudly at the front of the mansion has wilted, leaving just bare earth. The tepees are collapsing in on themselves and a tent covering the bumper cars is falling to bits..." As a snapshot metaphor for the tragic demise of Michael Jackson, ERIC MUNN's 2008 piece about the ruins of his Neverland playground is hard to beat. The aerial photographs of the ranch show a deserted and lifeless playground, with scorched earth and untended gardens, an abandoned circus, tumbledown and sad. In this blasted, dusty landscape, the only game was courtesy of a tennis court – its net wilting under the harsh Californian sun. The elephants, giraffes, lions and monkeys were all gone, the horses were at a nearby children's riding school, and Jackson's own pet monkey, Bubbles, was in a sanctuary.

But then you squint, flex, and start moving your toes from left to right, as "Rock With You" starts folding out of the iPod dock, followed by "Billie Jean", "Off The Wall", "Wanna Be Startin' Somethin'", and the greatest dance record ever made, "Don't Stop 'Til You Get Enough" (as good a piece of work as anyone has produced in the entertainment industry in the last hundred years), and the vision becomes blurry, and all you can do is dance.

MICK JAGGER

Over the years I've spent a fair amount of time with the photographer David Bailey, and during our various interviews he has often talked about Mick Jagger. He painted the Stones' front man as someone who initially needed Bailey as a cultural and societal tour guide.

J "Until the Sixties, the class structure in Britain was almost like the caste system in India," he said, "and if things had gone on as they were I would have ended up as an untouchable. But the Sixties broke all that down, at least for a few of us.

"Swinging London just sort of happened by accident, as everything appeared to in those days. Everything was sheer coincidence. It's almost existential that all the people I knew at the time became famous overnight. There was JEAN and CHRISSIE SHRIMPTON, MICK JAGGER, MICHAEL CAINE, TERENCE STAMP, TERENCE DONOVAN – suddenly all the people I knew were in the same position I was, which was on the verge on being successful. So in some respects being at the centre of so-called 'Swinging London' was no different than being around before it. Britain was still living in the Fifties. It *was* the Fifties. Things only started to change in about 1962, when *everything* started to change. Before 1962 you didn't go out and buy six pairs of jeans, you saved up for one pair and then wore them forever, because you couldn't afford to buy a second pair. But there wasn't a sense of desperation, and London wasn't full of people who were jealous of each other. Working class people knew they were different, but they weren't obsessed with people who had money.

"It was a bloodless revolution, but in reality the whole thing was something of a myth. You have to be careful not to write your own fiction, because a lot of what people say and write about the Sixties is simply not true. There were only about five hundred of us, but then there are only ever five hundred people at any one time doing something interesting. How many PICASSOS are there? How many BOB DYLANS? It was fine for five hundred of us, the lucky ones, but everyone else was still living in the Fifties. Apart from a few pockets of affluence and new money, London was not much different from what it had been at the end of the war. Everything was grey, dirty, cheap, miserable. Especially anywhere east of Tottenham Court Road, especially out in East Ham. London was also something like a different planet, because up in Liverpool or Manchester or Newcastle there was nothing happening at all. Nothing. I don't know if it was great for miners in Yorkshire, or machinists in the Rhondda Valley. For a lot of us in London it was like the rest of the country simply didn't exist. We weren't bothered by it at all.

"We started mixing with a lot of the upper classes, who I actually quite liked. It was the middle classes I found odd, because they put on such funny voices. I thought the upper classes talked like us in a way, just normal. I just got on with it... It was always MICHAEL CAINE who sort of carried a flag for the working class. I think he always felt a little bit patronised. But I didn't care, I just took people for what they were. I also didn't like people who glorified their cockney accents, or wallowed in all of that. To me it was the same as the gays who went over the top, who acted as though they were on stage. So you're gay, so what? For a while cockney accents became not only acceptable but desirable.

According to Bailey there was the gay crowd, and the old upper classes, but what comprised so-called Swinging London was a couple of hundred people at best – BAILEY, DONOVAN, BRIAN DUFFY, CAINE, STAMP, MARY QUANT, PETER SELLERS, JOHN BARRY, ANDREW LOOG OLDHAM, BRIDGET RILEY, ROMAN POLANSKI, NUREYEV, JAMES WEDGE, VIDAL SASSOON, NICKY HASLAM. And they all knew each other. PETER SELLERS used to hang around the scene a bit, along with LORD SNOWDON. Sellers tried to sue Bailey once, after a picture he'd taken of him. He didn't like his nose, apparently. BAILEY said, "Well Pete, you're blaming the wrong person. You should be blaming him upstairs!"

London at this point was like one long party that no one thought would ever end, especially those who had been recently emancipated. In some respects it was inevitable that something like this should have happened after the war; it was like MICHAEL CAINE said in *Goodbye Baby And Amen*: "To me it was unavoidable justice. It had to happen. It was all a question of the human spirit: you can keep it subdued for 1,960 years and suddenly there comes a time when you can't keep it subdued for another New Year's Eve. We suddenly realised that all these people for whom we had respect not only didn't respect us but didn't respect

J

themselves. So all the old values were out of the window." There was a sense of entitlement.

And everyone met everyone else in the space of five minutes. BAILEY met Mick Jagger because of Chrissie, Jean met TERRY STAMP through BAILEY, and BAILEY met MICHAEL CAINE through Stamp. But there was little competition between them because they were really just starting out. When Jagger was studying at the London School of Economics he needed to find a way to help pay his way, but he didn't become a cleaner like people often say he did. The story is that Jean's sister Chrissie put an ad in the *Evening News*, and that Mick replied and became her maid. But how on Earth was CHRISSIE SHRIMPTON going to get the money for a cleaner?! She actually met Jagger on Eel Pie Island, when the Stones were playing there one night. She told BAILEY they were going to be huge. "Mick's great," she said. "He's going to be bigger than the BEATLES!" And Bailey said, "There's no way that long-haired, scruffy git's going to be more successful than the Beatles!" He said he was winding her up. Jagger quickly fell in love with her, and so they all started to hang out together. At the time Jagger always wore stripy T-shirts and tight-fitting suits, and boots from Anello and Davide, the dance shoemaker in London. This was where the BEATLES started going later.

Jagger and Bailey became friends, and they even lived together for a while, though Bailey thought that he was somehow lacking in Jagger's eyes, bas he wasn't a musician. In a way Bailey became his link to another world. When Mick and Keith's Hampstead flat was broken into, they both went to live in the Hilton, but then Keith moved out to St John's Wood, and Jagger stayed with Bailey. If it hadn't have been for BAILEY, Jagger would probably have been homeless —Jagger was apparently impressed by the fact Bailey had three bathrooms. Bailey was travelling a lot at the time, and Jagger once went to Paris as his assistant, primarily to pick up girls. They behaved so badly and made so much noise they were actually thrown out of the hotel.

Jagger was extremely middle class, and he was unsophisticated without having the street smarts – a grammar school boy who didn't really know his way around. "Shortly after we met, Mick asked me to take him to a 'posh' restaurant," said BAILEY. "I think he liked my lifestyle. He kept pestering me to take him somewhere nice, because he'd never really been anywhere that wasn't a coffee bar or a club. Anyway, I decided to take him to a place called Casserole in the Fulham Road. This was the only other place that was as cool as the Ad Lib, and was run by a gay New Zealand guy who we called Casserarsehole. I, being working-class, noticed bad manners more than most people. I remember he paid, which was unusual because back then Mick never paid for anything. I told him to leave a tip and he said, 'Leave a tip? What the fuck for?' I told him it was customary to leave a ten-shilling note, one of those old brown banknotes. He put the note on the plate, but as we were putting our coats on I noticed he put it back in the pocket.

"Mick was already in the Stones, although no one really knew who they were. What struck me about Mick was his lips. I used to wind him up by saying his mother used to stick him to store windows while she went shopping. But I liked the Stones as I've always liked the blues, and here was a band playing WILLIE DIXON's 'Little Red Rooster' and stuff like that, stuff you could buy in record shops like Dobell's in the Charing Cross Road. I always liked the Stones more than the BEATLES, because the BEATLES were a bit naff, a boy band from the north. The Stones were cool. I thought the BEATLES were very manufactured when they started out, and they only got interesting around *Sergeant Pepper*, the "White Album", and *Abbey Road*. Jean had bought the BEATLES' first release and I thought it was really naff. Even though I quite liked them I thought they were a bit square – a good word that's sadly fallen out of use. The Stones were always laughing at themselves, always charming and funny, whereas the BEATLES were very controlling and protective of their image. Paul was always so earnest, and John was always quite rude. I liked

J

John because he was so rude; he had very definite opinions and certainly knew where he was going. The band were really just too worthy.

"The Stones have had a much longer career than anyone expected. They're like blues artists. Just before he died, JOE STRUMMER told me he was worried that he was too old to be doing what he was doing. I told him it was a racial thing, and that if he had been black and ninety-years-old then nobody would care. Which is what the Stones have done. But because Joe was white and middle class, he was hung up about the concept that old white people can't play rock'n'roll. But if he had been a BB KING, or a WILLIE DIXON, or a JOHN LEE HOOKER, nobody would think twice. That's where the Stones have carved out for themselves, and they can carry on until they die.

Swinging London soon became a theme park, a way of selling the Union Jack as a pop art symbol. Soon there were clubs such as the Bag O' Nails and the Scotch Of St James, although the only club with authenticity was the Ad Lib in Leicester Place, the tiny cut-through between Leicester Square and Lisle Street, right above the Prince Charles Theatre. This was where *everyone* went, the only place they'd play proper imported blues and soul. It had previously been called WIP's, with a fish tank full of piranhas and fur on the walls, owned by LORD TIMOTHY WILLOUGHBY D'ERESBY and NICHOLAS LUARD from the Establishment Club. However it didn't really take off, and it was bought by BOB BURNETT, who also owned the Stork Club and Pigalle, who reopened the place as the Ad Lib.

"I actually first went there with Jean and TERRY STAMP at the very end of 1963, the week it opened," said BAILEY. "It was a real place in the sky, a Soho penthouse converted into a discothèque with loud music, mirrored walls, and huge floor-to-ceiling windows looking down on London – you could see right across Soho, Mayfair and Piccadilly. The DJ wore a tuxedo, and the dancefloor was the size of a cocktail napkin. They served drinks like you got on an airplane – in little bottles with mixers on the side. They had a black chef called Teddy

J

– which was very exotic at the time – and people used to take their food out on to the balcony and smoke joints. There was even a doorman to park your car for you, which was unheard of for a place like that. There were photographers, singers, young actors and actresses, artists, models. There was the art dealer ROBERT FRASER, Indica's BARRY MILES, the BEATLES, the HOLLIES, MARIANNE FAITHFULL, NICKY HASLAM, MICHAEL FISH, OSSIE CLARK, PETE TOWNSHEND, CHRISTOPHER GIBBS, MICHAEL COOPER, everyone who was anyone.

"I came out of the Ad Lib one night, and got into my convertible Rolls Royce – there were only two made. ELIZABETH TAYLOR had one and I had the other – I bought it at auction after the owner, a property dealer called Claude, had died. I had spent all day photographing Jean with a python around her neck. The snake needed to be back at London Zoo by five because that's when it closed, so I had to keep it until the zoo opened again in the morning. It was only round the corner from where I lived in Primrose Hill, but I had no idea what I was going to do with it until then. The python was about twelve-foot long, and after the shoot we put it in a weightlifter's grip and put it in the boot of the car. Obviously that night I went to the Ad Lib, and had come out about midnight a little bit worse for wear. I was driving quite erratically and was stopped on Tottenham Court Road by a policeman. He asked me whose car it was, what the registration was – I didn't know – and then asked what was in the boot. Which is when I remembered the snake. And so I told him.

"'A snake? What do you mean a snake? Are you having me on?'

"'No, it's a snake.'

"And so he opens the boot, opens the grip, and out curls this twelve-foot python, frightening the living daylights out of him.

"'You're telling the truth!' he squealed. 'Are you in show business?'

"'Sort of,' I said.

"'Well, drive more carefully then.'

J

"And with that I drove off. I was stopped all the time because I was young, and in those days young people didn't have cars, especially not convertible Rolls Royces.

"In 1965 I was asked by *Vogue* to take some photographs of SOPHIA LOREN for the PETER USTINOV film *Lady L*, and so I asked if I could shoot Ustinov too, because I wanted to meet him. Anyway, I was driving up the A1 in my E-Type on my way to photograph her in Scarborough, where she was filming, when I was stopped by a policeman on his motorbike. He said someone had phoned through about me because I had been doing 120mph, even though there was no speed limit.

"'Who's car is it?' he asked.

"'Mine,' I said.

"'Where you going,' he asked.

"'Scarborough,' I said.

"'At three o'clock in the morning?'

"'Yes.'

"'OK, why are you going to Scarborough?'

"'To photograph SOPHIA LOREN.'

"'What's your name?'

"'DAVID BAILEY...'

"'Of course, and I'm Napoleon bleeding Bonaparte. Now get out of the car, and show me your driving licence.'

"And so I showed him my licence and he says, 'Oh, you're telling the truth, you really are DAVID BAILEY. My wife's a big fan of yours! Will you say hello to SOPHIA LOREN for me and please drive a bit slower...'

"I really wasn't Swinging London, I only photographed it. Mick was there, though, right in the thick of it."

THE JAM

PAUL WELLER's finishing school made some of best singles ever, and some of them still sound good when they're played really loud ("All Around The World", "Down In the Tube Station at Midnight", "Start", etc). 1978's *All Mod Cons* was also a pretty good LP. However, as someone I know said not too long ago, if you still like the Jam then you're probably the sort of person who wears sunglasses and chews gum at weddings and funerals. You might also be wearing white winklepickers. With black laces. And all the scuffed bits covered in Tipp-Ex.

JAY-Z

First a drug dealer (is this part of the script?), then a rap superstar, and now a music industry executive: SHAWN CARTER's journey has taken him from the ghetto to the boardroom. And he has made the journey with finesse and style. A hip-hop powerhouse, Jay-Z's on-stage persona is not exactly demonstrative, yet in person he is so far away from the image it makes you think you may have imagined the persona in the first place. He is polite, unassuming, effervescent even – hardly character traits one typically associates with rap superstars. But then that's what makes Jay-Z such an important cultural force, and such a great ambassador for his craft.

In his book *Decoded*, Jay-Z describes one of his raps as ending with "a dizzying carousel of conversations", which is how you could describe many hip-hop raps, the constant rat-a-tat-tat of street slang, abuse and code, a deliberately disguised language built as an alt Esperanto. PUBLIC ENEMY's CHUCK D famously called hip-hop the CNN of the ghetto, and he wasn't only right, he was profoundly right. This way of communication created a parallel world immediately, a revolutionary's paradise, a rebel's quarter, and a world that could also be aspired to by every fifteen-year-old suburbanite.

The rules were simple: lionising the gangsta, demonising the police, and painting the hustler as some sort of ROBIN HOOD anti-hero. If you're a drug dealer, you're dope, and your lot is inevitable. Even when they're barely out of school, rappers

J can come across as old sea dogs, trading stories of woe, in a constant reel of one-upmanship. It's tiring. "In hip-hop, top artists have the same pressure a rock star like BONO has – the pressure to meet expectations and stay on top," wrote Jay-Z. "But in hip-hop there's an added degree of difficulty. While you're trying to stay on top by making great music, there are dozens of rappers who don't just compete with you by putting out their own music, but they're trying to pull you down at the same time. It's like trying to win a race with every runner behind you trying to tackle you. It's really not personal – at least it shouldn't be – it's just the nature of rap. Hip-hop is a perfect mix between poetry and boxing. Of course, most artists are competitive, but hip-hop is the only art I know that's built on direct confrontation."

Like many hip-hop artists who have embraced the luxury world without irony, and who have built considerable businesses on the back of their success, Jay-Z has created his own social ladder. His world is bigger now than ever, a world where he can claim to be the 21st Century FRANK SINATRA. Sinatra's epic "New York, New York" is probably the best-known New York song (even though it was originally written for LIZA MINNELLI, for MARTIN SCORSESE's much-neglected film of the same name, from 1977), but it has actually been usurped by another anthem, Jay-Z and ALICIA KEYS' "Empire State of Mind", which is the best New York song of the new century, so far. The song became so iconic so quickly, it even attracted its own feature in the *New York Times*, written by BEN SISARIO. "The song, 'Empire State of Mind,' breaks down as roughly fifty percent rote Jay-Z chest-beating ('I'm the new Sinatra'), thirty percent tourist-friendly travelogue ('Statue of Liberty, long live the World Trade'), and the rest a glorious ALICIA KEYS hook." As Sisario eloquently points out, "New York is all about scale, from the skyline to the ambitions it frames, and like other great NY songs, Jay-Z's anthem offers a panoramic, postcard view of the city, leaping from landmark to distant landmark – 'Now I'm down in Tribeca, right next to DeNiro, but I'll be hood forever. I'm the new Sinatra, and since I made it here I can make it anywhere.'"

This is more than an attempt to draw comparisons to the baritone from Hoboken, as "Empire State of Mind" is Jay-Z's way of trying to take ownership of his town, using the city as his own personal playground, an aural smorgasbord of his own predilections, power and personality. Or, to put it another way, ego.

The thing you have to understand about New Yorkers is that they tend to have a sense of destiny. By dint of their location they think they are invincible, indestructible. Impervious to pretty much anything and everything you care to throw at them. Consequently it is the only city in the world that not only entertains anthems, it demands them. On a regular basis. And they are especially welcomed when they suggest a redemptive journey. Which is why Jay-Z's "ride in the back of a Maybach" resonates so much.

The Maybach is one of hip-hop's obvious measures of success, like wearing Tom Ford suits (in Jay-Z's case), and drinking vintage champagne. Although possibly not Cristal anymore. Rappers have long proclaimed their love for Cristal, frequently mentioning the high-end champagne in songs and popping the corks of the clear, gold-labelled bottles in music videos and at nightclubs.

But that all changed in 2006 when the makers of Cristal made the mistake of distancing themselves from the hip-hop community. In *The Economist*, FREDERIC ROUZAUD, the then managing director of Louis Roederer, the company that produces Cristal, said the company viewed the affection for his company's champagne from rappers and their fans with "curiosity and serenity". Asked if the association between Cristal and the "bling lifestyle" could be detrimental, Rouzaud said, "That's a good question, but what can we do? We can't forbid people from buying it. I'm sure Dom Perignon or Krug would be delighted to have their business."

Unsurprisingly, the comments didn't go down especially well in the hip-hop community, and certainly left a bad taste

J

in Jay-Z's mouth. The rapper stopped drinking it, stopped eulogising it, and pulled Cristal from his small chain of popular sports lounges.

"It has come to my attention that the managing director of Cristal, FREDERIC ROUZAUD views the 'hip-hop' culture as 'unwelcome attention'," he said. "I view his comments as racist and will no longer support any of his products through any of my various brands including the 40/40 Club nor in my personal life."

Again, unsurprisingly – didn't Cristal think of this? – Jay-Z began endorsing another brand, Armand de Brignac, and soon started a mutually beneficial business relationship with them. He launched his association with the brand in London in 2007, and saw fit to ask me to co-host a dinner with him. It's not everyday that I'm asked to host a dinner with Jay-Z – in fact every time the superstar hip-hop impresario had been through London in the past he had rather pointedly failed to make contact – and obviously I was flattered (in fact you could have knocked me down with a gold-plated bulletproof feather).

The negotiations for the dinner were all fairly straightforward, although it soon became apparent that he had surrounded himself with a lot of people who didn't necessarily feel the need to respond to telephone calls or emails. Hip-hop time is different to ordinary time, and while the rest of us tend to adhere to our own particular time zones, the "raperati" tend to ignore it completely. In my experience, the "hip-hop delay" is rarely the fault of the talent, but usually the result of over-protective flunkies: the people who get in the way of the people who say "Yes", basically by saying "No." All the time. Hip-hop minders have appropriated the old-school intransigence of hard-line Hollywood agents, and they take great delight in telling you things aren't possible, even when it's so blatantly obvious that they are. They compound this by doing everything at least an hour after they are meant to, making a mockery of pre-arranged business meetings. You want to meet at noon

on Wednesday? Sure, but don't expect to see us before lunch
on Thursday.

But although Jay-Z resolutely runs on hip-hop time, we
only got to the restaurant an hour late, which in his world is
tantamount to arriving early. And the fault I'm embarrassed
to say, was mine. When I pitched up at his hotel to pick him
up – dressed in Ede and Ravenscroft – he spied my pocket
square, realised he wasn't wearing one himself, and promptly
sent a flunky back to his room to pick it up. Which – obviously
– took forever. It took so long I thought he must have hidden
it behind the ceiling tiles.

On the way in the car, as we discussed being "dissed"
by Noel Gallagher about the decision to ask Jay-Z to play
Glastonbury ("The crazy thing is, 'Wonderwall' is one of my
favourite tunes"), his performance at the festival ("There
were so many people I couldn't see the end of them"),
his appearance on Jonathan Ross's television programme
("People said he's tricky, but I got him good"), and his friends
Coldplay ("Their new album is just a fantastic piece of work"),
he suddenly burst into song, singing the new Coldplay song
"Lost" at the top of his voice, causing his security guard to
turn round from the front seat, wondering if his boss had
suddenly – and convincingly – morphed into Chris Martin
(albeit Chris Martin dressed head-to-toe in Tom Ford).

When we arrived at the restaurant, the paps acted as though
Elvis Presley had arrived, drowning him in a blaze of flashbulbs.
Most of the evening was spent discussing Barack Obama, who
at the time Jay Z had met twice, and who had completely won
over the forty-year-old rapper. "It's not so much a case of if he
can do it – he has to do it, because if he doesn't then I don't
know where America is going. Black kids in the ghettos don't
have anyone to look up to in the political world. In the absence
of families their gangs become their families and they need
people to look up to. Barack is that man."

But that was hardly surprising, I said. It would be fairly
remarkable for a black role model like himself to vote for John
McCain.

J "I'm not voting for him because he's black," said Jay Z. "I'm voting for him because of what he stands for. And he stands for change. We didn't have anyone like Obama when I was running round as a kid. I did crazy shit, but I never looked up to a politician because they never addressed us, never spoke to us. With Obama you get the sense he's gonna talk to everyone. And for a black man that's a very powerful message."

And how happy was he to see the back of Bush?

"No happier than anyone else in America. Look what Bush did about New Orleans – nothing. That's how much Bush cares about black people."

Just as we were getting to the heart of the matter, several large white men of a certain age sidled up to Jay and started talking about the "vibe" and the "respect" and I could see Jay-Z's eyes begin to glaze over. The wiggas were advancing and the black Sinatra was trapped.

JAZZ-ROCK

HENRY MANCINI was still relatively unknown, the conjurer of heavily jazz-oriented soundtracks, when he was asked to score ORSON WELLES' *Touch Of Evil*. He had previously scored biopics of GLENN MILLER and BENNY GOODMAN, which made Welles wary. He didn't want jazz, nor any of the faux "mariachi" or "rancheros" numbers usually associated with scenes where traditional Mexican music was wanted.

What Welles wanted was "a great deal of rock'n'roll". "Because these numbers invariably back dialogue scenes, there should never be any time for vocals," Welles wrote in a memo to the composer. "The rock'n'roll comes from radio loudspeakers, jukeboxes and, in particular, the radio in the motel... What we want is musical colo[u]r, rather than movement – sustained washes of sound rather than tempestuous melodramatic or operatic scoring."

As CLINTON HEYLIN writes in his biography of Welles, *Despite The System*, "Mancini was allowed to give vent to a form of fusion in the motel scenes, where an ersatz jazz-rock (long before the term was coined) plays interminably through the hotel intercom. Only after the gang members enter Susan's room, confirming that she has entered her worst nightmare, is the music finally shut off. All that remains is a claustrophobic silence."

GORDON JENKINS

Cult records rarely live up to expectations, especially those which have become cyphers in the increasingly crowded world of kitsch'n'camp nostalgia. *Manhattan Tower* has managed to avoid this treatment, principally due to its scarcity. *Manhattan Tower* is a paean to New York, a musical by composer Gordon Jenkins which charts the romance between two young city dwellers. Part narrated, part orchestrated, the ten songs on *Tower* are a guide to the Manhattan of the late Forties/early Fifties – "music and romantic comedy; modern Americana full of the life and love and lore of a big city".

This love song to a city began in 1929 when Jenkins, an underemployed musician, arrived in New York and was bewitched by the skyline, people, moods, and rich twenty-four-hour life. Sixteen years later, he returned as a successful composer to work on *Manhattan Tower*.

It was originally twenty minutes long; the full forty-five minute version was recorded in the Fifties by Jenkins with his orchestra and the RALPH BREWSTER SINGERS for Capital Records. Though tremendously popular in its day, it's now almost impossible to find. As homages to Gotham go, Gordon Jenkins' creation is a towering achievement.

J JOAN AS POLICE WOMAN

Her moniker is fairly unprepossessing (doesn't she want a serious career?). JOAN WASSER started calling herself Joan as Police Woman to distinguish her solo singing career from her work as a violinist. Obviously. And it gives no indication as to what her music – or indeed her voice – might sound like.

Her music – and indeed that voice, that beautiful voice – has been described variously as soul, jazz and thrift-store rock, and a mixture of all three. Examine her lyrics, or listen to her talk about what she does and you'll discover a woman who is passionate about what she does, passionate in her espousal of her craft, and dedicated to finding hope in despair. So she's big on redemption. She does it so well.

By rights she should be a much angrier performer, yet her songs are curious arranged lullabies, sombre tunes with complex lyrics, delivered in a haunting and often exquisite voice. She is the alt LADY GAGA – less dramatic (well, a bit), with better pipes, and a sweeter disposition.

Her forte is the melancholy piano ballad, and it all comes from the heart: her mother's death, being in love, trying to figure out all the stuff in her head (and having seen her interviewed a few times, she certainly appears to have rather a lot of conflicting stuff going on up there). She has played with RUFUS WAINWRIGHT and ANTONY HEGARTY, had a three-year relationship with JEFF BUCKLEY (she addressed him in song on her debut album, *Eternal Flame*: "Just in case you never knew, I won't be the fighter for your eternal flame"), and has composed string arrangements for SCISSOR SISTERS and played violin for NICK CAVE, and LOU REED.

Overtly happier than she used to be, she still stands behind her electric piano on stage, as though she's reluctant to embrace being a proper performer, yet she is mesmerising.

Playing with ANTONY AND THE JOHNSONS in 1999 was a huge turning point for her. "Joining that band changed my life. It gave me a lot of hope when I was a little bit lost." Then, in

2004, Wainwright encouraged her to tour in his band and debut her Joan as Police Woman guise as his support act. Her stage name is a reference to her supposed resemblance to the actress ANGIE DICKINSON, star of the Seventies US cop series *Police Woman*.

J

ELTON JOHN

Los Angeles for me is forever associated with one image, the photograph – taken by TERRY O'NEILL – of Elton John on the blue-carpeted stage at Dodger Stadium in 1975. Elton is sitting at his piano (also covered in blue carpet), wearing a sequined Dodgers baseball kit and is about to launch into "Benny And The Jets" in front of the 80,000-strong crowd. The picture is so vivid you almost expect it to start playing the song, like a musical birthday card.

At the time Elton was the biggest star in the world, and his two shows at the home of the LA Dodgers that year were the pinnacle of his early success. As PAUL GAMBACCINI once said, no single photograph better demonstrates the hold a rock star can have over the public.

"Benny And The Jets" is also the quintessential LA record, and you can guarantee you'll hear it on the radio whenever you visit the city. You'll also hear every other great Seventies song. Most of the great "landscape" driving music was made in the Seventies, so it feels completely natural when the likes of AMERICA's "Ventura Highway", the DOOBIE BROTHERS' "Long Train Runnin'", or LYNYRD SKYNYRD's "Free Bird" come hurtling out of the rental car's speakers – accompanied, of course, by a flash of neon light, a plume of purple smoke, and a wash of dry ice.

Some say that Los Angeles is just New York lying down, although it's a hell of a lot younger; in fact in LA, by the time you're thirty-five, you're older than most of the buildings. You'll certainly be older than the cars, because LA is the

J most car-obsessed city in the world. (The cars are so cool in Hollywood that children don't wear masks on Halloween. Instead they usually dress up as valet parkers.) And if you haven't got a white Range Rover or a Mercedes S65, then frankly you're nobody.

There are more cars in California than people in any of the other states of the United States, while the Los Angeles freeway system handles over twelve million cars on a daily basis. The lucky residents of LA County spend an estimated four days of each year stuck in traffic. Everything revolves around the car here (why else would someone open an all-night, drive-in taxidermist?), and whereas most European films usually involve a small boy and a bicycle, all decent American films involve a car chase (these days with one driver steering the car with his knees because he's got a non-fat double decaf cappuccino in one hand and a cell phone in the other...while the other driver has a brick on the accelerator and a gun in his lap).

There are now so many purpose-built digital radio stations that it's possible to choose what you want to listen to for any journey, whether you want to listen exclusively to music made in the Nineties or the Thirties. On a recent trip to LA, as I drove through Bel Air, past the mansions and the gate lodges of Beverly Hills, past the exotic Chandleresque haciendas, rustling palms, lawn sprinklers, and chirruping crickets, and up into the Hollywood Hills (where it's still possible, if you're wearing a patchwork denim waistcoat and a pair of purple velvet loon pants, to catch a whiff of 1972 patchouli oil, joss stick, and body odour), I found a station pumping out an assortment of Elton John songs, including a few from one of his semi-great forgotten albums of the Seventies, *Rock Of The Westies*.

This is the great lost Elton record, an alternative *Goodbye Yellow Brick Road*, an uneven but fascinating album containing half-a-dozen classic songs: "I Feel Like A Bullet (In The Gun Of Robert Ford)", "Dan Dare (Pilot Of The Future)", "Feed Me", "Street Kids", and "Grow Some Funk of Your Own".

As I listened to the songs in my car, gunning it down Sunset Boulevard with the midday sun and the palms above me, I felt myself being transported back to the Los Angeles of the mid-Seventies. Suddenly I was driving through a bright blue Hockney dreamscape, surrounded by Cinemascope billboards for *Shampoo, Tommy*, and *One Flew Over The Cuckoo's Nest*. All of a sudden my trouser bottoms got a little wider, my lapels turned into aircraft carriers, my cologne became a little more pronounced, my shoes sprouted three-inch stack heels, and my denim waistcoat was suddenly made of silver lamé. Oh, and guess what? I was now sporting a pair of tinted spectacles the size of Texas. There was a copy of *Rolling Stone* on the passenger seat, along with a packet of More cigarettes, a paperback of ROBERT PIRSIG's *Zen And The Art Of Motorcycle Maintenance*, and an Eight-Track cartridge of SUPERTRAMP's *Crisis? What Crisis?*

The early Seventies are always held up as the decade in which Elton made his best records, that collection of extraordinary albums recorded between 1970 and 1975 – *Elton John* (1970), *Tumbleweed Connection* (1970), *Madman Across The Water* (1971), *Honky Chateau* (1972), *Don't Shoot Me I'm Only The Piano Player* (1973), *Goodbye Yellow Brick Road* (1973), *Caribou* (1974), and *Captain Fantastic And The Brown Dirt Cowboy* (1975) – and taken as a whole it is an impressive body of work. But he has had a forty-year career since then, producing another body of work that any major (and we're talking *major*) recording artist would be more than proud of. The thing is, Elton is in it to win it. He thinks you either go for it, or you bow out. There is nothing half-hearted about his appetite for success, which is why he has applied himself to each sector of the entertainment industry with such force. Think of *The Lion King, Billy Elliot*, the Vegas residencies, the soundtracks, the duets, and all the awards – the Oscar, the Golden Globe, the Tony, the Grammys, and the rest. Elton has had more careers than his roadies have had hot dinners.

And then there are the songs, the ones that came after the "canon", all the greatest hits sequels: "Sorry Seems To Be

J

The Hardest Word" (*Blue Moves*, 1976), "Song For Guy" (*A Single Man*, 1978), "Little Jeannie" (*21 At 33*, 1980), "Just Like Belgium" (*The Fox*, 1981), "Blue Eyes" (*Jump Up!*, 1982), "I Guess That's Why They Call It The Blues" (*Too Low For Zero*, 1983), "Sad Songs (Say So Much)" (*Breaking Hearts*, 1984), "Nikita" (*Ice on Fire*, 1985), "Sacrifice" (*Sleeping With The Past*, 1989), "The One" (*The One*, 1992), "Believe" (*Made In England*, 1995), "Something About The Way You Look Tonight" (*The Big Picture*, 1997), "This Train Don't Stop There Anymore" (*Songs From The West Coast*, 2001),and "Tinderbox" (*The Captain And The Kid*, 2006)... for instance. And that's forgetting the 2003 remix of "Are You Ready For Love".

Songs From The West Coast is a particularly good record, a collection of stark, plaintive, piano-led tunes that harks back to classic Elton albums such as *Madman Across The Water* and *Tumbleweed Connection*. Many of these songs echo the mood and arrangements of hits such as "Tiny Dancer", "Someone Saved My Life Tonight", "Levon", and "Mona Lisa's And Mad Hatters"; these include "I Want Love", which sounds like the great lost JOHN LENNON single, and "This Train...", which is as good a song as Elton and BERNIE TAUPIN have ever written. The sound on...*West Coast* is closer to Lennon's *Plastic Ono Band* than any previous Elton John album, and is as far from the PRINCESS DI version of "Candle In The Wind" as the chalk hills of the South Downs are far from the Cheddar Gorge.

"I decided that recording wasn't as much fun as it used to be," said Elton. "I thought if I was going to record again then I'd better be enjoying it. I also wanted to go back to recording just piano, bass, drums, and guitar, just a four-piece, analogue, with hardly any overdubs. I also thought it was really important for the piano to be featured much more than it had been. We got away from synthesizers and went back to being, I hate to use the word, but a bit more organic."

The use of "Tiny Dancer" (possibly Elton's very best song) in CAMERON CROWE's *Almost Famous* also introduced Elton to a whole new audience, one perhaps ignorant of his massive troubadour status in the early Seventies.

I've interviewed Elton many, many times, but when I looked back at all my old interviews with him, I was struck by how much I focused on the luxuriant trappings of fame – the clothes, the houses, the art gallery, the excess. It's easy to get sidetracked by the things surrounding Elton, and always important to remember that he is – first and foremost – a songwriter and piano player. You only have to see him perform once to understand this. The acclaim, and the attention, and the fawning he expects – as one of the most famous men in the world it would be surprising if he didn't– but the real thrill he gets on stage is not from recognition, it's from his own performance, and from watching his fingers run up and down the keyboard, making people smile and cry and dance in the process. Elton is never happier than when performing, losing himself in the moment.

At the turn of the century, he began making more naturalistic records, albums that reflected his growing disaffection with the pop industry, records that echoed earlier records like *Tumbleweed Connection* and *Madman Across The Water*. And in 2010 he started working with LEON RUSSELL, one of the men who inspired him to play piano in the first place.

In 1970, Elton played Los Angeles for the first time. In several landmark gigs at the city's notorious Troubadour in August that year, the piano man became a star in the space of forty-eight hours. It was a true overnight sensation, one that he would never recover from. First came acclaim, then commercial success, and sooner than he could ever have envisioned, global cultural supremacy.

The Troubadour concerts were also important for Elton as it was here that he met one of his heroes, the legendary pianist LEON RUSSELL. "In the late Sixties and early Seventies, the one piano player and vocalist who influenced me more than anybody else was LEON RUSSELL," said Elton. "He was my idol." Shortly afterwards the pair went on to play together at New York's Fillmore East, although it wasn't until 2010 that they actually made a record together.

J

The Union was an album of original material produced by T-BONE BURNETT and featuring songs by Elton and Leon, as well as Burnett and BERNIE TAUPIN. Having been out of touch for the best part of four decades, Elton listened to Leon's music while on safari in Africa in 2009 (he heard a vintage Russell song on his partner DAVID FURNISH's iPod), and was inspired enough to try and reconnect with his idol. The result, *The Union*, was a wonderful piece of work, and a real surprise. The album built on the sound, spontaneity and artifice-free feel of Elton's previous three albums – *Songs From The West Coast* (2001), *Peachtree Road* (2004), and *The Captain And The Kid* (2006) – relying more on artistry and musicianship rather than radio-friendly pop hooks. And because the album was written, sung and performed with LEON RUSSELL – a man for whom gumbo funk had been a calling card for four decades – the record was a genuine evocation of early Seventies West Coast rock, the sort that finds space for R&B, country rock and gospel funk.

The LA sessions for *The Union* (which included BOOKER T, BRIAN WILSON, NEIL YOUNG, and DON WAS) were complicated by the fact that Leon was only just recovering from brain surgery ("because he had spinal fluid pouring out of his nose," said Elton). This was a man who had already had a hip operation, and who walked with a cane. "I was an hour late the first day [of recording]," Russell said. "By then Elton had already written five songs."

Leon Russell was taught to play guitar by ELVIS PRESLEY's guitarist JAMES BURTON, and was a member of the famous WRECKING CREW, the LA session men who played on records produced by the BYRDS, PHIL SPECTOR, the BEACH BOYS, the MAMAS & THE PAPAS, and dozens more. He played on IKE & TINA TURNER's "River Deep, Mountain High", the BYRDS' "Mr Tambourine Man", and HERB ALPERT's "A Taste Of Honey". He wrote "Superstar" for the CARPENTERS, wrote "This Masquerade" (covered by GEORGE BENSON), and played with JOE COCKER (who had a hit with Russell's "Delta Lady", ERIC CLAPTON, and GEORGE HARRISON. He co-owned Shelter Records, and in the early Seventies was rock royalty, "the most luminous of LA luminaries". On his solo records he would mix gumbo with rock'n'roll, mix R&B with gospel, to produce his own type of Americana.

He was sixty-eight when they recorded *The Union*, and before getting the call from Elton, hadn't made a major-label studio recording in nearly two decades.

"I don't know why he just fell of the radar," said Elton about Russell. "It's like *Crazy Heart*... only without the drink and the drugs."

Still passionate about music the way that few big stars are, and passionate in his espousal of everyone from HOT CHIP, ROYKSOPP, and CROWDED HOUSE, to ARCADE FIRE, the SCISSOR SISTERS, and LAURA MARLING, Elton still gets a new batch of CDs from HMV every Monday, and he still plays them all. "I know what makes a number one record," he said. "I have a film company, a record company, an Aids foundation, a publishing company, a management company. So, I have to know what's going on. I'm probably more informed than most heads of any other companies in the entertainment business. I have to be."

ROBERT JOHNSON

King Of The Delta Blues Singers, the 1961 legacy collection of Johnson's work, is still talismanic for many, almost regardless of how old they are. He recorded barely thirty songs, a miniscule, yet somehow perfect offering. As someone said recently, he can't get any more legendary than he already is, and his importance remains forever undiminished. He's just there, like the Mississippi Delta, the twelve-bar key change, or air. "The Stones weren't formed yet, we were just a loose bunch of musicians eyeing each other," said KEITH RICHARDS. "When BRIAN [JONES] pulled out that Robert Johnson, I immediately said to myself, I want to work with Brian. He

J had come up with a record that I had never heard, because Robert was still so obscure at the time. The subject matter of his songs took you into another area of possibilities. That you can write a song about anything, you don't have to confine it to the popular norms, and that was a turn-on with Robert. He almost disappeared, which is amazing for a talent like that, but I guess he's like a shooting star, so briefly on the horizon."

GRACE JONES

"I'm a man-eating machine," sang Grace Jones on her 2009 album *Hurricane,* and anyone who has ever met her will agree. The woman who famously slapped chat show host RUSSELL HARTY across the face on live television in 1981, who starred in the Bond movie *A View To A Kill,* and who not only recorded "Slave To The Rhythm" (one of the greatest singles of the Eighties), but also *Nightclubbing* (the third best album of the same decade) is back with something of an androgynous vengeance.

For many she has always been an acquired taste – there are those who say that her voice has always had the animation of the Speaking Clock – and while others thought her little but a hollow gourd, just a voice-piece for others people's ideas (notably art director JEAN-PAUL GOUDE), for some she will always be the ultimate disco queen, a mirrorball icon.

Even for those who have met her.

I interviewed Grace Jones back in 1986, at the height of her fame, and it's an experience I've never forgotten (well, it left more of an impression on me than my encounters with BIG COUNTRY, or the ROARING BOYS). I was meant to meet her three months previously, when she was due in town to promote her album *Inside Story,* but eventually got to meet her when she came to London to have a cast made of her body for Madame Tussauds. Which obviously made it easy for me to accuse her of being self-obsessed.

"You think I'm narcissistic?" she growled at me, "Well thank you very much. For a while I was terribly vain, but not anymore. When I was modelling I spent half my life staring at thousands of perfect reflections. It got to a stage where I was losing all sense of reality – so after I quit modelling I took all the mirrors out of my house."

Feeling emboldened by too many cups of coffee, I asked her if this hadn't caused havoc with the way she looked.

"That's why I started dressing like a bum. I'd be walking around the house in rags and then I'd go out without stopping to look at myself."

For journalists of my generation, an interview with Grace Jones was always a poisoned chalice, because while you would certainly come away with great copy, there was always the danger that she might belt you round the face, bite your head off, or simply shout at you for being less than expected. Only four days before my interview she had supposedly punched a French journalist for probing too deeply.

For men, of course, there was also the frightening possibility that she might take a shine to you, forcing you to either perform like a Viking, or make your excuses and leave (quickly). I was certain she wasn't going to be interested in me, although when I arrived at her hotel suite that morning she had already drunk half a bottle of champagne... so anything might have happened.

I wanted to ask Grace Jones if she ever shopped in Woolworth, but she was so jet-lagged that the question might have provoked the sudden cancellation of the photo session for the magazine I edited at the time. Instead I asked her if she shopped in London. She didn't. Didn't like London much at all in fact, especially the press. "I've had more misrepresentations than I can handle, and people have told the wickedest lies about me," she said, as I nodded understandingly. "A lot of them have taken their frustrations out on me, and I don't like that because it can wound. Not necessarily me, but those around me. Journalists can be so bad." The Woolworth question moved itself further down the

J

list. "I don't take the English press seriously at all because all they want is dirt... I hate them."

So that certainly put me in my place.

She was, however, extremely beautiful. Still is, I think, even in her sixties. She was outrageously thin, with an AZZEDINE ALAIA waist and beautiful chiselled legs, although her voice was disconcertingly masculine, with an odd cockney lilt – "Alroit?!" She smoked incessantly, too, ate her club sandwich with both hands, and stirred her champagne with one of last night's dirty chopsticks.

At that time she had just finished shooting three films, one of which, *Vamp*, was generally considered to be the worst film anyone had seem since God was a boy, though it was difficult to find anyone who would own up to seeing it. Her film career has not always inspired the most flattering reviews, and one man in particular – the American critic REX REED – had taken it upon himself to carve a career out of carving up Grace's. And Ms Jones wasn't exactly thrilled when I brought him up.

"He says things like, I wouldn't wash my windows with Grace Jones, Grace Jones hisses like a radiator, there is a part of Grace Jones that is always in heat. He even compared me to the she-monster that fights SIGOURNEY WEAVER at the end of *Aliens*." A few months previously JOAN RIVERS had invited both Jones and Reed on the same edition of her TV show. Throughout the Reed interview Grace sat opposite him and drummed her gloves against her tights – Reed, Rivers and the audience all expected her to whack him around the face à la RUSSELL HARTY, but Grace kept her cool whilst Reed probably ruined his boxer shorts. "You should have seen his face, boy was he worried."

But it's hardly surprising, I said, because you are known for your intimidation. Did she need constant recognition?

"No, not constantly. I like a bit of honesty every now and again."

But not too much.

"But not too much."

And that's where I should have left it. Unfortunately, I made some lame joke about her newly-opened restaurant in New York, and she threatened to smash her champagne glass in my face.

But I'm sure she was only joking.

QUINCY JONES

Quincy Jones' most vivid memory of his mother is perhaps not one that many of us have when thinking about our parents. I'd say it was so rare that its lingering existence – burned into Jones' hard drive, no matter how hard he has tried to bury it – would have driven most people to the brink. Of addiction, of aggression, of suicide, of madness.

It was madness where it all started.

When he was ten years old, Quincy and his younger brother Lloyd were taken by his father to see his mother in an asylum, where she had been since she was incarcerated two years previously. One morning they left their home on the south side of Chicago, and drove out to the country. Once inside the hospital, Quincy immediately smelled something putrid, "like sheets soiled with urine and sweat". There were people lying all over the floors, writhing, screaming, curled up into balls. The patients were muttering to themselves, pointing at each other and laughing inanely, making funny, but not-so-funny noises. And then, standing quietly against one of the hospital's interior walls, Quincy saw his mother, Sarah. After acknowledging their presence with a small nod, she began ranting, about Jesus, the Pope, about the boxer JOE LOUIS. Her voice got louder, until she was almost hysterical, waving her arms around in the air.

And then it happened. She stopped throwing herself around, and squatted down on her haunches, before putting her hands behind her knees. Then she defecated into one palm, drew her other hand out from beneath her, and pushed

J

a finger into her own faeces. Then, using her finger as a fork, she lifted it to her open mouth.

Quincy, Lloyd and their father left soon after, driving back to Chicago, crying all the way. Left to fend for themselves in one of the roughest parts of one of the roughest cities in North America during the Depression, with a feckless father and an institutionalised mother, Quincy and his brother ran free, doing small errands for gangsters – "Until I was eleven a gangster was all I wanted to be," Quincy told me – without anything approaching a family life.

"I saw some terrible things back in Chicago," he said when we met last summer. "Dead bodies, piles of bloody money lying on basement tables, dirty cops, dirty women, dead bodies, Tommy guns. I saw it all." He calls the South Side of Chicago, "the biggest ghetto in the world". This was the great iron city, the dangerous, impersonal, mechanical city, a place where your neighbours would kill you if the weather didn't. His brother Lloyd once said, "On the way to school one day when we were six or seven, we stopped and saw this guy hanging by the back of his coat on the first rung of a telephone pole, with an ice pick stuck through his neck. We checked that out and went right on to school."

When Quincy was ten his father remarried, and moved west to Bremerton, near Seattle in Washington. Quincy was now the only black child in his class, exacerbating the sense of alienation he was already experiencing in his new extended family. He took refuge in work, delivering newspapers, shining shoes, picking strawberries, washing windows, and running errands for pimps and prostitutes. He would also hang out at the Sinclair Heights Barbershop, captivated by the voices. He would soon be seduced by all kinds of sounds, and learned to play the trumpet, the drums, the saxophone, and the piano. Inevitably he was soon playing in bars and clubs. He was arrested for smoking grass at the age of fourteen, but was more interested in music than drugs.

Quincy's story has the inevitable epiphany, one that involves him stumbling upon an upright piano while involved in a break-in. "As soon as I hit it, I knew I was gone. The concept of a human being playing music never occurred to me even though it was around me all the time in Chicago. And I knew right there and then that this was what I wanted to do for the rest of my life. It saved my life."

J

Quincy Jones' fingers have touched pretty much every genre of black music since the Thirties, from swing, to jazz, to R&B, to soul, to disco, and most things that came after it. A definitive link between old and new schools (as the DJ ROBBIE VINCENT once said), Quincy worked as an arranger for DIZZY GILLESPIE, as a touring trumpeter, bandleader, composer, arranger and producer, and sauntered between bebop, funk and hip-hop. If the music police ever land on earth, they're going to find Quincy's fingerprints on everything. Known as "Q" to his friends, Quincy, born during the Great Depression, has never stopped working. The man with more Grammy Awards (twenty-seven) than anyone else in pop music, Quincy Jones is a musical FORREST GUMP. He has also composed nearly forty film scores, including *In The Heat Of The Night*, *The Italian Job*, *Body Heat*, *The Pawnbroker*, and *In Cold Blood*. He has worked with RAY CHARLES, MICHAEL JACKSON, LENA HORNE, SARAH VAUGHAN, DUKE ELLINGTON, DIZZY GILLESPIE, FRANK SINATRA, MILES DAVIS, and GEORGE BENSON. He founded *Vibe* magazine, co-produced *The Color Purple*, executive produced *The Fresh Prince Of Bel-Air*, wrote the themes for TV series such as *Ironside* and *Roots*, and has released dozens and dozens of his own records. When NEIL ARMSTRONG and BUZZ ALDRIN landed on the moon in 1969, Aldrin played Quincy's arrangement of "Fly Me To The Moon". To put Quincy Jones in context, BONO says he's the coolest person he's ever met. Which is a bit like LANCE ARMSTRONG telling someone they're the best cyclist he's ever met.

Quincy is the only man to have worked with FRANK SINATRA, MICHAEL JACKSON, and AMY WINEHOUSE, the only man to have successfully used his diplomatic skills on the world's most irascible crooner, the world's most demanding pop icon, and one of the world's most troubled chanteuses.

J

Quincy Jones' emotional jukebox is full and comprehensively compiled. As a musical encyclopedia of the 20th Century it couldn't be more complete. The arc starts in the jazz clubs of Chicago, Seattle, and New York during the late Forties and early Fifties.

"Night after night, as I wandered in and out of clubs, bars, and jook joints with my trumpet beneath my arm and my scores tucked beneath my shirt, a tiny glint of something new began to emerge in my life, something I'd never had before," he wrote in his autobiography. "I had no control over where I lived, no control over my sick mother, no control over my hard-hearted stepmother and my overwrought father. I couldn't change the attic where I slept, or stop the anguished tears of my little brother Lloyd, who sometimes cried himself to sleep at night; I couldn't control the angry whites who still called me nigger when they caught me alone on the street, or the bourgeois, high yella blacks who considered me too poor, too dark, and too uneducated to be a part of their lives. But nobody could tell me how many substitute chord changes I could stick into the bridge of 'Cherokee'. Nobody could tell me which tempo to play 'Bebop', or 'A Night In Tunisia' in."

His first proper band was the CHARLIE TAYLOR BAND, where the prime aim was looking cool. Band members were fined twenty-five cents if they didn't look sufficiently cool. And Quincy was never fined. He was enjoying himself too much.

"Music was the one thing I could control," he said. "It was the one world that offered me freedom."

When he finally got to New York, his eyes were opened wider than they had ever been before. When he was introduced to CHARLIE PARKER, "the four of us took a cab to 139th Street. Bird was sweating a lot. He had a white shirt on and a big belly. One button was off his shirt and I could see some of his meat. We got out of the cab in front of a beat-up tenement and I felt like a million dollars. I was hangin' with Bird. I couldn't believe it. Bird and me." And then Parker conned some dollars out of him to score some heroin, and promptly disappeared.

He travelled all over America, visiting the South for the first time. In Texas, the band he was with pulled into a little town around five in the morning; hanging from the steeple of the largest church in town was an effigy of a black man. On the bus, the musicians sat in four groups: the nod squad, or junkie mainliners; the potheads; the juicers; and the gamblers. Quincy, meanwhile, was a ladies man, ladies of any age – "I loved me some thirty-five and forty-year-old ladies too..."

Quincy lost his virginity at the age of eleven, a fairly telling indication of how his life in this area would be spent. On the road, he had a girl in every town, every state, every country. There were many flings, including one with the singer DINAH WASHINGTON. One morning, having spent the night with Washington, Quincy's home phone rang, and his wife picked it up in another room at exactly the same time he did. "You know what, Mr Green-ass Grasshopper? In case you forgot, I got your li'l ass drunk last night and we did the doogie three times..." He went to Stockholm with Lionel Hampton in 1953, where the women were so intrigued by them that they ran their hands across their faces, to see if they were real. "The women thought we were made of chocolate... When I got back to the States... I kept going like I was in Europe, dogging it. I slept with women I was working with and those on the outside – black, white, Asian. Some turned me down. One woman, a Broadway star, told me, 'You're too short,' and another one said, 'No, baby, you ain't got enough money for me – I can't go there.' But most were game." There were groupies, hookers, Playboy bunnies, and girls of every hue who just wanted to sleep with a cool, good-looking musician with a wicked glint in his eye.

Travel and sex didn't just broaden his mind, it broadened his horizons, and soon he was arranging for FRANK SINATRA (at the age of twenty-five!), having hit records with LESLEY GORE, and eating lunch with PICASSO. It was one sunny summer afternoon on the Cote d'Azur. "He ordered sole meunière, ate the fish carefully, arranged his silverware neatly when he

J

J was done, and gently inched the plate with the fish bones into the sunlight, where it became parched enough to serve as the master's canvas. Then he took marker pens and turned the bones into a multi-coloured PICASSO design." When Quincy's wife asked for the cheque, PICASSO pushed his plate forward, as that was his way of paying. Quincy said to his wife, "That's who I want to be when I grow up."

These days, grown-up Quincy lives way up in the Bel Air mountains, in a 20,000-square foot mansion bought six years ago from JULIO IGLESIAS, far away from the hissing of summer lawns in Beverly Hills. This is real luxury, a proper Hollywood mansion with extraordinary views across Los Angeles that stretch all the way to Long Beach. The house is full of soul, as well as the trinkets of success. This is a house of spoils, a house of acknowledgement, the recognition of a creative life lived to the full. The walls of his screening room are covered by framed movie posters of many of the films he's scored, while the rest of this wing, the music wing, is full of gold discs, Emmy's, Grammy's, framed album covers, posters of everyone from FRANK SINATRA to BILL CLINTON, a couple of directors chairs, silver table frames containing photographs of Quincy with just about every Triple-A famous person in the world, art lying on the floor waiting to be hung or mounted, and framed caricatures. There is a huge wall-mounted presentation box from Epic Records, full of mini gold discs, "For being the No.1 producer in the world." You have to be careful how you tread in case you knock over an Oscar or ASCAP gong.

The main living section of this wing is an enormous circular room, surrounded by a tropical garden, containing over one hundred speakers, powered by his three Creston Sound Systems, which pump out jazz and classical music all day (from CDs, cassettes, DVDs, vinyl, DAT tapes, etc). At the back of the house, in the middle of the driveway, a leafless tree is covered in Chinese lanterns.

Did he have a hand in designing the house?

"Oh course I designed it," said Quincy, laughing. "I can see as well as hear!"

And did he record here?

"No man. I don't want a recording studio in my house, man, don't want dudes running round at three o'clock in the morning in their underwear. The studio is a sacred place, man. It's like a mosque, a church."

He had greeted me in prime cockney, taught to him by MICHAEL CAINE when he was scoring *The Italian Job* at the end of the Sixties. "He taught me so much rhyming slang, it's the damnedest thing." (Quincy and Caine were born in the same year, the same month, the same day and hour – "celestial twins".)

He is one of those people who tend to answer a dozen questions at once, probably because a) he's been interviewed so many times that he has a spiel that he uses on journalists and people he hasn't met before, and/or b) it's a defence mechanism. When I transcribed the tape, Quincy barely paused for breath, moving from problems in Darfur, his humanitarian escapades with BONO, BARACK OBAMA's budget problems, JOE PESCI's ability to sing jazz, gangsters old and new, black and white. It's almost a stream of consciousness that takes him around the world and in and out of the years, moving from Brazil to Paris with ease, via charity, philanthropic duties, campaigning, his various humanitarian projects, family tragedies, a pinball monologue masquerading as a conversation.

"I don't know if Obama is a two term President," he said at one point. "Obama has a lot of obstacles. He inherited a lot of stuff, and every President is always responsible for what was left behind by the last guy. Ten trillion dollars on Iraq? Come on, get out of here. However, I think there's a part of America that can't change its thinking, that can't handle having a brother in the White House."

Quincy Jones is his own soap opera. In the absence of emotional security, for years he buried himself in work. Running away from confrontation, death, family, responsibility, but without the means to do it. This absorption in his career has had a huge bearing on his personal life: he

J

has been married three times and has had seven children, six of whom are girls. He was married to JERI CALDWELL from 1957 to 1966; they had one daughter, JOLIE JONES LEVINE. His marriage to Jeri finally collapsed in 1966, shortly after Quincy moved west, to Los Angeles. He then married ULLA ANDERSON, fathering Martina and Quincy Delight III. Ulla and Quincy divorced in 1974. "I wasn't in any better shape for the second marriage," he said. "Probably just trying to create that next again." That year he married the actress PEGGY LIPTON, a union that lasted until 1990; they had two daughters, actresses Kidada and Rashida. He also had a brief affair with CAROL REYNOLDS which resulted in another daughter, Rachel. Between 1991 and 1995 he lived with the actress NASTASSJA KINSKI, and they have another daughter, Kenya Julia Miambi Sarah. Quincy has said his midlife nervous breakdown was due in part to a realisation that he had let certain members of his family down. In LINDA BAYER's book, *Quincy Jones: Overcoming Adversity*, she says, "Like jazz, friendship has a certain degree of improvisation, but in a marital context Quincy had more trouble with commitment than spontaneity. Likewise, Quincy made friends with ease and found plenty of brides." She rightly points out that he had never come to terms with his father's treatment of his mother, "which probably interfered with Quincy's own ability to establish a lasting marriage. As a child, Quincy blamed his mother for leaving but didn't question his father's conduct in abandoning a sick wife and carrying on with other women. Without the role model of a father to teach Quincy how to love and respect a wife, he had difficulty sharing his life with a woman and accepting the limitations marriage entails."

Obviously, what Quincy talks about more than anything is music. He even thinks about music when he's cooking, thinking about orchestration, thinking about the power of lemon: "It's like a piccolo in a symphony orchestra, it's the most dominant instrument. And lemon works in the same way. It takes out garlic, hot sauce, onions, everything. I'm always thinking about music. It all ties together. Whenever I think about melody I think about charcoal, then watercolours, then oils... it's crazy man."

His latest passion is the GLOBAL GUMBO GROUP, a joint venture with the United Arab Emirates entrepreneur BADR JAFAR, with a mission to develop multi-media opportunities "across all entertainment platforms" including music, film, television, publishing, and digital applications, in the Middle East and North Africa. The group includes a bunch of musicians that he is predictably enthusiastic about. It's a project that appeals to him because of the amount of travelling it involves, and if Quincy is addicted to anything it's probably music, women, and circumnavigating the globe. Hardly surprising when he has survived two aneurysms. They happened two months apart in the mid-Seventies, and he almost died. "I went to that place where your life flashes before you... My whole life was on its way passed my eyes, but then I drifted back to consciousness." He can't play the trumpet anymore because of this, and has a metal clip in his skull, meaning it's fun going through customs.

Humanitarian endeavours are rarely far from his agenda. In 2007, along with the Harvard School of Public Health, he advanced the health and well being of children worldwide through Project Q, challenging world leaders "to provide essential resources to enable young people to achieve their full potential". And through the Quincy Jones Foundation he tries to raise awareness and financial support for initiatives that support global children's issues in areas of conflict (particularly the Gulf Coast post Katrina). He is involved in dozens of such schemes, and they appear to take up most of his time.

"I've seen what happens to guys when they retire," he says. "They just dry up. But I feel like I'm just starting out. I really do. We made a lot of mistakes with Live Aid and 'We Are The World', so BONO and I decided to study this stuff to see if we could do it right. And so we studied it like it was a science, you know? I've seen a million dollars worth of food just sitting in the desert, spoiling, so unless you do it properly, you're doing it badly. And some of the stuff I've been doing on my own, well, it just seems like the right way forward.

J

"You know, jazz musicians have a tendency to shack up with music first and then court and marry it much later. We never cared about money and fame because jazz was the wrong kind of music for that. We just loved the music. But it was jazz that pushed me into becoming better as a musician and trying different musical styles. When I was young, guys like COUNT BASIE and CLARK TERRY took care of me so it's only natural that I should take care of the young ones, too."

For Quincy, it really is all about the kids.

"All the experiences with my mother were rough," he told me. "So rough it eventually killed my brother. You see the Korean lady who brought us our drinks, well she was married to him for thirty-three years. They took my mother away in a straightjacket when I was seven, and my stepmother was like the mother in *Precious*. I couldn't handle either of them, so I decided to make music my mother. I blanked everything out. My brother didn't do that and he died at sixty-five years old. He couldn't process it, and I understand that man. We didn't have a relationship with our mothers so we had to discover who we were, you know? Maybe that's why I feel so passionate about kids in similar situations. Because the kids don't cause all this shit, it's their parents."

Quincy is a keen – no, a *huge* – student of musical history, and unlike most people from his generation, adores hip-hop. "Rap comes from way back," he said recently. "It comes from the word *imbongi*, which is a poet/praise shouter who is the go-between from the leader to the people. In 1994 NELSON MANDELA had an *imbongi* at his inauguration, but they go a long way back in African history. It also goes back to the *griots* that ALEX HALEY talks about in *Roots* – the oral historians. It's old, man! It also comes via all of the American black music and the INKSPOTS, and the MILLS BROTHERS, and even Motown; they all have talking things. Even though it wasn't rhythmic rap, you can still see the connection."

He continued in this vein with me, "Rappers are geniuses, just like the bebop musicians were. I could feel this urban thing building up back in the Seventies, saying that if you won't accept me in your society then we're going to start our own society. They're brilliantly creative people. MELLE MEL – who I think is the CHARLIE PARKER of the hip-hop world – RUSSELL SIMMONS, RUN DMC, ICE T. KOOL MOE DEE, the SUGARHILL GANG, all the originals. It's the same attitude as bebop – jamming, rapping freestyle, improvisation, just like a bebop trumpet solo. It's a third genre, it's not the same as a singer or a musician."

Obviously, in some people's eyes, Quincy's career has been defined by his work with MICHAEL JACKSON. When Jackson decided to make his first proper solo album, there was one man whose advice he sought first. He had worked with Quincy on *The Wiz*, and had started to put his trust in him. The two met on the set on the day that Jackson had to rehearse a scene in which he read a Socrates quote. When the crew started stifling their laughs when he spoke – he pronounced it "Soh-crates", to rhyme with "low rates" – he knew he'd screwed up. It was Quincy who whispered the correct pronunciation in his ear. And when Jackson asked Quincy to recommend someone to produce his record, the producer naturally suggested himself.

They started making the record in earnest in LA, with Quincy indulging his young protégé, taking his ideas seriously, and making sure he was comfortable in the studio. He also surrounded him with experienced, non-confrontational musicians, and offered Jackson hundreds of songs to choose from. Weirdly, their work ethics dovetailed, almost perfectly. "Now I'm a pretty strong drill sergeant when it comes to steering a project," said Jones, "but in Michael's case it's hardly necessary."

When *Off The Wall* was eventually released, in August 1979, the extraordinary collection of songs – "Don't Stop 'Til You Get Enough", "She's Out Of My Life", the title track, and Stevie Wonder's "I Can't Help It", etc – showed an entertainer coming of age, wrapped in the kind of sophisticated packaging (Jackson was wearing a tuxedo) that was automatically going to appeal to an older, wider demographic than before.

J   This wider demographic turned out to be a lot wider than either of them imagined, although the album's success was nothing when compared to the success of its 1982 follow-up, *Thriller*, which would go on to become the bestselling album of all time, with sales estimated in excess of fifty million copies worldwide. Containing some of the most famous songs of the Eighties – "Billie Jean", "Beat It", "Wanna Be Startin' Somethin'" – the album still resonates, and was only recently re-released. These were the first "black" records to be played on MTV, being so successful that mainstream media couldn't afford to ignore them. (Perversely, Quincy initially didn't want to include the album's second single "Billie Jean" on the record – it was once eleven minutes long – not least because he thought some might think Jackson was singing about the tennis player, Billie Jean King.)

They worked together on *Thriller*'s successor, *Bad*, released in 1987, an inevitable disappointment that still ended up selling over thirty million units. (BARBRA STREISAND was offered the album's big duet "I Just Can't Stop Loving You", but allegedly turned it down on account of the age gap between her and Jackson. PRINCE was also going to be involved at one point. After a first meeting, PRINCE said to Quincy, "This is going to be a hit with or without me, man.")

By the time of 1991's *Dangerous*, Jackson had tired of Jones – foolishly, in many experts' opinions. In J. RANDY TARABORRELLI's biography, *Michael Jackson: The Magic & The Madness*, he writes, "...Michael no longer wanted to work with Quincy because he felt that the producer had become too possessive of him and his work, and had taken too much credit for it. Michael was still miffed that Quincy gave him a tough time about 'Smooth Criminal' – Quincy didn't want it on the *Bad* album. For Quincy's part, he felt that Michael had become too demanding and inflexible. With emotions running so high, the partnership that had once sold millions and millions of albums had soured. Still, Quincy figured he would work with Michael, again. He was never informed otherwise."

Although they fell out, Quincy never stopped being in awe of Jackson's talent, his myopic dedication to his craft. Initially, he couldn't believe Jackson's professionalism, his devotion to study (for instance he would watch tapes of gazelles and cheetahs and panthers to imitate their natural grace). In his autobiography, Quincy talks about Jackson's dedication at length. "At his place in Havenhurst, he used to have a mouthy parrot with a lot of attitude as well as a boa constrictor named Muscles. One day Muscles was missing. They looked all over the property, inside and out, and after two days they finally found him dangling from the parrot's cage, with the parrot's beak sticking out of his mouth. He'd swallowed that sucker whole and couldn't back his head out of the bars because he hadn't digested the bird yet. In a way, that's a metaphor for Michael's life after *Thriller*, because at a certain point, he couldn't get back out of the cage. It all became overwhelming for him."

Up in his Bel Air mansion, surrounded by the dozens of gold and silver discs celebrating Jackson and Jones' success, Quincy was sanguine about his relationship with his former protégé. "You know, I always deal in forgiveness and I'd forgiven Michael a long time before he died. We did some amazing work together, produced some remarkable, special records, and you can never forget that. You shouldn't. I forgive people because I expect people to do the same with me. If you don't forgive then it's a poison, and it eats you up and takes hold of you. Me and Michael had some amazing times together, unforgettable times."

At the end of 2010, Quincy released *Q: Soul Bossa Nostra,* one of those albums that pairs a living legend with contemporary stars, the type of record that's been attempted by FRANK SINATRA, TONY BENNETT, SERGIO MENDES – or anyone who obviously has more behind than in front of them (it's to their credit that the ROLLING STONES haven't done this – yet – as it would hardly be unexpected to hear of a new collection of "classics" reinterpreted by the band, helped along by the likes of JOHN LEGEND, LENNY KRAVITZ, FOO FIGHTERS,

J

J

JOHN HOMME, CALEB FOLLOWILL, or LADY GAGA). The album is a compilation of new versions of some of his more well-known recordings, by AKON, LUDACRIS, MARY J. BLIGE, SNOOP DOGG, USHER, AMY WINEHOUSE and, judging from the sleevenotes, seemingly hundreds of others. If it weren't so engaging – AKON's version of the SHUGGIE OTIS song "Strawberry Letter 23" that was made famous in 1977 by the BROTHERS JOHNSON (produced by Quincy) is one of the best covers of the last ten years – it would be gauche and so terribly self-aggrandising. Strangely, most of it works, the producers treating the material with enough reverence to make the juxtapositions seem perfectly natural.

The album also contains the last song AMY WINEHOUSE released before she died, a version of LESLEY GORE's "It's My Party", which was originally produced by Quincy in 1963. Winehouse's version is pretty dismal, and one wonders how long MARK RONSON, who produced it, had to spend in the studio with his editing tools to get something that was just about good enough to release.

Quincy first experienced Winehouse when he appeared at the NELSON MANDELA 90th birthday tribute concert in London, in 2008. He was backstage and a man came up to him and asked if he would mind meeting his daughter. "I had no idea who it was," he said at the time. "She got on her knees and she kissed my hand. It was AMY WINEHOUSE, and she started talking music, music! I had no idea that she was that astute; she was amazing. Reminded me of NAOMI [CAMPBELL] a little bit, my baby. Sweet as she could be. I told her, 'Why are you treating your life like this?' I've got six daughters so... we bonded. Everybody back here said, 'There's no way you'll get AMY WINEHOUSE on this record.' And we just let it go. Amy did it herself. At first she was going to do 'You Don't Own Me'. Then she changed her mind and wanted to do 'It's My Party'. It touched me very much."

"*Soul Bossa Nostra* was started about three years before with TIMBALAND," Quincy told me. "In Florida he gave me a big dinner party and said he'd like to do a hip-hop tribute

to me, opening it up to all of the hip-hop community. And
so everybody was picking their own songs, what they liked,
even the sweet little AMY WINEHOUSE. When I met her at the
Mandela concert she said, 'I've known your music ever since
you were my age, twenty-four years old, when you did "The
Swinging Miss D" with DINAH WASHINGTON.' I was absolutely
shocked by her knowledge, but then I was shocked by what
happened to her. I saw the sweet side of Amy, as I always
try and go for the sweet side of people. Naomi, who has been
like my daughter for nineteen years, she has lots of anger
management issues, but I always look for the sweet side, like
I did with Amy. It was kinda creepy in a way that her last
release was on my record. Even weirder that MARK RONSON
was almost my son-in-law, because he nearly married my
daughter, Rashida. When he proposed he filled out the *New
York Times* crossword puzzle with the words, Will you marry
me? But Amy? Well, she was going through a lot of changes."

The album's title is apt, as Quincy Jones is nothing if not
the Godfather. I remember once when NAOMI CAMPBELL was in
my office in London trying to get hold of PRINCE for something
or other she was trying to do for *GQ*, and for her the Route
One option was to call Quincy on his mobile. It was the wrong
time of day (Quincy was probably asleep), but the message
she left was indicative of the relationship she shares with
him, and probably indicative of the relationship he has with
hundreds of others. "Hi Q, it's Naomi. How are you, Daddy?
I need your help so please call me back. Love you, miss you."
Quincy is not just the conduit, he is the switchboard, the
hub and the nub, the control tower. And you're in a holding
pattern until it's time for Quincy to bring you in. You come to
Quincy for introductions. You come to Quincy to get things
started, to make things happen. You come to Quincy for
advice. And to have doors opened and shut. The Godfather.
It's a sobriquet the man wears lightly, knowing perhaps that
he's in this position by dint of still being around.

When he was the music editor of *The Face* back in the
Eighties, DAVID TOOP said that it wasn't unusual for people

J to come up to him at parties and gigs and discuss whatever it was he had written about that month. They might discuss the nuances of an album's production, songwriting structure, TROUBLE FUNK's ability to make an entire audience bounce up and down as one, blah blah blah. And invariably they'd end the conversation with, "So, is it any good?"

After all the spinning adjectives, the hand-finished opinion, and the hours and hours of typing, he felt all his readers really wanted was a thumbs up or a thumbs down. Well, you could spend weeks trawling through the highs and lows of his long and labyrinthine career and come to the conclusion that – simply put – Quincy's had more thumbs up than most people who have had careers of his length. Having said that, there aren't many people who have *had* careers of such length. This is the man who has touched the lives of LIONEL HAMPTON, RAY CHARLES, CHARLIE PARKER, DIZZY GILLESPIE, TOOTS THIELEMANS, MICHAEL JACKSON, STEVEN SPIELBERG, FRANK SINATRA, EDDIE VAN HALEN, DINAH WASHINGTON, SIDNEY POITIER, STEVIE WONDER, PATTI AUSTIN, MARVIN GAYE, WILL SMITH, TUPAC, OPRAH, and hundreds, thousands more.

As MILES DAVIS once said, Quincy is a man who can walk into any room without being phased, "Certain paperboys can go in any yard with any dog and they won't get bit. He just has it."

"In 1999, Quincy and I travelled to meet POPE JOHN PAUL II together," said BONO. "We were involved with the Jubilee 2000 Drop the Debt Campaign, a worldwide attempt to get governments to cancel the old, unpayable debts of the poorest countries. We headed for the outskirts of Rome on a mission to enlist the Pope's support. I cannot speak for Quincy, but I confess I was a little intimidated as we entered Castel Gandolfo, impressed by the sense of mystery and authority, by the Swiss Guard with their muskets and their uniforms designed by LEONARDO DA VINCI. The Pontiff was very frail. I was moved by the heroic effort he made just to stand and greet each one of us. Amid all the grandeur and trepidation, Quincy whispered to me, 'Check... out... the shoes.' The shoes of the fisherman on this particular day were burgundy wingtips with light tan ribbed socks. Q said softly with admiration in his voice, 'The cat is wearing pimp shoes. Stylin'!'"

J

JANIS JOPLIN

Janis was noticed during that period in the late Sixties when self-expression started to be graded in the same way as talent. She used all her internal problems to fuel her external expression of self, and so became notorious for making a spectacle of herself. She had a black voice, a taste for men and drugs, and perhaps the industry's largest inferiority complex. A sad role model, she died aged twenty-seven, before she had the opportunity to reinvent herself as – oh, let me see – BARBRA STREISAND, STEVIE NICKS, KATE BUSH, whoever. People love "Piece Of My Heart", but then everyone does.

JOURNEY'S "DON'T STOP BELIEVIN'"

If you are ever asked about television's greatest moment, there obviously can only be one answer: the final two minutes of the final episode of the best programme ever broadcast, *The Sopranos* (first shown on June 10, 2007). In the final scene, when TONY SOPRANO glances upwards and the screen falters and turns to black, many of us thought our Sky+ facility had decided to implode at the least opportune moment in TV history. Although, as the credits began to roll, we realised that this was perhaps the only way for DAVID CHASE's epic family saga to extinguish itself. Chase says that the show's audience was always bifurcated, and that on one sofa you had a small army who only wanted to see the Bada Bing mob

J whack people, while on the other you had another bunch that were far more interested in the family dynamic.

"I sort of knew that the people who wanted the big bloodbath at the end were not going to be thrilled with the ending, but what I did not realise was how angry those people would get," said Chase. "And it was amazing how long it went on. Especially when you figure that we had a rather significant war going on, and still do."

Ultimately the show's finale was all about the conflict. The theme of the final episode, No. 86, was "Made In America", as much of a reference to Iraq as it was to the financial comfort zone many US citizens found themselves in. Chase says he didn't want to be didactic about it, but all we needed to know about the subtext was there on Tony and Carmela's faces when their son AJ tells them he wants to join up. And the final song in the final episode of the greatest television show ever made, the record that will forever be synonymous with closure? Journey's "Don't Stop Believin'", the hugely successful single from their 1981 album, *Escape*. Which certainly confused the hell out of me.

"It didn't take much time at all to pick it, but there was a lot of conversation after the fact," said DAVID CHASE. "I did something I'd never done before: in the location van, with the crew, I was saying, 'What do you think?' When I said, 'Don't Stop Believin',' people went, 'What? Oh my god!' I said, 'I know, I know, just give a listen,' and little by little, people started coming around." When the episode was aired, reactions to the denouement were mixed. "I hear some people were very angry, and others were not," said Chase. "Which is what I expected."

Since *The Sopranos* has ended, "Don't Stop Believin'" has become a karaoke classic, as popular as any ABBA, or TAKE THAT song. Journey's lead singer, STEVE PERRY, refused to let Chase use the song until he knew the fate of the leading characters, and didn't give final approval until three days before the episode aired. He feared that the song would be remembered as the soundtrack to Tony's demise, until Chase assured him that this would not be the case. Strangely, he was right. In 2009 it was performed on the pilot episode of hit US TV series *Glee*, and has now become the bestselling digital song not released in the 21st Century.

Joy Division/New Order

The journey from 1981's "Ceremony", the first New Order record, which was really the last Joy Division record, to 1983's "Blue Monday" was a transformative one, taking them from concrete underpass guitar rock to a weird disco mélange that had its roots in Sparks' "Beat The Clock", and Sylvester's "You Make Me Feel (Mighty Real)" – raincoats to ironic sequins in a twenty-four-month swoop. Like the Smiths, New Order always attracted their fair share of tearaways, and their gigs were often raucous affairs; whereas being at a Joy Division gig was a bit like finding yourself in a huge Lowry painting, surrounded by stooping young men with intense looks, choppy fringes and Doctor Marten shoes.

MILES KANE

K

Him out of the LAST SHADOW PUPPETS (the superduo he formed in 2007 with his friend, ALEX TURNER of the ARCTIC MONKEYS), Kane released his debut album *Colour Of The Trap* in the spring of 2011, a frenzy of snappy pop songs that channelled the spirit of HANK MARVIN, the YARDBIRDS, SCOTT WALKER, and early Motown. The music appeared to make perfect sense, even if it felt a little secondhand, and appeared to hover in a world that had yet to experience the Seventies, the Eighties, the Nineties, or the Noughties.

NICK KENT

It's not so surprising that rock stars are often disparaging about journalists. After all, having been courted and feted early in their careers, it's natural for them to feel betrayed when these self same writers start clinically monitoring their descent. "Journalists are a species of foul vermin," said the fleetingly equable LOU REED once. "I mean, I wouldn't hire people like you to guard my sewer."

But then there are journalists, and there are journalists called Nick Kent.

Towards the end of the Eighties I became involved in writing a book about the legacy of JIM MORRISON, and spent over six months travelling to Paris, New York and back, meeting Morrison's common-law wife (who at that time had yet to be interviewed by anyone about the singer) as well as many of his friends, colleagues and associates. I also spent days hanging out at the singer's grave in Père Lachaise, interviewing backpacking Norwegians who'd come to pay homage to him. But one key figure proved elusive: the rather self-aggrandising biographer DANNY SUGERMAN, who co-wrote the notorious DOORS tome *No One Here Gets Out Alive*.

Having created his own little industry from posthumous DOORS-related material, he didn't appear inclined to help any rival biographers. Understandable, really.

I persisted, as there were certain questions about Morrison that I thought only Sugerman could answer. Having tried unsuccessfully to get through to him, I asked a friend to help. This he did by drafting a letter – back then, actually a fax – to Sugerman, a letter than began: "Dear Danny, You might remember me. I once OD'd in your bathroom with IGGY POP in 1974..." Only Nick Kent could have started a letter like that.

One of the foremost music journalists of his generation, Kent made his name as a writer on the *NME* in the early Seventies, alongside CHARLES SHAAR MURRAY, IAN MACDONALD, and PETE ERSKINE. FRANK ZAPPA famously once said, "Rock journalism is people who can't write, preparing stories based on interviews with people who can't talk, in order to amuse people who can't read." He wasn't far wrong, though Kent was never just a music journalist. Like HUNTER S. THOMPSON, NIK COHN, and LESTER BANGS before him, there exists around Kent an almost mythic glow. Degenerate poseur, celebrity drug addict, and genius wordsmith, he is a man who has lived rock'n'roll to the full. ("I could tell you stories about Nick Kent that would uncurl the hair in your Afro," said MORRISSEY in 1990.) During the Seventies, Kent was as famous for his drug intake as he was for his journalism, and from 1974 to 1988 was addicted to heroin, cocaine, methadone and various tranquilisers. "At the age of nineteen I started smoking hashish in earnest," he says, "and then moved on to speed and cocaine. Finally I was offered some heroin, and that was it for me. It was like being in heaven, it was ecstasy. I thought: this is worth getting lost for. But I got hooked and it took me fourteen years to kick it. The drug robbed me of my writing talent [not true] and I'm still angry at myself for getting so involved, but it was so seductive. I was on a death trip – if I hadn't got myself off I would be into crack by now. I should be insane. Or dead. I've always felt a bit like Blind Lemon Kent, you know, always second best [patently not true]."

If you were a rock writer in the early Seventies then sex and drugs came with the territory, as they still do to a certain extent (standing in a toilet cubicle with a girl in one hand and a rolled up £10 note in the other). When Kent kicked into gear – so to speak – rock journalism was going through one of its golden periods. Due largely to *NME* editor NICK LOGAN, during the Seventies the paper became legendary in Britain for its acerbic, cynical and occasionally puerile attitude towards the music industry in general and rock stars (any rock star) in particular.

In 2010, Kent finally published his memoir, *Apathy For The Devil*, an extraordinary recollection of his own Seventies, the decade that made him famous, the decade that caused him all the problems. In 1994 Kent published *The Dark Stuff*, a collection of his finest music journalism, a book to rank alongside GRIEL MARCUS's *Mystery Train*, NIK COHN's *Awopbopaloobop Alopbamboom*, and JON SAVAGE's *England's Dreaming*. *Apathy For The Devil* might even be better than that, charting, as it does, Kent's tawdry tales of sex and drugs and rock'n'roll with – among many others – the ROLLING STONES, DAVID BOWIE, LED ZEPPELIN, and the SEX PISTOLS. As he says himself, his story would come to mirror that of the decade itself, as he slipped into excess and ever worsening heroin use.

With a knack for decoding those stars who display little but a desire to be famous, and who rebel against nothing but personal imposition, Kent himself has rarely hidden his light under a bushel. "I happen to believe," he once told me, "that *The Dark Stuff* contains some of the greatest, most truly heroic stories of my time and generation... and no-one else has written them quite like me. This book has authority."

Good rock journalism should highlight the power, the glory and the depravity of rock music, not just the theory. It should concentrate on the flavour of rock, not just the aftertaste. It's all very well getting in a tizzy over the "validity" of DAVID BOWIE's *Station To Station*, or discussing its place in the "rock canon", but what kind of drugs was the Dame taking when he recorded it? And whose drugs?

K   It goes without saying that not all rock stars take too kindly to this type of speculation, increasingly viewing it as some kind of gross intrusion, incompatible with their own POV. But if journalism doesn't offer to say the unsaid (if not always the unspeakable), then it is little but PR. And as for Lou Reed, well, to hell with him (and his dreadful records). Compared to Reed, Nick Kent was always more fascinating, and certainly better company.

Kent is, when all is said and done, the definitive rock'n'roller. Towards the end of 1986, Nick was dining with his friends David Bowie and Iggy Pop in a little Chinese restaurant in Gerrard Street, in London's Soho. Confronted with a triumvirate of pop icons, the confused, if star-struck, waitress approached the man who most looked like a rock star for his autograph. Bowie and Iggy were shocked. Nick was flattered.

The Killers

Inspired by Oasis, and obsessed with the E-Street Band, Brandon Flowers' band will be remembered in part for bringing the refrain "I've got soul but I'm not a soldier" (from "All These Things That I've Done") into popular parlance. Flowers was always a more than elegant frontman, and the band were robust, metallic, and careful to invest everything they did with the required amount of magic and stagecraft. Almost accidentally they came up with the best Christmas song of the 21st Century so far: "A Great Big Sled". Oh, and Flowers is a Mormon.

The Kills

Once called *Gossip Girl*-endorsed reps for an underground sound and a fashionably sleazy aesthetic, Jamie Hince and Alison Mosshart's band were a photo-fit example of noir

pop: the skinny, sulky, edgy genre that has a through-line
that goes back all the way to GENE VINCENT via the VELVET
UNDERGROUND, JIM MORRISON, PATTI SMITH, the CRAMPS, the
JESUS AND MARY CHAIN, and everyone else.

Having made three fairly well-received albums – 2003's
Keep On Your Mean Side, 2005's *No Wow*, and 2008's
Midnight Boom (what awful titles) – Mosshart wandered off
to work with JACK WHITE in the jam band, the DEAD WEATHER.
She came back two years later and in 2011 she and Hince
released the grimy *Blood Pressures*. "The reason people like
our records and like to see us play is that we make them
uncomfortable," said Mosshart. "I'm not trying to be a safety
band. We're doing something that's a little dangerous, and
I'm sorry if anyone gets upset. I'm not REALLY that sorry."

The Kills are a standard issue alt prototype, and the
oddest thing about them is Hince's marital status: he is KATE
MOSS's very own WAG. JAMIE HINCE is a HAB.

KINGS OF LEON

They are a classic example of a hot band with scale. It's
more difficult to dance to a Kings Of Leon track than, say,
something by KYLIE MINOGUE or HOT CHIP, yet they have such
cross-gender appeal that dancing is mandatory wherever
they play. Whenever I think of the band, which, I have to
admit, is not often, I think of the epigram at the start of ROB
SHEFFIELD's *Talking To Girls About Duran Duran* –it was
said by the keyboard player for LCD SOUNDSYSTEM, "Look at
the two people dancing on either side of you. If you don't see
a girl, you are dancing incorrectly."

K

ROLAND KIRK

Kirk played soul jazz, hard bop, and many standards, before wandering off into the scary woods of fusion. He was a showman, a virtuoso who revelled in improv, and would play three horns at once, or play the flute through his nose. *Rip, Rig & Panic* (from 1965) was his first big album, and then came *The Inflated Tear* two years later, one of the most haunting jazz albums of the time – Creole-inspired. This album is his reaction to his blindness: on being diagnosed with an eye disease at the age of two, he was given the wrong medicine and was blinded. He said he could remember the last minute he could see, and the first minute he couldn't. And both are on this record. It is a favourite of BJORK's – "primitive and instinctive," she calls it. Note: Kirk played the flute on "Soul Bossa Nova" by QUINCY JONES.

KOOP

In 2001 Koop released *Waltz For Koop*, a lounge-core cash-in that nevertheless was so full of jazz it almost felt "genuine". Koop were another example of PoMoMoR (PostModernMiddleoftheRoad), a musical genre you may have heard in the last branch of the Body Shop you inadvertently wandered into. After the easy listening revival of 1994, the likes of KOOP, ZERO 7, AIR, ROYKSOPP, GROOVE ARMADA, and LEMON JELLY seemed content to lay muted trumpets over hip-hop beats until the cows came home (around five in the morning, bleary-eyed and looking for milk). The often redoubtable NICK HORNBY called this, "A cliché, lazy shorthand for a sort of vacuous, monied-up hip."

KRAFTWERK

The best passive-aggressive dance band since the age of swing. Have never made a bad record and probably never will.

LENNY KRAVITZ

A friend of mine who used to work at MTV used to enjoy calling Lenny Kravitz a wuss – a man too in touch with his own sensitivity. "He's the wimp from hell," he'd say. "No one buys that peace and love thing anymore."

While the US critics were reserved in their praise for the half-black half-Jewish singer-songwriter, at the time – 1989 – he had become an MTV staple, and the videos from his debut LP, *Let Love Rule*, were in constant (if not heavy) rotation. In Europe, and particularly Britain, Kravitz had become something of a star, and very quickly became a bona fide rock'n'roll celebrity. He was young – twenty-six – hip, introspective yet outspoken (perfect mix), and not without talent. He had, said one notable British record company executive, "marketable sincerity".

The son of middle-class liberals – his Russian-Jewish father was television executive SLY KRAVITZ, and his mother, ROXIE ROKER, was the star of the American sitcom *The Jeffersons* – Kravitz spent his childhood in New York. "My parents exposed me to everything," he said. "We lived across from the Met [New York's Metropolitan Museum Of Art], so I had this uptown, ritzy thing happening on the weekdays, but then I spent my weekends with my grandparents in Bed-Stuy [in Brooklyn]. In this society, if you have a drop of black blood, you're black, and my mother taught me to be proud of that, rather than confused."

Kravitz was obsessed with cool from an early age, teaching himself piano and guitar, and later mastering drums and bass.

K "I just picked up everything I wanted to play and spent the time to learn how to play it," he said. His parents encouraged him to act, and he started appearing in TV commercials when he turned eleven. But things weren't always that simple: sent to a Hebrew school, the young hipster revolted when they tried to put a yarmulke over his Afro. "I only went twice, because they couldn't deal with it, and me, being a kid, I couldn't deal with them not being able to deal with me. I was Jewish, but everyone else was white, and here I was, black with thick hair."

In his early teens his family moved to LA, after his mother was cast in *The Jeffersons*. There, ensconced in Beverly Hills High School, he started singing with the world-class CALIFORNIA BOYS CHOIR, and, during his three years with them, appeared with the Metropolitan Opera and performed with conductors ERICH LEINSDORF and SIR DAVID WILCOX. But he was still obsessed with pop, and when he graduated, in 1982, his parents, instead of forcing him to go to college, gave him a cash sum, which he used to give himself three months in a recording studio, desperately trying to turn himself into a rock star. "That was my education," he said.

Kravitz soon decided to foist himself onto the unsuspecting public, and so invented a whimsical pseudonym, ROMEO BLUE. "It was a phony time for me. So I know what posing feels like. I was a dick then. I wanted to be DAVID BOWIE more than anyone else in the world." ROMEO BLUE wore YOHJI YAMAMOTO suits, sky-blue contact lenses, and liberal amounts of hair straightener. Professionally, he couldn't get arrested. "Nobody wanted to know," he said. "The record companies would tell me, 'We like your music, but we can't help you because you don't sound black enough.'" And then he met LISA BONET.

The couple met backstage at a concert by BOBBY BROWN's old band, NEW EDITION, in 1985, and became immediate friends, though he says it took them nearly two years to become lovers. "We were feeling our way about. I was in love with her from the moment I saw her, but everyone was after her then and I wanted to show her that I really did love her, so I didn't push. We acted like brother and sister; we grew totally open with each other and got so damn close we just fell in love." They were married in 1987, in Las Vegas.

K

When they met, Bonet (whose parents were the exact inverse of Kravitz's: she has a Russian-Jewish mother and a black father) was making a name for herself in *The Cosby Show*, at the time America's favourite sitcom. She soon became one of the most talked-about women on American TV, and her highly explicit and disturbing love scene with MICKEY ROURKE in ALAN PARKER's 1987 movie *Angel Heart* (in which she played a beguiling voodoo princess with a name worthy of a Bond girl, EPIPHANY PROUDFOOT) confirmed her as Hollywood pin-up material. Unsurprisingly, Kravitz felt out in the cold, caught in her shadow. The press started calling him Mr Bonet, and in a particularly disparaging piece in *People* magazine, he was referred to as a "rock'n'roll imposter... a dreadlocked ring-through-the-nose-hipster".

But all things must pass. Virgin Atlantic signed Kravitz in 1988, and the following year he released the largely self-written, self-produced, and self-performed (who said self-regarding?!) *Let Love Rule*. Here was an egotistical new-age rocker in the style of PRINCE, or TERENCE TRENT D'ARBY, a loud-mouthed hipster who could write black pop for white hearts. Critics called him a nouveau hippie, a bogus hipster with more talent than sense. But if his wishy-washy lyrics left something to be desired, behind all the belligerent idealism and knee-jerk peace signs, there were some fine songs, particularly "Sitting On Top Of The World", "I Build This Garden For Us", and "Living In Fear". Without sounding in the least bit ironic, Kravitz said, "With *Let Love Rule*, I *arrived*."

He was compared to everyone from SLY STONE to JIMI HENDRIX, from STEVIE WONDER to CURTIS MAYFIELD, and there were traces of them everywhere on his records. Like them, Kravitz successfully ignored the traditional boundaries of rhythm and blues, creating a sound that owed more to the English singer-songwriter tradition than it did to urban North American funk. Those who didn't like his music called it derivative, and you only had to listen to his "homage" to "Poison Ivy" ("Mr Cab Driver") to see what they meant. He was also more than fond of Beatlesque harmonies:"I've always heard the BEATLES," he said, "because their music is in the air – it's part of the planet." Strangely (especially considering his love of the BEATLES), though the LP bore the same sparse production as JOHN LENNON's early solo work, Kravitz claimed not to have heard this until after *Let Love Rule* was in the shops.

"I was amazed by how similar it was. I mean, it really blew me away. I hadn't heard any of that Lennon stuff until then, it was so weird. My manager said the LP sounded like the PLASTIC ONO BAND, and I said who the fuck are they?! You know? It freaked me out. So after that I went out and bought everything by *everyone* – I ain't gonna get caught again.

"It's bullshit the way I'm compared to PRINCE, or TERRY D'ARBY, or any of those guys, because I'm nothing like them. Sure, I'm more like them than I am GEORGE BUSH, but anyone with black skin who plays a guitar is always compared to the last black guy who played a guitar. Of course it annoys me. There's five million white bands where the lead singer looks exactly the same, with his long blonde hair and tight ripped pants, T-shirt and leather jacket... and they all sound the same. No one says shit about that. Blacks invented rock'n'roll anyway. What I could never understand is why people say my shit sounds like ELVIS COSTELLO."

I got the impression that Kravitz had delivered the main points of his soliloquy before. He read all his press, and knew the gripes his critics had. As he did in his songs, in conversation Kravitz strained for significance. He was no wallflower, and was at pains to let his freak flag show.

"I don't care about criticism," he lied, "the whole world can laugh at me, what do I care? People try and say that my act is a put-on, and stuff like that. But I'm in touch with myself, and people can see that. I believe in it, so they do too."

It was early September, and the micro-megalomaniac was "holed up" (his term) at Waterfront Studios, in Hoboken,

New Jersey, with two young but grizzled engineers recording the follow-up to *Let Love Rule*. The studio was part of an old warehouse that sat by the Hudson River, where they filmed *On The Waterfront* all those years ago. He'd been taking the subway out here for the last two months, painstakingly working on his new collection of songs (which would become his 1991 album, *Mama Said*). Kravitz was very much into sound, and for one song had tried out over thirty snare drums. He was nothing if not diligent. A Hofner bass lay in the corner of the studio, and a CD of the BEATLES "White Album" sat on the mixing desk, next to a half-eaten carrot muffin and a pile of DAT tapes. The new-age rocker sat on the other side of the glass, vamping on an old Steinway, staring into space. Two teenage etiolated girls in embroidered waistcoats were lying on the studio couch, nodding along with their eyes shut, as one of Kravitz's new songs boomed through the speakers. The experience was a bit boring.

LISA BONET was nowhere in sight. She was there throughout the recording of *Let Love Rule*, but was now in Los Angeles, filming. The couple still shared property in LA and New York, but their separate careers forced them to spend long periods apart. There had obviously been some speculation about their marriage. "Me and Lisa both think the same about this," said Kravitz. "Our careers are important, but they're not going to tear us apart." They would finally split two years later.

Kravitz's "new shit" (as he referred to it), took up where *Let Love Rule* left off. "This one is from the pit of Lenny," he said, rather preposterously. "It's a lot more personal than the first record." He might have had an over-inflated sense of his own importance, and words like "rebirth" and "transcendence" may have rolled off his tongue a little too easily, but he could still write a mean tune. So mean, in fact, that MADONNA had asked him to pen a song for her. The result was "Justify My Love", an enormous worldwide hit.

Kravitz looked like a *hedonist*, an unreconstructed hippy in tie-dye Hendrix T-shirt and brown winklepickers. Wasn't he just an Eighties throwback? Watching him at work in the studio I was made painfully aware that securing a good "vibe" was as important as finding the right snare drum. This was a bit boring as well.

The thing was, Kravitz was actually there the first time around. "Even when I was four or five years old, I was aware of the Sixties. I was aware of the vibe, and the feeling of living in New York in the Sixties, living near Central Park and going to hear my mother and her friends read poetry. She had cool friends, Afro people, you know what I mean? They dressed real hip in dashikis and Afros and big cool beards... it was cool. I had a great childhood; I was like some LITTLE LORD FAUNTLEROY.

"I love the sound of the Sixties more than anything else. I've got nothing against electronics, I just don't like the way technology has changed the sound of recording. I'm quite a snob about it. I hate all this modern bullshit, and as far as I'm concerned 'state of the art' was in 1967. You know, I didn't ask to be called retrogressive – I hate all this Sixties throwback shit. You see all these bands who are walking around in Sixties clothes, you can tell a stylist went and bought them, they look brand new. They don't live the lifestyle. I've been wearing this shirt for three fucking months, every fucking day [and let me tell you, I could tell he wasn't lying]. I don't aspire to be a bohemian, and I certainly don't think you have to be a bohemian to be a rock star. Any yuppie can be one."

Kravitz talked about changes – political, social, environmental, spiritual – but, like most pop musicians, always in the vaguest of terms. "People are changing now," he said, "and they're not into all that plastic stuff. People want freedom, change, and happiness. And I think my music reflects that change." His own personal idea of change seemed to be wearing a kaftan instead of a tuxedo. And though he was keen to point out his bohemian qualifications, he too had a stylist, as well as a masseuse, and a dietician.

But what could have been more Nineties? Here was a young, half-black, half-Jewish, new-age showbiz flower child with stars in his eyes, and some talent at his fingertips. Ostentatious, self-assured, almost unbearably ambitious,

Kravitz was trying to snatch pop away from the ironists. But is self-aggrandisement a way of life?

"Self-praise is no recommendation, my dad told me that. I'm a very humble person, I don't blow my own horn. I do? Yeah? I suppose you're right, I'm not humble. But that's OK. It's better than being a wimp."

Kravitz would go on to have many, many hits, and win the Grammy for "Best Male Rock Vocal Performance" four years in a row from 1999 to 2002, breaking the record for most wins in that category and most consecutive wins in one category. His hits include: "Are You Gonna Go My Way", "Fly Away", "Always On The Run", and his masterpiece, "It Ain't Over 'Til It's Over."

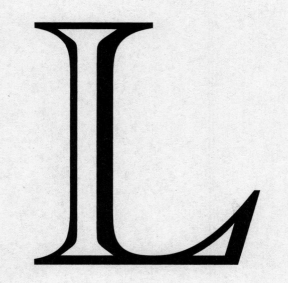

LADY GAGA

A while ago *The Economist* ran a whimsical column comparing Lady Gaga with MOTHER TERESA, and not just because both are venerated, driven, and have achieved success on a global scale. No, they were both identified as role models for corporate leaders, having turned themselves into brands, with appealing back stories, easily digestible messages, and brilliant communication skills, ensuring maximum reach. Reinvention has been key to their success (MOTHER TERESA starting out as AGNES GONXHA BOJAXHIU, Gaga as Stefani Germanotta), with Gaga using this as a barometer of her success. She has described herself as "a freak, a maverick, a lost soul looking for peers", assuring her fans that it is generally OK to be odd (a fortifying message for everyone from teenagers and fashionistas to beardies and weirdies).

She has been told she has "leadership projection", or what *The Economist* simply called charisma. Her biographers JAMES ANDERSON and JORG RECKHENRICH (of Antwerp Management School) and MARTIN KUPP (of the European School of Management and Technology) say she tells three universal stories by asking three fundamental questions: 1) "Who am I?" – the creative weird kid at school. 2) "Who are we?" – she calls her fans "my little monsters", automatically imbuing them with outsider status. 3) "Where are we going?" – together, Gaga and her acolytes can change the world!

Her concerts are like Broadway shows, or at least what Broadway shows might be like if they were performed in football arenas. What surprised me was how effective her ballads were in a live setting, putting them across with the same skill and stagecraft used by veterans like ELTON JOHN and PAUL McCARTNEY. She is probably built to last.

L LANDSCAPE (THE IMPORTANCE OF)

It's perhaps not wise to contradict someone like PABLO PICASSO, but on this occasion I have no choice. "Painting is not done to decorate apartments," he said in 1945. "It is an instrument of war." He was referring, obliquely, to his enormous canvas capturing the agony when the Luftwaffe, at General Franco's behest, carpet-bombed the Basque town of Guernica. *Guernica* is one of the painter's most enduring works, its emotional charge still so strong that in the months before the official start of the Iraq war, a tapestry copy hanging in the UN building in New York was tactfully covered over.

On the subject of painting, PICASSO was just about as wrong as a genius can be. Painting, in common with all of the arts, invariably acts as an accompaniment or a counterpoint to its locale, a way of lifting the spirits in a darkened room, or giving a Caribbean sunset extra gravitas. It's why we buy prints of famous paintings, why wallpaper was developed, and why furniture designers now have egos the size of GEORGE SHERLOCK sofas.

This is particularly true of music. While pop records that aspire to great art could conceivably be listened to anywhere, a lot of very good pop music (even great pop music) has the effect of making a landscape look even grander than it does already, a blue sky appear even richer, painting a suburban landscape in the correct hues of Fifties' Americana, or underscoring the intensity of a Chicago backstreet. Great pop music, whether it was designed to or not, expresses an abnegation of responsibility. And this is especially true if you are on holiday or at leisure – that moment when a searing power-chord shooting across a cloudless sky fills your heart with whatever you want it to, and encourages you to lean your foot a little more heavily on the accelerator pedal. If you've ever chosen the scenic drive home then you'll know the feeling.

Which means, I suppose, that music is a decorative art. While many of us buy records because we have a fundamental attachment to the preoccupations of the people who make them – when we're young, at least, or pretending we still are – at other times we buy them simply because we happen to like the way they sound: they encourage us to engage with our surroundings, but also allow us to distance ourselves from them.

If you're driving just north of Los Angeles, say, climbing up the Pacific Coast Highway on your way to Santa Barbara, hearing "Sleepwalk" by SANTO & JOHNNY will not only transport you out of California, it might just lift you right into outer space. Music and landscape make perfect bedfellows. JOHN PEEL's perfect dovetail of sound and vision appears on page 153 of his part-autobiography, *Margrave Of The Marshes*. It is 1961, and Peel is driving from New Orleans back to Dallas. "The drive gave me one of the greatest musical moments of my life. I had been driving for some time and it must have been two or three in the morning as I started through the richly-forested area of East Texas known as Piney Woods." There was hardly any traffic on the road, and as the highway rose and fell through the trees, past tiny little towns that were barely shacks and shop fronts, "the moon, which shone brilliantly directly in front of me, turned the concrete to silver". Peel recalls that he was listening, as everyone did in that area at that time, to WOLFMAN JACK, the maverick DJ who broadcasted from a station called XERB, over the border in Mexico. The Wolfman was just about the most exotic man in pop at the time (he is immortalised, for those that care, in GEORGE LUCAS's love letter to the period, *American Graffiti*), and as Peel came over the top of yet another hill, "to see another tiny town below me, he played ELMORE JAMES's 'Stranger Blues' and I knew that I would never forget the perfect conjunction of place, mood and music. Nor have I."

For music and landscape to co-exist in a perfect state, everything needs to work in 5.1 surround sound, the sort that makes you jump when the drums come in, the sort that sends

L you careering down a ravine after a particular key change. That notion of perfection is embodied, for me, by the BEACH BOYS – especially their more maudlin music – and the golden dunes of California. I close my eyes and I could be kicking sand on Malibu beach; clench them a little tighter and I'm transported to a ROUSSEAU painting, walking between 2D tigers and palm-trees.

Now if, like PICASSO, you like your entertainment confrontational, or if you think that entertainment shouldn't be entertaining at all, or that art, music, literature, and everything else should never be considered to be entertainment, then you'll hate the idea of a perfect sunset anyway (and I'm fairly sure you won't be having much truck with Caribbean holidays, either), but if you're the type of person who looks forward to having a perfect sunset unfold in front of you (I like mine about ten yards in front of me), and you want something that complements it perfectly, turn off your mind, relax, and hit play: "I'm a cork on the ocean…"

LAST.FM

If the prefix du jour in the Eighties was designer, and if the prefix du jour in the last decade was luxury, then the current prefix with the most traction is bespoke. Bespoke clothes. Bespoke music. Television. Holidays. Food. Books. Magazines. Blah. Using your iPod, Sky+, recipes created via social networking, and a society driven by flexible working hours, for many of us the world looks like a very different place to the one we knew even five years ago. And thanks to the joys of ABC (Automatic Bespoke Culture), it will look even more different in five minutes time.

The wireless (as my father still calls it) hasn't escaped this spring-clean, either, and just when I thought I had outgrown music radio, nearly a decade after it was launched, Last.fm started dictating the soundtrack of my life. On my second outing with it, as I was compiling a playlist to accompany a business trip (the MACCABEES, JEFFREY FOSKETT, JOEY SCARBURY, JEFF LARSON, MILT JACKSON, etc) I punched BURT BACHARACH, the EAGLES, and HALL & OATES into my Last.fm radio, and my bespoke station began pumping out LITTLE RIVER BAND, PETER THOMAS, DAN FOGELBERG, and CHICAGO. Suddenly, the light that traditionally pours into a southern Californian garden came pouring into Bayswater, as my room swelled to the sounds of DENNIS WILSON, CROSBY, STILLS & NASH, and GLEN CAMPBELL.

Now, while I realised that early adopters had been all over Last.fm since it launched, it made Apple's Genius function appear rather old-fashioned. Founded here in the UK in 2002, Last.fm is one of the best Internet radio sites, and currently claims over forty million active users based in more than two hundred countries. Users can create custom radio stations and playlists from any of the audio tracks in Last. fm's music library, and are able to listen to some individual tracks on demand, or download tracks if the rights holder has previously authorised it. Occasionally it thinks I'm too perverse for words (or music), and when I recently punched in STEELY DAN, MILES DAVIS, KRAFTWERK, and MALCOLM MCLAREN, it rather annoyingly said my station didn't exist. I had better luck with DAVID BOWIE, DIONNE WARWICK, and SERGIO MENDES & BRASIL '66, and my computer offered up everything from EXAMPLE and BOB SEGER to LADY GAGA and TRAFFIC.

THE LAUREL CANYON COUNTRY STORE

The Sixties are still very much alive and kicking in Los Angeles. If you know where to look, that is. Laurel Canyon is often written about as the place that gave the world CROSBY, STILLS & NASH – which is obviously why a lot of people hate it – the place that inspired JONI MITCHELL's "Ladies of the Canyon", DANNY SUGERMAN's *Wonderland Avenue*, and the neighbourhood

L

of benign bad behaviour and clandestine misdemeanours. Everyone from CLARA BOW and CHRISTINA APPLEGATE to FRANK ZAPPA and MARILYN MANSON has lived there, and it retains a genuine local feel – which is an almost implausible ambition in LA. This being Los Angeles, the area has also had its fair share of dark moments, not least the Wonderland murders, which happened in 1981, when four people were bludgeoned to death with striated steel pipes in a drug-related plot that involved the porn star, JOHN HOLMES.

Despite being the subject of standard-issue gentrification, the Canyon has kept the funky, rainbow-coloured charm of the Love Generation, something that is most apparent when visiting the Canyon Country Store, the neighbourhood social hub still. Wedged along the twisting Laurel Canyon Boulevard in the Santa Monica Mountains between West Hollywood and the San Fernando Valley, this is the place mentioned in JIM MORRISON's "Love Street" ("I see you live on Love Street, There's this store where the creatures meet..."). The wooden-floored grocery shop/deli/liquor store/café is still the place to go for canyon dwellers with the munchies, or for those in the industry who aren't working, and who need somewhere in the morning to stop for an espresso having spent all night partying in the Valley. Here they'll find Dandy Don's ice cream, Dave's Kombucha (fermented tea), bespoke sandwiches, hearts of palm salads, and the almost-but-not-quite-legendary decaf almond milk latte. Run out of Californian chardonnay, Heinz Baked Beans, Daddy's Sauce or patchouli incense? Look no further.

The Country Store is also the site of the annual Photo Day each October, where the residents of the Canyon all come together to have a group picture taken. The tradition dates back to the late Eighties, a celebration of the sort of community spirit you don't find anywhere else in LA.

Over the hill, the temporal nature of Hollywood is in full effect. Here, in the village of bougainvillea and watery melodies, time stands still. And if you want to wear your bellbottoms and feathers, don't think twice, it's all right.

HUGH LAURIE

L

New Orleans is the syncopated city. Music is everywhere here. Walk the streets and you feel as though you're moving around inside a giant iPod. The music in the Big Easy is like the food, a haute Creole mix of mambo, twelve-bar rumbas, boogie-woogie, Cajun blues, zydeco, Cuban habanera styles, and more. FATS DOMINO was pouring out of the airport public address system as I arrived, brass bands were playing in the street as I walked around the French Quarter in the late afternoon light, second generation gangsta bounce poured out of an old Escalade as I walked along Canal Street, and, as I watched a black transvestite built like a linebacker in the Double Play bar, LED ZEPPELIN's own version of the blues blew across the room in the form of "Dazed and Confused". It's also impossible to eat here without some form of musical accompaniment; order your gumbo and you'll find a double bass in your face. Hoover up a po-boy or some shrimp Creole and it will arrive from the kitchen with a banjo salute. In New Orleans, music travels via osmosis, drifting around the streets like seeds in the wind, blown in from across the Mississippi. SAMUEL CHARTERS, the biographer and custodian of the city's huge musical heritage, says that back in the Fifties, when New Orleans was quieter than it is today, if he found the place where the EUREKA BRASS BAND was meeting for a parade, "but I got there after they'd already started, if I just stood still and listened, I could hear a trumpet around the corner..." And there are trumpets around the corner still. "Nawlins" has what oenophiles call "terroir" – the theory that the place where a great wine's grapes are grown should be evident in every swallow. So when you hear *The River In Reverse,* ALLEN TOUSSAINT and ELVIS COSTELLO's 2006 album (one of the first major studio sessions to take place after Hurricane Katrina), you are hearing New Orleans, 2006 vintage – even though some of the record was made in Hollywood.

L New Orleans is also where Hugh Laurie chose to launch his first proper music project, in 2010. Laurie signed to Warner Bros Records that year, and *Let Them Talk* was his first release for the label, a celebration of New Orleans blues, a genre that he is more than passionate about. Laurie is a lifelong fan of the blues, ever since hearing "I Can't Quit You Baby" by WILLIE DIXON as a child. "I don't recall where I was when I heard that JOHN LENNON had been assassinated," he said, "but I do remember where I was when I heard MUDDY WATERS had died. I was driving down the A1 from Lincolnshire and had this awful, selfish reaction: 'Now I'll never get to see him play live.'"

On March 22nd the following year he performed songs from the album at one of New Orleans' most architecturally significant buildings, Latrobe's, the Louisiana State Bank built by BENJAMIN HENRY LATROBE; with its wrought iron balconies, cypress woodwork and stuccooed brick exterior, it's become one of the most famous addresses in the French Quarter, an area which is positively heaving with architectural wonders. On the day of the concert – the same day that legendary bluesman PINETOP PERKINS died of a heart attack at the age of ninety-seven – in the sun-drenched garden of Soniat House, a small boutique hotel just three city blocks from the Mississippi, Laurie – looking elegantly gaunt, unshaven, and studiedly dishabille in the dappled afternoon sun – painstakingly explained his long, devotional, and seemingly exponential relationship with the blues.

"The essential element of this whole project is my genuine love for this music, and my wish to communicate this and the music to other people. Obviously I was worried that some people might think I was involved in some sort of pastiche – especially the musicians I was working with – but I think they very quickly realised this was not the case. This is not tourism. If it is honest then nothing bad can happen – the worst that can happen is people say that it is terrible and that they hate it and will not buy it and go 'Ha Ha'. I don't really care if that does happen of course, but then I say that without anyone from the record company in earshot as they will obviously care very much. I certainly hope that if it pays its bills."

L

Laurie recorded *Let Them Talk* at Ocean Way studios in Los Angeles, singing and playing guitar and piano, and surrounding himself with some of the best musicians in the business, including the great drummer JAY BELLEROSE, who played on the ELTON JOHN and LEON RUSSELL record, *The Union*. He was also accompanied by IRMA THOMAS (often called the "Queen of New Orleans"), R&B legend ALLEN TOUSSAINT, cult hero DR. JOHN, and even Sir TOM JONES – who, the last time I looked, didn't appear to have any relationship with New Orleans, but who obviously has a good set of pipes. But it's easy for mediocre talents to surround themselves with virtuosos with the aim of disguising their weaknesses. What's so surprising about Laurie's record was not just how good it was, but also how good he was. He very carefully chose the right material, and interpreted it in a way that paid homage to the genre, while giving the songs, if not an extra dimension (that would be too post-modern), then at least a 21st Century polish. Suffice it to say, it worked, and there are some seriously good tracks on the album: "St James Infirmary" (made famous by LOUIS ARMSTRONG, and later covered brilliantly by ALLEN TOUSSAINT), "The Whale Has Swallowed Me" (recorded BY L.B. LENOIR, who was featured in MARTIN SCORSESE's epic series *The Blues),* ROBERT JOHNSON's classic "They're Red Hot", "Joshua Fit The Battle Of Jericho" (recorded by everyone from SISTER ROSETTA THARP to ELVIS PRESLEY), and many more.

His interpretations were reassuringly impressive, and often quite moving. Surprisingly so. But this still begged the question, why the record?

The record was actually the brainchild of Warner Music Entertainment President CONRAD WITHEY, a long-term fan of *House*. "I loved it whenever I saw Hugh play on *House*, and thought it would be a great idea to get him to record an album. The original idea was to do a BUENA VISTA SOCIAL CLUB type thing." Encouraged by his wife, Withey contacted Laurie's management, expecting to be rebuffed. But the idea

L was embraced with open arms. Of the three hundred ideas he had been pitched in the last five years, this was the one he wanted to do the most.

And so it happened.

Laurie's rationale is reassuringly matter-of-fact, and is perhaps best explained in a photocopied letter from Laurie that arrived at my office at *GQ* a few months before the album's release."I was not born in Alabama in the 1890s," wrote Laurie. "You may as well know this now. I've never eaten grits, cropped a share, or ridden a boxcar. No gypsy woman said anything to my mother when I was born and there's no hellhound on my trail, as far as I can judge. Let this record show that I am a white, middle-class Englishman, openly trespassing on the music and myth of the American South... The question of why a soft-handed English schoolboy should be touched by music born of slavery and oppression in another city, on another continent, in another century, is for a thousand others to answer before me: from [ALEXIS] KORNER to [ERIC] CLAPTON, the ROLLING STONES to the Joolsing Hollands. Let's just say it happens.

"Worst of all, I've broken a cardinal rule of art, music and career paths: actors are supposed to act, and musicians are supposed to music. That's how it works. You don't buy fish from a dentist, or ask a plumber for financial advice, so why listen to an actor's music? The answer is, there is no answer. If you care about provenance and genealogy, then you should try elsewhere, because I have nothing in your size."

For his role as DR GREGORY HOUSE in the medical drama series *House*, fifty-something Laurie is paid a staggering $400,000 a week, and is the highest paid actor on US television. *House* is the world's most-watched TV show, making Hugh Laurie the world's biggest TV star. His role has won him two Golden Globes, two Screen Actor Guild Awards, two Television Critics Association Awards and five Emmy nominations. The director BRYAN SINGER, one of the show's original producers, had made it clear he didn't want to hire a Brit for the role of the determinedly irascible doctor, but as he didn't really know who Laurie was, and not being *au fait* with British television comedy (and never having seen *Blackadder, A Bit of Fry and Laurie*, or *Jeeves and Wooster*), insisted on casting the actor after seeing his audition tape. And he worked. Immediately. Captivating the Fox audience so much that, seven seasons in, Laurie was Triple A famous. To some Brits, who catch the show on Sky, Laurie's performance is still rather incongruous – a reinvention comparable with STEPHEN FRY turning up as a Russian mafia boss in the next installment of the *Die Hard* franchise, or indeed, becoming BRUCE WILLIS himself.

So, having learned to talk American, he then decided to sing American, too, by turning himself into ROBERT JOHNSON because Laurie is a man who has never bought a DAVID BOWIE record, never bought a WHO record, who was untouched by punk, and, one assumes, any pop cultural splurge that came in its wake. Not for him the rallying call of insurgent pop, the rebellion of youth, or the allure of soiled satin and tat. No, what spoke to Laurie was the crawling king snake noise made by the likes of WILLIE DIXON, LEAD BELLY, and ROBERT JOHNSON.

The record was produced by JOE HENRY, the two-time Grammy Award winner who has previously worked with ALLEN TOUSSAINT, ELVIS COSTELLO, AIMIE MANN, TEDDY THOMPSON, SOLOMON BURKE, and MADONNA. Saliently, Henry also produced the 2009 ALLEN TOUSSAINT album *The Bright Mississippi*, the jazz album that went some way to helping Laurie form the record he wanted to make. Along with Toussaint's 2006 collaborative piece with ELVIS COSTELLO, the Grammy nominated *The River In Reverse*, this record set the tone for *Let Them Talk*. "I'm sincere when I say I think people will be stunned, not just at how much time he's devoted to his musical life but how interesting his take on the music is," said Henry.

Like any North American city, New Orleans has the duality of mirrored skyscrapers and weed-infested parking lots, but it is also a mythological city, the blues' Brigadoon – a fantastical city full of its own realities: the streets are full of hustlers, tourists, mid-city workers, conventioneers, drunken frat boys

L looking for cheap drugs and salt-shaker dancers, hip-hop souljas, and those who have been smoking "too much of too strong". While there continues to be criticism of both the Bush and the Obama administrations' attitudes towards the city since Katrina decimated New Orleans in 2005 (flooding eighty per cent of the city), there has actually been some much-needed and significant reinvestment, and people are moving back in serious numbers. Also, Louisiana's film and television tax credits have created a huge spike in the number of movies and TV shows made there. There is a real sense in New Orleans that the city is finally being rehabilitated, and while there are pockets that have not had as much love as others, New Orleans is moving forward. A recent spate of murders in the previously relatively peaceful St Roche neighbourhood notwithstanding, violence in the city is generally on the decrease, and optimism is in the air.

Laurie first made the pilgrimage to New Orleans last year. For him it was his Jerusalem, his Valhalla. And he was worried that it might not live up to expectations. "I dreaded coming here in the same way that you might dread meeting SEAN CONNERY, just in case he may not actually be like SEAN CONNERY. But when I eventually came it exceeded my expectations by some margin. My first impression was smell. It smelled right. It smelled sweet, with a very slight overtone of decay. It was a wet smell, of beautiful flora just turning. Sound and music were the second, sound and music on an astonishing level, and life almost bursting out of every building. You think that some of it must be recorded but then you turn a corner and see that it is actually two guys playing live... it is fantastic! First time I was here we went to a club to see WALTER 'WOLFMAN' WASHINGTON – great show! And we had been on the road for twelve hours and we went in at midnight and it was just so intoxicating. And I am still that way... I am still intoxicated."

Commercial expectations for the record were high. Initially there was a concern at the record company that, due to his dislike of publicity, Laurie would make the record and then simply retire to his hotel room, never to be seen again. But he was so proud of it that he went out of his way to sell it.

"I don't want to be artificially coy about it, and I'm not holding a gun to anybody's head," he said to me that day, squinting in the sun. "I am just saying, yes this is my thing and I am proud of it. This is the music I love and it is not necessarily music people get to hear these days. We were rehearsing on Sunday at Pine Street Studios, and I felt these songs were as alive as animals, sort of moving around the room. You know, the song would go up and lick the drummer's face and prop himself against the guitarist, and I completely felt those songs like actual living things. Some are close to a hundred years old but I felt them living in the room. And I am not claiming that I brought those songs to life but just as soon as we started I thought, Oh my God this is a living thing right here and I just desperately hope that other people will be able to listen to some of these songs and hear things that they have not heard before. If people buy this record because of *House* then it will obviously be successful, but I can only really count it a success if I encourage people to rediscover the likes of LEAD BELLY, ALLEN TOUSSAINT, and WILLIE DIXON. Then the whole thing will have been worth it."

LED ZEPPELIN

Think of the gatefold sleeve, think of the violin bow power chords, think of the head-thrown-back wail, and think of the most important Neanderthal noise made since ELVIS fused country and rhythm and blues. In their sonic pomp, Zeppelin were the mothership of motherships; what was extraordinary was how similar they sounded when they made their comeback in 2007 at the O2 in London. It was the gig of gigs, full of expectation and – who knew? – satisfactory delivery. They sounded just like did thirty-five

L years earlier; sure, if you looked at the mammoth screens in front of you you'd see The Oldest Men In The World, but it didn't matter, all the men in the audience (and, apart from NAOMI CAMPBELL – who I remember getting rather agitated as she'd lost her mobile – I don't think there were actually any women there) loved every second of it. Not just because they could say they were there, but because it was very, very good. In the years since, JIMMY PAGE has repeatedly tried to convince ROBERT PLANT to go round once more, but sensibly Plant has decided to let sleeping black dogs lie.

THOMAS LEER

Thomas Leer was responsible for kick-starting the DIY indie techno boom. His single "Private/Plane"/"International" (Oblique Records) was released in September 1978, over six weeks before "T.V.O.D."/"Warm Leatherette" by the NORMAL. "International" is my favourite post-punk single, but more importantly it encouraged a whole generation to explore electronics in a completely new way. This was cut and paste music in a cut and paste sleeve, a lo-fi masterpiece recorded in his bedsit without a synth. Not only did he have to sing in a hushed voice so as not to wake his girlfriend (Leer was "the original one-man bedroom band," according to the *Independent*'s ANDY GILL), but also the music was created by heavily processed instruments, tapes and extremely primitive electronic gizmos. Released on his own label, it was *NME*'s Single Of The Week, and caused a stir throughout the industry: "compelling pop with a dark heart, swooping between the pretty and the pretty disturbing," according to one review. It influenced the HUMAN LEAGUE, ZTT, THE THE, THROBBING GRISTLE, THOMAS DOLBY, and everything that came in its wake.

Born THOMAS WISHART in Port Glasgow, in October 1953, Leer played in several local experimental pop groups in the early to mid-Seventies, moving to London during punk and forming the punk band PRESSURE. Influenced by KRAFTWERK and CAN he recorded "Private Plane", and in 1979 released the album *The Bridge* in collaboration with ROBERT RENTAL. He later formed the duo, ACT, with ex-PROPAGANDA singer CLAUDIA BRUCKEN, released a bunch of singles and then retired. Inspired by a new generation of electronic whiz-kids, he reappeared like a Time Lord around the turn of the century, and still dabbles inquisitively.

L

JOHN LEGEND

So: two parts JAMIE CULLUM, one part SMOKEY ROBINSON, this former choirboy honed his performing and composing skills through working with KANYE WEST and LAURYN HILL, becoming a multiple Grammy-winning crossover sex symbol en route. He was once a management consultant, eventually learning to manage his own super-smooth skills to great effect. I saw him support SADE at the Staples Center in LA once, and when he stood on his Yamaha piano during his final song, the crowd went berserk, and we were suddenly all misbehaving in a secular church, as though we'd been doing nothing but knocking back boilermakers for the previous eighty minutes. Songs: "Let's Get Lifted", "Ordinary People".

JERRY LEIBER & MIKE STOLLER

Leiber & Stoller composed hundreds of simple, classic and tightly-wound hit singles in the Fifties and Sixties, including "Jailhouse Rock", "Yakety Yak", "Stand By Me", "Love Potion No. 9", "Fools Fall In Love", and PEGGY LEE's semi-autobiographical "Is That All There Is?". They often

L wrote their songs in near-real time: commissioned to write a song for BIG MAMA THORNTON, they completed "Hound Dog" in twelve minutes.

JOHN LENNON & YOKO ONO

The first thing you notice as you enter Yoko Ono's seventh-floor apartment in the Dakota, the huge gothic block on New York's Central Park West, is John Lennon's white baby grand, the celestial piano on which he wrote "Imagine" and many of his other classic songs from the early Seventies. Though it has been home to Ono since the couple bought it in 1973, to a visitor the gigantic nine-room apartment feels somewhat like a private chapel. I was asked to remove my shoes, and the sensation was intensified as the afternoon sun caught the piano's white keys and the silver picture frames on top of it.

Lennon is everywhere: staring down at you from the Warhol painting in the "black" room, in the photographs on the walls in the kitchen, and in those silver picture frames on top of his piano. Apartment seventy-two is something of a museum too, since apart from the acres of Egyptian antiques and dozens of Ono's own installation pieces, it is littered with paintings, lithographs and famous silk screens: a de Lempicka here, a de Chirico there. It was here on 72nd Street that John and Yoko spent their five years of role reversal, until Lennon's death at the hands of MARK CHAPMAN in 1980. While Yoko spent her days in their office on the ground floor, John would be upstairs, attending to their son, Sean, and "watching the trees change colour" in Central Park.

"This is where John used to bake bread," said Ono as she showed me into the kitchen, with its spice jars, chopping boards, and the unremarkable detritus of domesticity. "Every day he'd get up and make Sean's breakfast while Sean played on the floor. The he'd get up and make bread while I went to work downstairs. Often I'd work at the kitchen table just to be near them. We were a family and this was our home, Sean's home, and because of that I'll never leave."

Ono has had more than her fair share of bad press in the years since she first met Lennon. Since his death, her press initially appeared to actually get worse, as if we somehow couldn't bear the thought that she was still alive while he wasn't. (One of her American publicists even asked if I had any deep-rooted animosity towards Yoko, as though it were a given.) This vilification is a cross she'll probably have to bear until she dies, much like LINDA MCCARTNEY, who until her death was also, rather disgustingly, considered to be Paul's undoing, at least creatively.

In person, Ono certainly didn't seem like a business barracuda, but then it was obvious from the way in which her underlings scattered from the apartment with the wave of her hand that she is a formidable boss. Tiny, dressed entirely in black, she was extremely birdlike, talking in short, staccato sentences. She seemed endearingly dotty rather than demonstrative, often repeating herself or misunderstanding questions. I'm sure she's acutely responsible when studying the bottom line, but then, as the custodian of John Lennon's estate, she ought to be.

The office on the ground floor of the Dakota is crammed with all sorts of valuable BEATLES memorabilia and is where Yoko sits with her assistants, approving advertising artwork and plotting her husband's online future. In her private office next door, fluffy white clouds float across the sky-blue ceiling. There is a bronze sculpture of an apple with two bites out of it and, on her desk, a framed blank cheque, made out to Yoko and signed by John; I'm sure to some it would be an apposite approximation of their relationship.

JULIAN LENNON

L

Being Julian Lennon hasn't been easy. Wasn't easy at school, hasn't been easy since. He'd have found it easier had he chosen another career, but as it is the ancestry refuses to be shaken. When he is captured by the tabloids, the captions are invariably the same: "Julian Lennon seen at the Los Angeles opening of *Titanic*. Julian was only seventeen when his father, John, was tragically shot outside the Dakota Building on New York's Central Park in December 1980."

It's not as if he hasn't had a lot to live up to. The first words his father said to him, just a few hours after he was born at Sefton General Hospital in April 1963, at the height of Beatlemania, were, "Who's going to be a famous little rocker, like his dad?" Although his father officially left him in 1969, when Julian was just six, marrying YOKO ONO four months after the divorce from Julian's mother, Cynthia, John had been an absentee parent almost since his son's birth. It was Cynthia who brought him up, Cynthia who dragged him from Liverpool to London, then Weybridge, and Wales. And it was PAUL MCCARTNEY who taught Julian to play the guitar, not his famous father, Paul with whom he played cowboys and Indians. In 1980, John recorded the song, "Beautiful Boy" for Sean, the son he had with Yoko in 1975, yet he was so anxious about the reaction to the lullaby he wrote for Julian – "Goodnight", from the BEATLES' "White Album" – that he badgered RINGO STARR into singing it. For most of his life, Julian has suffered the consequences of his father's pronounced neglect, yet people still approach him as if he were a shrine, whispering "I loved your father" before he has a chance to say anything. Not that he would, of course: "I'm too nice not to be nice," he likes to say.

John effectively cut off relations in the early Seventies when he moved to New York to go and live with Yoko (or Hokey Cokey as Julian likes to call her). A house husband for most of the next ten years, he brought up Sean while his wife took care of business affairs. In recently unearthed letters to Cynthia in the Sixties, John admits to being a "thoughtless bastard" where Julian was concerned, and only started making contact when his son was in his late teens.

In the famous *Newsweek* interview conducted just before his death, asked why he hadn't made a record for five years, John said, "Because I wanted to give [Sean] five solid years of being there all the time. I hadn't seen my first son grow up, and now there's a seventeen-year-old man on the phone talking about motorbikes. I was not there for his childhood at all. I was on tour. I don't know how the game works but there is a price to pay for inattention to children. And if I don't give him attention from zero to five then I'm damn well gonna have to give it to him from sixteen to twenty, because it's owed, it's like the laws of the universe." Tragically, with Julian at least, he never got the chance. His son last spoke to him by telephone, two weeks before he was shot.

You could say it's a wonder the boy's still sane, but then he very nearly wasn't.

Having decided to enter the music business, he had huge success with his first LP, *Valotte*, which made the Top 20 in 1984, and a single, "Too Late for Goodbyes", which reached No.6 the same year. This success opened up new worlds for him, particularly the world of drugs.

In the Eighties he turned into a ferocious party animal, and spent several years in a haze of cocaine and booze. If you had dinner with him during this time you'd be eating alone, as he rarely strayed from liquids, spending most of the time in the loo. "I went mad for a couple of years, I admit," he said. "Thank God for self-restraint, that's all I can say. I've got far too much self-respect to go beyond where I was. It's common sense. You've got to remain in a situation where you can continue to be motivated. I was never going to experiment with anything else.

"It was my lifestyle. There were too many people around who took advantage of me, who used and abused me, for years. I took care of everyone's bills, paid for meals, drink,

L everything. I attracted the wrong kind of people, hangers-on, and I did that a lot. I had my fair share and still do from time to time, but I now feel I am wearing the cap of responsibility. I still drink and I feel fortunate that I am able to control that, because a lot of people lose it with drugs and drink. I think I'd be in a worse place if I'd had more success."

Since those early days his career has been rather a grab bag, with his follow-up LPs *The Secret Value Of Daydreaming, Mr Jordan*, and *Help Yourself* all selling less than their predecessor. This made him feel like something of a has been, although now he says he can't afford music to take over his life, filling his time with sailing, cooking, painting, sculpting, photography, and poetry, all the leisure pursuits of the artist in recovery. The one constant has always been his mother. "I think things would have been very different if Dad had been around, but I have to thank Mum for who I am. She has played the biggest part in my life, keeping me together in the way that I am and the way I treat people. She knows, she knows. She has always been the most important thing in my life, and will always be. Mum is the kind of person who likes people to make their own mistakes, and I think she would only have got involved if she had seen me at death's door, which I was close to, but thankfully I pulled back."

Musically, Julian burnt himself out, his lack of success pushing him into dozens of ancillary projects. He tried to open a chain of charity-based theme restaurants that paid homage to revolutionaries, built a multimedia centre in the south of France, and has involved himself with a software company, as well as assorted environmental projects.

The offspring of Sixties and Seventies rock stars who have decided to join the family business are many (ZIGGY MARLEY, ZAC STARKEY, JAKOB DYLAN, EMMA TOWNSHEND, etc), but Julian Lennon is in a different league. His father burst into a world that he made up as he went along, whereas Julian has simply to live in it. It has been a hard call. Not only do people still feel guilty about what happened to his

father, wanting to protect Julian in some way, they also want
to castigate Julian for following in his father's footsteps. It
would have been easier for him if he had chosen to make
cutting-edge dance music or form a heavy-metal band, but
instead he chose – rather bravely, I think – to make the
type of music his father excelled at: simple, straightforward
pop music featuring voice and piano. His ambitions to be a
songsmith have proved to be his undoing, and he has been
goaded almost beyond endurance by critics who feel that,
because his talent is perhaps not as great as his father's, he
is somehow sullying the family name by inflicting it on the
public. Julian, they say, was unlucky enough to inherit his
father's looks but his mother's talent.

"Hey Jude" was written by PAUL McCARTNEY following a
visit to Cynthia and Julian soon after the divorce. McCartney
knew it wasn't going to be easy for the young boy: "We'd
gone on this Greek Island once to buy an island, and Julian
and I spent a lot of time playing around on the boat," said
McCartney. "I used to play cowboys and Indians with him. I
remember John coming up to me and he took me aside and
said, 'How do you do it?' I said, 'What do you mean?' He
said, 'With Julian. How do you play with kids like that?' I
remember feeling a wave of sorrow coming over me. Then I
tried to give, like, the potted version: 'Play, pretend you're a
kid. Play with him.' But John never got the hang of it."

The younger Lennon has been involved in legal wrangles
with his father's estate almost since his death. In the original
divorce supplement, Julian was to receive £2,400 a year in
maintenance, and to inherit a £50,000 trust fund when he
was twenty-five. Quite rightly, he thought this wasn't fair,
so in the early Eighties he began lobbying to get more. "After
Mum and Dad separated, the only settlement she arranged
with him was that I had enough for food, clothing and
school – that was the only obligation Dad had. So the only
money I had I earned. Unfortunately, in the past, people
took great advantage of my age and inexperience, and the
majority of what I earned disappeared. I guess I was partly

L

to blame, but when you are making a lot of money at the age of twenty, twenty-one, you never think of the consequences of who's paying for the first-class accommodation or the Concorde tickets."

In August 1996, sixteen years after his father's death, following exhaustive legal work, he finally received a multi-million-pound settlement from the Lennon estate, an endowment bestowed by his stepmother in order to "clean up the books". While it is nothing compared to the £250m fortune Sean will inherit, the settlement is said to be in the region of £20m. "One of the things agreed is that we wouldn't talk about it," said Julian. In her defence, Yoko Ono said she had been waiting until he was "mature" enough to cope with the money.

Julian Lennon still makes the occasional record, gets involved in the stewardship of some of his father's archive, and in 2010 produced a book, *Beatles Memorabilia: The Julian Lennon Collection.*

RAMSEY LEWIS

This man was an instant party, or at least his records were. Clap hands, here comes Ramsey! Turn on one of his tunes and the room suddenly looks like a scene from a hipster film set in the Sixties, where sophisticates hover around kidney-shaped swimming pools in the type of places that wish they were a little bit closer to Palm Springs. Lewis' best records always had a jaunty, uplifting feel to them – his piano to the fore, hand claps in the background. This was crossover jazz, offering "the uninitiated an enticing gateway into the jazz idiom," in the words of writer, BILL DAHL. The standout tracks on *Finest Hour* (Verve, 2000) include lackadaisical versions of "Wade In The Water", and DOBIE GRAY's "The In Crowd".

THE LIBERTINES

L

The music hall punk of their first album *Up The Bracket* (2002) is the one that archivists and aficionados root for. I only cared for two (great) songs from the self-titled 2004 follow-up: "Can't Stand Me Now" and "What Katie Did". PETE DOHERTY's tabloid travails eventually overshadowed anything the band did musically, yet for a short while they were all anyone in the UK could talk about. We can't stand them now.

LINKIN PARK

You're driving across Southern California (Linkin Park's home state), it's late, and there's a big black sky stretching from the hood to the trunk. All above you is night, and all around you are the tempered sounds of nu and rap metal, bouncing off the car walls, rattling the CDs in the pocket of the driver's door, and making you think of the beach. Actually, the thrashing has stopped, and you're actually listening to "My December", from Linkin Park's 2000 debut album *Hybrid Theory* (the original band name, before they changed it to the alternative version of Santa Monica's Lincoln Park). Known for their junior LIMP BIZKIT nu metal "chops", their collaboration with Jay-Z, and for being poster boys of hard-core Noughties rock, this – in truth, a rather traditional six-stringed ballad – is their best song. It's unrepresentative of their early work, but a taste of where they would end up. If LYNYRD SKYNYRD had started making records thirty years later than they did, this is what they would have sounded like.

The Hometracked website identified the typical Linkin Park song structure. To wit: 1) Quiet intro: Each song has a relatively quiet two-measure intro. 2) The instrumental kicker: The full band come in together on the down-beat, and play two or four high-energy measures, usually instrumental. 3)

L

Quiet verse: The song eases off for a verse or two, heightening the dynamic contrast between the song's sections. 4) Heavy chorus: Usually the same chords established in the kicker, with Chester screaming over the top for added emotion.

"My December" is somewhat different. Not much, mind, but enough. And it still sounds good in a car if you're driving around Santa Monica at night, at Christmas.

LITTLE RICHARD

Looking the wrong way through the telescope, these days Little Richard is the black LIBERACE, the Saturday night turn with the whitey teeth and the gaping mouth and the greased-back pompadour.

"Awopbopaloobopalopbamboom" might still be the original clarion call for adolescent delinquency, but these days it's as though we're hearing it through glass. Did it really happen? Was it really as shocking as people made out? Were these really the stem cells of rock'n'roll?

LIVING COLOUR

According to a 1993 CNN and *Time* magazine poll, one American in five thought that ELVIS PRESLEY was or may be alive. The survey said that while seventy-nine percent of Americans believed that Presley died in 1977, sixteen per cent said he was still among the living, and five percent were not sure. Not only is ELVIS the most enduring American icon of the post-war years, he is the pop god by which all others are measured. ELVIS was there first, before the BEATLES, the ROLLING STONES, the SEX PISTOLS, or NIRVANA. But then of course he wasn't, as anyone with a passing knowledge of pop history will know.

This hadn't escaped the attention of VERNON REID, guitarist and self-appointed leader of black New York rock band, Living Colour: "The whole ELVIS thing makes me mad," he said, the same year. "ELVIS – the king of rock'n'roll. Where does that leave CHUCK BERRY? Where does that leave LITTLE RICHARD? Does that mean these people serve under ELVIS? You hear about CARL PERKINS and 'Blue Suede Shoes', right? But you never hear about OTIS BLACKWELL and 'Love Me Tender'. Do people know that OTIS BLACKWELL was from Brooklyn? Do people know that OTIS BLACKWELL wrote 'Love Me Tender' and 'Great Balls of Fire'?"

The reason Reid used ELVIS as a hobbyhorse was because of Living Colour's chosen method of making money: they are a black, hard rock band, a rare enough thing in itself. Record conglomerates have never been happy with the term black rock, preferring more classifiable genres like jazz, reggae, rap, funk, or soul. For them rock is not a mongrel genre, and since ELVIS it has been marketed almost exclusively to white youth.

But Living Colour are a link in the chain that connects CHUCK BERRY, LITTLE RICHARD, JIMI HENDRIX, SLY STONE, FUNKADELIC, PRINCE, and LENNY KRAVITZ – black acts who have incorporated "white" rock styles in their music. The crossover, though, from cult status to mainstream acceptance, is rarely easy. In CHARLES SHAAR MURRAY's Hendrix biography, *Crosstown Traffic,* he points out that a lot of rock fans don't consider Hendrix – possibly the greatest guitarist to walk the earth – to be black at all.

"What Living Colour have done is to re-establish rock music's links with its origins," said Murray, when I spoke to him in 1993. "All through the Fifties and Sixties there was an intense relationship between black and white music which was effectively silenced by the Seventies, when rock and soul had grown apart. Living Colour essentially completed the circle. Along with PRINCE, they brought it all back home."

"The same thing that started in the Fifties with me," said LITTLE RICHARD; "they took through the Nineties. And God

L

bless their souls. They are keeping it alive." VERNON REID was adamant: "A certain era of rock'n'roll is over. The whole idea of rock as spectacle – where you go to a stadium and worship a rock god – that is dying out. There's so much more interactive media these days that we're witnessing a real sea change. But I believe rock is still a viable medium for self-expression; you don't have to divorce yourself from the past."

Sitting in the Acme Bar & Grill on the edges of the East Village in downtown Manhattan (there are still as many "Acme Bar & Grills" in New York as there are pizza parlours called "Ray's Famous"), VERNON REID, singer COREY GLOVER, drummer WILL CALHOUN, and bassist DOUG WIMBUSH pledged allegiance to their own personal race against rockism, their *agenda*. Glover (formerly an actor – he had a featured role in OLIVER STONE's *Platoon),* Calhoun (who studied drumming at college), and Wimbush (as a member of the in-house rhythm section for Sugarhill Records he played bass on most of the important rap records of the early Eighties, including "The Message" by GRANDMASTER FLASH) chatted away amiably as Reid crouched at the end of the table, picking at his food.

Reid has never walked the straight and narrow. He has a history as an avant-garde jazz guitarist, played with arty New York band DEFUNKT, and in the mid-Eighties co-founded (along with *Village Voice* writer, GREG TATE) the BLACK ROCK COALITION, a New York-based umbrella organisation dedicated to exploring the parameters of non-Caucasian pop, "to produce, promote and distribute black alternative music... to disseminate information, and to network". And to reclaim their heritage. They stated in their manifesto: "Rock and roll is black music and we are its heirs." Living Colour owe their success in part to MICK JAGGER, who, back in the early Eighties, as well as producing their demo tapes, volunteered to approach record companies on the band's behalf (Reid worked on Jagger's *Primitive Cool* LP while Wimbush worked on *Wandering Spirit).* Epic Records (now owned by Sony) took the bait, and resigned themselves to the marketing of the unprecedented: a black rock act with a sociological heart. The band also supported the ROLLING STONES on their 1989 world tour.

Until Living Colour came along, most people thought that a black rock'n'roll band was a contradiction in terms. Ironically, when the band first appeared, they had the kind of reception that ELVIS encountered back in the Fifties. Not the wild sexual adulation, not the widespread disgust, but a perturbed, quizzical reaction: why would anybody want to do such a thing? Consequently they were ceremoniously ignored by American FM radio. "A black rocker is anathema," said CHARLES SHAAR MURRAY, "considered ludicrous, demeaning and – worst of all – inconvenient!"

But the worm turned. Their debut LP *Vivid* was released in 1988, and went on to sell nearly three million copies. In 1990 they followed this with *Time's Up,* one of the most impressive records of that year. The funk-rock fusion of songs like "Love Rears Its Ugly Head" and "Type" signified a commitment to hip-hop and bebop, as well as hard rock. And there was even the Soweto Pop of "The Solace Of You". "To me," said WILL CALHOUN, "there's nothing weird about having an African song and a thrash song on the same record. I wish more bands would do it." "Black music shouldn't be sacrosanct," said Wimbush. "Musicians ought to be adaptable."

Their record *Stain* (released in 1993), was produced by RON ST GERMAIN, who has worked with many white rock bands, including SONIC YOUTH and SOUNDGARDEN. The music is leagues away from the brute force of MEGADETH, ANTHRAX, IRON MAIDEN, DEF LEPPARD, and other leather-clad, nimble-fingered numbskulls. If anyone was going to bridge the gap between PUBLIC ENEMY and LED ZEPPELIN, it was Living Colour.

And the lyrical content was stridently uncompromising – attacking liberals, racists, etc – yet one song stood head and shoulders above the rest, a tongue-in-cheek snapshot of bisexuality. Like everything else on the record, "Bi" – "It's an homage to NOEL COWARD," said Reid – had a slightly acidic tone.

Unlike most militant rap, there was no racism or homophobia: they didn't write songs about cars and girls,

L contrive macho poses, or advocate drugs. Politically correct? These boys made STING look like LUCIFER. Literate, smart, and thoroughly un-rock'n'roll, they even spelled their name with a "u" – going against the Native American spelling. They were grammatically correct, too.

Reid was almost evangelical in his espousal of "black rock". "This is my music and I don't see why anyone can't accept that fact. If I want to play thrash metal, country, R&B, hip-hop, that is *my* prerogative. It's my right, our right, because the music belongs to us. I banged my head on so many walls for such a long time, that I don't see why I should stop now." But at the time hard rock fans still couldn't completely come to terms with them. When the American heavy metal magazine *Rip* featured members from Living Colour and white metal band ANTHRAX together on its cover, the editor received an avalanche of hate mail; one reader claimed the magazine had faked the picture, while another returned his copy with the faces of each Living Colour member burnt out.

"So there was a new breed of adventurers, urban adventurers who drifted out at night looking for action with a black man's code to fit their facts," wrote NORMAN MAILER in his 1957 essay, *The White Negro: Superficial Reflections On The Hipster*. "The hipster had absorbed the existentialist synapses of the Negro, and for practical purposes could be considered a white Negro."

Since then, the white emasculation of black pop has somehow been vindicated. The history of pop is the history of the white exploiting the black, never more so than during the Eighties, when seemingly every black musical genre was plundered by pop groups in desperate need of reinvention. We took this as a given. What has always been preposterous, though, is the white pop star's appropriation of the black experience – at great pains to empathise and "understand" – while denouncing their own race. As the Disneylandisation of America continues apace, so radical pop is pushed to the margins, in a desperate search for identity. These days the margins are overcrowded, as every seventeen-year old with a guitar or a drum machine tries to redefine rebellion. Duh – one way to do this is to think *black*.

L

The music business has had this weird racial subtext since the dawn of rock'n'roll. JANIS JOPLIN: "Being black for a while will make me a better white." MADONNA: "If being black is synonymous with having soul, then, yes, I feel that I am." THIRD BASS: "Yo! White people are wack. We're kind of embarrassed to be white." ANNIE LENNOX: "When I was singing I'd think of myself as a very old black man – I stepped into that persona."

In an article in the premier issue of *Vibe*, the American glossy magazine dedicated to hip-hop culture (the first magazine of its kind, *Vibe* was published by QUINCY JONES in conjunction with Time Publishing Ventures), JAMES LEDBETTER bemoaned this renouncing of race: "American writers, sociologists, and armchair sociologists have long spotlighted black wannabes, arguing that their desire to be black has some tenuous connection to Africa-American social oppression. [But] the disgust with wannabes comes from the sheer vulgarity of the white who cavalierly adopts the black mantle without having to experience life-long racism, restricted economic opportunity, or any of the thousand insults that characterise black American life."

"So what?" said DOUG WIMBUSH, when I quizzed him about the ELVIS-factor. "We're not trying to reinvent the wheel here. Some things you'll never change. White bands have always ripped off black bands. Like, big deal. We just wanted our shot."

LOUNGE

"Into Vienna" (2.44) by JOHN BARRY (*The Living Daylights*, Warner Brothers) 1987; "La Femme D'Argent" (7.08) by AIR (*Moon Safari*, Source) 1998; "Largo" (2.58) by the SWINGLE SINGERS (*Going Baroque*, Philips) 1965; "Up Up And Away" (2.10) by RAY DAVIES & THE BUTTON-DOWN BRASS (*Star Tracks*,

L Philips) 1971; "Shoreline Drive" (5.41) by KARMA (*The Chillout Lounge,* ilabelweb.com) 2009; "Wives & Lovers" (2.46) by BURT BACHARACH (*Hit Maker!,* Kapp) 1965; "At The River" (3.13) by GROOVE ARMADA (*Vertigo,* Pepper) 1997; "Casino Royale" (2.37) by HERB ALPERT & THE TIJUANA BRASS (Single, A&M) 1967; "6 Underground" (3.48) by SNEAKER PIMPS (Single, One Little Indian) 1996; "Mas Que Nada" (2.39) by SERGIO MENDES & BRASIL '66 (Single, A&M) 1966; "That Day In Monterey" (6.00) by JOHN BELTRAN (*Human Engine,* Exceptional) 2006; "Milk" (4.46) by GARBAGE (*Garbage,* Mushroom) 1995; "Brazil" (3.28) by GEOFF MULDAUR (*Brazil,* Milan) 1992; "Exotique Bossa Nova" (2.20) by MARTIN DENNY (*The Versatile Martin Denny,* Liberty) 1966; "Inner Flight" (5.02) by PRIMAL SCREAM (*Screamadelica,* Creation) 1991; "State Of Grace" (5.22) by CHILLED BY NATURE (*The Chillout Lounge,* ilabelweb.com) 2009; "Man Alive" (2.00) by TONY HATCH (*Downtown With Tony Hatch,* Pye) 1967; "The Odd Couple" (1.16) (*Television's Greatest Hits Volume II,* Tee Vee Toons Inc.) 1986; "Love Is The Word" (4.34) by SWEETBACK (*Stage (2),* Epic) 2004; "A Swingin' Safari" (3.07) by BERT KAEMPFERT & HIS ORCHESTRA (*A Swingin' Safari,* Polydor) 1962; "Tokyo Melody" (3.06) by HELMUT ZACHARIAS (Single, Polydor) 1964; "Pure Pleasure Seeker" (6.30) by MOLOKO (*Things To Make And Do,* Echo) 2000; "Sleepwalk" (2.23) by SANTO & JOHNNY (*Mermaids,* Epic) 1990; "Robinson Crusoe" (3.49) by the ART OF NOISE (*The Best Of The Art Of Noise,* China) 1992; "Protection" (7.51) by MASSIVE ATTACK (*Protection,* Circa) 1994; "Our Prayer" (1.06) by the BEACH BOYS (*20/20,* Capital) 1969; "Shiver" (2.53) by VIRNA LINDT (*Shiver,* Compact) 1984; "Music To Watch Girls By" (2.57) by RAY CONNIFF (*It Must Be Him,* CBS) 1970; "Underneath The Weeping Willow" (2.23) by GRANDADDY (*The Sophtware Slump,* V2) 2000; "Un Homme Et Une Femme (2.34) by FRANCIS LAI (*Un Homme Et Une Femme,* United Artists) 1966; "Pacific Coast Highway" (3.20) by BURT BACHARACH (*On The Move,* Chevrolet) 1970; "4th Chapter" (5.17) by ORG LOUNGE FEATURING COCO STREET (*ORG Lounge,* Water Music Records) 2001; "Novio" (2.35) by MOBY (*I Like To Score,* Mute) 1997; "Lolita Ya Ya" (3.20)

by NELSON RIDDLE (*Lolita*, MCA) 1961; "The Return" (3.25) by
RITHMA (*Las Salinas Sessions*, Jockey Club Salinas) 2004;
"Desafinado" (2.16) by DUNCAN LAMONT (*The Best Of The
Bossa Novas*, MFP) 1970; "Fool On The Hill" (2.53) by ALAN
MOOREHOUSE (*Beatles, Bach & Bacharach Go Bossa*, MFP)
1971; "I Have Seen" (5.04) by ZERO 7 (*Simple Things*, Ultimate
Dilemma) 2001; "Theme From A Summer Place" (2.25) by
LIBERACE (*The Best Of Liberace*, MCA) 1972; "The Warmth Of
The Sun" (2.13) by MURRY WILSON (*The Many Moods of Murry
Wilson*, Capitol) 1967; "Follow Your Bliss" (4.10) by the B-52s
(*Cosmic Thing*, Reprise) 1989; "Theme De Catherine" (2.50)
by FRANCIS LAI (*Vivre Pour Vivre*, United Artists) 1967.

COURTNEY LOVE

I don't often find women scary, but I saw Love at the private
view of an art show in London about ten years after Kurt
Cobain died, and she looked completely intimidating – she
reminded me a little of NANCY SPUNGEN, and appeared to be
possessed of a similar unpredictability. I've never been much
of a fan of her or her music, and probably because of that
have never really found her intriguing. However, I enjoyed
this alleged exchange between her and NEIL STRAUSS that was
reprinted in his book *Everyone Loves You When You're Dead*:

"The place was Courtney Love's house in Los Angeles. The
time was very late. The moment was when she leaped off her
bed and suddenly said...
COURTNEY LOVE: Say hi to Kurt.
She walks to a dresser, pulls open a drawer, and removes
a square-shaped tin. She removes the lid, revealing a plastic
bag full of white ashes. A faint smell of jasmine emanates
from the tin.
LOVE: Too bad you don't do coke. Otherwise I'd suggest
taking a metal straw to it."

411

Lyle Lovett

L

A quarter of a century after becoming country music's new big thing, "God Will" is still the record which exemplifies what Lovett does best. The long, tall Texan with the broccoli hair was at the vanguard of the new country boom, adding blues, swing, R&B, jazz and a large pinch of barbeque salt (with enchiladas and a guacamole salad on the side) to his sound. His first three records might be the best place for a primer – his eponymous debut album from 1986, *Pontiac* from the following year, and *Lyle Lovett And His Large Band* from 1989 – all of which displayed a healthy disregard for the traditional country legacy of melancholy and aw-shucks pomposity. Songs such as "L.A. County", "If I Had A Boat", "She's No Lady", "Cowboy Man", and "Here I Am" ("Hello, I'm the guy who sits next to you and reads the newspaper over your shoulder/Wait, don't turn the page, I'm not finished...") showed he was no C&W journeyman or down-home lone star, but a pragmatic troubadour mixing up a potent brew of expedient country (perhaps not surprisingly, he has a degree in journalism). "I really just write from a common emotional perspective. I just write songs to represent my feelings as accurately as I can," he said. "That's all." That's not all at all, and he keeps an arsenal of one-liners stashed in his ten-gallon hat (on the title track of his eleventh album, *Natural Forces*, he rhymes these words with "home is where my horse is").

John Lydon

One wonders what the 1976 Johnny Rotten would have made of the 2009 version – John Lydon, the sometimes lovable eccentric and occasionally great British institution who appears in advertisements for Country Life butter, stars on reality TV shows and in documentaries (he has presented programmes on bugs, gorillas, and sharks), and re-records the SEX PISTOLS' most famous songs for video games ("Pretty Vacant" for Skate, and "Anarchy In The UK" for Guitar Hero III), and yet who treats Britain with the same comical disdain as he did when he first became infamous. Would he have been pleased by his curmudgeonly elder self, a figure who has turned from spiky little street urchin into quintessential grumpy old man? Or would he be appalled that he had faded away rather than burnt out?

Back in the day I used to see Lydon all over London – down at the Roxy, the Marquee and the Nashville, or walking, sullenly along the Kings Road, trying to avoid curious policemen and the attentions of those Fifties throwbacks and youth culture dinosaurs, teddy boys. And in 1986, ten years after doing my punk National Service I met Lydon again, in a rented house in West London, and spent an afternoon with him, belching Red Stripe, listening to him swear, and watching him recite passages from WINSTON CHURCHILL's memoirs. He was back in town to fight – and win – the SEX PISTOLS VS MALCOLM MCLAREN, their former manager, High Court case. Lydon, STEVE JONES, drummer PAUL COOK, and ANNE BEVERLEY (SID VICIOUS's mother) each walked away with a cool £250,000.

He was openly contemptuous of McLaren with me, and spent nearly an hour assassinating his character, demonising him as a particularly unpleasant FAGIN for our times, a carpetbagger of ill repute.

"I learnt nothing from Malcolm," said Lydon. "He learnt from me if anything. I wrote the songs, I gave it all the direction, I was the brains. Not him. In hindsight he claims it was all him, but then he conceded so badly in court that he obviously knows he was wrong. Malcolm wouldn't know one end of a console from another. To him it's a big lump of metal with flashing lights... and he's got a cheek putting his name to all those records that were made by TREVOR HORN and all the rest."

When we met, far from being the miserable guttersnipe, Lydon adopted the wisecracking lush stance, jumping around the room in his over-sized baggy tartan suit shouting abuse at anyone or anything that occurred to him – journalists, tabloid warmongering and critical pomposity. At the time Lydon was

L worshipped like a god in such unlikely places as Japan and Australia, and had even built up a considerable fan base in North America, where he was thought of as the patron saint of punk, a sort of British IGGY POP. But without such a good torso. Or the sex appeal. Or the pecs. Or the sonorous voice.

Predictably, he reserved the most bile for journalists, a species he never had much time for, before or since.

"I've been way over the top with most of the journalists I've seen this time, playing up the nasty image, and I'm amazed at how many of them eat it up. More, more, more they say! However I've learned more from them than they have from me, which is that basically nothing is happening in this country. Because [the SEX PISTOLS] were so adamant and took such a definite stance, it was obvious that the backlash would be dreary, wimpy homosexual disco music – nail varnish on the keyboards."

In the years since, John Lydon has become something of a reductive idea, and unfortunately the lasting impression he leaves is of someone who has inherited the least exciting and least ambitious virtues of the punk ethos, someone for whom brute strength and vulgarity are benchmarks of cultural sophistication. For John Lydon, a belch is an acceptable form of rebuke, while insolence and wilful ignorance is something to be celebrated.

Regardless of his loutishness, his boorishness, and his bizarre attempts to behave as unpleasantly as possible, Lydon can, occasionally, still give good gab – as anyone who saw his appearance on *I'm A Celebrity Get Me Out Of Here*, or his performance in the documentary sections of JULIEN TEMPLE'S DVD *There'll Always Be An England*, will know. My favourite quote that afternoon, back in 1986, came when I asked Lydon what he thought of Red Wedge, the socialist musical collective spearheaded by the likes of BILLY BRAGG, and initiated to try to propel NEIL KINNOCK to power. "Red Wedge? It's the last resort of the gambling man. Save the Labour Party! Don't you think it's tragic that they can't save themselves?"

M

Paul McCartney

CHARLES SCHULZ's *Peanuts* cartoon strip is something that tends not to resonate very much with me. I doubt if it resonates with many men. After all, its rather trite homilies are the sort of thing appreciated by a select bunch: largely by overly-sentimental senior citizens, lovesick teenagers or prepubescent girls looking for scrapbook alternatives to their torn-out photographs of ZAC EFRON or ROBERT PATTINSON. Come to think of it, maybe *Peanuts* isn't so popular with them either, any more.

However, there is one strip that has always stayed with me, even though I haven't seen it for over thirty years. This is the one where the much-beleaguered LINUS says to his pal CHARLIE BROWN: "Charlie, you know that one day of your life will always be better than any other?"

"Sure," says CHARLIE BROWN, "everybody knows that. Why do you ask?"

"Well," says LINUS, "what if you've already had it?"

If you were a cynical person, you might think that this is a question PAUL MCCARTNEY asks himself on a regular basis. Come on, what could possibly top having five records in the American Top Ten? What could top playing Shea Stadium to the loudest crowd in history? Or making *Sergeant Pepper*? Or "Hey Jude"? Or "Let It Be"? What on earth could possibly top being revered by an entire generation? Or two. What could top being – along with DAVID BAILEY, the ROLLING STONES, and MICHAEL CAINE – pretty much responsible for the Sixties? What could top being a Beatle? Here is a man who gave his name to the RAMONES (PAUL RAMONE being McCartney's old stage name), who bought the rights to "Chopsticks" and "Happy Birthday", who effortlessly recorded duets with MICHAEL JACKSON (even though they weren't very good), whose "Yesterday" is the most popular of all time (2,400 mangled cover versions and counting), who conjured up the bass part for JOHN LENNON's "Come Together" in a jot, whose performance at Superbowl XXXIX was watched by a live TV audience of 145 million, whose first concert in Moscow took on all the trappings of a state visit, including a more-than-warm welcome from VLADIMIR PUTIN.

I think it's fair to say that there have always been more John people than Paul people. At least since 1970, when the BEATLES split, and especially since 1980, when Lennon was shot.

Lennon is untouchable now, immortal. His myth can be flattered in perpetuity because he is no longer with us. McCartney meanwhile has had to be content with growing old, happy, and saggy around the middle, not least metaphorically. And while it would be pointless to say that Lennon was the weaker half of the Lennon/McCartney partnership, at his worst he was certainly the more excessive sentimentalist, yet it's his former partner we like to dismiss; McCartney who tends to come off worse in comparisons.

At first sight there is certainly enough to criticise him for. He is, after all, the man who was blamed for splitting up the most important group in the world; the man who put his family before ambition and who rested on his laurels for longer than most artists have careers; the man responsible for some of the most fatuous pop songs of the last thirty years, songs that could easily accompany TV advertisements for deodorant or sanitary towels.

McCartney has released a sufficiency of unpalatable material in the last thirty years, displaying a surprising gaucheness rarely seen in pop: he wrote "Ebony And Ivory", "Mull Of Kintyre", and plenty more nursery rhymes loitering on the outskirts of awful. Like his Sixties contemporary BRIAN WILSON, in his thirties McCartney seemed to rush into the kindergarten, hastened by a belief that the key to his success lay, simply enough, in simplicity. And whereas Wilson's twee meanderings were the result of deadening medication and a wandering mind, McCartney's seemed willed by an arrant desire to turn his domestic life into his career. What else can explain the lurid nonsense of "Mary Had A Little Lamb",

"Wonderful Christmas Time", "We All Stand Together", or "The Girl Is Mine"?

If, in the early days of their partnership, Lennon and McCartney were sparks and petrol threatening to mix (McCartney jealous of Lennon's cynicism, Lennon mindful of McCartney's commercial sense of purpose), by the time they had been unleashed from the BEATLES both were eager to wallow in the joys of domesticity. With Lennon this decision was almost militant – John and Yoko against the Man! In Bags! In Bed! In The Amsterdam Hilton! – but in McCartney's case it was exactly the opposite. If YOKO ONO was Lennon's way of shouting at the world, LINDA EASTMAN, the photographer whom McCartney married at Marylebone Registry Office in London, in March 1969, was the ex-Beatle's means of settling down. Both men flaunted their women on their record covers, recording with them, performing with them. They showed enormous arrogance in thinking the world would be interested in their respective spouses, but the truth is that it was. Commonplace now, three decades ago this type of personal publicity was a novelty and, as Beatle Paul and Beatle John brandished their women on their arms, we sat up and listened.

McCartney's first records after leaving the BEATLES were slight affairs, brimming with melody if not meaning. After years of wanting more and more and more and more, McCartney suddenly wanted less. Furious that Lennon and GEORGE HARRISON had allowed legendary producer PHIL SPECTOR to remix his beloved "The Long And Winding Road" on *Let It Be* (layering it with a wash of JAMES LAST-style strings), McCartney released his first solo album – *McCartney* – three weeks before it in the spring of 1970, hoping to steal its thunder. At the time the album was considered a disappointment – the makeshift quality and conspicuously handmade nature of his early work annoyed those who were acclimatised to sophisticated BEATLES' product – though in hindsight, its almost scatter-shot celebration of "home, family, love", as McCartney called it, seems remarkably tender and unequivocally sincere.

M

Critics like to say that McCartney's career is analogous to ORSON WELLES', who started out with *Citizen Kane* and ending up doing sherry commercials. (The same could be said of FRANCIS FORD COPPOLA. I overheard him in The Carlyle Hotel in New York a few years ago, telling an admirer that, 'I've had my brushes with creativity. I used to make films to make art; now I make films to make wine.')

But McCartney carried on regardless, releasing album-after-single-after-album of homegrown paeans to love and marriage. If the most evocative pop music resembles westerns – epic, grandiose, an assault on the senses – then McCartney's early records were more like home movies, with the same bad editing, half-hearted ideas, and 'little moments' that often mean little to those uninvolved with the subject. They did, however, overflow with charm. His songs are often little more than doodles, but as the late, great *New Yorker* cartoonist SAUL STEINBERG once said, 'The doodle is the brooding of the human hand.' And, in McCartney's case, the human heart.

McCartney saw himself as a variety artist, a music hall tinker able to knock off a ballad as well as a sweaty R&B workout; an all-round entertainer firmly rooted in the tradition of the music hall and early American rock'n'roll. Always a staunch traditionalist, the man responsible for some of the most far-reaching and influential music ever recorded has, in following years, often seemed tyrannically nostalgic for the early days of pop – his neon-garlanded world little but a giant replica of a jukebox.

To paint him as pop's first real slacker is a mistake, though, as his extraordinary sequence of solo albums proves. When he formed the lamentable WINGS at the end of 1971, he again put his head above the parapet, and so risked constant comparison with his "previous group". McCartney wanted success. Badly. And during the Seventies he turned WINGS into a stadium-filling supergroup. Releasing seven albums, from the sublime (*Band On The Run,* 1973) to the ridiculous (*Back To The Egg,* 1979) via the merely ordinary (*Venus*

And Mars, 1975). And though this was almost beyond the call of duty, for some it was never going to be enough.

M

Having said that, many of McCartney's post-BEATLES songs have been criminally undervalued, and it's possible to imagine lots of them sitting quite happily next to Lennon's abrasive psychedelia, or Harrison's partially composed complaints on any number of BEATLES LPs. Try replacing "Good Day Sunshine" with "Let 'Em In" (*Wings At The Speed Of Sound,* 1976), say, or "Martha My Dear" with "Girlfriend" (*London Town,* 1978). Imagine "Monkberry Moon Delight" (*Ram,* 1971) on the "White Album", or "Letting Go" (the 1975 single) on *Abbey Road.* With iTunes you can do just that. Some of the things McCartney's written in the last thirty years are easily as good as anything he wrote in the previous ten. Is there really so much wrong with "My Brave Face" (*Flowers In The Dirt,* 1989), "Every Night" (*McCartney, 1970*), "Young Boy" (1997's *Flaming Pie*), or "Some People Never Know" (*Wild Life,* 1971), "This Never Happened Before" (*Chaos And Creation In The Back Yard,* 2005), or "Ever Present Past" (*Memory Almost Full,* 2007)? What about "Dear Friend", about which the *Independent* journalist RICHARD WILLIAMS said: "If 'Dear Friend' had been the first track on the 'White Album' instead of the last track on his least successful post-BEATLES effort [*Wild Life*], it would be as well know as 'Yesterday'." Personally, I think he can be forgiven anything for writing the exultant brass coda at the end of his 1982 hit "Take It Away", one of the most glorious, epiphanic forty-two seconds you'll find on a record anywhere.

MALCOLM MCLAREN

When Malcolm McLaren died in April 2010, at the age of sixty-four, he had already embarked upon a project that would have seen his legacy burnished even more. McLaren was some way into his autobiography, a book that would

M

have no doubt acted as some sort of Situationist tip-sheet, a manual of subversion using the many highlights of his extraordinary career as blueprints for causing chaos.

As it is, it will probably never see the light of day – if you went to McLaren's website in the weeks after his death, it simply said, somewhat predictably, "Malcolm will return shortly..." – although there is one hell of a story to tell.

McLaren's career was one of haphazard provocation, a career that pinballed around the entertainment industry without apparent rhyme or reason. He was a shopkeeper, entrepreneur, fashion designer, impresario, cultural theorist, showman, pop manager, singer, television presenter, writer, and agent provocateur. Oh, and the manager of the SEX PISTOLS, the most incendiary British pop group of all time. But most of all he was an iconoclast, one whose legacy and influence can be seen in everything from DAMIEN HIRST'S guerilla art to the quasi-punk clothes in Top Shop.

McLaren's only proper job was in 1962, when he was sixteen, and went off to work as a trainee taster for GEORGE SANDEMAN, the wine merchant. "The occasional glass of sherry on religious days was the only wine I'd tasted. But my mother, a walking cliché of nouveau riche, thought this sounded respectable enough to boast about at cocktail parties," he said. He hated the job so much he eventually got himself fired by smoking Gitanes, prompting a letter from Sandeman to his mother: "Your son is not fit to work in this firm. He's smoking foreign cigarettes, preventing other boys from tasting and smelling our wines. He's a saboteur!"

Wasn't he just.

When he drank Bordeaux or Burgundy later with his fellow students at St Martin's School of Art, he'd find himself saying, "This one's got a big back on it: older it is, bigger the back. A truly heroic, masculine body." Or that a cheap Beaujolais was, "young, frilly, got to watch her – she'll betray you." His friends would look at him, bemused, as if he were an intriguing, slightly exotic being, just off the boat from Burma.

McLaren claimed to have conducted his life by two rules: "Turn left, if you're supposed to turn right; go through any door that you're not supposed to enter." Proving that he had lost none of his relish for a stunt – or a press release – in 1999 he announced that he was going to run for London mayor on a manifesto that included legalised brothels and selling alcohol in libraries. The journalist JULIE BURCHILL once said that, "We are all children of Thatcher and McLaren," and in some respects she was right; his entrepreneurial spirit, and the way in which he was obsessed with harnessing Britain's innate counter-cultural street style, influenced an entire generation of media-savvy boulevardiers. McLaren's girlfriend, YOUNG KIM, compared him to ANDY WARHOL, describing him as the ultimate postmodern artist: "I think Malcolm recognised he had changed the culture, he saw he had changed the world."

And didn't he like talking about it – McLaren could talk for Britain. Could talk for hours on end. He didn't need an audience, as he was usually so pleased with himself that his conversations were just extremely long soliloquies.

It was nearly twenty-five years ago but the memory still lingers. The venue for my interview with Malcolm McLaren was the Hiroko sushi bar in the Kensington Hilton, next to Shepherd's Bush roundabout in west London. McLaren had just flown in from Los Angeles, where he was living at the time with LAUREN HUTTON, for a business meeting. He was spending a lot of time lecturing on the American college circuit, and had come to see his agent about more bookings. We drank and talked for nearly three hours, about his passion for Hutton ("She's a tough old girl, you know, but I love her..."), his mother ("I never spoke a f****** word to her, I just considered her to be one of those mad older sisters that you'd look at out of the corner of your eye..."), and – at length – VIVIENNE WESTWOOD, from whom he was then estranged ("Looking back I think I was in love with her, but I don't think I did her or the relationship justice, in fact I know I didn't...").

That night McLaren became quite emotional about Westwood – boring, even – and at one point even started

M crying. Due to the sake I eventually had to find a loo, which was situated somewhere over on the other side of the hotel lobby, a good fifty yards away. When I eventually returned I saw McLaren – who, by this stage was quite astonishingly drunk – babbling away into my tape recorder. When I transcribed the tape a few days later, I found more than babble. Malcolm – who was oblivious to most people at the best of times – had obviously not realised, or cared that I had taken my leave, and had continued talking away as though I was sitting next to him all the time. The tape had it all: "You know man, I really loved that girl. I loved Vivienne so much, man, you know? I really, really loved her. She was the love of my life, and I never ever should have left her. I was crazy, but there were so many things I wanted to do..."

A few years later I went out with McLaren again, to a small private members bar called Fred's that used to be in the building next to *Private Eye*, deep in Soho. We spent the first hour or so talking about a LED ZEPPELIN project that he was trying to get off the ground. Essentially it was a biopic of the hoary old rock'n'roll Vikings, and he said he had already secured MIKE FIGGIS to direct it, and BARRY KEEFE (who had scripted *The Long Good Friday*) to write it. Impressive? It certainly sounded so. We were soon interrupted by various people wanting to shake McLaren's hand, and so we spent much of the night separated from each other. But Fred's was quite a small club, no bigger than most people's kitchens, and every time I bumped into McLaren he would be telling someone his LED ZEPPELIN story. However the drunker he got, the more he would embellish it, and by the end of the evening, DANIEL DAY LEWIS had agreed to play ROBERT PLANT, ROBBIE COLTRANE had apparently signed on to play the group's legendary manager PETER GRANT, and – who knew?! – STEVEN SPIELBERG had signed up to direct. He looked like a cross between ARTHUR DALEY and FAGIN, and when I gave him a knowing wink, looked at me as though he were simply selling a secondhand car.

This was one of the many projects that McLaren failed to get off the ground, although to him they weren't failures, only intriguing departures, and in his eyes the fact that they didn't reach fruition – deep breath: a musical about the IRA; a movie called *Fashion Beast* based on the life of CHRISTIAN DIOR; *Rock'n'Roll Godfather*, a gangster movie about the first thirty years of pop; a stage show of *Fans*; *Surf Nazis*... etc, etc – was no reflection of his abilities, only a reflection of other people's misjudgment.

SHIRLEY MACLAINE

She was a man's woman with a big mouth and a cute smile, the occasional vamp with a firecracker wit and a wardrobe full of fishnets. Sexy, a kook, outspoken both onscreen and off, Shirley MacLaine had the ability to be both haughty and fun in the same instant – she had character and she had spunk and she looked like she could, if need be, party hard. For a while she appeared typecast as the "tart with a heart", and while not indelible, this gave her a patina of sluttishness which made her ever more appealing to men. She would have fitted into the TV world of *Mad Men* as easily as she once slipped into her red satin slip, the one she always seemed to find in her wardrobe. Back then, she played hookers, and don't they all wear red satin slips?

She was sparkle personified, a sexy little imp in a pencil skirt and heels, the cutest squinty smile, eyelashes worthy of a RISKO cartoon, playing shop girls and princesses with equal finesse. She was the same vintage as MARILYN MONROE, yet Marilyn's explosive mix of vulnerability and innate sexuality was almost the exact opposite of what MacLaine was all about. Deep down, ambition was a motive that MacLaine understood implicitly, and yet one that completely destroyed Monroe. DAVID THOMSON, the doyen of film critics, has been faint in his praise for MacLaine, but wrote, in his *Biographical Dictionary Of Film*, "MacLaine the beginner was very impressive: she had smart bounce, a sense of humour, and a wicked streak that made her short red hair seem tomboyish."

M Shirley MacLaine was always a hoofer, never a dancer. Her brother, WARREN BEATTY, summed it up when he told her, quite bluntly, "You were never a great dancer, but you were always terrific at the razzle-dazzle." As a singer, she was often marginalised, yet she was as good as many of her peers – just check out her duet with FRANK SINATRA on "Let's Do It" from the 1960 movie *Can Can*, her performance in *Sweet Charity* from 1969, or indeed the 1976 album, *Shirley MacLaine Live At The Palace*. As a child she was the neighbourhood tomboy; she hated dolls, fought with boys, emptied dustbins onto her neighbours' lawn. At fourteen she was playing for her school baseball team. But, tomboy or not, she always wanted to dance – and ballet, at that. "I kept telling mother, 'I want to be a little dancing girl.'" She was tenacious, uppity, determined: at sixteen she took the role of fairy godmother in the school's production of the ballet Cinderella, despite having a broken ankle. Even then she knew what she wanted.

Above all else, and there is a lot, Shirley MacLaine has always been a survivor – like her friend BARBRA STREISAND, one of the few elder stateswomen of American show business. Resilient star, jobbing actor (she was always too vaudeville to be a great actor), bestselling author, metaphysical oddball and, at times, fervent political animal – for years what MacLaine had more than anything was stamina.

She has played hookers and heroines and ingénues and blue stockings, and yet her defining role is probably the elevator operator she played in BILLY WILDER's bittersweet comedy *The Apartment*, first released in 1960. She starred opposite JACK LEMMON, an office clerk in a *Playboy*-era Manhattan insurance agency who lets the executives in his office use his apartment for the odd afternoon dalliance. Among them is his boss, who Lemmon eventually learns is using his place to sleep with MacLaine, who he has been worshipping from afar. Lemmon and MacLaine both gave "career" performances, and the film went on to win five Oscars, including Best Picture, having been nominated for ten (this was the last black and white film to win until *Schindler's List* in1993). Wilder's script was also justly celebrated, and it contains a payoff line almost as famous, and possibly funnier, than the last line of his previous film, *Some Like It Hot*. It was delivered by MacLaine.

M

In *The Apartment* she was sexy, vulnerable, coquettish, sluttish, and homely. Her character maybe wasn't the sharpest tack in the tack drawer, but then at the time – an era recently conjured up again so vividly by MATTHEW WEINER's *Mad Men* – this was considered an asset too. She writes about the movie on her website:

"We started filming *The Apartment* with twenty-nine pages of script and JACK LEMMON and I had no idea how the film would end and neither did BILLY WILDER. So he just watched our relationship to see how the chemistry would evolve. Everything was evolving. At the time I was hanging with FRANK [SINATRA] and DEAN [MARTIN], learning how to play gin rummy (that's why the gin game is in the apartment). BILLY WILDER was such a fabulous writer/director that the studio just financed the film without knowing what he would do, but they did know his reputation of creating great films and the studios knew their investment was secure. Billy could do a film on the phone book and studios and actors would stand in line to be part of the project.

"*The Apartment* was great... a wonderful shoot and it was one of the first pictures where we mixed comedy and drama together. And many of the people at the screening seemed confused as to whether it was comedy or drama. I remember MARILYN MONROE was at the screening. She had no makeup on and was wrapped up in a mink coat. In her low whispery voice she said... 'The picture is a wonderful examination of the corporate world.' My mouth flew open! She got it!"

She received her second Academy Award nomination for *The Apartment* (the first was for *Some Came Running*), losing out to ELIZABETH TAYLOR for *Butterfield 8*.

I interviewed MacLaine over fifteen years ago, at her ranch style beach house way up in Malibu, the celebrity playground ten miles north of Santa Monica on California's Pacific Coast Highway. Along with Beverly Hills and Bel Air, Malibu is where the real Hollywood money lives, or at least where it comes for the weekend. Sleek gunmetal Mercedes coupés, BMQ soft-tops, vintage Corvettes, and the occasional personalised Rolls Royce crowded the dirty beach road where MacLaine had her two-storey apartment. In the rarefied Malibu air, the signs on garages were unequivocal: unauthorised cars will be towed. Immediately. At the owner's expense. I'd just spent two weeks driving across America, from New York to LA, and had to spend an extra week in the city waiting to interview her because she was sick. She eventually agreed to see me on her birthday, so on the drive out from the city that day I stopped in Malibu village to buy her some flowers. Assuming the florist was probably as expensive as everything else in the area, I spent about twice as much on a bouquet as I normally would; silly me – when I turned up at her front door I was carrying a small garden centre in my arms, and probably looked to her like a rather enthusiastic stalker. She was about sixty at the time, and obviously couldn't care less about being interviewed. She had a film to promote – a rather lame affair starring Nicolas Cage called *Guarding Tess* – and was simply doing the rounds. But she couldn't have been more generous with her time or her anecdotes. She didn't know me from a hole in the Pacific Coast Highway, but she was never going to read the piece anyway, and having been interviewed thousands of times over the years, I'm sure was long passed worrying whether or not I was going to be kind or vicious.

Her house was on stilts, with the beautiful (and strictly private) Malibu beach to the front and a miniature Japanese garden, complete with ornamental wooden bridge, to the rear. In true Japanese fashion, it looked more like a hotel suite than a superstar's lair. She has always bragged that she is not interested in material goods, and her home was testimony to this.

There was carved oak furniture everywhere, with an enormous oak coffee table covered in crystals taking up much of the living room. Other tables were covered with African figurines, Chinese pots, Indonesian stone elephants and knick-knacks galore. There were Japanese

prints on the wall, big potted palms on bigger rugs, and
the obligatory wind chimes. Dozens of small, silver-framed
photographs showed MacLaine receiving her Oscar in 1983
(she accepted her long-awaited Academy Award, for *Terms
Of Endearment*, typically: "I deserve this," she said, to the
hoots of the assembled Hollywood big shots); MacLaine
with her parents, husband and daughter; with Beatty; and
with her many famous friends: JIMMY CARTER, LIZA MINNELLI,
JACK NICHOLSON, the DALAI LAMA, GEORGE MCGOVERN, FRANK
SINATRA and KHRUSHCHEV (same picture), FIDEL CASTRO and
the camp magicians SIEGFRIED AND ROY (different pictures).
On the forty-foot veranda overlooking the Pacific there was a
doormat. It was very Shirley MacLaine: "Welcome UFOs and
their crews," it said.

She paid for this view more than forty-five years ago with
money earned from her first flush of success, in films like
*The Trouble With Harry, Can Can, Around The World In
Eighty Days*, and *Some Came Running*. There are very few
accidental celebrities and MacLaine, who like her brother,
altered her name to make it sound more "sophisticated",
is certainly not one of them. She was always determined to
succeed. In 1950, having outgrown Virginia, she hightailed
it to New York, looking for luck. Chorus-line work came and
went, notably in RODGERS AND HAMMERSTEIN's *Oklahoma!* She
cut a dash with her long, wanton red hair, her 34-24-34 figure,
legs that put most dancers' to shame, and freckles. Lots and
lots of freckles.

Her break came early, in true fairytale fashion. In 1954, in
a bizarre stroke of luck, she was offered the job of understudy
to CAROL HANEY, the lead in the Broadway production of *The
Pyjama Game*. Shortly into the run Haney broke her ankle,
so MacLaine stepped into her shoes and was an overnight
sensation. Quickly signed up by the producer HAL WALLIS, she
was whizzed off to Hollywood, where she has stayed, off and
on, ever since.

Since Hollywood was born, women have been subjected
to the perverse and the mundane, cast as either hysterical

femmes fatales, or decorative, reactive adjuncts. But MacLaine was never really an ingénue, and she used her fame to forge her own on-screen persona – one that allowed her to wander through a succession of movies displaying a sparkly, soft-centred cynicism, always delicately mixing comedy with pathos. The tomboy always knew what she was good at. During her first screen test she was asked what she wanted to make of her career. Her reply was succinct: "To do comedy. Comedy with real good acting." So a kook was born, a kook who was to turn up in *The Apartment, My Geisha, Irma La Douce, Sweet Charity*, and dozens of other films requiring flirtatious, frowzy women. MacLaine has probably slept with as many people as her brother, but most of her indiscretions have been on screen. She has portrayed dozens of hookers, dancers, bar girls and molls. She played so many whores that she once said film studios did not pay her by the cheque: they simply left the money on her dressing-room table overnight. She was the girl next door all right, only she happened to live next door to a brothel. She gave birth to this character in the 1958 film *Some Came Running*, playing a prostitute called Ginny. The part was to guarantee her years of work playing archetypal tarts with hearts. There was a Faustian bargain to be made, but not one that troubled her when we met. "It wasn't the fact that I was playing hookers that worried me," she said. "It was the fact that I was playing so many victims. Then one day I turned around and became the victimiser."

For a while, back in the Fifties and Sixties, her image was bound-up completely with the Rat Pack. FRANK SINATRA and DEAN MARTIN were her "buddies", while she was their mascot. And although she was the only woman in their gang, she was treated just the same as the rest of them. She had no fear, and because of that was accepted as one of the boys. "They even teased me about it when I'd pull a water pistol out and point it at [mob boss] SAM GIANCANA." She remembers telling Giancana to go fuck himself when he tried to get her to eat his spaghetti, when she was on a diet. When he grabbed her arm, she kneed him in the balls. SAMMY DAVIS stopped the

skirmish and shoved her out of the room, but not before she
told Giancana to go fuck himself one more time. "The public
loves to fantasise about good-looking, dangerous teams of
men," she says, and she liked the attention and the acclaim
it brought her too. Who wouldn't? She said she was not
only flabbergasted by what she saw, but also by her reaction
to it. Once, when Sinatra, Martin and she were watching
television at two in the morning in a hotel in Vegas, Sinatra
suddenly got hungry and called the manager, demanding
that somebody wake up and fix them something to eat.
MacLaine could hear the manager mumble his irritation,
but knew that he probably liked the idea of seeing Sinatra
and Dino at two in the morning. The manager eventually
turned up with beer and sandwiches, walking into the suite
as Martin turned up the TV even louder. He started giving
Sinatra a hard time about his attitude, the noise from the TV,
and for ordering food at such a late hour (twenty-four hour
room service had yet to hit Vegas). Sinatra told the manager
to go fuck himself (a familiar refrain in the Rat Pack), the
manager called him a "skinny wop" and so Sinatra punched
him full in the face. Martin simply turned up the TV even
more, and said, "If you're gonna fight, do it on the other
side of the room." He then opened a beer, and inspected his
sandwich. "Too much mayo," he said. MacLaine stood there
aghast; was this appalling behaviour, or was this fun? She
soon realised that she was both intrigued by and attracted to
the unpredictability of their behaviour. "In much the same
way as the American culture is attracted to the Godfather
films of COPPOLA, I was attracted to observing the real thing
with Frank and company," she wrote in her 1995 memoir,
My Lucky Stars. "I admit to an interest in gangsters – almost
like a child watching a car wreck with my hands over one eye.
I couldn't stop gaping."

There have been rumours about her sexual involvement
with the group for decades, but although she readily admits
to having a crush on DEAN MARTIN, she denies ever having a
physical relationship with any of them.

M

The hoofer was not what I expected. I had imagined a bit of an ogre, an evangelical, an *Ab-Fab* virago. But there was nothing overwhelming or overbearing about her. Wearing a multicoloured pastel sweater over a striped cotton shirt, baggy blue jeans, and pink plastic shoes with dainty blue laces – that familiar red hair (which did not look dyed, though it surely must have been) falling over her face – she sat curled up in an armchair, looking crumpled and a little forlorn. She was not unreasonably defensive – having been dragged over the coals for some of the more preposterous stories in her autobiographies, she had obviously become resigned to criticism – though she was not all smiles. But then she has had to tell her story a thousand times or more.

She was born to middle-class parents in Richmond, Virginia, on April 24, 1934. Her schoolteacher mother, KATHLYN MACLEAN BEATY, had done her fair share of painting and acting but gave it up once she married, to devote herself to her family. Subsequently she pushed both Shirley and later the younger Warren to fulfil the ambitions she could only dream of. MacLaine's father, Ira – a strict authoritarian, a drunk and a bully, and the right-wing (some would say racist) headmaster of Richmond High School – was not always so encouraging. But Shirley and Warren became what they wanted for themselves; that was the motivation for their overachievement.

For MacLaine, stardom was followed by love, though not in the conventional way. In 1954 she married an actor, STEVE PARKER, whom she had met in New York and who was thirteen years older than her. There were problems from the beginning. Having been brought up in Tokyo, where his father was a diplomat, Parker was unhappy about the kind of life he was living in Hollywood and longed to return; he was also sick of being labelled Mr Shirley MacLaine, his plans forever subjugated to those of his wife. Soon he was on a plane bound for Tokyo, for good.

Before he went, MacLaine became pregnant. In September 1956, driving herself to St John's Hospital in Santa Monica, she gave birth to a daughter, SACHI, who was, in MacLaine's own words, an "accident"; she was cavalier about her maternal responsibilities. "I guess I wasn't an ideal mother," she famously said. "Maybe that is not one of my virtues. I had SACHI with me for most of the first six years of her life, but making movies took me away from home so much." SACHI lived with her mother until one day when MacLaine returned home to discover a drunken babysitter in bed with a boyfriend and SACHI sitting outside on the kerb watching the traffic. Not prepared to let go of her career to spend more time with her daughter, Shirley sent SACHI, aged six, to Japan to live with her father. There followed many years of trans-Pacific commuting for both parents until, in 1980 after twenty-five years of open marriage, they divorced. Little has been heard of Parker since. "I may not have a conventional marriage," MacLaine said during the Parker years, "but then a lot of people don't. Marriage is a very hard state as practised today. I just have done the best I could with the situations I have been given to deal with."

Her other relationships seem to pale by comparison: there was a long relationship with the American journalist PETE HAMILL, a romance with ROBERT MITCHUM, and an alleged affair with the Australian politician ANDREW PEACOCK. She also claimed an affair with a senior British politician in the early Eighties.

Hollywood never claimed her, she maintains, and the hoofer took it all in her stride. "I never had a hard time at the studios," she says, the Malibu surf crashing benignly in the background. "I was a star at nineteen, I was rebellious, iconoclastic, did what I wanted, was never chased around a desk. I used to think there was something wrong with me, you know. No one ever propositioned me. But I think because I'm so blunt and direct, and because men don't usually like to be laughed at, they left me alone.

"In the early days it was an adventure sure, but it was never special, not really. It was never a great party. I come from this middle-class Virginia background which always dictated

M

a sense of awareness never to go too far, a slight detachment so that you don't lose your balance.

"I don't go too far into reacting to tragedy, or too far in being ecstatic about joy: I find my balance. And I was fighting for my balance when I arrived in Hollywood. So I was never overawed. I had this talent to be myself in front of the camera, and it just came too easy for me to take it all that seriously." Many years ago she said it all when she wrote: "Being a film star is what I do, not what I am."

Interviewing WARREN BEATTY is like asking a haemophiliac for a pint of blood, whereas his sister will expose her innermost thoughts. She is what one might call self-absorbed, with an insatiable curiosity, particularly about herself.

Her ego is such that she once wrote and starred in a television drama about herself, based on her own book. After all, who could play Shirley MacLaine better than the woman who invented her? "My curiosity is rather relentless, I know," she says, "which is why I think I give the impression of being this terrible overachiever. But that will never stop, because I am endlessly and ceaselessly curious. Maybe I should have been a talk-show host. I'm a very good judge of human nature – I can really pick people apart. I mean, look at you: do you realise you don't smile at all? You've been here an hour and you haven't smiled. Why?"

I smiled.

"There you go. That's worth an extra forty-five minutes!"

This self-absorption has manifested itself in nearly a dozen hugely successful autobiographies which have covered everything from her early home life, marriage, Hollywood and Beatty, to her famous metaphysical proclivities: psychic healing, astral projection, trance mediums, reincarnation, spiritual realignment, and the fundamental search for inner peace. MacLaine has turned her memoirs into an industry. And she is far from discreet. She has rigorously catalogued her childhood (Beatty says: "I see it very, very differently...").Nevertheless, her books have been bought in their millions, particularly by those middle Americans who had taken MacLaine to their hearts decades earlier and who were prepared for yet more reinvention (through her experiments MacLaine claims to have discovered that in previous lives she had been a whore, a madam, and a dancer, roles she played with great conviction when she first made it to Hollywood). The critics, though, have rarely been kind, treating her books like the cod-psychological junk you find in American supermarkets. She has gained a reputation for being more than slightly unhinged.

"When I wrote my first book, I literally turned it in by the pound – I think it was 1000 pages," she says. "It was difficult at first and I wasn't sure if the public would like me for this... I'm not what you'd call a writer. I'm no WILLIAM STYRON or NORMAN MAILER, I know that much."

In Hollywood they have great respect for the dead but little for the living, which is perhaps why MacLaine began to look away from the town for solace. Throughout the Seventies she moved in and out of the movies, indulging her wanderlust by travelling to Asia, the Soviet Union, Eastern Europe, and all points in between. She lived with the Masai in Kenya and led a women's delegation to China. There was always a country to visit or a cause to embrace.

"Sit me down in a room with GANHDI, the DALAI LAMA, HITLER, TED BUNDY and I would have so much fun," she says. "More fun than filming, performing or writing. That's what I like to do. That's what motivates me – people. I love meeting all these people who say they've seen UFOs. I'd like to meet them all and crack open their case." She told me she'd "love to sit down with PRINCESS DIANA and ask her why she thought it was ever going to be any different."

MacLaine has adopted causes like MIA FARROW used to adopt children: civil rights (the Ku Klux Klan once burnt crosses outside her bedroom window when she was touring the South and branded her a "nigger lover"), feminism, abortion, overpopulation, health care and, particularly, the Democrats. She worked briefly for ROBERT KENNEDY, JIMMY CARTER and EUGENE MCCARTHY, though it was GEORGE MCGOVERN who really cast a spell on her. In 1972 she campaigned tirelessly on his behalf with Beatty, becoming a one-woman standard-bearer – occasionally, because of her vivacity, overshadowing

M the candidate – and was heartbroken when he lost in the landslide to Nixon.

"Supporting McGovern was the most important thing I've ever done," she said to me, animated at last. "To have Nixon become president and appoint people to the Supreme Court was more than I could stand. I gave up a whole year to work for George and I paid for it all myself, a couple of hundred thousand dollars. I insisted on that. I was heartbroken when it didn't happen. I remember watching the returns come in and thinking what a terrible disaster it was. He only won one state, Massachusetts. If George had won I probably would have quit show business and gone into government."

But he didn't, so the hoofer went back to Hollywood, her fingers burnt. She was reluctant to go through it again. "JIMMY CARTER saw himself more as a spiritual leader," she says, "and though I did some things for him, he wasn't as left wing as George was. And I've always been very left wing, though that's slowly changing. Our leaders aren't what they were, certainly." She said she liked Clinton, "but he's indecisive."

A difficult period followed. She was on Nixon's enemies list along with numerous other Hollywood liberals, including GREGORY PECK, and the CIA reportedly ransacked her New York apartment four times. Since then she has been a lot less important as a political ally, though reports of her allegiances can still make the front page. A week after our meeting in California, she called me up in London to refute some tabloid allegations that she had given up metaphysics in favour of working for HILLARY CLINTON.

"Warren was very passionate about politics at the time, but I think the Reagan years took it out of him. Now Warren's too busy raising a family to get involved with the Democrats, but for a time he could have done something."

MacLaine was a star before her brother, which undoubtedly contributed to some of the well-catalogued stories of friction between the two over the years. When Beatty won his Oscar for *Reds* in 1981, MacLaine famously quipped from the stage that if he had concentrated more on work and less on women he might have won it sooner. Beatty and his then girlfriend, DIANE KEATON, sat in the audience and squirmed.

And when Beatty was knocking around with MADONNA during the publicity blitz for the film *Dick Tracy*, MacLaine was again vocal in her disdain. When asked how easy it would be for her to have the singer as a sister-in-law, she replied, "I would say about as easy as it would be for me to nail a custard pie to the wall." Recently, though, it seems that the sibling rivalry has diminished and they have come to terms with each other's eccentricities. "He does his own thing and I do mine, and that's fine," she told me.

By the time the Seventies were over, with the film roles drying up, she decided to start exploiting her age. She was one of the first Hollywood actresses to treat the ageing process as a *fait accompli*, prolonging her career in the process (*Terms Of Endearment, Madame Sousatzka, Postcards From The Edge, Steel Magnolias*, etc). The move from leading lady to character actress may have been unavoidable but, if the truth be known, MacLaine was always a character actress, always prepared to play it for laughs.

"Now when I see one of my movies on TV I switch channels. It's embarrassing for me to watch what I was like as an actress. I can see the tricks, the falsity, and I can remember what was going on the day we shot the scene, and sometimes I don't want to relive that sort of thing."

Like MICHAEL CAINE – she starred with him in the caper movie *Gambit*, in 1966 – she has always been shockingly uncalculated about what would be a good move or not. "Sometimes it's stupid, but I'll go with a film because I like where it's being shot. The same thing applies to my stage work. When I decided to open in Los Angeles I chose the theatre that was nearest my freeway exit." But she continues to work. She has had enough careers for six people, yet still she carries on, pushing away at the tide, unable to stop that old razzle-dazzle. She has slowed down but is in no danger of stopping. There has recently been another book, *Sage-ing While Age-ing*, and there are more film roles she's discussing.

M

But it begs the question, why? Hasn't life offered her enough? Has her ego not been tamed? What is there left to prove?

"Proving anything never meant much to me," she said when we met. "Not even for my parents. What I was doing with them was fulfilling dreams they didn't have for themselves. But when my parents died, I did begin to wonder.

"With movies it's like giving birth: you forget about all the pain and the aggravation. I get seduced by the script and forget about the shoot. I think the psychological diversion of being someone else for a while still has a lot to do with it." But when she said, "I guess I still make movies because I like being other people," what she really meant is she likes being Shirley MacLaine. And as for the pain of giving birth, she has made a lot more movies than she has had children.

"A life without movies?" she says. "I can't see that. It's great to have a number-one movie for a couple of weeks, to be the new girl in the whorehouse again. I still get a buzz out of that. I'll continue to make movies and I'll continue to complain about it. I'd be very unhappy if I could not go away and be alone and write, but I'd be unhappier if nobody wanted me any more. But that's about rejection, not about being a movie star."

A few summers ago, I was interviewing TONY BENNETT in a restaurant in New York, and halfway through the meal an elderly couple came over to say hello. One half of the couple was MacLaine, and they embraced like old lovers. They chatted for a while, mainly about how old they were, and Bennett said, "You know Shirley, I've always loved your philosophy."

MacLaine beamed. "What, you mean, 'I don't give a shit'? Hell, I remember what BOB MITCHUM said to me one day. 'If I wake up and it doesn't burn when I pee, I'm happy.'"

MADNESS

M

London has been endlessly eulogised – in books, plays, film, and not least in song. No, there is nothing to rival "Paris In The Spring", "New York, New York", or "Napoli", but then songs about London are not usually moments of epiphany, and they tend to be colloquial, sentimental, cosy.

There is a through-line, though, a river that runs through the musical hall tradition of the capital, one that runs all the way from "Maybe It's Because I'm A Londoner" to SQUEEZE's "Up The Junction", via "A Nightingale Sang In Berkeley Square", "London Pride", "Chim Chim Cheree", and "Portobello Road" (sung by BRUCE FORSYTHE in the Disney film, *Bedknobs And Broomsticks*). During punk, the CLASH made a point of writing about London, often writing about little else, although they tended to concentrate on Notting Hill and all points west. Pop archeologist JON SAVAGE once called *The Clash* "virtually a concept album about North Kensington and Ladbroke Grove", containing "White Riot", "London's Burning", "48 Hours", and all the rest. While they soon cast their concerned eyes over the Middle East, South America, and any imploding quasi-Stalinist state they could find, for a while London was their world.

Then at the end of the Eighties came Madness. Most good pop has an air of melancholy about it, and Madness's paeans to north London are no exception. "Our House", "Grey Day", and "Cardiac Arrest", in fact most of their songs, manage to evoke the pathos of small lives lived in the big city. Their songs are euphoric and maudlin, odd little tales of woe spilling out of Camden Town, the backstreets of Somerstown, and the fields of Hampstead Heath. Madness were the consummate colloquial pop group, and their London is forever full of grey skies and Routemaster buses, small-time crooks and barstool philosophers.

Madness will always be the musical equivalent of an Ealing film.

MADONNA

M

In a thirty-year career that has encompassed every female contradiction from suburban sex kitten to lap-dancing virgin there seems little that Madonna could do to reinvent herself yet again – unless, perhaps, she were to find God (a move which temporarily killed BOB DYLAN's career), or to get monumentally fat (which killed ELVIS off entirely). And though both these options seem rather obvious – career options become tricky when you're a hydra-headed-hyphenate and you've done it all – I bet even Madonna hadn't anticipated becoming a fully paid-up member of the nouveau riche with a fascination for the British aristocracy. She's still not completely out of that phase – she still has two homes in London –although her peripatetic condition have certainly enabled her to produce better records than she has in years.

She was born in the disco, and she will die in it, too. It's where she drew her inspiration from, where she first had success, and where her enormous gay following still live. Madonna has always tried to escape the confines of the dancefloor and climb to what she considers more exalted levels, and in her time she's aspired to emulate a host of role models, from BARBRA STREISAND to FRIDA KAHLO. Yet she always returns to the disco as this is where she feels safe, where she has control, and where she has an amazing instinct about what will come next. And what will work.

Gossip still swirls around Madonna like dry ice, and seemingly inconsequential decisions are blown-up, pulled apart and taken out of context, so much that she lives in a parallel Madonna world, in the way that only the truly famous do (ELTON JOHN, PAUL MCCARTNEY, MICK JAGGER, and until his death, MICHAEL JACKSON). And while Madonna encourages it and can control it to a certain extent, her appeal is such that she can only really steer. Admittedly she can steer better than most, but when she gets beaten up by the reaction to her attempts to put her head above the parapet (acting, speaking, technically challenging ballads), she retreats to fashion, to the disco, where all feels warm and neon-lit. Home.

M

As a phenomenon Madonna has been consistently attracting attention since 1983, the year of "Holiday", "Lucky Star", and "Borderline". But it is for her music that she wants to be remembered, not as a human tornado. "I want my music to be reviewed, not my... ribcage," is a familiar refrain. And she is tireless in her quest for what she wants. "My person in the studio is, 'I'm in a hurry.'"

Her ambition might be her defining characteristic though, not her music. She wanted out from an early age, and never wanted to go back. "When I turned seventeen I moved to New York because my father wouldn't let me date boys at home [in Detroit]," she told me once. "I never saw naked bodies when I was a kid – gosh, when I was seventeen I hadn't seen a penis! I was shocked when I saw my first one, I thought it was really gross." In a way her younger, wilder days were nothing if not pre-ordained, the result of the misspent youth that happened when she left home. "It was just the rules. There were so many rules, and I just could never figure out what they all were. If somebody had given me an answer I wouldn't have been so rebellious. 'You can't wear make-up, you can't cut your hair, you can't, you can't.'"

So she did. Time and time again.

The Manic Street Preachers

Too many people whose opinions I respect tell me they are a seriously good band, so I am obviously wrong, as personally I've never liked them. I just don't get them. I wrote something about them in the mid-Nineties – when they were at their height – and they were so incensed that they apparently took issue with whatever it was I wrote from the stage of the Albert Hall. This isn't why I don't much like them – I just find

M

their whole attitude to be leaden and worthy. But like I say, I'm almost certainly wrong on this, and actually lucky to be surrounded by people whose opinions differ so much from my own. Even if they do like the Manics.

TANIA MARIA

Often when she spoke, Tania Maria would sound like GRETA GARBO in *Ninotchka,* a throaty voice with a heavy accent that oddly didn't sound that Brazilian. She swayed and semi-danced as she sang, moving with the perpetual rhythm, and piano-bench dancing. Her Portuguese scat was always one of her attractions, and she ad-libbed like a crazy person; ASTRUD GILBERTO she wasn't. Her music was the never predictable sound of Africa tempered by the Latin beat, a samba mixed with bebop, a complex mash of style. She once said it was important not to mix Brazilian music with other Latin sounds, yet her own mix is fused with many things. "In Brazilian music the most important [element] is the rhythm," she once said. "And in my music, I keep this. My harmony and melody are influenced by RAVEL and STRAVINSKY and Americans. But the rhythm is Brazilian. My music is not like notes, it's pure emotion." Highlights: "Don't Go", "Funky Tamborine", "Come With Me", "Made In New York".

BOB MARLEY

As the default colour-by-numbers symbol of global cultural rebellion, Marley long ago pushed JOHN LENNON into a distant second place. KURT COBAIN obviously became a popular poster boy when he killed himself at his home in Seattle in 1994, yet he wasn't really rebelling against anything other than his own personality. Marley is the face you see on undergraduates' halls of residence bedroom walls, Marley's music what you hear pouring out of Amsterdam coffee bars. And while it is really only the sweet sound of mild annoyance, the Rastafarian tropes (oppression, salvation, redemption, retribution, repatriation, etc) and an emphasis on social issues lends it weight. Which frankly makes him bullet-proof.

He is the universal symbol of benign rebellion. In 1986 I visited Leningrad on a Soviet Union Intourist tour, and one night ended up in the infamous nightclub (it cost me one Rouble and thirty-eight Kopeks to get in). There were carpets on the ceiling, a Russian band playing traditional folk music, and what seemed like an army of drunk Finnish teenagers, one of whom kept jumping in front of me, screaming "Bob Marley, yeah, rock and roll!" at the top of his voice, while flinging his right arm around in a PETE TOWNSHEND-style windmill, to the great delight of his friends. At the time I was dressed in regulation London streetwear: a black MA1 nylon flying jacket, Levi 501s and Doctor Marten shoes. And as I was so obviously a member of a decadent Western subcult, so my Finnish friend wanted to impress upon me how hip he was. Which obviously meant screaming "Bob Marley" at me as loudly as possible.

Indeed.

The son of a white Royal Marine father and black Jamaican mother, Bob Marley was so racially sensitised he apparently used shoe polish to blacken his locks, fearful he might be considered too white. His ex-wife, Rita, claimed he asked her to do this to "make it more African". She has also claimed that he raped her while they were married.

His hypnotic, aggressively commercial brand of reggae refuses to be diminished by time, and the likes of "Natural Mystic", "Stir It Up", "I Shot The Sheriff", "Waiting In Vain", "Jamming", "Could You Be Loved", and most of the rest are copper-bottomed classics.

Although if you hear a busker playing "Three Little Birds" (which I would suggest is one of the most irritating songs ever recorded by a professional musician), I would have thought it perfectly reasonable to mug them.

Marley died at the ridiculously early age of thirty-six, from a form of cancer, in 1981. Even looking at the material he was recording at the time, it's still difficult to know which direction he may have taken had he lived. At least he was spared to ignominy of the traditional glide into mediocrity, or any sugar-coated reprise of former glories. When this happens to other people – and technology has made the extravagant, late-period purple patch something of a foregone conclusion for those who have run out of talent – I now think of the anecdote in Christopher Hitchens' memoir, *Hitch-22*, in which he recalls the memo he received from the *Sunday Times* accounts department when he had just finished working on a story that would eventually lead to the imprisonment of a corrupt Labour mayor. "I've passed your Dundee expenses," wrote the editor, "but I couldn't help noticing that almost half the bills were for cocktails. I don't think any newspaper is entitled to this kind of loyalty."

Bruno Mars

As any semi-domesticated manager can tell you – as long as you appreciate the need for him to trouser the fifteen percent commission they're going to suggest for imparting such wisdom – the safest way for singers to protect themselves is for them to only open their mouths on stage. Safely cocooned within the confines of the klieg lights, with a click track behind them, a supplicant crowd in front of them, and a suite full of libidinous well-wishers ahead of them – who wouldn't want to play by the rules, sing along to the teleprompter, and simply get on with it? It's when they opt for Plan B – talking, on the record, to other people – that it can all go fabulously wrong.

Naturally what pop stars say off-mike doesn't actually matter if the records they made in the first place do the job for them. Think Simply Red. Think Nicole Scherzinger. Think the SPIN DOCTORS, VANILLA ICE, WET WET WET, or YANNI. Say. Not forgetting the teen heart-throb, 2011 vintage – little Hawaiian Bruno Mars. No, if your records are bad in the first place, no one is going to be listening to what you say anyway. Having said that, plenty of people were interested when, in the aftermath of the 9/11 attacks, LEE RYAN, – he of the boy band BLUE – said, in an interview on the BBC, that "This New York thing is being blown out of proportion", and asked, "what about whales?"

What about the whales indeed. Bruno Mars has yet to announce any fondness for the large marine mammal, although one suspects that if he did they would form a protest group and try to distance themselves from the singer, in the same way that BRUCE SPRINGSTEEN did when RONALD REAGAN tried to co-opt "Born In The USA" as a campaign anthem.

In the space of six months, from the autumn of 2010 to the spring of 2011, Mars had three humungous hits – "Just The Way You Are", "Grenade", and "The Lazy Song" (sample lyric: "I'll be lounging on the couch jus' chillin in my snuggie, Click to MTV so they can teach me howda dougie"), while his album *Doo-Wops & Hooligans* (a title which alone should have been enough of a health warning) was stupidly successful all over the world. Mars cleverly wove pop with soul, soul with R&B, and R&B with reggae, and came up with the sort of anodyne slop that gives Eton Mess a bad name.

Mars' lack of galactic talent was best described by a colleague of mine, who said that his oeuvre made one conjure up a kind of trainer-bra version of JACK JOHNSON's laid-back soft rock, with gentle reggae inflections, hang-loose sentiments and all. Although actually it was a lot worse than that. And as for being a knock-off JACK JOHNSON, Mars made Johnson seem like the bastard love-child of TED NUGENT, ALICE COOPER, and METALLICA (a union I'm in no hurry to imagine, either).

Little Bruno's undoubted gift for melody was offset by an inexplicable fondness for profanity that at times shamed OZZY OSBOURNE. Not only did "Billionaire", the song he helped write for TRAVIE McCOY, contain the "no-substitution" substitution

445

M

"freaking", Bruno also helped craft the nod to NOEL COWARD that was CEE LO GREEN's "Fuck You". But then Bruno appeared to also have a penchant for the violent metaphor: on "Grenade", he suggested he would jump in front of a train, throw his hand on a blade, take a bullet in his brain and – obviously – catch a grenade to show the object of his desires just how serious he was about her. It might be unfair to suggest that his inability to use more traditional methods of courtship might have contributed to this state of affairs, but then I reckon Little Bruno probably deserved all the criticism he could get. And as my colleague also mentioned, these acts of violence aimed at Mars became a lot less inexplicable if you'd actually heard his records.

One could say that Mar's ascendancy might not have been completely unrelated to his poster-boy good looks, although I like to think it was largely because of his winning ways with a simile.

Jump, you bugger, jump!

DEAN MARTIN

Thinking back, they were the first pieces of vinyl I ever remember holding. They were my parents', racked in a vinyl coated dark green box – with a cheap, goldish metal lock on the lid – just big enough to hold about forty 7" singles. There were all sorts of singles in there, all in thin, brightly-coloured paper sleeves, and most looked as though they'd been imported from America: FRANK SINATRA, the BEATLES, country star ROGER MILLER, folk "sensations" the SEEKERS, Dutch calypso duo NINA AND FREDERIK, one hit wonders ESTHER & ABI OFARIM ("Cinderella Rockafella"), R&B singer GEORGIE FAME, and my mother's favourite, Dean Martin.

Back in the Sixties, Dino was the man. Even though the world was being overrun with longhairs, guitar solos, free love, and dope, most people's idea of cool was bound-up in a six-foot, olive-skinned, Italian American called Dean Martin (that "personable baritone of Latin caste," as an early review referred to him). Girls liked him, guys liked him, and – more importantly, as far as I was concerned – Mum liked him.

He might not have been the Voice (he was never as dextrous as Sinatra), might not have been the King (although ELVIS copied his singing style wholesale), but he was the coolest man to ever wear a tux, and compared to him you look about as cool as Jabba The Hut in a hoodie. Or a shell suit. Or anything previously worn by JOHN MCCRIRICK.

Dean Martin invented cool. For twenty years, from the late Forties to the end of the Sixties, he was the epitome of louche sangfroid, a singer, actor and genuine star who conquered Hollywood, television and Tin Pan Alley. He was the first man to ever enjoy stardom on all four fronts of stage, records, television, and films. If anyone epitomised the age-old adage, "It's better to be born lucky than smart," it was Dean Martin. He liked a drink; indeed, towards the end of his career it was his defining characteristic, and he was rarely seen on television without a drink of some sort in his hand (his personalised number plate read DRUNKY). And he liked his women. But most of all he liked breezing through life without a care in the world. He was a star not just because he could sing well or act appealingly but because he was the epitome of relaxed, funny sexiness – in a word that first came into vogue during his rise, he was Cool. Cap C, double O. He dropped out of school because he thought he was smarter than the teachers, he delivered bootleg booze, served as a blackjack dealer, worked in a steel mill, and boxed as a welterweight. And then became one of the biggest stars in the world.

Other Italian-style singers of the time worked hard to seduce the women in the audience. To Dino, that came naturally – sometimes too naturally. He worked to seduce the men, winning them, bonding them to his side with the illusion of camaraderie. And scratch his flip, insouciant exterior... and you found a flip, insouciant interior. Which is probably why he felt so at ease with the way he dressed. His cool wasn't born out of arrogance, it was born out of indifference. And his uncaring air of romance reflected the flash and breezy sweet seductions of a world in which everything came down to broads, booze and money, with plenty of Amarone and linguine on the side – living high in the dirty business of dreams. During the Sixties he refused to rehearse at all for his ridiculously casual TV show, instead showing up for the taping after a round of golf and winging his way through it, reading off cue cards and pretending to be drunk (sipping apple juice instead of JD).

Happy days indeed.

So many men during the Fifties and Sixties had a seemingly inextinguishable need to be cool – MILES DAVIS with his green, button-down shirt, FRANK SINATRA with his cigarettes and hats, ELVIS PRESLEY with his pink pegs and truck-driver sideburns – but Dino had it (whatever it was) without ever trying. Martin was a hypnotically attractive figure, even though he was himself as unself-conscious as a performer could be. He didn't have a rigorous or unsparing approach to his art; anything but. Dean Martin swung not just because swinging was cool, but because it was easy. And Dean Martin was nothing if not easy. His singing style was practically weightless; disdaining obvious effort and explicit emotional involvement, it suggested the detachment of a new kind of hipster. When he sang, Dino unfolded with an exaggerated smirk, an effortless shrug of the shoulders.

I suppose my own infatuation with Dino stems from the fact that I grew up in a house where he was rarely off the turntable. From England's 1966 World Cup victory through to the first moon landing, my early memories revolve around listening to "Return To Me", "Volare", "Under The Bridges Of Paris", "You Belong To Me", and "Napoli", on the American air force bases of East Anglia. I also remember riding a chopper, reading *Goal!* and eating butterscotch Angel Delight, but for me my pre-adolescence was defined by smarmy Italianate men who never seemed to take their hats off. For me, those songs have always defined a certain kind of imported homespun sophistication, however ersatz it may have been. These guys were the business – cool, savvy, with the sort of dark brown voices which put you safely to sleep at night.

M

The Dean Martin records that I fell in love with when I was seven or eight were not only the ones that meant the most to me, but they were always the ones I kept. Whenever I went through a period of reinvention – pretty much every year from the age of thirteen to twenty-one – and parted company with a bunch of records which I thought had become embarrassing, the records that I would return to would be my soundtracks and my JOHN BARRY compilations and my Dean Martin records, the ones sitting stoically at the back of the record box, under the bed or under the stairs, quietly minding their own business.

It wasn't just the music, of course – it never was. Whether it was FRANK SINATRA or ALICE COOPER I was fawning over, the way they looked was always as important as the way they sounded. And Dino in particular pricked my interest. The man pictured on the single sleeves, and the EP sleeves, and the LP sleeves I found in my parents' record collection was like no man I had ever seen; you didn't get many Italian-Americans swanning around East Anglia dressed in herringbone sports jackets, open-neck shirts, pink v-neck cardigans, white slacks, white silk socks, and black suede loafers. Not even on the air-force bases where I grew up. But then that was the point, I guess. Dean Martin inhabited a world that wasn't easily accessible to an eight-year-old who had yet to buy his own trousers, let alone visit the Sahara Tahoe.

The image sank deep and took hold. I would never forget the louche, debonair gadabout who sang like an angel and dressed like a gangster on his day off. Soon enough, I realised that Dino wasn't alone in his sartorial elegance, and after discovering FRANK SINATRA – with his club bow tie and straw hat – and the rest of the Rat Pack (SAMMY DAVIS JR., PETER LAWFORD, JOEY BISHOP), I became quietly besotted with the surface smarts of Fifties' America. Tragically, I was a style obsessive before I was a teenager.

These days I bombard my kids with music, and they only have to spend an hour listening to my iPod to come into

M contact with a fairly comprehensive array of sounds from the last fifty years or so; but back then life was different, back then the only music you heard came from the radio, your friends' record collections, and the things you found secreted deep inside your parents' radiogram. The records I found there made me nostalgic for something I'd never experienced, and in a way they were like someone else's Madeleine, a reminder of somebody else's memories. They hinted at so many things, suggested so much. In a world where things you didn't know had to be imagined, before the click of a mouse brought everything to life instantly (in an ever-present present), these 7" black vinyl singles evoked a world of snap brim hats and patent leather booze: "No sooner had I heard the sound of 'Volare' than a shudder ran through my whole body, and I stopped, intent upon the extraordinary changes that were taking place... at once the vicissitudes of life had become indifferent to me, its disasters innocuous, its brevity illusory..."

And while the whole Rat Pack ethos endures because it represents adolescence in perpetuity, Martin was more adolescent than most. Among his Rat Pack buddies, Martin was always the joker, the martini-drinking lounge lizard with the laissez-faire attitude and an ever-ready excuse. Martin was also the author of some of the best remembered Hollywood *bon mots*: "I've got seven kids, and the three words you hear most around my house are, 'Hello, goodbye, and I'm pregnant (sic)...' You're not drunk if you can lie on the floor without holding on... I feel sorry for people who don't drink. They wake up in the morning and that's the best they're going to feel all day... It was a woman who drove me to drink, and come to think of it I never did hang around to thank her for that... Hey lady! Do I look all blurry to you? Cause you sure look blurry to me."

Dean Martin spoke only Italian until the age of five. Born Dino Paul Crocetti in Steubenville, Ohio, in 1917, his father was a barber from Abruzzo in Italy, his mother a local second-generation Italian American. Martin dropped out of school in the tenth grade because, in his own words, he thought that he was smarter than the teachers. This loose-limbed arrogance resulted in him working as a blackjack dealer, and boxing as welterweight ("Kid Crocett"), which earned him a broken nose and a lousy reputation. As he couldn't fight, he turned to singing, mainly with local bands, copying BING CROSBY (as everybody did in those days). In the early Forties he started singing for bandleader SAMMY WATKINS, and it was Sammy who suggested he change his name to Dean Martin. He also had a hand in Dino's singing style, too. Martin worked for various bands throughout the early Forties, but his appeal was based more on looks and personality than on his vocal ability until various bandleaders began encouraging him to focus on the way he sang. Soon after, he developed his own smooth singing style, taking the basic Crosby template and building a more bohemian shell around it.

This period of Dino's life has been condensed into legend: he met Sinatra, got married (to the author BETTY McDONALD) and, in a quest to secure more long-term engagements, started associating with the nightclub underworld. He ran with the mob – how could he not, he grew up with them? – but he never ran to them. Unlike Sinatra he deliberately kept them at arm's length, even when they were investing in one of his shows. There were rumours that it was Martin and not Sinatra who was the basis of the singer, JOHNNY FONTANE, in MARIO PUZO's *The Godfather*, who uses the Mob to get him a residency at a hotel in Vegas, but as the rumours passed, so the thought disappeared. To earn extra money, Martin repeatedly sold ten percent shares of his earnings in exchange for upfront cash. Martin did this so often that he soon found he had sold over one hundred percent of his income. Such was the power of his charm that most of his lenders forgave him his debts, while the ones who didn't had to wait and watch Martin get drafted. But having served a year (1944-45) in Akron, Ohio, he was classified 4-F (double hernia) and discharged. Then in 1946, at the Glass Hat Club in New York, Martin had his fortuitous meeting with a young

M

comic called JERRY LEWIS, and one of the greatest double acts in Hollywood history was born. Improvising their act, with Dino crooning and Lewis acting the fool, they created a unique blend of glamour and slapstick – sex and slapstick! – one that principally involved Lewis interrupting Martin while he was trying to sing. The secret, both said, was that they essentially ignored the audience and played to one another. Their show was such a success that from clubs they moved to radio and then to Hollywood, where, during the early Fifties, they became the hottest stars in town (eventually making seventeen films together). From a distance it's difficult to understand just how big the duo were, but in their day they were bigger than MORECAMBE & WISE, bigger than FRENCH & SAUNDERS, bigger than LAUREL & HARDY, NEWMAN & BADDIEL, the TWO RONNIES, PETER COOK and DUDLEY MOORE put together. Imagine the Mighty Boosh or Mitchell and Webb having the same sort of fame as TOM CRUISE or MADONNA and you can kind of imagine how ridiculously popular they were. But though they were more famous than HARRY TRUMAN or DWIGHT EISENHOWER, eventually Dean tired of being second fiddle to Jerry's antics (like Lewis pouring buckets of cold water over him whenever he tried to sing). The act broke up in 1956, ten years to the day after their first official teaming. Towards the end of their time together their combined jealousy was stultifying. One morning before filming, they had one of their increasingly regular arguments.

"Anytime you want to call it quits, just let me know," said Dean.

"But, Dean," countered Jerry, "what would I ever do without you?" And half meant it.

"Fuck yourself, for starters," said Dean.

Martin had recently experienced another split, divorcing his first wife Betty and then marrying JEANNE BIEGGER, a former Orange Bowl Queen of Florida. Betty began drinking so heavily that Biegger eventually took Betty's three girls in (Betty's son was living with his grandparents) and brought them up along with the three children she eventually had with Martin. And although he was settled at home, his first solo movie, the comedy *Ten Thousand Bedrooms* (1957), was a box-office flop. The following year, in order to establish himself as a serious actor, Dino took a starring role in *The Young Lions* (1958), for a mere $35,000; he was making more in nightclubs, but it launched his movie career, giving him the same sort of fillip that his pal Sinatra would experience after *From Here To Eternity*. In the following years, he would be making about ten times as much per movie, and starring with Hollywood legends like JOHN WAYNE, JIMMY STEWART, and ROBERT MITCHUM, and of course the Rat Pack. He would appear in highly-acclaimed movies such as the VINCENTE MINNELLI drama *Some Came Running* (1958), or *Rio Bravo* (1959), directed by HOWARD HAWKS, but then he would choose a fair amount of rubbish, too (albeit successful rubbish). Martin cared so little about his film work that he rarely looked at the scripts before agreeing to do them. It says something about Martin that he managed to appear in the basest rubbish and come out on top. In *Marriage On The Rocks* (1965) he walks into a pillar, falls over (twice), and engages in the following conversation with an equally bewildered DEBORAH KERR:

Dean: "I think I'll walk the dog."

Deborah: "We don't have a dog."

Dean: "I'll find one."

Critics would say he walked through his films as though he was "embalmed". He didn't care.

As the public would flock to pretty much any movie he chose to make, he tended to put more effort into the records he made, and in his thirty-year recording career made more than one hundred albums and recorded over six hundred songs. His signature tune, "Everybody Loves Somebody", knocked the BEATLES' "A Hard Day's Night" out of the number-one spot in the US in 1964. By 1965, some of Martin's albums, such as *The Hit Sound Of Dean Martin*, *Welcome To My World*, and *Gentle On My Mind*, were composed largely of popular country and western songs made famous by artists like JOHNNY CASH, MERLE HAGGARD, and BUCK OWENS. Martin hosted many country performers on his TV show and was named "Man Of the Year" by the Country Music Association in 1966.

For three decades, Martin was among the most popular acts in Las Vegas, both with and without the rest of the Rat Pack. People forget that the Vegas gigs were almost never preannounced, and the marquee outside the Sands Hotel would read: "Dean Martin – Maybe Frank, maybe Sammy". Sometimes one or two of the Clan might be too tired to turn up. On rare occasions, only one performer would show up. One show began with the MC asking over the loudspeaker, "Who's starring tonight?" Joey Bishop's world-weary voice then replied, "I dunno. Dean Martin is drunk, SAMMY DAVIS hadda go to da temple, PETER LAWFORD's out campaigning for his brother-in-law [JFK]." "What's Frank doing?" A knowing snicker. "Just say – somebody will go on." And eventually one of them would. The Rat Pack shows were comical anarchy. During one show, while Martin was singing, Lawford, Davis, and Bishop walked onstage wearing dinner jackets and boxer shorts, with their trousers folded over their arms. "We walked across the stage as if we were discussing business," Bishop said. "It got a scream – three guys in their shorts." Whether with JERRY LEWIS or the Clan, Dino spent his entire stage career being interrupted by comics. But Martin could be quick himself. Early in 1960, just after JFK had announced his candidacy for President, he attended one of the Clan's shows. When Sinatra introduced Kennedy to the audience, Martin watched the handsome young candidate as he stood and acknowledged the crowd's applause. Then Martin turned to Sinatra and asked, "What did you say his name was?"

The Rat Pack's self-deprecating humour was often hard edged, as when Martin picked up SAMMY DAVIS JR. and announced, "I'd like to thank the NAACP [the National Association for the Advancement of Colored People] for this trophy," or when Sammy told Lawford, "I know your kind. You'll dance with me but you won't let your kids go to school with me." In JAMES SPADA's PETER LAWFORD biography,

The Man Who Kept The Secrets, he recounts JOEY BISHOP saying that he thought their humour only crossed the line once, when Sinatra and Martin, improvising, started to call each other "dagos" onstage. Bishop walked off into the wings, and after the show Sinatra asked him, "What the hell happened to you?" "Frank, what happens after you leave the stage and somebody calls you a dago?" Bishop replied. "You're not gonna like it and they're gonna say, 'Well, I heard you say it yourself onstage.' I don't know how to act out there when you start that stuff. Am I supposed to think it's camaraderie? I can't stand out there on the stage while you're doing dago, dago, dago." Martin and Sinatra never used the word onstage again.

When Martin was introduced over the PA, the MC would say, "Direct from the bar..." He would then saunter on, holding a cigarette and a drink, turn to the conductor and ask, "How long have I been on?" Then he'd peer out across the crowd and ask, rhetorically, "How'd all these people get in my room?" And then, wandering off to a makeshift bar, "Oh well, I guess I'll fix me another salad." It was like an old-fashioned vaudeville act that never changed from year to year.

Sinatra used to say about performing: "The audience is like a broad – if you're indifferent, endsville", which is why the boys tried so hard to keep everyone happy.

Martin would turn to the Jewish Joey Bishop and ask: "Did you ever see a Jew jitsu?" Bishop, for his part, would turn to both him and Sinatra and reply: "Watch out. I've got my own group – the Matzia." Metzia is Yiddish for bargain.

"I want to talk about your drinking," Sinatra would say. "What happened?" asked Martin. "Did I miss a round?"

When they were in Vegas, the pranks never stopped. They would get weird stuff delivered to each other's rooms, cut the bed sheets in half, or cut off the legs of their pyjamas – little things that let them know that the other one hadn't stopped taking notice. In their prime, they knew they had a legacy, and all the boozing and the carousing and the playacting were fundamental to that. The joke was usually

M

perpetrated by Sinatra on one of the others, although Martin was the only member of the Clan who could take Sinatra to task, or who would slope off to bed in the middle of a drinking session.

There was a bond between Sinatra and Martin that couldn't be broken, no matter how hard they both tried. "Frank and I are brothers, right," Martin said. "We cut the top of our thumbs and became blood brothers. He wanted to cut the wrist. I said, 'What are you, crazy? No, here's good enough.'" Only Martin could get away with making a quip like, "When Frank dies they're going to give his zipper to the Smithsonian." Or, "Frank was an unwanted child. Now he's wanted in five states." At Sinatra's forty-second birthday party, at the Villa Capri in 1957, Dino sang a version of "He's The Top", changing the words to "He's The Wop". When Sinatra agreed to be the best man at Dino's third wedding, Martin gave him a silver cigarette lighter – it had Frank's initials engraved on one side and a heartfelt message on the other: FUCK YOU VERY MUCH.

The funniest gags always involved outsiders, or at least those not in the nucleus. One of Sinatra and Martin's greatest targets was MICHAEL ROMANOFF, the legendary Los Angeles restaurateur who imagined that he was Russian royalty (whereas he was in reality a Jewish orphan from Illinois). He was a small, meticulous man with a salt-and-pepper crew cut and a regal manner of speech; and both Sinatra and Martin loved him. It wasn't enough to nail his shoes to the floor of his wardrobe, or to cut his cigarettes to three-quarter size and reseal the pack. According to TINA SINATRA in her memoir, *My Father's Daughter,* the best jokes were more elaborate and required long-term planning. "Each week, wherever he might be, Michael would pack his fine laundry – from dress shirts and silk pyjamas to his shorts and handkerchiefs – in a strapped metal box, and ship it to Sulka in London. Dad intercepted the box, replaced Michael's clothes with rags, and sent it on to Sulka. It came back to its owner with each rag perfectly pressed. On one extended road trip, Dad and Dean got hold of Michael's walking stick after the 'prince' had gone to bed. Each night they shaved off a quarter inch of the stick. After a few days, Michael began hunching over. He was just about falling down when he finally caught on. "You know, old boy, I think I'm still growing.'"

TINA SINATRA is an official custodian of the Sinatra legacy, and she speaks – both in her book and in person – of the affection her father had for Martin. Far from being a hagiography, *My Father's Daughter* gives a fascinating insight into the warmth of the Clan's relationships.

For Dean, this sort of horseplay had started way back in the days of Lewis and Martin, when practical jokes were one of the few things that kept them entertained on the road (along with the obligatory booze and broads, of course). Once, when Lewis got sick of Martin arriving three minutes before showtime, slipping on his dance shoes and skipping on stage, Lewis filled those very same shoes with raw eggs, ketchup, broken biscuits, and cigar butts.

Dino's biggest success came with his own NBC TV show, which dominated Thursday nights at 10pm for nine years from 1965, and which exploited his public image as a lazy, carefree boozer. Few entertainers worked as hard to make what they were doing look so easy. He refused to rehearse, preferring to be out on the links. The way the producers got round this was by rehearsing all week with a stand-in, and then showing a tape of the final rehearsal to Dean on the day of recording, which he simply copied. And whenever a new writer would suggest that the show had maybe more drinking jokes than was strictly necessary, Dino would say, "Can't have too many, baby. How do you think I got this big house?" Another writer said that in order to write better material for him, he would have to get to know him closely. "No one gets to know me closely," said Dean, "not even my wife."

As SHAWN LEVY says in his definitive book *Rat Pack Confidential*, "Dean never wanted to get his hands dirty, so he learned how to deal cards and how to sing, and he made a living at it: he was too sanguine to chase women, so they threw themselves at him; he didn't have the fire in his belly to make himself a showbiz star, so he met a couple of wildly

M

ambitious guys – Jerry and Frank – who dragged him along."
But by dint of his relationships, and because he hung around
genuinely funny guys, he became funny himself, and during his
ten-year TV career, became one of the funniest straight men
of them all. Dean did the whole thing in a day: no meetings
with writers, no casting sessions, no extra rehearsals, nothing.
"I don't even breathe hard," he said. The atmosphere on set
was so louche, and Martin's boozy image so indelible that a
bar became a pivotal part of the set. As SHAWN LEVY writes,
Dean's lackadaisical mien was soothing, and as the principals
in the Rat Pack aged, Dino was the only member prepared to
become a caricature. People used to say that the WHO'S JOHN
ENTWISTLE walked on stage as though he was looking for his
dog; whenever Martin walked on stage, or on set, he looked as
though he had simply ambled on looking for his cheque. And
because the television show was so successful, and because
he kept making films – three JAMES BOND spoofs, with Dino
as an arch superdude called MATT HELM; what felt like dozens
of unaccomplished westerns; and lots of other nonsense –
over time he became so enormously wealthy he was reckoned
by many to be among the richest men in Hollywood. As an
example of how much they were making, in a fairly typical
four weeks in 1951, from touring alone, Martin earned over a
quarter of a million dollars. That's three million dollars a year
from just one revenue stream, forgetting the films, the records,
and the TV stuff; and this was sixty years ago. His work ethic –
doing what he had to to get by – paid off in spades.

"To my surprise, Dean, not Jerry, was the funny one to me,"
wrote Shirley MacLaine in *My Lucky Stars: A Hollywood
Memoir*. "His humour was subtle, spontaneous – a result of
the moment... Getting to know Dean was another story. The
words that come to mind are those that describe a person
cut OFF from feeling – purposefully cut off. Perhaps that
was why he seemed so devil-may-care and so coolly casual.
The Italians, I later learned, had a more apt word for it,
menefreghista, which means 'one who does not give a fuck.'
Dean Martin was basically a *menefreghista*."

Martin was cool incarnate, whether anyone liked it or not. Before cool became a commodity, he just sort of had it, basically because he didn't really care what others thought of him. And not only was Martin cool, he also inspired the coolest performer of the 20th Century: ELVIS PRESLEY. When ELVIS first auditioned for SAM PHILLIPS' at his Sun Studios in 1953, the office manager, MARION KEISKER, accused Presley of basing his entire vocal sound on Martin, and although it's assumed this was knocked out of him, if you study some of his early recordings you can tell that this influence didn't go away. In 1955 Martin had a huge hit with "Memories Are Made Of This", one of hisdefining moments, and one that resonated with the wider public. With its loping, easy swing it soon became a cookout favourite, the sort of song that appealed to everyone, both young and old. But compare it to ELVIS's "Don't Be Cruel" a year later and you see how easy ELVIS found it to appropriate Dino's style and mix it with a bit more of an R&B feel.

As the legendary guitarist-turned-journalist CHRIS SPEDDING said recently, "Apart from the fact that Elvis borrowed that descending-bass-run-followed-by-guitar-chord ending from the arrangement on Martin's record, other common elements are that sexy, wobbly, almost hiccupping baritone vocal not yet identifiably 'rock' until ELVIS made it so and Martin's novel use of a four-piece male gospel-type vocal group which we may assume helped inspire ELVIS, steeped as he was in traditional gospel music, to introduce the JORDANAIRES on his cut, effectively integrating them into a unique blend with his own lead vocal, thus establishing another rock archetype." ELVIS also copied the opening four-note motif from Martin's 1958 hit "Return To Me" on his 1959 song "My Wish Came True" (four syllables, same key); released "It's Now Or Never", an English-language version of the Italian favourite "O Sole Mio"; and covered the Martin throwaway "I Don't Care If The Sun Don't Shine". And if you study "Love Me Tender", it's actually closer to a Dino song. So while Tony Curtis may have inspired the famous Presley quiff, it was Dino who inspired his lazy baritone. "There are no less than seventeen references to ELVIS in NICK TOSCHES' 1992 *Dino* but for me the most telling is on page 394," says Spedding. "When ELVIS glimpses his hero in the audience during his show at the International in Vegas in January 1970: 'Seeing him at ringside, ELVIS, elated, sang "Everybody Loves Somebody" in his honour! This is the same guy who worried about forgetting the lyrics to his own hits but was confident enough in remembering his idol's latest hit to give an impromptu performance of it!'" When she was still a young girl, DEANA MARTIN met ELVIS in Vegas. "I love your dad," he told her. "You know, they call me the King of Rock and Roll, but your dad, he's the King of Cool."

Despite Martin's reputation as a heavy drinker he was remarkably self-disciplined. He was often the first to call it a night, and when not on tour or on location liked to go home to see his wife and children. What many thought was booze in his glass onstage was usually just apple juice, even though he gave a remarkable impersonation of someone gradually getting drunker and drunker. He borrowed the lovable-drunk shtick from the comic JOE E. LEWIS, while his convincing portrayals of heavy boozers in *Some Came Running* and *Rio Bravo* rubber-stamped the image. What few know is that "Dean the Drunkie" was a device conceived when Martin broke up with Lewis, a character that he could develop and have fun with, and one the audiences would lap up. His first night on stage by himself, at the Sands in Vegas in 1956, was also the first night he used his new persona. And his audience loved it. That night he tentatively walked on stage, and stood about a yard in, exactly where he used to stand when Lewis was monopolising the mike. "I'm just gonna stand here instead of there," he said, taking a long swig of J&B and making a face. He was laid-back and in command and the audience began to laugh. He took another sip, flicked ash onto the stage floor and, in a rare moment of lucidity, said to the audience, "Drink up. The drunker you get, the better I sound." The reaction was so enthusiastic that from now on he would use it every time he appeared on stage. Martin was both pretend drunk and committed drinker, and while his glass may have been full of iced tea or apple juice at the first show, at the second show it was bourbon or scotch. Later in their lives, when they organised two ad-hoc baseball teams, while Frank's team were predictably called Ol' Blue Eyes, Dino's were dubbed – maybe even more predictably – Ol' Red Eyes.

More often than not, Martin's idea of a good time was playing golf, watching westerns on TV and eating pasta fagióli. He was so distant he would even retire to his den when his wife Jeanne would be hosting a dinner party. He wasn't that well educated, didn't have the greatest vocabulary, and didn't keep up with what happened in the papers. Bizarrely, for one of the biggest entertainers of the 20th Century, he got intimidated easily. JOEY BISHOP said, after Martin's death, "I remember him most of all for his honesty. He hated anything that was phony and would not partake of it. He was one in a trillion." His daughter, Deana, said he gave new meaning to the expression "emotional detachment. We all would. It would have been great if, along with that legendary charm he could turn on like a lightbulb, he'd had the gushing warmth of FRANK SINATRA or SAMMY DAVIS JR. I would have loved to sit with him and listen to him talk freely about his own life and his choices and his loves. But Dad was simply not the type of man able to express himself."

He was a big benign presence, "warm and reliable", according to Sinatra's daughter, Tina. "He hugged like a bear. Though he had an air of authority, he was never intimidating – just the opposite, in fact. He loved to kid around. He approached young people at their level: he wasn't your typical patriarch." He also had these big hands, which was why he was such a good blackjack dealer when he was young (it was easier to palm the cards). But the warmth and the reliability tended to fade quickly, and then he'd be back in front of the TV, not needing anyone's company. He was everyone's friend, called every guy he met "Pallie". But not for long. SHIRLEY MACLAINE said of Martin, "He was nice to everyone, he just didn't want nice to go on too long."

M When asked once what he'd like written about him by way of an obituary, he replied, "Dean Martin? He was a good guy. That'll do just fine." He had a confident, rolling gait that told everyone he was perfectly happy, thank you very much, and didn't need any flattery, any conversation, or any intrusions at all. As one of Deana's friends once said, "Your dad walks like he's conserving energy." When he came home at night from filming, he'd sit and eat a sandwich still dressed in his slacks and v-neck sweater, play with the kids, watch TV, and then ask for a J&B (he claimed the initials stood for "Just Booze").

If Martin was going to make an effort, he wanted to get a lot of bang for his buck: he wanted it to be permanent. He wouldn't bother showing up for rehearsals, or learn his lines, or work up jokes for his stage shows – but during his years at the top he managed to find the time for a nose job, two operations to remove the bags under his eyes, and a regular visit to a hair colourist. His custom-made suits cost six thousand dollars. Each. In 1948!

By the early Seventies, Martin seemed to have the Midas touch, *The Dean Martin Show* was still earning solid ratings, and although he was no longer a Top 40 hitmaker, his record albums continued to sell well. His name on a marquee could guarantee casinos and nightclubs a standing-room-only crowd. He found a way to make his passion for golf profitable by offering his own signature line of golf balls. Shrewd investments had greatly increased Martin's personal wealth; at the time of his death, Martin was reportedly the single largest minority shareholder of RCA stock. But then Martin seemed to suffer a mid-life crisis. In 1972, he filed for divorce from his second wife, Jeanne. Less than a month after his second marriage had been legally dissolved, Martin married 26-year-old CATHERINE HAWN on April 25, 1973. Hawn had been the receptionist at the chic GENE SHACROVE hair salon in Beverly Hills. They divorced November 10, 1976. He was also briefly engaged to GAIL RENSHAW, Miss USA 1969. Eventually, Martin reconciled with Jeanne, though they never remarried. He also made a public reconciliation with JERRY LEWIS on Lewis' Labor Day Muscular Dystrophy Association telethon in 1976. FRANK SINATRA shocked Lewis and the world by bringing Martin out on stage. As Martin and Lewis embraced, the audience erupted in cheers and the phone banks lit up, resulting in one of the telethon's most profitable years. Lewis reported the event was one of the three most memorable of his life. Lewis brought down the house when he quipped, "So, you working?" Martin, playing drunk, replied that he was "at the Meggum", a reference to the MGM Grand where he was playing. This was a reconciliation of sorts, and the men kept in contact until Martin's death.

Towards the end of his life he'd play golf in the morning, watch TV in the afternoon, and then go to bed after a light supper and a couple of Camparis. He'd done working, done all the difficult stuff, and it was time for his abdication of ambition. Towards the end all he wanted to do was shuffle around at home, surrounded by his art, not knowing if he was looking at a CHAGALL or a MATISSE. "I just like the colours," he'd say. Martin was receding from work in a way that amplified his lifelong desire for peace and quiet. All his life he had wanted to do a GARBO, to go home early, and now, having passed retirement age, he was more than ready for it. Towards the end the stage boozing had turned into the real thing, and this, compounded by his Percodan addiction, made him something of a liability whenever he left the house. "I'm supposed to play golf tomorrow with Dean Martin," bragged one of the singer's less salubrious acquaintances, caught on an FBI wiretap. "But he's drunk as a fucking log. He wanted to play today. He can't. So he wanted to play the other day, forget about it."

Dino drifted in and out of everything – country clubs, restaurants, conversations, consciousness. For many, power meant money, sex, fame, security; for Dino, power was the ability to be left alone. His world was crumbling anyway: on March 21, 1987, his son, DEAN PAUL, was killed when his

M jet fighter crashed while flying with the Air National Guard. After DEAN PAUL's death, his father's eyes were not his own. Heartbroken, a much-touted tour with Davis and Sinatra in 1988 sputtered to a halt because Martin just didn't care anymore, and where once he had gone out of his way to appear as though he didn't give a damn, now he really didn't. On one evening, he infuriated Sinatra when he turned to him and muttered, "Frank, what the hell are we doing up here?" Martin, who always responded best to a club audience, felt lost in the huge stadiums they were performing in, and had no interest in the big booze sessions afterwards. His final Vegas shows were at Bally's in 1989, and by 1991 he was retired. In addition to never completely recovering from losing his son, Martin was suffering from emphysema, and, in September 1993, was diagnosed with lung cancer. He'd also been told he needed surgery on his kidneys and liver to prolong his life, but he refused. He'd had enough. It was widely reported, though never confirmed, that Martin had also been diagnosed with Alzheimer's around the same time. When Martin died, of respiratory failure, at his home on Christmas morning 1995, the lights on the Vegas Strip were dimmed in his honour.

Not only was King Crooner at rest, so was that innate ability to be genuinely cooler than anyone else in the room, that innate ability to just be, without pretending to. So the next time you go shooting your cuffs, rolling your shoulders, or pumping out your chest in a self-conscious display of cool, think again. Don't get above yourself buddy, because compared to Dino, in the grand scheme of things you're about as cool as a KULA SHAKER tribute band. And when you're next about to venture out on the town, do the decent thing and put on some Dino before you leave the house. You might never look like Dino, you might never have his luck with wine, women and song, but at least you can imagine what it once felt like to rule the world.

After all, if it was good enough for ELVIS then it's certainly good enough for you.

MASHUPS

"Smells Like Rockin' Robin" may not have troubled the MashUp charts (at the time it was popular, SQUAREPUSHER VS EMILIANA TORRINI was number one), but it was all over New York Fashion. It was used as a warm-up for the TOMMY HILFIGER show, and could be heard blasting out of iPod docks all over the city for at least six days. Produced by legendary bootleg/mash-up remixer MARK VIDLER (aka GoHomeProductions), "Smells Like Rockin' Robin" is an astonishing combination of NIRVANA and the JACKSON 5.

Having once been responsible for such acclaimed bootlegs as "Ray Of Gob", which spliced together MADONNA's "Ray Of Light" and the SEX PISTOLS' "Pretty Vacant" and "God Save The Queen", at the beginning of 2010 Vidler got the bug back and started mashing things again, producing this classic mash-up as well as a CARPENTERS' version of "Wonderwall", which has to be heard to be believed.

It's not so surprising to hear mash-ups at fashion shows, as the runway was always the best place to hear sonic juxtaposition. Back in the Eighties, when Bodymap were one of the most important design teams in London, their shows were always accompanied by an esoteric mix of sounds, with DJs mixing DVORJAK and the STOOGES with DINAH WASHINGTON and the DETROIT EMERALDS. Today's fashion show audiences take this sort of mélange as a given, and it's hardly a surprise when you hear the ROLLING STONES blended into the new DIZZEE RASCAL, or the RAMONES lovingly grafted onto something by Kylie or Britney.

"Smells Like Rockin' Robin" is something else again, a record that by rights should have been number one all over the world. It was in my house anyway. And we don't even have a catwalk.

M

MASSIVE ATTACK

"Unfinished Sympathy" from their first album *Blue Lines* (1991), is an almost talismanic song, as important to some people as anything by SOUL II SOUL, PRIMAL SCREAM, or ARRESTED DEVELOPMENT (who all released remarkable records around this time). Some even think it's the best single of the Nineties. Coffee table hip-hop, proto-chill, Massive Attack invented something very special, and followed up their debut with 1994's *Protection*, an equally stellar, if more downbeat collection. *Mezzanine*, even darker, came trundling after in 1998.

MEATLOAF

There are so many Meatloaf records that do the job they were employed to do (defining every minute of the arc of a paaarty), yet few of them rival *Bat Out Of Hell*, an album that demands to be listened to in a speeding car, driven by your designated driver, in the early hours of the morning, on the way home from a country ball, as you lie slumped in the back seat, your tuxedo covered in cold sweat, cheap red wine, and the lipstick of someone else's woman.

MELLE MEL

Hip-hop was so-named because of the US Army.

It was 1974, Melle Mel was thirteen, and there was a DJ in the South Bronx called KOOL HERC – he'd set up a microphone next to his turntable at parties and encourage everyone to dance. So Mel and his brother, nicknamed KID CREOLE, started embellishing this, as did another neighbourhood DJ, FLASH.

"No one called it rap then," said Mel. "It had no name. We got better at it and grew popular very quickly. Me, FLASH, KID CREOLE, and another kid nicknamed COWBOY got together and formed a group. We did our first house party in 1976. That night, a friend named COCOA MO came by. COCOA MO was leaving for the Army and COWBOY was on the microphone. When he saw COCOA MO dancing he said, 'Hip, hop, hibbit to the hip-hop,' like they do in the Army when they march. Somebody laughed and said, 'Y'all motherfuckers need to get a job. You can't make no money doing that hip-hop shit.' That's when we started calling it hip-hop. We never called it rap. The press called it rap later on."

LIZA MINNELLI

Meeting Liza Minnelli for the first time I was reminded of the scene in *Play It Again, Sam*, when WOODY ALLEN, in a desperate attempt to seduce DIANE KEATON, splutters, "You have the most eyes I've ever seen." Indeed, Liza Minnelli has always looked like a character from a Manga comic, her beautiful, bulbous, winsome peepers overshadowing every one of her other features. She has always had the eyes of a pop icon, for that is what she is; half close your own and she could still be Sally Bowles, the Oscar-winning role she played in BOB FOSSE's 1972 film *Cabaret*, the movie which made her a star.

And although she knows it – lives it, breathes it – the great star likes to pretend otherwise. Why? Because it would be rude and conceited to do anything else. "I'm a singer, not much else," she told me once. "Other people have been icons. I just get up there and sing and dance. I tread the boards for a living and sing my guts out. Sometimes my heart, too." Humility has become a major part of her make-up, yet another face to hide behind when the going gets rough. And for the last twenty years for Liza the going has been quite rough indeed.

M I met Minnelli in 1996, and my interview with her seemed somehow symptomatic of her life. After two aborted trips to New York (one cancelled because she urgently had to see her dentist, apparently), and one meeting in London – where she was recording *The Clive James Show,* on which she would appear remarkably articulate, if a mite insincere; obviously ignorant of the fact that James had once claimed she couldn't walk up a flight of stairs sincerely – I was granted an audience at The Savoy, her hotel of choice during a bout of promotion for an undistinguished album of torch songs, *Gently.*

It's not a word you could ever use to describe Minnelli's own life, and her arrival in London at this point was preceded by an unusual number of pejorative press reports. One piece in the *Daily Mail* suggested that she was giving cause for concern to family and friends by her erratic behaviour and washed-out appearance, and by a supposed rift with her half-sister, the singer Lorna Luft. This followed Minnelli's bizarre appearance on *Ruby Wax Meets...*, stories in the *National Enquirer* concerning her re-occurring drug problem, and a piece in the *Guardian* in which she appeared to have resigned herself to living her life in perpetual denial.

When I asked her about her somewhat negative press, she gave a good impression of having heard it all before. "I've always hung my ass out on the line, just waved it in the breeze waiting for someone to take me apart," she said. "Regret is a huge exercise in futility. There's no point in dwelling on the past, and the only thing is to take today and do it different, which is what I think most people try to do. I've made mistakes and I've done some dumb things, but I don't think there's any point in regretting anything. I'm far too old for that."

Minnelli was fifty at the time, and while she tottered because of her 1994 hip replacement – she's a hoofer, right? – the day we met she was as lucid as anyone can be with two-day-old jet lag. Although her smile seemed to kick-start itself every ten or fifteen seconds regardless of what she was saying, and she used the well-worn celebrity technique of plugging the product at every available moment ("I really don't think I've

ever sung better," she said, as I was halfway through asking
a question about ambition and regret), she was definitely
on-kilter (chain-smoking Marlboros throughout). Tiny, and
immensely quick, it was easy to imagine her scampering
around the lounge of a Sixties suburban dream home in a
pair of thigh-hugging slacks, her Alice band covered in swirls
of cigarettes smoke, arranging bowls of avocado dip as she
watched *The Dick Van Dyke Show* out of the corner of those
magnificent eyes. She looked like the kind of American woman
they don't make any more. Having said that, she was wearing
what all celebrities wear in hotel rooms: black T-shirt, black
Levi's, and white Reebok runners. Somewhat fond of shoes,
she proudly displayed a pair of stacked baseball boots she
had bought that afternoon in Covent Garden, "These are real
high-heeled sneakers, don't you think?"

There are dozens of stories concerning Liza Minnelli's so-
called addictions: to read between the lines of her profiles
you are encouraged to believe that she has been addicted to
everything from vodka and valium to cocaine and Prozac.
Some of these stories have a basis in truth: when her mother,
JUDY GARLAND, died in London in 1969, from an overdose of
sleeping pills after a lengthy bout of alcoholism, Liza was
prescribed tranquilisers in order to cope with the tragedy,
and in 1984 she was checked into the Betty Ford Clinic by
her friend, ELIZABETH TAYLOR, to deal with her addiction to
drugs. In reality, though, regardless of what else it is claimed
she has been partial to, what Minnelli is really addicted to
is attention.

Celebrity can be a dangerous condition, as it increasingly
destroys those whom it creates. This is something that
Minnelli knows only too well. Though her name is hardly
mentioned without reference to her mother, Minnelli was
actually closer to her father, the director Vincente, who made
Meet Me In St Louis and *Gigi* (he died in 1986, seventeen
years after her mother, thirty-five years after they separated).
It was he who pushed Liza into the movies, though apart from
Cabaret, the comedy *Arthur*, and her great lost performance

M

in MARTIN SCORSESE's masterpiece, *New York, New York*, it has been on the stage where she has truly shone. "Reality is something you rise above," she said once, and her stage routines have been testament to this: more extravagant, more melodramatic than anything conjured up by Streisand, Sinatra, or DIANA ROSS, for the past forty years Minnelli has been one of the few entertainers to bring a real sense of Forties glamour to Broadway.

In her fifties she was still doing one hundred and twenty-five shows a year, though the movie parts have been thin on the ground for some time. "I find it difficult to get the parts now, but then everybody does," she said. "You look at the best actresses in America and they're all playing someone's wife. But in music women are taking over the world. Look at JOAN OSBORNE and ALANIS MORISSETTE, SHERYL CROW, and TORI AMOS; these dames talk like people do on the street, they're making the folk music of today."

With media attention so finely focussed on the down escalator, it's easy to forget that Minnelli is still capable of the kind of nervous, fizzy energy which the likes of MADONNA and LADY GAGA have tried to emulate with only partial success. When Liza is "on" (her marvellous 1973 television special *Liza With a Z* is the personification of "on"), she makes all-comers seem like latecomers. When the King of Saudi Arabia went backstage to meet her after one of her many performances in Las Vegas she said, "Oh King, thanks *so* much for coming."

Her records have been very hit and miss, rarely reflecting her wonderful voice. You can't fault her dedication though. "It's a bit like being naked in Macy's window, you know?" she said about the sort of material she likes to sing.

I asked her if she still needed an audience. Was she as obsessed with being loved as she had once appeared to be? Her answer spoke volumes.

"I don't think I crave an audience, but the main thing I like is doing a performance live. I'm a road rat, and I just love getting out there. Singing is what I do, it's what I'm made of. You can't kill a good song, as it goes on forever."

BING CROSBY once said of JUDY GARLAND, "There wasn't a thing that gal couldn't do. Except look after herself." And while this has become a trite way of summing up Liza's own life, one wonders if it might be just true. Of course, she does go to great lengths to look after herself, but projecting a vision of yourself onto the world is always the very worst way of protecting what's underneath. However, if Minnelli has earned anything, it's certainly the right to do exactly as she pleases. She manages to cope, she said, because she has big *cajones*. "Very big *cajones*."

Just before she stood up to give me the kind of parting hug a mother gives her son, she told me her mantra – her way of dealing with her demons – in the form of a finely honed anecdote. "There's this guy who walks along the street one day and falls into a hole," she said, as another Marlboro took an almighty hammering. "And the next day he walks down the same street and tries to jump over it, but falls in again. Then on the third day he approaches the hole really slowly, and tries to walk around the edge but still falls in. The day after that, he takes a different street. You know what I mean? Sometimes it takes a while to learn how to deal with the world."

JONI MITCHELL

There is a misconception that many of the people who started becoming famous towards the end of the Sixties somehow got there through altruism, because they deserved to be there, or simply because they were around at the time. It's easy to forget that the Love Generation and many who came in their wake were desperate to get noticed. (Joni Mitchell was certainly driven, spurred on not least by the polio she contracted at the age of nine. Bizarrely this was the same Canadian epidemic – 1951 – in which NEIL YOUNG, then aged five, also contracted the virus.)

M

Which is one of the reasons ROBERTA JOAN ANDERSON was far happier using the name Joni Mitchell after she married the folk singer CHUCK MITCHELL in 1965. The same year she gave birth to a baby girl, and almost immediately gave her up for adoption.

An above-average singer-songwriter, she developed quickly, moving the genre on in a way never done before. She made sure she knew the right people to make herself heard, wrote a song about the Woodstock festival without actually being there, and hitched herself to GRAHAM NASH (which, in the late Sixties, would be like hitching yourself to MARK ZUCKERBERG these days).

There are many, many great Joni Mitchell records (including a few she has made late in life, where the voice has become genuinely world-weary), but the only three anyone really needs are *Ladies Of The Canyon* (classic happy folk-rock, from 1970), *Blue* (plaintive confessional ballads, from 1971), and *The Hissing Of Summer Lawns* (where jazz reared its ugly head, in 1975), all of which are extraordinary. She has described herself as a "painter derailed by circumstance", and although now retired, she sometimes still makes music (albeit with a very different, and much lower singing voice).

MOBB DEEP

"Q-TIP had taken them on as his baby brothers and he'd given them his library of drum samples," said MARK RONSON. "Q-TIP's drum sounds at the time [the mid-Nineties] were the equivalent of the QUINCY JONES of hip-hop, clear but incredible, and sounded amazing in a club... You'd have this raw, Queensbridge, nasally, eerie slowness that these guys had over this incredible production. Amazing." And he should know.

THELONIOUS MONK

M

Part bebopper, part free-jazz thinker, Monk was enigmatic in the extreme, the chancer. Years before ELTON JOHN, he persisted with the funny glasses, wore ecclesiastical robes, and played some of the strangest piano you'll ever be lucky enough to hear. Monk's tunes were, in the words of one critic, "rigorous investigations of musical ideas"; i.e. using the damping pedal to eliminate certain notes, using keys as a drummer might, and sometimes just wandering off stage in search of God knows what (although probably women, drink, drugs, and food, in that order), when he was supposed to be playing a solo. His 1951 album *Genius Of Modern Music Vol. 1* (Blue Note) includes "Round Midnight", by some distance the most recorded jazz song of all time.

ALANIS MORISSETTE

There's nothing wrong with her per se, it's just all the catch-up record company-led copycats who came in her wake. As DAVID NICHOLLS once suggested, in his book *The Understudy*, they all made "Music To Comfort-Eat By" – jangly, sub-JONI MITCHELL, college radio stuff. But a bit angrier – fuckingangryactually. There they stood, in their new boots and panties, waving a NAOMI WOLF book in front of you as you scurried down the hall, taking all your Spring Break preconceptions with you. *Jagged Little Pill* (released in 1995) sold over thirty million copies, and remains the bestselling debut album by a female artist in the US (even though it was actually her debut "adult" album – she had released various records in Canada while still at school), and the highest-selling debut album worldwide. It produced six hit singles, and was the angry-college-girl *Thriller* of its day. Sounds pretty dated nowadays, as does

M everything else she recorded. Download "Ironic", "You Oughta Know", or "Hand In My Pocket" if you must, but I don't think you must.

ENNIO MORRICONE

By its very nature, the soundtrack is a supplementary medium. It's intrusive and indistinct by turns, following its film like a shadow.

But if, like STEELY DAN's DONALD FAGEN says, good music should sabotage expectations, then it would be easy to say that there is very little good music in the movies. Aural clichés are as widespread as visual ones: jazz for the city; narcissistic flutes in the suburbs; AARON COPELAND-style orchestration for small-town Americana; scratchy guitars and piping horns for urban thrillers. For pastoral, copy DEBUSSY; for devastation, rework BARBER or ALBINONI; for a western, hire Morricone.

Ennio Morricone is one of those men who makes music to watch, one of those men who has conjured up something special from the dark. The godfather of film music, Morricone is the man who put the opera into horse opera. Having achieved fame with SERGIO LEONE's spaghetti westerns in the Sixties – he brought a surrealistic panorama of strange cries, savage guitar chords, jangling bells, and the cracking of whips to the films (once described as sounding like MITCH MILLER on dope) – he has since composed and arranged scores for more than four hundred film and television productions.

One of the most prolific and versatile composers in the business, he was responsible for the monumental *Once Upon A Time In America,* which, even more so than his *Once Upon A Time In The West,* is probably the greatest film score ever recorded, a real 20th Century masterpiece. Due to the film's unusually long gestation, Morricone had finished composing most of the soundtrack before many scenes had even been filmed. Because of this, some of Morricone's pieces were actually played on set as filming took place (a technique Leone used for *Once Upon A Time In The West*). "It's evident that Leone played Morricone's score on set in the daydreamy faces of his cast," wrote BILL CHAMBERS. "In so doing, the director transformed many a novice thespian, including a prepubescent JENNIFER CONNELLY, into someone more likely to register with the camera and less likely to be self-conscious performing for it."

Morricone is often asked when he is going to retire. It is a question he finds it difficult to indulge. "You go back to what BACH composed and how much MOZART wrote in thirty-three years, and you see I am unemployed compared to this," he said recently. "I would like to relax a bit, but this is not the right year to do it."

JIM MORRISON

At a typical DOORS concert, you had two types of crowd. You had the freaks, the heads, and the hippies, the longhairs who were tuning in, turning on, and nodding their heads in collective appreciation at the psychedelic din being made in front of them. And then you had the teenage girls, the ones called "snappers", the ones who sat in the front rows in their miniskirts, and schoolgirl bobbysox, banging their knees together as if they were fanning their insides, trying to get Jim Morrison to stare at their underwear, or – more usually – their lack of. If you look at film performances of the DOORS in concert during their heyday, you see a Sixties band in all their pomp, effortlessly working their way through their material, determinedly bringing the crowd to whatever climax they came in for. But study the performance a bit more and you see a charismatic front man and three wily musos bent over their instruments and probably wondering to themselves how they got so lucky.

Because the DOORS was always three plus one. And the one was always Jim Morrison.

"I think there's a whole region of images and feelings inside us that rarely are given outlet in daily life. And when they do come out, they can take perverse forms. It's the dark side. Everyone, when he sees it, recognises the same thing in himself. It's recognition of forces that rarely see the light of day."

Was Jim Morrison joking?

Morrison was the quintessential Sixties pop star, an enigmatic, egotistical playboy with a penchant for philosophical self-absorption and black leather trousers. A counter-cultural hero, he physically pushed himself to the limits, exposing his "dark heart" to an audience which had only recently recovered from the onslaught of BOB DYLAN and the ROLLING STONES. But Jim Morrison, the first rock'n'roll method actor, was something else again. Morrison was FRANK SINATRA in leather trousers, an overly theatrical figurehead whose influence can be seen in the personas adopted by everyone from IGGY POP to ROBERT PLANT, from PATTI SMITH and KURT COBAIN to MICHAEL HUTCHENCE, DAVE GAHAN and BRANDON FLOWERS, and every modern version thereof, and whose band delivered the best lysergic pomp if its day. (His band? Oh yes – even though RAY MANZAREK, ROBBIE KRIEGER, and JOHN DENSMORE were responsible for some haunting orchestrations, you only have to listen to the pitiful music on the two albums the DOORS released after Morrison's death to know that the DOORS belonged to Jim Morrison and to Jim Morrison only.) He was the narcissistic stuff of rock legend, a self-obsessed drunk whose ridiculous good looks and rich baritone contributed unduly to an archetype that would define Morrison and every copycat who came in his wake. Not only that, he was walking around topless while STING was still in school.

In 1989, I was commissioned by Bloomsbury to write a book about the life, death, and legacy of Morrison. Commissioned to commemorate the 20th anniversary of his death, *Dark*

Star – as it was eventually called – was meant to fill in the gaps not covered by Morrison's other biographies, celebrate his iconic status, and investigate the then still mysterious details concerning his death. I interviewed dozens of former Morrison associates in London, Paris, New York, and Los Angeles – girlfriends, musicians, managers, and journalists, including DANNY FIELDS, their legendary PR guru, and the man who would later sign the MC5 and the STOOGES to Elektra. I also spent days hanging around Morrison's grave in Père Lachaise, the 120-acre cemetery in the 20th arrondissement that also houses the graves and tombs of EDITH PIAF, OSCAR WILDE, PROUST, BALZAC, COLETTE, CHOPIN, and hundreds of other notables. With its carefully plotted street names, rolling hills, and elaborate sepulchres, it's easy to see why the cemetery has become one of the city's most popular tourist destinations, especially if you are a Scandinavian teenager intent on communing with the spirits of dead rock stars.

A war baby, born in Melbourne, Florida, on December 8, 1943, Morrison grew up amidst the headstrong affluence of the Fifties, only to rebel against his upbringing a decade later, like so many millions of others. But Morrison was unique, a singer who created a myth around him, a "dark star" whose shtick was opening up his psyche and inviting the uninitiated to come and peer inside.

With the DOORS – whom JOAN DIDION once called "the NORMAN MAILERS of the Top 40, missionaries of apocalyptic sex" – he created some of the finest pop music of the late Sixties, music which still sounds astonishing today, not least because of its lyrical content. Their first two LPs – *The Doors* and *Strange Days* – contain songs that are little more than cleverly constructed vignettes of nihilism set to jaunty tunes. The DOORS managed to marry sex appeal, musicianship, and a highly commercial exploitation of undergraduate sensibilities.

Morrison liked to think of himself as an intellectual in a snakeskin suit, thinking he deserved to be something other than a tawdry pop star – he courted film-makers and poets,

M

and saw himself as some kind of modern-day Renaissance man, a man with no peers. And that was ultimately his undoing: bloated by alcohol, despising his audience, he ended up hating the tormented Adonis image he created, the image that made him successful.

He was the first rock star to literally self-destruct. JANIS JOPLIN and JIMI HENDRIX both died before Morrison, but he was the only one who was really looking for an escape. Morrison was the first pop star to explore himself (as well as expose himself) in public and, in doing so, went just that little bit too far. With BOB DYLAN everything was about disguise. With Morrison it was the opposite. He crammed an awful lot into his twenty-seven years, becoming for some the most adored American entertainer since ELVIS. He had sex, drive and passion. He had brains, good looks, a voice, a talent for writing evocative, manipulative lyrics, and a fondness for Dionysian imagery. He was part poet and part clown – a man who, when he revealed himself, was often to be found simply acting out his own fantasies. A self-proclaimed "erotic politician", Morrison was as much a showman as he was a shaman – a sham shaman – an actor who pushed his persona, his creation, as far as it would go. By the time of his "retirement" in Paris, the DOORS were effectively over (something the group still deny) and – a sex symbol with a beer belly and a beard – Morrison was toying with the idea of reinventing himself as a poet.

Fat chance. He was found dead in his bathtub in Paris in July 1971, due to what increasingly looks like a heroin overdose. But death at least assured him an immortality, and a permanent place in the rock'n'roll hall of fame. Had he lived, he would surely have undone all he had achieved during the final five years of his life. As it is, he remains, along with JAMES DEAN, and JIMI HENDRIX, one of youth culture's most revered heroes.

By the summer of 1969 it was painfully clear to everyone who knew him that Jim Morrison was falling apart, lost in his own weird orbit of fame. His drinking was taking over his life, his pretty-boy looks had gone, and he was getting terribly fat: hardly an icon of the new age, he was an overweight soak. His face was puffy (he had developed several chins), his hair matted and dank. He hardly ever washed, and tended to wear the same pair of trousers for weeks on end. When the Doors realised his vanity had deserted him, it made them worry because they realised he didn't care any more. And that meant obsolescence. His life was turning into one long bar-crawl, beginning when he awoke and ending when he eventually fell over, some fourteen hours later, somewhere in Hollywood, with a beer bottle in one hand and blonde in the other (when asking for a blow-job he'd say, "Suck my mama").

His performances were no longer cathartic, only a slow form of public suicide. During concerts he would mercilessly taunt the squirming girls in the front rows with screams and torrents of abuse, often spitting at his astonished pupils. His sweat-blurred eyes would burn holes in their faces as he lashed them with his tongue. He'd stalk the stage with an erection plainly visible in his trousers, daring anyone to touch. Backstage he would flick lighted cigarettes at groupies and demand oral sex, regardless of who was watching.

Morrison's drinking bouts were now so extreme, and his alcoholic intake so huge, that the band were in constant fear for his life. He had turned into a perpetual drunk: he was abusive and violent, melancholic and tearful. He'd vomit in hallways, out of car windows, in people's apartments, at recording sessions, in bed, on the lavatory, in the bath – Morrison was sick everywhere.

One particularly brattish trick was urinating in public. At a film awards ceremony in Atlanta he emptied his bursting bladder into an empty wine bottle and put it back on the table where it was eventually (partially) drunk. Once, at Max's in Los Angeles, he peed in a wine bottle and presented it to the waitress, asking her to take it home as he couldn't finish it himself. One night in New York, in a small club off Columbus Circle near Central Park, drinking Mexican beer with STEVE HARRIS, he turned to the Elektra Vice President and said, "You

M

M

know the difference between me and you? The difference is that I could throw this bottle against that mirror, smash it, and in the morning I wouldn't have any guilt. None."

"He was an alcoholic – plain and simple," said Harris, when I spoke to him in his midtown condo in Manhattan towards the end of 1989. "He had the disease. It wasn't because of pressure – if times were good he drank, if times were bad he drank. If the sun was shining he drank, if it was raining he drank. It was as simple as that. And yet, he was obnoxious. Some people are sweet drunk, but Jim was a redneck – gross, obnoxious, and rude. You couldn't tell him anything, he was a complete sociopath."

With the band unable to tour he was free to indulge himself as much as he liked. PAMELA COURSON, his regular girlfriend, was also allowing him an unusual amount of freedom. Ever since the DOORS had become stars she had found herself unable to deal with the attention Morrison received – she disliked most of his friends, and was constantly on the lookout for girls trying to worm their way into Jim's affections. She also couldn't cope with his increasingly debauched lifestyle and, to compensate, had begun seeing a variety of different men. It got to the stage where she would go out with the specific intention of being picked up, solely to annoy him.

She felt unfulfilled, and by this time was already using, heroin, though she hadn't told him yet. He tried to please her by buying her endless expensive presents, by letting her go shopping in his chauffeured limousine, and even bought her a clothes boutique that she tried to run. But she still couldn't cope. There were always furious fights between them, after which they usually drove off in separate directions looking for someone to spend the night with. But the fights were getting worse, and while Courson would wander the bars of the Strip loaded on depressants and heroin, Morrison would trawl the other side of town, looking for his own action. (He once told fellow Door RAY MANZAREK that he wanted to contract syphilis and let it remain uncured, having the wild fits of insanity until he died.)

So instead of staying in with Courson, instead of going to the many record company meetings, photo sessions, and recording sessions that his band were obligated to, Morrison would spend his days cruising bars and joyriding up in the hills outside LA, or dreaming up obscure film projects for himself and his friends (he now saw film as one of the only ways he could truly express himself, and devoted much of his time to trying to organise his own production company, wary of the Hollywood producers who, he thought, "just want to hang my meat on the screen").

He also had a habit of playing the matador with cars on the freeway, and would drop in to see his new friend ALICE COOPER rehearse, often dragging one of Cooper's band out to his car, forcing him to race up to the hills. Once there, Morrison would demand whoever was driving to go as fast as possible whilst he threw himself out. This was how he liked to top off an evening, by getting involved in some foolish daredevil scheme that would invariably lead to a drunken act of student bravery.

Now that Morrison was relinquishing any interest he might have with the real world, Elektra found him impossible to work with. "He was such an asshole," former Elektra Press officer DANNY FIELDS told me, when I interviewed him in his Greenwich Village apartment in 1989. "But was that his problem or mine? At the time I wished it had only been his problem. But when you're working for someone, and when they're paying the bills, it becomes your problem." I interviewed Fields half-a-dozen times for my book, and he even spent an evening painstakingly going through some old filing cabinets in his office, pulling out unpublished photographs of Morrison, along with many handwritten notes from the singer.

"Of course there were worries about the way he conducted himself," said STEVE HARRIS, "because at that time FM rock radio had not really come into its own, and the AM stations liked everything and everybody to be hunky dory. After the New Haven bust [when Morrison was arrested for attempting

M to incite a riot after telling the crowd at a DOORS concert that the police had sprayed him with mace backstage], all the stations stopped playing "Love Me Two Times", which was out at the time. But the LP, *Strange Days*, kept selling, and after a while, people accepted him for what he was. So we went along with it, we left him alone."

With the world falling about his ears, Morrison sought refuge in the arms of PATRICIA KENNEALY, one of the shrewdest things he ever did. She was probably the most important influence on him during his last years. The couple had first met earlier in 1969 when Patricia had interviewed him for the East Coast rock magazine *Jazz & Pop*, of which she was editor-in chief. She had written extensively on the band before their meeting, and continued to afterwards. But while she was a fan she was no sycophant, pulling Morrison up on his verbosity and grandiose mannerisms in print long before she was doing it to his face.

Of course Kennealy was extremely attractive, but she had two other qualities which drew Morrison to her: she was his intellectual equal, and she wouldn't take any bull – if she thought he was stringing her a line, she told him so. Kennealy developed something of a reputation with the band and Morrison's record company, and as she had a reputation for being a practising white witch, for years after Morrison's death, no one would go near her. I needed to speak to her for my book, and so began looking for her in New York. I spoke with Elektra Records, and with the thirty or so people I interviewed for the book, in London, New York, and Los Angeles, but not only could none of them could point me in the right direction, some even advised me to steer clear of her completely. "She's dangerous," I was told. "She'll eat you alive." In the end it took me about forty minutes to track her down, simply by looking through the New York Yellow Pages.

"I was knocked out by his manners the first time I met him," she said, when I finally met her a few weeks later, in her East Village walk-up. "He stood up and shook my hand as I walked into the hotel room for the interview, and a rock

M

star had never done that before. I was obviously overawed because he was already a hero of mine, but I was staggered by how literate he was. I thought rock stars were mostly jerks before I met Jim. Music meant a lot at that point, and it was annoying to discover that the people making it were mostly dumb. Jim definitely had a brain. His songs were sometimes too contrived, but they had a certain quality that was different to everything else. He was funny too. He was much funnier when he was sober, but then I guess most of us are. Mostly when he was drunk with me he would get kind of quiet and surly. But he was never at a loss for words."

It took a while for them to become lovers – theirs was a strangely old-fashioned courtship – but when they finally did, they too became inseparable. "It was a very personal thing, and the fact that he was famous didn't seem to intrude upon it at all. I suppose that indicates a kind of ostrich mentality on my part, thinking we could walk around Central Park without anyone noticing. But for me it was as though we existed inside a bubble. Of course it wasn't true."

The bubble burst when Kennealy saw how he could behave in front of other people. "He gave people what perhaps he seemed to think they expected of him. He was rather obliging in respect of his drinking. I don't think the person I met was an act, I thought the Jim Morrison I knew was the real person. I might have been naïve as hell, but I thought that this was what he was really like, and the other stuff – the drinking and the drugs – was extraneous. I thought he was a genuinely shy person, and that the other stuff was a mask, a convenient persona for the people to relate to. It was self-defence. But this side of his character manifested itself in a totally outrageous and malevolent way, and it became larger than he was. His success magnified his human weaknesses."

Kennealy tried to pull Morrison back to earth, but as soon as she'd convince him to stop drinking, split from the band, and concentrate on living his life, he'd recoil and turn into the rock'n'roll pilgrim from LA. "At the time I thought, if this is as good as it can get, then this is what I'll have to settle for. I

M would have rather had what I had, than not have anything. He would always say that it was over between him and Pamela, that the relationship was half pity, but he never would have left her."

At this stage, Kennealy was one of the few people trying to get Morrison to slow down. To other people he was simply a wild rock'n'roller, one who was ever so slightly over the hill. "In those days," said Steve Harris, "people didn't think in terms of cleaning up their acts – record companies didn't ask bands to lay off the booze for a while because an important gig was coming up. There was none of that, basically because there wasn't the knowledge that there is now. That was the first period when people went for it in a serious way. Now, twenty years later those people are either dead, they've cleaned up, or they're vegetable. The records were still selling, so why should we have tried to stop them. We thought, so he drinks, everybody drinks, right?"

"I tried to stop him, but by then he was too far gone," said Kennealy. "It had got so out of hand. He was beginning to fall apart, on all levels, just sliding downhill. I felt useless, I would have sold my soul to stop it. It was like throwing yourself in front of a runaway bus – you can't do a damn thing about it. It was just so inevitable, it was like a Greek tragedy after a while. It just got worse, and worse, and worse. No one could do a damn thing about it. We'd talk, argue, scream, nothing would change. It didn't seem to be anything he could do anything about.

"He was too entrenched in all the bullshit. I would tell him he was surrounded by assholes, and he would laugh and say, yes, he knew. What can you do? You can't kidnap someone and deprogramme them. Maybe you can, but it wasn't something that would have occurred to me at the time. People can't be saved unless they want to be saved, and Jim didn't. I think he had this idea that once he was saved he wouldn't be an artist any more. It was this whole romantic Hemingway thing.

"He thought he could become a serious artist by being a rock singer, but just found the whole thing relentlessly trivialised by his fans. It depressed him when he realised that people only saw him as a rock star, and that he probably didn't control his own life or destiny any more. It was really sad – he should have cut out a hell of a lot sooner."

M

By the end of 1969 Jim Morrison was a sex symbol with a beer belly, a beard, and a serious attitude problem. He was fat, drunk, and unhappy. Strapped to a rollercoaster that showed no signs of slowing down, he was rushing through his life with no sense of purpose, all his sensibilities blurred by drink. As all around him the pressure and tension built up, he became a frenzied zombie, a walking corpse, a man who only wanted escape.

This was hardly surprising, as Morrison's life had recently become a litany of disasters: during November he had entered a not guilty plea in Miami, and was released on $5,000 bail. He had been arrested earlier in the year for exposing himself at a concert there. Two days after this, he was arrested after flying to Phoenix with TOM BAKER and a few drinking buddies, ostensibly to see the ROLLING STONES; he was charged with being drunk and disorderly, and interfering with the flight of an aircraft (i.e. being rowdy and molesting an air stewardess). The charges were eventually dropped.

The DOORS' movie, *Feast Of Friends*, was finally released, and was described by *Variety* as a failure, "Made either from the outtakes of some larger project or an unsold try at daytime TV slotted to meet the kids home from school." *Rolling Stone*, meanwhile, simply called it pretentious (for some reason the film did win an award at the Atlanta Film Festival). And *HWY*, an experimental film project close to his heart, was screened to a resolutely unenthusiastic reception. He was courted to appear in several movies – including one marshalled by STEVE MCQUEEN – but nothing came of them.

To console himself, Morrison continued on his drink and drug binges (taking Trimar, which was basically an epidural), though increasingly he was unaccompanied. His twenty-sixth birthday was celebrated at a friend's house in Manhattan Beach, just south of LA, where Morrison repaid

M

his hospitality by falling asleep on the couch, his penis poking out of his trousers, soaking the carpet with urine. Because he was turning into such a behemoth, and because the paranoia surrounding the band's performances had led to so many concerts being cancelled, the rest of the band kept asking him to get his act together, to shave, and shed a few pounds for their forthcoming dates in LA; but Morrison just ignored them.

The arrest in Miami had really taken its toll, and a string of paternity suits only made him more insecure. Morrison began to look vulnerable. It was now that he first began mentioning a move to Paris as a possible means of escape. Elektra tried to combat the steadily increasing bad publicity by relaunching Morrison as a "renaissance man", and various press releases outlining Morrison's raison d'être were drawn up for his approval. Predictably the singer wanted nothing to do with it: he didn't want the people told he was a superman, he wanted them to discover it for themselves.

The one thing which did please Morrison was the publication of *The Lords And The New Creatures* poetry collection by Simon & Schuster, even though it was credited to Jim Morrison, and not James Douglas Morrison, as he'd requested.

Then in February 1970 the group released a new LP, *Morrison Hotel* (named after a $2 skid-row hotel in downtown LA). After the disappointment of their previous record *The Soft Parade*, this was almost a return to form, though by no means a complete success. The record contained some strong, evocative songs – "Peace Frog" contained references to the witnesses of a car accident in his youth ("Indians scattered on a dawn's highway bleeding, ghosts crowd the young child's fragile eggshell mind"); "Queen Of The Highway" was inspired by Courson; and "Roadhouse Blues", with its flagrantly ironic blues lyric ("Well, I woke up this morning and I got myself a beer") was the story of his own life – but somehow everyone expected more.

A note of bitterness had begun to creep into Morrison's interviews. He told *CREEM* magazine at the time, "The music has gotten progressively better, tighter, more professional, more interesting, but I think that people resent the fact that three years ago there was a great renaissance of spirit and emotion and revolutionary sentiment, and when things didn't change overnight I think people resented the fact that we were just still around doing good music."

Two months after its release, *Morrison Hotel* was awarded a gold disc, making the Doors the first US rock group to achieve five gold albums in a row.

During the spring of 1970, Morrison renewed his acquaintance with PATRICIA KENNEALY. They had not had much contact since their first meeting a year or so earlier – only exchanging the occasional letter, phone call, or gift – but it was Kennealy whom Jim called when he doubted himself, and needed to be told he was a God or a schmuck. And Patricia would tell him in no uncertain terms.

His relationship with Courson might have been more habitual, but it was Kennealy who offered the intellectual firepower, who challenged him. When Morrison showed Courson the lyrics to a new song, she'd tell him how marvellous he was, when he showed Kennealy, she'd point out its pretentious literary references. He was as abusive to her as he was to Courson, but Kennealy saw sides of him, which no one else did.

"I saw him be a terrible pig," she told me. "He was a pig to me and he was a pig to Pam, but I have the other stuff to balance against that. I was honest with him. Apart from me I don't think anyone was honest with him at that point. And because he couldn't trust anyone, he covered up. He had this really vulnerable psyche, this inner self that he genuinely wanted to protect, the way we all do. He threw up screens to protect himself, and sometimes he was successful, sometimes not."

On Midsummer's Night 1970, at 10:30pm, after spending the day together, Morrison and Kennealy were married in her gothic East Village apartment in New York. But this was no ordinary service: it was a wicca wedding. A ceremony based in white witchcraft. At this period in her life Kennealy was a

M practising member of a New York coven, and the ceremony was conducted by the founders of that coven, a high priest and priestess.

"What I practise is witchcraft, for want of a better word," she told me the first time we met. "It's esoteric Christianity. I've fallen out of the habit of covens and all that kind of stuff, but I would characterise myself more as a pagan than a Christian. When I pray, it's not always to Jesus. I told Jim the first time I met him that I was involved in witchcraft, I was either so anaesthetised by drink or so incredibly comfortable that it just came out. He was surprised, sort of how you might be surprised if your cat suddenly started talking: you might be a bit intimidated, but on the whole, you'd rather like it. I suppose he felt a need for some kind of avowal of his feelings, a formalised connection, however unorthodox it might have been. The drama of the ceremony certainly appealed to him. It was an extraordinary experience, it was magical."

Morrison and Kennealy took part in the ritual hand fasting, and drew each other's blood as part of the Celtic tradition. They mixed a few drops of their blood with consecrated wine, which they then drank, and then proceeded to sign the two official documents, one written in English, the other in witch runes. Jim and Patricia signed their names in blood, after which Morrison fainted.

"He fainted because he came into the presence of the goddess, one of the ancient forces of nature, and one of the people to whom we pray. Being in a magical circle takes an awful lot out of you – it's very intense. It's an actual physical thing, and if you're not prepared for it – which Jim obviously wasn't – it's very powerful. Magic is a very real thing... it's a draining of energy."

Life sped on. There was no time to think, only drink. Soon after the bizarre marriage, Morrison visited Paris, scouting the city for apartments as well as visiting the bars. A week later he was back in LA, where he continued his excessive behaviour: one week being arrested for public drunkenness, the next catching pneumonia.

At a time when live performances by the group were sporadic, in July Elektra decided to release the Doors' first live LP, a two-record package called *Absolutely Live*, which had been recorded in New York during January. It contained some good performances, but was only noteworthy for the inclusion of a fully blown version of "The Celebration Of The Lizard King". The cover was a dead giveaway, featuring a photograph of Morrison which was at least eighteen months old; there was little point using a recent picture of the singer, he was too wan and fat.

The Miami trial began in August and was a farce from the outset. The prosecution paraded a seemingly endless procession of witnesses claiming to have seen Morrison expose himself, even though one hundred and fifty photographs taken at the concert contradicted this. Miami vs James D. Morrison was a sham of a trial. Maybe because the odds were stacked against him from the start. Morrison's attorneys tried to sidestep the issue by comparing his stagecraft with other forms of contemporary art: things like *Portnoy's Complaint*, *Hair!* and *Woodstock,* which included nudity, swearing, or purposeful exhibitionism. It was a cunning ploy, but nevertheless the judge threw the idea out of court, declaring that examples of "community standards" would not be admitted for evidence. "He was a scapegoat," said Kennealy, "taking the heat for a lot of other people."

Morrison's problems were compounded when, on August 14, Kennealy called him from New York to tell him she was pregnant with his child. After inviting her down to Miami, he systematically avoided her and refused to have anything to do with the impending baby. After a while he relented and they talked it through, though they couldn't agree to keep the child. In the end he offered to pay for an abortion, and promised to be with her when it happened.

"We talked about having the baby for quite a while," said Kennealy, "which is why it went as long as it did [twenty weeks]. I had to face up to the fact that he probably wouldn't be around much, and really neither of us wanted the child

M

anyway. It was terrible timing all round. I only really wanted the child because it was Jim's, and as he wasn't crazy about it, well..."

In the middle of the trial, the DOORS flew to England to appear at the Isle of Wight festival, which turned out to be one of their most shambolic performances. Morrison had been up for thirty-six hours when he went on stage, and his drinking had affected him so much he could hardly stand. The band hated the experience, hated playing outdoors in front of thousands of people they couldn't see or hear, and Morrison hated it so much he claimed he would never appear on stage again.

By now, the whole band were sick of performing. Guitarist ROBBY KRIEGER: "At that time we didn't think we'd ever go out on the road again. We were content to stay in LA and cut records. We'd had it with the police, hall managers, narcs and the vice squad. They were always there – with tapes, cameras, microphones. They were ready for anything."

In September, after more than a month, the trial was finally over, with Morrison found guilty of indecent exposure and profanity, though acquitted on the charge of "lewd and lascivious behaviour". He was released on $50,000 bail. He said to reporters after leaving the courtroom, "This trial and its outcome won't change my style, because I maintain that I did not do anything wrong."

Things went from bad to worse. JIMI HENDRIX and JANIS JOPLIN had just died, and Morrison would sit in the bars along Sunset Strip saying, "You're drinking with Number Three."

What if he was next? He'd sit alone by the jukebox and ponder the question. Paranoia was getting the better of him: his life was no longer worth living because it had become a living nightmare. He'd alienated most of his friends, the arguments with Courson and Kennealy were getting more intense, and as for the rest of the band, well he just couldn't talk to them anymore.

In Miami in October he was officially sentenced, receiving eight months hard labour and a $500 fine. He appealed.

In November in New York, Kennealy had the abortion. Morrison was not present. There were no flowers, and he didn't even call.

"Looking back I'm astonished at what I let myself be put through," said Kennealy. "But I'm twenty years older now. He was only about the third boyfriend I'd had in my whole life, and I didn't have a whole lot of experience. Obviously he made me happy or else I wouldn't have put up with it for as long as I did."

On December 12, the Doors played their last concert, in New Orleans. It was a shambles, with an almost unrecognisable Morrison stumbling about the stage, mumbling. He had lost patience with himself and with his audience. Then, living alone in LA, he was a danger to himself – he needed either Courson or Kennealy, to round off the edges. What he didn't need was both of them at the same time; but, when Courson returned from Paris and Kennealy flew in from New York, this is what he got. Morrison went to Pamela's apartment that night, only to find his two regular girlfriends deep in conversation. The two adversaries had met and, having tried to sort out their differences, ended up talking, drinking and smoking grass together for over three hours.

After the three of them spent the evening together, he ended up sleeping with Kennealy, having refused to stay with Courson. For Kennealy this was only a fleeting success, as Morrison spent most of January living with Courson.

But on St Valentine's Day, 1971, Courson left for Paris to look for an apartment. Kennealy, back in LA, stayed with Morrison for a week, seven days of idyllic drunkenness and their last together.

In the final week before leaving for Paris, Morrison left Kennealy and slept with a different girl every night, even seeing one through an abortion. Considering his intake at this time – rumoured to be three bottles of Scotch a day – it is doubtful whether he managed to have sex with any of them.

For Morrison, Paris was a city of dreamers, of romantics, of poets; his mind raced with thoughts of Rimbaud, Baudelaire,

M CELINE, of HEMINGWAY, SCOTT FITZGERALD, PICASSO, and GERTRUDE STEIN. He imagined the Paris of the Twenties, of Montmartre and the Latin Quarter, a Paris of the mind, driven by noble, artistic fervour. It was March 1971.

This was to be the last stage of Morrison's journey into hell. Sometimes with Courson, sometimes alone, he'd wander the city, sightseeing, shopping, and stopping at dozens of bars. He gained some anonymity, yet his lifestyle hadn't really changed. He felt relieved, but also lost and alone, as though he was waving to a crowd which had long since moved on. On Friday July 2, he went alone to a cinema. At five the next morning, Courson found him in the bath, dead. He had earlier complained of stomach pains, throwing up blood-flecked vomit. Courson had offered to call a doctor, but when Morrison said he felt better and went off to have a bath, she went to bed. When she awoke a few hours later and couldn't open the locked bathroom door she called her friends AGNES VARDA and ALAIN RONAY. Having broken open the door they discovered Morrison lying dead in the bath, with a trickle of blood dripping from one nostril. Due to certain intricacies of French law an autopsy was never performed, although unless he had a bad reaction to his asthma medication (which would have been extremely toxic mixed with alcohol), it is assumed he died from a heroin overdose. He was buried four days later in Père Lachaise. The cause of death will probably never be known as Courson herself died from a heroin overdose in Los Angeles, in 1974.

Today his grave is covered in graffiti, surrounded by the detritus of visiting rock fans, who come in their backpacked thousands each year to pay homage to their dead icon. The grave has consistently caused the authorities problems due to the number of people who congregate there every day. A bust of Morrison, put there by the Croatian sculptor MLADEN MIKULIN in 1981, was stolen seven years later, although it has been replaced with various alternative ad-hoc versions. There have been so many conspiracy theories surrounding not only Morrison's death but also about the whereabouts of his body – was it stolen? shipped back to America? burned? – that the state once considered moving his tomb to another cemetery, but in 1996 the French Minister of Culture announced that it was to be a permanent cultural monument. I last visited in January 2010, and it didn't look much different to how it had looked over twenty years previously. There was a similar smattering of poorly-dressed students, a few sixty-something hippies with a bottle of cheap wine, a few tramps, and a charming middle-aged couple from New Zealand who insisted on offering their sandwiches around – the only real difference to 1989 being the number of mobile telephones used to commemorate the visit.

Had he lived, and had been able to come to terms with his success, it's possible that Jim Morrison would have become a happy, more complete person. For his fans this would have been a disaster. Rock'n'roll obsessives don't want career plans, they want starbursts and crash landings. For them, Jim Morrison will always be twenty-something – he'll never have to denounce the booze nor give up the high life. Time didn't allow Morrison to grow old in public, and so his life remains a prototype of immaturity. In death he is, in his own phrase, "stoned, immaculate". Morrison will never change, and that's the way the fans like it.

VAN MORRISON

Like any true fanatic, I came to this thing rather late. I had bought Van Morrison's *Veedon Fleece* back in 1974, when I was barely a teenager and, although I liked it, at that time it was just another weird record by another weird, long-haired visionary. In those days they were ten a penny. No, this Van thing came to me in my thirties, when I had all but exhausted any fascination I might have had for short, balding, irascible visionaries. But when it finally hit, it stung. Obsessions tend to be things you grow out of, but Van Morrison was one I definitely grew into.

M Over the years he has been called everything from Van the Man, to Van the Mystic, to the Belfast Cowboy, but in reality he is the scowling sage, a difficult old goat with a belligerent streak in him as wide as the Irish Sea. To say that Van Morrison is terse would be like calling ALAN CLARKE promiscuous or CRISTIANO RONALDO prolific. "I never said I was a nice guy," he once told the hyphenate publicist, BP FALLON. "OK? Never. I'm not a nice guy... If somebody says I'm grumpy, I'm a c*** or whatever, that's OK, because I don't profess to be an angel."

A typical example of his irascibility apparently happened some years ago when Van was involved in the making of a short film for a television arts programme. Having communicated to the presenter his customary distaste for talking about himself, the producers wisely took him through a dry run on the morning the programme was due to be recorded. Afterwards, the presenter appeared satisfied if not a little relieved.

An hour later, when recording began, Van was asked his carefully rehearsed question, only to reply, "You must be mad if you think I'm going to answer that..."

Stories attach themselves to Van Morrison like lint: he was apparently so alarmed by an unofficial biography in 1993 that his management team offered to buy up all 25,000 copies from the publisher, Bloomsbury. And he allegedly instigated legal proceedings against the Belfast Blues Society in 1991 for attempting to place a commemorative plaque by the door of the house where he was born (prompting a cartoon in a local newspaper showing a Belfast City Council plaque inscribed with the words "Van Morrison Was Miserable Here, 1960"). Stories of his ill temper are so legion, and so oft-repeated, that it's difficult to doubt their veracity or their provenance. A musician who once played with Van – "a notoriously intense thundercloud of a man" – remembers an all-night bar-stool argument with the portly, obstinate Ulsterman. Morrison apparently argued his case, an arcane philosophical point, with such force and gusto that the musician eventually caved in, conceding defeat, and siding with Van.

"I agree with you, Van," he said.

"You what?" asked Morrison, somewhat perplexed.

"What you said. I agree with it."

M

"Well in that case," the singer shot back, "in that case, you're wrong." Not only is this typical Van Morrison, but as anyone who has ever spent time in a pub in Dublin will tell you, typically Irish.

Morrison is a grump in a hat. He reserves much of his wrath, predictably, for the fourth estate. One writer said that while every rookie music journalist is given the same piece of advice – never meet your heroes – what this actually means is, never meet Lou Reed, Morrissey, or Van Morrison... "Because unless you enjoy frosty recalcitrance during an interview, and gnarling grumpiness afterwards, you'll wish you hadn't even tried to eke words from Belfast's least chatty son." Marianne Faithfull, who has spent a lot of time in Dublin, and used to bump into Morrison all the time, says, "Van can be difficult, I'm sure, but belligerent? No. Anyone who says otherwise is probably a journalist – I'm sure he gives them a hard time. He's a creative artist; what the f*** do journalists expect them to be? Van is really a very good friend, almost like a counsellor, or a priest. With Van it's a bit like having a hotline to God."

For Morrison, success has rarely been more important than achievement. His is not the world of *OK!*, *Hello!*, or *Heat*, but then their world isn't his either. He regards music as a vocation, not a step towards celebrity. "I believe that an artist does not belong to the public but to himself," he'll say. "I don't want anyone to know about my personal life because it is my personal life." His aversion to the press is legendary – particularly to those who try to stifle him by definition. "Nobody asks a bricklayer about laying bricks," he once said, "why ask me about writing songs? There's no difference. I just do what I do." "It ain't why," he once sang, "it just is."

Can you blame him for being so difficult, so shy, so definite in his desire to remain private? Not me. I've still got a few heroes left, and past experience has taught me that meeting them can be terribly anti-climactic. Although it might be

M

fascinating to sit and talk to him and find out more about this tortured soul of his, I would be quite happy to know no more about him than I do today. As long as I could still listen to his records, that is.

And the work, as Van would be keen to point out himself, is the most important thing.

Successful musical miscegenation is rare, yet Morrison is one of the few people who has convincingly fused rock, soul, blues, R&B, jazz, and traditional pop styles (including doo-wop), with the result always being more than the sum of its parts. His music has always bypassed current trends; it hasn't just co-existed in some quasi-spiritual parallel world – one filled with haunting keyboards, onomatopoeic vocals, brushed drums, acoustic bass, and barely perceptible wind instruments –it's always been the canon to curl up with after a night on the tiles. And it doesn't matter how ingrained your musical allegiances might be, whether you like garage, alt country, or nu-metal, in the privacy of your own home the Man conquers all. After all, Van Morrison was chill out before there *was* chill out. His records have replaced those of MARVIN GAYE as the most popular tools of seduction. Even celebrities use them: to help Glenn Close relax for the sex scene in *Jagged Edge*, co-star JEFF BRIDGES played her Van's "A Sense Of Wonder"; to do the same for RACHEL WARD in *Against All Odds* he used "Inarticulate Speech Of The Heart" (well, you wouldn't use PHIL COLLINS, now would you?).

GEORGE IVAN MORRISON first achieved fame nearly fifty years ago with the Belfast-born THEM, an Irish ROLLING STONES, whose love of rhythm and blues never resulted in the kind of Faustian bargain that put paid to the careers of some of its peers. A grunt R&B band whose members' unlikely telegenic qualities helped propel them into the homes and hearts of Sixties' teenagers, in its time, THEM was as popular as the KINKS, say, or the MONKEES. Having unwittingly conquered popdom ("Here Comes The Night", "Gloria", "Baby Please Don't Go", were all big hits of some sort in the mid-Sixties), Van soon flew the coop, recording a series of solo pieces of varying quality under the guidance of producer BERT BERNS (the most famous of which is "Brown Eyed Girl", a record you can still hear in heavy rotation on Radio 2, though always with the "offending" lyrics referring to "making love" edited out). Then, suddenly, it all went horribly right; an album that belonged to no time and no genre, the legendary *Astral Weeks* – recorded in New York in forty-eight hours in 1968, when Morrison was just twenty-two – turned Van Morrison into a man, in the words of writer MICK BROWN, "whose sense of self was [suddenly] unassailable". Displaying a sense of abandonment seldom heard in rock music, with *Astral Weeks* Van Morrison somehow managed to define the unimaginable.

According to *The Mojo Collection* (2000), which is one of the dozen-or-so encyclopedias of pop albums you can buy at your neighbourhood corporate megastore, *Astral Weeks* has an "eerie nostalgic mood that makes [it] so enduringly fascinating". The *Rolling Stone Album Guide* (1992), meanwhile, is even more fulsome in its praise, "...blue, wise and yearning, its music combining jazz rhythms and freer structures, impressionist strings and woodwinds... Morrison voicing his lyrics like a misty, Celtic soul singer gifted with a virtuoso sense of drama. *Astral Weeks* is dense and complex, rich with private symbolism and cryptic suggestion."

Some critics believe Morrison has spent the last thirty-three years trying to better this LP, and that his frustration at being unable to do so has led to a rather jaundiced world view. I wouldn't believe it. Nostalgia is usually a little more than a stick with which to beat the present, and, in fact, Van's very best work came five years later. *Astral Weeks* was certainly a milestone in terms of broadening the parameters of rock, but it is not Van's finest work, not by a long shot. No, Morrison's masterpiece is 1974's *Veedon Fleece*, a record of such pastoral beauty it puts ALBINONI, CHOPIN, and MENDELSSOHN to shame. One critic described part of the record as the sound that grass makes when it's growing and if there was ever a musical equivalent of WALT WHITMAN, then this is it. As LIAM NEESON once said, "The guy can take

M

a walk through a meadow and go home and write an album about it."

In between these two records came *Moondance*, *His Band And The Street Choir* (both 1970), *Tupelo Honey* (1971), *Saint Dominic's Preview* (1972), and *Hard Nose The Highway* (1973), a remarkable body of work that would have lasted other artists a lifetime. Since then, there have been dozens of records (he has made more than thirty albums) which range from the prosaic to the bewildering – every one exploring Morrison's obsessional quest for personal enlightenment. Along the way he has written the occasional pop classic too: "Jackie Wilson Said", "Bulbs", "Bright Side Of The Road", "Have I Told You Lately". Lyrically he has been obsessed with the lost, legendary dreamland of Avalon, and the rain-soaked Irish countryside. As befits an Irishman, he worships the rain, and it's rare to find a Van Morrison record that doesn't mention something about "gardens wet with rain after a summer shower". In Morrison's world, every day is a grand, soft day.

It is too easy to dismiss the effect that music can have on you. For some it is the BUZZCOCKS, for others it's HANK WILLIAMS, for me it is Van. He strikes chords in me I didn't know I had. Of course it is possible, while listening to some of his work, to feel consumed by peace and completeness – Morrison "concentrates on capturing the evanescent quality of the moment through impressionism", writes his biographer, JOHNNY ROGAN –but it can also be disconcerting. Listen to "Across The Bridge Where Angels Dwell", "Into The Mystic", "Hymns To The Silence", or "Flamingoes Fly" (one of Van's lost tracks from *The Philosopher's Stone*, recorded in 1974 but only released in 1998), it can all well up – euphoria, melancholy, and all points in between. Listening to Van Morrison is sometimes like life squared.

Like any maverick, Van Morrison has done some odd things. As well as being overwrought and pompous he has embraced scientology, dabbled with Gestalt therapy, recorded a duet with CLIFF RICHARD, and covered a song made famous by KERMIT THE FROG ("It's Not Easy Being Green"). But hell, you expect this kind of nonsense from your heroes. After all, he's a soul in torment, isn't he? Isn't that what it says on the tin? Like his good friend, BOB DYLAN, Morrison seems to hate the way he looks, determined to contort his face and body, no matter how ludicrous he appears. His suits are usually too pinched, his body constricted, and when he does dress well, even then he tries to disguise himself, slipping onto stage in his dark, velvet-collared JOHN ROCHA jacket, pork-pie hat (he loves a hat does our Van) and sunglasses, looking not unlike a Belfast Blues Brother.

The very idea of being a pop star is just anathema to him. He is genuinely enigmatic, and goes to great lengths to distance himself from the world of pop. Some years ago he wrote a letter to the Irish *Sunday Independent*, complaining about their constant references to Van Morrison the Rock Star, "To call me a rock star is absurd," he wrote, "as anyone who has listened to my music will observe. On the one hand I am flattered by the sudden attention, having spent most of my life living the role of anti-hero and getting on with my job." On the other hand... In Morrison's eyes, being a troubadour is a noble vocation, like being a craftsman or a poet – someone who works with their hands, if only to lift a pen.

Morrison's influence has never been in doubt, and he's been an inspiration to BRUCE SPRINGSTEEN, MIKE SCOTT, RYAN ADAMS, TIM and JEFF BUCKLEY, KEVIN ROWLAND – the list just goes on. (Incidentally, Morrison's 1972 single, "Jackie Wilson Said [I'm In Heaven When You Smile]", failed to chart until ten years later when it was revived by DEXY'S MIDNIGHT RUNNERS. The song confused the *Top Of The Pops* production staff so much that they screened a backdrop of darts player JOCKY WILSON during Dexy's performance.) Morrison has become something of an establishment figure, too. His song "Days Like This" became the unofficial anthem of the Irish peace process after being licensed by the Northern Ireland Office in 1995, and this autumn his face is due to appear on a stamp issued by the Republic. Morrison's Irishness is something he

M

wears like a badge; it's not just manifested in his music but in everything he does. Stephen Pillster, one of Morrison's tour managers, witnessed the beginnings of his search for his heritage when he knew him in Dublin years ago. "I always thought Van had a tough time finding his centre," he says. "It really came to me in Dublin that he's really a mad Irish poet. That's his genetic make-up."

Morrison's "job" doesn't seem as important now as it once did, and Van hasn't really surfed the Zeitgeist for some time now. He still makes records, and some of them are very good, yet he seems to have drifted off the cultural radar a little. His last truly great record was *Hymns To The Silence* in 1991, a double CD characterised by nostalgia and gospel. The blues seem to be his current obsession, and, again like BOB DYLAN, he feels obliged to embrace it in a bid to dignify his old age. As KEITH RICHARDS always likes to say, if the bluesman is still allowed to perform in his sixties, then why can't the white man? Van Morrison is one of those Sixties musicians who once saw themselves as menaces to society but now look upon themselves as an endangered species. "I don't think I will ever mellow out," he says. "If you mellow out you get eaten up."

By the Nineties, Van Morrison was considered to be a grumpy old goat resting on his laurels. During this period, whenever I heard a new Van song, I would think about an old RAY LOWRY cartoon showing a nurse wheeling a stereo-system towards an elderly man in a bathchair, with the words, "Time for your Van Morrison, Mr Smith..."

But if you're keen on music, then you never stop rooting. Which is how I discovered Morrison's "Blue and Green", which is as good a blues record as you're likely to hear, or indeed deserve to hear, this century. It is, quite simply – in at least two senses of the word – brilliant, and has certainly restored my faith in the bitter, curmudgeonly old cove.

There I was, driving at speed through Herefordshire, seeing if I could keep ahead of the rain, and working my way through *The Best Of Van Morrison Vol. 3*, which is less a greatest hits collection and more a selection of the less offensive records he's released these last fifteen years. As any half-hearted fan will know, in his dotage, Van has been "harking back to his roots", knocking out dozens of rudimentary and pretty mediocre jazz and blues tunes, often accompanied by clunky, ill-suited cohorts such as RAY CHARLES, TOM JONES, and GEORGIE FAME, thinking – perhaps – that unadorned roots music will somehow afford him the critical acclaim that began deserting him in the Eighties. But seeing that most of the records he's made in the last decade and a half have been not so much curate's eggs as scrambled eggs (all mixed up and nowhere to go), it was a surprise when "Blue And Green" started wafting through the in-car stereo. In fact it was less of a surprise and more of a revelation – spare, seductive and even-tempered, it's one of those songs you could play repeatedly for an hour and not get tired of.

The song was previously included on the little-known charity album *Hurricane Relief: Come Together Now*, which raised money for relief efforts intended for Gulf Coast victims devastated by Hurricane Katrina – which is probably the reason I'd never heard of it. But I implore any disillusioned Morrison buff to seek it out, as it will restore your faith in belligerent, claret-jowled old men in ill-fitting leather jackets and inappropriate hats. As one contented Amazon customer said, "Despite having most of this already I paid out my money and what did I get? A reasonable overview with some obscurities, one of which 'Blue And Green', is worth the cost on its own."

As I understand it, most reviews on Amazon tend to be written either by the people responsible for the product, or by their friends and relatives (allegedly), although something tells me this one perhaps wasn't written by Van himself.

I've bumped into Van Morrison a few times, once at a private benefit concert in aid of Tibet he gave at London's Grosvenor House (where Morrison, in typically contrary fashion, turned a twenty-minute showcase into a glorious two-hour set that belied the anodyne location and weathered the interruptions of RICHARD GERE, who insisted on jamming with

Morrison and his band), but I've never particularly wanted to approach him as I figure he deserves his privacy. I've never really seen the point of just hurling yourself at a celebrity. If you're introduced, fine, but otherwise it's just embarrassing. Plus, you obviously run the risk of being blanked, like the journalist who approached RUSSELL CROWE recently at a party in London. "How are you?" the journo asked. "I'm not doing interviews," Crowe allegedly replied. Cheers. In Van's case, who needs another starfucker asking you to explain the lyrics to "Linden Arden Stole The Highlights", or "Caravan"? (It's music of love and devotion, what else do you need to know?) But Lord knows I've had my chances; I'd often see him in the Nisa supermarket in Notting Hill Gate (he had a house near there in Holland Park for a while). I'd be sifting through the microwave pizzas and Super Tuscans only to turn around and see Van's taciturn face staring back at me; dressed only in a baby-shit-brown leather jacket, voluminous dirty jeans, a pair of battered cowboy boots, and a scowl, looking rather like a cab driver who has just been poorly tipped.

He is not just the VICTOR MELDREW of rock, a few years ago he even banned his audience at a Texan music festival from having a drink. The bars remained closed throughout his performance, bearing signs explaining that this was "at the artist's request".

Which brings me to my favourite, though surely apocryphal, Van Morrison story. A few years ago, to celebrate the end of another successful WOMAD festival, a famous rock star threw a party in a barn near the festival site down in the West Country, inviting all the artists who had performed at the festival, plus any celebrity who happened to be passing through. Said rock star invited Van, telling him that it would be a low-key affair, and that his presence would be most welcome. Van, who at times can be pathologically antisocial, said that he'd try to come. Secretly both the rock star and Van knew that he would be unlikely to turn up.

Anyway, the party was a raging success, full of the great and the good, and all those in the smiling and nodding bracket.

But, unsurprisingly, no Van. At two in the morning, with only a handful of punters remaining, there was a quiet knock on the big barn door. The security guard opened it slowly, took a look at our badly-dressed hero, a more taciturn than usual Van Morrison, and turned to face the stragglers. "Anyone order a minicab?" he said.

It would be heart-warming to think that Van Morrison would have seen the funny side of this, but as the man knows himself, things are rarely that easy.

MORRISSEY

I've only ever interviewed three people who insisted on recording the interview themselves, just to make sure there weren't any "mistakes": the film director MICHAEL WINNER, the politician OLIVER LETWIN... and Morrissey. This was in the mid-Eighties, when he was as famous as he was ever going to be, and although his outspoken nature had helped him become probably the biggest rock star in Britain at the time, there were things which Morrissey had taken exception to, journalists who had taken "liberties" (ooh, how Morrissey loved a mockney).

But then Morrissey himself was his own creation, so he couldn't really object to other people trying to embellish the legend a little. Ever since the SMITHS became successful – 1983, a year when the charts were owned by the likes of CULTURE CLUB, WHAM!, THE THOMPSON TWINS, and HOWARD JONES – critics have taken pot-shots at Morrissey, taking him to task for being a miserable "celibatarian aesthete", for being a dangerously ironic racist, for wallowing in his own shambolic melancholy.

And he bounced it all back, safe in the knowledge that his legion of fans were happy to endorse a man who made public his disillusionment with the rampant permissiveness of pop.

M

The SMITHS themselves were the perfect pop group – a tight-knit group who made a splendid guitar-heavy noise, fuelled by a songwriting team who very quickly became as loved by their fraternity as Jagger and Richards, LAUREL AND HARDY, and Grand Marnier and Lucozade. Morrissey and Marr – Morrissey playing the librarian, and Marr the rock'n'roll groupie. Was there a better song in 1985 than "How Soon Is Now"? An hypnotic and solemn whirligig, it made JOY DIVISION seem like KYLIE MINOGUE.

Since the split – which was, lest we forget, way back in 1987, when MARGARET THATCHER was still PM – Marr has had a fairly peripatetic existence, as his ex-partner has tried to relive past glories, occasionally writing a classic song – "First Of The Gang To Die", "You're Gonna Need Someone On Your Side", "Suedehead", etc – but usually just sounding like a lyricist without a genius. So, you're big with the LA Latinos – we thought you wanted the world!

THE MOTOWN SNARE SOUND

One might think that the sound of the snare drum on Motown records was something arrived at by method, process, by developing systems, engineering, and – most importantly – shopping for the right kit. One of the label's regular drummers was URIEL JONES, who was a crucial member of the Motown session band known as the FUNK BROTHERS: "They were good drums, but they were second-hand," he said. "They were also a mix of brands. They also had another set of drums down there that they bought a few years later, but those drums were only used when we had a double drummer session. That second set was also just thrown-together stuff." Jones was a key component of the "psychedelic soul" sound of the TEMPTATIONS, including "Cloud Nine". He also played on "Ain't Too Proud To Beg", "The Tracks Of My Tears", by the

MIRACLES, "What Becomes Of The Brokenhearted", by JIMMY RUFFIN, and "Ain't That Peculiar", by MARVIN GAYE.

M

As Motown's studio technology was constantly evolving, drum recording techniques down in "Studio A" – where the bulk of the recording happened – were an ongoing experiment. Like other studios of the time, they moved from two- to four- to eight- and then sixteen-track technology. On early recording sessions, like the one for MARTHA & THE VANDELLAS' "Heat Wave", it was standard procedure for a percussionist to shake his tambourine into a microphone that was already being shared by the hi-hat and the snare (and, in the early days, guitars, bass, keyboards, vocals, horns, and strings).

To keep the sound of the snare crisp but not too sharp, the drummers – and there were a pool of four – would put electrical tape on the bottom skin, and then tape a pad of Kleenex to the top skin, the skin they hit. That's the sound you hear on the old SUPREMES, FOUR TOPS, and TEMPTATIONS records. The snare skins would become covered in McDonalds' grease and tomato ketchup, but the Kleenex was rarely changed; who knows what would have happened to the sound?

MUMFORD & SONS

Down on the farm people are still talking. Some say they are T.S. ELIOT set to music, others that they're just FLEET FOXES knock-offs. Donning old-man waistcoats, granddad shirts, Hackett jackets, rolled-up trouser legs, and more than their fair share of facial hair, Mumford & Sons kicked up dust aplenty. As the Noughties gave way to the Twenties, there briefly appeared to be only two dominant forces in music: dance-pop performed by teenagers sounding like chipmunks, and folk-rock bashed out by earnest young men and women with wistful looks in their eyes. So Mumford & Sons certainly weren't alone, although they were obviously one of the best: rabble-rousing on their way to work, hedgerow grazing on

M the way to the bar, and with as much pain and remorse as you felt you needed. They backed BOB DYLAN at the Grammys, won a Brit, and were feted by bright young things in common rooms and campuses (and farms!) from Oxford to Berkeley. Best song without a doubt: "Winter Winds".

MUSE

One of the few bands able to hold a candle to U2 where live performances are concerned, Muse can make a stadium feel like your front room. They make adrenaline space rock, classical punk opera – OK, OK, it's neo-classical bombast – crystallised by singer MATTHEW BELLAMY's falsetto. Influenced by the SMASHING PUMPKINS, NIRVANA, and RAGE AGAINST THE MACHINE, Muse are better than all of them.

THE MUSEUMS OF ROCK

Rock'n'roll was always going to be institutionalised, although the very thought of it still seems rather silly. Celebrating the ephemeral and the peripheral became a popular late 20th Century pastime, but the more ways in which pop started to be curated eventually gave the whole genre more gravitas. It shouldn't have done, but it did.

The further we get from the mid-Fifties and the birth of pop, the reasons become clearer; namely that, more and more, we are starting to believe that there was a "golden age" of post WWII pop, and, in particular, the media icons of the Fifties, Sixties, and Seventies. It's all very well, we say, claiming that the WHITE STRIPES and the LIBERTINES are as important as the ROLLING STONES and LED ZEPPELIN... but – alone at night, with our heads full of God-knows-what – we simply just don't believe it.

But then what do we know?

The Rock and Roll Hall of Fame in New York should really be the Madame Tussauds of the air guitar, the Disneyland of the drum solo, the Legoland of the leopardskin pillbox hat. But, situated bang in the middle of SoHo, adjacent to all the fancy dress shops and downtown "spaces" that give a very good impression of not knowing whether they're meant to be selling LICHENSTEINS or latte, this relatively new annex of the Cleveland-based museum is incongruous to say the least. Had it been set down in midtown, or even over in the East Village – where distressed black leather still has some sort of kudos, and not necessarily ironically – it would have made more sense. As it is, it looks about as comfortable as a cowboy boot in the Four Seasons.

It doesn't get any better inside, where, before you are allowed to wander round by yourself, and after handing over $25, you are forced to stand in a mausoleum covered in metal plaques which have all been etched with a rock star's signature. Look, there's MARVIN GAYE over by FRANK ZAPPA, DINAH WASHINGTON hunkering down with JOHN LENNON. Each time a plaque lights up, the artist's music blares out of the wall-speakers, presumably to make us marvel at the technological wonder of it all. But then you're ushered into a small cinema to watch a patronising film meant to encapsulate the fifty-year history of rock'n'roll, before being allowed to stalk the Perspex containers and gawp at a bunch of costumes, guitars, posters, and other uninspiring memorabilia.

There are some highlights, but they are few and far between. I enjoyed seeing JOHNNY CASH's boots, EDDIE COCHRAN's stage jacket, and CHUCK BERRY's waistcoat, as well as a flight bag used by JIMI HENDRIX, and a life-size 1957 Chevrolet Bel Air Convertible bought by BRUCE SPRINGSTEEN back in the Seventies for just $2,000. However, I had the most fun trying to decide whether ELVIS PRESLEY's white rhinestone-encrusted Vegas-era jumpsuit had a larger waist than the enormo-suit worn by DAVID BYRNE in *Stop Making Sense*. Byrne won by a whisper (or a Snickers).

M The curators have saved the best for last though, which you'll see if you nip to the loo after spending forty-five seconds in the world's worst museum shop. There, in the hall outside the gents, is a urinal that was installed in CBGBs in 1975, and which was probably used by everyone from LOU REED and TOM VERLAINE to IGGY POP and JOEY RAMONE.

Having had my patience severely tested in New York, the thought of going to the British Music Experience at the O2 in London (actually "the tent in Kent") made my heart sink more than a little. After all, rock and roll really needs to be experienced in all its sweaty, sexy, sequined glory to make any sense, doesn't it? I mean, what's the point of looking at ELVIS' rhinestone Graceland loo seat, JIM MORRISON's broken zipper, or MARC BOLAN's driving licence, in the confines of a large Perspex box? None? Well, that's about the size of it.

But the BME, which is situated in the dark recesses of the often-overpowering O2, somewhere between an outpost of Nando's and the flagship premises of a new restaurant chain called Pikey's Sushi (I think), is refreshingly entertaining. Which it needs to be, because let's face it, if you're going to go all the way down to the O2, you need to know that PRINCE is playing in the round, or that LED ZEPPELIN are reforming.

At the fully interactive British Music Experience you can see them both, and more. It actually has some coveted music memorabilia (DAVID BOWIE's ZIGGY STARDUST costume, NOEL GALLAGHER's Union Jack guitar, ROGER DALTREY's Woodstock outfit, and a vintage– and dry-cleaned – AMY WINEHOUSE dress) as well as the sort of audio-visual trickery that can transport you back in time by being in the crowd at legendary gigs or eavesdropping on fantasy dinner parties. You can also develop your skills on guitar, bass, drums, and in the vocal booth at the Gibson Interactive Studio, and even hone your dance moves (honestly, it's not as naff as it sounds). Plus there are the by-now inevitable download facilities, allowing you to log into your MyBME library and access all of your favourite bits of the exhibition. If, indeed, you can be bothered to do such a thing.

But what about Los Angeles? Shouldn't California by rights have the best rock'n'roll museum? Shouldn't the land of champagne, colitis, and guilt-free dirty sex inspire its own kind of R&R heritage theme park? You would have thought so, but maybe not in downtown LA.

Now, downtown Los Angeles is not known for much. I stayed at the old Biltmore Hotel there back in the Eighties and it felt as though I was in a different city, a different state completely. On my first night in LA I'd taken friends to dinner in Hollywood and then cockily started driving back downtown, thinking it would take me ten minutes.

In the end it took me three hours, as I drifted in and out of Watts, Compton, and many other places a white boy in a rented Mustang shouldn't be at two o'clock in the morning. I felt as though I were in a West Coast sequel to *The Bonfire Of The Vanities*, and I was so scared to stop the car that by the time I got back to the hotel I thought my bladder was going to explode.

Heigh ho.

I went downtown a few years ago to visit the Standard Hotel, which has the most magnificent rooftop bar – and until the Soho House opened a few months ago, it was the best rooftop bar in LA – and nearly totalled my Bentley as I drove back to Beverly Hills (we spun the car 360 degrees as though we were in a BUGS BUNNY cartoon). But until 2010 I hadn't been down there for five years. Honestly, why would you?

But I went to visit the Grammy Museum – 30,000 square feet of interactive rock'n'roll situated bang in the middle of L.A. Live, the gigantic, and rather ugly, sports and entertainment centre. It houses some interesting exhibits, not least the stage outfits of most of the important artists from ELVIS to BEYONCÉ. When I visited there was a touring exhibition devoted to flower power, including JANIS JOPLIN's lovingly restored 1966 Porsche 356c cabriolet, covered in swirling psychedelic graphics. It made me want to jump right in and drive myself to the Sixties, although all I really needed

M

to do was walk back upstairs and see Joplin on film, along with JIMI HENDRIX, MICHAEL JACKSON, and everyone else who has ever made a half-decent record.

My favourite room was the hall where they play a loop of noteworthy acceptance speeches. Along the middle of the hall are half-a-dozen glass cabinets containing various different incarnations of the actual award. The fifth design (1991 to the present day) has a base made out of a patented zinc alloy called Grammium.

Just so you know.

MUSIC IN CARS

While I have never really been in love with the car, per se, I have been in love with the idea of the road trip since I was still playing with Hot Wheels. I had no interest in trains, motorbikes, or pushbikes – I wanted to sit behind the wheel of a Mustang, driving along the California coast, listening to BOBBY DARIN, the REGENTS, BUSTER BROWN, JOEY D AND THE STARLIGHTERS, and all the other songs on the *American Graffiti* soundtrack. OK, I'll admit that I once owned a Chopper, and just after the moon landing I spent at least six months wanting to be an astronaut, but then I've always been a fan of thermal micrometeoroid garments that offer limited shielding against particle radiation.

Who hasn't, huh?

Just a few years after I eventually learned to drive, I organised a road trip across the US with a friend of mine, Robin, a journey that would take us all the way from New York, Philadelphia, and Washington, down through the Blue Ridge Mountains, Nashville, and Memphis, before joining Route 66 and continuing on to LA, via Texas, Arizona, New Mexico, and Nevada. And, of course, I made an individual mix-tape for every state, starting off on the Eastern Seaboard with lots of BRUCE SPRINGSTEEN AND THE E-STREET BAND, BOB SEGER AND THE SILVER BULLET BAND, and SOUTHSIDE JOHNNY AND THE

ASBURY DUKES, before moving onto the Southern States with plenty of NEVILLE BROTHERS, DR. JOHN, and ALLEN TOUSSAINT, and then joining the dustbowl motorway accompanied by fairly generic Seventies FM rock (the STEVE MILLER BAND, the EAGLES, FOGHAT, BOSTON, etc).

I had failed to understand that the radio stations in the States are built for long journeys, and that the soundtrack to my journey would be supplied whether I liked it or not. There was no need for me to make a cassette compilation of STEELY DAN's "King Of The World", ROBERT PLANT's "Big Log", or NEIL YOUNG's "Powderfinger", as they – and everything else I'd recorded for the journey – was on the radio every half-an-hour anyway.

"Good job you recorded this," deadpanned Robin as we trundled through New Mexico, after we'd listened to "Take It Easy" by the EAGLES, "because they've only played it six times on the radio today."

"Take It Easy" mentions Winslow Arizona, and it was just outside Winslow that we found the journey's own Holy Grail. The sun was falling in the sky, promising a rich, dark sunset as we sped along the highway towards Two Guns. In the distance the Juniper Mountains cut across the horizon like tears of pale blue tissue paper. As we gunned towards them we looked to our left and saw a deserted Drive-In, standing forlorn in the dirt, casting shadows that stretched all the way back to town. Suddenly I felt like an extra in *American Graffiti*, sitting in the custom-built benchseat of a Hot Rod, my cap-sleeved right arm around my girl, my ducktail brushing the rear-view mirror, and DEL SHANNON's "Runaway" pouring through the dashboard speaker.

Here was the true spirit of Route 66 in all its faded glory. Like the highway itself, the Tonto Drive-In was a totem of America's glorious past, a testament to the new frontier, the freedom to travel, and the democratised automotive dream of the Fifties, when a car was still every American's birthright. This deserted cathedral, standing stoic and proud in the burnt sienna sunset, was, quite literally, the end of the road. Suddenly, California – with all its promises of eternal youth, and "two girls for every boy" – seemed a long, long way away.

I drove down the California coast two years ago, from San Francisco to LA, en route to a party at Soho House, and I listened to digital radio all the way, moving the dial through "stations" that played music from every decade from the last eighty years. If I'd have been driving long enough I probably would have heard everything that's ever been recorded, from Louis Armstrong to Cee Lo Green, from the Andrews Sisters to Tyler, the Creator, from Big Bill Broonzy to Death Cab For Cutie. It was a joyous experience, but it could have been anyone's. It certainly wasn't mine.

So the last time I did a Californian road trip, from LA to San Diego via Santa Monica and Palm Springs, the soundtrack was worked out in some detail: I started off with some Erin Bode and Nightmares On Wax, followed swiftly by Example, Midlake, and Ed Sheeran, before moving onto Bon Iver, Here We Go Magic, and Ducktails.

Sure, I could have simply listened to the radio, and probably enjoyed myself just as much. That wasn't the point. This was my journey and I was the one who was going to decide what it sounded like.

Music in Shops

Let me offer you some quiet words of advice: never, ever buy clothes in a shop where there's loud music playing. Not only will you suffer temporary sensory distraction, but it will seriously affect your critical faculties, and you'll end up at home with two tight brocade vests embroidered with badly drawn caricatures of albino stevedores fashioned from interwoven burgundy and puce corduroy. And that's on a good day.

Many's the time I've been in a store when the music has convinced me that I'm at least a dozen years younger than I actually am. When OASIS were hip, I bought a wildly inappropriate white denim jacket only to find, when I got home, that it made me look as though someone had thrown a billowing denim tent over a pole. And all because a defeaning "Supersonic" was playing at the time. Earlier still, when CULTURE CLUB were big in the Eighties, I came out of a shop just off Carnaby Street with a bag full of trendy ecclesiastical T-shirts that made me look like BOY GEORGE's personal rabbi. And all because "Do You Really Want To Hurt Me?" was on constant rotation.

Music in shops can do many things. It can make you feel younger, older, taller, trendier, cooler. And, on occasion, it can make you feel like MICK HUCKNALL (and then you really know you're in the wrong place). If JIMI HENDRIX is playing when you walk into a shop, it will make you want to look like him; if JUSTIN TIMBERLAKE happens to be playing, it will probably make you want to dance like him, and if RADIOHEAD are playing, it could cause you to crawl home, throw all your clothes away and climb into the oven. All of which are unwise. The problem with music in shops was pointed out to me some time ago by someone who remembered the classic JERRY SEINFELD quote: "Buying clothes is always tricky. But when there's loud music playing, it really throws your judgement. You look at stuff like, 'Hey, if there was a cool party and I was a cool guy, this might be a cool shirt.' Then you get it home, there's no music, there's no party, and you're not a cool guy. You're the same chump, seventy-five bucks lighter."

WILLIE NELSON

A DAVID SEDARIS joke:

> Q: What's the worst thing you can hear when you're blowing Willie Nelson?
>
> A: "I'm not Willie Nelson!"

NEUROTIC BOY OUTSIDERS

A Neurotic Boy Outsider is palpably unhappy, willfully odd. Continually wrestling with those damn internal demons, the NBO displays an obvious nervousness, particularly concerning his own body; with NBOs there is always a hint of sexual ambiguity (with MORRISSEY there has always been more than a hint).

"NBOs all had problems because they were rather artistic, talented types," wrote PETER YORK in his classic essay on the subject. "People didn't understand them sometimes because they couldn't always *explain* how they felt, not in prose anyway. It was too intense. This meant they became very touchy and gestural. NBOs had to show how they felt by what they wore. This meant they went in for a lot of black, because it showed that they were moody, and deep."

Although most youth cults are about gang mentality, power in numbers, the NBO style centres around the individual, around not belonging; there is, as York says, "the battle to be different". ALBERT CAMUS' 1942 blueprint of defiant alienation, *The Outsider*, was interpreted on screen by the first great NBO, king baby himself, JAMES DEAN in *Rebel Without A Cause*. An NBO can never be too thin, too nervous, or too aloof. This is what distanced Dean from ELVIS PRESLEY, who was too dumb, too smug, and too sexy (and later too fat) to be decent NBO material; Dean was angst-ridden, yearning for attention. If ELVIS threw his jacket to the ground he was probably about to burst into song; when Dean did the same he was probably about to burst into tears.

Since then, the NBO Hall of Fame has got mighty crowded: Hollywood icons such as ANTHONY PERKINS (before he discovered television), MONTGOMERY CLIFT (before *and* after the accident), Brando (up to and including *On The Waterfront*); and introspective pop stars such as SCOTT WALKER, IAN CURTIS, MORRISSEY, Berlin-period DAVID BOWIE (and with hindsight you could make a pretty good case for CHATTERTON, BYRON, KEATS, and SHELLEY). Meanwhile, the queue outside stretches all the way to Carnaby Street. When JOY DIVISION's Curtis died in 1980, his legacy was seized upon by a host of gangling, anguished young dudes in dark grey Macs, Dr Marten shoes, Oxfam suits, and very small lapel badges pledging allegiance to PERE UBU, ECHO & THE BUNNYMEN, PATRICK MCGOOHAN, SARTRE, CAMUS, and JP DONLEAVY's *A Singular Man*. Almost every group signed to factory records or Rough Trade had an NBO in their ranks.

The NBO has become a recognisable youth icon, which is the ultimate contradiction: can outsiders join gangs, and if so, are they still outsiders? If you're not the only NBO in town, then how can you guarantee attention? Because NBOs have to go public about being private (they are nothing if not show-offs). Recent big time NBOs: THOM YORKE, CHRIS MARTIN (although you can tell his heart's not in it), and FRANZ FERDINAND's ALEX KAPRANOS. The 21st Century NBO is more likely to be a Woodsman, a bearded baldy in a check shirt who sings of lost love, lost ideals, and lost tress. Canadians are especially good at this, as are certain North Americans, and Scandinavians; the Brits less so (Woodsmen can't convincingly live near Norwich or Swindon). *See page* 821

HARRY NILSSON

For many, Harry Nilsson will always be known as the singer/ songwriter whose two biggest hits were written by other people ("Without You" was penned by BADFINGER'S PETE HAM and TOM EVANS, while FRED NEIL wrote "Everybody's Talkin'"). Others may remember him as the man who led JOHN LENNON astray during his protracted lost weekend in Los Angles in the early Seventies – when Lennon hit the city like a truck crashing into a distillery.

For others, Nilsson remains one of the most gifted songwriters of his generation, responsible for a string of mild-mannered classics such as "Me And My Arrow", "Without Her", "Coconut", "One", "Cuddly Toy", and "I Guess The Lord Must Be In New York City" (originally written for *Midnight Cowboy*). He signed to RCA Victor in 1966, releasing his debut album, *Pandemonium Shadow Show*, a year later. The BEATLES' press officer, DEREK TAYLOR, fell in love with it, and bought an entire box of copies to share with friends and acquaintances. Including the BEATLES. Having spent a marathon thirty-six hours listening to it, JOHN LENNON called him to offer his congratulations, while PAUL MCCARTNEY called a few days later, offering the same. At the time Nilsson said he was disappointed not to get any calls from George or Ringo. Nilsson could be as blunt as he could be sentimental, as one of his most famous lyrics can attest: "You're breaking my heart / You're tearing it apart / So f*** you."

Nilsson was the subject of a fascinating and rather affectionate 2006 documentary, *Harry Nilsson (And Why Is Everybody Talkin' About Him?)* produced by DAVID LEAF and JOHN SCHIENFELD. Screened at various film festivals, the movie was subsequently re-edited using previously unseen footage of Nilsson, along with further interviews and home movies, becoming a treat in the process.

"I do believe that most men live lives of quiet desperation," he once said. "For despair, optimism is the only practical solution. Hope is practical. Because eliminate that and it's pretty scary. Hope at least gives you the option of living."

NIRVANA

When KURT COBAIN killed himself in 1994, I have to say it felt a bit pat – I was in the US at the time and the media predictably went doolally, projecting Cobain as an unwitting spokesman for his generation. I don't want to minimise his death, or treat him or his family with disrespect, but it felt as though it was all part of the script. Obviously it wasn't, it was a tragedy, but his death was a defining moment for grunge, the musical genre Cobain's band Nirvana had been standard bearers for. And bizarrely, his death didn't enhance or maximise grunge, it minimised it, and a year later the world was idly wondering whether it would be OASIS or BLUR who would get to No.1 in the British charts. Nirvana? Who were Nirvana?

I was as intrigued by "Smells Like Teen Spirit" as everyone else, nevertheless, when I first heard it I kept thinking I had heard it before. What did it sound like? And then, after a few days, I realised it reminded me of BOSTON, and their massive 1976 hit "More Than a Feeling" – a song which also sounded like something of an homage to the KINGSMEN's "Louie Louie", with a little bit of ROXY MUSIC's "Love Is The Drug" thrown in there for good measure. Nirvana had other great songs – "Come As You Are", "Lithium" – and as a poster boy for his people, Cobain was perfect, with his skanky blonde hair, his lumberjack and denim clothes, and his decidedly slacker attitude, he was the perfect antidote to Eighties excess – a rock star who wasn't really a rock star.

Thing is, he hated the attention, the acclaim, and the feverish phony acclaim that came with it. He was weak, liked his drugs, knew his persona was as persuasive as his songs. And as soon as he died, the whole thing was over, seeming more like a fashion fad than the things it had supposedly come to replace. In a nutshell: Kurt Cobain killed grunge.

GARY NUMAN

N

Like many critics, I tend to have an aversion to any hysterical celebration of the new and the fashionable, often choosing to be contrary just for the hell of it. The tendency is to assume that the standard-bearers haven't studied their history, and that if they were to turn the heavily-bejewelled stone over for a second they would probably find an old MUDDY WATERS riff or a yellowing and slightly soiled KASABIAN B-side (God forbid that anyone would want to copy such a thing).*

But these days there is such a consensus surrounding what is "good" and "bad" in the world of entertainment (especially in the music business), such a consensus regarding the "canon" - *The Dark Side Of The Moon, Sign O' The Times, (What's The Story) Morning Glory?*, etc – that being contrary can often just make you look willfully difficult.

And being willfully difficult is one of those things – like expressing a fondness for the work of SALVADOR DALI, the films of KENS RUSSELL and LOACH, and the entire science fiction genre – that we are meant to grow out of by the time we are old enough to vote.

Some things, mind, are just too wrong to be right. No matter what the consensus is.

Now, I know that these days I am meant to take Gary Numan rather more seriously than I once did, and I am fully aware (being a keen fan of revisionism, obviously) that time and tide should by now have weakened the critical response to all but his most egregious recordings. I also know from experience that the older one gets, the easier it is to find redemptive qualities in almost any form of entertainment – even the sort you passionately, instinctively, and innately dislike. Over the years I have had many of my prejudices confounded and convictions overturned, so to speak. I no longer baulk at the collective work of NICK CAVE – I heard a recording of his song "Into My Arms" at a wedding a couple of years ago, and it almost made me well up (I was three glasses of prosecco in, and it made me feel the same way I did the first time I heard "A Whiter Shade of Pale", or MARSHALL CRENSHAW's "Fantastic Planet of Love"; "morbidly enjoyable", someone said). I no longer laugh at BILLY JOEL (and haven't for some years), and have learned to love the occasional nugget from BOB DYLAN's many "difficult" periods... Not only this, but I should come clean and admit that, to my shame, I was once oblivious to the obvious genius of NEIL HANNON, whose work with the DIVINE COMEDY deserves far more attention than it usually gets from snarky people like myself.

But still I have a problem with poor old, Tory-before-Tory-was-cool, sitting-in-the-pub-with-a-white-rat-on-his-shoulder, Gary. The new romantic star with a hod-carrier's moniker, the futuristic nerd, the third-generation Bowie clone, who looked like a man who wanted to look like a member of KRAFTWERK but who made the mistake of starting the process by shopping at C&A.

It would be easy to say that the entire British charts of the first three or four years of the Eighties were full of young men and women either pretending to be DAVID BOWIE, or using one of his many characters as a blueprint for their own tawdry space-faces, but few copied so poorly as Numan. DEPECHE MODE managed to emerge from the nightclubs of Basildon and Soho with their dignity intact – having stolen Bowie's old wardrobe along with his brightly-coloured austerity – as did HEAVEN 17, the HUMAN LEAGUE, BAUHAUS, and the PET SHOP BOYS. But not dear old Gary.

Before going solo, Numan (who was basically what Bill Wyman would have been like had he become famous in 1979 rather than 1963) was in TUBEWAY ARMY, who had a surprise UK number one with a wonderful creation, "Are 'Friends' Electric" (silly words, great tune, awesome production), but then he went and ruined it all by sticking his funny short-back-and-sides above the parapet.

In subsequent years, when the early Eighties have been fleetingly fashionable again (and this happened just a short while ago), Numan has been treated with almost as much reverence as DAVID BOWIE, which, frankly, is preposterous (and proof that some people haven't studied their history). And if anyone ever needed any evidence concerning Numan's unwarranted position in the pop pantheon, they need only look at the cover of his 1979 album, *The Pleasure Principle*. He stands behind a shiny counter wearing a badly-cut, double-breasted suit, a convention-ready tie of indeterminate hue... and (obviously – doh!) eyeliner. And the way in which he tries to impart his enigmatic qualities to his fan base, the way in which he attempts to semaphore his post-modern otherness, his colour-by-numbers existential angst? Come on, come on!

That's right. He's staring at a small illuminated plastic pyramid.

Job done, Gary, job done.

Numan does have a legion of hard-core devoted fans, who appear en masse online, whenever anyone mentions their leader in a disparaging way. They crawl up from their subterranean lairs, like slugs after the rain, and rail against whoever has been silly enough to criticise their metronomic boss. Mobilised, they would be an impressively large bunch, and almost worthy of conscription; if they could pass the written examination, that is.

* Apologies to KASABIAN: I rather like "Thick As Thieves".

LAURA NYRO

In this case I think it's fine to take a steer from ALICE COOPER: "I can't really remember how I discovered her, but I think it was through a girlfriend. I just went WOW. It reminded me of Broadway – sort of. She was a street singer, and she was a white girl singing with all these black girls. It just so happened that she could sit down at a piano and write those songs – she's as pure a songwriter as I've ever heard. I'm just addicted to her stuff, everything from 'Eli and the Thirteenth Confession' to 'New York Tendaberry'."

OASIS

O

They were all about the joy of crowds. Speak to anyone who saw Oasis in their prime, or indeed just before it, and they don't talk longingly of seeing them in a small club, or above a pub, far from it. The Oasis experience was the stadium experience, particularly the football stadium experience. Their songs were built for chanting – pretty much anything on the first two albums stand up to repeated singing – with "Wonderwall" being possibly the most anthemic song in British pop.

They were of course subject to the law of diminishing returns, and if *Definitely Maybe* and *(What's The Story) Morning Glory?* remain almost perfect examples of what happens when songwriting, performance, swagger, and Zeitgeist all genuinely harmonise, the five albums they released subsequently are all surplus to requirements (apart from the wonderful compilation, *The Masterplan*). Each album contains good songs – for example, "Do You Know What I Mean?" from the disowned *Be Here Now*, "Go Let It Out" from *Standing On The Shoulder Of Giants* (which is possibly the worst album title of all time, and certainly one of the most reductive*)*, "Little By Little" from *Heathen Chemistry*, "The Importance Of Being Idle" from *Don't Believe The Truth*, and "Falling Down" from *Dig Out Your Soul* – but they're not at all good records.

Oasis swept into power on a wave of laddishness, defining Britpop in an instant, revered by the Polo Geezers and jacketless Untuckables who swore by them. Anti-bourgeois, anti-alternative, their brethren celebrated ordinariness to an almost pathological degree, brethren who acted in a way that exposed them as vending machines of predictability. The massive were Mad For It, and if they hadn't been so intractably, hopelessly male, you'd have thought they were Valley Girls, speaking in a code mutually understood and made more effective by exaggeration and repetition.

O NOEL GALLAGHER remains a national treasure, his media highlights being a redemptive performance on MICHAEL PARKINSON's television show, and the totally brilliant live album he released in support of Teenage Cancer Trust, 2009's *The Dreams We Have As Children – Live At The Royal Albert Hall*.

PHIL OCHS

BARACK OBAMA has never spoken of his fondness for Phil Ochs, and it is completely possible that he has never heard of him. One of America's foremost protest singers (though he preferred being called a topical singer), he described himself as a "left social democrat", and during the Sixties became a staple at civil rights rallies, student sit-ins, and anti-Vietnam marches. Originally a political journalist, when he was introduced to the music of WOODY GUTHRIE, PETE SEEGER, and the WEAVERS, he started writing political songs. He would later call himself "the singing journalist", in much the same way that ALLAN SMETHURST would later call himself "the singing postman" – once, when riding with BOB DYLAN, he criticised one of this songs, at which Dylan kicked him out of the car, saying, "You're not a folksinger, you're a journalist."

Ochs always had a hint of TOM LEHRER about him, and in spite of "Is There Anybody Here?", "I Ain't Marching Anymore", "Here's To The State Of Mississippi", and "Here's To The State Of Richard Nixon", the song for which he ought to be remembered is "Love Me, I'm A Liberal". In this lovingly constructed rant, rather than assailing conservatives, Ochs castigates instead those who claim liberal status but who fall short of affecting social change: "I cried when they shot MEDGAR EVERS," he sings. "Tears ran down my spine, I cried when they shot Mr Kennedy, As

though I'd lost a father of mine... But MALCOLM X got what
was coming, He got what he asked for this time. So love me,
love me, love me, I'm a liberal..."

There is a great YouTube clip of Ochs introducing the
song at a concert, in which he says, "In every American
community you have varying shades of political opinion.
One of the shadiest of these is the liberals... Ten degrees to
the left of centre in good times. Ten degrees to the right of
centre if it affects them personally." These words, and Och's
lyrics, started to gain traction in the blogosphere in 2010, as
it became fashionable to accuse Obama of reneging on his
campaign promises. Personally, the attacks seemed trite,
although I wouldn't have been be surprised if NICK CLEGG
had been made aware of Phil Ochs shortly afterwards.

As for Ochs himself, in the Seventies his career went
into free-fall, he was diagnosed as bipolar, and eventually
hanged himself in 1976.

ORBITAL

It takes a certain kind of British self-deprecation to name
yourself after a motorway (the M25, the ring road around
London which was so important to rave culture in the late
Eighties), although there was little self-deprecating about
their music. Confrontational? You could say so, in spite of
you being able to dance to it.

OUTKAST

ANDRÉ 3000 and BIG BOI's 2003 double album *Speakerboxxx/
The Love Below* was essentially two solo albums, and
consequently would have benefited from an independent
producer, or a powerful referee. Like most albums since

the birth of the CD, it's at least twenty minutes too long, but contains such a varied assortment of delights it makes it easy to forgive. Contains the globally addictive singalong "Hey Ya".

P

CHARLIE PARKER

P

Parker was the king of bop, the fastest saxophonist in the west, and at the time – the mid-Forties – one of the coolest men in America. *The Yardbird Suite* (Castle Pie), released in 2000, contains many of his classics – "Ornithology", "Ko-Ko", "Groovin' High", etc – as well as his greatest ever recording, the incomparable "A Night In Tunisia", which must rank as not only just one of the greatest jazz records of all time, but one of the greatest records, period. Parker had a terrible impulse towards self-destruction, and before his untimely death in 1955 (from a heroin overdose: he was thirty-four, although the coroner thought he was sixty), became quite adept at burning candelabra at all ends. He had the most dissolute lifestyle it is possible to imagine, fuelling the cliché that to be acknowledged as a genuinely gifted jazz player you needed to be perpetually living on the edge. He may have left some astounding recordings, but he really did live a terribly incomplete life. He suffered marriage failures, the tragic death of a daughter, and various substance dependencies. As well as being responsible for recording some of the finest music of the 20th Century, he also came up with the ultimate jazz truism: "If you play something that seems to be wrong, play it again, then play the same thing a third time. Then they'll think you meant it."

VAN DYKE PARKS

Known principally for his cypress-scented work with BRIAN WILSON (for instance, he wrote the convoluted "Surf's Up" lyrics that so incensed MIKE LOVE), there is also a fair body of solo work too, most notably 1975's *Clang Of The Yankee Reaper*. A Warner Brothers PR man once organised a Parks interview on National Public Radio's *Fresh Air With Terry*

P

Gross. When he rang the next day to find out when the piece would air, he was told, "Never". "Seems they determined that there was no way to edit VDP's responses – his language was so rich and his digressions so entertaining – and keep a modicum of coherence."

TONY PARSONS

Anyone who knows anything about journalism will know that Parsons started his career at the *NME* in 1977, escaping the gin factory to be one of NICK LOGAN's infamous hip young gunslingers. The paper knew that it needed some young blood to write about the burgeoning punk scene, and having interviewed dozens of potential young hacks, hired JULIE BURCHILL and Tony. The *NME* was where he made his name, interviewing everyone from the SEX PISTOLS to IGGY POP, from the BUZZCOCKS to JOHNNY THUNDERS. Tony became synonymous with punk, although ironically his career has lasted a lot longer than most of the people he interviewed back then. In the last ten years, BLONDIE have had one number one, and Tony has had eight.

That career took on another dimension in 1999 when Tony wrote *Man And Boy*, a publishing phenomenon that was voted Book of the Year in the UK, and has been published in over forty countries. Since then, he has written *One For My Baby, Man And Wife, The Family Way, Stories We Could Tell*, and many others. To date he has sold over five million copies of his books in the UK, and another six million worldwide. That's a remarkable achievement for someone who used to interview SID VICIOUS in the toilets of the Marquee.

One should never forget that Parsons made his name as a columnist, a journalist who has never suffered fools gladly. Whether he is writing about the CLASH or DAVID CAMERON, Tony will always have a definitive view. Like all good columnists, Tony's world is a black and white world, one unencumbered by indecision, confusion, or compromise.

I was reminded of this once back in the autumn of 1992. Some of you may remember that Parsons was once married to JULIE BURCHILL, and in the autumn of 1992 she was about to publish her second novel, the follow-up to *Ambition,* a pretty dreadful affair called *No Exit.* I'd just joined the *Observer,* and we had been offered an interview with Julie to publicise the book. The same day I had lunch with Tony in the Groucho Club, to discuss some of the features I was going to try to get him to write over the next few months.

We had a perfectly convivial lunch, as usual, but it was only on my way back to the office in the car that a light bulb went off in my head (sort of). Why not ask Tony to interview Julie? What a brilliant idea! Yes, I, like everyone else knew that they had famously fallen out, and that there was a terrible war of attrition between them, but wouldn't this be a great way for them to make peace with each other?

So, as soon as I got back to the office, I rang Tony and left a message on his machine, explaining what a good idea I thought it would be if he interviewed his ex-wife.

A couple of days later I received one of Tony's traditional handwritten postcards, of which I probably have several hundred at home, with a message that not only reinforced yet again how Tony has the ability to distil emotion into just a few words, but also illustrates why he is so loved by so many:

Dear Dylan,

Thank you for lunch, it was lovely as always.

And I would love to interview Julie... only I make it a policy not to interview fat, untalented cunts.

Love,

Tony

It seemed from Tony's comments that my career as a peacemaker had some way to go.

535

P DOLLY PARTON

After all the fame, the smash records, and the hit movies – there was a time when you couldn't turn on the radio without hearing "Jolene" or "9 To 5" – the country girl with "busty substances" moved away from commercial music and successfully reconnected with the music she grew up with, bluegrass. "If I could have made a living, and still had the career, doing this kind of music, I would have done that. I had to get rich in order to afford to sing like I was poor again. Isn't that a hell of a note?"

KATY PERRY

Like the former *New York Times* critic FRANK RICH (the Butcher of Broadway) once wrote about the stage musical version of *La Cage Aux Folles*, "as shamelessly calculating as a candidate for public office." But this time with added hotness.

LEE "SCRATCH" PERRY

The CLASH only recorded their cover of JUNIOR MURVIN's "Police And Thieves" because they had only recorded twenty-nine minutes-worth of material for their first album. Having added it to the final running list, *The Clash* (1977) now lasted nearly thirty-six minutes, and so was finally fit for purpose. The original falsetto version was one of those records on heavy rotation at the Roxy, the 100 Club, and at house parties all over London, one of a handful of popular reggae tunes that were soon to become classics of their kind. The CLASH's PAUL SIMONON had grown up with rock steady in his teens, had learned to play bass from listening to the *Tighten Up* series of albums, and had an almost encyclopedic knowledge of reggae; luckily reggae was one of the few types of music it was acceptable to like during these "Year Zero" days.

The original "Police And Thieves" was produced by Lee Perry, the legendary Jamaican who had steered records by everyone from the UPSETTERS to BOB MARLEY. He thought the CLASH had ruined Murvin's record with their almost glam rock cover, but was sufficiently intrigued by them (and the proposed financial arrangement) to agree to produce the band's third single "Complete Control". Simonon was instrumental in this: "I see Lee Perry as the ENNIO MORRICONE of Jamaican music." Simonon said Perry had scant creative input in the final record, save from encouraging JOE STRUMMER and MICK JONES to turn their guitars down in the studio (who knows what it would have sounded like if this hadn't happened: the single is not only the CLASH's best record, not only the best record made during the entire punk period, but is also one of the most spirited guitar-driven anthems ever made by anyone anywhere ever). Perry did, nevertheless, compliment Jones by saying he played with an "iron fist".

To call Perry "wayward" would be something of an understatement (others like to say he's mad as a cut snake): asked by the CLASH to support them when they were booked to play at Bonds on Broadway in 1981, Perry ruined his performance by emerging from his dressing room fifteen minutes late, and then proceeding to wander around placing various artifacts (including, apparently, a caped Action Man figure) on the stage while saluting the rest of the band.

Born almost unbelievably in 1936, Perry worked for various sound systems and studios before branching out by himself. He recorded one of the first samples (a baby crying), and worked as a writer, producer and performer, working with the WAILERS, MAX ROMEO, the HEPTONES, GREGORY ISAACS, and hundreds more, all of whom were subject to his unique brand of Rastafarian psychedelica. His pseudonyms include the UPSETTER, the SUPER-APE, PIPECOCK JACKXON, INSPECTOR GADGET, and the FIRMAMENT COMPUTER. In 1980, the diminutive (5' 2") producer was seen walking backwards around Kingston,

537

P

Jamaica, bashing the ground with a large hammer. Witnesses who knew him might not have been surprised by this – after all, this was the man who supposedly planted the records he produced in his garden, before watering them – but they were rather shocked by what happened next. Ending a six-year period of extraordinarily prolific recording, Perry burnt his Black Ark studios to the ground. It was probably accidental, although to cover his embarrassment Perry has claimed he did it on purpose.

In 1998 Perry reached an even bigger audience when he appeared as the guest vocalist on the hilarious "Dr. Lee, PhD" from the BEASTIE BOYS' *Hello Nasty*. Perry turned himself into a work of art, appearing in public festooned with reflective mirrors, patches, wires, and what appeared to be engine parts. For those who want a Perry primer, the best place to start is *Arkology* (1997).

In *Brideshead Revisited*, CHARLES RYDER – when discussing the various merits of the Bacchic and the Dionysian – says he drinks "in the love of the moment, and the wish to prolong and enhance it". I have often thought about reggae in a similar way, and while it is obviously fuelled by a different, and more soporific tonic, and lyrically often concerns itself with oppression, the overall feeling one gets from listening to reggae is a sense that the party isn't about to stop just yet. (Note: Perry got his nickname after recording "Chicken Scratch" for Clement "Coxsone" Dodd, the creator of the legendary Studio One sound.)

PET SHOP BOYS

NEIL TENNANT once said that the Pet Shop Boys (the definite article has always been optional) are "the SMITHS you can dance to". He wasn't wrong, and Tennant and CHRIS LOWE's ability to juxtapose clever, world-weary lyrics with stirring, melancholy disco-pop continues to produce something very singular.

They wrote one of the best ever songs about London, "West End Girls", and have made films, produced a ballet, a musical, worked with MADONNA, ELTON JOHN, DAVID BOWIE, DUSTY SPRINGFIELD, JENNIFER SAUNDERS and JOANNA LUMLEY, ROBBIE WILLIAMS, KYLIE MINOGUE, SAM TAYLOR WOOD, architect ZAHA HADID, and film director DEREK JARMAN, performed a brand new soundtrack to accompany the seminal 1925 silent film, *Battleship Potemkin*, and been more productive and more inquisitive in their thirty-year career than most of their peers.

Theirs is a very particular English brand – self-deprecating, camp, quite stoic – with Tennant acting as a loquacious QUEEN MOTHER figure, and Lowe his grumpy mate ("I don't like country and western, I don't like rock music, I don't like rockabilly or rock and roll particularly," Lowe reportedly said once. "I don't like much, really, do I? But what I do like, I love passionately").

I know it might be heresy to say so, but in their day they were better than the SMITHS – smarter, more inclusive, funnier, warmer – and occasionally still are. NEIL TENNANT has always been a better lyricist than MORRISSEY, and it's a wonder that he hasn't been celebrated in the same way as the dour Mancunian indie darling. Tennant could be a Laureate, whereas MORRISSEY will always want to be an adolescent. Some like to say that we've had enough Pet Shop Boys records, and that all that's left for them to do is produce identikit versions of their previous incarnations, administered with their usual hyper-real irony, and the latest trendy disco beat (what BPMs are we eating today?). And yet, and yet... every now and then they produce something so clever, so funny, so lovely to listen to, to dance to, that you have to slap yourself for thinking such cruel thoughts. Who else would write songs called "You Only Tell Me You Love Me When You're Drunk" (*Nightlife*, 1999), "How Can You Expect To Be Taken Seriously" (*Behaviour*, 1990), "Opportunities (Let's Make Lots Of Money)" (*Please*, 1986), "I Wouldn't Normally Do This Kind Of Thing" (*Very*, 1993),

P

or indeed their take on the fraught relationship between TONY BLAIR and PETER MANDELSON, "I Get Along" (*Release*, 2002) – "I get along very well without you..."?

Their continued presence is often taken for granted, yet in a world awash with flat-pack pop, their sense of proportion, knowingness, and respect for the very idea of pop is something we should treasure. For me, their two best songs are both from *Behaviour*, the massively popular and totally defining "Being Boring", and "My October Symphony", Tennant's own Russian odyssey.

Note: in 1986 I wrote a long, rather inflammatory, and not especially good piece in *i-D* about a silly Italian urban youth cult called the Paninari. In my over-excited way – in those days my enthusiasm for things like this was boundless – I catalogued the Paninari obsession with casual sportswear, their predilection for riding little motorbikes through the narrow, winding streets of central Milan, wearing sunglasses (I think it was decreed that no member was allowed to leave the house unless they were wearing a pair of Aviators), hanging out in sandwich bars (hence the name, a *panino* being a bread roll), and, of course, their reactionary pre-pubescent machismo. Acting on disinformation, I also wrote that the Pet Shop Boys – who were apparently huge fans of Paninari fashion – had even recorded their own paean to the cult, called, simply enough, "Paninaro". As the song eventually appeared a few months later, I thought nothing of it. Until about three years later, that is, when I read an interview with the Pet Shop Boys in *Rolling Stone*. They had read my piece: "We read that we'd recorded this song," said Lowe. "Of course we hadn't but we thought it was such a good idea that we soon did." And the song? Well, it was better than the article. But not much.

TOM PETTY & THE HEARTBREAKERS

P

Like feathers on a freeway, Tom Petty's songs are meant to bounce around your car as you cruise down the highway on a journey to the past. They actively encourage nostalgia, songs you're meant to play as you're driving home from work. Or out into the desert. Or, like I said, back to the Sixties. Petty took a bit of the BYRDS, some power chords (when they emerged in the mid-Seventies they were practically considered punks in their homeland), and built a sound based on the Big Jangle. It was corny as hell, but the tunes were good, even the ones produced by JEFF LYNNE (the only man who can make a snare drum smack last four beats, and not in a good way). It didn't hurt that Petty looked cute (a bit like BRIAN JONES crossed with a chipmunk). The first album is the best (*Tom Petty & The Heartbreakers*, 1976), but then none of the following should be ignored: *You're Gonna Get It!* (1978), *Damn The Torpedoes* (1979), *Full Moon Fever* (1989), *and Into the Great Wide Open* (1991).

PINK FLOYD

Sometimes the public really knows what they're talking about. And in 1973 they knew that space was the place. *The Dark Side Of The Moon* is the sound of pop music getting long. Not stretching wildly in the studio, turning licks into jams into interminable solos, not the inexpert extrapolation of progressive rock. No, this is a journey on a rocket ship, shooting way out into the farthest reaches of the galaxy, to a place where sound doesn't sound like it does at home, where it bounces around between the planets, pinballing about in one big echo box.

P "Moon" has become one of the bestselling albums of all time, a populist concept album that emerged at a time when the counter-culture started greedily moving into the mainstream, and when a gatefold sleeve meant a cool sophistication rather than a Pandora's Box of rebelliousness. It's an incredibly slick, rich record, timeless in its own way. There were lots of cute sound effects, gospel vocals, angst-ridden lyrics, fiery guitar solos, even a saxophone, and all beautifully produced. It captured our imagination because it felt expansive, yet most of the songs were actually quite short. Clever boys, the Floyd. Space was the place, but it felt like home. They would make one more masterpiece – 1975's *Wish You Were Here* – and achieve global fame with *The Wall*, but "Moon" is the one.

PORTISHEAD

The Bristolians' 1994 CD, *Dummy*, was as inventive as anything during the Britpop boom years, even if it wasn't much fun to listen to. This was the bleak underbelly of low-tempo British hip-hop, a sullen post-MASSIVE ATTACK collective that made trip-hop famous. Journalist GARRY MULHOLLAND had it right when he said Portishead resembled "...hip-hop on a life-support machine... a late-night jazz set from the subterranean factory tunnels of DAVID LYNCH's *Eraserhead*, maybe even DE LA SOUL drowning in squid ink."

PREFAB SPROUT

"I work to the point of monomania," said the band's leader PADDY MCALOON once, "mainly through the fear of not writing anything." This paid dividends, though rarely of the commercial type. Best songs: "Cars And Girls", "Hey Manhattan".

ELVIS PRESLEY

Teenage is all about hair. Although Elvis Presley's haircut is considered to be one of the most influential pop icons of the 20th Century, it was actually copied from TONY CURTIS. Presley wore Royal Crown hair products during high school to make his blondish locks appear darker, but it wasn't until he saw Curtis in the 1949 film, *City Across The River*, that the singer adopted the greased duck-tail. Dyed blue-black, covered in grease, with truck driver sideburns trailing his cheeks, Elvis finally had his five inches of buttered yak wool.

To middle-class white America, Presley was the devil incarnate, a southern white boy who danced and sang like a black. He was threatening because he was so flagrantly dirty, owning, among other things, the world's sexiest haircut. His hair was Presley's trademark, his strength, and an accessory that only added to his animal sexuality. In *Elvis World*, JANE AND MICHAEL STERN's 1987 homage to the King, they describe his crowning glory: "Like the man to whose scalp it is attached, the hair breaks loose onstage. Appearing first as a unitary loaf of high-rise melted vinyl etched with grooves along the side, it detonates at the strike of the first chord." While many continue to endure plastic surgery in order to look like Elvis, no one has even been able to reproduce his thatch.

Famously, when he appeared for the third time on *The Ed Sullivan Show* on January 6th, 1957, Elvis was shot only from the waist up, because his wild, erotic dancing had caused such an uproar all across the US. In reality it made hardly any difference at all, because libidinous teenage girls could still see Presley's hair.

Elvis kept his mousey hair dyed black all through his career (using everything from Clairol Black Velvet to L'Oreal Excellence Blue-Black), originally to carve himself an image, then because he thought it photographed better on film (it did), and then finally because he started to go

P

grey. When Elvis died, the hair underneath his blue-black dye was almost completely white.

As for TONY CURTIS, well, he came to detest the attention paid to his looks. "I thought my very gift was something so mystical and magical that by cutting my hair I thought I would be gone. I could understand what Samson felt. I was afraid if they cut my hair too much they would cut my talent."

THE PRETENDERS

We have reached a stage in the development of pop when a group can sound almost exactly like they did when they were starting out. This is not just the result of rapidly improving studio wizardry – proving to their fan base that they can still sound like they did the day they first rushed out of the traps – but also the desire to recapture that first flush of fame, when their records had the blessing of novelty as well as distinction.

The Pretenders are one such example, and their 2010 record, *Break Up The Concrete*, doesn't sound so very different from their first, thirty years ago. The album came with a "doubled-up" best-of CD, containing everything from "Back On The Chain Gang" and "Kid", to "Message Of Love" and "I'll Stand By You". It also contained a song that had previously passed me by, a small masterpiece (well, a masterpiece if you like the Pretenders) called "Night In My Veins".

In 1994 CHRISSIE HYNDE – who to all intents and purposes is the Pretenders – felt the band needed a hit, and so drafted in seasoned songwriters BILLY STEINBERG and TOM KELLY, who wrote songs to order (they were responsible for "True Colors" for CYNDI LAUPER, and "Eternal Flame" for the BANGLES). Their biggest success was the worldwide hit "I'll Stand By You", although that always sounded a little too much like BRYAN ADAMS for my liking; it's a revelation that they also co-wrote "Night In My Veins".

With lines such as "He's got his hands in my hair and his lips everywhere, he's got me up against the back of a pick-up truck, either side of the neon glare, It's just the night under my skin... slippin' it in..." it sounds as though Hynde is lost in a maelstrom of lust, a rare and very welcome display of female sexuality.

"'I'll Stand By You' felt a little generic," said Steinberg, "and I know that Chrissie felt that way, too, to some extent. But 'Night In My Veins' really felt like a great Pretenders rocker." Not just that, but one of the most vivid, as well as libidinous songs she has ever sung. It's as though she suddenly walked into one of those photographs by GREGORY CREWDSON, a seemingly ordinary suburban landscape masking nefarious goings-on. It whispers sex.

Oh, and yes, just in case you were in any doubt, it sounds just like any other song the Pretenders have recorded in the last thirty years.

PRIMAL SCREAM

The STONE ROSES had done it, as had the HAPPY MONDAYS, but no British rock group embraced club culture with such fervour. Until they started recording *Screamadelica* (1991), Primal Scream had been a fairly mediocre and traditional rock band; after working with DJ ANDREW WEATHERALL (alongside veteran ROLLING STONES producer JIMMY MILLER) they turned into indie dance fiends extraordinaire, while leader BOBBY GILLESPIE became a drug rock swami. It was a classic album that still stands up to repeated plays (highlights: "Movin' On Up", "Come Together", "Higher Than The Sun", and the majestic "Loaded").

P

PRINCE

Until he started throwing his toys out of the purple pram, rowing with his record company, and embarking on a ludicrous strategy of flooding the market with product (most of which could be filed under Too Much Information), Prince was The Man, and for much of the Eighties he was The One To Watch. Sexual chameleon, JAMES BROWN clone, enigmatic imp, and near-genius songwriter, Prince (once called "the JOE STRUMMER of orgasms") treated his acclaim seriously, continually using his own success as a benchmark, forcing himself to top himself with each subsequent album. And for a while it worked.

"I hate the word experiment," Prince once said. "It sounds like something you didn't finish." He was a repeat offender. *Sign O' The Times* began as *Dream Factory* in 1986, a triple album that Warner Bros, Prince's record company, understandably refused to release (his recent sales had been poor). He had a couple of other stillborn projects, too (over five hundred unreleased songs, according to those who would know), so in early 1987 Prince picked the best bits from all of them, and assembled an album that took diversity to new margins, bouncing between sex and religion, between JONI MITCHELL and SLY STONE, via searing funk, coy ballads, rap, prog, and the obligatory drum machine. It was the perfect rock'n'soul interface, a record of vaulting ambition.

Prince was the TODD RUNDGREN of his day, a funky little polymath, quixotic to the core. The album features all the standard accoutrements of the decade – the Linn drum, the Fairlight – yet it has fared well. His alter-ego, Camille, duets with him on "If I Was Your Girlfriend", he duets proper with SHEENA EASTON on "U Got The Look", and elsewhere largely plays with himself (he sacked his band before going in to assemble the record). The songs here are as varied as any he recorded – some as stark and as minimal as a Seventies video game, others as extravagant as a Lacroix frock. It's all here, and so is he: Prince, the Cobb salad of the studio.

Prince enjoyed his fame, but didn't feel the need to engage with his greater public, becoming a notorious recluse. He made a lot of records, but didn't like talking about them too much. The paradox is that, for all his warts and insecurities, he was adored as much as the likes of MADONNA, BRUCE SPRINGSTEEN, and MICHAEL JACKSON – the other stadium giants of the Eighties – who all had a far more urgent need to manipulate their audiences.

P

P.J. PROBY

P.J. Proby was one of the most outrageous performers of the Sixties – kitsch, crude, and wildly excessive. In 1965 he was at the height of his career, and then... tragedy.

1989: P.J. Proby was teaching me to sing "Somewhere", explaining when he came up with this version, the definitive version, of the *West Side Story* ballad. With a disconnected stare he was looking in my direction, singing at the top of his voice, somehow managing to wring four bruised syllables from the song's title: "Sum-mah-way-er, Sum-mah-way-er!" He looked pleased with himself for getting this far.

"I made a bastard version of that song, mixing BILLY ECKSTEIN with DELLA REESE, making it a little black in the process. I could never figure out why no one could get a hit with 'Somewhere' – you had the JOHNNY MATHIS version which was very pretty, you had the MATT MONRO version which was very FRANK SINATRA, but still very good... I couldn't understand why no one had ever had a hit. Then I was laying in bed one night and it struck me like a shot: no one had ever hit with that song because they'd all been too good! The public doesn't like perfection, so I figured the way to get a hit with 'Somewhere' was to fuck it up a little, play it down. I fucked it up and it became a monster."

At the beginning of 1965 P.J. Proby was flying high. With three Top Ten hits under his black patent leather belt, he was the biggest male singer in Britain. A protégé of pop Svengali

P

JACK GOOD, he had become the most desired pop performer in the country in a matter of months. His brazen sexuality, explicit way of dressing, and husky, sensual voice made him the hippest thing to hit the country since ELVIS. And – unlike Presley, who never came to the UK – P.J. Proby was here in person!

On record, with his impassioned, swollen singing, he sounded like a possessed JOHNNY RAY, his intense ballads and raucous rock'n'roll picking up where ELVIS left off. But it was his live performances that brought the myth to life, his savage yet girly sexuality causing hysteria among his pubescent female fans. ("Those girls would tear their knickers off," he once told a journalist, "throw them on stage, and I thought they were handkerchiefs. I'd pick one up, wipe my face with it and then realise I was bathing my face in piss.") He pounded his way through the coarse, melodramatic songs, offering his moans of despair and relief.

Proby was the embodiment of rock'n'roll burlesque, a singer who bridged the gap between pop and cabaret before either TOM JONES or, indeed, ELVIS himself. He was a performer who spanned light and dark, good and bad. He performed a surreal collection of songs – a bit of rock, a bit of music hall, mixed up with more than a hint of melancholy. For some he was a mesmeric performer, his self-obsessive, self-destructive persona showing itself to full effect when Proby was hamming it up in the spotlight. And Proby was always good at hamming it up.

His clothes were the ultimate in daring: tight, white satin hipsters, white satin shirt, and white satin Anello & Davide shoes, with little gold buckles. He had a false ponytail made by Bermans & Nathan, which he had safety-pinned into his own hair at the back. He had his suit copied in ten different colours of velvet, with matching velvet shoes, and he eventually grew his own ponytail. At some of his early personal appearances he would get his dresser to split his shirts down the seams with a razor blade, and lightly tack them together with thin spread, so that the seams would pop open at appropriate times in his set, leaving him free to walk about the stage naked from the waist up, while adoring nymphets soiled the seats below.

Proby came to Britain instead of ELVIS, and to a lot of people he was as good, if not *better* than the King... Proby was *live*, he was in the flesh. He personified the glory days of Sixties pop frenzy, the shining star with the dark underbelly, the complete showman, lusting after wine, women, and immortality. Proby was the basis of the hero of NIK COHN's rock'n'roll novel *I Am Still The Greatest Says Johnny Angelo*, the portrait of a doomed rock star.

But it all came to an end on January 29, 1965, at the Castle Hall, Croydon, on the first date of a nationwide tour that also featured CILLA BLACK. During the climax to one of his crowd pleasers, Proby's blue velvet trousers split wide open. They split again two days later at the Ritz Cinema, Luton, and then again a few days later. That night the curtain literally came down on his career, and he was thrown off the tour, to be immediately replaced by TOM JONES.

In a fit of moral panic, what seemed like the entire British establishment came down on him like he was the embodiment of the devil himself. He was banned from performing in every major venue in Britain, and then, on February 8, was banned from any show on the old ATV television network. The BBC soon followed suit. In America, ELVIS PRESLEY was once only allowed to be filmed from the waist up; ten years later in Britain, P.J. Proby wasn't allowed to be filmed at all. Confronted with this media blackout, Proby went underground, where, for the most part he has remained ever since.

The man who became P.J. Proby (real name James Marcus Smith) was born into a wealthy Texan family on November 6, 1938, in Houston. Mollycoddled as a young child, his parents separated when he was nine, he was made a ward of the State of Texas, and was forced into military college, where he remained until his mid-teens. On leaving, at seventeen, he made the first big decision of his life – to move to Hollywood. But his regimental upbringing had hardly prepared him for the debauchery and skullduggery to be found in California. "Normal relationships just didn't exist there," he once said,

P "all you had were homosexuals passing themselves around all
the directors and the girls doing the same thing."

He soon fell in, and in no time was recording rock'n'roll
under the name JET POWERS. He became a Hollywood
hyphenate – recording his own songs, writing songs for
other people, singing on other people's records, and acting
in B-movies and TV westerns. In the early Sixties he even
recorded demos for ELVIS, having been befriended by him
when Presley dated Proby's sister. The songs Proby ghosted
turned up on the soundtracks of Presley's many movies of
that period.

In 1963, Jet Powers was quietly getting on with his life
when EDDIE COCHRAN's ex-fiancé, SHARON SHEELEY, introduced
him to producer JACK GOOD, and P.J. Proby was born. Good
was so impressed with Proby's long hair (the only other singer
at the time to have long hair was PHIL MAY from the PRETTY
THINGS) and his "baroque vocal talents and dark charisma",
that he immediately signed him up.

Good originally wanted to cast him in a rock version of
Othello, but instead put him in the pilot for his TV pop show,
Shindig, before bringing him to London to appear with John,
Paul, George, and Ringo on the huge TV special, *Around The
Beatles*. Proby, a heavy drinker since fifteen, was habitually
inebriated, and he arrived in Britain completely drunk,
wearing tatty jeans, a cowboy hat and (as legend would
have it) a pair of TUESDAY WELD's knickers. He was met by
a rented Rolls Royce and a gang of reporters who had been
rounded up by Good, and for the next year P.J. Proby was to
experience what it's like to be a full fledged star – a man with
the entourage, a man with money, a man with good suits and
bad women, a man with an audience. His first week in London
was a nightmare, living in Earl's Court with no money, riding
the bus to learn the currency ("I used to watch the conductor,
as that was the only way I could get used to it"), but as soon as
his first record hit, he was swept up into the laps of the gods.

Like many people who hit success on the Sixties, Proby's
life moved at a fairly rapid pace. In the next eighteen months

Proby had seven Top Thirty hits in Britain, starting with the up tempo "Hold Me" (his biggest hit, it went to No. 3 in May 1964), through "Together", "I Apologise", "Let Water Run Down", and "That Means A Lot", to his classic, enigmatic ballads "Maria", and "Somewhere", the two LEONARD BERNSTEIN/STEPHEN SONDHEIM songs from *West Side Story*. But the trouser-splitting experience all but finished his career, and though he continued having the occasional hit right up to spring 1968, his time as a pop star was effectively over. Proby went from being a star to someone of whom nothing was expected.

The moral panic surrounding P.J. Proby's thighs now seems ludicrous, but at the time the Grades, the Delfonts, MARY WHITEHOUSE, LORD LONGFORD, and every righteous theatre owner in the country were up in arms about this shocking, degenerate Texan. Proby has persistently said the promoters ganged up on him because he blabbed to the press about the dirty deals they were involved in (scalping tickets, overcrowding venues, etc), but the fact remains it was Proby's crotch, not his mouth, that got him into trouble.

When the sexually provocative on-stage antics of nineteen-year-old American soul star BOBBY BROWN upset the police in Columbus, Georgia, a few months before my interview with Proby, he was fined $652 and held in custody for an hour. The next day he was pulling exactly the same stunts somewhere else; at the time, for BOBBY BROWN to have been hounded out of the entertainment industry like Proby was he would probably have had to bugger a dead pony on stage. And although bad things happened to him later, in 1989 he might have even got away with that.

In February 1968 Proby declared himself bankrupt, with debts of over £80,000. He returned to America, but was lured back to Britain in 1971 by JACK GOOD to play IAGO in his rock version of *Othello*, now called *Catch My Soul*. The years that followed, though, were a litany of unfulfilment. Though he spent most of the time wandering the north of England in abject poverty, he did find time for the occasional live

P performance ("I was the first person to bring a Las Vegas-style show to northern clubs," he said), in 1977 took up with Good again, taking the starring role in the West End musical, *Elvis*. He had a brief dalliance with the SEX PISTOLS, though inevitably nothing came of it; and in 1978 even recorded with the Dutch rock group, FOCUS.

For most of this time Proby's life was rather small– during the Eighties he was a caretaker, a janitor, and a farm hand. Disillusionment, lack of foresight, and a taste for alcohol played havoc with his life. His newspaper appearances at the time were usually because of his wives, all six of them. He married his third wife, Dulcie, a Mancunian croupier, in 1975 – "He wanted Westminster Cathedral, we got Bury register office," she said. After three years together he was prosecuted for shooting her five times with an air pistol (he was acquitted). In the mid-Eighties the tabloids understandably went wild when they discovered he had married a sixteen-year-old farmer's daughter called ALISON HARDY (in fact she was only fourteen). Shortly afterwards he was in the papers again as he had allegedly mauled a young researcher when appearing on a Sky TV chat show. "All bullshit," P.J. insisted.

When we met he was a fifty-year-old man, an alcoholic, living alone, in Bury, near Manchester, and supported by his Social Secretary payments, the occasional royalty cheque, and handouts from his friends at Savoy Records. DAVE BRITTON and MIKE BUTTERWORTH set up Savoy Books in Manchester in the mid-Seventies, to produce new imprints of neglected books, re-issuing works by HENRY TREECE, JACK TREVOR STORY, NIK COHN (the rights to *Johnny Angelo* cost them £500), HARLAN ELLISON, and MICHAEL MOORCOCK. They also experimented with new books, and later comics and children's books, often publishing what was unlikely to be published anywhere else. They were obsessively underground, dedicated to "soliciting moral outrage". Savoy were labelled both neo-fascists and pornographers (they were raided following personal instructions from Chief Constable JAMES ANDERTON), while others found them seedy, odd, or just immature. There was certainly no other company like them in Britain. In 1981, as a result of continued police harassment and the collapse of their distributors, New English Library, Savoy's book operation went into liquidation. Undaunted, Britton and Butterworth continued to publish, pursuing different imprints and widening the scope of their activities.

Britton had met Proby in 1982 – ostensibly with the idea of writing his biography, which he still intends to publish one day – and wondered if it might be possible to get him back into the studio. In the course of this fifteen-year decline, Proby had found that people who made themselves available to him wanted one of two things: to fuck him or manage him. Britton didn't want either.

"It struck me as really sad that there was this great voice, this legendary singer, who couldn't get a deal anywhere," said Britton. "So we threw ourselves in at the deep end and dragged him into a studio with some musicians to do 'Tainted Love'. It was farcical, SPINAL TAP wasn't in it. But it worked in an odd kind of way, and we took it from there."

Their strategy was to take classic songs, and warp them, debunk them, using only Proby's voice and the limited technology available to them. They chose songs that meant a lot to people, in the hope of offending as many people as possible. Thus, the 1985 release of "Tainted Love" was followed by JOY DIVISION's "Love Will Tear Us Apart" (1986), DAVID BOWIE's "Heroes" (1986), the SEX PISTOLS' "Anarchy In The UK" (1987), and PRINCE's "Sign O' The Times" (1988). Proby also covered songs by IGGY POP and ROXY MUSIC, as well as a truly manic version of T.S. ELIOT's "The Wasteland".

Depending on your tastes, these records are either deconstructed classics or pathetic junk. But to dismiss them as junk is to miss the beauty, and the joke, of the exercise. These songs have been fed through a blender, and stuck together again, and then had Proby's ferociously drunken vocals laid over the top.

"It's a serious business, it's serious *outrageous* art," said Britton. "We're not messing about. Jim's always taken songs and warped them, only we're maybe warping them a bit more – we are trying to create the aural equivalent of the DENNIS

P

HOPPER character in *Blue Velvet*. We're carrying on in the great Proby tradition. He was always butchering people's songs. It's not a frivolous thing – it takes an awful lot of money to make these records, money we can't really afford. Maybe when we've stopped doing them and Jim's under the ground, people will realise that they are quite remarkable records, quite strange, but different."

A lot of Proby's Savoy records are horrific, great slabs of fierce, scary pop; often, however, he sounds quite silly, like a little boy shouting a dictionary of obscenities or an incoherent drunk singing an ABBA song. "Hardcore" is a pornographic rap which Savoy released as a "duet" between Proby and MADONNA. A kaleidoscope of monotony, it nevertheless created a certain amount of controversy; they were told they would be sued by her record company, but nothing ever came of it. The best response came from Madonna's fan club, wanting to know where and when it had been recorded.

Proby followed this with another Savoy production, a surprisingly subdued version of the PHIL COLLINS hit "In The Air Tonight", although it was yet another Proby record that Savoy failed to find a distributor for.

Savoy did not have a great relationship with music journalists, who either found the records distasteful, or regarded them as some kind of exploitive wind-up – Savoy as post-McLaren art guerrillas. Britton steadfastly refuted this: "If we weren't using him, someone else would be. We are using him to make art. The alternative to us being here is five years of nothing. What's better? Of course it's our perception of him, but we believe we're making great records in the Proby tradition. Occasionally I do feel guilty about it, because Jim hates the records – he particularly loathed 'The Passenger' (originally by IGGY POP), he kept shouting, 'Fucking shit, what a load of crap, fucking awful, fucking awful song' – but Jim's never been happy with any of his stuff; he hated 'Hold Me' and a lot of his other singles, so are we really doing any harm? We pay him for his work; we're always slipping him money. Is that really so bad? He can walk away any time he likes. He's quite free. I'm doing this because I believe in him, because

I'm trying to draw on his talent. And yes, in my madness, I really think he could come back."

In the time he was with Savoy, Britton and Butterworth supported him as much as they could, paying the occasional bill, and trying to wean him off the booze. "We've tried time and time again to dry him out, but he's not interested. He's too far gone – he says he wants to die through alcohol, and he knows what he's doing so that's his right. Maybe I lack courage to really take him in hand, but I wouldn't be that presumptuous, really. It's a man's right to die how he likes."

A short while later, Proby entered the small, cluttered Savoy office cleaning phlegm from his throat.

"... haaaaa-aaaarrrrkaaaah!" He stumbled into the room in a plastic anorak, his denim dungarees disappearing into oddly immaculate cowboy boots. Apart from the boots, he looked terrible, just like he had spent the past four days curled up in a cold flat with nothing to eat or drink. Which is precisely where he had been. Without a penny to his name, he had to wait for Butterworth to pick him up that day for this interview. He clutched a carrier bag full of Special Brew that Butterworth had given him. Pulling one open he coughed again.

"I've been flat on my back in my room for four whole days, without even enough to buy a stamp," he said, shaking his head and slurping his beer. "I've lost my house! No more phone, no more electricity, and they've cut my water off. I've been through hell." And not for the first time.

"I've had to go through days of withdrawal, all by myself, and that's very, very dangerous. You can have a heart attack. I didn't know what I was going to do. I kept repeating to myself, I can make it, I can make it... but I really didn't think I could."

He took another slug of beer. Today's intake would consist of the cans of Special Brew, a bottle of cheap white wine, and a bottle of Canadian Club mixed with half a litre of Seven-Up; and this was all before five o'clock in the afternoon.

"I was so desperate for a drink I was gonna pawn this ring [brandishes ring] – it's the last one I got. It's worth quite a lot of money, but I don't give a shit. But I couldn't get out of bed."

P

P Proby's face didn't just look lived in; it looked as though that same person died in it, too. He still had his Texan drawl, and though he mumbled unevenly, it was with determination. He was a sad figure, a broken man, and I felt a bit ghoulish for treating him like a freak. But undoubtedly, his behaviour during his time with Savoy had turned him into one. When everyone else had left the room, he made his feelings known about the "freakish" records he'd made with Savoy.

"I think they're awful, I think they are the worst things I've ever done in my life. They're goddamn awful, they don't say anything, they're rude, they're vulgar, they're not commercial – no station will play them. I liked 'Heroes', the PHIL COLLINS thing, and the PRINCE song's OK, but most of the stuff I have done with them is too filthy to be played. And you know what? I wrote it all. They'd call me up and say, 'Write some more filth, write us some more dirt!'

"But Mike and Dave, they're my friends. Ever since I met them they've been very kind to me. Every time I've been really down they've always helped me financially, giving me five or ten pounds or something like that. When I was living up on the mountain, out in the country, in the winter when there was five feet of snow outside my door, I'd have to call them and they'd come up in a Land Rover with food and money.

"But why'd I make the records? Money. My wife and I were starving. Why does a whore fuck on the streets with a mattress on her back with roller skates underneath – she's hungry."

Proby said he'd like to get into a studio with a proper orchestra and record country songs, but not only could Savoy not afford this, they didn't think it would work anyway. "He'd either never turn up," said Britton, "or he'd try and conduct, or he'd get into a fight, or if he organised it, no one would turn up. We tried it a few times, but it was a nightmare."

After twenty years of failure and missed opportunities, Proby knew more than most about the real nightmare, that huge abyss of regret, into which everyone peers occasionally.

"If I had everything I had between... say '64 and '66... along with all this computer bullshit, well, I'd be better than anybody. It's difficult, but I couldn't do it. All I need is one hit record... just one hit... but nobody will give me a chance. Those years, I didn't give a shit. I was making a name for myself instead of living up to one. Now I have to love up to something that's already in the past. In the old days, if nothing happened, nothing happened. Who cared? I could always go back and be a stunt man or ride my motorcycle... but I can't do that because P.J. Proby was born and now he's my responsibility."

How would he describe himself?

"I'm a very jaded person, but not to the point of hate towards the many people who took advantage of me. Bitter? I don't feel bitter, I just feel sad. JACK GOOD invented me, and if he'd stayed with me and guided my career none of this would ever have happened, and Tom Jones would still be in the working men's clubs."

Seemingly oblivious to his own shortcomings, he continually mentioned the managers, the agents, the promoters, the friends, the lovers, and the record companies who let him down. He told me his biggest regret, though I felt the answer would have been different yesterday, and would be different tomorrow:"I think back to 1957, when two guys came to my house on Mulholland Drive and wanted me to sign up. I said 'Why me, I'm nobody? Wait till you've got a product to sell.' They said they wanted me there and then. Well, I regret not signing with the mafia, I really do regret it. At the time I was nineteen and my idea of the mafia was big men stomping on little men, killers and everything like that. My Hollywood mind was going back to the days of Capone. I'd forgotten it had become very, very big business. That was the biggest mistake I ever made. I should have signed up, because almost everyone is now. If I'd signed up I'd have had great representation, great management, no matter how they got it for me... and I'd have had someone working for me, except myself, and I've had to learn the hard way. I've had to bullshit since I was seventeen. I was thrown in at the deep end too soon, with no guidance. That is the main word of my life – 'guidance', no guidance. I have had to play it by ear all the way.

"What I really wanted out of show business, the reason I put so much of me in to it, I never got out of it. I am not talking about money, I am talking about a stable marriage, a home, and children. Those were my goals. You can tell that by how many times I tried – six times."

In 1985 he had flown back to Texas, to die. Ten days later he was back in Manchester. He had been arrested for vagrancy, and his stepmother had put him on the next plane for Britain. To his family Proby was an outlaw and an embarrassing drunk. He wanted to be buried by his father in Texas, something his stepmother apparently opposed.

He had been diagnosed as having some form of stomach cancer, and, though his liver was shot, he refused to give up drinking. The rest of him was in remarkably good shape, but I wondered for how long. He had been drinking every day for the past thirty-five years, a staggering amount of booze, which would have killed stronger men. All the other big boozers of the Sixties, people like PETER O'TOOLE, RICHARD HARRIS, RICHARD BURTON, had either stopped, or were dead. All except P.J. Proby. His drinking had affected him so much that his vision of the world bore no resemblance to reality. There didn't seem to be much that was dignified about the decay of Jim Proby.

His anecdotes, like his muse, were on tap, though they were largely unreliable, as they started and finished (if they finished at all) in different decades, different countries, and often involved different people. He could be lucid, and some of the early stories – like how he initially met JACK GOOD – had been honed to a fine art, but they had been embellished so much that it was impossible to decipher the truth.

"I am a very unhappy person, but a person who is ready in a couple of months, to check out," he said at one point during our interview.

It was unnerving to sit in a room with someone who was telling you that they were going to kill themselves, but as Proby had said this before, to other journalists, it was difficult to take him seriously. "I'm gonna blow my head off on stage. ELVIS was gonna do that, but he died on the toilet, ha, ha, ha! ELVIS planned to die on stage, but he had a heart attack and keeled over. I wanna die on stage; I'm just gonna end it with the greatest stage finale the world has ever seen. And this will be in about two months..."

He was talking about a forthcoming date at a nightclub in Wakefield; though the Savoy bunch seemed convinced it would never happen. "He's working out his set for the night, writing down all his favourite songs," said Britton, "but it will never happen, he'll have forgotten about it next week."

"You know," said Proby, "I don't fear anything anymore. I have had too much of life to fear, I have had everything. I have had it all... but no guidance to keep it all. It will be a grand finale. It will be the happiest place I have ever wanted to be in my life."

He coughed one last time.

"Right up until the end I had a deal with [British] *Vogue* – They were selling these exclusive little P.J. Proby shirts for the men and nightgowns and false hair extensions for the girls, and buckle shoes for the boys and girls. I became a designer label but when the pants split they dropped me like a hot rock. These days, the more clothes you wear the less you get paid. These days, the boys all wear ponytails and all the stuff you see in *Vogue* magazine is ripped anyway. Every mistake I made is now a design."

Proby eventually stopped drinking, made a record with MARC ALMOND, toured with the WHO (playing The Godfather in a production of *Quadrophenia*), and still tours occasionally.

P

P

THE PRODIGY

When KEITH FLINT reinvented himself as a comic book villain, the Prodigy suddenly had themselves a Brit rave image, becoming pop stars and tabloid pariahs in the process. Extraordinarily shouty, "Firestarter", "Smack My Bitch Up", and all the other fun-lovin' Prodigy toons made the band punk heroes for a generation not born when JIMMY PURSEY and CHARLIE HARPER were in their prime. Officially the oldest noisy teenagers in town.

PUBLIC ENEMY

This was not crossover music, not the sort of black music intended to appeal to anyone other than its core constituency. Which is why it was so influential. *Yo! Bum Rush The Show* was the 1987 sound of black consciousness, a torrent of unambiguous anger. With this, and 1988's *It Takes A Nation Of Millions To Hold Us Back*, and 1990's *Fear Of A Black Planet*, Public Enemy became the most politically charged group in hip-hop's short history. They turned confrontation into an art form – not in a post-modern SEX PISTOLS way, but in a genuine call-to-arms way. Made a generation of suburban white boys rather too desperate to be black.

PUNK SINGLES (1976-1979)

The early days of punk were analogous to present-day activity on the web – scattershot releases, limited edition rather than viral, but still with an urgent guerilla sensibility. Records were released without great fanfare, and often you only knew where to buy them... if you knew where to buy them. You needed to read the right papers, know the right people, and shop at the right stores.

P

Singles were the only recognised currency. Oddly, albums, LPs, were for a while considered to be distinctly "old wave", an indulgence too far. It was decreed by the cognoscenti that everything had to be short, Spartan, and almost devoid of adjectival subjectivity. Pop culture appeared to be moving so quickly that each new release came complete with its own promise of Zeitgeist-defining authority. And so in that spirit, here are the most representative, the most "winning" punk and punkish (new wave, etc) singles, 1976-1979 (one each).

Note: 1976 is now regarded as the Year Zero of late 20th Century music, a metaphorical line in the sand. This, of course, is bunk. 1975 and 1976 were two of the greatest years for rock music, and the likes of DAVID BOWIE, the ROLLING STONES, BOB MARLEY, LED ZEPPELIN, LITTLE FEAT, and ROXY MUSIC were still making great records. In fact, there is a case to be made for 1976 actually being the end of modern rock culture rather than the beginning; music almost had to start again after punk, but while those involved were keen to complain about the previous generation's protagonists staying around forever, a lot of punks stayed around for over thirty years, banging on about anarchy and revolution to an ever-decreasing audience of balding nostalgia groupies.

"Dirk Wears White Socks" by ADAM & THE ANTS, "Gary Gilmore's Eyes" by the ADVERTS, "Love Lies Limp" by ALTERNATIVE TV, "X-Offender" by BLONDIE, "The First Time" by the BOYS, "I Don't Mind" by BUZZCOCKS, "Right To Work" by CHELSEA, "Complete Control" by the CLASH, "Fuck Off" by WAYNE COUNTY, "Human Fly" by the CRAMPS, "Killing An Arab" by the CURE, "Neat Neat Neat" by the DAMNED, "Satisfaction (I Can't Get Me No)" by DEVO, "Baby Let's Twist" by the DICTATORS, "Sweet Gene Vincent" by IAN DURY & THE BLOCKHEADS, "Watching The Detectives" by ELVIS COSTELLO & THE ATTRACTIONS, "Bingo-Master" by the FALL, "Safety-Pin Stuck In My Heart" by PATRIK FITZGERALD, "Feel A Whole Lot Better" by the FLAMIN' GROOVIES,

P "Damaged Goods" by the GANG OF FOUR, "Your Generation" by GENERATION X, "Blank Generation" by RICHARD HELL & THE VOIDOIDS, "Empire State Human" by the HUMAN LEAGUE, "I Got A Right" by IGGY POP, "All Around The World" by the JAM, "Transmission" by JOY DIVISION, "International" by THOMAS LEER, "Saturday Night Beneath The Plastic Palm Trees" by the LEYTON BUZZARDS, "I Love The Sound Of Breaking Glass" by NICK LOWE, "Shot By Both Sides" by MAGAZINE, "Where Were You?" by the MEKONS, "The Sound Of The Suburbs" by the MEMBERS, "White Mice" by the MO-DETTES, "The Monochrome Set" by the MONOCHROME SET, "Warm Leatherette" by the NORMAL, "Another Girl, Another Planet" by the ONLY ONES, "Don't Dictate" by PENETRATION, "Non-Alignment Pact" by PERE UBU, "Roxanne" by the POLICE, "Public Image" by PUBLIC IMAGE LIMITED, "I Remember You" by the RAMONES, "I Can't Stand My Baby" by the REZILLOS, "Rich Kids" by the RICH KIDS, "Roadrunner" by JONATHAN RICHMAN & THE MODERN LOVERS, "2-4-6-8 Motorway" by the TOM ROBINSON BAND, "Do Anything You Wanna Do" by the RODS, "In A Rut" by the RUTS, "This Perfect Day" by the SAINTS, "No More Heroes" by the STRANGLERS, "God Save The Queen" by the SEX PISTOLS, "Hong Kong Garden" by SIOUXSIE & THE BANSHEES, "Borstal Breakout" by SHAM 69, "Tell Me Your Plans" by the SHIRTS, "Typical Girls" by the SLITS, "Because The Night" by PATTI SMITH, "Seventies Romance" by SPHERICAL OBJECTS, "Where's Captain Kirk?" By SPIZZENERGI, "Another Nail In My Heart" by SQUEEZE, "Suspect Device" by STIFF LITTLE FINGERS, "Ambition" by SUBWAY SECT, "Psycho Killer" by TALKING HEADS, "Do The Standing Still" by the TABLE, "Marquee Moon" by TELEVISION, "Chinese Rocks" by JOHNNY THUNDERS & THE HEARTBREAKERS, "Teenage Kicks" by the UNDERTONES, "Police Car" by LARRY WALLIS, "I Am The Fly" by WIRE, "Whole Wide World" by WRECKLESS ERIC, "The Day The World Turned Day-Glo" by X-RAY SPEX, "Are You Receiving Me?" by XTC, "Suffice To Say" by the YACHTS, "Keys To Your Heart" by the 101'ERS, "Emergency" by 999.

QUEEN

The writer SASHA FRERE-JONES – who, unlike many of his peers, has a radar acquired from the very top shelf – has a word for it. "Squinting", the act of peering at a musician you fell in love with when you were much younger, to try to remind yourself why you found them so fascinating. "The relationship grows through awkward phases," he writes, "nautical dress, orchestral arrangements, dodgy collections of poems. Along the way, you find yourself squinting to keep seeing what made you fall in love; you will need to pretend that the accordion and the Balkan song cycles are something else. (Fans of BOB DYLAN have unusually deep creases.) In pop music, which is a worse deal for the ageing than painting and fiction are, there can be a fair amount of effort involved."

And although Queen only really had a career that lasted twenty years, and whose oeuvre was crowded but not exactly perverse, their fans were always completely forgiving. As they started out as a rather orthodox (if flashy) rock band, this was even more unusual, but as the band pinballed between theatrical ballads, disco, and high camp pop, their legions of admirers blithely followed along (honestly, if you liked "Seven Seas of Rye", you weren't programmed to enjoy "Killer Queen"). The band got away with it as they wrote the sort of tunes you couldn't shake, even if you wanted to.

Their fans tended to be rather orthodox, too, and for a while appeared to be in some sort of collective denial concerning FREDDY MERCURY's sexuality. I always think of Freddie in the same way as the ROBERT DeNIRO character in the 2007 movie, *Stardust*. DeNiro plays a gay pirate called CAPTAIN SHAKESPEARE, who tries to hide his sexuality from his crew. When he is eventually outed, his men give a collective shrug. "We always knew you were a whoopsie," says one.

Queen's twenty-minute appearance at Live Aid, at Wembley Stadium in the summer of 1985, was one of the most captivating performances of the decade (in 2005

Q

Channel 4 voted it the greatest gig of all time). It was also great television. Seen by over two billion people, they stole the show, and completely revitalised their career. In the weeks following the event, all of Queen's albums tumbled back into the charts.

Queen's Greatest Hits is the bestselling album of all time in the UK; released in 1981, it has sold 5.8 million copies – THE BEATLES' Sgt Pepper's Lonely Hearts Club Band (1967) has sold 4.9m, ABBA's Gold (1992), 4.6m, (What's the Story) Morning Glory by OASIS (1995) 4.4m.

QUEENS OF THE STONE AGE

OSCAR WILDE once said that he liked WAGNER's music better than any other as, "It is so loud that one can talk the whole time without people hearing what one says. This is a great advantage." Queens Of The Stone Age were loud, thunderous, and made traditional rock sound important again. When they appeared, in 1998, out of the ashes of stoner rock band KYUSS, there was nothing around that compared, and JOSH HOMME's band went out of its way to keep it that way. Their 2002 album, Songs For The Deaf, has been called the best heavy metal album since LED ZEPPELIN's Physical Graffiti (1975), and with good reason. It is so loud, that, played on the right equipment, it could probably be heard in space.

QUINTESSENCE

Prog rock born in Notting Hill, Quintessence were London's GRATEFUL DEAD, often making a dreadful, protracted noise. They played jazz-rock, noodled, wore sheepskin, aped traditional Indian music. They rehearsed in All Saints Hall, the converted church near Portobello Road (of course they did!), played Glastonbury twice, recorded three albums for

Island, and played a benefit for Bangladesh at The Oval, in Kennington, appearing on a bill that included the WHO, MOTT THE HOOPLE, LINDISFARNE, ATOMIC ROOSTER, the GREASE BAND, and AMERICA. A lot of their stuff is still unlistenable – I would venture that more than ninety percent of it is – although one song (well, "track") is still a favourite in the Jones home, a wistful instrumental called "Prisms" which you can easily find on both iTunes and YouTube (two things which wouldn't have made any sense to anyone when Quintessence were actually making records).

RADIOHEAD

They have always understood their constituency extremely well, aware that every move they make is subject to the ridiculously high standards of their fans. Radiohead have had integrity thrust upon them ever since they started, and they know that their success is based on them living up to expectations. They might say – as all artists do – that they are determined to live up to their own high standards, but that's a fallacy: Radiohead are successful because their supporters believe they care more than anyone else about what it is they do.

Starting out as a sort of thinking man's Brit NIRVANA, they quickly rubber-stamped themselves as the sullen flip-side of Britpop, a raggle-taggle band of grumpy, bedsit, sonic innovators. Radiohead World is like *The Truman Show*, an enormous artificial dome where instead of Seahaven you have one giant hall of residence, with hundreds of different types of mournful, ambient music seeping out from underneath each door.

"A tired snarl, a reedy drone, and a light falsetto," was how *The New Yorker*'s SASHA FRERE-JONES described Thom Yorke's voice, and I think it's fair to say this isn't the group's most appealing ingredient. Although what that is, exactly, is harder to pin down. As Frere-Jones wrote once, Radiohead sound like an instrumental band that happens to have a singer, and their manic collages, their complex melange, is almost like soup. On a good day, they sound like the band the BEATLES were trying to be when they disappeared into the studio in the post *Sgt Pepper* bunker years, something best heard on their most popular record, 1997's *OK Computer*, an album that regularly tops polls of the best/most influential album of the last twenty-five years. Often referred to as this generation's *The Dark Side Of The Moon*, it was inspired by MILES DAVIS' *Bitches Brew*, and is often as satisfying – sometimes more.

Favourite Radiohead songs? Well, JAMIE CULLUM once covered "High and Dry" and I have to say he did a very good job.

THE RAMONES

In 1976, punk was a stance that encouraged rejection. And rather than the aggressive guttersnipe persona the media encouraged (as personified by the SEX PISTOLS, the CLASH, and everyone else), before the movement became commodified, punk literally meant punk – weedy, unformed, an outcast. Unlike most other acts of the mid-Seventies – when the Ramones evolved – the band had no interest in being either nice or erudite (they celebrated a *Mad* magazine world inspired by cartoons, B-movies, TV, and surf culture). Commonplace now, the Ramones were a law unto themselves: nerdy.

Which is why the Ramones were the perfect punk group. They looked like failures, sounded like Vikings.

And, even though they made ridiculously fast (for the time) buzzsaw rock, audiences could relate to them because of how they looked. And although their demeanour was strange to them – why would you want to paint yourself as a dweeb when our entire adolescence is spent trying to show everyone else how smart and sexy and cool we are? – the Ramones looked like their audience: long hair, T-shirts, sneakers, and jeans. The only difference was the widths of their 501s.

On their 1977 British tour they were supported by the TALKING HEADS, who were far more alien to the crowds as they looked like the people they'd just spent five years avoiding at school. The Heads' arch persona was helped along by leader DAVID BYRNE's insistence in saying – and only saying – "The name of this song is...." between songs, leaving the audience unable to figure out how sincere they were (which was maybe the point).

And then the Ramones hit the stage. We had been half-expecting their own monosyllabic performance, and JOEY RAMONE's exchange with the audience consisted entirely of repeating "1-2-3-4" before each song, in a weird approximation of their support group's tactics.

Both performances were extraordinarily dynamic (the gig I saw, at Friars in Aylesbury, still sits in my Top Ten of all time), although the Ramones' blitzkrieg bop was an extraordinary, almost frightening, tour de force. Sure it had comic elements, but the ferocity with which the entire band played made you think they'd been saving up to play like this since having sand kicked in their faces at Coney Island when they were kids.

Best song? "I Remember You" from *Ramones Leave Home* (Sire, 1977).

CHRIS REA

Ibiza is a great leveller. It's the random island. Spend any time in the beach bars here – especially in the north – and you'll hear it all: low-fi hip-hop, classic chill out, chillwave, aquacrunk, scratchy old soul, edgy film noir soundtracks… and Chris Rea. I've lost count of the number of times I've heard "On The Beach" on the island – OK, I wasn't actually counting, because that would be silly – and I've heard it on boats, in bars, in clubs, in cars, and in villas. It's just one of those things you hear, like "Rose Rouge" by ST. GERMAIN, the GIPSY KINGS, or FC KAHUNA's "Hayling". Rea's record makes perfect sense here, as it fits the constant low gears of the island, dovetailing perfectly with the glacial Balearic lifestyle.

Now, Rea isn't cool; never has been, never will be. Occasionally his records nod vigorously towards it, and some of his records have such an overwhelming sense of well being, even when expressing a world-weary disappointment, that you can't fail to like them. Personal favourites include "Girl In A Sportscar", "Loving You Again" (which I will always remember as the song that my friend Robin and I listened to most as we toured the battlegrounds of the Somme one sunny afternoon – along with *Saturday Night Fever*, obviously), and "The Chance Of Love", from the generally uninspiring 2011 *Santo Spirito* box set.

R RED HOT CHILI PEPPERS

Funky-punky Californification band who wore socks on their cocks and wrote some memorable tunes ("Under The Bridge" on 1991's *Blood Sugar Sex Magik* being the best). Should have been bigger than GREEN DAY but were a lousy live act. And while they made cool their thing, were occasionally rather naff, too.

Sartorially, one of the most ridiculous things I ever saw was in the Wag Club, in London's Wardour Street, back in 1982. This was the time of "hard times" chic, when the look du jour was a pair of thoroughly distressed Levis, a studded leather belt, a pair of black Chinese slippers, a wife beater (a.k.a. a plain white vest), and a bottle of Pils grafted to each hand. One night, as I pushed my way to the bar, I had to squeeze passed two loudmouth Americans who had – get this – painted tin cups hanging from the epaulettes on their cheap, imitation leather jackets – both of them with one on each shoulder. They looked so ridiculous they may as well have had "gormless" written across their backs in toothpaste.

But what do you know? A few years ago, as I was eagerly making my way through *Scar Tissue*, the breezy and rather salacious autobiography by the Chili Peppers' lead singer ANTHONY KIEDIS (someone who appears to have based his entire career on IGGY POP), I came across a passage detailing the band's brief visit to Europe in the early Eighties. "We had a great time exploring London, Paris, and then Amsterdam. In Paris, I ditched (band member) FLEA for a few days to hook up with a beautiful Danish girl. He gave me the silent treatment when I got back, but then I bought some beautiful, painted, powder-blue tin cups off a street vendor and put them in the epaulettes of our leather jackets, and we instantly became the Brothers Cup."

Lou Reed

Am I alone in believing that Lou Reed hasn't made a good record since 1972? Such a lot of fuss was made about *New York* when it was released in 1989, but I have to say all the acclaim passed me by.

Like any sane, sentient human I bow with great reverence before the edifice that is the VELVET UNDERGROUND. They were inspirational, they were first, and they were seriously good (best VU album? A tie between their third, *The Velvet Underground*, and the live double, *1969*), yet the only Lou Reed record I like is the one rescued and produced by DAVID BOWIE, *Transformer*. It's extraordinarily rich, camp, and full of good tunes. Like any Bowie record of the time.

Berlin? No thanks. *Coney Island Baby*? Pass. The only Lou Reed song I've enjoyed that's been recorded in the forty-odd years since *Transformer* is "Some Kind of Nature", the GORILLAZ track that Reed sings on *Plastic Beach* (and even then he's outshone by BOBBY WOMACK and SNOOP DOGG).

Many feel the same. Many critics (as well as civilians) certainly feel antipathy towards Reed himself. But then he only has himself to blame. If you spend your professional life being unpleasant to people (not that I think Reed thinks of journalists as people) then they're going to start being unpleasant back. You can only kick a dog so many times, after all (for instance: "They are a species of foul vermin. I wouldn't hire people like you to guard my sewer. Journalists are morons, idiots. I don't perform to idiots. Journalists are ignorant and stupid"). Hilariously, Reed studied journalism at Syracuse University.

Reef

A band defined by one song, "Place Your Hands", the DNA of which is so similar to the DNA of so many things that came before it, any decade from the Sixties onwards could

R

have spawned it. Was it made by a West Coast jam band in 1968, was it left off an ARGENT album in the early Seventies, was it recorded by a band in the early Nineties who for some bizarre reason wished they were the BLACK CROWES? Were they actually JET?

DELLA REESE

Della's accelerated version of IRVING BERLIN's "Blue Skies" on *Della* (RCA, 1960), is one of the most exhilarating two minutes in all jazz – it pops like a champagne cork on repeat. In its own way it is as ebullient as "Complete Control" by the CLASH, or "Shake Some Action" by the FLAMIN' GROOVIES. She has tended to be forgotten, and her name is absent from three of the so-called classic texts (*The Penguin Guide To Jazz On CD, LP and Cassette* by RICHARD COOK and BRIAN MORTON; *Jazz: The Rough Guide* by IAN CARR, DIGBY FAIRWEATHER and BRIAN PRIESTLEY; and *The Virgin Encyclopedia Of Jazz* edited by COLIN LARKIN).

REGGAE'S GREATEST HITS

1. CULTURE *Two Sevens Clash* (Joe Gibbs), 1977. During the summer of hate, this was the reggae record on everyone's turntable, a record so full of propaganda it made the CLASH's album seem wishy-washy by comparison.

2. JACKIE MITTOO *The Keyboard King At Studio One* (Universal Sound), 1977. This is the funkiest reggae ever made. He was the musical director of Studio One during the mid-Sixties, however, it is for his funky instrumentals that he will be remembered.

3. AUGUSTUS PABLO *King Tubbys Meets Rockers Uptown* (Rockers/Jetstar), 1998. Recorded between 1972 and 1975, this is dub at its best – moody, mellow, scary, and Oriental.

R

4. EASY STAR ALL-STARS *Dub Side Of The Moon* (Easy Star), 2003. A totally serious (well...) interpretation of the Pink Floyd classic. In dub. And er, that's it.

5. THIRD WORLD *96 Degrees In The Shade* (Island), 1976. Often dismissed as inauthentic by purists, this, their best LP, includes a cover of BUNNY WAILER's "Dreamland".

6. DOCTOR ALIMANTADO *Best Dressed Chicken in Town* (Greensleeves), 1978. A DJ and toaster, Alimantado (born WINSTON THOMPSON, Kingston, Jamaica) was loved by punks and Rastas alike, not least for his forthright and often ironic lyrics.

7. U-ROY *Super Boss* (Nascente), 2007. "The Originator" wasn't the first deejay to rap over existing reggae songs, but he was one of the best. This includes his version of "The Tide Is High".

8. BOB MARLEY & THE WAILERS *Songs Of Freedom* (Island), 1992. The biggest-selling CD box set in history (1.5m copies and rising), this is the all-encompassing, definitive overview of Marley's career, with highlights and lowlights.

9. SHABBA RANKS *Golden Touch* (Two Friends), 1990. Ragga's one true international superstar, Ranks' "rockstone" voice was perfectly equipped to deal with "slack" (sexually explicit) themes.

10. TOOTS & THE MAYTALS *Funky Kingston* (Trojan), 1975. This compilation brings together most of their best-loved songs, and is both sublime and uplifting.

11. LEE PERRY *Arkology* (Island Jamaica), 1997. This triple-CD, fifty-two track set has about as much Lee Perry as you need in your life. Contains five versions of JUNIOR MURVIN's quintessential "Police And Thieves".

12. THE ABYSSINIANS *Satta Massagana* (Heartbeat), 1993. The Abyssinians' vocal style was not only responsible for redefining Jamaican "close-harmony" singing, it also developed its own sense of gravitas.

13. BLACK UHURU *Guess Who's Coming To Dinner* (Taxi), 1980. SLY & ROBBIE's finest hour or so, a collection of their best work for the band, including "Shine Eye Girl", "Leaving To Zion", and "Plastic Smile".

14. BARRINGTON LEVY *Collection* (Greensleeves), 1990. This houses many of his big dancehall hits, including the absolutely essential single "Here I Come", a 12" masterpiece in which Levy claims to be "broader than Broadway".

15. BIG YOUTH *Screaming Target* (Trojan), 1973. The big toasting disc of the early Seventies, for years this was the yardstick for roots style.

16. PETER TOSH *Legalize It* (Island), 1976. Pass the bong, old boy. As much as the roots movement of the Seventies called for a re-evaluation of Rastafarianism, it also espoused the "religious" aspect of smoking an awful lot of ganja.

17. THE CONGOS *Heart Of The Congos* (Black Ark), 1977. Produced by LEE PERRY, the standout track here is "Fisherman". (Note: the CD re-release contains an extra disc of dub and 12" versions.)

18. BUNNY WAILER *Blackheart Man* (Island), 1976. A founder member of the WAILERS, this was produced during reggae's golden spell and remains one of the best releases of the period.

19. STEEL PULSE *Handsworth Revolution* (Island), 1978. Closely aligning themselves with Rock Against Racism, they signed to CHRIS BLACKWELL'S Island and released this, their defining moment. They may have played at BILL CLINTON'S inauguration in 1993, but they'll be remembered largely for "Ku Klux Klan", included here.

20. THE SLITS *Cut* (Island), 1979. Labelled punk incompetents by the music press, who were belligerently sexist towards them, their avant-garde reggae became a delight, and their debut album contains their finest five minutes, the single "Typical Girls".

21. VARIOUS ARTISTS *Dread Meets Punk Rockers Uptown* (Heavenly), 2001. A bunch of classic tracks selected by DON LETTS, the DJ at the Roxy. This is the stuff he used to spin: KING TUBBY, BIG YOUTH, HORACE ANDY, the CONGOS, JUNIOR MURVIN, CULTURE, U-ROY, and the like.

22. VARIOUS ARTISTS *Tougher Than Tough: The Story Of Jamaican Music* (Mango), 1993. Unashamedly populist, this vast four-CD collection is book-ended by the FOLKES BROTHERS' original version of "Oh Carolina" from the late Fifties, and SHAGGY'S raga update from 1993.

R

579

23. VARIOUS ARTISTS *Hardcore Ragga: The Music Works Dancehall Hits* (Greensleeves), 1990. Produced by AUGUSTUS 'GUSSIE' CLARK, and including the work of GREGORY ISAACS, J.C. LODGE, SHABBA RANKS, and REBEL PRINCESS, this heralded the arrival of digital recording and reggae embracing new technology.

24. VARIOUS ARTISTS *The Harder They Come* (Island), 1972. "Every day hundreds of kids flock into the slums of Kingston from the hillsides of Jamaica – drawn by the promise of the transistor – sure that they can get it if they really want."

25. VARIOUS ARTISTS *Lovers Rock: Serious Selection Volume 1* (Rewind Selecta), 1995. The genre got its name from a label that devoted itself to the soft, lilting sounds of "reggae lite". Early lovers rock tunes were criticised for being "sung by girls who sounded as [though] they were still worrying about their school reports".

R.E.M.

Did we need any more R.E.M. songs? Surely when we thought of R.E.M. we thought, "Great, and enough". Most of us probably only have a finite amount of space for R.E.M. songs in our brains (and maybe even our iPods), and it's already full of "The One I Love", "Electrolite", "Orange Crush", and everything on *Out Of Time* and *Automatic For The People*, records that still, rather remarkably, have an ability to sound fresh and innovative even if you've heard them hundreds of times. *The Word*'s DAVID HEPWORTH once said that the reason R.E.M. were not as loved as they once were was because they simply hung around too long. We knew they were there, over in the corner somewhere, beavering away on another record that tried to make fifty-five-year-old men sound as though they were thirty years younger, but we were not actually that bothered. I think the moment the band started to mean a lot less to us all was when MICHAEL STIPE started walking around with a painted face, as though he was a kind of fancy nightclub shaman. Oh, don't be so silly, man, you felt like saying. Go back in the studio and try a little harder with the songs. But then thankfully they called it a day and wandered off into the distance.

KEITH RICHARDS

Who would have thought that Keith Richards would turn out to be one of the defining musical icons of the last twenty years? Who would have thought that, decades after first achieving success, he would spend the Nineties and Noughties being revered as not just an elder statesman of rock, but also something approaching a national folk hero? An ancient guitar hero with slurred speech, inconsistent playing, and arthritic joints. Seriously now, who would have thought it? Yet here he is, the most iconic musical entertainer of his generation, a man who looks like Leatherface in the original *Texas Chainsaw Massacre*.

He no longer falls asleep on stage (which he did once while playing "Fool To Cry" – "It's a very boring song," said Keith in his defence. "Mind you, I was pretty out of it"), and he no longer stays up for days on end (his record was nine, over two hundred hours). Nevertheless he still has his quintessential bad boy haircut, these days accessorised with coins and small animal bones, and he still smokes with the commitment of a lifer. While he is hardly beyond parody, his gift to the world – as well as over a hundred great riffs – is the rock'n'roll blueprint. Affecting a rock'n'roll stance is one of the great enduring clichés of the last fifty years, but Keith Richards

R will forever be the real deal. "He's never changed," said DAVID BAILEY, who has photographed him dozens of times over the last forty-five years (and who famously shot the covers for *The Rolling Stones No.2, Out Of Our Heads, Get Yer Ya-Ya's Out,* and *Goats Head Soup*). "He is just rock'n'roll, that's what he is. Rock and roll."

The journalist NICK KENT, who has probably come as close to the real heart of the Stones as anyone, said that Richards, "Consumed drugs like other humans consume air, which is to say, unceasingly... There was talk... that he might indeed be possessed of super-human faculties. Roadies whispered in hushed tones about Keith's latest hedonistic marathon and several firmly believed he was blessed with two lives." Nick lived with me briefly in the early Nineties, and whenever talk turned to Richards – and it tended to three or four times a day – he would become agitated and testy. "Keith Richards, man, now there is a dude who has seen the dark side. I mean, I've seen a lot of bad shit – IGGY POP, SID VICIOUS, SYD BARRETT, LOU REED – but never have I see anyone like Keith. All the stories? They're all true..."

Richards says that with three months being the longest he has spent in one place in the last twenty years, his life feels rather like that of a whaling captain. Some whaling captain.

A reductive view of the Stones is simple: MICK JAGGER stars as the aloof corporate Svengali; CHARLIE WATTS plays the quiet man in a Savile Row suit (who loves jazz and never listens to the band's records); RONNIE WOOD plays the perpetual adolescent, the reformed Jack-the-lad who many people think isn't even a proper Rolling Stone even though he's been with the band for over thirty years; and Keef, the rock'n'roll axe hero incarnate, a cosseted renegade, a musical gypsy, and a man who has somehow successfully cheated death, time and time and time again.

The most marked difference between Jagger and Richards, according to the latter, is the fact that, "Mick has to dictate to life. He wants to control it. To me, life is a wild animal. You hope to deal with it when it leaps at you. He can't go to sleep without writing out what he's going to do when he wakes up. I just hope to wake up, and it's not a disaster." Asked if his relationship with RONNIE WOOD has changed since he gave up drinking, and whether he misses having a drinking partner, Richards says, "I am my own drinking partner. Intoxication? I'm polytoxic. Whatever drinking or drugs I do is never as big a deal to me as they have been to other people. It's not a philosophy with me. The idea of taking something in order to be Keith Richards is bizarre to me."

Perhaps unsurprisingly, most interviews with Keith these days focus almost exclusively on the fact that he isn't dead; there was even an interview with him in a US magazine recently in which nearly every question concerned death. It's now just about the only thing you interview Richards about – "Why do you think you're still alive when you shouldn't be?" – and he comes armed with dozens of coy *bon mots* to offer in response. He would probably be irritated if you didn't ask him about death, come to think about it, as his very existence is one of the things which contributes to his legendary status. "I feel like I have to defy it now," he said, in response to yet another question about his mortality, recently. "There were plenty of times I could've given up the ghost. But it just seemed such a cheap way out."

The culture of excess has followed Richards around like a stale, musky vapour trail since the band's earliest successes, and his narcotic-driven extravagance has filled book after book after book: Altamont, Redlands, recording *Exile On Main Street*, the fictitious blood transfusions, the guns, the six-day parties, the private jets full of hookers and groupies. In 1977, Richards carried two grams of heroin and cocaine on a flight to Toronto, during which he spent three hours in the toilet, hoovering up as much as he could. After eluding Toronto customs, Richards quickly scored another ounce of heroin and five grams of cocaine and then retired to his hotel suite. Hours later, fifteen Mounties burst into the room, found the drugs but couldn't wake Richards up. They slapped him so hard his cheeks were scarlet when he

R

finally roused. Predictably, his surprise was only matched by his indignation.

Like many addicts, he was devious, and although he was protected from so much of the real world, would go to extreme lengths to get himself into the place he needed to be. "I was staying in the Plaza once in New York; I would fly with a needle and just put it in the hat to fix the feather. I wasn't going to fly with syringes. So the minute I got the shit, well, now I need the syringe, right? My trick was, I'd order a cup of coffee, because I need a spoon, right? And then I go down and FAO Schwarz [the American Hamleys] was right across the street from the Plaza. And there, if you went to the third floor, you could buy a [children's] doctors and nurses set that had the barrel and the syringe that fitted the needle that you'd brought. 'I'll have three teddy bears, I'll have that remote control car, oh, and a doctors and nurses kit. My niece, you know, she's really into that. Must encourage her. Oh, actually, give me two.' Rush back to the room, hook it up and fix it."

These days, largely free from the excesses of his middle youth, self-awareness has enveloped him. "The image is made up of a kaleidoscope of other people's ideas of me," he told his biographer, JAMES FOX. "I could surprise them all, still."

And, remarkably, he does. The ROLLING STONES franchise was kick-started again recently with MARTIN SCORSESE's extraordinary concert film, *Shine A Light*, a genuine cinematic tour de force that managed to do for the Stones what he did for BOB DYLAN in *No Direction Home* (rubberstamp the legend for a generation of pop consumers who weren't aware they were interested).

Scorsese has used the Stones' music in so many of his films it sometimes feels he is more wedded to them than he once was to ROBERT DENIRO. In this context their music doesn't just complement the narrative of his films, it runs through them like a highlighter, somehow perfectly contextualising them. *Shine A Light* however isn't a documentary, and doesn't try to contextualise them in any way at all; it simply captures them doing what they've spent the best part of the last fifty years doing, playing live. "The Stones are the most documented band in history," said Scorsese – what more do we need to know about them? I had to keep telling everybody, 'The history of the ROLLING STONES is right there onstage in their faces, in the way Mick is moving and the way Keith is handling that guitar and the way CHARLIE WATTS plays the drums and the way RONNIE WOOD is working. So why don't we see how they work with each other onstage?' Maybe we get caught up in that very primal euphoria."

Ironically, Richards had already become something of a movie star himself. Having based his character CAPTAIN JACK SPARROW in *Pirates Of The Caribbean* entirely on Richards, it seemed only polite for JOHNNY DEPP to actually ask him to appear in a sequel – which he eventually did, playing Depp's father in *At World's End*. He wasn't diminished by the caricature, either, didn't demean himself like most rock stars playing at being actors. (Depp, meanwhile, gave up copying Keef a few years later, and for his portrayal of SWEENEY TODD in the TIM BURTON film appeared to spend his entire time on screen aping late Sixties DAVID BOWIE, the demon cock-er-ney of auld Fleet Street, me auld china.) "The connection that I made when I was thinking about Captain Jack was that pirates were the rock'n'roll stars of their era, of the 18th century. First and foremost, the myth or the legend would arrive months before they would make port, which is very similar to rock'n'roll stars," said Depp. "He was definitely one of the main ingredients for my character, and you'll definitely recognise some Keith in Jack Sparrow. It was a long shot that [Keith] agreed to do it, [as] it was above and beyond. It was a dream come true. When he arrived on set, suddenly every single person from the crew that you hadn't seen for ages, guys you hadn't seen for years showed up to see the maestro. He just turned up and did it. Two take Richards [we called him]." Having met Richards recently I can confirm that there is little difference between his on-screen performance and the role he plays in real life, while a brief conversation with Depp in the film could be a précis of Keith's own time on earth.

"You've seen it all, done it all, and you've survived. That's the trick, isn't it?" says Depp's Captain Jack. "To survive."

R "It's not just about living forever, Jackie," says Richards as CAPTAIN TEAGUE. "The trick is living with yourself forever."

Keith Richards will never again be the man who lolled around the harbour in Villefranche in the summer of 1971 – the year of his creative peak, and the year he looked his very best – but he wasn't a legend then. By 1988 – the year he released his first solo album, the much derided but actually rather good *Talk Is Cheap* – there was no rock and roll legend bigger.

One of the main reasons for this was the launch of MTV in August 1981, when the channel began its twin-track approach of showcasing new video-friendly acts and celebrating the iconography of pop. The Stones were instantly introduced to a new generation, a generation that while it enjoyed the reruns of all those ancient pop promos and TV appearances from the Sixties and Seventies, was actually far more intrigued by the contemporary videos for songs such as "She Was Hot", "Undercover (of the night)", "Start Me Up", and "Waiting On A Friend". It was via MTV that the band's logo became truly ubiquitous, the international sign of stadium debauchery (intriguingly, Keith once said that the logo was originally meant to mutate into other forms: in one incarnation there were going to be two pills on the tongue, and in another it was going to transform itself into a penis).

To paraphrase RALPH WALDO EMERSON, the religion of one age is the entertainment of the next, which is exactly what happened with the Stones, and those who saw the band in their prime in the Sixties and Seventies would have been astonished by the display of corporate rebellion on display at their stadium gigs of the Nineties and Noughties. Not that the gigs are bad – at their best there is nothing to top them – but for the last twenty years people have been going to see the Stones for the same reason they visit Venice: they want to see both before they crumble into oblivion. Their concerts are like church services, feeding the congregation exactly what they came for, an entertainment blueprint that is still frowned upon in the old-fashioned "rock" world, where improvisation and impetuousness are everything.

It used to be said that he had been chiselled by rock'n'roll but not yet ravaged by it (think Mount Rushmore rather than PETE DOHERTY). But anyone who has seen him posing for the ANNIE LEIBOVITZ pictures in the Louis Vuitton campaign will have seen a man who looks more like luggage than his luggage, with a face that looks like it has seen everything that life has had to offer these last forty-five years or so. It's fair to say that Keith Richards has lived the life, bought the T-shirt, and lived to tell the tale. On April 27, 2006, nine days after leaving New Zealand, where the Stones had been performing, Keith fell out of a tree at the Wakaya Club on Fiji. Having tried to pick some coconuts, he fell sixteen feet to the ground, suffered mild concussion and was flown to Ascot Hospital in Auckland. There he underwent surgery to relieve a blood clot on the brain, an operation that usually involves drilling a hole through the skull to drain the clot. This incident was a bizarre echo of one that took place in 1998 in Keith's Connecticut home, when he broke three ribs and punctured a lung when he plummeted from a ladder while trying to retrieve a book (ironically, a copy of LEONARDO DA VINCI's book on anatomy) in his library. It was just as well he didn't have access to a quad bike.

Perhaps the incident that best encapsulates the way in which Keith Richards has become such an icon of preposterous legend is the incident concerning his father's ashes, and whether or not he snorted them. At the time – May 2007 – there was wild tabloid speculation about what Richards actually did, and only recently did the real story surface. "I opened my dad's ashes, and some of them blew out over the table, just because of the suction of the lid – you know what I mean?" says Keith. "And I no longer do cocaine – I'm not allowed to since I broke my head open, otherwise I'd be right in, baby! Nothing stops the old snorter! But I can't do it; I didn't do it. I looked at my dad's ashes down there and – what am I gonna do? Do I desecrate them with a dustbin and broom? So I wet me finger, and I shoved a little bit of Dad up me hooter. The rest of them I put round an oak tree, which is coming up a treat."

R

And then we had The Book. *Life*. In 2007 it was announced that Richards had signed a deal worth more than £4.5 million to write his autobiography, a tome that would trace his trek from cherubic choirboy to rock'n' roll survivor (this to add to his cut of the £275 million the band made from their last tour, *A Bigger Bang*; after U2's 360° tour, the biggest-grossing tour in rock history). Richards was collaborating on the book with JAMES FOX, author of the 1982 murder mystery, *White Mischief*. He was only the second member of the venerable band to write his memoir, following former bassist BILL WYMAN, who wrote *Stone Alone* in 1990. Jagger started to write an autobiography once, but soon got bored and abandoned the idea. "Keith Richards has stood cool at the centre of the hurricane for nearly fifty years," said MICHAEL PIETSCH of Little, Brown, who won the right to publish the book, when the deal was announced. "His story, in his own words – the band, the songs, the tours, the life – will be the most eagerly awaited book ever to come out of the hallowed halls of rock and roll." And for once, the hyperbole was justified. *Life* turned out to be the best rock'n'roll memoir ever, even better than Bob Dylan's *Chronicles*.

Perhaps unsurprisingly, the deal was brokered by ED VICTOR, the world's most influential publishing agent (who, again unsurprisingly, was also responsible for the recent ERIC CLAPTON autobiography, which is currently the bestselling rock biography of all time). Victor said, "This was the smallest, longest, and biggest auction I've ever run." Only three publishers were allowed to see the twelve-page synopsis, which had to be read in the presence of Victor, JAMES FOX, and Richards' manager, JANE ROSE.

"We had three meetings – three long meetings – in which we allowed the publishers to read it, in front of us, and we took it from there," said Victor at the time. "I didn't want the manuscript all over town, as it would have been on the internet in seconds. James' proposal was one of the most stunning I've ever read, and there is going to be some really surprising material in the book. It wasn't going to be a difficult book to sell but I wanted to keep it manageable."

The three publishers that Victor chose were Doubleday, Harper Collins, and Little, Brown. Doubleday blinked first, making it a two horse race. Apparently both publishers offered the same amount, with Richards himself involved in the final decision.

Back in 1999 we photographed Keith on the rooftops of midtown Manhattan for a twelve-page story in *GQ* for that year's Men Of The Year issue (in his case actually "Maaaan Of The Year"), with the Human Riff showing off his GIANFRANCO FERRE overcoat and black Gucci jeans against the Gotham skyline. I was interviewing him in a hotel in San Sebastian in Spain for the accompanying article, and when he looked at the pictures taken by PETER LINDBERGH, his jaw ever so slightly dropped. The legend set down his rather large tumbler of vodka and fizzy orange and looked in my direction, if not fairly squarely in the eye. Because of the hastily arranged drapes covering his windows it was difficult to make out his mood, but his mouth said it all. "Hats off, man, they rock. You know what I'm saying? These pictures really rock." And he wasn't wrong. "You know what, man?" he said, playing with his pirate rings as he absent-mindedly sprinkled the pristine hotel carpet with cigarette ash. "You've made me look like Keith Richards. And believe me, that's not as easy as you might think."

Every flat surface in his hotel room appeared to have been covered with a scarf of some description. In fact, the photograph of Keef in the Louis Vuitton ad is a pretty good approximation of the generic Keith Richards hotel room, with scarves draped over the lights, several piles of books, a magnifying glass (which he now uses to read) and a small skull on a side table, and a glass of vodka and fizzy orange standing by the phone.

I met him at dusk, and he looked like something out of a gothic horror movie, a man – if that is indeed what he is – who lived according to his own particular timetable within his own parameters. Forty-five years of fame had allowed

R

him to indulge himself to the extent that he operated on Keith time and on Keith time only, GMT being strictly for squares, you understand.

His simian good looks and delicate little body should have been diminished by his habits, but they had actually, largely, been strangely enhanced – even if he did still have the nonchalance of the dead. He famously had a decade-long heroin odyssey during the Seventies and, although he admitted to having had "a little taste" of it on the Stones tour at the time, seemed remarkably compos mentis. He was sipping vodka and was apparently still smoking grass (he was carrying some extra-large Rizlas "more in expectation than anything"), yet he was sprightly on his feet.

And he still looked great in a Versace coat.

At the time the lolloping libertine had been the most elegantly wasted man in rock for well over four decades. If MICK JAGGER still seemed like an over-wound toy, Richards was still the quintessential urban cowboy; his gait that of a bow-legged junkie looking for his horse (or his guitar, which he once never slept without). He was fifty-five yet his skin was clear and the lines he carried on his face were, in his own, rather elasticised words, "built from laughter". This was even more remarkable seeing that the ROLLING STONES had been on tour for the previous twenty-four months, playing over a hundred and thirty concerts in a hundred cities to six million insatiable customers, and earning more than £200m in the process. He talked a little like the legendary British journalist BILL DEEDES, or the PAUL WHITEHOUSE creation ROLLY BIRKIN QC, though if Keith were to complete a story with the words "...but I must say I was very, very drunk", then you know he almost certainly would have been. Very.

"I've been an amateur chemist, a 'drugologist'," he said, of his thirty-five year relationship with drugs. "I always went by this old 1903 medical dictionary, which was produced before such drugs were considered bad for you. If you were constipated you were told to go to the chemists and get a little tincture of cocaine. If you had diarrhoea then it was a grain of heroin. I've abused drugs, but I didn't go into them without boning up on them first."

The Dartford-born axeman had already outlived three generations of rock'n'roll bad boys, intent, it seemed, on emulating the wizened old bluesmen who originally inspired him. The Human Riff was a werewolf in black leather, scuffed bovver boots, and skull rings, his fingers resembling nothing more than overcooked Lincolnshire sausages: "I play the guitar, what can I tell you." In his Spanish hotel room he was also sporting some slightly odd dreadlocks, which his assistant had plaited during the recent tour. "It's something of a fetish," he said, rather unnecessarily.

He was more than intrigued by his own image, happy in the knowledge that no one else had ever looked quite like him. When he was young, he wanted to look like ELVIS and Little Richard, then Buddy Holly and then finally, forever, himself. "I don't really study my legacy," he said, in his increasingly macabre-looking hotel room in San Sebastian. "It's got to the point where it's like a shadow that you drag around behind you. Now and again I just pull the Keith Richards look and scare the living daylights out of somebody just because they're in my way; it's just a little something you have in your locker. It's a look and a quick move. I don't have a fixed image of myself. You know, 'cos every time I see myself it's in a slightly different shade. Each tour produces its own outfit. At the moment I'm wearing this jacket that was bestowed upon me by some biker friends in Germany. Fighting colours they are. Heavy dudes.

"My lifestyle and the way I look evolved out of being on the road, my semi-nomadic life. I carry my own home furnishings with me, a few rugs, a few rags, things that can be packed up. If you're going to be in hotels for two years on the trot, I've got to transform a room immediately. I even do it at home, but then in the last twenty years I've never lived anywhere for longer than three months."

When he's on tour, Keith is constitutionally incapable of anything resembling normal behaviour, while his world is

R

almost hermetic in its isolation from the one outside. The vampire will party 'til dawn, then sleep 'til the middle of the afternoon (often curling-up with one of his beloved guitars or an unread history book), eventually stirring and "swimming through his scrambled eggs and vodka breakfast". After a gig Keith will hang out in a specially designed after-hours area that he still occasionally shares with fellow Stone RONNIE WOOD (even though Ronnie has given up the booze) and which looks exactly the same at every venue in every city in every country.

Planet Keith must be a fun place to live, though for the man himself it is not the only place. He has two grown-up children as well as two from his relationship with his current wife PATTI HANSEN (the American model whom Keith married in 1983), and when not on tour will "hang" with them at their homes in Connecticut, Sussex and Jamaica.

"After a tour I'll pop down to Sussex for a couple of weeks and decompress with the family. That way they'll semi-domesticate me again. I find it difficult to get to grips with the idea of daylight, but a little sojourn in the tropics usually helps. It's not easy coming off a tour and come dinner time – and this is something that really pisses off the old lady – I'm wondering where the gig is."

Perhaps no other living rock star has lived so excessively and, judging by the kind of publicity that he generates, for the last quarter of a century Richard has consistently been only a rumour's distance from the grave. But if it's all true – all the cascading stories of horrendous excess – then why isn't he dead? Because if Keith pushed the envelope, then the envelope has certainly pushed back.

"There are lots of people who say I should be dead by now, and I do feel blessed in a way. I watch it myself with amazement. I mean, it never ceases to amaze me. I weigh the same as I always have. I've been blessed with an amazing constitution, I guess – it's been tempered in the fires of hell! The human body is incredibly adaptable, especially mine. I never exercise. I would say that if you tried two-and-a-half hours with the Stones three or four times a week with a guitar round your neck, that would do it for you. Just about. You sweat off maybe a pound and a half every show. I dread thinking about my body I mean, I take it for granted. But I don't have a death wish, I like life too much."

Now, maybe, but in the past his lust for life has been almost libidinous. "I never liked speed," he said, as he sipped vodka and orange in San Sebastian, back in '99, "and that's probably why I go more for depressants, because my natural energy is very high. In the old days I really didn't want to deal with being a star everyday and you could kind of hide inside heroin, it was like a cocoon; a soft wall between you and everything else. Probably not the best solution to the problem, but at the time I didn't think about that. It's an experiment that went on too long – getting heavily busted, blowing it for the Stones and for my family. I had to stop. So I did. People talk about cocaine addiction all the time, but I know what addiction is: opium, heroin, you know? That's when you're climbing the walls and you see your own fingernail marks 'cos you think there's something behind the wall. Cocaine is just a bad habit."

Over forty years ago he squinted into the sun at Villa Nellcote in Villefranche, where his band were recording their greatest record, *Exile On Main Street*, and asked: "Who says you've got to live three score and ten years? There's only one source of information I know that says that and even that doesn't say everybody's got to make it. Everybody can't make seventy." But for a man who –perhaps even more than PETE TOWNSHEND – was meant to die before he got old, he seems as though he might outlive us all.

And as for retiring, Keith was having none of it. "If I was a plumber I would still be playing guitar," he said. "I feel very much the same as MUDDY WATERS. Why stop? People reach creative peaks at different times and you never know when it's going to come again. Especially with a team, with a band. So in a way, I suppose the quest is: 'Lets find out how long a rock'n'roll band can go.' Nobody knows because the music's not been around for that long. There's a certain missionary sense that goes unspoken amongst us. And I've always felt that there's a slightly racial bias because if you're white you're not supposed to do it. If I was black, nobody would go on about how old I was, they'd say wonderful that he's still going. They wouldn't go on about thinning hairlines and wrinkles and all that crap."

This is a theme he returns to constantly, enjoying the comparisons to old blues masters. "The media's perception of longevity is you're supposed to be able to do this from eighteen to twenty-five, if you're lucky," he said recently. "In 1956, rock and roll was like calypso – a novelty. They said, 'None of it will last' – without realising that all of the music behind it was not a novelty."

When we met, he was particularly disparaging about one review that had suggested that he might be too old for his game. He was referring specifically to a review of one of the Stones' Wembley concerts that summer by the *Observer*'s wickedly perceptive LYNN BARBER. "She's just an old, bitter hag who should leave her photograph off her by-line if she wants to criticise people," said Richards, somewhat ungraciously (and somewhat out of character). "She belongs to the 'Would you let your daughter marry one?' school. Her piece could have been written thirty-five years ago, you know? It would have been knocking these slobby young kids instead of knocking these slobby old men."

He had less harsh words for his old partner in crime, the recently detached MICK JAGGER. "I find it quite easy to distance myself from Mick's private life," said Keith, "but then it's ludicrous because it's not private at all. I sometimes see what the old bugger wants in life, he's intent on being CASANOVA or DON JUAN. He's always looking for it, which is a little cruel on his loved ones. But he has always been like that. I don't talk to Mick about his love life because it's like, 'Whoops! You've skidded on another banana skin!'"

A slobby old man indeed. Keith Richards is now so entrenched in the public imagination that his iconic status is protected by unspoken decree. We like him because he fulfils all our expectations of what someone like Keith Richards should be. He is Keith, and we are not. And we seem to like it that way. And not just because he looks great in a Versace coat. And his health, and his persistent refusal to slip off this mortal coil? "I must be fine," he says, "because I'm not seeing any doctors."

Would we like the records to be better? Of course we would. Would we like to slip a new Stones CD into the car stereo and be blown away by the dazzling mixture of crunching guitar and studio wizardry, of vaguely pertinent lyrical imagery and insolent misogyny? Silly question. Of course we would. What man wouldn't want to drive home listening to the ancient art of weaving wrapping itself around songs no one could afford to ignore.

However, much of the Stones' output in the last twenty years stands up against their "canon", but neither the band nor radio programmers seem much interested in it. *Steel Wheels*, their 1989 "comeback" album produced three classic songs: "Between A Rock and Hard Place" was a great generic Stones single, if a little blandly produced, as was Keith's "Can't Be Seen", a song that still sounds perfect blasting out of a car on a summer's evening, and then there was another wistful Keith ballad, "Slipping Away". (The first single from *Steel Wheels,* "Mixed Emotions", was not only mediocre but contained an unusually terrible CHARLIE WATTS drum roll, although the 12" version, available on *Rarities (1971-2003)* is worth finding, precisely because everything has been metronomically cleaned up.) Then there was "Sex Drive", a great dance number from the semi-live 1991 album, *Flashpoint*, that probably disappeared from memory so quickly as it was almost never performed live. The next album, 1994's *Voodoo Lounge*, featured not only "Love Is Strong", "I Go Wild", and "Out of Tears" (a critics' favourite), but also "Thru and Thru", with Keith's melancholic wail and CHARLIE WATTS' gunshot snare, which had a second life on television, being prominently featured in the concluding episode of the second season of *The Sopranos*. Next came the band's extraordinary version of "Like A Rolling Stone"

R

from their 1995 live album, *Stripped*, and then, two years later, *Bridges To Babylon*, which featured "Anybody Seen My Baby?" (which owed so much of its melody to K.D. LANG's "Constant Craving" that she eventually got a writing credit on it) as well as the beautiful "Thief In The Night", which Keith he sings as though he's sitting on someone's porch at twilight, almost whispering the verses, as if he's trying to avoid amplification. And just recently there was "Rough Justice" on 2005's *A Bigger Bang*, a single that sounds as good as any generic post- prime Stones record.

Richards' somewhat solo records have also often been overlooked. *Talk Is Cheap*, from 1988, contains a gorgeous soul crawl called "Make No Mistake" that also features in *The Sopranos* (as well as another great Keith song, "Locked Away"), while 1992's *Main Offender*'s highlight is another ballad, "Hate It When You Leave". His offshoot band, the X-PENSIVE WINOS, recorded a great version of the Stones classic "Connection" on their *Live At The Hollywood Palladium* album, recorded in 1988 and released three years later. (Jagger has also been responsible for a couple of great solo singles, notably "Sweet Thing", the sub-"Miss You" dancefloor classic from his 1993 solo album *Wandering Spirit*, and "Old Habits Die Hard" from the 2005 *Alfie* soundtrack.)

Many of Richards' most successful songs – and they tend to be ballads – are gorgeously overwrought and proudly incoherent. Like many songwriters of his stature, his permission to write is guaranteed by his fame, so there is never anything self-conscious about his songs; they just are. "Blues and rock'n'roll singing is about style," he says. "It's about using the character of your voice to convey the song. You're not singing correctly, in fact you're probably breaking half your vocal cords. BUDDY HOLLY would have hiccupped himself to death had he stuck around a bit longer."

Some say that the reason Jagger and Richards don't write good songs anymore is simply because they have lost touch with reality – when their former manager ANDREW LOOG OLDHAM expressed to a friend how dismal *A Bigger Bang* was, the friend said, "But Andrew, these people don't even have to press the buttons on elevators" – but in fairness the Stones probably lost contact with reality about six months after their first hit, back in 1962.

Whenever critics start bleating about the Stones' lack of decent contemporary material, I'm reminded of what JOSEPH HELLER used to say when he was criticised for not writing another novel as good as his debut, *Catch 22*.

By all accounts he would nod sagaciously, look his accuser calmly in the eye, smile and then say, not without a soupcon of irony, "But who has?"

In the summer of 2011 I interviewed Keith again, in connection with his appearance at the *GQ* Men Of The Year Awards, as the winner of that year's Writer Of The Year Award:...

> *Keith Richards has a face that conjures up many things. When he walks into his manager JANE ROSE's downtown Manhattan offices, it strikes me that he looks like a slightly ruined country house, with a leathery and runnelled face. As I shake his hand I'm thinking that this is probably what W.H. AUDEN would have looked like if he had worn leather trousers, or a cape. In different dress, Keith could also pass for an Afghan tribal leader, something that would probably please him.*
>
> *We are meeting today, in early June, to talk about Keith Richards winning this year's GQ Writer Of The Year award for* Life, *the autobiography he crafted with the help of his friend JAMES FOX. Life is probably the best rock'n'roll memoir ever written, easily as good as BOB DYLAN's Chronicles: Volume 1, but six times longer. It is the result of painstaking research (one hundred and forty people are thanked in the book, many of whom Fox interviewed in order to fill in the hulking great gaps in Keith's memory), an eye and an ear for detail, and the sixty-seven-year-old's engaging way with an anecdote. Oh, and it is also one of the greatest rock'n'roll stories*

R

ever told, ever lived. Which is probably why the book has been so monumentally successful.

It's all here: sex, violence, drugs, myth-making, the character traits of some of the world's most famous people, and, of course, the truth about the ancient art of weaving. While it is written chronologically, it pinballs all over the place just when you least expect it, painting a believable, vividly colourful picture. There are some especially evocative passages about London after WWII, passages that go a long way to establishing why Keith ended up as "Keef".

The thing that struck me most when I first read it – and indeed, reviewed it at the time – was the refreshing way in which Keith discussed his monstrous drug-taking: not in a self-congratulatory way, but in extremely matter-of-fact terms. There are fascinating descriptions of what it's like to exist on heroin, extraordinary passages outlining his motivations for being under the influence, and wonderful accounts of Keef using drugs as though they were gears.

Keith and I chatted for two hours, in a suite of offices full of ROLLING STONES *paraphernalia: a doll based on his character in* Pirates Of The Caribbean: At World's End; *a poster advertising the* MARTIN SCORSESE *documentary* Shine A Light; *piles of tour T-shirts; acres of gold discs; a signed poster advertising their infamous 1972 tour; imprints of* Life; *a Diamond Award presented to* JANE ROSE *in recognition of* Hot Rocks 1964-1971's *twelve million American sales; and a huge painting of the world's greatest rock'n'roll guitarist, memoirist and raconteur. As we talked, I was overwhelmed by a very odd sensation, one I rarely experience: this, I thought to myself, is a privilege.*

Dylan Jones: Keith, we share an agent, the man you've rechristened ED "F***ING" VICTOR. Did you do a beauty parade of agents for the book?

> *Keith Richards: No. Ed was the person I wanted. Obviously, I drew up a shortlist, but it was always* ED F***ING VICTOR! *And then he went to work on it, which was amazing. I wasn't involved in the business end of it, but Ed did everything and more than was asked of him. And I have to tip my hat constantly to* JAMES FOX *for the way it was put together. They're my stories, but the way he crafted them, I couldn't have written it that way myself.*

R

Up until Life, BOB DYLAN's Chronicles had set a new bar for rock autobiographies...

> *That was the other thing I couldn't go through, trying to outdo somebody else's. Everybody's got a different way of telling a story – and has different stories to tell. But Chronicles was fantastic. That was the benchmark. When we started, I told James a few school stories and said this is what I remember. But within a week, James had found the guy I was talking about, and got the confirmation that this story would hold up. After that, I started to get more confidence in my memory. I mean, it's been pretty fried.*

Why did you decide to do the book?

> *The Stones had just finished the last tour, having been away for three years, and I knew there was going to be an inevitable gap where we would all be sitting around thinking about what's going to happen next. And the idea came up just at that moment, and it seemed the perfect thing to keep me occupied. It just seemed the right point in the story so far. And then other things fell into place and I knew that I had a couple of years to do it, basically.*

What did you want to achieve with the book?

> *I just wanted to tell it from my point of view, and the incredible escapades we got involved in. It would be*

R

enough for most people's lifetimes if just one of those things happened to them. But I wasn't expecting the incredible reception that it's got. It's got me into a semiliterate area – people thought I was just a moron. I've actually got to like critics in the last year! It's like, "Wow, thanks pal, let me buy you a drink!" I thought they were going to drag me through the mud, as I'm used to that, but in actual fact it sort of elevated my opinion of myself. I don't want to get bigheaded here, as I always play myself down, but I've been pleased. To me, my biggest fear is getting a bighead, and that is when I get the hammer. Because it's very easy in this game to believe you're something special. Just look at BRIAN JONES *– he died from it.*

You've been fairly transparent about the partnership between you and James, and that's earned you a lot of credit.

I couldn't have told the story without him. In some uncanny way he captured the strength and breadth of the story. I've been friends with James for years, so he was used to my rhythm of speech. It helps that he's also a very good blues guitar player. So when I'd run out of ideas or taped the stories, we'd sit down and play some blues. But it's weird to drag through your whole life, because in the process you're actually living the damn thing twice. As we went on, I was shocked by thinking, "How did one guy go through all this?" And then I realised it was me! It put my past into a more coherent perspective. Before doing the book I'd look upon my life as incredible, disconnected episodes, and in the process of doing the book I managed to make sense of it. When I finished I felt more exhausted than after three years touring with the Stones. I felt a weight had been lifted off my shoulders.

What did you learn about yourself writing the book?

That I'm a much meaner bastard than I thought. But

at the same time, I realised how much friendship had meant to me, and how much my friendship had meant to other people, which I hadn't thought about before. This is the rock'n'roll life, and you had to invent it as you went along. There was no textbook to say how you operate this machinery. You didn't know you were always walking on the edge of disasters, and there's nobody to turn to and say, "How did you feel?" because no one had been there before. It was very exciting. Still is, in a way. There are loads of things people wish I'd done, and some things I wish I'd done! You become a cartoon character, and I can play that to the hilt, and I know that people have come up with a great story and they go, "He didn't do it, but if he'd thought about it and he'd been there, he would have done it."

You spend a long time describing London after WWII.

Even though my memory of the war is pretty much nonexistent, as I was only eighteen months old, I still had a sense of sirens and collective fears. But as you're growing up in the Fifties, you're thinking this has got to change, it's too tight, the atmosphere, it's too restricted. The others running the joint want us to go back to the Thirties and we can't. And I guess as I was reaching the age of fifteen, sixteen, you've got the energy and you're bursting to escape. Plus, I fell in love with blues music, and that was where you found roots and a form of expression we didn't have in England. But as I was growing up, my mother was listening to a lot of BILLIE HOLIDAY *and* ELLA FITZGERALD... *You hear things on the BBC, and then you start to bump into other guys who are into it, too; you realise it isn't just you sitting in a council flat. There are other guys out there listening to music, and somebody's got a new record from America and you're immediately at their house. You bring a bottle of beer – that was your entrance fee – and you sit around and listen to records, which is nuts but it's beautiful. It was very innocent.*

In the book you describe using drugs as gears. What gear are you in these days?

I'm pretty much in neutral.

How many stories couldn't you include?

There were a lot for legal reasons. Especially concerning families who didn't even know that one of their relations was a drug dealer. A lot of my friends were very well brought-up boys, and I wouldn't want to upset the family just to name somebody. Everybody was experimenting and everybody was a pirate, especially in those days. In the club subculture, actually in every sort of culture, there are some very interesting people down there, but it's a great leveller where you find out who's one of your people or who's full of s***; who would stick by your side in a tough situation, and who would rat you out. It's not the most pleasant world to be in, but I do think it's kind of necessary to keep one foot in the gutter.

Why?

Because I never trusted the pavement.

Mick[Jagger] didn't love the book, did he?

Mick was obviously a bit peeved, but that was yesterday and this is today. We're two guys divided by life.

Did you read Ronnie Wood's book?

Well, I think he tossed it off. Even Ronnie would admit that. Ronnie's got a much better story to tell than that book, that's all I can say. Charlie's book is the one I really want to read.

R

Six months before the book came out I bumped into DAVID REMNICK, the editor of the New Yorker, and all he could talk about was your book. He said that he was hoping you were going to explain the open G tuning. Which you did!

> *I'm amazed by that part of the book, and how much response I've got from the guitar players of this world. It's so difficult to put on to the page how you play an instrument, and I was amazed by the fact that I can, and I apparently made it fairly comprehensive. It's got a lot of tips in there, and that was the one difficulty for me and James – I didn't know how to put it into words. I know you have to do this and put this there, but on the page that will look dopey. But the translation worked.*

And is there going to be a movie of the book?

> *Yeah, there are feelers out at the minute. I'm in no rush right at the moment. Also, how are they going to find me? The idea of a succession of Keith Richards coming down is horrifying. Maybe when I'm dead and gone they can make a movie of it.*

THE ROCK'N'ROLL T-SHIRT

Why do grown men wear rock'n'roll T-shirts? What possesses otherwise rational, sentient men to parade around in dodgy pieces of billowing, faded, flimsy, hundred percent cotton (if they're lucky), which prove that they saw the STONE ROSES at Spike Island or OASIS at Knebworth, or U2 just about anywhere? I mean, I saw DR FEELGOOD in the Nag's Head in High Wycombe, in 1975, when I was fourteen, but do I feel the need to tell everyone?

Like most men, I went through my T-shirt phase. This was some time ago, when I was a teenager and it was deemed acceptable to proclaim your love for the SEX PISTOLS, the CLASH, or the BUZZCOCKS. Such was their provenance and appearance that it seemed perfectly natural to shout about it. But I was sixteen at the time, not thirty-five. Or fifty. So why do grown-ups do it? Why do they have to prove so little to so many? I went to a BOB DYLAN concert at the Shepherd's Bush Empire a few years ago, and apart from the fact that every song was unrecognisable (par for the course in Bobland), the evening was notable because every member of the audience was a white, balding, male endomorph, each one wearing a BOB DYLAN tour T-shirt, as this was obviously the only way they could communicate with each other ("You saw Bob at Blackbush in '78?" "Er, yeah..." "Wow, cool..." End of conversation).

I was in a fairly fancy Italian restaurant off Baker Street in London a few years ago. It was your basic 21st Century trat: modernist concrete interior, impenetrable menu, and twenty-eight winning ways with burrata and aubergine. The sort of place where they mock you if you ask for butter. Anyway, there we were, three men in casual suits having dinner; three men who, at some point in their lives, had worn a T-shirt proclaiming their allegiance to a Zeitgeisty pop group (in my case the RAMONES, although I'm fairly sure my companions preferred A FLOCK OF SEAGULLS and CHRIS DE BURGH). But we'd stopped wearing them years ago, just as we'd stopped wearing lapel badges and baseball caps.

At the other end of the restaurant was a group of thirty-something men, all of whom were patently still afflicted. Three were wearing commemorative tour T-shirts: BOB MARLEY (always a favourite), RAGE AGAINST THE MACHINE (a touch idiosyncratic, I admit), and, of course, the ubiquitous U2 number (apparently celebrating some long-forgotten European jaunt of the late Eighties).

And they all looked like Very Sad Men, men whose arc of achievement hadn't quite got off the ground, whose benchmark of success was being in seat twenty-four, Row F, of the Hammersmith Odeon thirty years ago.

But it's not the unreconstructed childishness of this that intrigued me, it was the total banality. If men are prepared to do this – and I defy anyone to find three similarly attired women – then what stops us from applying this chest-beating to other seminal events in our lives: T-shirts that announce to the world that we ate in Granita in 1992, or moved to Paddington in 1998? How about The Groucho Club (back of the brasserie), 1985; Tuscany 1993; BMW 320SE 1991-1994; or, an idea I think might easily catch on, JEAN PAUL GAULTIER, the spandex years, 1983-1987?

But hold on. Did BOB DYLAN do that already?

THE ROLLING STONES' TATTOO YOU

When you reach a certain age in life – could be eighteen, could be thirty, could be forty-five – when you think you have found all the music you like, and when your computer and your shelves are heaving with your personal taste's greatest hits, you are often tempted to wander.

I know I am.

You get bored with the stuff you've got (the stuff you thought pretty much defined you) and start seeking out stuff you previously thought was naff, stuff you didn't think you'd like, stuff that always felt a bit old, pedestrian, ordinary, odd. Or simply stuff you've never heard before. Hell, you might even start to like NICK CAVE. This happens collectively as much as it does individually: how else can you explain the recent and decidedly curious veneration of LEONARD COHEN? Had we really exhausted every other potential cult hero? And could it really be the turn of the KAISER CHIEFS next?

And so, thinking back to a time when, say, you might have been passionately consuming JOY DIVISION, the HUMAN LEAGUE,

R the B-52s, and the CRAMPS (let's stamp it 1981), you begin looking around for other things you could have liked, another life you could have lived, searching for a parallel universe full of BRUCE SPRINGSTEEN, the BEE GEES, the PSYCHEDELIC FURS... the Rolling Stones, say. Maybe *Hi Infidelity* by REO SPEEDWAGON wasn't as bad as everyone assumed it was, maybe YAZOO weren't so rubbish after all. Uh-huh. (In their own way, the *Guardian* writers have already done this: in their 1976 end of the year review, they advised their readers to "ignore those boring SEX PISTOLS", for it had actually been "the year of JACKSON BROWNE".) And so you begin employing the same rationale you used at the age of thirteen, playing a record until you liked it, no matter how bad it was (in my case I give you exhibit A: *Ooh La La* by the FACES, and exhibit B: *Muscle Of Love* by ALICE COOPER). All those years you spent vacationing in Ibiza? Well, imagine instead you had gone every year to the Cote d'Azur.

In the summer of 1981, a new Rolling Stones album was released. Its title was *Tattoo You*. The album itself was a compilation of odds and sods from half-a-dozen previous recording sessions, some from *Some Girls*, some from *Emotional Rescue*, and some from the infamous *Black and Blue* sessions of the mid-Seventies – leftovers that had, as another critic would write, a "slovenly gait". And a rather wonderful one at that. The tracks selected covered the eight years since 1972, and featured such former contributors as BOBBY KEYS, BILLY PRESTON, WAYNE PERKINS, and MICK TAYLOR (fact: the Stones were at their prime when Taylor was in the band). And they had been recorded everywhere from Paris and Rotterdam, to Kingston, Jamaica, and Compass Point in Nassau. *Tattoo* was made possible by travel agents as much as anyone.

My sojourn with the record was kick-started by an article I read in *Entertainment Weekly* a few years ago, in which the director GREG MOTTOLA (*Superbad*) described his efforts at authenticity in his film, *Adventureland*. The movie is set in the Eighties, and Mottola wanted a specific Stones song included on the soundtrack, "Tops", and he wasn't going to accept any substitutes. Intrigued (I'd never heard it), I sought it out, and found it, slap bang in the middle of *Tattoo You*.

R

According to Stones biographer PHILIP NORMAN, "Like that of its predecessor, *Emotional Rescue*, [*Tattoo You* was] a vague, unrepentant swipe of male chauvinism. *Tattoo You* contained a track called 'Start Me Up', sung by a voice as snarlingly adolescent as if the past decade had never been, set about by plain guitar chords of dark lazy malignity. Among the prevailing aural high-tech, its effect was that of a cave painting, lit by primitive fire. All that was new and current could not suppress its Neolithic growl. For the first time since 'Angie' in 1973, the Stones were top of the American singles charts."

Some Girls, from 1978, had been the perfect Stones album, containing one genuine worldwide smash – the disco-themed, four-to-the-floor, harmonica-driven "Miss You" – and various solid-gold classics like "Respectable", "Beast of Burden", and "Shattered". It felt old and new at the same time, both modern and venerable. It was as surprising as it was refreshing, the record no one had any right to expect (and was one of the few "old wave" records it was OK for us punks to like). Yet its follow-up, *Emotional Rescue*, was a ragbag of not very much at all, and those of us who felt we shouldn't have liked *Some Girls* in the first place felt vindicated. So by the time *Tattoo You* was released, those of us of a certain vintage, with even a modicum of respect for the band, simply ignored it, thinking it couldn't possibly be any good.

Listening to it thirty years later, I realise how wrong we were, and although *Some Girls* is still considered *primus inter pares*, *Tattoo You* could be even better. I'm not holding it like a hymnal, but it currently gets more heavy rotation than any other non-current CD in the house (apart from the original cast recording of STEPHEN SONDHEIM's *Company*, of course – oh, and HERBIE HANCOCK's *Hear, O Israel*, and ENNIO MORRICONE's *High*). This record doesn't burn with intensity – and in true Stones style, a lot of its high points you can imagine

being the result of no more than a shrug of the shoulders —
but it's a great, old-fashioned party album, a bachelor pad
staple, a classic of its kind.

This wasn't the 1964 vintage of elephant-cord hipsters, tab-
collared shirts, and Carnaby Street suede lace-ups. This was
no *Beggar's Banquet*-era pageantry of death, no bohemian
requiem. This was a serious acknowledgement of stadium
rock, which "Start Me Up" quickly became a quintessential
example of (along with ELTON JOHN's "Benny And The Jets",
HALL & OATES' "Out Of Touch", PRINCE's "Purple Rain", and
U2's "I Still Haven't Found What I'm Looking For"). By 1981
the Stones were a generic top-down, rock'n'roll-by-numbers
outfit, delivering power-chord riff-rock for those in the cheap
seats behind the stanchions, fans for whom nuance was a fancy
French restaurant. We were entering a period when rock'n'roll
was squeezing itself into a brand new pair of training shoes,
and rolling the sleeves of its pale pink linen jacket up to the
elbows, when there was little in the world that couldn't be
solved by a Roland 808 and a 12" dance remix.

But although they had become an outfit committed
to celebration rather than introspection, the burden of
debauchery still sat lightly on their shoulders.

Tattoo You started inauspiciously, being initially cobbled
together in order for the band to have a new album to promote
for their massive worldwide 1981 tour (a record to go on the
road with, like REM's *Monster*, or the U2 album, *No Line On
The Horizon*). Initially MICK JAGGER was opposed to the tour,
as he was busy in the Peruvian jungle filming WERNER HERZOG's
Fitzcarraldo, but when his co-star JASON ROBARDS fell ill with
amoebic dysentery, and then Amazon head-hunters invaded
the set — much to KEITH RICHARDS' amusement — the film was
postponed and Jagger found himself having to tread the
boards once more. This wasn't the band that appeared dressed
as leather-clad hookers and paedophile Nazis in NIK COHN
and GUY PEELLAERT's *Rock Dreams*, this was a well-lubricated
corporate roadshow, a stadium behemoth. At this point in
their history the band didn't need to make another mark on

history, they simply needed content for their latest travelling carnival. This was pantechnicon rock.

R

According to the album's associate producer, CHRIS KIMSEY, "*Tattoo You* really came about because Mick and Keith were going through a period of not getting on. There was a need to have an album out, and I told everyone I could make an album from what I knew was still there." The gossip surrounding the Stones at the time suggested that Jagger and Richards were getting on so badly that they couldn't be in the same room together, let alone write songs, and although Richards was still adjusting to a life without heroin, RON WOOD was apparently near-incapacitated from freebase cocaine (by the early Eighties he was rumoured to be spending $5,000 a day on his habit).

However KEITH RICHARDS begged to differ: "The thing with *Tattoo You* wasn't that we'd stopped writing new stuff, it was a question of time. We'd agreed we were going to go out on the road and we wanted to tour behind a record. There was no time to make whole new album and make the start of the tour."

Maybe. One writer recalls visiting Richards' New York home in the early Eighties, and on entering the guitarist's pool room, seeing a hideous portrait of the owner: wild hair, a huge distorted nose, with one hand holding a cigarette. On the other hand sat a glove puppet, a tiny MICK JAGGER.

Either way, Kimsey spent three months with Jagger going through material that had been recorded for the previous five albums, finding stuff that had been either rejected or forgotten about. The album was primarily composed of outtakes, some dating back a decade, with new vocals and instrumental overdubs. Apart from two tracks, the songs were all written and recorded in the Seventies, and so were all of exquisite vintage.

Years before the remixed, amalgamated, sampled, digitised world would force old-skool rock to put on a pair of sneakers in order to dance in the modern world, *Tattoo You* feels like a collection of old songs that have been put through some sort of modernising blender: Rolling Stones 0.2.

R

"*Tattoo You* is basically an old record," said MICK JAGGER, matter-of-factly. "It's all a lot of old tracks that I dug out. They're all from different periods. Then I had to write lyrics and melodies. A lot of them didn't have anything, which is why they weren't used at the time, because they weren't complete. They were just bits, or they were from early takes. And then I put them all together in an incredibly cheap fashion. I recorded in this place in Paris in the middle of winter. And then I recorded some of it in a broom cupboard, literally, where we did the vocals. The rest of the band were hardly involved. And then I took it to BOB CLEARMOUNTAIN, who did this great job of mixing so that it doesn't sound like it's from different periods."

"Some tracks weren't quite ready [for] *Emotional Rescue*," said KEITH RICHARDS. "The music had to age just like good wine. Sometimes we write our songs in instalments – just get the melody and the music, and we'll cut the tracks and write the words later. That way, the actual tracks have matured, just like wine – you just leave it in the cellar for a bit, and it comes out a little better a few years later. It's stupid to leave all that great stuff just for want of finishing it off and getting it together."

One of the ways in which the band "tarted-up" the songs was by asking jazz legend SONNY ROLLINS to play saxophone on them, most significantly on "Waiting on a Friend". "I had a lot of trepidation about working with SONNY ROLLINS," said Jagger. "CHARLIE [WATTS] said, 'He's never going to want to play on a Rolling Stones record!' But he did, and he was wonderful." Rollins got the inspiration for the sax on "Waiting On A Friend" by asking Jagger to dance for him while he played. "He said, 'You tell me where you want me to play and *dance* the part out.' So I did that. You don't have to do a whole ballet, but sometimes that movement of the shoulder tells the guy to kick in on the beat."

For a certain generation of consumers, *Some Girls* could have been a debut album – the band were as engagingly obnoxious as they had been back in the early Sixties: back in 1978, when KEITH RICHARDS was asked why the Stones had called their new album *Some Girls,* he replied, "Because we couldn't remember their fucking names" – and in their eyes the three that followed (*Emotional Rescue, Tattoo You,* and *Undercover*) were as good as those early Sixties' records. As *Rolling Stone* said at the time, "*Some Girls* kicked off a five-year run ripe for re-appreciation: the Mall-Rat Years. The Stones seduced a new breed of Eighties parking-lot kids who didn't give a crap about the band's legacy but shook mullet when 'She's So Cold' or 'Little T&A' hit the radio in between JOURNEY and FOREIGNER."

Yet *Tattoo You* resonated with those it was least expected to. "By all rights the Rolling Stones shouldn't exist in 1981," wrote GIOVANNI DADOMO that year, in the October issue of *The Face*, "let alone be making the kind of noises that simmer through the hotter parts of *Tattoo You*, an album, which, true to its title, makes more than a few lasting impressions." He went on: "'Black Limousine' finds the ensemble doing what they do best, i.e. pretending to be Chicago niggers circa '62; the resultant blues breeze stands comfortably alongside similar ventures by the same group – on *Beggar's Banquet*, or the like." Dadomo loved the Stax references, Jagger's falsetto, the quasi-psychedelic "Heaven", the femininity of their arrangements, the machismo of their rhythm and blues. Their special sauce, basically, a sauce that was reduced splendidly by the amount of time the group had, over the years, spent touring and recording in the US (MARTIN SCORSESE, who would later film the band for the *Shine A Light* documentary, says for him the Stones never seemed like a London band, but a New York one).

The cover of the album was designed by PETER CORRISTON, who won a Grammy Award for it. This was just before the arrival of the CD, when album sleeves still meant something, before they became pauperised. Corriston had previously designed *Some Girls* and *Emotional Rescue*, and would go on to design *Undercover*. And although he has worked for BILLY IDOL, TOM WAITS, ROD STEWART, and the NEW YORK DOLLS, is probably best known for his Led Zeppelin cover, *Physical Graffiti* – which *Some Girls* was obviously influenced by. The cover is striking for many reasons, not least because it is one of the few to only feature Jagger on the front. Their tattooed faces served to disguise the ageing process, keeping the idea of Jagger and Richards as vibrant, priapic rock gods still viable. Forever obsessing about the group's virility, Jagger even considered decorating the back cover with a tattooed penis. "I'd been reading about Samurai warriors, and about how they would have tattoos in order to show they could endure pain," said Corriston. It was he who came up with the idea, and the idea of calling the album *Tattoo*. "Mick has the attention span of a fruit-fly, so it's very difficult to get him to approve anything, but he loved this."

Just before the album was pressed, at the last minute Jagger changed the title from *Tattoo* to *Tattoo You*, causing Richards to publicly fume, claiming he had never been consulted about this.

"Tops", "Waiting on a Friend", and the glorious "Worried About You" (which echoed elements of Wayne Perkins' "Hand Of Fate") were recorded in late 1972 during the *Goats Head Soup* sessions (and featuring Mick Taylor, not Ronnie Wood, on guitar; Taylor later demanded and received a share of the album's royalties); while the libidinous "Slave", with its elephantine riff, was recorded in 1975 during the *Black and Blue* sessions in Rotterdam. "Hang Fire" (originally recorded as "Lazy Bitch"), "Start Me Up", and "Black Limousine" (languid, funky, cool and sexy, this is possibly their most underrated song of the last thirty years, although it reminded some of Jimmy Reed's "You Don't Have to Go", as well as an old Hop Wilson tune) were originally recorded for *Some Girls*, and "Little T&A" (sung by Keith, this was an ode to his girlfriend Patti Hansen) and "No Use In Crying" came from the *Emotional Rescue* sessions. One reason why "Black Limousine" may have taken so long to be released was Ronnie Wood's insistence on receiving a writing credit. Jagger and Richards have always been loathe to give other band members credit on songs (this was one of the reasons their second guitarist MICK TAYLOR left), and were less than happy about Wood's request. "One of the lessons I had to learn was that if you want to get a credit, it has to happen there and then in the studio as you're recording it," Wood later said. "[Often] I didn't go about it professionally enough to get a credit, so I let it go." "Neighbours" (skinny tie "new wave" Rolling Stones) and the ethereal "Heaven" were the only new recordings. (Note: it was once said of Keith that when he sings, deaf people refuse to watch his lips move, but I've always been a fan.)

"On most albums there's one duff track," said IAN STEWART, the band's unofficial sixth member, in 1981, "but on *Tattoo You* they're all good."

"Start Me Up" had the sort of riff that, when you first hear it, will wake you up in the morning, competing with your heartbeat. It was released in August 1981, and was so infectious it reached the Top Ten on both sides of the Atlantic, helping carry *Tattoo You* to Number One for nine weeks in the States; the album was certified quadruple platinum in the US alone. The song had originally been rehearsed during the *Black And Blue* sessions as a reggae song called "Never Stop" (there were "forty or fifty" takes according to Richards), but was completely overhauled for its single release, a raunch-by-rote construction that would eventually become their most famous song (it was licensed by Apple for the launch of Windows '95). The infectious "thump" to the song was achieved using mixer BOB CLEARMOUNTAIN's famed "bathroom reverb," a process involving the recording of some of the song's vocal and drum tracks with a miked speaker in the bathroom of the Power Station recording studio in New York.

And when Jagger started dancing to the song on stage, you could still see the vestiges of the innate irreverence that made him famous in the first place. As the *Guardian* writer RICHARD WILLIAMS once observed, "Where PAUL MCCARTNEY grinned, shook his head and went 'Wooooo!', MICK JAGGER did a sinuous lithe Nureyev-goes-to-Harlem dance and shook his quadruple maracas like voodoo implements, a portrait of self-absorption." Oh, yes, please. The ten-week, twenty-eight-city tour grossed twenty-five million pounds, at the time it was the highest-grossing tour in history. It was said that the 1981 tour divided America into two camps: the two million people who saw one of their forty-six concerts and the two hundred and twenty-four million who wished they had. Whenever I think of Jagger I think of the brilliant quote of JESSICA MITFORD's: "I don't think I could ever take myself seriously enough to go grubbing about looking for my soul – that is, I couldn't get interested in it, hence religion, psychiatry, consciousness-raising and the like are all totally beyond my ken." JOHN LAHR once said that, "Style, it seems to me, is metabolism. If you can find the pulse of the artist, you can find the pulse of the art." With Jagger, the pulse had for some time been about little but showing off, which was why *Tattoo You* was a perfect Rolling Stones record: it was *all* about showing off.

It used to be said that a theatre director was someone who was engaged by the management to conceal the fact that his players cannot act (this was once attributed by newspaper legend HAROLD EVANS to the *Sunday Times* critic JAMES AGATE), and the history of popular music is full of record producers who have spent their careers turning chicken shit into chicken soup, making rose gardens using little but compost. With the songs on *Tattoo You*, all Clearmountain had to do was equalise everything so that it all sounded as though it were recorded for the same purpose. These days you could probably do it yourself on a Mac, but in 1980 this was a painstaking, if somewhat prosaic, job.

"The quality of the production was done in the mix," says Jagger. "You mix it brighter with more EQ and much more drum kick and a high-range on the high-hat. Then you screw around with the bass until it really tightens up."

A lot of the band's late Sixties, early Seventies work was quite baroque – grandiose in design and opulent in execution. But by the late Seventies, the work had become less versatile, less ambitious, and rather more straightforward. There was a corporate gloss to *Tattoo You* that was largely the result of Clearmountain's production sheen.

It was the Power Station where final touches were added to "Start Me Up", including Jagger's switch of the main lyrics from "Start It Up" to "Start Me Up". Richards fretted that the riff was just "Brown Sugar" in reverse yet it soon became a, if not *the*, signature Stones riff – a sticky, handclap-fuelled romp. And if anyone needed any empirical evidence, all they had to do was listen to CHARLIE WATTS' pedestrian and predictably inaccurate drumming (I've always lived by the maxim that, like Ringo, the better Watts's stick-work, the worse the record).

"Start Me Up" was recorded at the Pathé Marconi studio – Paris's Abbey Road – in December 1977, the same day they laid down the rhythm track for "Miss You" (proving to be one of the most profitable days in their entire career). At the time it was little more than a typical KEITH RICHARDS' ad-libbed riff with a reggae pulse, and there are innumerable "an-ting" takes languishing in the vaults

"It came together very quickly," said Jagger. They considered pursuing the song for *Some Girls*, but when Richards listened to the playback, as well as worrying that it was just a new version of "Brown Sugar", he thought it sounded too similar to something he'd heard on the radio – possibly JAY FERGUSON's "Thunder Island", a hit by the ex-Jo Jo GUNNE and SPIRIT guitarist whose same stop-start riff was in the charts at the time. And so CHRIS KIMSEY, the engineer, was told to dump it. Luckily Kimsey didn't wipe the tape, and the band took another stab at it during the 1979 sessions for *Emotional Rescue*, although again it was consigned to the shelf. Two years later they tried again.

"[The song] was just buried in there," said Jagger. "Nobody remembered cutting it… it was like a gift."

For the lyrics, Jagger used a glove compartment full of car metaphors ("My hands are greasy, she's a mean, mean machine", etc), while the line about the woman being able to make a dead man "cum" no doubt originated from LUCILLE

R

BOGAN's old blues number, "Shave 'em Dry" ("I got something between my legs can make a dead man come"), which Richards had been listening to for years.

"I never realised how loud he could sing," said Clearmountain at the time, marvelling at Jagger's raucous vocal. Still, he rendered everything box-fresh.

"The story here is the miracle that we ever found that track," said Richards. "I was convinced – and I think Mick was – that it was definitely a reggae song. And we did it in thirty-eight takes – 'Start me up. Yeah, man, cool. You know, Jah Rastafari.' And it didn't make it. And somewhere in the middle of a break, just to break the tension, Charlie and I hit the rock and roll version. And right after that we went straight back to reggae. And we forgot totally about this one little burst in the middle, until about five years later when somebody sifted all the way through these reggae takes. And he found that one in the middle. It was just buried in there. Suddenly I had it. Nobody remembered cutting it. But we leapt on it again. We did a few overdubs on it, and it was like a gift, you know? One of the great luxuries of the Stones is we have an enormous, great big can of stuff. I mean what anybody hears is just the tip of an iceberg, you know. And down there are vaults of stuff. But you have to have the patience and the time to actually sift through it."

In *Life*, Richards' extraordinary memoir, released at the end of 2010, he explained at length how he mastered the open G tuning on his guitar (removing the lowest string on his Telecaster), a technique he has used for dozens of classic Stones' riffs, including "Start Me Up".

"IAN STEWART [the Stones' unofficial sixth member] used to refer to us affectionately as "my little three chord wonders". But it is an honourable title. OK, this song has got three chords, right? What can you do with those three chords? Tell this to JOHN LEE HOOKER; most of his songs are on one chord. HOWLIN' WOLF stuff, one chord, and BO DIDDLEY. It was listening to them that made me realise that silence was the canvas. Filling it all in and speeding about all over the place was certainly not my game and it wasn't what I enjoyed listening to. With five strings you can be sparse; that's your frame, that's what you work on. 'Start Me Up', 'Can't You Hear Me Knocking', 'Honky Tonk Women', all leave those gaps between the chords... If it's Mick's song to start with, I won't start it off with five-string. I'll start on a regular tuning and just learn it or feel my way around it, classico style. And then if Charlie ups the rhythm a little bit or gives it a different feel, I'll say let me put this to five-string for a moment and just see how that alters the structure of the thing. Obviously doing that simplifies the sound, in that you're limiting yourself to a set thing. But if you find the right one, like 'Start Me Up', it creates the song. I've heard millions of bands try and play 'Start me Up' with regular tuning. It just won't work, pal."

"Start Me Up" is the first record that BORIS JOHNSTON bought, at the age of seventeen, and was the record that used to get ELTON JOHN up in the morning, when he was living temporarily in Paris in the early Eighties. It is a favourite with celebrities, with royalty, and with those whose musical appreciation rarely extends beyond what they once consumed as teenagers. It is also the record that *GQ* Contributing Editor PIERS MORGAN used to play every morning before he went off to edit the *News of the World*. "After I played it I was ready for another day in the war zone," said Morgan on *Desert Island Discs* last year.

The song has become a staple at sporting events, especially in the US, and is usually played before the start of a game, in the way that QUEEN's "We Are The Champions" still is over here. Ford used the song in 2003 as part of a campaign to reintroduce their cars to the American public, although eight years before this it was famously used by Microsoft for the launch of their Windows '95 campaign.

"We were struggling to find an ad campaign that worked," said BRAD CHASE, then a Microsoft executive. "The agency WK [Wieden+Kennedy] was well briefed, had a good understanding of our goals, was working hard and had a lot

R of creative ideas but we kept asking them to go back and try again as they just were not hitting the bulls eye. I am sure we were hard clients. Finally they presented the idea of a campaign based on 'Start Me Up'. I loved the idea, but then WK told me they had been unsuccessful negotiating the rights for the song so the campaign was a non-starter. The Stones wanted us to pay $10m to sponsor their next concert tour and then they would consider the rights to the song. WK knew we would not do that. That created a pretty big debate, as I wanted to know why they would present an idea if it wasn't possible to do. They told me the reason they pitched it was to see if I could negotiate with them myself – they figured we had nothing to lose."

When they finally reached a deal, the band sent Microsoft a live version of the song. According to Chase, he found out later that "the reason they gave us the live version was that it was recorded after Bill WYMAN had left the band. Giving us the original meant that Wyman got his allocation of the deal which of course meant that giving us the original version of 'Start Me Up' meant that Jagger, Richards and the rest of the band got less." Chase also maintains that the band was paid a lot less than $10 million.

"We may think of them as a rock band but they are really like a corporation, with Mick the CEO and Keith the president, whose product happens to be rock music," says BRAD SILVERBERG, another Microsoft exec who was involved in the deal. "Mick didn't want to do any licensing of songs as he felt it hurt their artistic purity. But it was at a time when their popularity had declined and so they were open to aligning themselves with new and exciting stuff. Plus, Keith did want to license. Apparently his burn rate was higher than Mick's, and he wanted the money. Keith pushed Mick hard and finally prevailed on Mick, who wanted to help Keith out. They agreed to license it to us and after long, painful negotiations, we reached terms."

Rather endearingly, the song still has the power to shock. During their half-time performance at Superbowl XL, Jagger was censored twice: once when he sang the word "cocks" in "Rough Justice", and once when he sang "cum" in "Start Me Up". Two years previously Janet Jackson had stunned the press by baring her right breast at the end of a less than remarkable duet with Justin Timberlake at the same event, so the organisers were taking no chances this time. When Jagger said the offending words, the microphone was simply turned down.

Jagger has always been keen to point out that the songs on *Tattoo You* are not rejects, but simply songs that just didn't fit on previous albums. "We tried to use them before but they didn't seem to work. They're good songs though. But you know every album has a lot of oldies on it, and has done for *years*. We've used, like, 'Sweet Virginia' which was on *Exile On Main Street*. That was recorded from before *Beggars Banquet*." In fact you wonder why the band don't do this now, simply cobble together a collection of outtakes every eighteen months or so, or whenever they're about to go on tour. They could simply give the CDs names such as *Rolling Stones 2010, Rolling Stones 2012*, ad nauseum.

Anyway, *Tattoo You* is there to be rediscovered, because if you like the Stones, then this is probably the last great record they made, probably the last great record they will make, and it deserves to be cherished.

Searching the internet late one night for reviews of the album, I came across a blog site full of comments about the album: many of which were full of praise – "This is an excellent buy for any age group to slam on at a party to get everyone rockin', or quietly sit back in a dim light with a joint and a bourbon on the rocks, and let the evening drift away!!!"; many of which were just statements of fact – "*Tattoo You* is a rather good album. It sort of 'Starts Me Up' and tries to bring me to 'Heaven'. The album is very lively and energetic, it kind of rocks" ; while an equal amount were fairly disparaging. To wit: "I took *Tattoo You* to my friend Brubaker's house because we were all gonna drink and watch the movie *Neighbors* with DAN AYKROYD and JOHN BELUSHI," wrote one

R

SHAWN KILROY. "They both came out at the same time and I associate them. *Tattoo You* is the last great Stones album as much as *Neighbors* is the last great Aykroyd/Belushi movie. My plan was to put the song 'Neighbours' on as soon as [the] credits [rolled], however, when I got up to get it, seems that Bru and another guy called Red Burns had put my LP in the oven and melted it into a shrinky dink. I was horrified and asked them why they would do such a thing. "Don't you love the Stones?" I shrieked? Bru said, "Yeah, but not that disco bullshit.""

Kilroy's passion was undiminished: "It's still my favourite Stones album," he wrote. He's not alone, and there isn't a disco song in sight.

MARK RONSON

An attractive Manhattan socialite, hip-hop aficionado, whiz-kid producer, and all-round cocktail-hour renaissance guy, Ronson had his fingers in all the pots of Noughties pop. He produced everything from ADELE's *19* (tick), to ROBBIE WILLIAMS' *Rudebox* (run for the hills, and hang your head in shame, young Ronson), via NAS, LILY ALLEN, CHRISTINA AGUILERA, ESTELLE, and the KAISER CHIEFS. Elicits jealousy among critics, who find him too talented and too connected. The nimbus of black hair accentuates his features, giving him the appearance of a cartoon character imagined by an illustrator trying to blend PEE WEE HERMAN with TINTIN. He is also blessed with an oddly individual mid-Atlantic accent, making him perhaps seem even more like some mid-Sixties keen-to-travel archetype.

In 2007 he released an unorthodox version of the Smiths' "Stop Me If You Think You've Heard This One Before", before going on to produce his album, *Version*, the same year. In 2007 he also produced most of AMY WINEHOUSE's *Back To Black*, for which he deservedly won three Grammys. His 2010 album, *Record Collection*, made with THE BUSINESS INTERNATIONAL, was a fairly extraordinary demonstration of Ronson's eclectic tastes – it cleverly weaved together all manner of pop styles, from traditional Fifties ballads to Eighties electro-pop via Nineties hip-hop and Seventies power pop. Every track is a small gem, and the album is as varied and as much fun as FLEETWOOD MAC's *Rumours,* or (even) CULTURE CLUB's *Colour By Numbers* (there were even contributions from BOY GEORGE and SIMON LEBON). If DE LA SOUL had been white, they might have sounded a little like this (favourite couplet: "I drive round cities in a chariot, I get preferential treatment at the Marriott"). DURAN DURAN were so flattered by Ronson's attention, they asked him to produce their 2010 album, *All You Need Is Now.* Ronson described it as the true successor to their 1982 album, *Rio.*

DIANA ROSS

If you were to complete a taxonomy of Diana Ross records, it would include most popular dance styles of the Sixties, Seventies, and Eighties, as she battled to stay popular. The "CHIC" records of the early Eighties were definitive in their own way, as were the dozens – some enormously sultry – she made in the Seventies, yet it will always be the Motown records of the Sixties that will define her, the little aspirational epiphanies that made the world dance (or at the very least, shuffle). Like a lot of mid-period Motown, the SUPREMES' music has lost some of its bite and sense of provenance due to its ubiquity in the advertising industry, yet there aren't many hotel lobbies that don't experience a sudden frisson as soon as "Stop In The Name Of Love" starts to do what it does best.

ROUGH TRADE

Before Rough Trade, most record shops in Britain were fairly anodyne places. In the Fifties you bought records at the back

R

of electrical shops, after you had made your way through acres of fridges and cookers, washing machines, vacuum cleaners, and televisions. But by the Seventies you bought them in places likes Our Price, which were basically just small supermarkets. Rough Trade changed the way record shops operated completely.

The first shop was opened in Kensington Park Road, near London's Portobello Road, in 1976, by GEOFF TRAVIS, a twenty-four-year-old Londoner with an obsessive vinyl habit who had just been in America amassing a huge record collection. He said he started the shop here because it was close to Powis Square, which was featured in one of his favourite films, NIC ROEG's *Performance*. And it was hugely influential. Rough Trade was where you went for anything independent, whether it was pub-rock, punk, or difficult-to-find singles from the likes of the MC5 or the STOOGES. Rough Trade was where you went for limited edition releases, for imports, samplers, record company promos, and gossip. If you were looking for something obscure, wanted to find something obscure, this was where you went. In 1978 the shop spawned Rough Trade Records, which would go on to sign the SMITHS, the LIBERTINES, the RAINCOATS, the YOUNG MARBLE GIANTS, and SCRITTI POLITTI. Rough Trade is one of those iconic labels that helped kick-start the post-punk era, a label that touched everyone from the FALL, PERE UBU, and STIFF LITTLE FINGERS, to CABARET VOLTAIRE, and JARVIS COCKER. The brand was so successful that at various times it had stores in Paris, Tokyo, and San Francisco (where NIRVANA played a gig in 1990).

NEIL TAYLOR's fascinating *Document and Eyewitness: An Intimate History of Rough Trade* is a lovingly compiled oral history, and he describes a landscape composed of the fragments of the fading London underground, the emerging international punk scene, the nascent fanzine culture, and a couple of nerdy music freaks who wanted to create the musical equivalent of San Francisco's City Lights. It is an essential purchase for anyone who was involved in, or influenced by, the punk maelstrom of 1976, a riveting evocation of a period in musical history that becomes more important the further we get away from it. 1976 might not have been year zero – far from it, in fact – yet it was the year that formed the basis of the thirty-five years of pop culture that was to come after it. There are some great vignettes here, including a recollection from cartoonist SAVAGE PENCIL, who used to write the "Rock'n' Roll Zoo" column for *Sounds,* one of the old music weeklies. He once put together a template for a fanzine based on the RAMONES, called Pinhead. Its genius? Well, it was going to have no dialogue and no narrative.

The book triggers many memories, including a couple of frequently forgotten ROBERT WYATT singles that Rough Trade released in 1980: 1) A haunting version of the CHIC ballad, "At Last I Am Free"; 2) "Caimanera", a post-revolution reworking of "Guantanamera" (the song concerned the US airbases at Guantanamo, which few outside Cuba knew about at the time).

BIC RUNGA

I first heard "Get Some Sleep" by Bic Runga sitting by the pool in the mid-century splendour of The Parker in Palm Springs. Originally opened as the first Holiday Inn in California in 1959, it was refurbed in 2004, overhauled by the gonzo-retro designer JONATHAN ADLER. This is where the recently coupled Los Angelenos come to party, and by noon on a Saturday the adult pool is full of the tanned and the beautiful, the lemonade stand surrounded by a delicate tableau of flesh and silicone. It's the kind of place that ought to sell stick-on tattoos, as you can feel naked without one. Strangely they don't look as awful as they might do on a Spanish beach, but then that's largely because no one by the pool is a Brit. Bic Runga fit right in: mellifluous vocals, low-level kidney-shaped production, and the kind of tune that moved across the water like a blow-up dolphin.

S

SADE

As a metaphor for the Eighties, the CD is as good as any other. Like MADONNA, the Filofax, MTV, privatisation, shoulder pads, or TERRY FARRELL's dreadful post-modern architecture (ladies and gentlemen I give you the TV-am building in Camden Town and the MI6 headquarters in Vauxhall), the CD is the defining symbol of the age, an age where presentation wasn't just paramount, it was everything. The compact disc compartmentalised its contents; cleaned it up, washed behind its ears, and then dressed it up for the market; it digitally improved it, shrunk it and then enshrined it in a transparent, pocket-sized jewel case.

Yes, the CD occasionally had a rather large and unnecessary photograph of MICK HUCKNALL on it, but let's face it, no decade's ever perfect.

Like the designer decade it would soon become synonymous with, the CD was an emblem of burnished success – a smarter, more upmarket version of all that had gone before it. The CD was a designer accessory like no other, and heralded an era where music became codified. Almost overnight, music became a lifestyle accessory, a muted background fizz to be played at designer dinner parties in designer lofts in designer postcodes. "CD music" became pejorative, as did the likes of SADE, ANITA BAKER, and LUTHER VANDROSS. Critics – the sweaty guys at the back with the bad teeth, the bad shoes and more opinions than they would ever have money – said that this was just music with the edges rubbed off, with the soul extracted. "Sade?" they said, almost as one. "Those guys are so boring their dreams have Muzak. And barely audible Muzak, at that." Aspirational in essence, if you didn't have the wherewithal to surround yourself with the occupational hazards of yuppiedom, then a few CDs left casually on the sub-MATTHEW HILTON coffee table would suffice.

What the critics didn't understand was that the Eighties generation wanted designer dreams just as much as their

S predecessors did – and what the market wants, the market tends to get. Or at least it did in the Eighties. Which is probably why Sade became one of the biggest bands of the decade, "designer" or not.

People weren't kind about them in the early days, but then most of the criticism came from those critics – yes, them again – who were championing the likes of the BIRTHDAY PARTY, "THE THE", and German avante-garde nonsense like EINSTÜRZENDE NEUBAUTEN. Elsewhere the band – and Sade was always a band, never just a gorgeous Nigerian-born singer called HELEN FOLASADE ADU – were welcomed with open arms, cutting through class, culture, age, race, and sex, while their first album (sorry, CD), *Diamond Life* (you remember: "Smooth Operator", "Your Love Is King", "Hang On To Your Love", "Why Can't We Live Together", etc), sold six million copies in the UK, and in the region of seventeen million in the US. Which, as ROBERT DeNIRO says at the end of *Midnight Run*, is a very respectable neighbourhood. One of the reasons they were so successful was because they slotted nicely into "Quiet Storm" programming, the sexy, late-night radio format featuring soulful slow jams, smooth R&B, and misty-eyed soul, pioneered in the mid-Seventies by DJ MELVIN LINDSEY at WHUR-FM, in Washington, D.C. Like NEIL DIAMOND knock-off ANDY KIM, Sade rocked, but gently.

The brilliant thing about the band was their almost total ambivalence towards success, and no sooner had they conquered the world, than they would run back home again (to London, Cheltenham, New York, or the Caribbean), only to emerge, sleepy-eyed, three or four years later when it was time for another record. They were seeking fame without the attention, and BOY GEORGE (sorry), they got it. In spades. And every other suit. In their twenty-six year career they have only released six studio LPs, and only three in the last twenty years. Their most recent, *Soldier Of Love*, was released on Valentine's Day 2010, and – sit down, all you lovers of EINSTÜRZENDE NEUBAUTEN – was as good as anything they'd ever done. Songs such "The Moon And The Sky", "In Another Time", and the title track make you want to slip away from work early, climb into a ridiculously expensive sports car and drive all the way to the south of France, hood down, stereo up all the way – only stopping to briefly sleep with an Italian princess at the Crillon in Paris on the way. Of course, the other brilliant thing about Sade is the fact that they really do sound good anywhere, and because of the mellifluous beats and insidious melodies, the songs sound just as good in your living room as they do in a lovingly preserved Ferrari Dino 246. There are some who will always be embarrassed about enjoying a Sade record, and there we are...

Robert Sandall

The writer, rock journalist, broadcaster, and wine expert, Robert Sandall, died on Tuesday morning, July 20, 2010, aged just fifty-eight, after a protracted battle with cancer. For many years he was the rock critic of the *Sunday Times*, and then wrote more generally for the Culture section, where he flourished until the very end of his life. He also wrote a wine column and features for *GQ*.

This is part of the eulogy I gave at his memorial service:

Where was God? Not a religious or metaphysical question, but rather a more prosaic one. Where the hell was God when you needed him? We hadn't seen him for over half an hour, and we needed guidance on what wine we should order for dessert.

Where was God? Well, God was actually over by the bar, ordering an above average claret while discussing the possibility of Ugandan affairs. This was a long time ago, back when we were all footloose and fancy free. When we would roam the pubs and clubs of central London without a care in the world.

S God was what we called Robert. I can't remember who came up with it, or when, or indeed where. But it was what we called him. Why? Because he was tall, good looking, smart, cultured, well-dressed (sometimes), and just generally rather wonderful. One drunken night we all agreed that if God had had a modern-day, living, breathing manifestation, then he would have looked exactly like Robert.

And so Robert became God.

God could write, too. In fact it was what God did best. I commissioned God both at the *Sunday Times* and at *GQ*, and I never had to worry about the brief. Robert was one of those rare writers who only had to be told once what was needed. Robert didn't need to be coaxed or cajoled or sent endless briefing notes. Yes, he might require a rather protracted and liquid lunch to discuss the matter, but after about four o'clock that day, you never needed to have any more contact. You discussed the idea, you gave him a deadline and a word-count, and he went away and did it.

He would always call you up after he'd interviewed someone to say that they had made some terrible faux pas, or had been terribly indiscreet, or had insisted on conducting the interview underwater, or at the top of the Empire State Building, but he never bothered you with nuance. Because to Robert nuance came naturally. It's what he did. In fact he could often conjure nuance out of thin air, especially when he had been to interrogate someone who was incapable of being interrogated, usually because they were too stupid, or just plain dull.

Simply put, Robert delivered. Time and time again.

He didn't need his hand holding, either. Whenever I asked him to do something, he would immediately come back with some theory or other about the subject of the piece – and Robert's favourite expression was "I have a theory about this" – that gave you the impression that he had been thinking about them at just that very moment. And that if you hadn't called him to commission the story then he would have called you to suggest it himself.

God was the consummate professional. A man who took his job far more seriously than most of his peers, a man who really cared if the latest R.E.M. record was as good as the last one. Who really cared if the production technique on the latest Lou Reed record warranted all the attention it was getting.

But Robert's death has proved that he wasn't quite all he was cracked up to be. Because Robert's death has put me at a terrible inconvenience, as I have to now find someone else to write about wine, and music, and politics, and science, and all the other things that Robert could write about at the drop of a hat.

Jon Savage

For two weeks in the spring of 2009 I trained myself to wake up early in order to plough through *The England's Dreaming Tapes* by Jon Savage, "interviews, outtakes and extras – the essential companion to *'England's Dreaming'*, the seminal history of punk". I woke up one morning at 5.45, to spend an hour with Chapter Four, which starts with an interview with Roger Armstrong, who was the manager of the Rock On stall in Soho market back in the mid-Seventies. Along with Ted Carrol's parent shop in Camden, this was a major catalyst in the revival of roots rock. Many punk bands bought their records there – "holy relics of mania on seven-inch vinyl". With Carrol, he also formed Chiswick Records, who released records by the Count Bishops, Johnny Moped, and the 101ers.

Savage's book has it all, in almost infinite detail. As a social history of London (and, in its way, Manchester, and New York) in the mid-to-late Seventies, Savage's original book is beyond compare, and though I'm a huge fan of his writing, sometimes the sociological contextualisation blurred what actually happened. So without wishing to disparage his original book – which is remarkably over twenty years old

S – *The England's Dreaming Tapes* are so gripping because they are simply transcripts of all the interviews that Savage undertook as research for that book; and so you see the history of punk unfolding before your eyes, an oral history of one of the most important periods in modern 20th Century music.

The book effortlessly builds a picture of London life in the Seventies, a time that was rather grey politically, and certainly socio-economically, a time when a generation of outsiders, oddballs and pop-cultural refugees were all searching for "the next big thing". It was also a relatively unmediated time, and as you read about the very genuine media furore caused by punk, as you listen to how the principals at the time were all intimidated by the press coverage (including MALCOLM MCLAREN, the so-called media manipulator), you remember what a totally different country we were then. Savage's book also shows that as well as being a good writer, he is also a very, very good listener.

Everyone is here – all the bands, protagonists, club-runners, journalists, shopkeepers, photographers, etc – and it is an absolute joy.

MIKE SCOTT

In case anyone was in any doubt, magazine cover-mounted gifts have always been subject to the law of diminishing returns. I have rather a lot of previous in this area, and in my time have stuck CDs, videos, DVDs, books, memory sticks, posters, leather wallets, even sunglasses on the covers of the various magazines I've worked for, and I've never known how effective they've been. Not only do many readers take free gifts for granted – is there any monthly music magazine that doesn't offer a free cover-mounted CD as a matter of course? – but as so many magazines offer them these days, they have long since ceased to be special. (Giving me a free memory stick? Can't I have a man-bag instead?)

Having said that, when I picked up a copy of *The Believer's* 2009 Music Special in a bookstore in San Francisco's Pacific Heights, I didn't realise it included a free CD. I eventually pumped it into the car stereo, but, having been let down dozens of times before, my expectations were understandably low. As it was, the CD wasn't too bad, with various songs destined to end up on my iPod (including those by BETH SORRENTINO and DAVID SYLVIAN).

One song, though, crept up on me – possibly because it runs to over ten minutes. "A Wild Holy Band" by former WATERBOYS frontman Mike Scott is a strange beast: minimally, almost sparcely produced, lyrically it is encumbered by cliché after cliché and sounds a little like an homage to any number of mid-Seventies epics (BOB DYLAN's "Idiot Wind", AL STEWART's "The Year Of The Cat", or ROY HARPER's "When An Old Cricketer Leaves The Crease"). And yet, and yet, somehow it works. Haunting, deceptive, and engagingly pretentious, this is an unapologetic road song that almost wills you to dislike it.

"I wrote this song in my bedroom in Scotland at six in the morning, just up, in a songwriting mood, trawling through old notebooks and journals from the late Nineties, looking for any ideas that might be lying there forgotten," said Scott. "To my surprise, I found the entire first verse intact on the page of a journal. I must have written it some years before, and had only the dimmest memory of it. The verse suggested more words, a lyrical theme, and in my head I heard a tune. The song followed." A song that sounds like someone wrote it forty years ago.

GIL SCOTT-HERON

"The Revolution Will Not Be Televised" is still probably Gil Scott-Heron's most famous song, a roughly-cut slice of stinging social commentary that very quickly entered the

S vernacular of black agit-prop: "You will not be able to stay home, brother. You will not be able to plug in, turn on and cop out. You will not be able to lose yourself on skag and skip out for beer during commercials, because the revolution will not be televised." In 2010 the song was listed as one of the top twenty political songs of all time by the *New Statesman*.

This was 1970, and is now recognised as the moment that kick-started rap, a genre which now dominates so much of the musical landscape. Heron's raps were fundamentally influential in the way in which rapping would develop in the late Seventies – not just in terms of its style, but also in terms of its politically-charged nature. Heron was traditionally more lyrical, more verbose, yet his topics were the bedrock of the style: black US radicalism, racism, political corruption (both micro and macro), alcoholism, and drug dependency. Scott-Heron was "one of the foundations that rappers could form themselves off of," said Chuck D, the former member of Public Enemy, one of the most militant rap groups of the Eighties. "I think a lot of it happened with the word, the meaning, the definition, the redefinition of the words he used. But also the pacing. Mr Heron delivered his words with a feeling and with a rhythm that was something that was a great basis for rap, a great fundamental start for rap to trigger itself off." Heron himself called his stuff "storm music" or "survival kits on wax".

To many, Heron was Curtis Mayfield, Malcolm X, and James Brown rolled into one, a radical campaigner, compelling poet, accomplished musician and professional nuisance.

The second half of his life was one in which his career imploded (he released only two albums in twenty years), and while he was prescient in his warnings about substance abuse, was unable to resist the temptations himself; he became a professional cocaine addict, wasting hundreds of thousands of dollars a year on his habit.

Shortly before his death in 2011, at the age of sixty-two, there was an extraordinary profile of Heron in the *New Yorker*. He was living in diminished circumstances in a ground-floor apartment in Harlem which he rarely left, and appeared to spend most of his time smoking crack. Without any gatekeepers to speak of, Heron allowed the writer an unusually generous amount of access. It was a terribly sad piece, one that accurately chronicled Heron's ignominious and somewhat tragic decline. When the writer – ALEC WILKINSON – phoned to leave him a message once, Heron answered by saying, "I'm here. Where else would a caveman be but in his cave?" Classic songs include "The Bottle", "Winter In America", and "Johannesburg".

SHABAZZ PALACES

"Facilitates nodding..." (Try "Black Up".)

GEORGE SHEARING

Many entertainers embellish their impoverished upbringing in order to heighten the drama of their success; with Shearing it was real. He was born on August 13, 1919, the youngest son of nine children fathered by a Battersea coalman, and went on to write "Lullaby Of Birdland" ("Not *the* COLE PORTER," Shearing would joke, "but *a* coal porter"). Blind from birth (he thought it was the result of a botched abortion), he enjoyed picking out songs from the radio on the family upright piano, and soon started having lessons at the Linden Lodge School For The Blind, in Wandsworth. He found sponsorship, went to America, and found success quickly. He deciphered be-bop for the general public without anaesthetising it, and people loved him for it. His music was criticised for being "bland and uninsistent in timbre", although that was the very core of its appeal. His party piece was playing the slow movement of BEETHOVEN's *Moonlight Sonata* and slowly allowing his right hand to stray into COLE PORTER's "Night And Day", until two became one.

S

JUDEE SILL

She called her music "country-cult-baroque", which considering she made it, she is perfectly entitled to. She had a rather pure prairie-style folk voice, a fondness for Bach-like melodies, and the sort of winsome librarian looks that could have easily cast her as a JONI MITCHELL wannabe. Judee Sill was never going to be a JONI MITCHELL wannabe.

The first artist to release an album on DAVID GEFFEN's Asylum label back in 1971, she wrote "Lady-O" for the TURTLES, "Jesus Was A Crossmaker" for the HOLLIES, and rather stupidly died in 1979 from a drug overdose. "I did heroin with gusto because I wanted to escape my torment and misery," she told *Rolling Stone* in 1972. "But then I figured if could maintain that kind of habit that long, the willpower I'd need to kick it would be a cinch." She was wrong. A substance abuser from an early age – both parents and her step-father had been heavy drinkers – she resorted to crime in her teenage years, and after developing a penchant for armed robbery (she carried a .38 and held up gas stations and drug stores), spent nine months in a state reform school in Ventura, California. On release, she got even more heavily into drugs, and, eventually, prostitution. "As a hooker, my heart wasn't in it... all I really cared about was getting that needle in my vein, squeezing off."

Not that you'd immediately know this from listening to her records. While her lyrics could only have been written in the late Seventies (where laborious introspection was something of a default option for any fledgling singer-songwriter), her melodies and arrangements sound like sophisticated alternatives to the sort of material being developed by RICHARD CARPENTER. And that's not a criticism. An exponent of "the Laurel Canyon sound", her music sounds as vital now as it probably did back then. It's consistently surprising, too, and unlike much of the material made by her Los Angeles contemporaries – CAROLE KING, JACKSON BROWNE, etc – hasn't been diminished by heavy, constant rotation.

Her best song, "The Kiss", from her second album *Heart Food*, is worthy of mid-period BRIAN WILSON, and dovetails perfectly with the BEACH BOYS' *Surf's Up*. Catch it now on YouTube, performed by Sill on *The Old Grey Whistle Test* (and where you can also find her signing a heartbreaking version of PAUL MCCARTNEY'S "Blackbird").

S

PAUL SIMON

At the turn of the century, JK GALBRAITH began lamenting the fact that old age had brought a rather annoying affliction. "Still Syndrome", he called it, a pejorative term for the way in which people would ask him if he were "still writing", "still interested in politics", or "still healthy". As he was in his dotage, so it was assumed that his interest was diminishing in everything that had once made him powerful.

It's the same with the likes of Paul Simon, formerly iconic musicians who have, for the last twenty-odd years (maybe more, in some people's cases), somehow slipped off most people's radar. Simon is "still" the brains and the nimble fingers behind "Bridge Over Troubled Water", "Mrs Robinson", "The Boxer", and all those other legendary Simon and Garfunkel hits, still the man who wiped ART GARFUNKEL'S vocals off *Think Too Much*, the Simon and Garfunkel reunion album that never was (it was released as a Simon solo record, *Hearts and Bones*, in 1983), still the man who lost a fortune putting on *The Capeman*, his Broadway musical, in 1998 (it initially ran for only sixty-eight performances); but he's also "still" a practicing musician, "still" someone who takes the actual process of writing and recording songs incredibly seriously. On March 1, 2007, Simon made headlines again when he was announced as the first recipient of the recently created Gershwin Prize for Popular Song. The Prize, created by the Library of Congress, was awarded to Simon during a Concert Gala featuring his music at the Warner Theatre in Washington, D.C., on the evening of May 23.

S A year earlier, I saw him perform in London, at the Bloomsbury Theatre, at a gig sponsored by Radio 2, the home of the seat belt, airbag, sat-nav rock fan (and that's a compliment, by the way). He was involved in a bout of dignified self-promotion, having just released a new CD, interfered with by BRIAN ENO, *Surprise* (which contained one of his most beautiful songs, "Father and Daughter", the theme song for the animated children's film, *The Wild Thornberrys Movie*, written in 2002 and nominated for an Academy Award for Best Song a year later). The audience was identical to the audience at a BOB DYLAN gig I'd seen a few months before, and the only male heads that weren't bald were covered with DONOVAN-like peaked caps, toupees or perfectly tilted yarmulkes. At Paul Simon concerts, the only people with hair are women.

I felt as though I were in church, as the audience was eager to suggest it was totally on his side, totally prepared to allow itself to be cosseted and charmed. Simon's voice was unable to disguise its scat doo-wop origins, his new songs solely dedicated to the art of amplifying "quiet".

Like many celebrities who have been around for a while, who have suffered the brickbats as well as the plaudits, Simon is a lot more self-aware than maybe people imagine. Yes, there were hilarious rumours back in the Eighties insinuating that he had a "rug" roadie on tour with him, whose job it was to ferry Simon's collection of wigs from one gig to another. But I don't know of a single journalist who was brave enough to ask him if it were true. Most of the time, however, the eyes are wide open. A while ago, a friend of mine was interviewing him for a music magazine, and made the mistake of mentioning the fact that Simon was, and I quote, "diminutive".

"What do you mean when you say the word 'diminutive'?" asked Simon.

"Well," said my friend, "I just meant that you were, are, er..."

"Short is what you meant, so why don't you say 'short'? I'm not diminutive, I'm short."

Still short, then, and still rather brilliant.

FRANK SINATRA

It's a fair enough assumption to think that everyone's been through a Sinatra phase at some point in their lives, a time when his experiences and his ability to express them has for some reason chimed with our own experiences and our inability to do the same. When we've needed him to, we've asked Sinatra to do the talking for us.

Personally I seem to go through my Sinatra phases fairly regularly, although my most recent phase started a few years ago, because of a present I received from my wife, a Sinatra boxed-set called, simply enough, *Vegas*. The Sinatra/Vegas Venn diagram traditionally throws up the Rat Pack, the singer's hard-drinking gang, co-starring PETER LAWFORD, DEAN MARTIN, SAMMY DAVIS JR., JOEY BISHOP, and SHIRLEY MACLAINE, and usually involves a lot of high jinx, a lot of horsing around and lots of lame gags about boozing. But this boxed-set focuses on Sinatra alone, and it's been an absolute revelation. The recordings are culled from performances at the Sands in 1961 and 1966 (the latter featuring COUNT BASIE & HIS ORCHESTRA, with a young QUINCY JONES conducting), Caesar's Palace in 1982, and the Golden Nugget in 1987 (the DVD features a complete and unreleased concert from May 5, 1978, at Caesar's Palace, one of more than 500 shows he performed there) – over a quarter of a century of saloon bar blues.

Vegas during the Fifties and Sixties was growing as a destination resort while also representing the surface smarts of American post-war prosperity, during a period when Europe was in the doldrums, and Britain in particular was experiencing the fall-out from the break-up of its Empire. Vegas was sexy. Vegas was the future. And Vegas had Sinatra. Here was a man in a tux holding a microphone and a glass of bourbon. And nothing else. His show didn't have pyrotechnics, or dancing girls, or lavish, expensive stage sets. There were no spinning orbs, no back-projection, no banks of neon, and no hoary old stage theatrics. There was a singer and some songs, and an orchestra that could blow your bow-ties off.

S "We're gonna take this here building and move it three feet that way... now!" he says with Count Basie's orchestra behind him. "Hold onto your handbags!"

These days, like a lot of men, I tend to listen to music mainly when I'm driving, and it was in the confines of the company car that I once again fell under Sinatra's spell. Traditionally live albums tend only to be interesting from an anthropological perspective, as snapshots of moments in time, and even the classics – James Brown's *Live At The Apollo*, the MC5's *Kick Out The Jams*, the Who's *Live At Leeds*, Isaac Hayes *Live At The Sahara Tahoe*, Nirvana *Unplugged*, Bob Dylan's 66 Manchester Free Trade Hall gig, and Bob Marley live at the Lyceum – are not exactly great listening experiences, not for very long, anyway. You simply don't play live albums. Well, not more than once anyway. But these Vegas recordings felt intimate, definitive, grand – feelings compounded by hearing them in an enclosed space. When I played them it was like Sinatra was there in the car with me, performing his well-worn songs for me and everyone else in the auditorium... or at least everyone else in the car.

Bill Miller, Sinatra's pianist, said, "Everything changed when Frank signed with the Sands. His career was on an upswing; he was confident, and it showed in his performances. Sometimes he would rehearse the same night another act would close. We would start around 2.30am, after they cleared the Copa Room, and Frank would rehearse the entire show with the band. That way he could choose the line-up of the songs for the show; we would rehearse until he was completely satisfied. When it came to the music, Frank was a perfectionist. Those were great days to be a musician and working in Vegas."

Sinatra has such a singularity that it's sometimes blinding. His voice, his image, the very idea of him, is such a cliché now that its difficult to imagine there's anything to him that we don't already know. The biographies keep coming – Bill Zehme's *The Way You Wear Your Hat*, Anthony Summers and Robbyn Swan's *Sinatra: The Life*, George Jacobs and William Stadiem's *Mr S: My Life With Frank Sinatra*, Will

FRIEDWALD's *Sinatra! The Song Is You,* and SHAWN LEVY's *Rat Pack Confidential* are all worth reading – yet the more we learn the more indelible the image becomes. Listening to him do what he did best – sing, live, in front of an audience – somehow brings out more of him. We know all about the wine and the women and the mob and the moods and the fights and the films and the booze and the broads and Capitol and the comebacks and the yada-yada-yada – but hearing these recordings made me understand more about him than I ever thought I would. And it's all in the voice, all in that uninsurable jewel of a voice, all in the way he interprets the songs, the way in which he reaches into himself to express fairly prosaic sentiments.

It was the first recording – made at the Sands in November 1961 – that struck me the most. Here was a man in his natural habitat, treating the stage as though it were his living room or his terrace, taking a small trip between songs to visit the wet bar, and chew the fat with his band. "Morning folk, it sure is early," he says during his first monologue – the one between "The Moon Was Yellow (And The Night Was Young)" and "You Make Me Feel So Young". "I don't know how you people can stay up till eight or nine in the morning in this town, I just don't understand it at all. We welcome you to the Sands, and hope that you're having a nice evening. Salut... Jeez, I fell off the wagon with a boom-bang last night. I woke up this morning, my hair hurt."

Then, two-thirds of the way through the set, the temperature steps down a notch, and Frank goes all gooey, but only in the way that a man's man can. "You know if you've seen us perform before, if you've seen me perform before, that we try to inject a little touch of this kind of song. It's what we call the saloon song, and I have a great reverence towards the saloon song... I guess I've been singing them in more saloons than any other singer I've ever known in my life. And I've had torches so high I've burned down buildings. Yeah, get that bum outta here!

"This is a song that you wouldn't consider a sad song, normally I mean, because of the way you hear it done – it's

S

usually done in jazz or Stork Club style... But when you hear it this way it really does have a different kind of taste..." And then he starts singing "Just One Of Those Things", and it just breaks your heart.

Immerse yourself in the songs and you hear the interesting way he plays with words, the way he comes down hard on his consonants (pronouncing hard "g"s in "Imagination"), and the way his brooding baritone bends sentences to suit his path. Listening to the boxed-set you hear this trait everywhere. He says "correk" instead of "correct" during a monologue in the 1978 Caesar's Palace show, taking great delight in deliberately screwing up his language. His free-form interpretations came in handy towards the end of his career, disguising the fact he couldn't reach certain notes any more, and his shorthand approach is noticeable on both the later CDs. His speech impediment is more noticeable too. During GEORGE HARRISON's "Something", he sings "a-twacks me like no other lover". The 1978 show is something of a spectacle, as not only do you see Sinatra's ease with an audience, and the way he adlibs seemingly without thought – muttering "Yeah baby" every couple of minutes, like a proto AUSTIN POWERS – but even when he's being harsh, and telling off-colour stories or berating his friends, he's genuinely funny. In a good-natured response to a request from the crowd he says, "Shhhh. When I want you to speak I'll turn the lights on you. No, I don't mean that facetiously, I mean it abruptly." The DVD is also special because towards the end of the show, when he's pointing out friends and acquaintances in the audience, he spies ORSON WELLES and asks him to take a bow. Sinatra and Welles in the same room – what more could a man want?!

The monologue from the Caesar's Palace show is typical: "Thank you ladies and gentleman, and I'd like to say an official good evening to you and welcome you to the palace of the Caesars," he says. "Where there are now thirteen – me! There were twelve before but we chased them out because they couldn't swing. I'd like also to propose a toast to you and wish you all the best in life, for you and your families. And

God bless us all. Cheers." Then Frank takes a sip of his JD. "You have no idea how nice that is," he continues. "To cool the throat [pronounced troat]. That's not a specimen folks, that's Jack Daniel's and soda in case you're curious about the colour of it. I think the guy who poured it had a boxing glove on when he poured the drink in here. Jesus, you could run your car with this mother I think... And I'd like to talk about Caesar's Palace for a minute because it's one of the finest hotels on this side of the street. I don't know about the other side of the street, I rarely cross that, because it's suicide to cross over there. They got some fine saloons in here, they got a lot of action and they got a couple of good restaurants. And then when we close here they're gonna renovate the joint. No they're not, they wouldn't do that. No, Ann Margret comes in and she renovates the place. She comes in and then Old Brown Eye comes in, Sammy comes in for a week. And at the same time Old Red Eyes works across the street at the MGM, and we got all the eyes around here...

"How many more nights we got here?" he asks the band. "It's like doing time." And then to the audience: "Why are you staring at me? I'm having a hell of a time I tell you!" And then it's straight into "Night And Day".

Sinatra always offered unique pleasures, and just when he appeared to be merely filling space, he would rescue everything with a perfectly timed key change or some weird lateral alteration to the melody. Even towards the end of his career – captured on the 1987 CD – when his voice has lost its edge, its character, its indelible ghostly character carries the songs. You can hear Sinatra walking through songs the way MICHAEL CAINE walks through films – not somnambulantly, but as though nothing really could be more natural. Sometimes he can't hit the notes too good, but it's still Sinatra.

After a while I realised that even though it was probably way past midnight, and that most of the boozed-up audience at the Sands had no doubt hoovered up a liquid smorgasbord of Casino-supplied martinis, high balls, vodka gimlets, and Gods-knows-what-else, and that they had probably blown half

S a week's salary on the tables on their way to the show; even though, at the time, Nevada could still be considered as one of the ungodliest places on Earth, these people weren't simply at a concert, weren't nonchalantly applauding some after-dinner supperclub hack, they were at church, their own church, and had come for an audience with their own personal deity.

There are still dozens of boil-in-the-bag supperclub crooners who regularly phone in their performances from whatever lounge bar or reality TV show they happen to find themselves in, but there will only ever be one Sinatra. These days people aren't famous for fifteen minutes, as ANDY WARHOL once said everyone would be, they're famous for fifteen Megs. In fact by the time you've finished this article, there will no doubt be another couple of hundred Zit-list celebrities trying to push their way into the virtual VIP room, elbowing Paris and Nicky and all the rest out of the way. This makes me long for the days when celebrities really were celebrities, when fame was an acknowledgment of talent rather than ubiquity (or access to a webcam).

The idea of a serious Sinatra biopic probably passes the desk of some TOM FORD eyewear-sporting Hollywood executive every couple of weeks, although even in the wake of *Walk The Line* (where JOAQUIN PHOENIX managed to play JOHNNY CASH without resorting to mimicry), the idea still seems fairly ludicrous. So bizarre, it reminds me of what SIMON WINDER writes about the cult of 'M' in his extraordinarily far-reaching JAMES BOND biography, *The Man Who Saved Britain*: "His power and meaning are such that we should think of M in the same manner that a small group of Hindus thought of GANDHI, trying to persuade RICHARD ATTENBOROUGH that for his film GANDHI should be played not by BEN KINGSLEY but by a pure point of light." Because Sinatra's core competency was being himself.

Frank Sinatra was better at being Frank Sinatra than anyone before, since, or ever will be.

In my teens, as I immersed myself in the starburst worlds of DAVID BOWIE and ROXY MUSIC, I came across my parents' copies of Sinatra's *Songs For Swingin' Lovers* and *A Swingin' Affair*, and even at that age I could tell that when The Voice sang "Stars fractured 'bama last night" he was being as irreverent as any glam rock star. "I've Got You Under My Skin" – unnegotiably Sinatra's best-ever performance – and "It Happened In Monterey" (the sort of glamorous travelogue that really kicks in with an adolescent) convinced me that Sinatra was the coolest man to ever walk the earth.

Frank Sinatra was a Leviathan. He only lived once, and the way he lived it, once was enough. Booze, broads, bespoke suits – in Frank's world there was always a silver lining if you knew where to look for it. He also had strict rules, maxims you ignored at your peril: "You treat a lady like a dame, and a dame like a lady." "Alcohol may be man's worst enemy, but the bible says love your enemy." "Cock your hat – angles are attitudes."

And what amber-drenched nights he had, after-hours marathons when he'd drink nothing but tumbler after tumbler of JD. He once went to see a new doctor who asked about his alcohol intake. Sinatra, somewhat taken aback, said he drank thirty-six drinks a day. The doctor, perhaps unsurprisingly, asked him to be serious. Sinatra said he was serious, and that he drank a bottle of Jack Daniels every day, which he reckoned was roughly thirty-six drinks. Appalled, the doctor asked him how he felt when he woke up every morning. Frank said, "I don't know. I'm never up in the morning and I'm not sure you're the doctor for me."

Sinatra didn't need logos to let you or anyone else know he was cool, he just wore a suit and simply got on with it. "When an invitation says black tie optional, it is always safer to wear black tie," he once said. "My basic rules are to have shirt cuffs extended half an inch from the jacket sleeve. Trousers should break just above the shoe. Try not to sit down because it wrinkles the pants. If you have to sit down, don't cross your legs."

His oddest idiosyncrasy, though, and one I heartily recommend, was polishing the bottom of his shoes. "If you're gonna look the business, then do the business," he said.

S "Any outstanding remarks about my Mary Janes?" he asked the Sands crowd in February 1966, referring to his new evening slippers. "That leather with little bows on them. You think I'm trying to tell you something? You know I took eight weeks of karate lessons before I had guts enough to wear these? I broke wood and windows and tables... they still hurt my feet. This one little mother has been biting me for five days..."

He liked the ladies, too, though at the time this was merely an assumption on my part. I later found out that Sinatra had an almost pathological need for sex, and when he wanted a girl, it didn't really matter who she was. It was like a food chain: when he was "dialling for pussy" as he called it, he'd start with the film stars, then work his way down through the ingénues, and finally the hookers. The only time he wasn't chasing the ladies was when he was "in training" for an album; then, he was a monk. When the legendary director JOHN FORD asked the equally legendary AVA GARDNER what she saw in her "one hundred and twenty pound runt" of a husband, she shocked the veteran Ford by retorting, "Well, there's only ten pounds of Frank, but there's one hundred and ten pounds of cock." Seriously, how could you not love this man?

For years this was a fairly one-sided love affair, although eventually I got the chance to live my own particular Sinatra anecdote.

Some years ago in our office there worked a lovely (if occasionally high-maintenance) girl called ANTHEA ANKA, a young Los Angelina whose father is PAUL ANKA, the hugely successful teen idol of the post-ELVIS era who went on to write the English lyrics to "My Way". I was in Los Angeles, in 2001, on business with some friends from work and Anthea arranged for us to see Paul one night. We booked his favourite table at The Ivy, dressed-up in our finest Savile Row threads, and turned up a respectable twenty minutes early ("Sir, you might be more comfortable in this seat, as Mr Anka likes to sit there," our server pointed out, before my RICHARD JAMES trousers had brushed the banquette).

Anthea had briefed us to not AT ANY POINT mention Frank Sinatra, or "My Way", or anything to do with the song or indeed her father's relationship with Frank. She was vaguely aware that there had been some sort of bust-up between them (singer and composer) and that we shouldn't tempt fate by reminding him of this (on one of the Vegas CDs Sinatra jokes about the "little Arab" only writing a song for him every ten years).

And so when Mr Anka arrived (even we were beginning to get reverential by now), we dutifully asked him how his Vegas residency was going, how his publishing was doing, and what life was like on the road ("Great," "Great," and "Great," I seem to remember the answers being). At no point did we mention Big Frank, the "song", or indeed anything of the sort. I think Alex at one point half-mentioned the fact that the Rat Pack were becoming quite popular again in London, although I'm not sure our guest heard (seeing that Alex's observations were curtailed somewhat sharply by both Bill and I kicking him sharply in the shins under the table).

But after only about ten minutes or so the Ankatola floored us all by asking, completely unprompted, "So, are you boys Sinatra fans?"

Well, you have never seen three grown men try and ingratiate themselves so much: "Yes Paul, I've got every original Capitol album before he left to set up Reprise." "Yes Paul, I actually saw him on his last trip to London." "Yes Paul, I especially like the bossa nova albums he made in the Sixties..." etc, etc. We were nauseating, but I think Paul was pleased. We'd loosened up, stopped acting like British stuffed shirts, and were still blowing smoke up his ass ("So Paul, what was he really like?" "Was he a shit in the studio?" "Were there, you know, always women around?").

I'm sure he could tell that we really were massive Sinatra fans because after a while he began telling us about... the "song". He told us that Sinatra had called him up and asked him to work on it, told us how he'd sweated for days to get

S the lyrics right, how Sinatra had asked him to tweak it, and, finally, how Sinatra had invited him to the session.

We were ploughing our way through the Pinot Grigio and the Barolo by this time, and we were all getting worked up, as was Paul, in the retelling of the story. Finally, he turned to me – maybe realising that, out of the three of us, I was the saddest, most obsessive Sinatraphile – and said, safe in the knowledge that he had the answer on hand, "Guess how many takes it took Sinatra to nail it?" I can't quite remember what we volunteered, but I think the responses were in the low numbers. But none of the guesses were right.

"You know how many takes it took Sinatra to nail 'My Way'?" asked the composer. "One, just one damn take. Now that man was a professional. That man was the man."

The night dragged on, and ended in the small hours in a cigar club somewhere in deepest Hollywood, where we all sat around smoking Silk Cut and Cohibas. As the three of us got up to leave Paul to his cigar (we all had jet-lag, although he was totally prepared for a night on the lash), he asked if I'd like to hear Frank's first take of "My Way". As rhetorical questions go, this was one of the best I'd ever had and I obviously said yes. "I'd love that Paul, that would be great."

"Well, I'll send it then," he said, as a curl of blue smoke coiled its way from his mouth to the ceiling.

Thirty seconds later, in the lift going down to the car park, Bill turned and said, "That, I guarantee, is not going to happen."

But it did. Ten days later a package arrived by FedEx from LA, inside of which was a freshly cut CD in a blank jewel case, and a little note from Paul. "Enjoy", it said, in case I had entertained the thought of doing otherwise.

And when I played it – on my Mac, about five seconds later – that's exactly what I did. The CD contained Frank Sinatra's very first take of "My Way", the one you hear on the record; although unlike the record, all you can hear is Frank. You can vaguely make out the backing track seeping from Sinatra's headphones, but for the purposes of argument it is only Frank's vocals that you can hear. The first time I played it, it was like some sort of quasi-religious experience, like listening to PAUL McCARTNEY first play "Let It Be" for the rest of the BEATLES (*Anthology III*), or watching the CLASH perform "Complete Control" in front of a captive audience (Victoria Park, East London, 1978). Considering how good studio jiggery-pokery is these days, it would be easy to assume that Paul had simply edited out the instruments, leaving Frank to sing to his heart's content, but this was an actual take – the first take, for fuck's sake! – of Frank Sinatra singing not only one of his trademark songs, but one of the defining popular songs of the 20th Century – live, by himself, unaccompanied!

Paul's CD has since become one of my most treasured possessions, which is ironic seeing that "My Way" was never one of my favourite Sinatra songs, not at all. For me "My Way" was always a prime example of Pub Frank, one of those obvious karaoke Sinatra songs such as "Strangers In The Night", or "Chicago", that over-refreshed Sinatra fans think they can get away with come closing time, one of the broader, more populist tracks from the Reprise years, rather than the classic Capitol years. But without the strings, the embellishment, the heavy-handed production, "My Way" becomes a plaintive letter from the check-out lounge, a poetic summation of a life lived large.

A few years ago I had an affair with hubris when I agreed to record a Sinatra song for a charity CD. Ignoring one of the cardinal rules governing cover versions – you don't mess with Frank – I decided to try my hand at "Learnin' The Blues", one of his lesser-known songs. I'd sung it enough times to my wife and children, I thought I'd let the world know how good a crooner I was. Encased in a cylindrical recording booth in north London, with my headphones on, and a Sure-esque microphone brushing my lips, I felt like I was deep in the Capitol Building in LA, in 1956; all I needed was a snap-brim hat, two fingers of scotch, and an unbelievable singing voice. But obviously I didn't have any of these things, and my version of "Learnin' The Blues" proved I was a worse singer

S even than FRANK SINATRA, JR., something I thought technically impossible. (I was, however, in good company, as the album also contained NIGEL PLANER ruining PAUL WELLER's "You Do Something To Me" and TRISTAN DAVIES, then the editor of the *Independent On Sunday*, and SIMON KELNER, then the editor of the *Independent*, performing major surgery on JIMMY WEBB's "Wichita Lineman" – without, I should add, an anaesthetic.) The reason Sinatra (Snr) was such a convincingly good singer was because he walked through a song, taking everything in his stride, and making every step his own. Every word was his. Whereas Sinatra was the only singer who could sing a semi-colon, I had trouble opening the dictionary.

But, like many before me, I wanted a bit of Sinatra magic to call my own, to somehow try and grab a small percentage of a hundred percent kinda guy. I found a similar sort of devotion nearly twenty years ago, when I visited the Sinatra Music Society, an independent non-profit making organisation that is still around today, albeit in a much smaller form. It was a quietly extraordinary experience, life affirming in its own small way. Google "Frank Sinatra Fan Clubs" today and you'll get 376,000 results (compared to PARIS HILTON's 173,000, JADE GOODY's 1,810,000, and GANDHI's 15,600,600), and the internet is awash with arcane and largely unwanted Sinatra trivia. The internet has empowered the marginal, the talentless, and the librarian in all of us. If punk gave everyone carte blanche to pick up a guitar and scream at the world, so the World Wide Web has allowed anyone and everyone the opportunity to share their small world view with anyone with time to kill. And so cyberspace is as full of Sinatra as it is full of child pornography or conspiracy theories.

However, real Sinatra freaks want to meet each other, to describe their experiences, and to actually listen to the records. It's all very well knowing where The Man bought his cufflinks, but if you can't hear him sing, then what's the point of being a fan?

"Will you be careful with Frank?" I remember a woman saying, to no one in particular, as a framed portrait of Sinatra fell off the ground-floor stage in Baden Powell House, deep in London's Royal Borough of Kensington. This was the third Sunday in August 1990, and the monthly meeting of the London branch of the Sinatra Music Society held a public meeting.

"You can't be treating Frank like that," said the woman, "not today you can't, anyway." This was Frank's day.

The Society was then in its thirty-sixth year. With nine other branches around the country – in Glasgow, Newcastle, Leeds, Merseyside, Manchester, Birmingham, Salisbury, Cardiff, and Sussex – at the time it was the largest easy listening club in the world. There are still other organisations, of course, for the likes of TONY BENNETT, JOHNNY MATHIS, MATT MONRO, and BING CROSBY – but no crooner has ever inspired devotion like Frank.

There were a hundred and fifty people, mostly white, middle-aged couples, and it felt like a youth club for the over fifties. There was a smattering of young people, most of them recent converts, and a suggestion box and small stalls selling records, tapes, CDs, and – shock, horror! – bootlegs of Frank and his pals, as well as signed black and white portraits, and colour snaps of the singer in concert. You could also buy the in-house magazine, *Perfectly Frank*, then up to issue No. 221. Around the walls were enlarged album covers and huge portraits mounted on polystyrene boards.

At the start of the meeting, someone from the committee read out some messages: "Toni and Alan have requested a song from the *Come Fly With Me* LP, which we'll play later. They apologise for not turning up today but Alan fell and hurt his hip. So he's a bit poorly." Then they started to play some records. When I visited, all the records had been pre-recorded onto tapes and played on an old reel-to-reel machine. Beside the guest speaker was a sign on which LP covers were placed: "You are now listening to..." it proclaimed, just in case there was likely to be any doubt.

The audience stared at the stage and tapped their toes, or swayed in their plastic seats. They had brought flasks and

S sandwiches and Kettle Chips, though tea was served at half-time (the meetings last for three to four hours). This was *Little Britain* without the irony, and the people here would never have imagined that ten years later Sinatra would be held up as a hero for a new generation of retro-hungry swinging frat-boys, for whom Vegas would become their new Valhalla. They passed around photo albums and talked of concerts past. A young girl got up and played her five favourite Frank songs. She was in the middle of her GCSE exams but was here instead of studying. Playing a song from *Ol' Blue Eyes Is Back*, she told us that this was the record her mother was listening to when she went into labour. Sinatra-ism runs in her family.

They played a few songs in tribute to SAMMY DAVIS JR. and talked about a trip to a Frank convention in Birmingham. There was an argument about spare places on the coach. They talked about what Frank means to them, about how they became converts.

The assembled fans mostly seemed like bright, broad-minded trainspotters, and not at all like the maniacal necrophiles who attend ELVIS conventions – none of these people came dressed as Frank during the Capitol years, with a pork pie hat and silk tie, nor did they come sporting unconvincing toupees. They came as fans.

To be honest, there wasn't a lot to do other than wallow in the music, but being forced to listen to Sinatra for four hours on end should hardly be anyone's idea of hardship. After a while it was impossible not to get lost in the music, swept up in its optimism and swing, Sinatra's voice taking you to places you've never been before, places which don't exist anymore. This is what they call the Sinatra magic. Even though I'd been listening to Sinatra since the age of five or six, it was here, sitting in a municipal hall surrounded by a bunch of people who probably had more in common with my aunt than with me or with anyone I knew, that I really came to terms with the subterranean supperclub of the world's greatest-ever popular singer. Sitting there on my orange moulded plastic seat, I realised – duh! – that there will never be a better singer, never a man like Sinatra who can wrap himself around a song and make it his own. As RALPH J GLEASON (the co-founder of *Rolling Stone*) wrote in the sleeve notes to Sinatra's *No One Cares* LP, "Sinatra can take lyrics that are in themselves and of themselves banal... and make them live and breathe and communicate emotion."

And it was also in Baden Powell House that I first realised that listening to Sinatra in this way was a lot like being in church. I wasn't at a meeting or a fan's convention. I was at the Church of St Francis. We were convening on a Sunday afternoon to worship at the altar of Sinatra; we were here to praise the God-like phrasing and saintly swing of the most charismatic singer ever to walk the earth. We were here – at this most famous church of light entertainment – to listen to sermons and prayers. The disciples, old and young, were here to pay respect. Most of them had met the great man one way or another – either backstage or outside the stage door – but even the ones who had never seen him, believed.

Jane, a twenty-five-year-old children's book designer from Dorking, had seen Sinatra seventeen times and had tickets for all of his forthcoming London shows, as well as one for his concert in Glasgow. She had travelled as far as Los Angeles to see her hero: "I first got into him back in 1974 when he made his comeback. I was influenced by my parents who liked him but also by what else was around. There was no one as good as Frank. I like TONY BENNETT, MATT MONRO, and JACK JONES but no one's as good as Sinatra, no one. I've met him half-a-dozen times after concerts – he once gave me a silk handkerchief."

Had she ever been disappointed by his performance? After all, here was man who wasn't exactly in the first flush of youth. "Never. I go expecting to hear a seventy-four-year-old man, not a seventy-four-year-old man singing like a thirty-five-year-old. The press expect miracles, but I don't."

What about his private life – was she ever appalled by his conduct? She must have read KITTY KELLEY's *His Way*?

"Look, no one's perfect, even Sinatra. And his private life is his business, it doesn't taint him in my eyes."

S Hang around Sinatra obsessives long enough and you'll be told that Frank peaked during the Capitol years, and that his best album was one of the early "concept" albums, *Songs For Swingin' Lovers*. And while this opinion has some veracity, playing the record in your home – or indeed Baden Powell House – when other people are there is a bit like playing SIMPLY RED's *Stars* or the second Oasis album: what do you want, a medal? Personally, I think the coolest Sinatra album is actually the *Francis Albert Sinatra & Antonio Carlos Jobim* record, released on Frank's own label Reprise in 1967, a shag-pile carpet of a record that manages to appropriate bossa nova without making it corny. It's an extraordinary album – "The Girl From Ipanema", "Quiet Nights Of Quiet Stars", "How Insensitive", "Baubles, Bangles And Beads", etc – and can he heard playing in the background on TONY SOPRANO's boat, in the final episode of the second series of *The Sopranos*, in the scene where Pussy gets whacked. The juxtaposition of silky-smooth bossa and shocking, personalised violence is incredibly powerful, and is one of the most operatic bits of television you could ever hope to see. There's a version of "Baubles, Bangles And Beads" on the 1978 Vegas recording, and although this one has a considerably different arrangement – jazzier, jumpier, dirtier – it has Sinatra's unmistakable insouciance, Sinatra's unique interpretation, Sinatra's innate style. Sinatra style.

Francis Albert Sinatra died at 10:50pm on May 14, 1998, at the age of eighty-two. His final words were, "I'm losing." Legend has it that Sinatra was buried in a blue suit with a flask of Jack Daniel's and a roll of ten dimes which was a gift from his daughter, Tina, along with a card that said, "Sleep warm, Poppa – look for me." The ten dimes were a habit dating back to the kidnapping of his son, FRANK SINATRA, JR., due to the kidnappers' demands that negotiations be made via pay phone. A Zippo lighter (which some take to be a reference to his mob connections) is purported to be buried with him, as is a pack of Camel cigarettes. The words "The Best Is Yet To Come" are imprinted on his tombstone.

One of Sinatra's favourite toasts, and one he made increasingly in his later years, always made with a full glass in his hand, was, "May you live to be a hundred and may the last voice you hear be mine."

Or, as I seem to remember him saying once, "Do be do be do."

S

SINGING IN THE SHOWER

If you ask me what we sing in the shower says a lot less about us than we've been lead to believe. We might think the shower test is a good indication of what we really really like (although I'd like to point out that I've never sung a SPICE GIRLS song when naked – come to that I'm fairly sure I've never sung a SPICE GIRLS song fully clothed, either), but that's never been the case with me. The reverse is true, in fact. For years I would sing "Synchronicity II" by the POLICE, not only a song I have no affinity or fondness for, but one I can safely say I actively dislike. (The only POLICE song I've ever really liked is "So Lonely", and only then because it sounds like "Sue Lawley".) But there we are. A few years after this affliction, I was hit by another, rather less infectious song, "Bull Rush" by PAUL WELLER. Again, a song that's not exactly close to my heart. I played it in the car a few times when it came out, but it's no Desert Island Disc. Not even for PAUL WELLER I would imagine. Yet I sing it every other time I have a shower.

Just about the only song I sing in the shower that I actually like is "Are You Ready For Love" by ELTON JOHN. The rest just seem to be things that have, possibly through osmosis, though more likely through repetition, lodged themselves in my brain (once even "Breaking Free" from *High School Musical*, a song that a few years ago was played on average ten times a day by my kids, and one on which I didn't so much hit the notes as wander round them).

Perhaps the one song I sing when wet, more than any other, is EDDIE MURPHY's "comedy-rap" record "Boogie In Your Butt", which contains the immortal lines, "Stick a telephone in your butt, Stick a dinosaur bone... in your butt, Stick a

S tree in your butt, Don't you wanna stick me in your butt?" I don't know why I sing it, but I do, and can often be caught in the office singing this to myself, much the embarrassment of any passing purveyor of luxury goods. The first time my new PA overheard me signing this, I caught her staring at me as though I had suddenly decided to cover myself in jam. It's certainly not the world's best record, and I can only imagine the reason Murphy agreed to make it is exactly the same reason he agreed to make the execrable *Best Defence* after the huge success of BEVERLY HILLS COP: "Three men walked into the room carrying a cheque."

THE SMALL FACES

Munchkin mods who conjured up playful, direct psychedelia, and who have an almost completely untainted cv (if one forgets the lamentable 1976 comeback, that is), one element of the band's success is often overlooked: pint-sized STEVE MARRIOTT's enormous voice. JERRY SHIRLEY played with Marriott in the band he formed after disbanding the Small Faces, HUMBLE PIE, and once discussed his secret: "He goes, 'Have a look at this,' and he opened his mouth. I looked inside. The back of his throat was literally enormous. The gap between the top and his tongue was inches wide, compared to a normal person. He must have been a freak of nature."

PATTI SMITH

There has always been a sense that Patti Smith peaked with her first record, the astonishing *Horses* (1975, Arista), and there is a lot to support this – namely everything she released afterwards. *Easter* had her cover of BRUCE SPRINGSTEEN's "Because The Night" (when he eventually released his unreleased version, it was immediately apparent she had simply copied this), and she has periodically been an interesting live act. Nevertheless she has a reputation for being difficult, and there is a sense that she has always thought more of her work than anyone who has actually listened to it.

She has perhaps been more influential in the archetype she created. When she started to be noticed, in New York 1974-5, her strikingly simple *androgynie* was surprisingly powerful, and it was copied by an entire generation of young boys and girls who wanted that sexy, EGON SCHIELE, tubercular look (we were more sheltered back then).

For those who thought she was washed up, redemption has come in the form of her ROBERT MAPPLETHORPE memoir, *Just Kids*, an elegantly written and beautifully observed book that has actually humanised Smith for those of us who weren't sure she was human at all.

SNOW PATROL

Great records, nice guys, worst marketing strategy since, well, forever. Why aren't they enormous?

STEPHEN SONDHEIM

According to Sondheim, a little authorship can be a dangerous thing. If a lyric is too full of itself, he says, music can make it muddy or grandiose. At their worst, these lyrics convey the aura of a visit: they announce the presence of the writer. He is strict: "There are only three principles necessary for a lyric writer, all of them familiar truisms. They were not immediately apparent to me when I started writing but have come into focus via OSCAR HAMMERSTEIN's tutoring, Strunk and White's huge little book *The Elements Of Style*, and my own

S

sixty-some years of practising the craft. I have not always been skilled or diligent enough to follow them as faithfully as I would like, but they underlie everything I've ever written. In no particular order, and to be written in stone:

- Content Dictates Form
- Less Is More
- God Is In The Details
- all in the service of
- Clarity
- Without which nothing else matters."

Sonic Youth

No, sorry, it's just too much, way too late. Oh my Lord, when will it end? Maybe with a one-way ticket to Dignitas.

Soul II Soul

It's been said that their debut album, 1989's sumptuous *Club Classics Vol. One*, single-handedly sparked a British soul revival, and to a certain extent that's true. More importantly they were responsible for producing two of the best dance records of the decade, "Keep On Movin" and "Back To Life", songs which not only defined the post-Buffalo West London sound, but which also continue to resonate on dancefloors from Tokyo to Mumbai.

SPA MUSIC

S

The music you hear in spas is massively underrated. Honestly, it's not the drugs talking here, I mean it. And anyway, I'm not on medication at the moment, not seriously.

Having had back problems for the last five years or so – if you've never had back pain you will have already turned the page, and if you have you probably can't bear to read on – I am used to lying in a small, darkened, candlelit room as various men and women work their magic. Or not, as the case may be. Recently I have been having a lot of acupuncture – Zen, in Notting Hill, seeing as you didn't ask – and as it seems to be working, I keep going back. A lot. And every time I visit they play the same tape, the same ethereal loop of panpipes, slowed-down drums, washes of angular guitar, and plinky-plonky strings. It's one of those pieces of music that personifies "tranquil", and as such, I can't really fault it. If you could drink it, it would taste of green tea, and if you could wash your face with it, it would smell of jasmine. I imagine that when these things are commissioned, the person writing the cheque says they need something that evokes Polynesian waterfalls, Maldivian sunrises, or Santa Fe sunsets, and I have to say the people they employ to do these things have no problem interpreting them.

Even though I'm a fan and aficionado of loungecore, easy listening, and supperclub crooners, it's never been suggested that I investigate "new age" music as it's always supposed to be rubbish. In fact I once heard it described to me as the sort of music you listen to as you're having acupuncture. Which, I have to say, is why I like it. But although it evokes a certain secular spirituality, a way of feeling good about yourself while distancing yourself from other people, in essence this is really travel music, which is where you should find it in iTunes or HMV.

Anyway, if I'm honest, I probably own the most "new age" CD of them all. In 1990 I visited Carmel in California, where

S CLINT EASTWOOD used to be mayor. In one of the many "new age" trinket shops in which I bought ergonomic table lamps and deleted recordings of JACK KEROUAC reciting dreadful poetry, I bought one of my most treasured CDs, a recording of the Pacific Ocean crashing against the northern Californian coastline (see VIRGINIA ASTLEY).

It is, like, totally rad. And it sounds great as someone's making mincemeat of your back.

SPANDAU BALLET

The first time most Londoners heard the words Spandau Ballet was on the London Weekend Television arts programme, *Twentieth Century Box*, in May 1980. Presented by DANNY BAKER, *Twentieth Century Box* was the place you went to for your youth culture fix, the TV spot where you expected to see for yourselves what or who had just crawled out of the latest nightclub.

Baker's programme that week was devoted to a new cult, The Cult With No Name, a bunch of soul boys and girls, disaffected art students, hairdressers, and apprentice advertising salesman who all wore clothes that referenced architecture rather than pop culture, and who frequented some of the more elite Soho nightclubs, and who had learned the art of reinvention at the knee of DAVID BOWIE.

Elegant, well dressed, and rather bizarrely obsessed with cleanliness (Spandau were even quoted on the show saying that they hated most gigs because everyone was so dirty), they were, to put a fine point on it, the In Crowd. And they were hated for it.

And Spandau Ballet were the In Crowd's band. And they were hated even more. Ushering in a new era of visually-dominated pop, their dissatisfaction with their musical peers manifested itself in a mechanical, stylised sound that was born and bred on the dancefloor's of the West End. They were

Bowie Kids, Blitz Kids, white soul boys who had rejected rock, choosing to embrace electronica and frilly shirts instead.

Amateurish? Ridiculous? Their adolescent pretensions represented a sensibility rather than a display of ability. "We're not just another band," said Spandau's occasionally ridiculous singer, TONY HADLEY. And they weren't, not by the longest piece of chalk in town.

When discussing the pantheon of Eighties pop, Spandau are usually ignored, but some of their early records remain some of the most resonant of the period, and "Chant No.1 (We Don't Need This Pressure On)" was, in its own way, nearly as important to the summer of 1981 as "Ghost Town" by the SPECIALS – a canny mix of contemporary funk and bottom-heavy agitprop, the perfect encapsulation of the new decade's obsession with fiddling while Brixton and Toxteth burned.

THE SPECIALS

A few years ago, towards the end of the Noughties, if you happened to be reading the classified ads in the arts pages of your favourite national newspaper, you would have seen that revival tours were all the rage (as they like to say in Chipping Norton). ABC, the HUMAN LEAGUE, The WHO, LLOYD COLE, ULTRAVOX, DEEP PURPLE, the EAGLES, GOLDEN EARRING, and SIMPLY RED were all treading the boards again, seemingly regardless of how these opportunistic outings would ultimately affect their legacies. And who could blame them? People will pay good money to see bands they enjoyed in their youth, sometimes regardless of how many original members they contain. And still it goes on. That weird little band from 1983 whose only hit you devoured as though it were the essence of life itself? Yup, well they're probably back too, playing the Shepherds Bush Empire the night after JOE JACKSON, and probably supporting ORCHESTRAL MANOEUVRES IN THE DARK, or the HAPPY MONDAYS. With all the original members, too, strangely – apart from the

S drummer, who died in a bizarre gardening accident in what the rest of the band at the time thought was a misguided, if not completely unfunny, homage to SPINAL TAP.

Oh yes, as far as music is concerned, there's nothing quite so au courant as nostalgia.

And, if you looked carefully, you would have seen that the Specials were back too, those advocates of late Seventies post-modern ska, the inventors of 2 Tone, and quite simply one of the coolest, most important British bands of all time. In the space of just two years, from 1979 to 1981, the original Specials managed to embody the new decade's violent energies, morals, and conflicts – though always with an ironic and often sardonic detachment that kept the band cool as the Eighties grew increasingly hot. "Gangsters", "Too Much Too Young", "A Message To You, Rudy", "Do Nothing", "Rat Race", "Ghost Town", records that defined a generation who weren't sure they wanted to be defined in the first place. Sure, the band were earnest, but they were studiedly sarcastic, too, which endeared them to everyone at the time who mattered. Not only that, but they came from Coventry, Britain's very own answer to Detroit, the epitome of the post-war urban wasteland, the quintessential concrete jungle, and felt they had a right to bleat about anything they wanted to, especially the onslaught of Thatcherism.

And on their return, thirty years later, churning out the old hits as though they were a human jukebox, they were greeted with open arms by the critics and public alike. Only they weren't really the Specials at all, because the most important member, JERRY DAMMERS, the man who invented them, who gave the band their edge, who wrote most of their songs, and who was responsible for making them truly memorable, was not encouraged to participate in the reunion ("I founded the Specials, and now they've excluded me," said Dammers when the band first reunited, in 2008). There had always been friction between Dammers and the group's singer – TERRY HALL, the most miserable man in pop – and that friction continues; obviously to the extent that they find it difficult to work together.

JERRY DAMMERS was the creative genius behind the Specials, the man who gave them their political edge, who gave them their idiosyncratic musical tropes, and who set them apart from the likes of the SELECTOR, the BEAT, or BAD MANNERS. The Specials without Dammers were like the DOORS without JIM MORRISON, QUEEN without FREDDIE MERCURY, WHAM! without GEORGE MICHAEL, or MORECAMBE AND WISE without Morecambe or, er, Wise.

I have to admit to a bit of previous here, and own up to the fact that I knew Jerry extremely well for about five years in the Eighties. Although we have lost touch now, back then he was a friend. I would regularly hitch up to Coventry to sit in sullen working men's clubs with Jerry and his extraordinary circle of friends and acquaintances, discussing socialism (we differed), the provenance of PRINCE BUSTER and the validity of HEAVEN 17. We went clubbing together, spent a few memorable New Year's Eves in Bristol (where Jerry's parents were from), spent birthdays together, and once DJ'd together at a miners' benefit at London's Wag Club in 1983 (he played politically correct funk while I played right wing disco). I even sat through some of the tortuous recording of the SPECIAL AKA's 1985 album *In The Studio*, the one containing Jerry's defining moment, the monumentally influential "Free Nelson Mandela". This ultimately led to the Mandela 70th birthday tribute concert at Wembley Stadium in 1988, and helped add to the groundswell of support that led to Mandela's release from prison in February1990.

Dammers was always a genuine bohemian, and it's no surprise to me the way his career has panned out (DJ-ing, production, forming various esoteric dance orchestras). However, I also thought he might turn out to be our generation's JOHN BARRY, scoring important movies with solemn yet iconic orchestral themes, balancing JACQUES DERRIDA with FRANCIS LAI, SCOTT WALKER with DR. JOHN. To me, Dammers was the Lennon and McCartney of ska, one of the most important voices of the post-punk generation, a man who always appeared to be carrying his generation's hopes and dreams on his shoulders, as well as his own. Quite simply, I thought Dammers was

S

something of a musical genius. A genius who has always followed his own path: that he didn't turn into JOHN BARRY was a disappointment to me, but probably not to him.

SHARLEEN SPITERI

On the face of it, she shouldn't have been a singer. A hairdresser, for sure, maybe even a make-up artist, or something back-room and creative that would have taken her from the Glasgow suburbs to the edges of the glamour business she fantasised about so much. But a singer? With a nose that's been broken four times?

Spiteri has always been a bit self-conscious about her nose, doesn't particularly like being shot in profile, and was initially wary of being the focus of her group, TEXAS. Out of necessity the band reinvented itself in the mid-Nineties, allowing Spiteri to properly blossom; against her better judgment, but with considerable success. When the band started, in the late Eighties, she was an androgynous waif, wrapped up in a leather jacket and a surly, angular fringe – but after her makeover, she discovered she could pout and flirt and wink without looking sappy. Suddenly she was Patti McSmith, a lollipop with a fishhook inside.

The band was never exactly flavour of the month, with most of their stuff being lumpen and callow. What people liked was Spiteri's voice, a voice that was pushed to the fore after the rejig, a recalibration that resulted in much, much better records: "Say What You Want", "Summer Son", "Black Eyed Boy."

BRUCE SPRINGSTEEN

As television moments go, this was one of the very best. In the fifth series of *The Sopranos*, in the episode "Long Term

Parking" (screened in the US on May 23, 2004), Christopher shows up late for a meeting with TONY SOPRANO and consigliere Silvio, in their back room office at Bada Bing. "You're late," says Tony, angrily. And Chris's explanation as to why? "Sorry. The highway was jammed with broken heroes on a last-chance power drive..." Not only are these obviously some of the most pertinent lyrics in Bruce Springsteen's "Born To Run", but Silvio – who doesn't acknowledge the reference – is played by Bruce's E STREET BAND member, "Little" STEVEN VAN ZANDT.

As was said when it aired, this was a vignette that spoke volumes about just how much Springsteen is woven into modern American mythology, maybe even more so than one of his idols, BOB DYLAN.

In America, Bruce Springsteen's fame has always been Presidential, where in Britain we've always been rather embarrassed about allowing ourselves to enjoy something so unambiguous, so prosaic. In the Seventies, when he was still in his larval stage, he used to throw his woolly hat in the air, turn towards the audience, put his hands behind his back, and catch it as it fell, just as the band cut the final chord. It was corny but fabulous. He was cornier in the Eighties, as the industrial-strength, muscle-bound, MTV hero of the Eighties – "Ah-one-two-*thray*!" – revelling in sweat-stained bandannas and air-punching aerobics (a man who could reasonably be blamed for BONO, JON BON JOVI, and BRYAN ADAMS).

Few would call Springsteen a grabby man, especially when compared with other icons of Eighties US pop, such as PRINCE, MADONNA, or MICHAEL JACKSON. Sure, he has the same career aspirations as any "artist" (i.e. immortality), but he's always known when to curb his excesses. Perhaps this is why he's had so much success: trying to capture the nature of Everyman is a daunting task, and Springsteen has endeavoured to do it time and time again.

For the best part of forty years he has imbued the aspirations of smalltown blue-collar America with a mystic glow. With a much-lampooned repertoire of songs extolling the virtues of pink Cadillacs, Jersey girls, and gimcrack

S homesteads, Springsteen has affected the American psyche in a way that WOODY GUTHRIE could only dream of. Take *Born To Run*, that glorious statement of intent from 1975: it's *West Side Story* on wheels, a ruthless pursuit of sensation that sounds like BOB DYLAN produced by PHIL SPECTOR, only much, much better. You only had to hear it once to know that no one believed in the redemptive power of rock music quite as much as blue-collar Brucey.

Automobile imagery was crucial to those early romantic notions of sex and freedom, and the heroes of his mini-parables were poets-cum-car mechanics – dreamers and schemers who linger aimlessly on the low-rise industrial park fringes of society, down in "Jungleland", "Thunder Road", "Spirit In The Night"s' Greasy Lake, or the infamous "rattlesnake speedway in the Utah desert". Most of the time, though, was spent on the Jersey Shore, drinking warm beer beneath rotary fans in dilapidated diners as their fuel-injected suicide machines sat patiently outside, gently humming after a 200-mile journey across a dozen county lines. Jesus, it was hard work being this disenfranchised.

Bruce would claim that he'd never had an image, though it would be hard to find another rock star so easily objectified, and it's as easy to distil the Springsteen myth from the way he looks as it is from listening to his music. In the early days – the long days and dark nights of *Greetings From Asbury Park NJ* and *The Wild, The Innocent And The E Street Shuffle* – Bruce's beard and pimp cap gave him the air of any self-important East Coast troubadour; but by the mid-Seventies he was starting to look even more generic: lumberjack shirt, faded blue jeans, leather jacket, and motorcycle boots. He perhaps looked his best towards the end of the decade – the time of *Darkness On The Edge Of Town*, which probably remains his defining statement and, along with four-fifths of *The River*, it's his best album – with his drawn, gaunt face, V-neck T-shirt, and windcheater making him seem more like JIMMY DEAN than BOBBY ZIMMERMAN.

Five years later it was ANNIE LEIBOVITZ's iconic cover of 1984's *Born In The USA* which rubber-stamped his image:

a white cap-sleeve T-shirt, a studded cowboy belt, and Levi's
501s with the red baseball cap hanging out of his right back
pocket. Looking at it nearly three decades later it doesn't just
look ironic, it looks stereotypically gay

During this period Bruce was briefly co-opted by the Right,
who not only misinterpreted the beleaguered irony of *Born
In The USA* itself, but thought that Springsteen's onstage
persona was comparable to SYLVESTER STALLONE's jingoistic
stooges, Rocky and Rambo. For some this was an easy
mistake to make, as Springsteen had been working overtime
in the gym, pumping up his body to beefcake proportions.
But Bruce never exploited his maleness, and although his
classic songs tend to celebrate the male experience, he has
spent equal amounts of time pondering his own masculinity.

In this way Springsteen has never been an especially
libidinous performer, and you'd never exactly call him a sexy
star, not compared to, say, STEVEN TYLER, MARVIN GAYE, or KID
ROCK.

His fanbase has always been more male orientated as he's
always appealed to boys who desperately want to be older,
as well as men who wish they were younger. Like the boys
in ALBERT CAMUS' *The Outsider* (another male adolescent
passion), who leave the cinema with affected gaits after
watching cowboy films, songs like "Thunder Road" made men
in Golf GTIs think they were driving souped-up Thunderbirds,
made men working in photocopy shops dream of cruising
down Route 66.

I didn't get Springsteen for years. Having been brought
up on a diet of glam rock, punk, and Sinatra, Springsteen's
overblown pomp seemed silly (how could a Home Counties
schoolboy identify with a lovelorn steelworker or a Vietnam
vet?). But then I went to America and it all made perfect
sense. The space. The sky. The open roads. A big country
demands big music, and that's exactly the sort of music Bruce
Springsteen made. Epic. Cinematic. Unashamedly unironic.
Never an inadequate like so many British pop stars – RAY
DAVIES, PETE SHELLEY, MORRISSEY, etc – Springsteen was a man
whose internal workings were all on the outside.

S Whereas punk celebrated the mundanity of urban, lower middle class life, Bruce helped me escape it. Springsteen sang about "highways jammed with broken heroes on a last-chance power drive", while all I was doing was driving to the off-licence

In 1987 Springsteen made an effort to escape his own environment and deflate the myth he had taken so long to build by releasing the decidedly low-key *Tunnel Of Love*, managing to distance himself from his enormous fanbase in the process (if BOB DYLAN could dismantle his image then surely Springsteen could too). The cover shot compounded the effect, Bruce's sombre black suit and faintly ridiculous bootlace tie making him appear more like the manager of some upwardly mobile cocktail and enchilada joint in the Midwest than an out-and-out rock god (he looked like he'd walked out of *Paris Texas* straight into *Miami Vice*). Literally and metaphorically, the shirtsleeves were back, the revisionism taking him from superstar Everyman to self-doubting thirty-something (intensely intimate, it's his most personal memoir, a divorce record about his failed marriage to JULIANNE PHILLIPS).

These days a lot of rock stars seem to use up the bulk of their inspiration by the time of their second CD, but with Bruce it took twenty years, when he moved to the West Coast after a lifetime based in New Jersey. He famously benched the E STREET BAND, got married again, had a bunch of kids, and started writing songs about watching television ("57 Channels (And Nothin' On)"). He swapped the gauche pink Cadillac for a $14m Beverley Hills mansion, parked the battered '69 Chevy in his double-fronted garage, hung up his cowboy boots, and settled down for a night with his wife and a couple of bottles of Californian Chardonnay. He indulged in self-parody, too: cavorting about the stage looking like a Rodeo Drive vagabond in neatly pressed jeans, gypsy shirt, and dagger-pointed boots; a rich man in a poor man's shirt. The idea of "Bruce Springsteen" became a bit naff, and for men over a certain age he became a guilty pleasure, like jumping up and down at a UK SUBS reunion gig.

Throughout the Nineties he made the long walk back from the wilderness. First came "Streets of Philadelphia" (which bagged him an Oscar), then the difficult but critically well-received album, *The Ghost Of Tom Joad*, in 1995. A dour acoustic record full of Steinbeck and Guthrie tidbits, devoid of artificial colouring, it sold around 120,000 in the UK, roughly a tenth of *Born In The USA*. Middle-age brought a fully-fledged reunion tour with the E STREET BAND four years later, along with the release of *Tracks*, a celebratory four-CD boxed set of mostly rejected material, followed by the release of *18 Tracks*, an edited version including a reworking of "The Promise", a song he wrote and recorded for the album that became *Darkness On The Edge Of Town*, but which lay around for twenty years while he decided what to do with it. It's considered by some to be the best song he's ever written, and its mournful romanticism – "two-bit bars", "broken spirits", and "broken cars" (any more clichés up your chambray shirtsleeve, Springsteen?) – was a reminder that what he did best was synthesise the pulp American experience. (It may be heresy, but I maintain the best Springsteen song was actually written by TOM WAITS, "Jersey Girl", to be found on *Live/1975-85*; not forgetting that Waits was also responsible for the best EAGLES song, "01'55", from *On the Border*.)

In 2010, he finally released *The Promise*, the album that would have come out after *Born To Run* if he hadn't been embroiled in a legal battle with his former manager. And, much to the surprise of even those who already had bootleg versions of the bulk of the material, it was an extraordinary record, easily as good as anything he has recorded in his forty-year career.

How good was it? Well, it was as though the BEATLES had decided not to release the "White Album" –preferring instead to offer a few of its songs to other performers, alluding to the album only in passing. Imagine the original version of "Obladi Oblada" was by the MARMALADE; imagine the only recorded versions of "While My Guitar Gently Weeps" were on ERIC CLAPTON live CDs. Yes, *The Promise* was not only as good as the "White Album", it showed such a love for the work

S

S

of ROY ORBISON, PHIL SPECTOR, and ELVIS, that it made some of the more nostalgic material on his recent records, *Magic*, and *Working On A Dream*, far more understandable.

The album had an edge, too. While he was recording it, punk was causing seismic ructions throughout the industry, and Springsteen would make regular forays to his local record store in Manhattan to buy all the latest singles from London, Manchester, and New York. "I took them home, heard something unique, undeniable, and not so foreign to my experience," he said. "My musical path had been chosen but the uncompromising power of these records found its way onto *Darkness* through the choices and themes of my material." Most of the tougher material found itself included on *The Darkness On The Edge Of Town,* but some of it found its way onto *The Promise.* In some ways this is one of the most generic records Springsteen ever recorded, with glockenspiel and saxophone to the fore, and because of the occasional punk influences, some of the songs sound like they were recorded for an IGGY POP Christmas record.

Bruce has never been what you might call garrulous, which in turn has contributed to his iconic status among the public, particularly in the States. Recently, though, he has loosened up a lot. A few years ago, when I saw him, he even started making jokes on stage. They were all quite ribald, and this is one of the few suitable to be told before the cocktail hour (not that Bruce would ever dream of having anything as affected as a cocktail).

A woman comes out of her house in the morning and there's a gorilla in a tree in her front yard. She goes, "Jeez, that's silly. You must have escaped last night from the zoo." Then a guy comes and knocks on her door. [Bruce makes a knocking sound on his guitar.] She opens the door and he says, "Ma'am, I'm here to remove the gorilla from your tree, and since this isn't really a normal day I'm going to need a little help." And she says, "Okay..." She goes out into the front yard and there's a stick, a pair of handcuffs, a Chihuahua, and a gun. "Ma'am, I'm going to go up into this tree and I'm going to poke the gorilla with this stick, the gorilla's going to fall out of the tree, and when he falls out of the tree this Chihuahua has been trained to bite him in the b****. Then when he covers himself you're going to throw the handcuffs on him." She says, "Okay, but I got one question: What's the shotgun for?"

"If I fall out of the tree first, shoot the Chihuahua."

STAPLE SINGERS

They started out gospel, then went secular. "When we started doing songs like 'I'll Take You There' and 'Respect Yourself', the church people got all upset, saying we were playing the devil's music and whatnot, but those songs are about the Lord."

RINGO STARR

An hour or so into my interview with Ringo Starr, as we were exploring the changing ambitions and motivations of the recovering alcoholic – a subject he had willingly brought up himself – the fifty-eight year old ex-Beatle stopped in mid-sentence and said, with surprising indignation, "Look, this is all very interesting, but if we could talk about the record for a while, if we could ever do that, that would be good."

He looked at his watch and then fixed me with one of his stares. Though we were in a plush suite in the Carlton Tower Hotel just off London's Sloane Street, I was suddenly transported back to school, half expecting the celebrity in front of me to don a mortar board and start lecturing me on the etiquette of mentioning "the product".

Ringo was present, under sufferance, so it seemed, to publicise his new record, his first since 1992, an album of fairly orthodox, inoffensive rock music called *Vertical Man*.

S

A record, he hoped, that could catapult him back among the big boys (it wouldn't, as it wasn't very good). He hadn't had a meaningful hit in Britain for a quarter of a century, and even Ringo thought this might be a little too long.

So what do we know of Ringo Starr? Well, in 1998 – when I met him – he was pretty much the same as he is today: he is still the ex-drummer of the most famous group there will ever be, an ex-Beatle who hates being know as such. For most of the Sixties we knew him as a cuddly, ugly-cute pop star, a happy-go-lucky imp, ever ready with a self-deprecating quip or nonsensical epigram. Then there's the nose, one of the many reasons he was so loved as a Beatle. He's been teased about it since he was a baby – his nickname for years was simply "The Nose" – yet even though he can appear a belligerent old bugger, he still seems good-natured about it. Why shouldn't he be? It endeared him to millions. When Beatlemania hit the States in 1964 it was Ringo who proved the most popular, Ringo who was considered the most lovable. My favourite "nose" story concerns a spelling mistake in an American tabloid newspaper: "Ringo Party Row: Ringo Starr had a visit from the police after his Los Angeles neighbours complained about the amount of nose."

But in 1998 – like now – Ringo Starr was not so cuddly anymore, not so self-deprecating. The moptop had long grown tired of being cast as the bumbling Beatle.

Previously the third most famous person in the world, Ringo has had his downs, and for a man who appears to have turned indolence in to an art form, he has certainly made life difficult for himself. There have been the drugs, the lengthy bouts with drink, the temper tantrums, and the professional failures. He has also turned into one of those pop stars – like LOU REED, say, or CHUCK BERRY – who are notorious for the disdain with which they treat the press. He loathes talking about the past, particularly the B-E-A-T-L-E-S, so interviewing him can be tricky. In 2008 he publicly said he was too busy to read his fan mail, and in the same year said that he missed "nothing" about Liverpool, sparking fury in the press and in his hometown.

When we met I was told that there was to be no booze or cigarettes around, although as the interview was scheduled to start at 9:30am, this wasn't too much of a problem. Ringo hasn't had a drink since 1988, and usually doesn't like to be reminded of the fact. He might have known he'd have problems with drink, as he had his first alcoholic blackout at nine. Being in the BEATLES didn't help; the band had always been partial to a few Scotch and Cokes, while Ringo's drinking started to get worse in the mid-Seventies, shortly after his solo career peaked. His cognac drinking became legendary, and he once said, "I wouldn't go out because you'd have to be in the car for forty minutes without a drink." Aware of his problem, he began replacing his beloved cognac with Brandy Alexanders and then, when his addiction really escalated, wine, often sinking sixteen bottles a day. He spent much of the mid-Seventies boozing away the Californian days with the likes of KEITH MOON, HARRY NILSSON, and JOHN LENNON – then enjoying a temporary split from YOKO ONO. "If you were straight I wouldn't have you in my house."

Finally, in October 1988, he sought professional help, and checked into an addiction clinic in Arizona. With good reason, he has become quite evangelical about his sobriety. "I just couldn't handle it, and those nights when you drink more than you remembered had become almost every night. The way I am now is a direct result of sobering up, as I was so busy getting drunk that I didn't take notice of anyone else, only myself. I think I am a nicer person since I stopped drinking."

Whereas he used to have a look of perpetual bewilderment, Ringo has developed a formidable poker-faced stare. He is not so obviously loveable these days, appearing rather curmudgeonly and curt. Somewhere along the road, probably when he was drinking sixteen bottles of wine a day, his laconic humour turned into an uncharitable surliness. He says he's not a difficult person to work for, but I have my doubts. He is edgy and self-absorbed, and gives the impression he expects to be treated as though he were still the third most famous person in the world.

S

When we met he looked elegant and approachable enough – as well as his two small earrings and tinted spectacles, he wore a black Nehru jacket, black tailored drainpipe jeans, black PATRICK COX boots, and a pink PAUL SMITH watch – but as soon as we started to talk it was obvious he considered it a publicity chore, not respite. His Pagliacci eyes looked you over, searching for indications of cynicism, and he continually crossed his arms. Oh, the body language! As for his speaking voice, he now possesses one of the world's unlikeliest mid-Atlantic accents, peppering his cumbersome Liverpudllian drone with Americanisms such as "guy", "chick", "todally", and "gotten". The voice is quintessentially Ringo, a noise it would be impossible to alter. "I have the range of a fly," he said once. "But a *large* fly."

"He can be a handful," said someone who used to work with him, "but if you steer clear of the BEATLES and the booze you'll be alright." As it was, Ringo brought these subjects up independently.

"Though he's still lumbered with the clownish image, I think he handles it quite well," said an executive who used to work at Apple in London. "With day to day matters he's always been easy to deal with – in fact, you get the feeling he's overridden by the others [the BEATLES] a lot of the time. It's only when he gets involved with those he doesn't know that his other side shows through. He can be mistrustful of people."

Did Ringo think he is difficult? "Well, I expect people to do exactly what I ask them to do, but I'm not difficult as such. I expect people to act professionally. If people don't pull their weight I just fire them, simple. Get out, get off. I've calmed down a lot these days, and that's a direct result of sobering up. Buddha has this great line: the hardest thing we can do is change our mind. And I had to do it, and I do it now on a daily basis. With drink I am not strict with other people, or those that work for me, I'm only strict with myself."

He didn't like reporters, though, did he?

"I can't answer that, I really can't. All I know is that I find it easier to deal with criticism now, I used to wake up in the morning and want everyone to love me and I wanted them to love everything I did. Now I know that they're sometimes absolutely right."

So what made him angry? "Oh anything, I just have to wake up."

He was a lot less difficult than I had expected him to be, but then this was his first print interview for over five years. After two hours with me he was already beginning to tire, and I can imagine him being a bit brusque at the end of the day. He made a big effort to be conciliatory, but every now and then a distinct edge came back into his voice, which made me think he could be highly demanding. This edge was disconcerting because Ringo's current state of mind – according to the man himself – was meant to be one of serenity and forgiveness. But if he was feeling so manifestly spiritual, so centred about things, why was he so spiky?

"I'm not sure it's spiritual; it's just that the gist of what I do now is peace, love, and understanding, and I surround myself with people who think the same," he said. "I had lunch with GEORGE [HARRISON] yesterday and we were laughing because he used to co-write my early songs, because I couldn't finish them, and he was into Krishna and God and whatnot in the early Seventies but I couldn't say that stuff then. I suppose I am practising to be more spiritual, to be a better human being. I try and do that more and more on a daily basis. But it was mainly, 'What about me?' And although it's still a lot of, 'What about me?' it's also, 'What about you?'"

He certainly had been of great help to PAUL McCARTNEY, who had been living with the tragedy of his wife's death. "I do what I can. It's hard, you know, it's hit him very hard and it'll take him some time to come to terms with it," said Ringo. "He's spending a lot of time with his kids, going to Paris to see Stella. He's taking their support. But it's tough."

As for himself, Ringo thought he was even more considerate than he'd ever been, more understanding of people's ways. "A lot of it's got to do with Barbara; she's a very forgiving person. To live with me for eighteen years you'd have to be forgiving."

S How times have changed. Once, when asked whether he had a message for his fans, he said, "Message? I'm not a post office." When the BEATLES visited the Maharishi in his Himalayan retreat back in 1968, Ringo, overly frank as always, said the place "was a bit like Butlin's".

It is now over seventy years since Richard Starkey was born in his parents' bedroom in their home in Dingle on Merseyside. Born into a close-knit if war-torn community, his was a world of barmaids, bakers and boilermakers, of house-painters and shipyards, where neighbours were considered extended family. It was a long time ago, a long time since CILLA BLACK – then Pricilla White – used to "do" Ringo's mum Elsie's hair. Dogged by recurrent ill health, little Richie spent more time in sanatoriums than he did at school, and when he eventually left at the age of fifteen he could barely read or write. His first jobs included messenger boy, ferryboat barman, and joiner, until the skiffle craze got him started as a drummer and something of a local celebrity. Richard Starkey then became Ringo Starr when RORY STORM – the leader of Ringo's first band, RORY STORM AND THE HURRICANES – rechristened him because of his habit of wearing lots of rings. "Ringo Starkey sounded a bit funny. Starr was a natural, it made sense to me and I liked it," said Ringo.

He was the Beatle with the drollest sense of humour, the one blessed with the most offhand resilience and self-deprecation. Like JOHN LENNON, who had a similarly sardonic view of the world, Ringo could always be relied upon to come up with the dead-pan one-liner ("I love Beethoven, especially the poems"), or a piece of Scouse fireside wisdom (Reporter: "Why do you wear all those rings on your fingers?" Ringo: "Because I can't get them through my nose"). Then there were the famous "Ringoisms" like "It's no different change, really" and "I haven't got a smiling mouth or a talking face." He famously came up with titles for various BEATLES songs such as "Tomorrow Never Knows", although 1964's "A Hard Day's Night", which has forever been associated with him, was actually coined by the singer EARTHA KITT a year earlier.

And DAVID BAILEY claims to have coined "Eight Days A Week" ("Because I was working so much, and when JOHN LENNON asked me one night in the Ad-Lib how I was I told him I'd been working eight days a week..."). Always demonstrably down-to-earth, during the BEATLES' heyday, when they spent fortunes everyday on everything from cars and cine cameras to bespoke suits and jewellery, Ringo favourably compared Asprey's to Woolworths.

Yet he was a star. While it is certainly true that he spent much of his time during those famous recording sessions playing cards with BEATLES' assistants MAL EVANS and NEIL ASPINALL, his is the happy voice-over we hear on "Yellow Submarine", "Octopus' Garden", and "With a Little Help from My Friends" and the other songs that turned the world's most famous drummer into the world's most famous pub singer. Even when he was attempting heart-rending ballads he still sounded as though he were simply reading the football results.

He married early, at the age of twenty-four, wedding MAUREEN COX, a hairdresser's assistant and his childhood sweetheart, in February 1965, divorcing ten years later. He has three children by Maureen: Zak, a drummer; Lee, a make-up artist who recently suffered a brain tumour; and Jason, also a drummer. In 1995 Maureen died of leukaemia, and Ringo was there at her bedside.

Bored by the BEATLES' obsession with recording, he began a secondary career in films, appearing in *Candy* (1968) with MARLON BRANDO, and *The Magic Christian* (1968) with PETER SELLERS. Then there was *200 Motels* (1971) with FRANK ZAPPA, *That'll Be The Day* (1973) with DAVID ESSEX, and KEN RUSSELL's ridiculous *Lisztomania* (1975). His acting wasn't at all bad, and one could have imagined him building on those early roles and developing into a reasonable character actor, but again he got bored. "I was a personality actor who was mucking about. I'm a drummer, not an actor."

Ironically, he was also the first Beatle to quit the group, leaving during the recording of the "White Album" when the

S band's tardiness got too much for him. He spent two weeks on PETER SELLERS's yacht before being coaxed back, only to have the group disintegrate two years later. Of the four, Ringo was the one who took the BEATLES' split the hardest, and who was the most often quoted wishing they could all be together again. "Just say the feeling is based on my natural optimism," he once said when asked why he thought they might re-form.

His solo career was initially as successful as any other Beatle's, giving him huge hits with singles such as "It Don't Come Easy", "Back Off Boogaloo", "Photograph", and "You're Sixteen". His albums didn't do too badly, either, and by the mid-Seventies he was as successful and as famous as he had been ten years earlier. But then his indifference to his career and his penchant for booze conspired against him, causing him to release some of the worst records of his life – or anyone else's career. He tried to diversify, launching a furniture company, in 1971, whose most photographed item was a coffee table fashioned from a Rolls-Royce radiator grille. The business was up for sale by 1976. After this he launched a record label, Ring O'Records, which lasted two years. There was the acting, the occasional record and cameo as a highly-paid session drummer, but the rest of the time the reluctant vaudevillian went on holiday.

He met his second wife, the actress and former Bond girl BARBARA BACH, in 1981, on the set of *Caveman*, a film in which the participants had little to do but grunt, scratch and gesticulate. Bach brought a passion to his life, yet she also became his drinking partner, something he could have done without. He eventually paid the price.

The rich and famous move in higher gears than most, their lives accelerated to the point of absurdity; their downtime is equally extreme, often involving months, sometimes years, of luxurious indolence. When they've stopped drinking, drugging, and generally abusing themselves, the tendency is towards extravagant pastimes while maybe pursuing a few ancillary projects on the side. Having dabbled in film production, acting, retailing, professional endorsements and

S

the like, and having drunk himself senseless for the best part of twenty years, Ringo now seems quite content to sit around the house and do not much at all. In reality, one supposes that he's always been fairly good at it.

"I don't fill every moment, it's easy for me to relax," he said when we met. "It's easy for me to just sit in the garden, or walk in the country. I don't have to be a busy person. I'm not a workaholic. My ambition is to have joy in my life, to sleep easy. I muck about on the piano, but I have to sit down many, many times before something happens."

His song writing has improved since the old days, when he used to present a half-written song to Lennon or McCartney only to be told that it was already a hit for someone else. "I wrote a lot of songs in the BEATLES but they were always variations of someone else's song. I'd hear a record on the radio and then subconsciously write it again!" By his own admission, even now Ringo can only write a few verses before he starts getting bored: "Ending is hard for me, I just repeat myself. I like giving someone the general idea and then let them get on with it. I'm not really a songwriter. My mum used to say that she's never seen me happier than when I was drumming, and I still feel like that."

In his time Ringo has done some odd things, but nothing you'd particularly begrudge him. He turned down a part in *Dallas* but accepted a role in the US mini-series of Judith Krantz's *Princess Daisy*. In the mid-Eighties he famously advertised wine coolers on American television and in 1996 was paid £500,000 for two days' work to appear in a Japanese soft drink commercial. In 1997 his image even appeared in *The Simpsons*. He also had a 3.2 percent stake in Britt Allcroft Productions, the company that licensed *Thomas the Tank Engine*, and made over £2m from his work as the former narrator of the series. By 2011 he was worth around £100m, netting further millions from the eight-hour BEATLES *Anthology*, plus a few more from the three double CDs, as well as all the BEATLES reissues up to and including the recent release of all their songs on iTunes.

S He has pharaonically extravagant homes in Los Angeles and Monte Carlo – where he has lived since 1989 – as well as a £2.3m penthouse in London, and in 1999 bought Rydinghurst, the two hundred-acre 17th Century mansion in Surrey. In 1998 I interviewed him for the *Sunday Times*, and I turned up with a photographer, an old friend from the Sixties, who greeted him as Rich; and as one of the assistants was also called this, Ringo suggested they refer to the ex-Beatle as "Very". When he said, "I'm not an extravagant guy, I did all that years ago... there's nothing I can't afford, but then there's nothing I particularly want that I haven't got," it was easy to believe him.

What he wants to do, he said, was drum, because that's what he does best. "I'm not too bothered about making records, I just loved playing live, it's what I do. I'm not a plumber, I'm not an electrician, I'm a drummer. I learnt to play drums in clubs and bars, but with the BEATLES, after a while, we just messed about in the studio. I play a lot more now."

While Ringo is undoubtedly the world's most famous drummer, he has never been the world's best drummer, and his style has often been called clumsy. In the Sixties, one critic said he made his drums sound like puddings, and when MUHAMMAD ALI first heard him, he gibed, "My dog plays better drums!" "Poor Ringo," it was whispered, as the bejewelled sticksman walked through the hallowed corridors of London's swankiest nightclubs. "He's not the best drummer in the world." "You know what?" said JOHN LENNON. "He's not even the best drummer in the BEATLES." Oddly, when Cirque du Soleil put on *Love* in Las Vegas, the subsequent remixed record showed Ringo in a completely new light, and if anyone ever wants to know what the BEATLES saw in the big-nosed Teddy Boy, then they need only listen to *Love* to find out.

For better or worse, you still can't mistake him, something he's enormously proud of. Proud and slightly resentful; if you mention that there might be drummers out there who are better than he is, he'll jump down your throat. "I'm the *only* person who can play like I play, but I'm a drummer so I need other people around me, I can't go on tour by myself. I'm sure I've evolved, but the actual rhythm pattern remains the same. I'm just a really good player."

The reason Ringo plays like he does, the reason he sounds so "Ringo-ish" on all those old BEATLES records and even on the new one, is the fault of his grandmother. Ringo was born left-handed but from an early age his grandmother forced him to become right-handed, so even now, although he plays a right-handed drum kit – "I play it backwards, really, moving around it in an anti-clockwise fashion" – he holds a cricket bat with his left hand, and signs autographs with his right. Semidextrous rather than ambidextrous, his left hand only has a slight idea what his right hand is doing.

"I play a right-handed kit with a left-handed heart."

Insecurity seems to be the motivating force behind much of his recent work. Having grown sick of being treated like a buffoon for much of the Sixties, and having been drunk for much of the Seventies and Eighties, in the Nineties he decided he wanted to be taken seriously. For the last decade and a half he has toured with his ALL-STARR BAND, a constantly changing group of session musicians and ex-rock stars (men like JOE WALSH, JACK BRUCE, and PETER FRAMPTON) who have learnt their "chops" in supergroups like the EAGLES, CREAM, and HUMBLE PIE. Ringo sets great store by virtuosity and likes to surround himself with it.

This insecurity was also possibly behind his decision to record a version of the BEATLES' first single, "Love Me Do", in 1998. "It may look odd," said Ringo, "but I'd always wanted to do that song properly. I was always adamant that I would never cover a BEATLES song, even when Paul asked me to, but I began to think that it was my legacy, too, so why not? Everybody else does them, so it was about time I grew out of it. I won't be doing 'Eleanor Rigby', or 'Hey Jude', or 'Glass Onion', but I can do 'Love Me Do'. People accuse Paul of sounding like the BEATLES, but shit, give him a break. Someone said the other day that my new record sounds a little Beatley, but shit, why not. I am one."

S Perhaps the real reason he decided on this particular song dates back to the BEATLES' first demos for GEORGE MARTIN at EMI in 1962. Martin wasn't convinced about PETE BEST's drumming abilities, so he brought in a session drummer called ALAN WHITE to work on the recording session. By then, Ringo had replaced Best, but Martin wasn't taking any chances. Ringo subsequently played on the album version, but the BEATLES' first-ever single will forever feature a session drummer.

The BEATLES' legacy is one he is increasingly tired of decoding for others. "I never read anything about the BEATLES, never," he told me. "A lot of people like to make stuff up and I'm sick of it. Doing the *Anthology* was our way of setting the record straight. Often our accounts of what happened would differ, but what it did show was how we loved each other. Then we grew up and we broke up.

"Thank God the BEATLES happened in the Sixties and not now. It was pretty tough on us but not as tough as it is today, particularly for groups like OASIS. There aren't any pictures of us in clubs, and the BEATLES were in clubs every night. We could escape, unlike this lot. I don't lie awake at night worrying about OASIS, though. The BEATLES had a couple of drinks, too, in the Sixties and we made it through. We're still here."

Which brings us back to Ringo's relatively newfound, if rather elastic, deistic beliefs. "Without any hesitation I'd say I was a lucky person," he said. "Things have happened which have brought me up short. My daughter's tumour, the death of my ex-wife, my wife's mother who died last year, and now LINDA McCARTNEY. Things like that make you look at yourself. I feel blessed."

It would be easy to see Ringo Starr's spiritual emergence as an exercise in redemption – born again as a teetotal sourpuss – although actually it has more to do with survival. In his own eyes, Ringo's very existence is essentially a homage to all those souls who have made it through the rough times – well, all those recovering, alcoholic, celebrity drummers who have made it through the rough times. It reinforces the fact that he is no rock'n'roll casualty. Unlike the HARRY NILSSONS, the

KEITH MOONS, and all the other hell-raisers he hung around with in the Seventies, Ringo is still with us, and that, plainly, is something worth celebrating.

"These days I live in the now," said Ringo, as he peered, rather bad-temperedly, from behind his tinted spectacles. "I've never written my autobiography because the publishers only want to know what happened in the BEATLES. But I'm not interested in any of that. I was born very young and had a good life. End of story."

STEEL PULSE

Originating from Handsworth, Birmingham, during the punk era, the band were named, rather prosaically, after a race horse. Closely aligning themselves with Rock Against Racism, they signed to CHRIS BLACKWELL's Island and released *Handsworth Revolution* (1978), which remains their defining moment. They may have played at BILL CLINTON's inauguration in 1993, but they'll be remembered largely for "Ku Klux Klan", the album's stand-out track.

STEELY DAN

You can tell almost all you need to know about a person by asking them what sort of music they like. And although that's the sort of question usually only asked (and answered) by boys between the ages of twelve and eighteen, I was asked it a while ago by someone I'd never met before. And even though I could have easily beaten it back by saying something flippant, or something that "would have done", I was stumped.

The American writer CHUCK KLOSTERMAN said that, having for many years experimented with a litany of abstract responses when asked this question, he started to say, with some honesty as well as accuracy, "Music that sounds

S like the opening fourteen seconds of HUMBLE PIE's 'I Don't Need No Doctor', as performed live on their 1971 album, *Performance: Rockin' the Fillmore.*"

Now, never having heard this record, I couldn't comment – although it certainly sounds like the sort of thing I wouldn't like at all – but apparently it has the desired effect, the reply having the added bonus of significantly changing the conversation, or ending it entirely.

Usually the answers to questions like these are either endearingly banal – "Oh, the usual, you know, ABBA, the BEATLES, a bit of COLDPLAY" – unbearably pretentious – "the first five FALL singles and pretty much nothing before or since" – or, in the case of a lot of politicians, simply lies.

Having thought about it myself, I've decided to adopt Chuck's policy. Initially I thought of just saying "Steely Dan", because it not only shows confidence (they're not really what anyone could call cool), but like Marmite, they are an acquired taste, and unless you're an aficionado, you'll probably hate them.

However, like Chuck, I've decided to be annoyingly specific, and while I thought about singing the praises, yet again, of their sixth album, *Aja*, the next time someone asks me what kind of music I like I'm going to say, having first locked them in with my most sincere stare, "Music that sounds like the second guitar solo in 'Green Earrings' (from *The Royal Scam*), the one that arrives after two minutes and seven seconds, the one that makes you feel as though you're cruising over the Florida Keys' Seven Mile Bridge in a rented Mustang."

And if I were asked what the best album of all time is? Well, it obviously isn't *Nevermind*, isn't *Revolver,* and isn't *Pet Sounds*. Strangely it isn't even *Sgt Pepper, London Calling*, or *Sticky Fingers*. No, the best album of all time was released at the end of August 1977, just as the sweltering Summer of Hate was beginning to wilt. But this record has nothing to do with the SEX PISTOLS, the CLASH, or the JAM (who all released classic LPs in 1977), has no affinity with the estuarial guttersnipe squall of punk. In fact this record is as far away from the insurgency of punk as Southern California is from the Westway.

S

The aforementioned *Aja* is as gentrified and as anal a record as you'll ever hope to hear. DONALD FAGEN and WALTER BECKER's masterpiece is an homage to passive aggressive studio cool, and in their own way the progenitors of the world's greatest record were as disdainful of the palm tree and flared denim world of Los Angeles as the whey-faced urchins from west London, and the band's nihilism is plain for all to hear, disguised as FM-friendly soft-rock. Their lyrics are dispassionate, the song structures ridiculously premeditated, the guitar solos ridiculously sarcastic. And yet they made, over a two-year recording period, some of the most sophisticated, the most polished, most burnished music ever heard: "Black Cow", "Deacon Blues", "Home At Last", and the rest.

Steely Dan weren't just up my street; they were, to paraphrase NICK HORNBY, knocking on my door, pressing the intercom and peering through the letterbox to see if I was in. Which I was, crouched over the B&O, devouring the pop art dystopia that was the DNA of the Steely Dan brand (also available in different forms on *Can't Buy A Thrill*, *Countdown To Ecstasy*, *Pretzel Logic*, *The Royal Scam*, and many more).

Aja was their high water mark. You can keep your *Zuma*, your *Veedon Fleece*, your *Blue*, your *Parachutes*, or your *OK Computer*. They might all be straight from the heart, but Steely Dan's *Aja* offers the delights of a world uncharted by pop groups, past or present. Those who hate the band call them sterile, surgical, cold. Which is sort of the point. Becker and Fagen – fundamentally sociopaths masquerading as benign dictators – like to give the impression they're being as insincere as possible, the very antithesis, frankly, of almost everyone else in the music business.

CAT STEVENS

S

For a music critic there are few things more excruciating or indeed more embarrassing than sitting through the playback of a new record in the presence of the person who has just recorded it. You sit there, just the two of you, in an anonymous recording studio, as the star proudly, painstakingly, plays you every song from his new CD, explaining his divine inspiration, his search for truth, and gleefully looking up at you after each track, awaiting your (no doubt) adulatory pearls of wisdom. Said star has probably just spent the best part of eighteen months recording this latest masterpiece, sometimes longer, and, if they're honest, are not looking for anything other than fulsome praise. A lot of it. They're certainly not looking for anything other than fulsome praise from you, anyway.

Having been in this situation on a number of occasions, there is little you can do but tell them that every song is little short of a masterpiece. "Brilliant." "Amazing." "Just wonderful." "Wow, I've never heard anything like this, this is just so... good..." But predictably, this is a process of diminishing returns, as not only do you soon run out of superlatives, it's also impossible to be objective.

I once spent a few hours in a New York midtown recording studio with DAVID BOWIE, as he played me every track from his *Earthling* album (the drum and bass one, the one where he wears an ALEXANDER MCQUEEN Union Jack jacket on the cover), and while it was easy to find nice things to say about the first few tracks, after half-a-dozen songs I felt my enthusiasm beginning to wane. And so I did what any self-respecting critic would do in my situation, I was honest. Which, given the circumstances, I'm not sure Bowie exactly wanted me to be. I wasn't rude – Bowie is a musical genius and even his less successful ventures tend to be better than anyone else's – but instead of saying "Brilliant", "Amazing", or "Just Wonderful", I said things like "Well, I like it, but I don't like it quite as much as the other ones", and "It's not exactly 'Life On Mars',

is it, Dave?" Actually I didn't say that at all – no one says
that to Bowie – but I was fairly circumspect. After which he
looked at me as though I'd just accused him of moonlighting
as a roadie for a GARY NUMAN tribute band. Anyway, the album
eventually picked up speed (and actually turned out to be one
of the best he recorded in the Nineties), so I'm glad I saved a
few superlatives till last.

My worst experience was with TERENCE TRENT D'ARBY, back
at the tail end of the Eighties. Having released an extraordinary
debut album in 1987, he decided to follow it with one of the
most perverse albums ever made, a pretty damn awful thing
called *Neither Fish Nor Flesh*. Having interviewed him at
the time – where he sat cross-legged in a completely white
room in a large rented St John's Wood house and laboriously
explained how he was channelling MARVIN GAYE and the Lord
Almighty (among others) – I knew he was also trying to evoke
WALT WHITMAN's *Leaves of Grass*, although it only took me
one listen to wonder whether he hadn't been smoking some
instead. The title was actually a complete misnomer, because
it stank like a six-week-old trout, and should have been called
Neither Good Nor Brief.

Occasionally, just occasionally, you go to a playback
that isn't embarrassing at all, and so it was when I went
to a playback of YUSUF ISLAM's new CD in Queen's Park, in
northwest London, in 2008. Sixty-one-year-old Yusuf – who
for many years traversed the globe as Cat Stevens – looked
lean, contented, well-groomed, and spoke in the same
dulcet north London tones he did when he was regularly on
television in the early Seventies, introducing such hits as
"Morning Has Broken", "Matthew And Son", "Father And
Son", and "Another Saturday Night". He not only played his
new CD (*Roadsinger*), giving a running commentary as to
how he came up with each song, but also, halfway through
the session, decided to pick up his guitar and actually play
the songs himself. And, having assumed he had turned into
a grizzly old polemicist who could neither write nor sing
anymore, I was assaulted by a singing voice that had altered

S not one jot in thirty-five years. Encouragingly, the songs weren't so far away from the sort of material he wrote before he turned his back on music in 1978 (deciding to devote himself to philanthropic causes in the Muslim community instead); with one song, the title track, already sounding like a classic. He enlisted the help of PAUL MCCARTNEY and DOLLY PARTON on one song, while another sounded like it could have come from a PAUL WELLER CD.

Part of Stevens' appeal was always his looks – he appeared at a time when girls in their late teens were buying records by sensitive, good-looking singer-songwriters – and while he was no longer a hirsute Adonis, he still had charm. Maybe I was biased: when I lived on the south coast when I was ten, I used to lie in the back garden staring at the sky and play a cassette of Stevens' early, Sixties songs, things like "Laughing Apple", and "Bad Night". I'm not sure if they were any good; they were there when I did what I did.

DAVE STEWART

The former Eurythmic is the man with everyone on speed dial. He has worked with more famous people than ZELIG – OK, deep breath, MICK JAGGER, BONO, BOB DYLAN, the NEVILLE BROTHERS, RINGO STARR, LOU REED, BRIAN MAY, JOSS STONE, TOM PETTY, TERRY HALL, DARYL HALL, JIMMY CLIFF, STEVIE NICKS, ARETHA FRANKLIN, BRYAN FERRY, and half the other people you can think of without really trying. As the journalist DAVID QUANTICK said not so long ago, "Dave Stewart is so much top-level, highest echelon rock superstar club that part of me is convinced he was in the TRAVELING WILBURYS." I was with him once, in his recording studio in London's Crouch End, when a personalised leather invitation arrived of such lavishness (private jets, luxury yachts, seven star hotels, etc) that it looked like a spoof, but then Stewart's life is so gilded that he even had the temerity to complain of Paradise Syndrome (feeling dissatisfaction, even though you have success and riches beyond your most imaginative dreams). His own records are scattershot, hit and miss, his one true classic being "Heart Of Stone", from 1994's *Greetings From The Gutter*.

S

ROD STEWART

Christmas records come and go, but there will always be SLADE. And WIZZARD. The seemingly ubiquitous POGUES. Again and again and again. Personally I have always preferred a bit of FRANK SINATRA at Christmas, or, perversely, the BEACH BOYS, as their Southern Californian harmonies always sound surreal wrapped around "Santa Claus Is Coming To Town", "Silent Night", or "White Christmas". The song that really sums up this time of year for me, however, is Rod Stewart's "Sailing". Not because it's the best song in the world, and not because it's Rod's best performance, but simply because of its ubiquity. When it first came out I was fifteen, and for two or three years Christmas never seemed to end, as that's all I ever seemed to hear on the radio. When people say the Seventies were grey, they're wrong: they were white.

I heard the record so much that after a while I began to hate it, in the way that every punk at the time was conditioned to hate anything that had preceded spiky hair and safety pins. But while I still don't love it, there are dozens of other Rod Stewart songs that I would take with me to a desert island (even some of his more recent ones, the ones we're not meant to like). Why? Well, we don't just like rock stars because of their records; we somehow have to like them, too, and who doesn't love Rod? He has, after all, always behaved like a pop star should. And like the best, has always been resolutely upwardly mobile. In the mid-Seventies, he moved away from the public bars and greyhound racing of grey old Blighty to the cocktail bars and manicured poodles of California, and swapped his leather coats and tartan

S scarves for fishnet T-shirts, spandex, satin shorts, and garish headbands. During much of the Eighties, his eyes lassoed by eyeliner, and believing that an old silk jumpsuit would never let him down, Stewart started to resemble OLIVIA NEWTON JOHN. But still we loved him.

Also, never let it be said that Rod hasn't done his bit for female emancipation – he has, after all, seen more sex than a policeman's torch. As DAVID WALLIAMS said once, "Rod Stewart is a man of principle – he will not go out with a woman with brown hair." And what a litany of women: Harrington (D), Ekland (B), Hamilton (A), Emberg (K), Hunter (R), and finally (for now), Lancaster (P). That's some alphabet. A blonde alphabet, if you will.

One of the reasons that Rod is still the man he is, one of the reasons he can still sell out Twickenham or the O2 in the time it takes him to sing "Maggie May", is his inelegantly coiffured barnet. Rod Stewart's hair has not only spent four decades defying logic as well as a good brush, it has also become his defining badge of cool. Take away the Stewart locks and you are left with a phenomenal singer in tight trousers. Take away the pineapple hair and all you end up with is an ageing lothario who also happens to sing a bit.

This is something that's rarely mentioned when discussing those singers who are knocking on a bit. Admittedly PHIL COLLINS still has something of a career, but would MICK HUCKNALL still be famous if he were bald? Would ROBBIE WILLIAMS? Would MICK JAGGER? Back in the Eighties there was an hilarious (and obviously untrue) rumour that PAUL SIMON used to have a "rug" roadie on tour with him, whose job it was to ferry Simon's collection of wigs from one gig to another, so that when he sang "Bridge Over Troubled Water" and "Mrs Robinson", his baby boomer audience didn't have to watch the spotlight bouncing off his forehead. Could anyone ever seriously imagine Rod doing the same? Not only is he gifted with the looks of a rock star, he's also gifted in the art of common sense.

The thing about Stewart, the reason he is considered as much of an institution as MICHAEL PALIN or STEPHEN FRY, is the fact that he's never taken himself too seriously, even during his spandex period. And while he is fiercely proud of his music, essentially he's a self-effacing crooner who has never forgotten where he came from. A few years ago a friend of mine interviewed him for a music magazine, and as their chat was coming to an end, they started talking about that particular male gene that causes us to take our trousers off when we're drunk. As if to illustrate the point, Rod then went off to find some photographic evidence – namely a bunch of snaps showing Rod the Mod and his mates in a state of celebratory undress.

And it all came with a running commentary. There was a photo of Rod posing saucily in a shrunken pair of lurid skimpies ("what a slut"); another showing him with his shirt undone having obviously polished off several magnums of good red ("that's me well p*****"); squashed into the electrical closet of a club with a saucepan on his head ("me in the electrical closet of this club with a saucepan on my head"); and one which even Rod seemed reluctant – or at least unable – to explain. This turned out to be a photograph of his ex-wife sitting on the loo, with, as my friend put it at the time, "a lacy suspension bridge of knicker between her knees".

As the soul singer supreme studied the picture, a frown gradually descended over his face, as though he were exploring a thought that had never occurred to him before.

"Hang on," he said. "I don't remember taking that one."

STING

On the wall in the ground floor lavatory of Sting's Highgate cottage there used to be (maybe still is) a framed newspaper cartoon of two tired businessmen sitting mournfully at a bar. One is saying to the other: "Oh, I'm pretty happy. I just wish my life was more like Sting's."

S Who wouldn't? Here is a man who appears to have everything: looks, talent, money, creative success, even – some would say – a conscience. But does he have respect? Though he is still enormously popular, he is also strangely reviled. He has become the man it's OK to hate, the pretentious rock star with an ego the size of Brazil.

He has it all. He has sold over seventy million albums during his career (both with and without the POLICE), and is apparently worth north of £80m. He is happily married to TRUDIE STYLER, and has five children, including two from his previous relationship with FRANCES TOMELTY. He is a committed, and very public, philanthropist, and has devoted a lot of time to the environmental pressure group The Rainforest Foundation, in which his wife has also been a driving force. ("Don't talk to me about saving the rainforest," the comedian DENIS LEARY used to say in his act, "Try saving your hair pal.")

There is the property, too – houses in London, Wiltshire, New York, and LA. The trappings of success seem to suit Sting perfectly. And why shouldn't they? Sometimes he has been his own worst enemy. In 1992, after twelve years, he finally married TRUDIE STYLER, the actress turned film producer, daughter of a packer in a lampshade factory. She attended the service dressed in a £20,000 Versace gown, riding on a white charger led by her fiancé. Sting wore a Regency Buck tailcoat nipped at the waist and cut away to reveal matching neckerchief – all designed by Versace. As an exercise in bad taste, it was exemplary.

Of course, he became a star in the age of presentation, and he took to this like a duck to water. After all, he is a pragmatist at heart: in the POLICE days, Sting had no qualms about dying his hair for a chewing gum commercial.

But self-deprecation is not his forte. "I have been perceived as an arrogant person, but I don't see that," he told me once. "I think I have a lot of self-esteem. I'm successful, I'm happy. I stand on my own two feet. I've always been confident, and even when I wasn't I could pretend that I was. I have always been able to mask my fears, which is what I suppose was perceived as arrogance."

And still is, I fear. Is this why we dislike him so? Is it simply envy, that particularly insidious English disease, or are we right to be annoyed by what appears to us to be his pomposity?

The man himself has heard it all before. "I react to criticism pretty well. It used to annoy me and I used to write back to the journalist involved, but not any more. Once you've done one interview you've signed a pact with the devil, so you have to take what comes."

Charmed, I'm sure.

Why is he so disliked? Well, it could be because he says things like this: "Mistakes? Well, I don't think I've made any, do you? I suppose I might have done things which were perceived as mistakes by my critics – the odd movie, the odd shirt – but musically I really don't think I've made any.

"Can you think of one?"

STONE ROSES

The disappointment that greeted the Stone Roses' second album, *Second Coming*, was similar to the confused and slightly embarrassed feeling some of us had about ten minutes into *The Godfather Part III*, when we knew it was an absolute stinker. I played the record more than I watched the film (I've seen the Coppola film twice, watching it again a few years ago just to see if it was as bad as I'd thought it was – and it was). *Second Coming* was released at the very end of 1994, a full five years after their extraordinary debut, and it seemed to make no sense at all. Whereas they had once been the BYRDS on ecstasy, now they appeared to want to be the baggy LED ZEPPELIN.

The Stone Roses epitomised everything that was good about Madchester, and were the first band to signal the

S end of the Eighties, an end to the designer culture that colonised music, fashion, design, cinema, and all points in between. 1989 was their year, when their single "Made of Stone" reminded many that pop was often at its best when it went hand-in-hand with insurrection. Refreshingly uninterested in anything around them, the Stone Roses were genuinely imperious. They rubber-stamped their brand when, one minute into a live 1989 TV performance on *The Late Show* on BBC2, the power failed, prompting singer IAN BROWN to repeatedly roar "Amateurs!" at the presenter, TRACEY MACLEOD. Oh, how we giggled. The Roses were belligerent, full of spunk, and wildly imaginative. When PETE TOWNSHEND saw an early Roses performance, he said that Reni was the most naturally gifted drummer he had seen since KEITH MOON.

But like I said, a few years later, having spent a lot of money and – so it is written – taken an awful lot of drugs, they made a mediocre follow-up, went heavy and eventually split up.

"Amateurs!"

BARBRA STREISAND

Barbra Streisand was the role model for every American hip-hop star worth their mirrored shades, white towelling jump suits, and costume jewellery. Her diva-esque traits – all of which I wholeheartedly applaud – have become a modern-day blueprint for excessive celebrity behaviour. The lateness, the – alleged – rudeness, the high-and-mightyness. Oh Babs, you were there first!

In REX REED's classic collection of profiles, 1968's *Do You Sleep In The Nude?*, Streisand is described thus: "One thing about Barbra Streisand: to know her is not necessarily to love her. Barbra is always late. She hates being interviewed, distrusts all photographers, and is as nervous about publicity as she is about her own performances." And there's more.

"Reporters covering her second CBS-TV special, *Color Me Barbra*, even had running bets on just how late she would be for each appointment. The answer, from every corner: very."

Boy could she get away with it. Principally, obviously, because she was very, very good at her job. Extraordinary, in fact. And anyway, after a while people – new people, people who didn't know Babs from Adam – started to expect the diva stuff, got disappointed if they didn't get it, went home happy if they did.

THE STROKES

Let's re-invent the Seventies and the post-punk pot pourri. Welcome to New York in 1998, and a skinny-legged band with a very appealing recipe: a dash of BLONDIE, a slice or two of TELEVISION, a splash of TALKING HEADS, the CARS (yes, the CARS!), and even a bit of the VOIDOIDS. Basically the Strokes sounded like CBGBs in the mid-Seventies, synthesised to sound as though everything were made five minutes ago (which it was).

JULIAN CASABLANCAS, NICK VALENSI, ALBERT HAMMOND, JR., NIKOLAI FRAITURE, and FABRIZIO MORETTI looked like the sort of men who buy dumb-bells in order to improve their physique but who are then too weak to carry them home; nerds who need to put a bit more thought into their cardiovascular health in order to improve their muscle definition.

The noise they made was great, a garage rock blend of NYC circa 1975-6. Their debut, *Is This It* (with its egregious lack of a question mark) in 2001, was a huge critical and commercial success, and it's still considered by many to be the best album of the Noughties (it's actually sold over four million copies). Pretty much everything they've done since then has been alright, while their 2011 album, *Angles*, is what critics still like to call "a return to form".

THE STYLE COUNCIL

S

I lost count of the number of times I saw the JAM. The 100 Club, the Marquee, the Nag's Head, the Red Cow... I probably saw them – and their support band, the decidedly mediocre NEW HEARTS – a dozen times, sweating through their suits, jutting their chins, and pumping out the likes of "In The City", "All Around The World", and "The Modern World" with the sort of sincerity that these days just looks forced and nostalgic. Then they ditched punk, became the most popular band in Britain, and bowed out in a blaze of retro-active glory.

Five minutes later, PAUL WELLER reinvented himself as the leader of the Style Council, a great band with a terrible name. When Weller finished off the JAM, he was looking forward, not only to a fresh start with new musicians (a new career in a new town), but also to a period of relative normality, for a superstar at least, where the paparazzi wouldn't be parked outside his Solid Bond studios, where he wouldn't be accosted in Oxford Street by hordes of Norwegian, parka-clad JAM fans. In 1983 Weller was looking forward to being an un-pop star. Much like PAUL McCARTNEY when the BEATLES split (and he would still hate the comparison), Weller surrounded himself with a few select musicians and started getting on with his life, making records every now and then, not really caring if his old fans warmed to his new direction. He almost took a perverse delight in refusing to have anything to do with his past, refusing to play any of the vast number of excellent JAM songs, or even talk about them. This was what Modernists did. And Weller couldn't resist telling you what a Modernist he was.

And the Style Council turned out to be one of the best things he ever did, better than the JAM (that's right, better than one of the best epoch-making singles bands), and almost as good as the solo career he would pursue in his thirties, forties and fifties.

Not that he was happy with his lot, oh no. Along with his partner in crime, MICK TALBOT (ugly mug, played keyboards),

Weller went out of his way to distance himself from the game of self-promotion. One way in which the Style Council combated their image as a "quirky Eengleesh pop band" – which is what they almost immediately became in the eyes of the press – was to send the whole thing up. Irony was always big in their world, and what was often seen as gross pretentiousness was actually a giant wind-up. It was in this way that Weller defused a lot of the contradictions thrown up by him being on the one hand a recognisable icon in *Smash Hits*, and an opinionated political animal on the other. For the maudlin pied piper, donning a silly hat let him off the hook, but for many of their fans the irony was lost. They just liked their records.

SUEDE

As BRETT ANDERSON showed me into his tiny, ramshackle west London flat, the strains of ACKER BILK wafted up from his record player. "Do you know anything about VERA LYNN?" he asked, stepping over a pile of decidedly shabby coats. "I tried to buy her version of 'The White Cliffs Of Dover' today, but I came back with this instead." He nodded his fringe at the stereo as "Stranger On The Shore" faded into nothing. Perhaps Anderson had discovered irony; one didn't expect the lead singer of Suede to have such peculiar weaknesses. But then maybe he *did*. "I like anything," he said, rather petulantly. "Pop music has become all about cool, about kids wearing sunglasses. We were never like that. Suede were never cool."

It was a cold, rainy February night in 1994, a Monday, just a little after seven. Bedsitland. These three small rooms were where Anderson, then twenty-six, had lived for the past two years, during which time he had unwittingly – some said undeservedly – become the most idolised pop star in Britain. He had recently acquired a larger home in north London, but for reasons of convenience we were sitting in Notting Hill, crouched on rickety chairs, drinking instant coffee from

S cocktail glasses, and trying to ignore the intermittent comings and goings of his neighbours. Tonight, like many before it, Anderson was surrounded by paper-thin walls.

Without so much as a backward glance, Suede had earned themselves a place in the pantheon of Great British Pop Groups. And, like all good things before them, they seemed to come out of nowhere. Two–and-a-half years before this they were just another low-rent glam rock group looking for a place to play, just another bunch of naïve hopefuls named after a fabric, like so many bands at the time (FELT, CORDUROY, DENIM, etc). Then, almost overnight, after a few good live reviews and the release of their first single – a shrill declaration of independence called "The Drowners" – the music press descended upon them like a pack of rapacious bloodhounds. In just six months Suede – purveyors of modern Nineties glam rock – got the covers of the *Melody Maker*, *NME*, *Q*, *Select*, and almost every other music magazine in Britain. There were twenty covers in all. Although the press were more than keen, with hindsight it was deemed to be a highly-orchestrated campaign by the group's publicist, JOHN BEST. So successful was Best's assault thought to be, that he won the *Music Week* award for press campaign of 1993. The judges said it "took Suede from obscurity to being hailed as the best band of the year". Given their enthusiasm, it is likely that the music press would have written about the band anyway.

These four skinny white boys were called The Last Great British Pop Group, The Saviours Of Rock, The Finest British Pop Group Since The SMITHS… four louche young men who had, according to one particularly smitten rock journalist, "single-handedly revitalised our faith in sexy, provocative English guitar pop". They had so much coverage that one began to suspect that very little else was happening in the British music scene. This was not altogether untrue. Even considering the tyranny of youth, in those days pop phenomena were few and far between, and Suede arrived at a time when the other icons of modern cutting-edge pop – MORRISSEY, the STONE ROSES, PRIMAL SCREAM, etc – were absent from the scene.

According to the then editor of *The Face*, "They came at a time when the music press were desperate for something to write about, so they smothered them with praise. The problem is that it's all been done before. But then Suede are not aimed at everyone who has seen it all before. They're aimed at eighteen- and twenty-year-olds, who haven't. Brett's feyness was certainly appealing to those who'd never experienced DAVID BOWIE."

Suede's music was certainly distinctive, if a little derivative. Brittle, overwrought guitar pop, it demanded attention. As did Anderson – who was unquestionably the group's leader – who employed the same strident mockney tones used previously by the likes of ANTHONY NEWLEY, BOWIE, and COCKNEY REBEL'S STEVE HARLEY. The sound of Suede was the sound of bedroom doors being slammed, and all the youthful market-town angst that went with it. This was rock music intended to mean more than life itself, to teenagers, anyway – music to get you through adolescence, however arch and mannered it may have been (typical song titles: "So Young", "Breakdown", "Sleeping Pills", "The Next Life", etc). Trying to find something which sounded uncontrived or unaffected in Suede's songs was like trying to find an Afro-American in a WOODY ALLEN film. Yet the fact that they *sounded* insincere did not necessarily mean they were.

"It'll sound pretentious if I try and describe it," said Anderson, "but Suede for me is something very young and beautiful and vital. Almost sort of silver. That's the colour I always think of, silver, something very shiny. Our music is the kind of music that should be listened to by one person in front of their stereo. It's not a gang thing at all.

"There's no arrogance with us, or even confidence, really. It just stems from an absolute love of music, and visions about how wonderful music can be. Things just jump into my brain sometimes which have a lot to do with sexuality and violence. I don't know, I just get a vision every now and then. I'm not talking about WILLIAM BLAKE or anything like that. It's only me." Aha.

S Anderson was even more melodramatic towards the beginning of the band's career, and quotes like these endeared them to their rapidly increasing army of fans.

Flailing about in a hyperbolic fug, Suede were the talk of the town. Two more singles followed – "Metal Mickey", "Animal Nitrate" – as did their first album, called, simply enough, *Suede*. Months before its release it was hailed as the most eagerly awaited debut since the SEX PISTOLS' *Never Mind The Bollocks*, back in 1977. When the record finally appeared it went straight to Number One. After that there was the Mercury Music prize (LP Of The Year), a live video, and a somewhat unsuccessful tour of North America (where they were overshadowed by their support band, the CRANBERRIES, a group without the camp excesses of Suede), along with preparatory work for the second album.

Then came a new single, the bombastic eight-minute "Stay Together", by which time Anderson had – almost by accident – become a spokesman for his generation. The twenty-three-year-old BERNARD BUTLER, who along with Anderson wrote all of the band's material, was the HARPO MARX of the group, refusing all requests for interviews, allowing his co-partner to enjoy the limelight. Cheeky, garrulous, and belligerently uncynical, Anderson quickly became an anti-establishment icon for disaffected youth. He was disarmingly attractive, studiedly introverted, and pointedly anti-consumerist. Most pop stars during the Eighties aspired to designer lifestyles, fast cars, supermodels (the trophy wives of the day), holidays in Montserrat, and pop-cultural world domination. Anderson appeared to aspire to nothing more (or less) than personal epiphany.

While it is rare to gauge someone's true personality after only a few hours of their company, Anderson did at least display the requisite celebrity persona. In order for people to want you, buy your records, chase you across crowded railway stations, and throw flowers at you on stage, you must have charm and magnetism. And Anderson appeared to have both. In the flesh he was far more masculine than he looked on stage, and yet the accoutrements were all there: black crew-neck sweater, black flared jeans, black socks, black clumpy shoes. Black! The colour of angst.

S

But angst didn't last. Butler left, the hits dried up, they were elbowed out of the spotlight by OASIS, BLUR, and every other Britpop spunk-bubble, and the band's relevance came into question. All in all Suede were a flash in the pan, but a very brilliant one at that.

SUGAR

Having disbanded the hugely influential (although never to my taste) HÜSKER DÜ in 1987, their guitarist and vocalist, BOB MOULD, embarked on a semi-functional solo career, and then, in 1992, formed this power trio, a rather sweeter sortie. They ended up making a couple of so-so records, but their debut, the awesome *Copper Blue*, is one hell of a barnstorming album, full of loud guitars and exhilarating hook lines. This is buzzsaw power pop, its stand-out track, the soaring "Hoover Dam". So many mediocre "alternative" rock bands sounded and looked like this in the Nineties – portly, shaven-headed guys in their thirties whose idea of deportment and sartorial elegance was defiantly wearing a black T-shirt with their legs astride, convinced they had found a legitimate form of expression.

SUGAR RAY

Sugar Ray bludgeoned everyone with mediocrity. They are to power pop what HOOTIE & THE BLOWFISH are to whatever music they try and approximate. *OC Weekly* once said of their song "Someday", that it was "a ballad that haunts the playlists of chain restaurants and grandpa-friendly radio stations,

S making it ripe for a sneering, mocking, high-speed punk rock or metal cover." Their song "Every Morning" is a great radio record regardless of their status, sampling both "Suavecito" by MALO, and "Grazing In The Grass" by HUGH MASEKELA. They also covered "Spinning Away", the 1990 BRIAN ENO and JOHN CALE song.

SUPER FURRY ANIMALS

We love the Super Furry Animals. With something of a passion. They made eccentricity fun. *Rolling Stone* called *Rings Around The World* (Epic, 2001), "A widescreen musical masterpiece with a knowing wink." Well, maybe not a masterpiece, but certainly something sketched from memory.

THE SUPREMES

Not only were the Supremes the first real queens of American pop – they may have been black, but suburban America liked their demure sensibility, their white clothes, the way in which they obviously wanted "in", rather than "out" – they were also some of the first BLAPS (Black American Princesses). Whereas a lot of pop stars in the early Sixties backcombed their hair, teasing it into the required shape (from the dawn of pop, television was instrumental in determining the way in which pop was presented and articulated), the Supremes took the easy way out – they wore wigs. It was towards the end of 1964 – the year in which the Supremes had their first real smash hit, "Where Did Our Love Go" (no question mark: odd) – that FLORENCE BALLARD, MARY WILSON, and the force of nature that was DIANA ROSS began accumulating wigs.

After their first appearance on *The Ed Sullivan Show*, their career took off, and, finding themselves with a full calendar for the next twelve months, the girls stocked up on wigs of all shapes and sizes. They had a lot of songs, a lot of costume changes, and a lot of vanity. "It was easier to change wigs than to change hairstyles," said MARY WILSON in her autobiography, *Dreamgirl*. "We each had dozens of them, all expensive, handmade human-hair pieces in a variety of styles ranging from mod-ish VIDAL SASSOON cuts to high, elaborate flips. In fact, the bulk of our luggage was made up of huge wig boxes." During this period, Motown's most popular female singing group also wore padded bras, false eyelashes, hip pads, false nails, and padded bottoms.

Did this ever happen to the SMITHS?

SWING OUT SISTER

They have, it must be said, a truly terrible name, yet so did the BEATLES. They can be forgiven, though, at least in my book (literally). For certain types of people, there is no greater epiphany than driving along California's Pacific Coast Highway as NEIL RICHARDSON's "Riviera Affair", WALTER WANDERLEY's "Rain Forest", or ALAN HAWKSHAW's "Girl In A Sportscar" magically erupts from the car stereo.

It certainly works for Swing Out Sister's CORINNE DREWERY and ANDY CONNELL. During their nearly thirty-year existence, they have dedicated themselves to fusing electro-pop, jazz, and funk with their first true love, easy listening. They have moved from clinical pop-funk to free-form soul and back again, while always retaining a keen pop sensibility. Their first LP, 1987's *It's Better To Travel* (another terrible title), contained a clutch bag of singles – "Blue Mood", "Breakout", "Surrender" – though it was 1989's euphoric *Kaleidoscope World* which firmly established their lounge credentials. With such beautiful songs as "You On My Mind", "Forever Blue", "Where In The World", and "Coney Island Man", the album was a love letter to luxury, a paean to the five-star pop days of yore. "Coney Island Man" was almost an homage to

S

Bacharach himself, and worthy of inclusion in any great Sixties espionage thriller involving a coastline drive (the Riviera, the Santa Monica Freeway, Sorrento, whatever), an implausibly sunny day and a flame-coloured open-top sportscar driven by a wispy blonde in a JACKIE O headscarf and Argentine air-hostess sunglasses.

"Personally I have a real problem relating to things like JAMES BROWN or Motown because it's nothing to do with me," said ANDY CONNELL. "I never listened to that when I was growing up. I bought records by BURT BACHARACH." "Forever Blue" even uses a refrain borrowed from JOHN BARRY's *Midnight Cowboy*. "We called him up and told him what we were up to and he said he didn't mind," said Drewery. On this track, and another from the same album, "Precious Words", SOS drew on the talents of JIMMY WEBB, and Connell was in shock for weeks afterwards, "He was astonishing; he took these songs and transformed them... when he was in the studio I was literally speechless."

If this is your type of thing, all their albums are essential: *Get In Touch With Yourself* (1992), *The Living Return* (1994), *Shapes And Patterns* (1997), *Filth And Dreams* (1999), *Somewhere Deep In The Night* (2001), *Where Our Love Grows* (2004), *Beautiful Mess* (2008), *Les Etrangers* (2009), and *Private View* (2011).

THE SWINGLE SINGERS

BACH has always been enthusiastically adapted by the lounge fraternity, and the Swingle Singers almost made a career out of it. Their first album, *Bach's Greatest Hits*, established WARD SWINGLE's singers as the most adventurous vocal group of the Sixties, while in 1965 they recorded a bizarre "convergence" album with the MODERN JAZZ QUARTET, *Place Vendome*, a collaboration that would later inspire PAUL WELLER during his last days with the STYLE COUNCIL. The octet now comprises two tenors, a couple of basses, a pair of altos, and two sopranos, and although Bach covers remain their signature sound, they have a hundred and fifty songs committed to memory. In 2005, JEM sampled the Swingles' recording of BACH's "Prelude In F Minor" for trip-hop hit, "They".

T

T. Rex

Having spent the Sixties unsuccessfully trying to get arrested as a dandy, MARC BOLAN eventually started getting some traction when he tried turning himself into a visionary, and began making folkie records with TYRANNOSAURUS REX. Then, still feeling frisky, needing greater success, he went "electric" (ooh, get him!), had a massive hit with "Ride A White Swan", and helped invent glam rock in the process.

In 1971, the year he really took off, he said that, "The majority of pop hits that make it are a permutation of the twelve-bar blues, and I've found one that works." Hadn't he just, pumping out a succession of brilliantly conceived trashy pop singles that all sounded terribly on-message. For a few years he was the most famous entertainer in Britain – bigger than DAVID BOWIE, bigger (if you can believe he was ever mentioned in the same breath) than GARY GLITTER – then succumbed to ego, cocaine, and the inevitable combination of both. His twelve-bar blues suddenly sounded like old CHUCK BERRY B-sides, he got fat, and was killed in a car crash. If the crash had happened two years previously he'd be as revered by some as JIM MORRISON or KURT COBAIN. Odd thought, but true. The nine singles from "...Swan" to "20th Century Boy" are all essential, as are "Child Star", "Cat Black (The Wizard's Hat)", "Life's A Gas", "Stacey Grove", "Baby Strange", and "Mad Donna".

TAKE THAT

The boy band as soap opera, just another on-off, will-they-won't-they story of everyday folk, conquering Britain not once, not twice, but thrice! Progress Live, their 2011 tour, was the UK's biggest stadium tour of all time, while the album it supported was the fastest selling of the century (it's been said

T that a crowd at a particular moment in history creates the object to justify its gathering, but, no, Take That were actually at all of these concerts). In some respects they have become like royalty, untouchable, and impervious to criticism. Forever reminding a large part of their constituency that they were once young, they are five little CLIFF RICHARDS, all taking it in turns to hold the flame of everlasting youth for whoever wants to watch. And, it has to be said, producing more than a manbag of great singles in the process.

TALK TALK

Lost in a cycle of drum machines and pop promos – the tyranny of the music business in the early Eighties – many bands struggled to cope. Talk Talk had some minor chart success, and then did a *volte face* and reinvented themselves with 1986's *The Colour of Spring* – which included what I still regard as one of the most transcendent singles of the decade, "Life's What You Make It" – before going deeper and deeper into their own thing. They're a favourite of ELBOW's GUY GARVEY: "You can hear on certain tunes the sound of someone desperately looking for something. I don't know what it was, but you've got to go somewhere to come back with that music."

TALKING HEADS

"Music," said W.H. AUDEN, "can be made anywhere, is invisible, and does not smell."

This was Talking Heads when they started out. They came from New York but could have come from any state, they were deliberately contrary, and decidedly anti "rock". Looking back now, it's difficult to imagine just how shocking Talking Heads were in 1976 and 1977, when they began supporting the likes of the RAMONES. For while the RAMONES were the perfect example of hard-core cartoon punk, they still looked like rockers, as many new bands did at the time: they wore denim jeans, leather jackets and skanky old T-shirts, and gave the impression of never being comfortable anywhere other than the subway, the street, or on stage. Talking Heads looked like architecture students, with button-down shirts, skinny ties, and square haircuts. At the dawn of punk, this was almost revolutionary (it was certainly confrontational), as by staring at them for the first time you really had no idea what they were or what they did.

DAVID BYRNE's band were intimidating on stage, too, as their only interaction with the audience involved Byrne announcing, in his clipped, deadpan voice, "The name of this song is..." (this strangeness was compounded whenever they supported the RAMONES, as their only communication with the crowd involved JOHNNY RAMONE shouting "1-2-3-4!" before each Blitzkrieg – see THE RAMONES).

Critics like to say that *Fear Of Music*, their third album from 1979, and *Remain In Light*, their fourth from 1980, are the key texts, but neither has the immediacy of their eponymous debut from 1977. Sure, both records show the band getting funky (they were one of the first "punk" band to successfully take ownership of black music), getting African (thanks to BRIAN ENO), yet their debut still sounds as though it were made in a bubble. It could have come from anywhere, it was invisible, and it didn't smell.

TAME IMPALA

Occasionally – very occasionally, mind – a group's self-awareness is acute. THE PET SHOP BOYS have always had a keen sense of themselves, probably because they didn't become famous until NEIL TENNANT and CHRIS LOWE were approaching their thirties.

T Tame Impala hail from Perth, in Western Australia, and perhaps have the distance to know exactly who they are. They describe themselves as a band that makes "steady-flowing psychedelic hypno-groove melodic rock music that emphasises dream-like melody" (music which sits on the edge of ethereal "dream pop"). Which is actually bang on the impala – they seem adept at layered sonic exploration, the sort that's filtered through sepia gauze, the sort that was big in the late Sixties, coming back in a fairly substantial way in the Nineties, when no one really cared what type of music anyone made anymore.

They formed in 2008, which means that whatever they do is seen through a prism of half a century of pop, meaning every mark they make is drawn over a mark that has previously been made and rubbed out by someone else. But to their credit they appear to know that. After all, Perth does boast about being the most isolated city in the world. Some suggests it's so isolated, in fact, that no new music has reached the city since 1969: which is certainly reflected in Impala's pitch-perfect recreation of a world that almost existed.

"I can't stress enough how insignificant Tame Impala is," said band leader, KEVIN PARKER. He created Impala's 2010 debut, *Innerspeaker*, largely by himself – writing, playing, and eventually recording himself at a house near Perth (with some mixing help later from FLAMING LIPS and MGMT producer DAVE FRIDMANN in upstate New York).

Tame Impala sound like the GRATEFUL DEAD may have done if they'd been born in Japan, hired GEORGE HARRISON as a singer, BURT BACHARACH as a songwriter, and GEORGE MARTIN as their producer. And then formed a supergroup with BIG STAR. Oh, and then spent a month in Ibiza with a bunch of SPIRITUALIZED and AIR CDs.

Miles from civilisation? Well, while their music is a weird, if oddly topical mix of the old and the new (Tame Impala's music is the most modern old music I've ever heard), *Innerspeaker*'s cover is about as Zeitgeisty as possible, looking not a little like ARCADE FIRE's *The Suburbs*.

Self-awareness in excelsis.

JAMES TAYLOR

T

Taylor started life as the patchouli lothario, painted as a stud-muffin troubadour and designed to appeal to teenage college girls in their bedsits and dorms. He had the long hair and the good looks and the mellow, silky, low-fat singing voice. And he wrote and sang some beautiful songs. As well as the obviously famous ones, these are essential: "Copperline", "Frozen Man", "Blossom", "Country Road", and "You Can Close Your Eyes" (from the recent CD/DVD he did with CAROLE KING, *Live At The Troubadour*). And if you like JT, there are many, many more. When BOB DYLAN turned sixty, his voice was shot – "idiosyncratic", "symptomatic of"... whatever – JT sounds just like he did when he was the poster-boy for sophomore sweethearts.

These days he's bald and wears a hat, a comic look almost permanently spread across his face (he looks a bit like a hippie ALFRED E. NEUMAN). But he's still got that amazing singing voice, and occasionally writes another beautiful song.

He is extremely matter-of-fact, even sanguine, about his songwriting, and whereas most songwriters go out of their way to tell you that, "Actually, I think this is probably the best material I've ever written" – even when everyone else, including the people paid to look after them, know it's junk – Taylor is admirably self-deprecating.

"In the beginning, when I was writing, the songs were forcing their way out," he said. "I've written most of these songs two or three times now. And that's fine, to have the same dozen songs you write over and over. There are some odds and ends – a song about Australia, a song about a traffic jam – but generally there are just a dozen or so themes. There are love songs, songs of unrequited yearning, songs about going home, songs about my father. It takes a little bit of material to assemble a decent father cycle."

T TELEVISION

TOM VERLAINE's band were a fetishist's delight. They were at the apex of the hip New York downtown scene as punk broke, and their 1977 debut album, *Marquee Moon*, was a splendid lurch away from the Neanderthal hubba-hubba-1-2-3-4 of bands like the RAMONES and the HEARTBREAKERS. Duelling guitars ("Marquee Moon" itself was over ten minutes long), desperate vocals, and proper outsider status (they were photographed by ROBERT MAPPLETHORPE, hung with PATTI SMITH, got properly reviewed by NICK KENT!), Television were pounced upon by any old hippie who couldn't quite cope with the likes of the SEX PISTOLS and the DAMNED. If you had spent the early parts of your adolescence trying to build a carapace of cool, there was no way you were suddenly going to pretend to like the oiks who bounced up and down to EDDIE AND THE HOT RODS, so Television were the perfect respite, looking like new wave, sounding like old wave.

TINIE TEMPAH

The first thing I realised was that he's not so Tinie. I met him in June 2011, and as he arrived for his photo session – in a railway arch in Hackney – with a suit bag and a smile, Tinie Tempah (his name is an homage to his hero DIZZEE RASCAL; he was born Patrick Chukwuemeka Okogwu on November 7, 1988, and was raised in South London) came over like Gentleman Jim. Only a year or so into his career, he was taking success in his stride, and apparently without a hint of arrogance. He introduced himself to everyone on set – photographer, stylist, wardrobe ops, film crew, assistants, magazine staff, everyone (even those who were simply there to see what this hugely popular celebrity looked like) – and told anyone who would listen (everyone) how pleased he was to be there.

Tempah's debut album, *Disc-Overy*, debuted at number one in October 2010, and was preceded by the number one singles "Pass Out" and "Written In The Stars", and by the top-five "Frisky" and "Miami 2 Ibiza". At the time he was about as hot as it was possible to be for someone making uncompromising British hip-hop with a transatlantic swagger. He was something of a dandy, too, and had fostered a reputation for the Big Look: the TOM FORD spectacles, the Nikes, the Rolex.

That year it was difficult to find a festival that didn't have Tempah on its bill, and he used the festival circuit as a marketing exercise, trying to convert those customers who may have turned up to watch someone else completely. "People discover you at festivals. They come to see COLDPLAY or whoever, and then wander over and catch your act. Festivals make a lot of sense to me."

Having just returned from a two-month tour of the States, he had been exposed to the inner workings of the machine. His schedule was so full that one afternoon he had some sort of meeting every twelve minutes. Being in the US had also made him aware of the global potential for – and yes, he mentioned the word before I had a chance to – "the brand".

And how was success compared to what he imagined it might be? "There's so much business. The meetings. The marketing. The tours. The sponsorship. The publishing. The lawyers. The accountants. The deals. The budgets. The all of it. But it's all part of the brand." A brand he is so immersed in that even his mother calls him Tinie.

THROBBING GRISTLE

I remember going to a TG concert in London in 1977, and the atmosphere was so aggressive, so disturbing, and the music so unnerving, that when dry ice started to slowly swamp the stage, there was a collective and irrational feeling we were about to be gassed with something. I used to listen to their

T

records a lot, during a period when I obviously felt that the unpleasant needed to be embraced, nurtured, and celebrated. TG were a noir narcotic, and I began feeling a lot better when I moved on to the B-52s.

TONTO'S EXPANDING HEAD BAND

Algorithms plus algorhythms equals space-age funk. Tonto's early Seventies electronic albums are long-deleted, absent from iTunes, and seemingly only available illegally, yet MALCOLM CECIL and ROBERT MARGOULEFF's "band" remain hugely influential, having created a soundtrack to techno-utopia. Their work with STEVIE WONDER also contributed to this, and they helped define his futuristic swampy sound during his purple patch.

ALLEN TOUSSAINT

Being just under the radar often pays dividends. It can certainly extend the career. I was first made aware of Allen Toussaint in 1977, soon after GLEN CAMPBELL had covered – not fantastically well, I might add – his song "Southern Nights" (Toussaint calls himself the "Southern Knight"), which led to a circuitous and frequently interrupted journey of discovery that took me from "Fortune Teller" by the ROLLING STONES (he wrote it), to "Lady Marmalade" by LABELLE (he produced it), via the BAND's "Rock Of Ages" (he helped arrange it). Constantly running between the control booth and the studio, and never comprehensively defining a career in either, has probably been responsible for Toussaint's cult status, but it also helped him become one of the most respected musicians of his time, among other musicians, at least.

The record he has become known for most this century (his first in ten years) is the JOE HENRY-produced mini-masterpiece, *The Bright Mississippi* (2009), one of the funkiest records you'll ever hear without a drum machine, a record that feels, sounds and tastes as though it were made from the very finest gumbo. Paying homage to the likes of DUKE ELLINGTON, DJANGO REINHARDT, SIDNEY BECHET, THELONIOUS MONK, and other jazz legends, it offers an alternative take on tradition.

Perennially understated, he tends to look a little like the best-dressed bartender of the slowest hotel in town, a man who might easily put down his cocktail mixer, walk across the lobby and start playing the piano as though he were LEON RUSSELL, DR. JOHN, RAY CHARLES, or ELTON JOHN ("When I meet someone like Allen Toussaint," said Elton, "that for me is like meeting, you know, someone the equivalent of the DALAI LAMA because for me, he influenced the way I played the piano. He's a historical part of rock and roll"). Or indeed, Allen Toussaint. He has the air of someone who always has a dry-cleaning bag hanging in his room, a man who lives for work. A man who doesn't understand why you wouldn't want to shine your shoes before blowing your socks off.

I saw him at the Brecon Jazz Festival in 2011, when he was seventy-three, and a better raconteur you'd be hard-pressed to find. He managed to be funny and self-deprecating while quietly letting the audience know exactly who they were dealing with. "I wrote 'Working In A Coal Mine' for LEE DORSEY, but I saw TOM JONES do it once on TV, and he was surrounded by all these girls in bikinis and pick-axes. That was a show. Nice work. I thought, way to go dude."

Paying tribute to others who have recorded his songs, he said, "I was so glad when the [ROLLING] STONES recorded my song 'Fortune Teller' – I knew they would know how to roll it all the way to the bank." He kept saying he had no idea where he was, but indulged the audience by going on to say, "It's so beautiful here. You people have nowhere to go when you die."

His singing voice was pitch-perfect too, even if his duster coat looked like it had been borrowed from either a SPANDAU BALLET tribute band or a roadie who once worked for ALI BONGO, or SIEGFRIED & ROY.

TRAVIS

Everyone thought they were going to be the new BEATLES and then they turned out to be nothing but Travis. They made some great records, with "Sing" (from their third album *The Invisible Band*, 2001) being the very best.

TWIN ATLANTIC

"Free" by Twin Atlantic was the impassioned sound of young Glasgow – fast, furious, and repeatedly championed by *Kerrang!* The band had been around since 2007, playing festivals, getting sticky on YouTube, touring the US, and making the sort of baby pop metal that goes down well at uni. But until 2011's "Free" (the title track of their first proper album, two years on from the critically acclaimed mini-album *Vivarium*), they had yet to come up with a hook that might hint at immortality. As they use so much that has gone before them (their line-up, the genre, the form itself), these days groups like this – and it has to be said that there are many groups like this – find it difficult to get the traction they need.

The big problem here is equity, and the difficult in building it. The problems are manifold.

1. Even when they have three sixty deals, record companies don't invest in groups like they use to.

2. Because of the lack of music on television, advertisements in newspapers, and the small size of CDs, it's hard for bands to market their image.

3. Talking of CDs, we all know that no one is buying them anymore (physical is dead).

4. Because of this, artists need to go out on the road more to raise funds; consequently the market is swamped, with too many acts going out too often (and newer acts finding it difficult to fill the schedule gaps).

5. Music no longer plays the role it once did as a formative teenage experience.

6. Everything is now immediate and consumed instantly, and career arcs now last weeks not months.

7. Oh, and the stuff itself: there will always be those who can write songs and come up with marketing gimmicks and costumes... But we really are talking about the law of diminishing returns here.

8. It's no good simply saying you'll play festivals, as there are now far too many of them.

9. For some time now, being in a band has been a career choice rather than a vocation.

10. Finally, you can't put your arms around a download.

11. Twin Atlantic's way of trying to stave off the inevitable was by sticking to their roots, refusing to opt for the traditional mid-Atlantic vocal style, and preferring to sing in a pronounced Scottish accent. It might sound inconsequential, but so far has proved to be anything but.

T TWO DOOR CINEMA CLUB

If you see their jaunty pop promos – old-fashioned, so weirdly refreshing – or ever watch them live, County Down band Two Door Cinema Club (so named when guitarist SAM HALLIDAY mispronounced the name of the local Bangor cinema, Tudor Cinema), sort of crouch down, curling over their instruments, as though they've possibly only just learnt to play them, carefully watching their fingers crawl up and down the fretboard, not entirely sure where they're going to end up. This is engaging, and makes them appear even younger than they are (and they're young), the best boys in their class, beavering away under an imaginary glass ceiling, effervescent and jangly in equal measure. In preppy jumpers, plimsolls (Converse, in all likelihood), and sports jackets, with floppy fringes and smiles, looking not unlike HAIRCUT 100, ORANGE JUICE, or any other floppy-fringed boy band of the last thirty years.

Their music is still sparky, the kind of sparkling indie-pop that makes sense played between the FEELING or FRANZ FERDINAND – their influences sound like the constituent parts of a heritage music magazine, one with a news section for new bands at the front: BROKEN SOCIAL SCENE, STARS, STEVIE WONDER, AT THE DRIVE-IN, IDLEWILD, DEATH CAB FOR CUTIE, JOHN DENVER, KYLIE MINOGUE, and MEW. And "Something Good Can Work", their landmark single, "I Can Talk", and "What You Know" are almost as good as anything by any of them. Their publishers and record company didn't shy away from obvious marketing ruses either, and their songs were used on soundtracks, video games, TV shows, and ad campaigns (including one for French bank Credit Agricole).

Starting off with the jangle is fair enough – it's where a lot of bands start, as we know, honouring their record collections, wanting to sound a little like the BEATLES, the BYRDS, MARSHALL CRENSHAW, or indeed FOALS – but it's where the jangle leads that turns the idea into a journey. This band, like others, should perhaps be mindful of Saul Bellow, when he said "any artist should be grateful for a naïve grace which puts him beyond the need to reason elaborately." Which actually means keeping the jangle.

U

UNITED SERVICES
ORGANISATION

U

GEORGE BUSH's golden presidential cuff links were glinting as the sinking Persian sun made its way behind the USS Enterprise, while five thousand expectant American troops, huddled on the ship and in front of the makeshift stage, looked on. It was December 1998, and the seventy-four-year-old, 41st President of the United States had just been delivered by motorcade to Dubai's principle loading dock, one of the American military's Gulf headquarters, where the Enterprise, one of the world's largest active aircraft carriers, had been docked since September. Five days later it would be catapulted into action in the furious if somewhat truncated Gulf war sequel, launching dozens of aircraft in the quick-fire assault on Iraq, but today it would resembled a benign mother ship, cooling in the bay. Bush was here at the request of the United Services Organisation (USO), to address the troops and introduce the entertainment, and he was already an hour behind schedule. The 4pm heat had forced the former President to take off his jacket as soon as he left the Mercedes, though his armed bodyguards, who were whispering to each other through their ear pieces, their hands nervously stroking their ties and ready to grab their pistols, were using their own jackets like camouflage.

Bush was blanketed by his secret-service security detail, as well as a dozen members of the Enterprise's shore patrol. All former Presidents are treated like precious cargo by the American security forces, but none more so than Bush. Firstly, he was a Republican; secondly, his predecessor, RONALD REAGAN, was largely incapacitated so didn't travel well; and thirdly, Bush not only was still a huge supporter of his country's armed forces, but continued to visit troops overseas. He was in the Emirates this week largely as a guest of the military, and in Dubai – the Dallas of the desert – to rally the throng.

U As he made his way through the sea of crew cuts and tattoos towards the tiny floorboard stage that had been hastily assembled in front of the Enterprise, the former President leant towards me, in a way he must have done hundreds of thousands of times in the hope of seeming conspiratorial, and whispered in a decidedly stentorian fashion, "You know I'm not really doing this for the USO, I'm doing it for myself, for my own morale. The Unites States Navy has always been close to my heart and I think it's important to fly the flag." As Bush wandered off, sound bite over, pressuring the overstretched flesh, the USO's main attraction, HOOTIE & THE BLOWFISH, ambled onto the makeshift stage. America's biggest rock group at the time had been invited to tour the Gulf by the USO, and the Dubai concert team was the second to stop in a short trip that included concerts at US army bases in Bahrain, Saudi Arabia, Bosnia, and Hungary. The Dubai gig was the biggest, a good-natured romp in front of a forty-year-old, five-acre, 280,000-horsepower behemoth carrying eighty personal carriers, reconnaissance, early warning, and attack planes – F-14s, F-18s, S-3Bs, ES-3As, E-2Cs, and EA-6Bs – their wings folded over like sleeping blackbirds; in front of 4880 stir-crazy servicemen and 120 stir-crazy servicewomen. "It's the biggest thing to hit the Gulf since the Scuds," said one moustached, tattooed pilot. "We're really gonna party tonight, you betcha, m'boy."

As the band began their set, lurching into a stirring a cappella interpretation of the Star-Spangled Banner, Bush leant over again. "I probably shouldn't say this about Hootie," he said, as though it were of great import, "but I gotta admit it's my first time. Having said that, I'm willing to be converted. I'm sure I'm gonna enjoy them."

But if GEORGE BUSH was ignorant in the ways of Hootie he was in the minority, as their brand of wholesome, fad-free, full-bodied, big-hearted rock had captured the imagination of Middle America like no other band since FLEETWOOD MAC invaded every white-picket-fenced house in the Seventies. They had also been given several political seals of approval.

BILL CLINTON had posed for pictures with the band on more than one occasion and embraced them at various Democratic party conventions, and TONY BLAIR (never shy about jumping on a bandwagon) had then told a BBC radio presenter how much he'd like to see them play live. Not only were they DAVID LETTERMAN's favourite group for a while, but such was their magnitude that the day the band were due to fly to Bahrain for the first concert in their USO tour, HILLARY CLINTON appeared on the *Today Show* in New York, officially wishing them farewell. At the time this was tantamount to CHERIE BLAIR going on *The Big Breakfast* to wish JIM DAVIDSON all the best for entertaining the British troops in Bosnia.

MARCEL DUCHAMP once said that the fame of an artist is reliant on the multiplication of small anecdotes, and in HOOTIE & THE BLOWFISH's case the anecdotes were already part of rock'n'roll lore. Singer DARIUS RUCKER, guitarist MARK BRYAN, bassist DEAN FELBER, and drummer JIM SONEFELD met in 1986 as undergraduates at the University of South Carolina, Columbia, starting a bar band a few years later, naming it after the nicknames given to two university classmates, one with owl-like glasses, and another with full, bulbous cheeks. The band began touring seriously at the scraggy end of the decade, when they'd completed her studies, along with a lot of other weirdly monikered local bar acts called things like GRACIE MOON, COWBOY MOUTH, DILLON PENCE, and TREADMILL TRACKSTER. Hootie were nothing if not diligent, performing over three hundred gigs a year in places such as the Variety Playhouse in Atlanta, Georgia, and Green Streets, in Columbia, South Carolina, playing cover versions of songs by everyone from R.E.M. and the POLICE, to SQUEEZE and the EAGLES, and selling home-made tapes and CDs off the back of a truck. "We'd play anywhere," said the band's unofficial spokesman, Rucker, "birthday parties, frat parties, fairs. We'd drive twelve hours to play twenty minutes for a few bucks and free beers." During this time they were making perhaps $5000 a year each, yet none of them got disillusioned, because they were enjoying themselves so much. "We tasted enough of real life

U

to realise that being a poor musician in HOOTIE & THE BLOWFISH is so much better than getting a pay cheque and working in a bank," said Felber.

When they eventually secured a record deal in 1993, their debut album *Cracked Rear View*, released towards the end of 1994, took seven months to reach the top of the American charts, where it stayed for over a year, selling a staggering seventeen million copies in the States alone and becoming the bestselling debut of all time. In America it has sold more copies than any single album by the BEATLES, the ROLLING STONES, or U2. The record company suggested the band pull more singles off the album and let it sell for another year, but as they spent so much time playing live, they needed more material to play – songs that the audience knew. Consequently they needed another album. This follow-up record, *Fairweather Johnson*, however, only sold a measly four million. Their third album, 1998's *Musical Chairs*, tried to emulate the band's debut, at least where sales were concerned; by the time they played Dubai it had already matched the success of *Fairweather Johnson*. As the millennium grew near, HOOTIE & THE BLOWFISH, whether you liked it or not, were officially America's band.

Musically they were something of a hotchpotch – a little country, a little R&B, a little bluegrass, a little rock'n'roll, a little bit of everything, in fact. Their sound was homogeneous, and occasionally bland – but it was never reductive. As *Time* magazine said on its release, the band's first album came across as something fresh and different because it *didn't* try to come across as something fresh and different. The American public were tired of angst-ridden diatribes from the likes of NIRVANA and PEARL JAM, were sick to death – in KURT COBAIN's case, literally – of grunge, sick at the sight of Generation X-ers invading the charts with their mordant tales of adolescent ennui. After complaint rock, here was compliant rock. Hootie, for their sins, offered an alternative to the alternative – breezy, melodic, optimistic, heartfelt songs that reminded many of the EAGLES, the band they used to cover in college.

For this they were severely criticised, accused of being sophomoric dullards producing unchallenging, soporific soft rock. The Stepford Rockers. This, even though they'd won the validation and friendship of the hippest mainstream band in America at the time, REM. "They're a difficult band to promote because they're so normal," one of their phalanx of British publicists told me. "They're undemanding, ordinary guys who make undemanding, ordinary music. Who wants to write about that?"

This carping still rankled. "It makes us laugh, I mean it's just so shallow, but what can you do?" said Rucker, as he huddled together with the other band members in a Portakabin next to the stage on the Dubai dock. "Some press people meet us and like us and realise we're not so dull, but a lot of them just read other people's articles and take their lead from them. I'm not gonna become a heroin addict just to please some dumb journalist.

"The bad press has helped in a way, because now no one expects anything from us. We can just be ourselves, I didn't go and put my make-up on, or my sulky mood before this interview. I like being me, I've always liked being me. We always liked being ourselves. The defining characteristic of most rock bands is the fact that they don't like themselves, which is why they develop an alter ego. We're not like that. We know it's not cool to look like the guy who buys your record, but we do."

This much was certainly true, as HOOTIE & THE BLOWFISH looked like walking Gap ads, sporting the regulation twenty- and thirty-something uniform of khaki combat trousers or shorts, loose fitting T-shirts and polo tops, workmen's boots and baseball caps. Walk through the downtown area of any large American town and you'll still see thousands of young men dressed this way, while the only men wearing suits will be those unlucky souls working in the service industry, in a hotel maybe, or a photocopy shop. Rucker and the boys were the epitome of ordinariness, the revenge of the normal, as American as cherry pie, chewing gum, and fast food, making

U them perfect fodder for the USO, the everyman uber-settlers drank a lot of beer, talked a lot of beer, and seemed quite proud of their embryonic beer bellies. They even golfed!

They were also, obviously, racially mixed, and though they were criticised – preposterously – for being a white band with a black singer, they endlessly repeated the maxim: "Everyone says we're one black guy in an all-white band, but we're actually three white guys in an all-black band." They were verbally attacked by everyone from the extreme right – Rucker had death threats from the Ku Klux Klan for suggesting that the Confederate flag should be removed from his local town hall – to progressive liberals who wrote the band's success off to Rucker's "beigeness". "White America wants to see the one side of black," said Rucker. "I guess they [rappers] are probably more acceptable black figures to white America as they are more threatening."

However, this might have been one of the reasons Hootie were so popular with Clinton; they came from the South, made pleasant if undemanding music, and had an apposite racial demographic. Wouldn't you know it, they also did a lot for charity. Band member Felber thought it had more to do with the fact that they'd achieved the American dream. "We didn't come from money, we struggled for many years and we had to live on very little money, so for us to actually make it, to make our dreams come true, and have money to give some to people who need it, that means a lot to us, to have that power. It's something that should be respected. I should think that appeals to him. It doesn't make us a better band or better musicians or even better songwriters..."

"...or help us sell more records," said Rucker.

"It's just one of those things that makes you smile," continued Felber.

Since the Second World War, or at least since 1941, when the Americans pitched in, the USO has brought a "touch of home", largely in the form of celebrity entertainment, to America's transient military personnel. A non-profit, non-governmental organisation, it receives no direct government funding, though it manages to deliver its programmes and services to millions of active servicemen in more than a hundred and fifty locations worldwide. The USO thrives on conflict, and whenever peace has broken out – after 1945, or the Korean and Vietnam evacuations – the organisation has been virtually out of business, though in 1998 it was once again in huge demand due to the enormous military build-up in the Gulf.

During the Forties, Fifties and Sixties, the USO was like a star-studded Red Cross, worshipped by American servicemen, and lionised on the covers of *Life* magazine and the *Saturday Evening Post*. And while it organised food canteens, community centres, and large-scale accommodation, it was as a glorified booking agent that it made its name, bringing superstars to entertain the troops. From Guadalcanal to the frozen mountains of Korea, from the jungles of Vietnam to the deserts of Saudi Arabia, the USO pitched its tent and brought on the dancing girls – What the heck! Let's do the show right here! In its time it has persuaded most of Hollywood to don combat gear and travel: SAMMY DAVIS JR., JOHN WAYNE, ERROL FLYNN, JIMMY STEWART, BING CROSBY, DANNY KAYE, CLINT EASTWOOD, and on dozens of occasions, BOB HOPE, the USO's most famous advocate. Recently the stars have included STEVE MARTIN, JAY LENO, BILLY JOEL, EARTH, WIND & FIRE, and JIM CARREY, while – alarmingly, perhaps – the cast of *Happy Days* travelled to Europe for three consecutive years. And HOOTIE & THE BLOWFISH were something of a coup, as so often the boys overseas have to make do with fourth-rate Seventies funk bands and forgotten country-and-western singers.

The soldiers, sailors, marines, and airmen always liked the comedians, the singers, and the song-and-dance men, but it was the girls they loved, women such as MARILYN MONROE, ELIZABETH TAYLOR, SHIRLEY MACLAINE, GINGER ROGERS, NANCY SINATRA, ANN-MARGRET, JAYNE MANSFIELD, BROOKE SHIELDS, and cheerleaders galore, particularly those belonging to the Dallas Cowboys. MARLENE DIETRICH was also something of a hit, not least because her idea of entertaining the troops was rather more specific, not so much in the way of boosting morale but rather to satisfy her capacious sexual appetite. There were no cheerleaders on this trip, but there were rumours about a forthcoming appearance from those belonging to the Miami Dolphins, and there was a sense of anticipation in the air. In the smoking room at a cocktail reception for Bush on the USS Enterprise after the show, one pilot said he was happy to see Hootie "and his boys, but what we really gotta get is some pussy out here, man, we gotta let the bone see some real fish. Now that'll be something".

The USO continues to support the US troops in Afghanistan, as well as the various other places they're stationed around the world. In 2009 STEPHEN COLBERT filmed *The Colbert Report* in Iraq as part of a USO-sponsored event, and other entertainers who've made the trip to the Middle East include CRAIG FERGUSON, GARY SINISE, CARRIE UNDERWOOD, and TOBY KEITH. The really big stars don't travel now, though, which I've always found very odd. In the spring of 2010 I spent a week in Afghanistan, and spent four days in Camp Bastion, in Helmand, where surprisingly few entertainers have visited. The troops I spoke to were not disappointed as such, because there was little expectation in the first place. I would have thought the likes of CEE LO GREEN, RIHANNA, the BLACK EYED PEAS, LADY GAGA, or the GLEE cast would have made the journey, but no.

Well, the organisation has always struggled for funding, and its organisational capabilities have rarely been slick – BOB HOPE used to say that the USO planes he travelled on were turned down by kamikaze pilots. JEFF SMITH, Hootie's perpetually beleaguered tour manager, was eager to concur. Like all grade-A stadium bands, Hootie planned their tours with surgical precision, and they were not used to the USO's old-fashioned, lackadaisical attitude. "They make two telephone calls and then say they've done everything they can; they're hopeless," said Smith. "We do this kind of thing for a living, so we know the logistics, but if we had relied on the USO to get us to the Gulf, none of this would have happened. We've had to shadow them every inch of the way."

Here there were no landmines to deal with, no air-to-shore missile attacks, but the USO did experience its own minor catastrophe, albeit at the fourth hole on the main course at the Dubai Creek Golf and Yacht Club. The official USO photographer on this trip was CHESTER SIMPSON, a veteran rock photographer who had done twenty-nine USO tours since 1990. He'd been shot at by snipers in Somalia and chased by Serbian rebels in Bosnia but he'd manage to escape serious injury until the day of Bush's arrival. Earlier in the day the Hooties had been playing a full round of golf in the 110° heat at Dubai Creek, with the heads of various Dubai-based companies who were helping sponsor the USO concert. This was not just another PR exercise but a long-anticipated payback to all those oil-rich bigwigs who had funded the shebang. And as Simpson positioned himself on a benevolent-looking mound to catalogue the tee-off at the fourth, one of the bigwigs drove his ball straight at him – accidentally, of course – causing the war-torn photographer to lurch off to hospital with a sprained wrist, all the while muttering to himself like some addled DOONESBURY character.

Having missed their flight from Bahrain the night before – "another USO f***-up", according to JEFF SMITH – the Hooties were bushwhacked, but had agreed to the game not just because they're nice guys – oh, if you only knew! – but because they were, to a man, completely obsessive about golf. It was, according to DARIUS RUCKER, something of a religion, "the only thing we really believe in". And though they could have done with some sleep, and less severe heat, there was no way they were going to miss it. As golf is a game that requires a certain amount of commitment – not least time – they rarely get to play on tour, so this was a bonus, albeit a hot one.

The Hooties had first played a USO gig two years previously, in Hungary, when US troops were being deployed in Serbia and Bosnia, and they enjoyed it so much they asked if they could come back. Due to the impending hostilities the tour was nearly cancelled the month before, but they were here and, much like their five thousand-strong audience, they couldn't quite believe it. "I'm flabbergasted,

U totally psyched," said Rucker. "It's such a blast to be here. Not many people come over and do this, so the crowds are always incredibly receptive. It's tough for these guys, so this is our way of saying we haven't forgotten about them. We're not trying to make any kind of political statement, we're just over here playing shows and trying to give these people a slice of home for a while. If people look at it politically, then they're missing the point."

And they meant it. The band talked as if they still couldn't quite believe their immense good fortune, making constant references to the fact that they never wanted to do desk jobs and how the band's success had enabled them to carry on doing what they enjoy – playing live music as often as possible. At the time they played over two hundred and fifty gigs a year. They were a genial bunch, and it made a change to meet pop stars who were so effortlessly charming. Hardly social butterflies, they continued to live in Columbia, within walking distance of each other, and seemed to treat fame with a bashful indifference. This perspective was helped by the fact that they didn't become truly successful until their early thirties, by which time most rock stars have burnt themselves out and subjected themselves to rehab.

By the time HOOTIE & THE BLOWFISH had finished their set, the sun had sunk below the horizon, and the five thousand-odd troops, both on the Enterprise and on the deck in front of the stage, were a quivering mass of khaki, blue and white, a captive audience grateful for any entertainment. Some of them were hysterical, even the men. "My wife and I spent our courting time listening to Hootie," said one of the shore patrolmen guarding the stage, beaming, "and you never forget somethin' like that. It's great to see these guys. I really mean that. I haven't had such a good time in three months. And I'm not even supposed to be enjoyin' myself."

"What I'd really like to do it go kick Saddam's ass. We know where they are and what they're doing, it's all on radar, but they won't let us near them," said his partner, not knowing that five days later he would have his wish. "But standing here and listening to Hootie ain't so bad."

After being called back for the inevitable encore, the band whizzed through half-a-dozen cover versions, and when they careered through the DOOBIE BROTHERS' "Long Train Runnin'", and SANTANA's "Black Magic Woman", it was easy to understand why they were so popular – they were the biggest bar band in the world. They even made DAVID BOWIE's glam-rock classic ZIGGY STARDUST, with its latent androgynous overtones, seem like perfect bar-band fodder – an achievement in itself. "Go Hootie!" cried a drunken voice in the mass. "Go rock the boat, baby, let's rock Saddam's ass!! Let's kick it, m'boy!! Let's Hootie!!"

By this time George Bush's motorcade was a long, long way away. Nobody had thought to ask him if he'd been converted.

Hootie and his pals still tour extensively. Their best record is their cover of ORPHEUS's 1968 hit "Can't Find The Time To Tell You", produced by JERRY HARRISON, and which appeared on the soundtrack of the 2000 movie, *Me, Myself & Irene*.

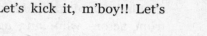

U2

In the world of rock'n'roll I have paid my dues. I have bought the T-shirt. I have been in more dingy basements, more dodgy lofts than anyone I know. I have been in clubs above pubs that were the size of wardrobes. I saw the JAM at the 100 Club, saw ELVIS COSTELLO & THE ATTRACTIONS at the Nags Head, saw the BUZZCOCKS at the Roundhouse, and saw the CLASH in a room smaller than the smallest room in the house (I even once had an altercation with SID VICIOUS in the toilets at the Rainbow, halfway through a RAMONES show, but that is another story altogether...)

Back then, back in the day, small was good. Big was not only bad, it was the manifestation of evil. Big meant "the Man". Who wanted to see a band in an aircraft hanger? Who wanted to see a band from the last row in the stalls, when they looked so small they could have been anyone?

No. Back in the day, small was cool.

U But not any more. Today in the world of rock'n'roll big is beautiful, big is best. And U2 are the biggest band of them all. In fact they are so big they are the only band you can see from space.

In the era of mass communication, when scale means so much more than secrecy, U2 are pretty much lords of all they survey – which, from the stage of the claw-like platform on their most recent show, was rather a lot. In fact I wouldn't be surprised if Bono could see his house most nights.

A lot of bunk is talked about "owning the stage" (especially from actors who long ago gave up the hope of owning anything else), but U2 paid off their mortgage a long time ago. Over the years I must have seen U2 over twenty times, more than any other band I've ever seen. I saw them in the early Eighties, saw them in their pomp on *The Joshua Tree* tour, saw Zoo TV, and at every stage since. I even saw them at Live Aid at Wembley back in 1985, where at one point we were so far away from the stage my girlfriend thought the band were playing via satellite from Philadelphia.

SIMPLE MINDS used to think that they made the kind of noise that was designed solely for stadiums, as did OASIS, and for a while they did, but usually bands only play big venues because they're too popular not to. And most of them simply can't hack it. MADONNA might make great dance records, but she dies in a stadium. MICHAEL JACKSON was the same. Not even the Stones can do it any more.

No, just about the only people who can rival U2 on a big stage are BRUCE SPRINGSTEEN, ELTON JOHN, PRINCE (when he's playing in the round), and MUSE. And when MUSE supported the band on their North American tour in 2009, BONO and co deftly kicked them into a cocked hat. Without even appearing to try.

The only time you realise you have a reputation is when you're not living up to it, and U2 have spent the last thirty years making sure their reputation comes before them. Becoming the greatest rock and roll band in the world wasn't as easy as it may have looked, and they've taken the job seriously: they probably care more about their success, their legacy, and their fans than any of their peers.

And when you see them live... it shows. BRENDAN BEHAN may have said that a job was like death without the dignity, but U2's shows are imbued with as much dignity as you could hope to find in a sports stadium.

Of course the band are relentlessly criticised for being rather too demonstrative for their own good – pompous, imperial, self-regarding. BONO is slapped down by the right-wing media for daring to have an opinion about politics – even though TONY BLAIR implied in his memoirs than he would have made a better Prime Minister than either JOHN PRESCOTT or GORDON BROWN. But then you either buy into the dream or you don't.

U2 are one of the few acts in the world who have got better the bigger they've become, and whose relationship with their audience has actually improved. U2 always wanted to be scalable, and they've done it with considerable style. Their 2009-2011 one hundred and ten date 360° Tour was not only the biggest ever staged by a rock band, but would eventually gross more money than the ROLLING STONES' *A Bigger Bang* extravaganza, and by the end of their two years on the road, the band would have performed in front of a staggering seven million people. Initially designed to support their 2009 album, *No Line On The Horizon*, the tour had taken on a life of its own, one that looked as though it might dwarf everything else the band had ever achieved. While the album hadn't captured the Zeitgeist like those before it (the album's signature single "Get On Your Boots" has all but been disowned), the tour was the most extravagant thing they'd ever attempted. Playing inside a massive architectural wonder nicknamed, much to the band's consternation, "The Claw" (based on the Theme Building at LAX, and inspired by a design that BONO originally tried to describe on his kitchen table in Dublin using three old forks and a grapefruit), featuring a hundred-ton steel construction using a conical 500,000-light LED screen display conceived especially for the show, videos beamed direct from NASA's International Space Station, a light show not seen in a rock show before, and the sort of pyrotechnics usually reserved for Olympic ceremonies, BONO, THE EDGE, ADAM CLAYTON, and LARRY MULLEN, JR., put on their version of the greatest show on earth.

"We want to connect, and our whole thing is about connecting," BONO told me, in the summer of 2011, as the tour was winging its way to a close. "We go out of our way to do that. Punk was all about the guy on top of the speaker stack or in the middle of the crowd who gets on stage, and that's what we're about. We're about community."

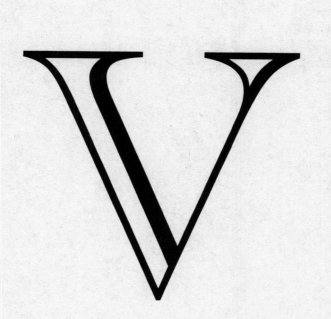

VAMBO!

Alter ego created by ALEX HARVEY. Once acclaimed as "The TOMMY STEELE of Scotland", Gorbals-born Harvey metamorphosed into a back-street vaudevillian (vaudevillain?) via his theatrical hard-rock ensemble, the SENSATIONAL ALEX HARVEY BAND. In the early Seventies his portrayal of a flamboyant, thuggish raconteur earned him and his group (including the demonic guitarist ZAL CLEMINSON) a devoted following, particularly on the terraces. Harvey's studied tenement operas included such rabble-rousers as "Framed" and "Sgt Fury"; his cover versions included TOM JONES' "Delilah" (derivative) and JACQUES BREL's syphilitic "Next!" (definitive). On stage, Harvey had "Vambo Rools" spray-painted behind him, while several songs incorporated this alter ego.

SUZANNE VEGA

She had problems with her teeth, and so went to see her dentist in Greenwich Village. She was grinding her teeth in her sleep, traditionally a sign of tension, a trait not uncommon among singer-songwriters. One wonders whether AIMIE MANN did the same thing, or JOAN OSBORNE. Her fixed teeth still wrap themselves around "Luka", "Tom's Diner", and "Small Blue Thing."

VELVET UNDERGROUND

The orthodoxy of rebellion always starts somewhere, and in the world of the transgressive teen, there is nowhere else to look but here, right here, at the Velvet Underground, in New York, in the mid-Sixties.

The music – the sound – they made is a whirlwind of subversion that manages to epitomise the immortality of youth – with the Velvet Underground you can either live or die forever – while producing blueprints that will be copied by teenage start-ups for as long as they continue to manufacture guitars.

Their look was extraordinary, a stylistic idea that has probably been more influential than any other in pop – and that includes beat groups, long hair for men, punk, the B-Boy look, everything. It was all here: skinny jeans, Breton tops, plastic jackets, winklepickers, sunglasses. Black.

The Velvets crystallised the idea of the genuinely bohemian, urban, narcissistic art school gang. They were born in New York, were sucked into the art scene, the drug scene, and were the talismanic pioneers of what we all now think of as "white cool". They even had a difficult German in the band, and a Welshy. And a girl!

There is no call these days to walk into common-rooms, or coffee bars, with albums under your arm that alert your peers to your marvellous good taste (it would be like carrying around a framed poster, or one of those cardboard cut-ups they used to have in record shops – remember record shops?), but for years the first two Velvets albums were considered to be the ones that exemplified what they were all about; maybe so, but probably their best record, and latterly their most influential, was their third, simply called *The Velvet Underground*, released in 1969. In contrast to those groundbreaking albums, this is a quiet affair – due in part to JOHN CALE's departure. From "Candy Says", about transvestite CANDY DARLING (sung by Cale's replacement Doug Yule), to "After Hours" (sung by drummer MO TUCKER), via "Pale Blue Eyes", and "Beginning To See The Light", VU3 is forty-three minutes of the most understated music of the Sixties. This is the sound of the loft, the squat, or the bedsit at three am.

THE VERVE

Out of context, RICHARD ASHCROFT's band will be remembered for the elegiac "Bittersweet Symphony", a genuinely epic single that forever sounds good pouring out of a radio. The looped orchestration was a sample from ANDREW LOOG OLDHAM's version of the ROLLING STONES' "The Last Time". Former Stones manager ALLEN KLEIN owned the rights and promptly sued. In context, The Verve were a shouty Britpop band with a ridiculously self-opinionated singer, but then none of this matters as this song is a good enough legacy.

THE VILLAGE PEOPLE

A boy band born in a fancy dress shop, this lot were like a gay BANANA SPLITS. Everyone knows the karaoke hits – "YMCA" and "In The Navy", only to be sung having drunk your body-weight in Slippery Nipples – while "Go West" remains something of a camp classic, like the RITCHIE FAMILY's "American Generation", LIME's "Your Love", or SYLVESTER's "You Make Me Feel (Mighty Real)", a tantalising celebration of expectation (Castro Street, here we come!). It was famously and rather brilliantly covered by the PET SHOP BOYS in 1993, using the break-up of the Soviet Union as its leitmotif (see what they did there?).

Having flirted with the New Romantic Movement, in 1985 the Village People attempted another comeback, with a preposterous Hi-NRG single called "Sex Over The Phone". I was flown to Paris to interview them, and on the night we arrived, spent hours in a rowdy restaurant, and then hours more in a gay club in the middle of *Dieu sait où*. The next morning, when I arrived at the dance rehearsal rooms where we were to conduct the interview, I realised that in my hungover state I had left my questions, my tape recorder, my pens and any other form of recording our chat back in the hotel, and so had to talk to them for forty-five minutes or so, without taking a single note. They were either too polite or too stupid to say anything.

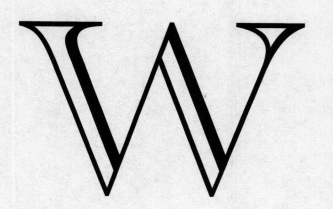

TOM WAITS

W

There is a scene in JENNIFER EGAN's *A Visit From the Goon Squad*, when record producer BERNIE SALAZAR and his wife Stephanie are finally invited to a party a year after moving into a new area in upstate New York. The host, a hedge-fund manager known as DUCK, had invited them only after hearing that Bernie had discovered the CONDUITS, DUCK's all-time favourite band. At the party, DUCK asks Bernie what became of the band's wayward guitarist.

"'Bosco? He's still recording,' Bernie said tactfully. 'His new album will be out in a couple of months: A to B. His solo work is more interior.'"

Personally, I can't think of a more appropriate description of Tom Waits' recent work. I think of him in the same way as I think about WOODY ALLEN – I actually did prefer the earlier, funnier films, and I much prefer Waits' early work, too. His finest record – by some distance – is the soundtrack to FRANCIS FORD COPPOLA's 1982 movie *One From The Heart*, when he duets with CRYSTAL GAYLE on such varied songs as "Broken Bicycles", "I Beg Your Pardon", and "Picking Up After You".

W.G. "SNUFFY" WALDEN

US television's alpha male composer of (often sentimental) theme tunes. Did *thirtysomething, Roseanne, Ellen, The Wonder Years, My So-Called Life, etc.* Oh, and *The West Wing,* probably the most stirring small screen title music ever written. In ROB LOWE's autobiography, *Stories I Only Tell My Friends*, he describes Walden conducting a full orchestra on Warner Bros' giant dubbing stage. There is the timpani rumble, the cymbal clash, the explosive strings, and snatches of French horn. Lowe then goes on to describe a vision he has while listening to this: "We are in black tie. This song is being played by another orchestra and now we are standing and people are applauding. We leave our seats and walk to a podium and walk to another, rising and walking, and now I know this is an awards show, and so is this one and that one and the next one. We rise and walk again and again, always with music, always in black tie. And I can see AARON [SORKIN], and he's holding a statue. I see this as clearly as if watching filmed footage."

As the music soars to its crescendo, Lowe's reverie is broken by his co-star, JOHN SPENCER. "Well, what do you think?" he asks.

"Johnny, I think this is walkin' music," says Lowe.

SCOTT WALKER

It used to be that there was nothing more fashionable than outsiders, those misfits on the margins who avoided convention like the plague. Their trajectory was simple: starburst entry, rapid disillusionment, then a life spent in the shadows producing work which in years to come is seen as their most challenging and enlightening. Cult heroes, they were called, and though most of them have by now been exposed to daylight (a process starting with lavish journalistic praise and ending in histrionic biopics), some are still with us, lurking in dark corners of their own making.

Scott Walker has spent most if his career on the margins, certainly on the edges of the pop world and seemingly on the verges of the real one, too. He has honed torture, existential angst to such a degree that his haunting, desperate records can alter the mood of a room as surely as a power cut. His is a twilight world, but hardly a pretentious one; dozens of devotees have tried to emulate Walker's style and attitude over the years, yet Walker remains a true original. Whereas you get the sense that the people who try and copy him are just affecting a pose, with Walker it's difficult to imagine him doing anything else. "I do believe I'm an artist," he once told me, "and what I do is important. But not everyone has to hear it, and I don't need to do it all the time."

In the mid-Sixties the WALKER BROTHERS were about as big as a pop group could be. Ohio-born SCOTT ENGEL teamed up with GARY LEEDS and JOHN MAUS to form the WALKER BROTHERS in 1964, but it was only when they left California for England, twelve months later, that they had any kind of success.

During the next two years they became as famous as the ROLLING STONES, the KINKS, or the WHO, recording a series of spectacularly successful melodramatic torch songs which owed much to PHIL SPECTOR – "The Sun Ain't Gonna Shine Anymore", "My Ship is Coming In", "Make It Easy On Yourself" – all sung in Scott Walker's soaring baritone. Their material was a manageable mix of the light and the dark, but when Walker went solo in 1967, the dark side came to the fore. His first solo singles were hits, though the success tailed off as he found it increasingly difficult to balance the Radio 2 ballads which he performed on the TV show he fronted, with the maudlin and esoteric workings of his LPs (he became obsessed with JACQUES BREL, recording dozens of his songs). Devastated by the commercial failure of his 1969 LP *Scott 4*, he all but walked off into the sunset. In the process he became the cult hero to end them all.

"There was drink and lots of other stuff," he once said. "I used to really go for it, drinking more and more just because I hated what I was doing. It started towards the end of the [WALKER] BROTHERS but continued right into my solo career as I battled against people trying to push my career in directions I didn't want it to go. They wanted me to be PERRY COMO and I wouldn't do it. They wanted me to be MICK JAGGER – I wouldn't do it."

Walker went solo not only because of the increasing squabbles within the group, but also because he was ill-equipped to deal with the demands of pop celebrity; he had a pathological fear of performing live, and recoiled from the "screamagers" – as he called them – who fell adoringly at his feet.

Towards the end of 1966, at the height of the group's fame, Walker moved to a Benedictine monastery on the Isle of Wight, but within days the island was awash with teenage girls, demanding their idol. "I loathe the show business ladder and the way it operates," he said at the time. "I only do it for the bread."

"I was always more interested in following a pure path than most people," he said later (when I interviewed him once he spoke so carefully that I began to think he was wondering what I was going to do with this information]. "To me, singing like Sinatra or TONY BENNETT was more of a divine path than anything the hippies got up to in the Sixties. All those longhairs were morally bankrupt, they were acting as though the real world didn't actually exist. I wanted to be a totally serious torch singer, someone who is dedicated to their craft; I didn't want to stand in front of thousands of young girls, whipping them into a frenzy, nor did I want to pretend I came from Mars. All I wanted to do was sing my songs."

Along with DAVID HEMMINGS, SIMON DEE, and DAVID BAILEY, Walker once seemed the epitome of mid-Sixties chic, but he soon retreated into himself, shunning his fans, his fame, and eventually himself. There were reports of heroin addiction and attempted suicides... but above all else was the music, at least the music he liked. The WALKER BROTHERS reformed in the middle of the Seventies, having some success with the song "No Regrets", but after another few years of intermittent recording, Walker drifted off again. He went back to art school – the Byam Shaw School of Art in South London – travelled, and cut down on his drinking. Then, in 1984 he recorded another solo album, *Climate Of Hunter*, which caused a flurry of activity in the press. By then he was being looked after by DIRE STRAITS' manager ED BICKNELL who, after the record's release, tried to get his charge to record an album of songs written by the likes of CHRIS DIFFORD and GLEN TILBROOK from SQUEEZE, MARK KNOPFLER, and BOY GEORGE. Predictably this came to nothing, as did a collaboration with BRIAN ENO and DANIEL LANOIS.

"A lot of people have tried to reactivate my career, but I always found them too contrived," said Walker. "I've got no interest in nostalgia. There was a misunderstanding between Eno, Lanois and myself on the particular record. I spent six months writing material and then brought it to the studio to record with them, but I found their way of working too scattered, and Lanois I found totally useless. So one night in the early stages of making the record I just stood up and walked out."

Walker's most recent records – *Tilt*, from 1994, and *The Drift*, from 2006 – are challenging things, and although not without their charms, in no way pander to anyone who might have enjoyed any of his records made prior to 1984.

When I interviewed him, in the mid-Nineties, in his manager's four-storey terraced house in the heart of London's Holland Park, surrounded by the clutter of children's toys, pop videos, and overburdened bookshelves, he explained what he had been up to in the ten years since his last record. He was actually quite charming, but after about an hour, he leant forward and asked, "Have you got enough?"

DIONNE WARWICK

That she is the greatest interpreter of BURT BACHARACH and HAL DAVID's material has never been in any doubt, yet over the years Dionne has appeared to be rather resentful of this, almost as though she feels her success has been tied to theirs exclusively, and that without them she would still be struggling. "I have been asked by many of my peers," she said in 2010, "'How do you sing that stuff?' When presented with Burt's music, I did feel sometimes as if I were taking an exam. But, since he wrote the songs for me, I felt I was meant to be able to sing it. People have at times assumed that I wrote or co-wrote many of the songs that I have been singing for years. Well, I certainly wish I had. I was the interpreter of songs written by Bacharach and David, as well as other composers. To me, those who have the ability to put words and music together, giving pleasure to the listening ear, have a very special talent. Also, those who are able to sing and record their works have an even more special talent."

So there.

DINAH WASHINGTON

"Dinah was a star. She had a voice that was like the pipes of life. She could also do something a lot of singers then and now could not do: she could take the melody in her hand, hold it like an egg, crack it open, fry it, let it sizzle, reconstruct it, put the egg back in the box and back in the refrigerator, and you would've still understood every single syllable of every single word she sang. Every single melody she sang she made hers," QUINCY JONES

WEATHER REPORT

Oh my word, life was so much simpler in the Seventies, when there were still properly observed demarcation lines on the beaches of pop. In 1976 Weather Report released *Heavy Weather* (on Columbia, no less), the greatest fusion album of all time, one of the bestselling jazz albums of the decade, and an alternative soundtrack to the summer of punk. They were a supergroup – WAYNE SHORTER, JACO PASTORIUS, etc – who turned elaborately arranged songs into FM-friendly hits, "Birdland" included. The album would spawn a new genre of radio broadcasting, "smooth jazz", just as SADE would define another a decade later with "quiet storm".

JIMMY WEBB

A songwriter friend of mine was visiting a Los Angeles recording studio in the late Sixties when a young, Nehru-jacketed Jimmy Webb pushed his head around the door. Would Doug [Flett, who wrote "The Fair Is Moving On" for Elvis Presley] like to hear a demo of "Wichita Lineman", this new song he'd written? Would he? Would an eight-year-old boy want to meet Wayne Rooney, Ryan Giggs, Eric Cantona, or Bobby Charlton? Can blue men sing the whites? Quick as a flash, Doug followed Webb into his own studio, where he was afforded the luxury of hearing Webb belting out his demo version of the song which was made famous by, among many others, Glen Campbell.

"It wasn't just the song," said Doug. "It was the voice, a beautiful, haunting thing." Unfortunately, so far as most people are concerned, Webb's voice has never really lived up to expectations, because although he has written a handful of the most evocative torch songs of the last forty years (by the time he was twenty, Webb was a millionaire with as fistful of Grammies), he has rarely been able to give them the interpretations they deserve. Like Burt Bacharach, he has had to accept the fact that his songs work best when they are sung by other people (even, in the case of "Didn't We" and "MacArthur Park", by Richard Harris – what Christopher Hitchens once referred to as "the horror song").

For three weeks in 1994, Webb, then a sprightly forty-eight, gave Londoners a chance to experience his voice in person for the first time in over a decade. The Café Royal's Green Room had been operating as a supper-club venue for just over a year, hosting small, personal concerts by the likes of Eartha Kitt, Michael Feinstein, and Sacha Distel, where dinner and cabaret would set you back £48 per person. The mood was certainly intimate, but then you could be unlucky enough to be seated in front of one of the Green Room's many pillars, which is taking intimacy a little too far. Having said that, it was the perfect place to see someone like Webb, who is ostensibly a songwriter, not a performer.

He was obviously experienced at this cabaret kind of thing, as he made a point of trying to build a Vegas-style rapport with the audience from the first song in. There were small jokes, witty asides (OK, not so witty), and plenty of music industry anecdotes. (In the previous year's *Archive* compilation, Webb had displayed this dubious gift with his sleevenotes: introducing "Lady Fits Her Blue Jeans", he wrote, "And she did.") A tall man, Webb spent most of the concert crouched over his keyboards, his ponytail bouncing behind him, with his eyes shut and his head pointing heavenwards, as if leaning towards divine inspiration. As a pianist he had a deft touch, though as he has never really excelled as a singer, some of the versions of his own remarkable songs made me long for the FIFTH DIMENSION, JOE COCKER, or GLEN CAMPBELL.

He begun with an uplifting version of his first proper hit, "Up, Up And Away", before leaving the Sixties behind and moving into cooler and less charted waters, singing various Seventies ballads, including "The Highwayman" and "The Moon's A Harsh Mistress". There was, however, no "PF Sloane", "Where The Universes Are", or "Where's The Playground Susie", and not enough of the songs he wrote for LINDA RONSTADT; instead we got half an hour of twee, maudlin show tunes (including a paean to Converse All Star training shoes), for shows which never got off the ground in the first place. Webb described this part of the evening as "completely off Broadway".

The home stretch started with fulsome versions of "Didn't We", "If These Old Walls Could Speak", and "MacArthur Park". He then finished with a disappointing medley of "By The Time I Get To Phoenix", "Galveston", and the obligatory "Wichita Lineman". Obviously these songs have haunted him down the years, and he perfunctorily bashed them out on a baby grand as though there were a man behind the curtain with a very big stick. Like DAVID BYRNE with "Psycho Killer",

RAY DAVIES with "Lola", and TONY BENNETT with "I Left My Heart In San Francisco", these are the songs which Webb feels he cannot get by without playing. As swiftly as possible.

It was an uneven evening, as I assumed it would be, though there was the occasional chilling moment – especially in "Wichita Lineman" and "What Does A Woman See In A Man" (from his 1993 comeback LP, *Suspending Disbelief*) – when Webb's compassion and latent melancholia seemed to overshadow his inadequacies as a vocalist, causing ripples and fleeting epiphanies all over the Café Royal.

Jimmy Webb has never been the greatest singer in the world, but when it comes to a maudlin refrain, there are few to touch him.

KANYE WEST

There is no denying that Kanye West has produced some amazing records. To wit: "Diamonds From Sierra Leone" from *Late Registration*, 2005, and including a massive sample from "Diamonds Are Forever" by SHIRLEY BASSEY; "Stronger" from *Graduation*, 2007, which included a vocal sample from "Harder, Better, Faster, Stronger" by French house duo DAFT PUNK; "Paranoid" from 2008's minimalist *808s & Heartbreak*; and "Dark Fantasy" from 2010's *My Beautiful Dark Twisted Fantasy*. Determinedly inventive, West has continually pushed the boundaries of hip-hop, making records that have rarely sounded like anyone else's (ignoring the dozens of samples on them, of course).

His ego, however, undermines him time and time again. "If I was more complacent and I let things slide, my life would be easier," is a typical Kanye quote. "But you all wouldn't be as entertained. My misery is your pleasure." And he isn't immune to the attractions of bling: early in 2011 he spent $180,000 (£135,000) on an 18-carat gold, diamond-encrusted timepiece emblazoned with an image of his own face (this just months after splashing out on some custom-made gold and diamond teeth).

Embarrassment likes to follow him wherever he goes. His biggest faux pas of 2010 was trying to get *My Beautiful Dark Twisted Fantasy* banned by the US supermarket chains. Its cover featured an image of West having sex with a naked white angel, a heterogeneous coupling so vile it was sure to get banned. "Yoooo they banned my album cover!!!!!," tweeted West. "Banned in the USA!!! They don't want me chilling on the couch with my Phoenix." But it appeared that no one cared about Kanye chilling on the couch with his Phoenix, as no one batted an eyelid.

I spent a weekend with Kanye once, in Paris, during the men's collections in 2010. He was a huge enthusiast, and went to every show with the expectation of the innocent. He knew how to work the paparazzi though, and after each show would be ferried back to his hotel to change outfits. Huge, JOAN CRAWFORD-style glasses would be exchanged for a hat, a loud foam bomber jacket would be swapped for a yellow jumper. Etc, etc. I saw him go to around eight shows a day for two whole days, which means he worse at least sixteen different outfits. He could talk the talk, too, and ingratiated himself with the fashion fraternity extremely successfully (actually this is never so difficult, as celebrity has greater currency than almost anything else apart from a blood line), although he was a real pain to talk to. When you are that famous and that successful there is a tendency to think that everyone is at your beck and call, which makes even-handed conversation quite difficult. Kanye, my friend (actually not my friend), take your sunglasses off – you're indoors! – and stop talking about yourself in the third person. You sound like a fool!

I think he showed what a narcissist he is at the 2009 MTV Video Music Awards, when he stormed on stage – drunk on Hennessy cognac – to unleash an astonishing rant during an acceptance speech by TAYLOR SWIFT. The nineteen-year-old singer, who was collecting Best Female Video for "You Belong To Me", was left humiliated as West snatched the microphone from her hands and shouted that the award should have gone to his friend Beyoncé, for "Single Ladies".

What a charming man.

WEST SIDE STORY

It's 1957 and the opening night of a new show at the Winter Garden theatre on Broadway. The curtain comes up and you're greeted by a row of dancers frozen against a stark, stylised representation of a city playground, the only noise being rhythmic finger snaps. What comes next is a "serious" musical, stylishly staged in fluid, semi-abstract patterns, by turns romantic, funny and savage: a blue-collar tenement opera.

These days, *West Side Story* seems almost as much a romantic exercise in nostalgia as *Oklahoma!*, or *Fiddler On The Roof*. In fact, we now think of it as a classic Broadway musical rather than a genre-busting phenomenon. But in 1957 musicals like this just didn't exist. We had *The King and I*, *South Pacific*, *Can-Can*, and *Kiss Me Kate*, but nothing as incendiary as *West Wise Story*.

Look at *West Side Story* now and it looks like a collection of blueprints for pop promos. It would be easy to imagine anyone from LADY GAGA to U2 climbing up the set's zigzag fire escapes, their bodies swathed in the harsh white streetlight. But in 1957 the idea of a musical set against a backdrop of stylised urban violence was anathema to the theatrical establishment.

While it might seem to be an exaggeration to say that *West Side Story* had the same effect on the world of the American theatre as the SEX PISTOLS and punk had on the British rock establishment in 1976, after its first staging, in 1957, Broadway would never be the same again. Indeed, the show's prologue – "Listen to the finger snapping pulse of life of the West Side of New York City, where a lifetime can be only 48 hours long" – is echoed in the CLASH's 1977 paean to teenage hedonism, "48 Hours". Without *West Side Story*, we wouldn't have had the *Rocky Horror Show*. Without *WSS* there would be no *Rent*.

Not only that, it also made way for stage shows such as *Grease* and films such as *Saturday Night Fever*, as well as all the other musicals that shamelessly exploit the subcultural world of the adolescent American misanthrope. Admittedly, without *West Side Story* we probably wouldn't have had JULIEN TEMPLE's botched *Absolute Beginners* and PAUL SIMON's over-reaching *Capeman* either, but then the less said about that the better. It pre-empted the video era, too, as *WSS* contains nearly twice as much music, and much less dialogue, than the average Hollywood musical of the period. And whereas dancers usually had to be content with providing a chorus line for the stars of the show, *WSS* was a real ensemble piece: because so much of the action is gang-related, with all the principals mixing with the crowd, each cast member was required to sing and dance as well as act, including the lead characters, Tony and Maria.

The show opened in New York with what WALTER KERR, the critic of the *Herald Tribune*, called "a catastrophic roar". With the likes of *My Fair Lady* still packing them in at neighbouring houses, Broadway was ill prepared. A contemporary interpretation of *Romeo and Juliet* set against a background of juvenile warfare between rival Puerto Rican and American gangs on the west side of Manhattan (the Latino Sharks vs the squeaky-clean Jets), the musical was a snapshot of America's emerging teen culture, and was the first time that cinematic hoodlums found a voice in the theatre, the first time that Brandoperatics and Deanisms found their way onto the Great White Way.

Its creators were already renowned, and together they formed something of a dream team; JEROME ROBBINS as director and choreographer, music by LEONARD BERNSTEIN, a script by ARTHUR LAURENTS, and lyrics by a young STEPHEN SONDHEIM. Robbins was one of Broadway's most established figures and had worked with Bernstein on the enormously successful *On*

The Town, while Bernstein had found a distinctive place in the nation's heart through his ability to appeal to the popular as well as the classical audience, scoring musicals, symphonies, and song cycles galore, while famously conducting the New York Philharmonic. As for Sondheim, this was his first taste of success, having previously only written incidental music for a now forgotten show called *Girls of Summer* – although as an OSCAR HAMMERSTEIN protégé he had always been destined for big things.

The music itself was contemporary in the extreme, an orchestral interpretation of a flick knife, though it was all immensely palatable. Because of Bernstein's orchestral sweeps, coupled with Sondheim's uncharacteristically uplifting lyrics (he tends to disown them now, thinking them too saccharine), the songs are as energising as any you'll find in the theatre, and it still feels that way: "Something's Coming", "Maria", "America", "Tonight", "Gee, Officer Krupke!", "I Feel Pretty", etc. The show's cleverness was in mixing traditional American homilies with the cut-and-thrust of New York street life. In "Something's Coming", Sondheim mines the familiar bourgeois dreams of hope and attainment (what the writer JOHN LAHR calls "that peculiarly American expectation of a magical insulation from life"), while most of the other songs are fantastically upbeat. (The show even contains one copper-bottomed, spine-tingling standard, the sublime "Somewhere", an epiphanical song that has withstood interpretation by such diverse bedfellows as BARBRA STREISAND, P.J. PROBY, the PET SHOP BOYS, and TOM WAITS.

WHAM!

Where chart sensations are concerned, it's always easy to dismiss all that went before them, difficult to imagine any one pop phenomenon being able to inspire the same kind of national, if not quite global, loyalty. With pop it's always Year

Zero. Think of TAKE THAT, BROS, CULTURE CLUB, or T. REX, and we automatically think of bargain basements full of discarded copies of "Back For Good", "I Owe You Nothing", "Karma Chameleon", or "Jeepster".

As built-in obsolescence always seems to be the order of the day, apart from TAKE THAT (who have a bizarre and yet fascinating hold on the nation's throat) it is unlikely that a greatest hits collection by any of the aforementioned teen dreams would stand much chance of making it to No.1 in the UK any time soon. Yet Wham! were always different, and while they never had the kind of long-term Queen Mother appeal of TAKE THAT, during the rashly extravagant Eighties, GEORGE MICHAEL and ANDREW RIDGELEY were treated by press and public alike as minor royalty. Maybe there were some who actually thought they were minor royalty. Their records were insanely popular, and although *NME* critics dismissed them as formulaic pop, they were anything but: our radios rattled to the sub-Motown sound of "Wham Rap!" (No.8, January 1983), "Wake Me Up Before You Go Go" (No.1, May 1984), "Freedom" (No.1, October 1984), and the rest. Wham!'s controlled exuberance epitomised everything that is good about pop, and though they were in the charts for just four years, from "Young Guns (Go For It)" (No.3, October 1982) to "The Edge Of Heaven" (No.1, June 1986), during that time they hardly made a duff record.

The late Seventies and early Eighties were not exactly giddy times in Britain, yet out of the recession came dozens of smart young pop groups willing to dance while London, Coventry, or Sheffield burned. None was smarter than GEORGE MICHAEL's Wham!. They were part of the biggest British pop explosion since the mid-Sixties, as FRANKIE GOES TO HOLLYWOOD, CULTURE CLUB, DURAN DURAN, and SPANDAU BALLET broke the American charts, paving the way for such unlikely glamour kids as the THOMPSON TWINS and the EURYTHMICS. When we think of a Wham! song, we tend to think of a rose-tinted illusory past. And we rather like it. George's "Careless Whisper" (No.1, August 1984) sounds like our past, even if it had nothing to do with it. The duo also had the perfect pop divorce: George being granted ascension to the very top of the pop hierarchy, Andrew having faded from view like a GTi-driving Garbo.

I first saw Wham! in July 1983 at the launch of their debut LP *Fantastic* (such confidence!), in a small suite of offices just behind Fulham Broadway Tube station in London. While dozens of sneering music journalists and record-company bigwigs stood about, working at being brilliant, the two nineteen-year-old soul boys, dressed in Hawaiian shirts, cutaway jeans, and deck shoes, jived together on the dance floor, jitterbugging along to their own version of the MIRACLES' "Love Machine". Rarely had I seen two men enjoying themselves so much. To be dancing to one of their own records! At their own party! In front of other people!

Suburban boys with West End aspirations – second-generation immigrants, Andrew coming from Italian/Egyptian stock, and George (real name Georgios Panayiotou) was Greek – they were high street through and through: their white T-shirts and socks came from Marks & Spencer, their blue jeans from Woodhouse. They hailed from Bushey in Hertfordshire, in the heart of the disco belt. For years they danced themselves stupid at the New Penny in Watford High Street, moving on to the Camden Palace as soon as it opened in the spring of 1982, immersing themselves in London's holier-than-thou nightlife. To west London sybarites they looked oddly naive in their quasi-naff clothes and floppy fringes, yet anyone with eyes in their head and loafers on their feet could tell that they had a very spangly future ahead of them.

After they became famous they still went out dancing, and it was not unusual to see Andrew on display at the Limelight, or George down at the infamous Taboo nightclub. For about eighteen months "Everything She Wants" (No.2, December 1984) was the hippest record to be seen dancing to, and George could often be seen doing just that, right in front of the DJ booth. Even at 3am in the bowels of some

W

sweaty West End nightclub, he looked as though he'd just stepped off the plane from Ibiza: tandoori tan, summer whites, designer stubble (something the singer invented), and perfect PRINCESS DIANA hair. He was always serious about his hair. "Some days I made the covers of the tabloids. Some days PRINCESS DI made the covers of the tabloids," he said. "Some days I think they just got mixed up."

George was less home-boy than homely boy. If he was the suburban sonneteer, happy in his bedroom writing tearjerkers, then Andrew was the quintessential party animal, the LIAM GALLAGHER of his day, unable to leave a party without a bottle of Moet in one hand and a bottle blonde in the other. It was Andrew who realised George's pop ambitions, Andrew who acted the extrovert to George's shy loner. George might have written the songs – in four years Andrew only gained three co-writing credits, for "Wham Rap!", "Club Tropicana" (No.4, July 1983), and "Careless Whisper" – yet it was his partner who looked the part when they sang them. Andrew's image was crystallised on the 12-inch version of "I'm Your Man" (No.1, November 1985): a racing car is heard careering through a plate-glass window, followed by the sound of its driver cackling with laughter as he asks, "Where's the bar?"

The boys were managed for a time by Sixties impresario, SIMON NAPIER-BELL, but it was always George who had the vision thing, even at school. There was nothing haphazard about this affair, and Wham!'s seemed organised with staggering efficiency. Their songs were hardly arch (unlike, say, the PET SHOP BOYS), but even to the untrained ear one instinctively knew the people behind them weren't stupid. Not only were they perfect fodder for twelve-year-old girls, but they also had a superior ironic quality: whether you were an art student or an estate agent, you knew they were cool.

It all ended in the most spectacular, and – for a pop group – impressively orchestrated manner. Displaying unusual sagacity for a twenty-two-year-old, Georgios decided the clock was nearing midnight, and that Cinderella really ought to go home. Ziggy Stardust-style, he broke up the band to go solo, organising one last showbiz gesture, the final farewell triumph at Wembley Stadium in the scorching summer of 1986.

One gets the feeling that Andrew could have carried on forever, but for George there were only so many shuttlecocks he could put down his tennis shorts. Andrew gradually disappeared, moving to Cornwall and dropping out. George decided he wanted to be a sex god, then he changed his mind (changing the name of his second album *Bare* to the slightly more off-putting *Listen Without Prejudice Vol.1*), then he started smoking a lot of weed, hanging out in public lavatories, crashing cars, and generally making a nuisance of himself.

White Man's Overbite

The unfortunate by-product of going to see a heritage act is the audience, which almost always contains a small bunch of pot-bellied fifty-something men who can't dance. They sit there as though they were glued to their seats, trying to summon up enough courage to nod their heads, twists their shoulders, or – heaven forbid! – bob up and down. The thing is, it's only ever the upper half of their bodies they move, scared to move their legs in case anyone laughs at them. They twitch, fidget in time, minutely jutting their chins out, like very timid pistons, each and every one of them practising the white man's overbite.

What these men do – and I fear I have to say that these men are almost always white – is chair dance, twisting and turning their upper bodies as though they would be whipped if they moved their legs. Chair dancing can only really be convincingly executed in cars, and even then it looks a bit silly. There they sit, in their archaic rock'n'roll T-shirts

("Radiobed & the Eiderdowns: No Sleep Till Chipping Norton!"), with their manbags, their combats pants, and their funny shoes, all nodding in earnest, as though they were human metronomes. Some might throw caution to the wind and start tapping their hands on their thighs, hitting imaginary cymbals, approximating paradiddles, and playing air snare.

I saw a heritage act play the BBC studios in Maida Vale once, and while the ageing rocker went out of his way to look and sound like a twenty-something, a portion of the audience descended into cliché. There were plenty of people under forty who were swaying away at the back, and plenty of young girls down the front who couldn't stop dancing. Yet there was a group of twenty or so chair dancers in the middle who refused to do anything but gyrate their necks and bite their lower lips. As said heritage act worked his way through an encore, the twenty-something girls danced as one, the thirty-something men swayed from side to side, and even the BBC mice were up on their feet, all of them oblivious to the bunch of balding, pot-bellied chair dancers in the middle of the room. But boy were those guys jutting their chins.

The White Stripes

With the White Stripes, every day looks like Christmas, a red and white fiesta of blues. MEG WHITE wore her NANCY SINATRA hipsters, or a skirt the size of a beer mat, along with her resigned, slightly nervous smile, the rictus smirk that often made her look ill at ease. JACK WHITE looked like JOHNNY DEPP, in red strides, a cocky rock star grin on a face that sometimes made him look a little like MARY-LOUISE PARKER, when she was playing JOSH LYMAN's strident fuck-buddy in *The West Wing*. They were the co-dependent LED ZEPPELIN.

Together they made a primeval, leviathan noise that actually moved the blues along, picking up a narrative many thought had died with the Mississippi riverboats, making the blues relevant and sexy and vital. Two garage-blues fanatics from Detroit went from playing low-ceilinged basements to headlining Glastonbury, playing melodramatic music (strangled vocals, methylated guitar) that sounded as though it was being forced from the band by a series of heavy and merciless blows to the stomach. *White Blood Cells* (2001), *Elephant* (2003), and *Get Behind Me Satan* (2005) are all good, as are all the rest, a legacy it's nigh-on impossible to puncture, a collection of analogue Mephistolean tinctures that will guard against most things, not least mediocrity.

They could just as easily have been called the Black Slacks.

THE WHO

For years I had one of KEITH MOON's drumsticks, thrown into the audience at a Rainbow gig in 1975. It moved everywhere with me, from bedsit to flat to – oh, damn, where did it go? I'd kept it as it was always the drums that I liked the most about the Who, the drums which first appealed to me, the drums that I thought made the band sound so wild, so anarchic, the drums that filled me with such an urgent sense of immortality. If you listen closely (in truth you don't have to listen that closely) to the drums on *Who's Next*, it's not only "Baba O'Reilly", "Bargain", or "Won't Get Fooled Again", that sound so important, it's the weaker songs too, "My Wife", "Going Mobile", and "Getting In Tune". Take away Moon's feverish bashing and the songs sound almost ordinary. On some songs, you can even imagine Moon sitting down, picking up his sticks and starting to drum away on his own little journey, obviously never oblivious to what was going on around him, but knowing he could make it to the end without needing to turn himself into a human metronome. "6.34? Sure, I'll set off now and see you at the end." Moon's magic was actually gold dust, adding a sparkle and at least an extra forty percent to every record he ever played on.

PETE TOWNSHEND wrote generation-defining songs, sung by someone who had no problem singing them, yet – like no other band before or since – the Who were defined by their drummer. KEITH MOON's style was so idiosyncratic, so brutal, and so surreal, that it became impossible to imagine the band without him. Which is why is was so difficult for them when Moon died in 1978, why their frenzied noise was never the same again.

The best way to understand the Who's very particular dynamic is to read JAMES WOOD, writing in the *New Yorker* in 2010: "The Who had extraordinary rhythmic vitality, and it died when KEITH MOON died, thirty-two years ago. PETE TOWNSHEND's hard, tense, suspended chords seem to scour the air around them; ROGER DALTREY's singing was a young man's fighting swagger, an incitement to some kind of crime; JOHN ENTWISTLE's incessantly mobile bass playing was like someone running away from the scene of the crime; and KEITH MOON's drumming, in its inspired vandalism, was the crime itself. Most rock drummers, even very good and inventive ones, are timekeepers. There is a space for a fill or a roll at the end of a musical phrase, but the beat has primacy over the curlicues. KEITH MOON ripped all this up."

We love the power chords (how easy it is to drown in the aural pyrotechnics of "The Kids Are Alright", "Substitute", "Pinball Wizard", "5.15", "How Many Friends", and all the rest), we love Townshend's stripped down ballads ("Blue, Red and Grey", "Too Much Of Anything", "They Are All In Love", etc), we love the studied belligerence of the microphone-flailing Daltrey, and we love the way JOHN ENTWISTLE used to walk on stage as though he were looking for his dog. Most of all we love the mad man on the riser, eagerly creating harmony from chaos.

BRIAN WILSON

Over fifty years after inventing the Californian Dream, Brian Wilson is finally living it. In his primary-coloured Hawaiian shirts and standard-issue Ray-Bans, he can be found cruising along Mulholland Drive, high up in the hills above his sprawling adobe-style Beverly Hills home, listening to oldies stations, and wallowing in the security of the present and the serenity of the sunshine. Having survived half a lifetime of drug abuse, drug damage, psychoanalysis, and stultifying medication, Wilson is now trying to enjoy all the things he espoused when he first started making music with the BEACH BOYS fifty years ago. He still suffers from a schizoaffective disorder, a mental condition that means he hears voices in his head and suffers terrible bouts of depression... So he lives day to day, trying to replace all his bad old memories with bankable new ones. He rarely listens to his old records, as he's unsure what sort of memories will cloud his mind. But when the good ones come, and when a record comes on the radio he likes, he embraces them: "Each one brings back a different kind of memory," he says. "Sometimes sadness, but most of the time it brings back a good feeling – sunshine and ocean. The BEACH BOYS were all about sunshine and ocean."

The ocean was such a defining trope of Wilson's songwriting that he has all but abandoned it – "I don't need to think about the ocean" – and sunshine is the thing that keeps his dark moods at bay. He rarely visits the beach, as he doesn't know what it holds for him, unsure of his ability to cope with it. Instead, he embraces terra firma, his car, and the Southern California sunshine, visiting the past only when he feels like it, in his imagination. Wilson is a big man, six foot four, with broad shoulders, but the gentle giant has a weathered face that makes him seem critically vulnerable. He has full salt and pepper, JEFF BRIDGES hair, but again this is incongruous; he is about as emotionally fragile as a seventy-something-year-old man can be.

"He needs a real comfort level," said his second wife Melinda. Not only is she responsible for his new spiritual well being, she's also the one largely responsible for his creative rebirth, and for getting him back into concert halls ten years ago. Melinda and Brian share their Beverly Hills home with their adopted daughters, Daria Rose and Delanie Rae, and a son, Dylan, as well as an assortment of dogs. The past doesn't exist here, only the now, and there are no mementos from the past, no reminders of the life he knew before he started coming back to the relative normality he enjoys these days. And instead of gold discs or photographs of the BEACH BOYS, there are Toby jugs, Victorian dolls, and twee shop-bought paintings (Wilson was always criticised for having poor taste in this respect – he was always too bound-up in himself and his art to worry about what paintings might be on his wall).

When he's interviewed these days he tends to sit bolt upright, as though he's there under duress, and walks in and out of rooms as though propelled by remote control. Wilson can appear absent-minded at the best of times, although there is always a strange logic underpinning his actions. He was having dinner in the Wolseley, in London, a few years ago, eating steak with a famous friend of his, and their respective spouses. Having finished his meal, he simply stood up, announced he wanted to go, and started walking towards the door. Once he got there, he stood, implacable in his own way, and waited for his companions to finish their meal. Having spent half his life at the beck and call of others – his father, his band, carers, doctors, dealers, therapists – Brian Wilson now tends to do things his own way.

"Brian Wilson's psyche is now a fragile and uncertain thing, stabilised on a variety of legally prescribed mood-dampening and -altering drugs," wrote GQ's MICK BROWN when he interviewed Wilson for the magazine on the release of Smile in 2004. "In profiles he is sometimes described as 'child-like' – an apt description. Wilson lacks the easy felicities of normal conversation: he has the child's way of replying to any question with no more than the question demands – talking with him can be like navigating a map of cul-de-sacs. It can sometimes seem as if he is not quite in the present; yet he remains capable of pulling the most surprising recollections from his past."

He now plays more concerts than he's played since the early Sixties, and the songs that nearly killed him are now keeping him alive. "I sit down on stage because I feel more comfortable sitting," he said. "I move my hands around to try and look alive. I'm looking at the front row and I'm looking up in the air, but I can't see without my glasses and I don't remember any faces."

But he's enjoying himself.

While it is true that Brian Wilson helped invent California – a neo-Polynesian paradise conjured up by an overweight, puppy-faced adolescent – up until recently he had never been able to fully enjoy its spoils; trapped, seemingly, in an internal – and eternal – world of foreboding, panic, and insecurity. The only thing that has saved him from true madness is his awesome talent for sweet music.

Like BURT BACHARACH, Brian Wilson had the ability to mix euphoria and melancholia in the space of a single song, often the same melody, and occasionally the same note. Given his history of personal problems (an aggressive and belligerent father, a dysfunctional family, a fragile mental state, addictions, weight problems, and a long-standing over-bearing therapist), it's hardly surprising that Wilson's best music always had an innate sadness, a tender quality which can be found in such diverse BEACH BOYS songs as "Our Prayer", "Wind Chimes", "The Lonely Sea", "Melt Away", "Caroline, No", "Surf's Up", "The Warmth of the Sun" (written in response to the JFK assassination), and his greatest triumph, "Till I Die" (a version of which appears on their 1971 LP *Surf's Up*, though a vastly superior extended instrumental version was released on *Endless Harmony* in 1998). As legendary rock journalist NICK KENT has so eloquently written, Wilson wrote "harmonies so complex, so graceful they seemed to have more in common with a Catholic Mass than any cocktail a capella doo-wop." Wilson called his work "rock church music", while every one of his classic songs contains a "money chord"; MARK ROTHKO, eat your heart out.

The remarkable thing that Wilson achieved was to create a world that wasn't there before, a world that not only celebrated a Californian dreamworld, but also invented an inner world where Wilson – and anyone who ever listened to a Wilson record – could go and be comforted. In this case his music acted as medication, therapy, or in Wilson's case, a piano standing in a box full of sand. The other remarkable thing is the way in which Wilson's world connected with so many millions of people. The awful irony of Wilson's fabulous invention was his complete inability to enjoy it, even though it gave so much enjoyment to so many others. In BARNEY HOSKYNS' gripping book *Waiting For The Sun: Strange Days, Weird Scenes And The Sound of Los Angeles,* the songwriter JIMMY WEBB says, "I don't think that the Californian myth, the dream that a few of us touched, would have happened without Brian, but I don't think Brian would have happened without the dream." Wilson fuelled a fantasy and surf pop was born.

When Wilson was at his very lowest ebb, in the late Sixties and early Seventies, having suffered more than one nervous breakdown, and having taken far too many illegal drugs, his behaviour was so strange it soon became legendary. In the grip of one of his many mental breakdowns he would regularly insist that business associates attend meetings in the deep end of his swimming pool, where, he believed, it would be impossible for anyone to bug them (a true paranoiac, he believed he was being listened to all the time). And because he wanted to recreate the feeling of being at the beach, and wanted to feel the sand beneath his feet when he was composing, Wilson had a huge sandbox built in his living room and a truckload of sand shovelled in to fill it up. This ruse worked – "Heroes and Villains", "Surf's Up", "Wonderful", and "Cabinessence", were all written in it – although Wilson's dogs started using it for their own purposes, and it soon began to stink of faeces. For a while though, "It created a mood that was magic," says Wilson. There was also an Arabian "inspiration" tent pitched in an adjacent room, where he went to smoke dope. Every day. And having achieved a temporal state of nirvana, he would then trundle off to record a backing track at the bottom of his pool.

For much of the Seventies, the bloated musical genius was "brain-fried", in a world of his own. So much so that he's spent a good portion of the last forty years being discussed in the past tense: "I was a useless little vegetable. I made everybody very angry at me because I wasn't able to work, to get off my butt. Coke every day. Goin' over to parties. Just having bags of snow around, snortin' it down like crazy."

Wilson was so strung-out on drugs that he basically went to bed for four years. And what did he do in bed for those four years? "Beat off. Watched TV. I didn't read. I couldn't see, my eyes [were] too bad. I could have gotten a pair of glasses. That would have helped me. I stayed in my room and wouldn't see anyone. I reclused, definitely. I don't know how, but I somehow got into weird stuff in my head. All mind and no activity."

And how did it feel to be a recluse?

"Pretty powerful. I felt power, but I didn't know what it was about. I couldn't relate it to anything. Maybe it wasn't my power. I could have been feeling somebody else's power."

When the near-legendary British publicist KEITH ALTHAM represented the BEACH BOYS as the Sixties turned into the Seventies, he was initially kept away from Wilson. On one visit to LA to see the band, he asked brother Dennis to take him to see Brian. The following day he was taken to a health food restaurant called The Radiant Radish that Brian had an interest in. As Dennis and Altham sat in their car in the car park, waiting for a visitation, eventually Brian shuffled into view, a huge, bloated figure dressed only in a bathrobe and a pair of dirty slippers.

"There," said Dennis, pointing excitedly. "There he is." Brian was now in the store, manically taking tins and bottles of honey from a shelf, and Altham wanted to pounce. "Great," he said. "Let's go and talk to him."

"Talk?" said Dennis. "You don't talk to Brian. No one 'talks' to Brian. I thought you just wanted to see him."

One day Wilson turned up at drummer HAL BLAINE's house – the same HAL BLAINE who had played on many PHIL SPECTOR and BEACH BOYS records – and forced him to take his gold discs. Wilson didn't want anything in return, just wanted rid of the memories. And if Blaine didn't take them, he figured they could easily just end up in a ditch.

The BEACH BOYS myth, however, is an enduring one, even though it has been disproved time and time again. And while any history of the group must now include sibling rivalry, domestic violence, appalling drug abuse, death, madness, and internecine lawsuits, the popular images of bronzed beach babes, hot-rods, and roller-skating carhops at the Wilshire Boulevard Dolores Drive-In have become as iconic as those grainy black and white photographs of the Cuban-heeled, black-clad BEATLES rushing through the streets of London pursued by hundreds of screaming schoolgirls; none of it was particularly true, though now it's almost too late to deny.

The songs, though, are as true as anything cast in vinyl: everything from "Surfin' USA", "California Girls", and "Spirit of America", to "Fun, Fun, Fun", "God Only Knows", and "I Get Around" epitomising all that was once white and willing about American youth – real sonic sunshine. The success of the BEACH BOYS' early records – all of which eulogised life on the California beaches – encouraged the rest of America to vicariously enjoy this new "layabout" lifestyle. "The records would have been effective advertising jingles for mail order catalogues, for surfboard hire companies, or for travel agencies looking to attract the nation's youth to Santa Monica," wrote CHARLIE GILLETT in his definitive history of the early days of rock'n'roll, *The Sound Of The City*. The West Coast idyll of "two girls for every boy" was apotheosised in a catalogue of extraordinary songs that celebrated happiness, and happiness only. Initially, at least. Wilson's reaction to living in a world without love was to write and inspire some of the loveliest songs ever recorded: "In My Room", "Don't Worry Baby", "Please Let Me Wonder", "And Your Dreams Come True", and dozens and dozens more, songs that managed to say so much with so little. (JOHN PEEL once wrote that a lot of groups write songs that have revolution in their lyrics but not in their music, although where the BEACH BOYS were concerned, the opposite was usually true.)

LEONARD BERNSTEIN once called Wilson one of the greatest composers of the 20th Century, while BOB DYLAN said Wilson's one good ear should be donated to the Smithsonian Institution. PAUL MCCARTNEY has famously acknowledged that it was *Pet Sounds* that "was probably the big influence that set me thinking when we recorded [*Sergeant*] *Pepper*." At the ceremony inducting Wilson into the Songwriters' Hall of Fame, McCartney called Wilson "one of the great American geniuses" and paid succinct tribute to his friend by saying, "Thank you, sir, for making me cry." He's been called rock and roll's gentlest revolutionary, a songwriter whose body of work contains real humanity – vulnerable and sincere, authentic and unmistakably American. "What Brian came to mean," said the VELVET UNDERGROUND'S JOHN CALE, "was an ideal of innocence and naivety that went beyond teenage life and sprang fully developed songs –adult and childlike at the same time. There was something genuine in every lyric. And it was difficult for me not to believe everything he said." He could write instant epiphanies (using a sound as big as Niagara Falls), sad songs about happiness, and most things in between. According to ART GARFUNKEL, his voice was "this unique, crazy creation, a mix of rock and roll and heartfelt prayer." He wasn't so much the nabob of sob, as the nabob of male neuroses.

Brian Wilson's more obvious influences have been well documented (the FOUR FRESHMAN, PHIL SPECTOR, mid-period BEATLES), though a lot of his orchestration and arrangements owe much to MARTIN DENNY and LES BAXTER (and in particular tracks such as "Misirlou" and "Voodoo Dreams/Voodoo")

W as well as other exponents of exotica, like YMA SUMAC (Amy Camus) and TAK SHINDO. Even Wilson's most innocent and naive melodies have a hint of pathos about them, and using exotica's bizarre array of references (eerie choral repetition, jungle noises – "Pet Sounds" – staccato keyboards), he found himself able to conjure up the most sublime parables of hope and desperation (*Pet Sounds*, in the words of *GQ* journalist PETER DOGGETT, "conjures up the volatile ecstasy and despair of teenage romance within the context of loss, love and self-awareness that can only come from the experience of adulthood"); music which seemed like it had spent a thousand years 20,000 leagues beneath the surf. The BEACH BOYS became teenagers when the teenager was suddenly something, when teenage emancipation was big news. They inspired generation envy: how colourless were their parents' times – born too early... too early to be a Beach Boy. If you believe that the adolescent environment as represented by the comfort of pop music is little more than the prolonging of childhood, then the world imagined by Brian Wilson was the epitome of that – a self-contained club that took care of its members. At their core the BEACH BOYS really represented Fifties' ideals, and although the imagery surrounding them was quintessentially Sixties, they were reassuringly old-fashioned; which made the lurch from their Beach Blanket Babylon early days to the drug-induced weirdness of their post-1965 period even more pronounced.

Wilson's CV has been truncated into legend: after a difficult childhood, the shy fat boy creates a hit factory, then produces the best record ever made (*Pet Sounds*), takes drugs and goes mad, living in a vegetative state for thirty years before an unlikely creative comeback. What this version of his life fails to acknowledge are all the little masterpieces he made during his hiatus, all the little anguished missives, the fragile sketches of a better life buried on mediocre BEACH BOYS albums and solo records. No rendering of Brian Wilson's life is complete without a soundtrack that includes the likes of "This Whole World", "Sail On Sailor", "Still I Dream Of It", "Love and Mercy", etc. The extraordinary thing about

Wilson's most successful work is the unnerving way he manages to evoke physical landscape while at the same time painstakingly exploring his interior world. How to describe Wilson's music to someone who's never heard it before? Well, how about you imagine you're dreaming about paragliding over Big Sur – and really, really worrying about it. Many have written songs about being mad, and some have written songs while actually being mad, but none have done either with as much finesse as Wilson.

Up until a few years ago, Wilson's official releases tended to sound unnervingly like nursery rhymes (particularly some of the more arcane material on *Orange Crate Art*, his 1995 VAN DYKE PARKS collaboration), and for a while his legacy was in the hands of people like the HIGH LLAMAS, who once had a remit to finish the album he found himself unable to complete until 2004, *Smile* (back in the Seventies Wilson said that attempting to finish *Smile* would have been like "raising the Titanic"). A decade ago Wilson was all washed up, an empty Coke bottle on Venice Beach, and there was little hope that the tortured genius would – with the help of some descending minor chords, some cascading strings, soaring horns, and the fat twang of a cheap guitar – ever finish *Smile* himself; but then with the help of SCOTT BENNETT and the WONDERMINTS, the LA-based BEACH BOYS' style band he accidentally hooked up with in the mid-Nineties, in 2004 he did just that. I have an ungovernable appetite for the BEACH BOYS, and like many, I had spent thirty years collecting the various bits and pieces required to build a decent version of *Smile* – an honourable task, I thought, and one that had occupied considerable amounts of my time; but having got there, having achieved my goal, when Wilson finally released his rerecorded interpretation, all I felt was a massive sense of deflation. It was all right, I thought to myself, but a) It's not quite as good as the original, b) Now everyone's got it, and c) What do I do now?

Brian Wilson's *Smile* is a remarkable achievement, but when I first heard it in 2004 I almost felt like a light had been turned on in a basement I had been very happy to wander around, in the dark, for over twenty years. But this wasn't about me, or any other BEACH BOYS obsessive, it was about Brian Wilson.

Like many BEACH BOYS obsessives, I've spent hundreds – maybe thousands - of hours immersed in their music, seeking out bootlegs and alternative versions, looking for those maudlin little songs that are the true reflection of Brian Wilson's psyche (even at the height of punk, when everyone else was searching out rare STOOGES releases). These days, unsurprisingly, the internet is where BEACH BOYS obsessives like to hang out (where did you think you'd find them, down at the beach?), and you can get lost in all the noise made by these cyber cicadas, noise made almost exclusively by men. On one site's message board I found the following tag: "Why don't women like the BEACH BOYS?" posted by "Jeff" on Saturday, September 25, 1999, at 11pm. Three hours later he got a carefully considered response, from one "MCP": "One possible reason is that the early BB stuff was male focused, surf, cars, etc. Then there is the *Pet Sounds* period... singing about what all young men go through. Thirdly, women are inferior to men."

Brian Douglas Wilson was born on June 20, 1942 in Hawthorne, California, a barren, treeless, and smog-filled sprawl, an hour from LA ("The City of Good Neighbors") and more than a world away from the Malibu surf, a suburban backlot that was also the home of MARILYN MONROE, singer CHRIS MONTEZ, and OLIVIA HARRISON, Beatle George's second wife. Hawthorne was not and never will be La Jolla. Sixty years ago the only thing to do here was go and watch the planes take off at LAX. Decades seldom start on schedule, yet Brian Wilson ushered in the American Sixties in 1961 by forming a garage band in Hawthorne with his two brothers Dennis and Carl, his cousin MIKE LOVE, and family friend DAVID MARKS (soon to be replaced by another friend, AL JARDINE). When the brothers were lying in bed at night, having been scolded again by their father for some minor misdemeanour, Brian would lead his brothers in three-part renditions of famous hymns. The songs were learnt at Sunday services where they were taken by their mother, and maybe the reason Wilson – who was at heart a suburban misfit – used to describe his BEACH BOYS songs as "modern hymns". Wilson was the songwriter, mixing the tried and tested rock and roll of CHUCK BERRY with the production style of PHIL SPECTOR and the harmonies of the popular vocal group, the FOUR FRESHMAN. They started singing about cars and girls, until DENNIS WILSON inadvertently stumbled across the focus of their sound, brought alive by his experiences surfing the waves down on the coast. (Brian would never surf, and when, years later, JOHN BELUSHI "arrested" Wilson for not even climbing on a board in the classic *Saturday Night Live* sketch, the sight of the whale-like Beach Boy being forced into the sea was more than a lot of fans could bear.)

The BEACH BOYS were the most important American band of the Sixties, reinventing the music industry in the way that the BEATLES would soon do in Britain. They wrote their own music, they produced their own music, and they had a keen idea of exactly what they wanted to be.

The biggest influence in Wilson's life was his overbearing father, Murry, a frustrated musician who would live vicariously through his sons' success. From a very young age, Murry insisted the boys follow his orders with rigid precision. Confronted by a child who had violated one of his orders, he would yell "I'm the boss", before whacking them with his belt. He had an artificial eye, and would regularly remove it, forcing his sons to stare into the jagged inside of the socket. He actually had two glass eyes – one for normal use and a special bloodshot model for when he was hungover. Dennis once stole the bloodshot model after Murry had spent the evening drinking, and took it to school the next day. Unsurprisingly he was soundly beaten on his return. Stories of the tensions between Brian and his father are legion, including one apocryphal tale of Wilson defecating on his father's dinner plate – at Murry's behest, to punish him for some small misdemeanour. "No, that's absolutely not true," Murry told *Rolling Stone* in 1971. However, it appears to have been Murry who was responsible for ruining his son's hearing: Murry once hit him so hard that he destroyed all the hearing in his

W

eldest son's right ear, and consequently Brian only ever heard his records in mono. One of his father's most brutal acts of cruelty was to "appropriate" the copyrights to Brian's songs, selling them in 1969 for $700,000, a pitiful sum. Twenty-one years later, the younger Wilson won millions of dollars in back royalties after arguing in court that he was a casualty of drug abuse at the time. When Wilson senior finally died of a heart attack aged only fifty-five in 1973, neither Brian nor Dennis attended his funeral. As dysfunctional families went, the Wilsons were in a league of their own. (A decade later, Dennis was also dead, drowned while diving off the side of his boat, his body ruined by alcohol. Carl followed him in 1998, stricken by lung cancer.)

Wilson suffered his first nervous breakdown in 1964, just a few years after his band's first success, so unable was he to cope with the pressure of recording and touring. And so the dense forest of Wilson's professional history began, the damaged genius using alcohol, food, and drugs to try and alleviate his emotional pain. He started taking acid in 1965 at the age of twenty-three, and it changed him forever. As NICK KENT wrote in his classic 1975 piece in the *NME*, "The Last Beach Movie", "His personality, always as fitful as it was fanatical in any given direction, was supposedly weighed down by brooding hermetic traits, and he was often erratic, paranoid, crazed – cursed by a weight problem that had ultimately got out of all proportion and which consequently seemed to be reinforcing his numerous complexes."

By 1966, Wilson had moved from surf, cars, and beauty queens to a less specific absorption in sensation, what the exotica specialist DAVID TOOP once called, "the magic of nonsense, the power of the elemental".

He was only twenty-four by the time he'd finished *Pet Sounds*, but when Wilson heard *Sgt Pepper* he abandoned *Smile* and went to bed for two years. He spent years laying inert in his bed, his weight ballooning up to twenty-four stone. He admits he was a child during these years, unable to cope with even the most ordinary, menial day-to-day things.

Shy and socially awkward as a boy, Brian's battle with his demons and insecurities grew more acute with age. *Smile* was meant to be a celebration of Americana, a panoramic commentary on America's tangled past: "I was there to support his 'dreamscape'," says Wilson's collaborator on the project, Van Dyke Parks. "He wanted to make the American saga a legitimate currency in this new global music market that had just defined itself since 1964."

But the making of the original *Smile* literally sent him mad: one night, while recording a section of his "Elements" suite about fire, called "Mrs O'Leary's Cow", Wilson distributed plastic fireman's helmets to the orchestra and lit a small fire in the studio to feel the heat and smell the smoke. When Wilson learned that later the same night a building near the studio had burned down and that there had been several other fires across Southern California, he abandoned the entire project. The music was just too powerful. Wilson was scared of his talent, scared of what he could produce, scared of the reaction his music caused in other people. To understand the tragedy of *Smile*, you could maybe try to imagine PAUL MCCARTNEY, say, having a nervous breakdown after recording "Yesterday", scared that having created something so perfect, he might never be able to match it, and then withering on the vine, unable to cope with the burden of topping it. "I'm getting there,"Wilson said, back in the mid-Nineties, from the one side of his mouth that still seemed to want to talk to the world. "I'm forcing my way out. It's almost as though I went into an egg and just had to poke my way out of it." *

---

*(The actual "sound" of *Smile* has become something you try to approximate when you run out of ideas in the studio – just listen to the hash of it that R.E.M. made on their *Up* album in 1998 – which made it even more strange when Wilson did the same thing when he eventually rerecorded it. Its influence

is all over the place – a glockenspiel here, an oboe there, a theremin thrown in for good measure over there in the corner, plus marimbas, wind chimes, and jewellery percussion. It's there in the intro – Wilson *is* the intro – to "This Life", track six on BRUCE SPRINGSTEEN's *Working On A Dream*; there's nothing wrong with it, but it's an unnecessary homage. The post-*Pet Sounds* "sound" has become a template, a trendy cliché: I was watching a TINA FEY film on a plane to Hong Kong a few months ago and one of the "sequence-blending" songs was little but a BEACH BOYS song full of glockenspiel and trippy organ, an atmospheric melange that sounded as though it had been made by a bunch of Japanese high school kids with access to little but BEACH BOYS records and their parents' collection of loungecore. It's difficult to imagine NICHOLAS STOLLER's film *Forgetting Sarah Marshall,* which is set in Hawaii, without some mention of the BEACH BOYS, and it doesn't take long – thirty minutes to be exact – for there to be one.)

Wilson's excessive drug taking often ended with him wandering semi-comatose down the highway dressed only in his bathrobe. "The big disappointment I feel about my life is that I didn't have more wisdom when it came to taking drugs," he said recently. "Drugs laid me out for years." Asked once if he'd prefer to come back free of his mental handicaps but also free of his talent, or spend his time again with the same mix of musical genius and mental anguish, Wilson said, "You know what? It would take me a year to answer that question..." When pushed he answered, "I would take being a songwriter with the handicap. I wouldn't be able to live without music."

By the early Eighties, Brian weighed over twenty stone and was consuming a dozen eggs and a whole loaf of bread for breakfast. He refused to wash or dress and rarely rose before six in the evening. With his children and first wife Marilyn gone (they were divorced in 1979), there was little to distract him from his demons.

In desperation, his family gave him over to a psychiatrist called EUGENE LANDY, a man who appointed himself as Brian's unofficial "creative" father. Like Murry before him, Landy had no intention of letting go once he had a hold of Brian. For eight years he milked his charge of millions of dollars, controlling his every move – even down to choosing which women he was allowed to date. It eventually took a judge to remove the psychiatrist's grip from his life. Life became more stable for Wilson when he met MELINDA LEDBETTER in a Cadillac dealership in the mid-Nineties (she was trying to sell him a car). They married in 1995.

The ORSON WELLES of rock still has anxiety attacks, but he has learned to walk between the raindrops. "I'll tell you something I've learned," he said not so long ago, "It's hard work to be happy."

The Wilson brothers' boyhood home in Hawthorne was demolished in the late Eighties during the construction of the Century Freeway, although it was eventually honoured by the dedication of the Beach Boys Historic Landmark (California Landmark 1041) in May 2005. The monument is somewhat underwhelming, being little more than a small wall of bricks with a rectangular white stone in its middle, featuring a carving of the boys carrying a surfboard (inspired by the cover of their *Surfer Girl* album). It sits exactly where the curb of their front lawn used to be, and looks as surreal as it looks drab.

It's somewhat ironic that the Wilson family home – a home where Brian first crafted those teenage hits about surfing and hot-rodding – should have made way for eight lanes of the I-105 freeway, where many of the cars will be tuned to oldies stations pumping out Wilson's songs... about surfing and hot-rodding. "If you tip the world on its side," said FRANK LLOYD WRIGHT, "everything loose will end up in California." This, everyone now seems to agree, is how the Golden State turned out the way it did, how it became North America's repository for the eccentric, the esoteric and the extravagant... the larger than life. To live in California means to live in italics. It's difficult to write about the state without compiling a list of the absurd and the fanciful: the pet cemeteries, gaudy museums, and beachfront fashion parades – the wicked kitsch of the West. Eventually, everything in America becomes entertainment, and often the celebration of hyper-consumerism seems the metier of the whole country. In his essay, "Travels in Hyperreality", UMBERTO ECO pinpointed the appeal of America's seemingly unquenchable thirst for the extravagant and the preposterous: "American imagination demands the real thing," he wrote, "and, to attain it, must fabricate the absolute fake." And in their own way the BEACH BOYS were as fake as anything else here, because not only were they the first American boy band, but underneath the classic karaoke pop hits was a world of heartache, a dark underbelly of disappointment, thwarted ambition, violence and madness. With the BEACH BOYS the revelry was always countered by a tragic back story, a duality highlighted by Brian Wilson's inability to surf. Ironic? At the time, at the birth of the Sixties, when Wilson was the man most able to articulate the teenage dream, this handicap was like discovering that MICK JAGGER was impotent.

But Wilson's music, like much of California itself, is breathtakingly beautiful. The Californian coast is a celebration of fantasy, a Pacific kingdom of sunshine, sand and surf, a reconstructed world of wonder where plastic palm trees sway beneath artificial moons, and where DAVID HOCKNEY paintings come to life. This post-industrial landscape aspires to being a terrestrial paradise, a near-tropical dreamland where vistas of magnificent natural beauty vie with car parks full of neo-Mexican shopping malls; where giant redwoods and valleys of golden poppies surround the state's popular cathedrals of kitsch. This is a life of abundance, where anything is possible, and little is real. A lot of California looks like a grandiose campsite, a frontier state, where much looks as though it was thrown up overnight. Here, little looks permanent, making the landscape look as untamed as it looks manicured. But there are few things more enjoyable than hurtling down the Pacific Coast Highway in a rented convertible, few things better than the California sun hitting your ERMANNO SCERVINO sunglasses, the spray from the surf hitting your windscreen, the wind rushing across your face, and the sound of the BEACH BOYS blasting through the in-car stereo. For California, Brian Wilson always had unlimited praise.

As it leaves Carmel, Route One climbs up through Big Sur. The highway soars high into the sky, and you're rewarded with eighty miles of stunningly beautiful coastline: sharp, sheer drops where mountains hit the water in dramatic fashion, where the rocks are so high you feel as though you're driving through cloud, as sea otters and grey whales thrash about in the Pacific below. The route is surprisingly tortuous, a narrow winding road that follows the wild and underdeveloped coast up and down the Santa Lucia mountains, in and out of canyons, like the oldest, slowest rollercoaster in the world. It's easy to see why the BEACH BOYS wrote a hymn to the Big Sur hills: "Cashmere hills filled with evergreens flowin' from the clouds down to meet the sea/ With the granite cliff as a referee..."

But then the BEACH BOYS wrote so much about California, a state that wouldn't have existed in its current form unless Brian Wilson had reinvented the American Dream, moving it from New York just a few years after the Brooklyn Dodgers uprooted their team and moved themselves to LA. Eventually everyone comes to California, in the short term looking for fun, perhaps in the long run for rebirth, to be creatively born again. Brian Wilson has certainly had a rebirth, and his God-like genius is not quite as diminished as you might think it is, as anyone who has seen him perform at London's Royal Festival Hall in the last few years will know. Having seen him perform *Pet Sounds* there in London in 2002 (it was like seeing J.D. SALINGER turn up for a recital, as though ROBERT JOHNSON had suddenly descended from the Gods in his button-down and braces, and yup, I blubbed like a baby), and *Smile* two years later (how did he do that?), two of the best concerts I've ever seen, two performances so heartbreakingly perfect, so moving, both left me sort of numb for days afterwards – when it was announced that he'd been specially commissioned to write a piece to be performed there, my heart sank. After all, it's all very well reproducing "Girl Don't Tell Me", "Lay Down Burden", "I'd Love Just Once To See You", and "She Knows Me So Well" live on stage – the extraordinary thing about "the Brian Wilson Construct" is the way in which the music is replicated with such precision without it sounding in the least bit hokey-karaoke – but could he write a modern-day song cycle that lived up to (or at least wasn't embarrassed by) the various high bars set by *Smile*, *Land Locked*, and all the rest? Was *That Lucky Old Sun* going to be any good?

Wilson's life has been so tragic, so fractured, that even the giddiest of Beach Boys' songs now seems to have a dark, maudlin underbelly, every silver lining we now know to have some sort of cloud. Wilson literally suffered for his art – suffered because of his art – which is obviously one of the reasons we revere him so much. And one of the reasons we expect everything he records these days to be tinged with the same sense of pathos, even though we almost always expect to be disappointed (his 2004 CD *Gettin' Over My Head* wasn't exactly his finest hour). The Festival Hall concerts underscored the great pathos in his work. There was something joyous about watching a man emerging from a long night of the lost soul. There was a sense that when he wrote and performed a lot of his songs the first time around, that he was anticipating loss, wallowing in heartache; now, as he approaches his dotage, that loss, that heartache, has become part of his legacy. The most pertinent quote I've ever read from Wilson is one he gave just before his first performance at the Royal Albert Hall in 2007. It says all you need to know about an introverted teenager who would rather commune with the elements than go surfing, a boy in love with sensation: "When I was sixteen, I had a Woolensack tape recorder and I taped the wind. I lost it and those tapes. I don't know where the hell they are."

Surprisingly, rather wonderfully, Wilson and his band of upward managers (last time, there seemed to be twenty of them on stage) somehow pulled it off, with at least half a dozen of the songs on *That Lucky Old Sun* (which was released last summer) being worthy of inclusion on your Big Sur iTunes playlist (mine is a hundred and forty-nine songs, just over seven hours, 471.2 MB). Written with his old sparring partner (when you say that these days people automatically assume you've been to a spa together) VAN DYKE PARKS and Wilson band member SCOTT BENNETT, *That Lucky Old Sun* evokes – once again – his deep love of Southern California, and at times you can almost feel the mid-afternoon sun bouncing off your forehead (and at Brian Wilson concerts, there is always a lot of forehead in the audience). And if you ask me "Midnight's Another Day" and "Southern California" are two of the best songs Wilson has written in the last twenty years. One critic suggested that the listener could have been forgiven for thinking Wilson had been meddling with a computer randomiser, because the album is essentially a "treasure trove of BEACH BOYS buzzwords and almost-familiar melodies rearranged into a meticulous suite about – what else? – California." It is always with trepidation that lifelong fans listen to another Brian comeback, because for so long his albums have been curate's eggs, only offering glimpses of his former genius. But these songs are life affirming. Nowhere can you hear the resigned indifference of old age, nowhere can you sense he's going through the motions. These songs are wistful reminders of what went before: there is so much pathos attached to almost every song written and performed by Wilson after *Pet Sounds*, and these new songs are no different; however because he has been through such a fundamental rite of passage – one that has taken up pretty much his entire adult life – these latest songs appear to suggest some sort of genuine redemption (just listen to his heartbreakingly cracked melancholy voice). If a Brian Wilson song has ever touched you, then you should go back and buy *That Lucky Old Sun*. If you're disappointed, then you probably never understood the BEACH BOYS in the first place. And should be banned from driving in California. For life.

Twenty years ago, the day I left California for the first time, I thought back to the afternoon I arrived. Climbing into my rented black convertible Mustang at San Francisco airport, groggy from twelve hours of travelling, I pushed a button to drag back the top, and turned on the radio. In a moment of unprecedented giddiness, I pushed myself deep into my seat, smiled at the sinking, squinting sun, and pondered the road ahead. As BILLY IDOL, then the prince of plastic pop, poured his tiny heart out of my dashboard speakers, I sat there, just wallowing in the moment, listening to song after song after song, until, inevitably, after about fifteen minutes, the DJ played the BEACH BOYS. "Well she got her daddy's car, And she cruised through the hamburger stand now, Seems she forgot all about the library, Like she told her old man now..." This, I thought to myself, is it. This is most probably it...

It still is for Wilson, too. He's working on ideas for yet another stage in his rehabilitation, this time a concept album called *Pleasure Island: A Rock Fantasy.* "It's about some guys who took a hike, and they found a place called Pleasure Island," says Wilson. "And they met all kind of chicks, and they went on rides and – it's just a concept. I haven't developed it yet. I think people are going to love it – it could be the best thing I've ever done."

AMY WINEHOUSE'S "ME & MR JONES"

Where sex is concerned, we all know that one person's meat is another's meat loaf. It's the same with music, especially with "sex" music. All of us, I'm sure, have a record that has the ability to make us go a little haywire downstairs, a song that makes us arch our back a little more as it sends expectant signals to the groin. Could be DUSTY SPRINGFIELD's "The Look Of Love", could be "Let's Spend The Night Together" by the ROLLING STONES, could be any number of dirty bump-and-grind records, records whose libidinous lyrics successfully coalesce with the sensual nature of the music.

Or it could be – if you've got the musical appreciation of a Flanimal – MOUSSE T's "Horny", or COLOR ME BADD's "I Wanna Sex You Up". Then there are those records that simply sound like sex – LED ZEPPELIN, JAMES BROWN, PRINCE, BILLIE HOLIDAY, PINK – the sort that make your mind wander (though hopefully not your hands) when you hear them on the radio.

For years I vacillated between MARVIN GAYE's "I Want You" and DAVID BOWIE's "Drive In Saturday", two songs that, while not exactly acting as seduction tools, are both possessed with an innate lasciviousness. But when Amy Winehouse released *Back To Black* in 2006, both were replaced in my affections by the most libidinous song I think I've ever heard. "Me & Mr Jones" is a song about revenge, and it oozes blood, sweat and tears, sounding like a collision between Forties jump blues, Fifties dirty doo-wop, and slick Sixties soul, all mixed together with predictably unselfconscious postmodern panache (this is the 21st Century, after all, and all records these days reference the past in some form or another). Winehouse's voice is a completely surprising appropriation of black torch singing, the sort of voice that JOSS STONE might have if she didn't try so much to be liked. And as the noise of it all begins to perk you up, the words fold in like a litany of complaints – funny, wanton lyrics that manage to acknowledge weakness while being sexually aggressive at the same time, words that could only have been written this decade, and only by a woman.

STEVE WINWOOD

It is often said that the 1958 Newport Jazz Festival in Rhode Island – as filmed by photographer BERT STERN for 1959's *Jazz On A Summer's Day* – was the greatest outdoor concert of them all, while jazz aficionados always cite it as the acme of cool, the perfect paradigm of music, fashion, attitude, and weather, an example – *the* example, perhaps – of post-war modernist chic. Steve Winwood would even name-check it in his 1982 hit, "Valerie".

But although Newport had THELONIOUS MONK, ANITA O'DAY, and GERRY MULLIGAN (when I first saw the film, when I was about twenty, I thought that ANITA O'DAY's performance was probably just about the coolest thing I had ever seen), many think the BLIND FAITH gig in Hyde Park in London in front of 100,000 people on June 7, 1969, was better. As the band tear through a selection of songs that immediately became classics – "The Presence of the Lord", "Can't Find My Way Home", and "Sea of Joy" – the crowd (including, on film, MICK JAGGER and his brother Chris, DONOVAN and FLEETWOOD MAC's PETER GREEN) sip wine, hold up buckets of homemade dry ice, and dance erratically as boats slowly glide on the Serpentine in the distance (like a lot of things in the Sixties, everything here seems to happen in slow motion). They took the stage at 5pm, careering into BUDDY HOLLY's 'Well All Right", as people clambered on car roofs and climbed up trees in order to get a better look at them. Another reason the Hyde Park film feels so much like the BERT STERN film is the "Do What You Like" jam, which has a time signature almost identical to DAVE BRUBECK's "Take Five", and gives the impression that the Newport and Hyde Park concerts had somehow been contracted into one. Winwood himself is obviously a fan of the Stern movie. "I was eleven when the film came out. It opened a whole Pandora's Box of music for me. I just liked the way the film brought together so many different elements, from blues to modern jazz."

Born out of the ashes of CREAM and the original incarnation of TRAFFIC, BLIND FAITH were heralded as the world's first supergroup, the Justice League of rock, a four-piece featuring ERIC CLAPTON, Steve Winwood, GINGER BAKER, and RICK GRECH (formerly of FAMILY). Because both Clapton and Winwood had felt compromised by their previous groups, they wanted

BLIND FAITH to be more adventurous, more like the BAND. They lasted barely seven months, fell apart after an extraordinary debut album of progressive blue-eyed soul (released later in 1969), and have been unfairly criticised for leaving a rather lacklustre legacy. But what a band their were, and what a gig this was.

Since watching the concert on Sky Arts in 2007 I've watched it dozens of times. I've watched it so many times I have a fairly comprehensive topographic memory of Hyde Park, and I know where every tree is positioned (and even what some of them are called). To read old reviews on the concert you'd think that it was little more than a soundcheck, and even Clapton has been disparaging about the event (claiming their PA wasn't big enough) – diehard fans of Clapton screamed "We want CREAM back!" as the bands left the stage – but watching the film now, the concert seems almost magical, and has a timeless quality, as though it happened in a vacuum, or some sort of parallel universe – which ironically is precisely why BERT STERN's film is held in such high regard.

Winwood is something of a revelation, too, and watching him sitting behind his electric piano in the mid-afternoon sun, in his Breton T-shirt, his purple linen ranch-style shirt, his red hipster trousers, and his Cuban heels – with his impossibly boyish face, oriental eyes, perfect teeth, and thin lips, his mouth wrapping itself around BLIND FAITH's expertly crafted blue-eyed soul, he looks like nothing but a genuine pop icon. Forget ELVIS, forget Hendrix, forget JIM MORRISON – for one day, forty years ago, in the summer of 1969, Steve Winwood was the coolest man on God's earth: a rock star mod with the voice of a black angel.

He is a joy to watch: as the band strive for unanimity around him, his fingers dart over the RMI electric piano and his huge industrial-strength organ, his head swaying in the Hyde Park haze, drawing attention to himself in that way piano players are forced to. It's all about the voice, all about the mouth – the shape his mouth makes when he sings makes him look a little like a fish just caught on a line, but even then he manages to look ineffably cool.

Who cared if he had a white man's overbite? Who wouldn't have wanted to look like Steve Winwood at the age of twenty-one? PAUL WELLER certainly did, and when the ex-JAM frontman was looking for a new direction after the STYLE COUNCIL fell apart at the end of the Eighties, found inspiration in both Winwood's sound and look. Indeed, you could say that the last twenty years of Weller's career owe more to Steve Winwood than is dignified (it's been said that Weller has based so much of his solo career on his hero, his album *Wild Wood* should have been called Winwood). Weller even asked Winwood to play on his watershed *Stanley Road* album: "Stevie played keyboards on 'Woodcutter's Son' and piano on 'Pink on White Walls'. We called his manager and asked if he'd like to do it. I had read somewhere that JIM CAPALDI [Winwood's partner in TRAFFIC] had liked *Wild Wood* and phoned Steve, telling him to check the album out because he'd like it. That gave us a way in. He was great; very humble, modest, quiet, and an immense talent. I was a real trainspotter, asking him about all his TRAFFIC recordings. I'd ask who played bass on this track and he was like, 'I did', so I'd say well who played lead guitar here, and it would be him again. He seemed to do most of it."

Steve Winwood is the man, who if ERIC CLAPTON had had his way, would have been the fourth and most prominent member of CREAM: "The band sounded a bit empty to me, as if we needed another player," wrote Clapton in his autobiography. "I had someone in mind from day one, Steve Winwood, who I had seen play at the Twisted Wheel and other clubs, and who had really impressed me with his singing and playing. Most of all, he seemed to know his way round the genre. I think he was only fifteen at the time, but when he sang 'Georgia', if you closed your eyes, you would swear it was RAY CHARLES. Musically, he was like an old man in a boy's skin." Clapton wanted Winwood to front the band, which, given Winwood's soaring choirboy voice, is hardly surprising. Chris Blackwell, who signed the Spencer Davis Group to Island Records, says Winwood "sang like Ray Charles on helium". According to Spencer Davis himself, "He was able to copy Jimmy Reed, and I thought, 'Where the hell is this voice coming from?' From a diminutive guy, at that age, how can he do it? But he did it."

Didn't he just.

By his own admission Steve Winwood has led something of a charmed life, but he carries his contentedness lightly. In the last thirty years I've interviewed hundreds of people who have good reason to feel blessed, but I don't think I've ever seen someone with so many laughter lines, or who smiles with such sincerity. Even the spectre of a rather delicate lawsuit involving Island Record's Chris Blackwell doesn't appear to have dented his optimism.

Winwood is the musician's musician. He is anything but the archetypal cult artist, not an avant garde performer at all. He has soul in his voice as well as his heart, and you can tell this every time he opens his mouth to sing. For the last forty-five years Winwood has sought to perfect his own very particular mix of rock, jack, folk and "world music" (a term he was using twenty-five years before it became fashionable), and while the different types of music he has created in that time might initially lead you to think he has swung back and forth like some sort of wayward metronome, his course has always been clear. Take the Spencer Davis Group: while he may have originated a very particular kind of driving Soho soul with the band – recording some of the most well-known R&B hits of the Sixties – his unmistakable voice and keyboard skills would stand him in good stead for the rest of his career. Then, with Traffic, he rebelled against their initial pop sensibilities – "Hole In My Shoe", etc – by fusing his rhythm and blues skills with the free-form experimentation that the period required. And having disbanded Traffic, his solo years display a similar catholic taste – from the blue-eyed soul of *Steve Winwood* and *Arc Of A Diver*, through to *Back In The High Life*.

All of it is Winwood and Winwood is all of it.

"I've never consciously tried to go in any one direction, never particularly thought about the commercial appeal of anything I've done," Winwood told me, sitting in one of the voluminous sofas that pepper his recording studio, which sits on a hill not more than a mile from his home, deep in the middle of the English countryside, in the Cotswolds. "My goal has always been to make classic records, classic albums. Sometimes the recording process and the era it was recorded in means the production leans in a particular way, but to me they are all part of the same process."

"In some respects I'm quite easily lead, so I have to make sure I've got my own space, and that I feel comfortable in my working environment. It's very important for me to work with the right collaborators, as I can easily get lead into a corner where I'm not comfortable. There have been periods in the past when certain record executives have felt that they wanted to point me in a certain direction, and I can be quite susceptible to that. Having said that, I'm quite good at getting out of the corners..."

"There are some basic principals that I've always tried to adhere to, ever since the end of the SPENCER DAVIS GROUP, my training ground, where I was learning the business, and where I learned playing skills, singing skills. We played songs we'd heard on the radio, songs we heard in clubs, songs we liked – blues, R&B, lots of black music from America. And we were desperate to play it. Because we enjoyed it so much we wanted other people to hear it as well. But when I left the group I made a definite decision to make music that was a hybrid of rock, jazz, folk, and ethnic music. This was the plan I made with JIM CAPALDI and CHRIS WOOD specifically in TRAFFIC. It was a pact. And that fusion, that mix has gone all the way through my career, even in the heady days of the Eighties, where perhaps it's easy to think I went down a more pop route. Pop was never meant to be part of my agenda at all, and you study the elements that were in the music, it was the same stuff I'd always done.

"Like I say, it's all part of the same story."

And what a story it is. He was born in Handsworth, Birmingham, in 1948, and grew up in a semi in the suburb of Kingstanding, "right where Birmingham ended. There were fields with duck ponds out the back," says Winwood. Steve and his older brother Muff were born into a family with parents who encouraged musical evenings at their home. He learned piano and guitar from an early age and could pick up anything by ear after hearing it played just once. And then, like many young boys of his generation, he picked up on nascent rock'n'roll by listening to Radio Luxembourg, obsessing about FATS DOMINO, BUDDY HOLLY, and LITTLE RICHARD. He now he was playing guitar with Muff and their multi-instrumentalist father in the RON ATKINSON BAND – playing big-band and Dixieland jazz – soon mastering both the piano and drums ("We played town halls, weddings, the lot," says Winwood). This led to THE MUFF WOODY JAZZ BAND, who gained a fanatical following in the Midlands after broadening their repertoire to include R&B covers. Winwood soon began playing in other bands, and by the age of twelve had written his first song, "It Hurts Me So", later recorded by the SPENCER DAVIS GROUP. Around this time he also encountered the voice that was to change his life and determine the way he would sing for the rest of his career – RAY CHARLES. "Steve's voice was breaking around the time he got into RAY CHARLES," said his record executive brother Muff, once, "so he was already singing in that style as his voice matured. He just naturally sang like a soul man." Like so many of his black soul heroes, some of Winwood's earliest singing experiences were on sanctified ground, at St Johns in Perry Bar in north Birmingham. After the church organist had left for the day, Winwood would climb into his seat and start playing the pump organ, his voice carrying the strains of "What I'd Say" way up to the rafters. "I thought he had the greatest voice," said BILLY JOEL, "this skinny little English kid singing like RAY CHARLES."

Having joined the SPENCER DAVIS GROUP when he was barely out of puberty, the band had huge success with "Keep On

Running", "Gimme Some Lovin", "Somebody Help Me", and "I'm A Man", before he formed Traffic with Chris Wood, Jim Capaldi, and Dave Mason (writing their debut hit "Paper Sun" among many others), and then Blind Faith, before embarking on a benchmark solo career, the sort of dignified solo career you don't see too often in the music industry.

"In a way my career has been a series of happy accidents, because as far as I'm concerned my goal has always been to try and use all the elements of rock and jazz and folk to try and make something unique, and that has often been through experimentation, jamming, and spending time in the studio. Everything is a consequence of that. Since I was nine years old I knew I wanted to be a musician, and so I used every opportunity to get up on stage, or in the corner of a room and play with other musicians. But the goal for me was not playing live – even though I probably play more now than I ever have done – the goal was making great records."

But how does the studio whiz-kid equate with the live performer. After all, are they not two completely different animals?

"I suppose I've always been a band leader, rather than a virtuoso, like Eric Clapton. Interestingly, since I've been working with Eric he's become a great band leader and a good accompanist, which he never was in the early days. But that was what I did, that's what I learnt from my family, playing swing and jazz and adapting myself to whatever was required. I've never been a particularly outgoing stage performer, I just love playing music.

"I've never wanted to force music on people, and have always been rather sensitive about being too aggressive, wanting to push music on people. Years ago we opened for Tom Petty, which was slightly odd because I thought his audience was a bit more middle America than mine. Once we started the tour it soon became apparent that it wasn't really working just announcing us and then going on stage, and so each night I got them to leave the house lights up and the house music on before we walked on stage and started fiddling around with the equipment. And of course the audience think we're the road crew, until the lights shut down and we launch into a song. People were looking for their seats with drinks and hot dogs in their hands and theatrically it worked perfectly. We'd open with 'I'm A Man', 'Different Light', 'Pearly Queen', anything we fancied. It's much better for me to go on and to try and draw them in, rather than try and be extrovert about it."

With TRAFFIC – who he would reform every now and again throughout his career – Winwood would go on to explore folk, Latin, jazz, and R&B, as well as the more traditional forms of late Sixties longhair music. He could take the music of the tenderloin and give it airs and graces without emasculating it. He could give it an air of sophistication without castrating it. Though he would hate the very idea of it, he gave his R&B class. Winwood called his own blend of rock and jazz "headless horsemen" music – you couldn't identify it. TRAFFIC were the first band to "get it together in the country", to just disappear into the countryside to write and play music... fuelled, obviously, by the traditional late Sixties longhair substances. They were the British version of the BAND, and instead of BOB DYLAN, they had Winwood. His love affair with the countryside would soon manifest itself in other ways, because in 1970 he was one of the first rock stars to properly decamp, buying a 50-acre 17th Century manor house in the wilds of Gloucestershire. He quickly embraced the huntin', shootin' and fishin' country lifestyle, a green-wellies-and-beagle-puppies-and-clay-pigeons world that would soon be embraced by the likes of his friend ERIC CLAPTON, PINK FLOYD, and other copper-bottomed Seventies rock stars. These days he is also a keen supporter, along with BRYAN FERRY, Clapton, and COCKNEY REBEL'S STEVE HARLEY, of the Countryside Alliance.

One of Winwood's career highs remains his eponymous first solo album, which was largely ignored when it was released in 1977, arriving in an era of three minute insurrection and glottal stops ("Punk frightened me because although I didn't really get it, I thought I might never work again"). Even those critics who applauded it were still fairly circumspect, misunderstanding Winwood's attempts to mix experimental rock with blue-eyed soul (when you read a critic saying that there was an "unfortunate tendency for songs to run beyond their most effective length", it's easy to interpret this as a singular misunderstanding of soul music). *Steve Winwood* mined the sort of material that TRAFFIC had perfected on their 1971 album *Low Spark Of High Heeled Boys*, but was fused with deceptively sophisticated R&B – Winwood's wailing, fragile voice becoming even more distinctive as the instrumentation became less strident. One critic said his voice had "maintained the innocent and inquisitive tremor of a romantic while developing an edge of experience," and it is the singer's natural instrument that has obsessed journalists for his entire career. Recently one said it was "like glue. It can hold a song together where other less talented, less gifted voices would merely sound like cats crying outside your bedroom window at three in the morning." Reviewing his recent *Nine Lives* CD the critic said, "[His] voice is his primary instrument and its saving grace."

The best song on the album, "Vacant Chair" (about death), was co-written by VIV STANSHALL, of BONZO DOG DOO-DAH BAND fame, and the maverick genius responsible for *Sir Henry At Rawlinson End*. Stanshall also wrote the lyrics to two of the songs on the follow-up, *Arc Of A Diver*, including the title track (a song about perfection). Interviewed eight years before his untimely death in 1995, on a rainy September evening in 1987 in his Muswell Hill flat, Stanshall explained his unlikely relationship with Winwood. At the time he had been pursuing his portfolio career with the usual randomness, extolling the virtues of Cadbury's Creme Eggs on television, and writing a libretto to a collage of animal sounds which, according to the *Record Collector* journalist who interviewed him, "hinted at an aesthetic, if uncommercial, brilliance". Stanshall and Winwood struck up a relationship while the singer was still in TRAFFIC, and Winwood was one of the few people Stanshall could write straight (i.e. not comic) songs for. "I can sing in tune and I've got quite a big range, but there are not many people that I've ever wanted to put my words in their mouths," said Stanshall. "Steve Winwood and JOE COCKER are two. I admired CHRIS FARLOWE, and DICKIE PRIDE, and DAVE BERRY, but I'm not sure how much that had to do with their voices. I wrote MATT MONRO a song called 'Blind Date'. I sang it to his manager, who collapsed under the desk. I just couldn't write a straight song." But he did with Winwood, writing over a hundred altogether, almost all of which remain unreleased.

In the Eighties Winwood had something of a comeback, some would say a creative rebirth, having huge hits with *Talking Back To The Night, Back In The High Life*, and *Roll With It* – almost single-handedly creating adult contemporary rock programming in the process – and massive chart singles like "While You See A Chance", "Valerie", "Higher Love", and "Back in the High Life Again".

"In the forty-five years I've been in the music business, my popularity has gone in and out like waves, and it's never been my own doing. I just do what I do and hope people like it. People catch up with me like a spring tide. It first happened in the mid-Sixties with the SPENCER DAVIS GROUP, and then in the early Seventies with TRAFFIC. At that point we'd gone off to the country to make music that basically pleased ourselves. We weren't accountable to anybody. We were making these long jams based in rock and jazz with African percussion that didn't sound like anything else around. We were content to do this for our own enjoyment, I suppose because we were more idealistic and couldn't really care what anyone thought of us. And this was just at the time that in America FM radio was starting to replace AM, and they wanted long, high-quality pieces of music for the new underground stations. And so we had a readymade audience without knowing anything about it.

"By the Eighties the production process of making records had changed so much that they started to sound very different, but the principles were basically the same. The music hadn't changed much at all. It was the technology that had changed."

And what about the marketing, the videos, the whole MTV culture?

"To tell you the truth I left that to other people."

Winwood's music has become part of our subconscious in a way that a lot of popular music has – on some radio stations you hear his songs as often as you hear the weather forecast. In fact, you even find his music in the homes of people who usually have no truck with pop at all, and would rather curl up with a sonata or a symphony than anything as vulgar as electrified music. His career ever since has been blue chip all the way. Just two years ago he released the magnificent *Nine Lives*, which included one of his finest songs in years, the focus track "Dirty City". Having built his second career on radio-friendly production-heavy adult-soul, it is extraordinary that, on "Dirty City" (an ERIC CLAPTON collaboration), he can still conjure up the harder, almost swampy sound of BLIND FAITH. In fact, if you close your eyes and open the window, you can imagine them playing the song in Hyde Park in 1969.

Winwood today is the quintessential country gent, and tends to wear Barbours, woollen shirts, v-neck sweaters, and gentleman jeans. However, while he may look like an off-duty landowner, and while be may *be* an off-duty landowner, like many of his generation he is living testament to the maxim that if you can remember the Sixties then you weren't really there.

"It's all a big blur," said Winwood, with his customary smile, "and if I'm honest I can't remember much. For me it was just about the music. What people forget about the Sixties is that as well as enjoying all the things we'd been promised since the war – the freedom, the breakdown of class, the excitement of being young – for lots of us musicians it was all about playing, about pushing the boundaries. Eric and I didn't think that BLIND FAITH would be this big, momentous thing, it wasn't cynical in that way at all. We just wanted to play together and see what happened."

And it just so happened that a lot of other people were interested to see what happened too.

"Our music was the soundtrack of the decade, and that applies to anyone who was in a band at the time. We were just genuinely obsessed with making music, which hadn't happened before in this way. A lot of people think that the music was responsible for a lot of changes in the Sixties, but I think the music came out of it. The music wouldn't have happened without the social changes. It happened in America first – before the Fifties every son wanted to be like his father and every daughter wanted to be like her mother... but the Sixties changed all that. In the Sixties you didn't want to be like your parents at all."

Unlike many of his generation, Winwood doesn't appear to have much of a demonstrative ego, and doesn't seem overburdened by a sense of his own importance; he is the quintessential quiet man of rock. Since his commercial heyday in the Eighties, Winwood has had rather a steady, low profile, but this again is one of the reasons why Winwood is considered to be so cool, because his talent was never forsaken or overrun by ambition. The fact that he has been a journeyman for much of his life is testament to that. He just sort of gets on with it. When he is interviewed, journalists like to point out that he always appears to be looking over their shoulder, towards the direction of Gloucestershire, where he's got his farm, his wife, his family, and his recording studio. He always seems to be a rather reluctant interviewee, and if he could give away even less about himself, then he probably would (direct answers tend to collapse with exhaustion before they're finished). "Steve Winwood would rather be ritualistically disembowelled than give a quote," wrote one. "Like a native who won't have his picture taken for fear of fading his soul, he sits there, already too pale, muttering monosyllables in monotones."

However, prick his interest and get him on music and he won't stop talking. He is also one of those rare musicians who genuinely believe that they are a musician rather than an entertainer, and listening to him discuss his passion is enthralling. "Musicians and music lovers are completely different," he says, sitting upright in his seat. "I mean I don't really listen to music all the time, whereas my wife is a music lover, and has music on whilst she's cooking in the kitchen. I can't possibly do that – I even have trouble listening to music when I'm driving because I tend to make wrong turns when I'm not concentrating. Like a lot of musicians I'm not really a music lover, and I don't listen to music for fun. Consequently it's very difficult for me to be objective, and to see how I fit in with anyone else – with a U2 or a BOB DYLAN. I suppose I've always been niche, unusual, out of the ordinary.

"Listening to music for me is like homework. Music will give me enjoyment, but as soon as it's giving me that enjoyment I want to analyse it, and then it becomes work. Why does it sound like that? How? Then I dissect it... but then I think most musicians are like that."

He says his career has been based more on what he wants to play rather than what his audience might want to listen to. When most musicians say this they can appear disingenuous, but with Winwood you believe him. Our relationship with music is often more personal than we might think, as are our motivations for listening to it. "Music was my accomplice," said MICHAEL PHELPS, after winning eight gold medals at the Beijing Olympics (listening TO LIL "WEEZY" WAYNE, YOUNG JEEZY, EMINEM, OUTKAST, and USHER), a word that infers collusion as well as emotional support. With Winwood you get the sense that music might determine nearly everything he does, while his relationship with it seems strangely co-dependent. You have to remember that this is a man who enjoys session work like no other, and who over the years has recorded with MARIANNE FAITHFULL, STOMU YAMASHTA, DAVID GILMOUR, GEORGE HARRISON, BILLY JOEL, LOU REED, TALK TALK, TOOTS & THE MAYTALS, JIMI HENDRIX, JOHN MARTYN, and the WHO.

These days the founder member of the rocktocracy regularly tours the world in style. His voice hasn't changed in forty years, and neither have his aspirations, or his partners in crime. He stills plays gigs with ERIC CLAPTON, and regularly plays double-headers where they effortlessly breeze through "Presence of the Lord" and "Can't Find My Way Home", as well as a few other BLIND FAITH classics.

As for his 2010 boxed set, *Revolutions*, he was tinkering with the track listing for months, and remastered, remixed, and tweaked a few things here and there. Because much of his music was recorded for vinyl, a lot of the sound was originally modified and compressed in order to fit, and because of the limited bandwidth the music had less body. This has obviously now been altered. "I went to see my sixteen-year-old son play in the school orchestra recently, and they were playing VAUGHAN WILLIAMS' *London Symphony*, and in the programme it said that although he wrote it in 1914, in 1933 he was still tinkering with it. I thought to myself, if it's good enough for VAUGHAN WILLIAMS, then, who's to say it's not good enough for me."

Steve Winwood is not the sort of man who harbours regrets. The have been a few contractual issues along the way, but contractual issues and the music industry go hand in hand, like sex and drugs. Does he regret anything?

"Not really. I possibly smoked a bit too much weed in the early days, but then that did lead to some interesting records, so I can't even regret that. However, I was in a situation once where we had just spent a day recording, and then sat around with the band afterwards talking about the session. We ended up having an argument because they all thought the drums were too loud, and I didn't. Everyone had gone home apart from me when the cleaning lady came in. I was still listening to the song, and she said, 'That's sounds good but the drums are too loud.' That remark kept me up all night."

You see, with Steve Winwood, it's all about the music. Always was, always will be.

STEVIE WONDER

BARACK OBAMA is the first truly funky President, the first President not to get an aide to compile a list of his favourite records for him, or to load their "personalised" iPod. BILL CLINTON may have played the saxophone, but he was hip in a slightly apologetic way (and how can you blow if you don't inhale?). No, the Big O is down with his tunes, and hip to that kind of trip.

And in case you hadn't noticed, he is also Stevie Wonder's biggest fan. And we're talking Big. "When I was at that point where you start getting involved in music," Obama said just before winning the election last year, "Stevie had that run with *Music Of My Mind*, *Talking Book*, *Fulfillingness' First Finale* and *Innervisions*, then *Songs In The Key Of Life*. Those are as brilliant a set of five albums as we've ever seen." The feeling is mutual: taking hyperbole to new heights, Wonder has described Obama as a cross between JOHN F. KENNEDY and MARTIN LUTHER KING JR., and played at various Obama rallies, as well as the Democratic convention, and eventually the Presidential Inauguration. Perennially sought-after, Wonder also played before GEORGE BUSH at a presidential gala in 2002, an event that saw Dubya, who was sitting in the front row, wave at Wonder as he took the stage. The story of the President waving at a blind man obviously delighted the nation. But then everyone loves Stevie, and he is, by some distance, the elder statesman – he's in his sixties – of American black music, a genuine national treasure. However, he is now officially the court musician to the Sun King, and not only is he Obama's favourite musician, Michelle loves him, too.

Wonder is the go-to guy when you need a heavyweight, a living legend with global reach, limitless scale. When he sang "I Never Dreamed You'd Leave Me In Summer" at MICHAEL JACKSON's memorial service at the Staples Center, it was a genuinely – if predictably – moving moment. It might not have been his finest performance, but it was the only reasonable dénouement. Seriously, when you book Stevie Wonder, you book dignity. Serious dignity.

You can tell a lot about someone from their cuts. You can tell a lot about the journalists who interviewed them, too. Look at most interviews with Stevie Wonder and they rarely mention his blindness. Perhaps they think it causes too much embarrassment, might think it is a bit like asking PAUL MCCARTNEY whether he'll ever re-form the BEATLES, or like asking GEORGE OSBORNE about the economy or NICK CLEGG about his sexual conquests. Anyway, it is a strange thing, like meeting an alien and not asking where they come from.

Having been blind almost since birth – he was premature and lost his sight after receiving too much oxygen in the incubator as hospital staff fought to save his life – darkness has always been Stevie Wonder's world. He says he is resigned to his condition (a condition which has informed all his work), yet for years rumours persisted about the amount of money he spent trying to regain his sight. Twenty years ago he even volunteered to be a guinea pig in a series of eye transplant experiments which had only previously been performed on animals. When I last saw him, fifteen years ago, he said that other things were occupying his mind, and his response to questions about his sight echoed this: "I don't care about it. I'm alive and I'm doing the best that I can in life, given what I have to work with. I'm not going to tell you that I wouldn't care if I was able to see, but I'm not going to spend my life saying how good it would be if I could. I've learned to cope."

In late December 1994, Wonder arrived at London's Lanesborough hotel, en route from Ghana, where he was looking for a house, for a short promotional bout publicising *Conversation Peace*, his first bona fide album in eight years.

You wait three hours to talk to Stevie; his concept of time is different from other people's, making no particular distinction between night and day, and he will sometimes sleep for three days solid. He can stay awake in the studio for even longer, doodling on his custom-made computers and banks of high-tech keyboards. When he was recording his breakthrough album, *Talking Book*, in 1972, in Greenwich Village's legendary Electric Lady Studios, surrounded by his ARP and Moog synthesisers, he often became so immersed in his new-found creativity that he would forget to eat or sleep. So fertile was his imagination, and so eager was he to master this new technology that he would work for days at a stretch. As one writer put it, "In the face of boring, day-to-day stuff like time and place, Wonder has repeatedly shown himself capable of an indifference bordering on the heroic." Wonder is obviously forced by his condition to live a fairly sedentary life, though it is difficult to imagine him any other way than pottering about his various recording studios like some madcap inventor. He always has a keyboard of some description to hand, and has an extravagant ritual involving his various synthesisers, wherever he goes; his assistants have to be sure that he can touch one whenever he feels like it, doodling on the keyboard absent-mindedly as others might scribble on a notebook. The singer SYREETA WRIGHT, whom he married in 1971, divorced him eighteen months later, because "He would wake up and go straight to the keyboard. I knew and understood that his passion was music. That was really his No.1 wife." She died in 2004, around the same time as Wonder's brother, Larry.

Wonder was led into his suite at the Lanesborough by two large aides who hung around for a while after seating him to make sure their boss was happy. Wherever the star goes he is followed by a cavalcade of minders, assistants, press officers, fixers, friends, and helpers. So protective are these people that you imagine this to be the kind of entourage that ELVIS surrounded himself with in the Seventies. He treats his gofers with care, and they seem to reciprocate. When we met there were plenty of pleases-and-thank-yous, and when Wonder asked for some peppermint tea and some "biskits" in his faux cockney, the assistants laughed benignly.

He said hello politely and extended his hand, asking me various questions without seeming particularly interested in the replies, and then spent some time messing about with one of his aides, guessing coins by the way they fell on the floor ("That's an American coin... that's an English coin..."). When he was much younger, Wonder used to feel people's faces when he met them, and Motown boss BERRY GORDY claims that when he met young women he would "let his hands walk". Wonder would always say this was purely accidental. (In the Eighties the author and comedian LOUISE RENNISON had some success with her stand-up show, *Stevie Wonder Felt My Face*.)

The image you expect is of a large, egg-shaped black man dressed in loose-fitting, oddly-coloured leisure clothing, a man with space age dark glasses weaving his head from side to side in time to some faraway metronome. His weight has fluctuated over the years, and during the Eighties he became so ample that it was necessary to dress him in a variety of ambulatory tents. At the Lanesborough, though, he looked if not svelte, then certainly fairly trim. He was wearing a purple Nehru suit and a pair of sci-fi glasses that certainly lived up to expectations (the only black celebrity to ever wear more extravagant eyewear was GEORGE CLINTON). His braids were pulled back to reveal a mass of scar tissue above his right temple – the result of a near-fatal car crash in 1973. Sitting bolt upright in the dining room in his suite he looked like nothing less than a Buddha, impervious to criticism, weather, or, come to that, time. He seemed regal – exacerbated by the fact that when you meet him you have to do all the running. I had to speak – filling those empty spaces usually taken up with gesture – or else nothing happened. Because of this my words hung heavy in the air: did I say the right thing? Did I mumble?

It is surprising just how much his blindness affects you, surprising how difficult it makes any kind of conversation. The only way you can force the pace or change the topic is by interrupting him, which, you begin to think, is a terribly rude thing to do to a blind person. To one of his replies I nodded furiously, then realised what a stupendously stupid thing this was to do.

One wonders what he sees, so to speak. I wondered, perhaps presumptuously, what he imagined I looked like. White, British, skinny hands. Could he tell that I'm tall even though I was sitting down? And quite awed by his presence? His demeanour suggested that he could see as much as he wanted to, and one got the impression that he didn't want to know any more about me than he could sense already. Having no doubt been interviewed by thousands of hapless hacks, he was probably accustomed to using his blindness not only as a shield but also as a weapon, a particularly intimidating one at that. He has fun with it, too: he habitually talks about "seeing", and often catches people out by walking into unfamiliar rooms and saying, "Hey, nice place you have here."

But oh, how he has suffered. The Stevie Wonder interview has unnerved many a seasoned journalist, and the faux pas are legion. One writer went to interview the star in a hotel in downtown Los Angeles. Walking into the penthouse suite, said writer looked out across the Hollywood Hills and forgoing all formalities, immediately said, "What a fantastic view!"

"So they tell me," said Wonder, wistfully.

Once, at a Wembley Arena gig, he asked for the house lights to be turned off, all of them, bringing blindness to everyone in the room. Those who were there say it was an extraordinary, if somewhat unnerving moment.

He can be stubborn, stern, and occasionally pompous. He says what he means, and makes no bones about it. When I asked him why *Conversation Peace* had taken nearly eight years to finish, he cut me up short. "The record is coming out now because I feel comfortable with it. I think it's complete, and before it wasn't. Simple as that." When he smiled, though, he beamed, and lit up the room.

From Motown marionette to soul pioneer, Stevie Wonder has – time and time again over the past forty-five years – helped reshape the face of pop music. Before PRINCE was PRINCE and MICHAEL JACKSON was MICHAEL JACKSON, there was Stevie Wonder, the original black wunderkind. He was born Stevland Morris in Saginaw, Michigan, in 1950, and grew up poor on the east side of Detroit during the infancy of Tamla Motown, the Motor Town record label that was to launch a string of successful black artists including DIANA ROSS, MARVIN GAYE, the FOUR TOPS, and the TEMPTATIONS. By the age of eight it was clear he was a genuine musical prodigy, a singer, and a natural performer already mastering drums, bongos, harmonica, and piano. Brought to the attention of Motown boss BERRY GORDY, Wonder had his first hit song, "Fingertips (Part 2)", at the age of thirteen, and his debut LP, *The 12 Year Old Genius*, made number one. Every day after school he would go to the Motown offices, hanging out with the stars and making his own recordings. He was a natural mimic, able to imitate most of the artists he worked with, and his BERRY GORDY impression was so good that he managed to fool Motown personnel with bogus phone calls offering them huge pay rises or cancelling their contracts.

But Wonder was cherished by Gordy, who made sure the Motown team of writers, producers and engineers gave him as much encouragement as possible. It worked: during the Sixties he had over twenty hits, including "Uptight", "A Place In The Sun", "I Was Made To Love Her", "For Once In My Life", "My Cherie Amour", and "Yester-me, Yester-you, Yesterday". He also wrote and produced many songs for other Motown artists, including "Tears of a Clown" for SMOKEY ROBINSON, and "Loving You Is Sweeter Than Ever" for the FOUR TOPS. By the time he was twenty-one, Wonder had sold more than 30m records.

For a former child star, Wonder is practically unique in that he has not disgraced himself, fallen foul of drugs or the law, or been embroiled in any kind of sexual deviancy. The only thing he has been guilty of is making a series of increasingly bland records. "This is Stevie Wonder," wrote the American music critic, ROBERT CHRISTGAU. "He is black and considers that an advantage; he is blind and given to mystic visions. His music is both meticulous and wildly expressionistic; his words combine a preacher's eloquence with an autodidact's clumsiness."

"I was blessed," Wonder said to me rather predictably, swinging his head from side to side, "that's why I haven't fallen by the wayside. When I was young, anyone who was older than me was my parent in my eyes, and they basically helped to discipline me. Not eating too much candy, getting some rest, keeping out of fights. My life hasn't been normal, and I've needed help. I've always been protected, I've needed to be protected."

At the beginning of the Seventies Wonder renegotiated his contract with Motown. He was in such a strong position due to his almost unprecedented success that this new contract gave him carte blanche to do whatever he liked. No black American musician had ever been afforded such freedom, and Wonder did not abuse it. Over the next few years he recorded some of the most remarkable, as well as some of the most successful, records of the decade. Inspired by the likes of MARVIN GAYE and SLY STONE, Wonder began mixing melodically sweet tunes with politically hard-hitting lyrics, exploiting the two predominant themes of black American music: the confrontational and the soulful. His socio-political lyrics were always accompanied by a sweet refrain ("You'll excuse me," he once said, "I don't consider myself to be a black performer. I consider myself to be a performer who is black"). Making full use of electronic wizardry (clavinets, synthesisers, etc) he created his own version of progressive rock, toured with the ROLLING STONES and soon became the pre-eminent black entertainer of the day. Motown even came up with a slogan for this reinvention: "If you liked the boy," they declared rather clumsily, "you'll love the man." His appeal was universal, being favoured by the mass middle-of-the-road audience as well as the white critical establishment who acclaimed him as an innovator and social commentator. Wonder has always been more pragmatic than people give him credit for, and it is a sign of his diplomacy and cunning that he could be on good terms with both LOUIS FARRAKHAN and JULIO IGLESIAS.

In this time he has preached insurrection, but never violence. "I'm not militant, and I've never believed in violence," he told me when I broached the subject. "That's not the key. But then oppression is not the key either. The reason there is so much violence in America right now is because people have been hurt and they're disillusioned. People have idle time because they don't have anything better to do, because people have made promises to them and not fulfilled those promises. Since that time [the early Seventies] my music has been devoted to changing the way people think, how they act."

Back then the albums came fast and furious. First there was *Music Of My Mind* (1972), then *Talking Book* (1972), *Innervisions* (1973), *Fulfillingness' First Finale* (1974), and then – after renegotiating his Motown contract again (it reputedly ran to a hundred and twenty pages), with a twenty percent royalty rate and a thirteen million dollar advance – his masterpiece, 1976's *Songs In The Key Of Life*. These groundbreaking LPs gave birth to such hits as "Superstition" (the opening bars of which are often cited as the perfect encapsulation of the term "funky"), "You Are The Sunshine Of My Life", "Higher Ground", "Living For The City" (a 7" Mean Streets), "You Haven't Done Nothin'" (written about RICHARD NIXON), "Boogie On Reggae Woman", "I Wish", "Sir Duke", and "Another Star" – all of them written, arranged, produced, sung and largely played by Wonder himself. For Wonder, making *Songs In The Key Of Life* was as happy an experience as a return to childhood. He immersed himself in the project for more than two years (employees at Motown took to wearing T-shirts with the logo "Stevie's Nearly Ready"), finally surfacing with a collection of twenty-two songs; too many tunes even for a double album, so four of them were included on a special EP that was given away with the record. Not only was *Songs...* thought to be Wonder's greatest achievement yet, it was widely considered to be one of the finest pop records ever made. It still is.

With these albums, he gave a public face to the ghetto-fabulous blaxploitation culture of the early Seventies, dusting the urban experience with Wonder's own sweet sweet sugar. He was bigger than Isaac Hayes, bigger than Sly Stone, bigger than George Clinton, bigger even than James Brown. Bigger than all of them. And oh, was he adored. Amongst black American role models he was unique.

Barack Obama has been careful not to alienate the hip-hop community (producers and consumers alike) but has been outspoken about the way in which rap culture feeds into a cycle of low self-esteem. And while it might be rather hard to believe that when Obama attended the stag party of his half-sister's fiancé he left as soon as the "entertainment" arrived, it's easy to see why he has railed against the reductive nature of rap culture, and specifically the way in which a lot of young black men dress. He especially dislikes the trend amongst black youths of wearing baggy trousers that sag way beneath the backside, a fashion that when taken to extremes makes the model look as though their waist has suddenly contracted by at least six inches, or that they have almost been injected with anorexia. "Brothers should pull up their pants," Obama famously told a reporter from MTV. "You are walking by your mother, your grandmother, your underwear is showing. What's wrong with that? Come on."

Seeing that Obama is such a bastion of *Mad Men* proto-yuppieness (the "dual heritage" black man in a grey flannel suit), the White House was never going to be turned into a P. Diddy-style crib, but his criticism of the homies was targeted at the homies themselves, rather than being solely for the benefit of the media. But he loves Stevie, because Stevie has dignity. He might deign to record with current hip-hop stars in the hope of getting a hit, but he's not going to start swearing or adopting sexist iconography. He is an old-fashioned Motown man through and through, and his upwardly mobile demeanour appeals to Obama in so many ways.

After *Songs In The Key Of Life*, Wonder was so hot that Motown would have released anything that he delivered.

They would have released a narrated shopping list, an album of baseball chants, or a largely instrumental concept LP about the secret life of plants. Which is just as well because that's exactly what he gave them. *Journey Through The Secret Life Of Plants*, released in 1979, was condemned by critics as being far too esoteric – "One of them even called it shrubbish," said Wonder – and was a lot, lot less successful than his previous albums. At a low point in his career, Wonder was intransigent. His critics were wrong, he said.

"Failure? I know it well enough to understand what it is," he said, "but I don't give up every time I see it coming. Failure is always relative, and like a lot of people when I look back at my life and work I judge things by how I was feeling at the time, how happy I was. And there are lots of records which you might think are great but were possibly made when I was bummed out. It's a state of mind kind of thing. Who can say that the BEATLES are better than MICHAEL JACKSON?"

During the Eighties, as his records became more innocent and bloodless, so his political activities became more strident, and increasingly he came out against racial injustice. He has campaigned against everything from the arms race and apartheid to drunk drivers, though of his various projects and pet causes he is most proud of the ratification of MARTIN LUTHER KING's birthday, January 15, as a national holiday. He lobbied the American government for years until he realised his ambition in 1986. In 1988 he was honoured by the United Nations Special Committee Against Apartheid for his commitment to "the uplifting of the oppressed and downtrodden of the world".

"I'm not satisfied yet with what the world is, as I'm sure none of us can be," Wonder said to me, "and that alone is what pushes me to create music which can hopefully add something to people's lives, that can bring on another train of thought. Many things make me want to make music. Since my last record [discounting the 1991 soundtrack of SPIKE LEE's *Jungle Fever*, this was 1987's *Characters*] there has been the fall of the Berlin Wall, the fall of communism... the whole situation with MIKE TYSON, MICHAEL JACKSON, RODNEY KING, O.J. SIMPSON... famous blacks, all in trouble. In the case of these people, and in particular MICHAEL JACKSON and O.J., they are guilty until proven innocent. With O.J. it's a trial by television, and in most people's eyes he's already guilty. There are still double standards in America."

In 1988 he announced that he would stand for mayor of Detroit. Three years later he rescinded this.

"I decided to run because I thought there was a desperate need for someone to take on that kind of responsibility," he tells me. "I felt that I could do it because I was passionate about the subject, about people. I didn't need the money or the fame, unlike a lot of politicians. But I also soon realised that as much as I like politics, music would always come first. Also, I knew that I would have to make the kind of compromises that politicians do, and I wasn't prepared for that. I think I would have been out of my depth. Plus, my family would have suffered."

And Wonder has a large, if unwieldy family. He has a daughter, Aisha Zakia – for whom he wrote "Isn't She Lovely" – and son, Keita Sawandi, the result of his relationship with the writer Yolanda Simmons. His other son, Mumtaz, lives in California with his mother, the singer MELODY McCULLEY. In 1971 he married SYREETA WRIGHT, a former Motown secretary who introduced him to transcendental meditation, and with whom he was to write several hits. They divorced amicably a few years later, before he set up house with Simmons, who had previously been his personal assistant. He lived with her for twelve years, then briefly with McCulley, and then in 2001 married the fashion designer Kai Milla Morris, with whom he has two sons – Kailand, who is now eight, and Mandla, four. Altogether he has seven children.

The click-clack "Stevie swing" is as closely associated with Wonder – although perhaps rather less celebrated – as the MICHAEL JACKSON "yelp" (the almost-falsetto noise he'd repeatedly insert into a song, seemingly at random, as though he'd been goosed). This is the way Wonder dances, his head bobbing, wagging, and weaving about, like a cross between the nodding dog in the back of the wrong car and the executive ballbearing toy on the wrong banker's desk. The "swing" always seems a genuine expression of Wonder's exuberance, of his unmitigated and almost child-like joy. It's also extremely infectious: on a speedboat a few summers ago in the Mediterranean, as an Ibezan loungecore cover of "Another Star" blasted out of the RIB's speakers, my head began swinging from shoulder to shoulder as though it were the most natural thing in the world, and I suddenly felt happier than I had any right to be. It was approaching sunset and I was doing the Stevie Wonder schwing! There never appears to be any artifice about the way he swings his head from side to side; one could never, for instance, imagine Wonder doing anything as vulgar or as premeditated as Jackson's "crotch-grab". In that respect he is one of the most sexless entertainers of all time. In Stevie's world – a world of constant supervision, a world of continual introspection – physicality is a different thing altogether. With Stevie, it's all about the love, LUV. Interviewed just a few months ago, he gave a good impression of someone so happy with his legacy that he doesn't concern himself so much with today's critics. Does he care that I don't think much of the records he's released in the last twenty-five years? Actually, not much. After all, he is Stevie Wonder, and I am not.

How different the stories of Wonder and Jackson. Both were anointed by Motown boss BERRY GORDY, both were driven by an innate desire for success, and both had achieved worldwide fame by the time the Sixties turned into the Seventies. But while Jackson, the boy wonder, allowed himself to be turned into a sex symbol, a solo artist whose oeuvre revolved around the aspirations of the upwardly mobile black urbanite, Wonder was simply the boy genius who turned into a grown-up genius, a studio-bound whiz-kid – the real Boy Wonder. If MICHAEL JACKSON was the butterfly on the dancefloor, Stevie Wonder was The Geek Who Could. It's impossible to think of Wonder succumbing to any form of cosmetic surgery; considering his affliction, it seems fundamentally pathetic. If Stevie Wonder succumbs to narcissism, it is of a far higher order.

Regardless of his diminishing musical prowess, it's his standing, Wonder's status that has changed recently. He may no longer be the world's pre-eminent African-American songwriter, but he's now got the ear of the most powerful man in the world.

Whether it's his penchant for MILES DAVIS, Bach and the FUGEES, or his dislike of Baskin-Robbins ice cream (he slopped out scoops in one of their shops as an impossibly good-looking teenager), the lifestyle choices and consumer habits of BARACK OBAMA have made headlines all over the planet. He has read all the HARRY POTTER books, he owns a pair of red boxing gloves autographed and once used by MUHAMMED ALI, he once kept a pet ape called Tata when he lived in Indonesia, has more than a fondness for BOB DYLAN, and obsessively collects Spider-Man comics.

Oh, and he really, really loves Stevie Wonder.

Wonder's ability to accumulate human experience, seemingly by osmosis, and articulate it in such an easily digestible, populist way is one of the reasons Obama likes him so. And the fact he's one of the most famous African-Americans in the world. Stevie Wonder communicates. He has proved time and time again that he can summarise the general and the personal – painting enduring images of both the (ever-changing) urban landscape and his (considerable) interior life. He appeals to everyman, and every man knows it. Obama certainly knows it. MICHAEL JACKSON might have been the black ELVIS but Stevie Wonder is the black Pope. And only churls don't tug their forelocks to the Pope. Ignoring Stevie Wonder would have been like ignoring NELSON MANDELA, AL SHARPTON, or – gulp – like ignoring Oprah.

"It's remarkable when you consider that Stevie has been putting politics into his music for three decades, starting – in the Nixon era, no less! – with 'Big Brother' and 'You Haven't Done Nothin',''' said LUCIAN GRAINGE, the Chairman and CEO of Universal Music Group. "Then, of course, we all saw the central part he played in the historic campaign to have Dr MARTIN LUTHER KING's birthday declared a national holiday in America.

"Everyone in music recognises Stevie for his extraordinary accomplishments and his influence on other artists. But I think that when BARACK OBAMA used 'Signed, Sealed, Delivered, I'm Yours' during his presidential primary campaign, it somehow brought time in a circle. It validated what both men mean to so many people around the world, and what they stand for: talent, hope, determination, excellence, possibilities – and no excuses."

Obama's patronage has increased Wonder's standing amongst a public who already thought of him as some sort of walking God. Astonishingly, he is now even more famous, and even more worshipped than he was before. Wonder's world has always been fairly intoxicating, but nothing beats the exhilaration of presidential patronage, and while dozens of African-American leaders have successfully pulled the entertainer into their orbit, nobody has the pulling power of the Prez.

But if Stevie Wonder is BARACK OBAMA's bitch, Obama is a Wonder geek – it's why he used "Signed, Sealed, Delivered" on the campaign trail, it's why he references him in so many interviews, it's why he hangs with him. He loves the man. He's expressed a fondness for many artists – some of whom, including JAY-Z and BRUCE SPRINGSTEEN, have shown him love with endorsements – but it's Wonder whom he loves the most.

In February 2009, the multi-Grammy winning soul star was presented with the Library of Congress's second annual Gershwin Prize for Popular Song during a concert at the White House hosted by the President and his wife. At the concert Wonder performed alongside TONY BENNETT, DIANA KRALL, and PAUL SIMON – the only other recipient of the Gershwin Prize. Obama described Wonder's back catalogue as "the soundtrack of my youth" while his wife used the opportunity to reveal that they chose the singer's "You and I" as their wedding song, claiming that *Talking Book* was the first album she ever bought. "Years later, I discovered what Stevie meant when he sang about love," she said, to a wildly appreciate audience (the other guests cried "awwww" as one).

Obama echoed his wife's sentiments. He said: "I think it is fair to say that had I not been a Stevie Wonder fan, Michelle might not have dated me, we might not have married.

"The fact that we agreed on Stevie was part of the essence of our courtship." Awwww.

The President's public love-in with Wonder had started a few months earlier, when, in an interview with *Rolling Stone,* the then senator said: "If I had one musical hero, it would have to be Stevie Wonder."

Accepting the award, Wonder said, "President and Mrs Obama, I'm so excited to know that I was part of... I needn't say more." He said he was looking forward to the President uniting the world, "so that in my lifetime I can write songs about love, about unity, and real songs of passion." Also in his speech, he added, "What is truly exciting for me today is that we truly have lived to see a time and a space where America has a chance to again live up to the greatness that it deserves to be seen and known as, through the love and caring and the commitment of a president – as in our President, BARACK OBAMA." The guests lapped it up when he said, "You know, maybe I'll be a part of creating some more of those babies."

When we met, in 1994, the singer was making a brief stopover in London on his way to his new apartment in Accra, in Ghana. He was one of a growing number of black Americans who were migrating to Ghana to try to find their "roots", encouraged by the country's then leader, Flight Lt JERRY RAWLINGS. At the time ISAAC HAYES was also moving back. "I have been crowned king, with all rights and privileges," said Hayes. "I'm a development king, which is my chance to bring in investors."

Wonder's move was first mooted in 1973. "I'd love to go to Ghana," he said at the time, "go to the different African countries and see how I'd like to live there."

"Ghana is going to be a full-time thing for me," he told me, rather indignantly, as though I was suggesting it was a mere whim. "I've been visiting on and off for the past few years, and soon I'm going to move there for good. I like the people, I love the country, and the place reminds me of what I remember from when I was very little in Detroit. There is more sense of a community than there is in Los Angeles [where he currently lives]. When an African-American makes any kind of pilgrimage, to try and find his origins, then you're going to get people coming to Ghana. Not because it was the centre of slavery, but going to any part of Africa is a pilgrimage in a way... because due to the slave trade none of us really know where we're from. There is such an enriched culture in that part of the world, and it's a culture that the West is still quite ignorant about."

Didn't he run the risk of appearing like just another rich tourist, culturally slumming?

"Number one, my richness is not in the amount of money that I have, but the richness that I have because of my experiences. I can be a teacher. Obviously when I become a citizen I'll get involved with local politics, and if there are areas in which I think I can help, then I will. Being a citizen of a country in a sense means you're part of a family, so if I don't express myself in the right way, then I'm doing myself a disservice and I'm just as irresponsible as a person who doesn't vote. I was born in the United States and a lot of my family are there so it's not like I'm going to abandon them or my culture because African-American culture is very unique and I don't want to leave anyone with the impression that I have decided that's not so."

The move to Ghana never happened.

In his biography of MARLON BRANDO, PETER MANSO asked a simple question: isn't a genius who has pushed the boundaries and probed the depths of our psyche obligated to the culture to continue his quest? While Brando gave up the quest decades before he died, Stevie Wonder believes that he is still carrying the torch. Push him and he will admit that his most recent records aren't quite as good as they might be, but he firmly believes that he is still making art. However, Wonder's most recent work has tended to focus on the twee, the childlike, and the sentimental, and in the past twenty-five years or so, he has seemingly concentrated on nursery rhymes – something epitomised by enormously successful, but quintessentially banal, songs such as the PAUL MCCARTNEY duet "Ebony and Ivory" and "I Just Called To Say I Love You"; this won him an Oscar for its use in the film *The Woman In Red,* and has been the subject of many a joke, like this one from a 1985 issue of the *New Yorker,* showing a secretary using the intercom to speak to her boss: "While you were out, Stevie Wonder just called to say he loves you...". He made some great records in the early Eighties – "Lately", "Happy Birthday", "That Girl", "Do I Do", etc – but towards the end of the decade he seemed to lose the plot somewhat. There were some nice songs on *Conversation Peace,* but that is all they really were – nice. They tend to sound rather too processed. They might include the odd polemic about gun control or the homeless, but in the main they are standard fare. Wonder's first new album in ten years, *A Time to Love,* was released in October 2005, and, apart from a typically sumptuous ballad, "Moon Blue", was a largely uneventful affair. He performs at every important opening ceremony, sporting event, gala dinner, charity bash, TV special (the Olympics, Live 8, Superbowl, *American Idol* – you name it, he's done it), and has kept his hand in, playing and recording with the likes of BABYFACE, BUSTA RHYMES, DR. DRE, SNOOP DOGG, STING, ANDREA BOCELLI, QUINCY JONES, TONY BENNETT, CJ HILTON, RAPHAEL SAADIQ, and more.

When we met, Wonder's thoughts often seemed confused, and he tended to wander off into cheap metaphor at every available opportunity. He excelled himself when I asked him how he answered those critics who persist in saying that nothing he has done since has equalled *Songs In The Key Of Life*: "It's like when you're a little kid and say, wow, that's my bedroom, that's my bed and I had the best sleep of my life in that bed. The best memories are in that bed, so it's got to be the best bed there ever was. And then you move on, you move out and you live in an apartment, and you sleep in another bed. But of course you're always thinking that your new bed isn't as good as your old one.

The memories of growing up and all the fun things that happened in your life you associate with that bed. Life is all about beds. Beds mean a lot to me. It doesn't mean that your old bed or your new bed are invalid... all the beds have an importance...

"I do not deny the fact that I enjoy *Songs In The Key Of Life* – it is my... favourite album. The longer I live and the longer it lasts the more I feel that it is my favourite. It withstands time... But should *Conversation Peace* become major, major, major successful, then there will be people who treat it as their favourite bed."

He had obviously been down this road before. When I questioned his commitment he got quite agitated, almost to the point of banging the table between us. "I am certainly not less interested in music than I was," he said. "Back then I didn't have children, back then I didn't have as much business stuff to deal with as I do now. In the Seventies I lived at a totally different pace. I don't find it more or less difficult to get motivated these days, or to be inspired, because for me life changes every day. I want to achieve more and more. I love music, and what I would like to do next is write a musical, something that hangs around as long as *Hair* or *Jesus Christ Superstar* or *West Side Story*.

"I'm never far away from music. I never sit down and compose, I move around too much to do that, but I'm always fooling around, making pieces of music, playing on the keyboard and just trying to come up with a new slant on something. There are times when I have sat down and written something just like that, but they're rare. There have also been times when I have had writer's block and haven't been able to finish a song... but I have never turned away from music. Never. I wrote most of the songs for this album in Ghana, but a lot of the lyrics were written in cars, on planes, in airports, at my mother's house... Basically this is what I do and I do the best that I can with it."

One wonders to what extent he is shielded from criticism. Surely it would be fairly easy to keep him away from unflattering profiles or vitriolic journalistic attacks? (As the comedian JOAN RIVERS once said about the headgear, "Who's going to tell him that he's got a macramé plant holder on his head?") If there is a particularly scathing review in a paper, do people just not show it to him? The singer says this is not the case: "For the most part I don't think people hide things from me. I hear what's going on, you know, I know what's going down. Not a lot gets passed me."

It was soon time for the benevolent enigma to go. But before another of his aides helped pull him out of his chair, I asked him to tell me the funniest joke he'd ever heard about himself. He looked in my direction, then smiled his big, cheesy grin, and said, "Jokes? Oh, there's been all kinds of silly things, you know. Let me see, I think it's the one that goes, Hey José, have you seen Stevie Wonder? No, not me, says José. Why don't you ask RAY CHARLES?"

Perhaps the jokes, like the records, were better in the old days. But Wonder is still the best-loved black musician in the world, a sixty-one-year-old musical genius (albeit a lapsed one) who generates more affection than PRINCE, MICHAEL JACKSON, WHITNEY HOUSTON, BEYONCÉ, and JAMES BROWN put together. Jackson might have sold more records, PRINCE might still be more funky, but Stevie Wonder is – by common consent – closer to God than any of them.

EDDIE MURPHY summed this up perfectly in *Delirious,* the film of his 1983 stage show: "I did Stevie Wonder on the show [*Saturday Night Live*] once, and black people lost their minds, I had brothers rolling up to me and going 'Hey, you the m*********** that been doing Stevie Wonder? That s*** ain't funny! Don't you never let me see you do that s*** again. I'll f*** you up! Stevie Wonder's a musical genius. That's terrible, that's terrible man. Your mother brought you up wrong, that's what it is...'"

It's a DVD BARACK OBAMA has seen, a sentiment he echoes. Is it still important for Stevie to be liked?

"I would like to be liked and I think it's pretty easy to like me," Wonder said, beginning to move his head from side to side again, "but if a person doesn't, what can I do? I'm not going to beg."

The Woodsman

COLIN WELLAND had it about right. The star of *Roll On Four O'Clock*, Welland's early-Sixties TV play about the staff and pupils of a Manchester Secondary Modern, was a teenage outcast called "Pansy" Peter Latimer. Wearing blue jeans, a fawn roll-neck sweater, a blonde fop fringe, and a black leather jacket with "Pete" written on the back in round silver studs, Latimer was the school odd-ball – tormented, bullied, and relentlessly beaten up.

"Latimer, he's a special case," says one teacher. "He's not a bad lad," says another, "for a creep."

Latimer was Britain's first homegrown Neurotic Boy Outsider who wasn't a singer or an actor. He was a bona fide internalised rebel; a teacher's pet who hates games, an outsider who longs for acceptance. It's not difficult to see where MORRISSEY drew his inspiration from, and it's surprising that "Pansy" Pete hasn't turned up on the cover of one of MORRISSEY's records, a Northern role-model to rival PAT PHOENIX in *Coronation Street*, or ALBERT FINNEY in *Saturday Night And Sunday Morning*.

There are few more classic pop archetypes than the Neurotic Boy Outsider. Continually wrestling with those damn inner demons, the NBO displays an obvious nervousness, often disguised with a hint of sexual ambiguity. He traditionally wears a frown and a leather jacket, tries to look like JAMES DEAN, MORRISSEY, or KURT COBAIN, conducts interviews in a mordant manner, and always looks concerned.

In pop promos he will be seen hitching along a lonely desert road, moody and alone (NBOs are always unaccompanied), gazing skyward, in search of divine intervention, or perhaps a new pair of sunglasses. He is, above all else, determinedly aloof, if not a little evangelical (NBOs are never far from displaying an unhealthy Messiah complex).

And now there is a new pop archetype, the Woodsman, the bearded loner in the lumberjack shirt and the scowl, a singer of indeterminate age who fronts a band of sullen subordinates who can't quite believe how successful they are. Woodsmen are everywhere. The big one is BON IVER'S JUSTIN VERNON, followed in no particular order by the DECEMBERISTS, FLEET FOXES, ARCADE FIRE, GREAT LAKE SWIMMERS, BEIRUT, BAND OF HORSES, VOLCANO CHOIR, IRON & WINE, MY MORNING JACKET, and all the rest. When the *New Yorker* published a piece about MY MORNING JACKET a while ago, they said, "You know these guys are bearded without seeing a photograph of them."

There is a snake-like litany of Woodsmen in pop, all the way from NEIL YOUNG to CALEXICO, yet there have never been so many of them as there are today, never been so many pop groups who talk wistfully of remote cabins in north-western Wisconsin or renovated chicken-shacks in the Californian woods, rather than infamous Hollywood groupies, and whose lyrics focus so much on isolation and displacement. There are no smiles, only far-away looks and FLEET FOXES fashion. As *GQ*'s JAMIE MILLAR said not so long ago, "Think lumberjack checks, waxed jackets and just generally looking as heritage as they sound." The music is often wispy, acoustic and decidedly lo-fi, music to look forward to a long hard winter to. Many find this sort of thing uplifting – "Listening to BON IVER'S *Bon Iver* is an activity comparable to lying in the grass of a vast garden replete with brightly coloured flowers," wrote one critic. "Patches of crimson, and marigold, and periwinkle, and violet, and peach on grassy beds, verdant and luscious with dew." And yet the enjoyment has to be solitary: "On a gently sunny day, with a cloud or two drifting by, and you are alone to observe this."

Given the success of modern folk in Britain – NOAH AND THE WHALE, LAURA MARLING, KING CHARLES – you might think there are Woodsmen here too, and yet we are too parochial to have spawned any convincing examples; our countryside is too manicured, and at MUMFORD & SONS gigs they tell jokes between songs.

Thankfully the Woodsman doesn't appear quite so desperate as the Neurotic Boy Outsider to tell everyone how unhappy he is, preferring to stare mournfully out at the world from publicity pictures and CD covers. NBOs always have to generate attention, and as they are nothing if not show-offs, always have to go public about being private. I remember a classic example of this. It was 1984, in the Soho Brasserie, in London's Old Compton Street. There he was, this lanky NBO, a throwback to the Seventies – all gaunt and secondhand – sitting by himself, surrounded on other tables by braying Eighties would-be whiz-kids – colourful young things with gaudy clothes and short attention spans talking about money, magazines, travel, and nightclubs. The NBO was a reading a Penguin Modern Classic.

As I passed him on my way out, I noticed that the book was upside down.

THE WORD PODCAST

At about four thirty on a Saturday afternoon, there are few things better than a very deep, slightly too hot bath, the sort of bath that will steam up your glasses so much that it makes it nigh-on impossible to read. Especially if said bath is accompanied by a bucket of robust tea. Or indeed your favourite radio show. Which, these days, will almost certainly come in the form of a podcast. And in my case will come in the form of *The Word* podcast.

I've been a fan of *The Word* since it launched, in 2003, but the delights of its regular podcasts had always escaped me. Until recently, that is, and having discovered them, I now find myself incapable of slipping beneath the meticulously scented bubbles in my tub – sorry, is this overshare? – without the dulcet tones of MARK ELLEN and DAVID HEPWORTH in the background, offering up yet another oddly fascinating piece of rock'n'roll trivia, or waffling on about nothing in particular (men walking onto tube trains carrying tubas, the minutiae of children's television in the Fifties, the provenance of R&B chord structures, the smell of old record shops, BRIAN ENO's a capella evenings, and the etiquette of demo tapes, etc). Sort of like radio, actually, but without any of the boring bits. If you're remotely interested in the lyrics to the Star Trek theme, if you care about CAPTAIN BEEFHEART's influence on TOM WAITS, or take an unhealthy interest in the interviewing techniques of music journalists of a certain age, then this is the place for you. Indeed, if you're vaguely aware of the phrase "I and I step forward for a sandwich," then you will soon be treating this podcast like your new home.

X-Ray Spex

X-Ray Spex had a saxophone. For punk rockers who had suddenly reinvented themselves – honestly, were any of them born that way? – this presented them with something of a problem. Was the sax punk? Wasn't the sax redolent of all-that-had-gone-before? The band also appeared to be obsessed with consumerism, and their records were smarter than a lot of the other stuff about at the time. On the release of their first and last proper album (which is pretty much indispensable from an archaeologist's POV), *Germfree Adolescents*, in 1978, the *NME*'s CHARLES SHAAR MURRAY wrote, "Smash the barriers and the truth shall make you free (as long as stocks last, anyway): barriers between humans and objects, between the natural (sic) and the Art-i-ficial (sicker). These barriers mark the world which X-Ray-Spex inhabit and the world about which POLY STYRENE writes with the sophisticated innocence that gives a tree and a supermarket equal value: never mind how it got here (grew/cloned/came in a box), the fact remains that it's here and what are we going to do about it?"

I saw them a few times, most memorably at the Rock Against Racism Carnival in Hackney's Victoria Park, in London, in the summer of 1978. They sounded a bit like ROXY MUSIC, looked a lot like a thousand bands that would come in their wake, and felt like dangerous fun.

XTC

ANDY PARTRIDGE's Swindon punk band were another group out of step with the times: in 1977 they made smart, funny, melodic, provincial pop (they were the epitome of New Wave Arch), and as they grew up and started having hits, were resolutely anti-commercial. Then, when they stopped touring – Partridge hated travelling with the band so much that for most of their career XTC exemplified the *ex-cathedra* recording principle – they went all Late Sixties British Bucolic Psychedelic. Basically they shifted from being the most "modern"-sounding punk band to one that wanted to sound as old and as distant as possible. The hits still sound good, as do the first four "pop" albums, despite Partridge being largely remembered for very British wistful Eighties ballads such as "Wrapped In Grey" and "Chalkhills And Children". In a parallel world Partridge would be considered a national institution, but he didn't have the thirst or the stamina for the fame, or the activity needed to pursue it. Like PETER COOK, who could have been a judge but who never had the Latin, so Partridge could have been MORRISSEY but didn't have the artifice.

Y

YES

In their pomp, they were the Princes of Prog, the Lords of Improv. It was always going to end in tears, and with 1974's *Tales From Topographic Oceans*, Yes italicised the end of an era.

NEIL YOUNG

Young Neil's greatest hits are the stuff of legend – at least among the converted. Young is a Marmite artist, and there are as many who recoil from his thin, whiney voice as those – like me – who find nearly everything that voice attempts (even the less successful stuff) fascinating. Of course, like any true Young fan I like the CRAZY HORSE material more than anything. I like the *Harvest* period enormously (check out cover versions of songs on that particular record by DOUG PAISLEY, KELLEY STOLTZ, VILLAGERS, and NEVILLE SKELLY), and "On The Way Home" on *Live At Massey Hall* takes some beating – nevertheless it's CRAZY HORSE who really kick up the dust, CRAZY HORSE who can make you feel as though you're sitting on the edge of the world, imported beer in hand, stick-cigar, sitting on a rock, watching all the madness below.

And for sure, the CRAZY HORSE classics are great outings – "Cinnamon Girl", "Cowgirl in the Sand", "Down by the River", "Cortez The Killer", "Like A Hurricane", "Powderfinger", etc – yet in my opinion the greatest NEIL YOUNG & CRAZY HORSE album is *Ragged Glory*, a CD that contains four solid gone epics: "Country Home" (7.05 minutes), "Over and Over" (8.28), "Love to Burn" (10.00), and "Love and Only Love" (10.18) – forty minutes of aural carnage that could change your life completely. It was around this time that Young started to be called "The Godfather of Grunge" (sloppy drums, unreconstructed chords, plus lank hair, anti-designer

Y jeans, trucker's T-shirts, sneakers, etc), although *Ragged Glory* was actually recorded in 1990, way before grunge's commercial high points, NIRVANA's *Nevermind*, and PEARL JAM's *Ten*. After the success of this album (his first great album after a decade in the experimental wilderness), Young embraced his own guitar histrionics, subjecting his audiences to mammoth one-note solos and acres of feedback. "It's not a macho display, like some bands have this strutting thing where they get up there and move around and they sweat and they pose," he said. "The sweating we do is because we're so far into it that we've forgotten how not to sweat. I start hyperventilating, my nose gets really cold and I feel this cool breeze blowing in my face when it's about 110 on-stage. You just get to this point where nothing else is there, it's just all gone and you're taking off."

When we describe the way music makes us feel, it's usually got something to do with abandon – feeling completely separate, cut-off, falling through the air, walking through the woods, flying way above everyone, standing on the cliffs looking at the midnight ocean, crouching in a cornfield and peering into the valley... Neil Young's searing guitar solos have the power to make us feel that way, and the guitar on *Ragged Glory* is some of the most evocative of his career. It was certainly some of his loudest: when an earthquake struck nearby San Francisco, on the last day of recording at Young's Woodside ranch, apparently no one noticed.

THE YOUNGBLOODS

Some old record reviews are priceless. The "scribes" who worked for the *NME* in the early Seventies could be spectacularly cruel – CHARLES SHAAR MURRAY and NICK KENT, I'm talking principally about you here – and that whole period was full of journalists who were taking out their anger on peers who dared to make music for money. I found this review of The Youngbloods' *Good And Dusty* on *Rock's Back Pages*, written by "METAL" MIKE SAUNDERS, in *Phonograph Record*, from April 1972. "There's really no way around it," he wrote. "The Youngbloods' career divides quite clearly into three distinct periods: 1) The Youngbloods with JERRY CORBITT, 2) *Elephant Mountain*, 3) the post-*Elephant Mountain* Youngbloods. Which is to say that if the early Youngbloods were one of the best rock groups in all of America, then the current Youngbloods are maybe the best group in Marin County. Maybe not even that. *Good and Dusty* is so lacking in any sort of energy that the comments about its being stoned Marin County living room music are all too true. Not that it's particularly bad; it just should have stayed in the living room, that's all."

Actually the only thing you need to know about the Youngbloods is that their song "Sunlight", from *Elephant Mountain* (once elegantly covered by JEFFREY FOSKETT), is one of the most beautiful songs ever written.

Z

FRANK ZAPPA

It is too easy to say that Frank Zappa was simply a satirist. The early MOTHERS OF INVENTION albums might still sound like TOM LEHRER made them on acid, and few people at the time were brave enough to disparage the counter-culture from such close quarters (let alone from within the citadel), yet in some ways Zappa was the quintessential comic – you know the guy, the one who makes his living from making people laugh, but who expects lavish praise, lots of enthusiastic and chin-stroking critical acclaim when he goes "straight". Zappa wanted – demanded – it both ways: he wanted to be acknowledged as the Grand Wazoo, the great oracle of sarcastic rock, and he expected to be revered by the masses for being a virtuoso musician, the noodly guy with a dry (in his case, unfunny) sense of humour.

"For the pop life of me, I cannot see why anyone past the age of seventeen would want to listen to Frank Zappa again, never mind revere him as a deep and important artist, never mind worship at the tottering edifice of his recollected, remastered and repackaged works," wrote IAN PENMAN in *The Wire*, in 1995. " Surely the only pertinent use for Zappa was as an interim stage for young lads – scared witless by what they suddenly perceive as the transience or hollowness of popular culture – for whom Zappa represents a gi-normous prefab sneer of self-importance behind which they can shelter for a while."

Along the way Zappa made some marvellous records, great washes of noise and commotion that were way above the pay scale of most of his peers (and indeed most of his collaborators). As a soundtrack to the frenetic urban experience, few pieces of music can match "Peaches en Regalia", the brilliant but incessant instrumental on his 1969 album, *Hot Rats* (it sounds like one big traffic jam, a bit like a non-linear companion piece to JIMI HENDRIX's "Crosstown Traffic").

Z   If he were alive today he would be writing a column for the *Onion*, leading the band on *The Late Show With David Letterman*, laughing loudly at the collapse of the music industry, but demanding absolute quiet during his solos. (His family and fans appear totally subservient to the myth, and pretty much everything he ever recorded, in whatever form or state of completion, is deemed important enough to be made public.)

Like MORRISSEY, Frank Zappa will be remembered as much for his song and album titles as anything else: "What's The Ugliest Part Of Your Body?", *Lumpy Gravy*, "Don't Eat The Yellow Snow", and *We're Only In It For The Money*.

Acknowledgments

I'd like to thank the following people for their help, support and encouragement: Sarah Jones, Edie Walter Jones, Georgia Sydney Jones, Jonathan Newhouse, Nicholas Coleridge, Ed Victor, Spas Roussev, Georgina Atwell, Martyn Luke, David Thomson, Stephanie Sleap, Luciana Bellini, Karen Dolby and Edina Imrik.

INDEX

Index

Index

Index

Index

Index

Index

Index

Index

Index

EAGLES, 50, 156, 229, 246, 277, 385, 511, 661, 669, 681

EARTH, WIND AND FIRE, 156, 731

EARTHLING, 686

EAST SIDE BEAT, 157

EASTWOOD, CLINT, 31, 660, 731

EASY STAR, 577

ECHO & THE BUNNYMEN, 143, 230, 518

ECKSTEIN, BILLY, 547

ECO, UMBERTO, 782

THE ECONOMIST, 327, 381

EDMONDS, NOEL, 131

EDDY, DUANE, 289

THE ED SULLIVAN SHOW, 543, 702

EEL PIE ISLAND, 230

EFRON, ZAC, 417

EG & ALICE, 96

EGAN, JENNIFER, 747

EINSTURZENDE NEUBAUTEN, 628

EISENHOWER, DWIGHT, 452

ELBOW, 232, 710

THE ELECTRIC KOOL-AID ACID TEST, 266

ELIOT, T.S., 505, 553

ELLEN, MARK, 250, 312, 823

ELLINGTON, DUKE, 79, 191, 232, 717

ELLIOT, GAIL, 295

ELLISON, HARLAN, 552

ELVIS '56, 41

ELVIS WORLD, 543

EMERSON, RALPH WALDO, 586

EMINEM, 233, 234, 800

ENERGY 52, 113

ENFIELD, HARRY, 274, 283

ENGLAND'S DREAMING, 367

ENO, BRIAN, 92, 113, 233, 256, 638, 750

ENTERTAINMENT WEEKLY, 607

ENTOURAGE, 79

ERASERHEAD, 542

ERSKINE, PETE, 366

ESG, 234

ESSEX, DAVID, 677

ESTELLE, 620

ESTHER & ABI OFARIM, 446

ESTONIAN TARTAR, 51

E-STREET BAND, 368, 665, 669

ET, 267

EUREKA BRASS BAND, 387

EVANS, BILL, 69, 78, 190, 234

EVANS, GIL, 194, 196, 197

EVANS, HAROLD, 614

EVANS, MAL, 677

EVANS, TOM, 519

EVENING NEWS, 320

EVEREST, 66

EVERS, MEDGAR, 528

EVERYONE LOVES YOU WHEN YOU'RE DEAD, 411

EVERYTHING BUT THE GIRL, 157, 220

EVITA, 186

EXAMPLE, 385, 512

EX-FRIENDLY, 48

EXIT THROUGH THE GIFT SHOP, 286

Index

Index

Index

Index

Index

Index

Index

Index

Index

Index

ORFF, CARL, 63
ORG LOUNGE, 410
OSBORNE, JOAN, 470, 741
OSBOURNE, OZZY, 153, 445
O'SULLIVAN, GILBERT
OTHELLO, 550, 551
OTIS, SHUGGIE, 96
O'TOOLE, PETER, 205, 558
OUTKAST, 159, 529, 800
THE OUTSIDER, 517, 667
OWENS, BUCK, 453

P. DIDDY, 810
PABLO, AUGUSTUS, 577
PACINO, AL, 73
PALIN, MICHAEL, 690
PALLENBERG, ANITA, 153
PALMER, HARRY, 57, 60
PALTROW, GWYNETH, 309
PALUMBO, JAMES, 290
PARIS TEXAS, 668
PARKER, ALAN, 373
PARKER, CHARLIE, 39, 62, 192, 193, 346, 353, 358, 533
PARKER, MARY-LOUISE, 764
PARKER, STEVE, 432
PARKINSON, MICHAEL, 54, 528
PARKLIFE, 187
PARSONS, GRAM, 121, 221
PARSONS, TONY, 212, 311, 534
PART, ARVO, 260
PARTON, DOLLY, 160, 536, 688
PARTRIDGE, ALAN, 6
PATTINSON, ROBERT, 417
PAUL, DEAN, 463, 464
PEACOCK, ANDREW, 433
PEARL JAM, 728, 832
PEARLMAN, SANDY, 118

PEARSON, ALLISON, 18
PEARSON, JAMES, 234
PECK, GREGORY, 74
PEELLAERT, GUY, 136, 609
PEEL, JOHN, 50, 242, 383
PEE WEE HERMAN, 125
PENDERGRASS, TEDDY, 255
PENETRATION, 562
THE PENGUIN GUIDE TO JAZZ ON CD, LP AND CASSETTE, 576
PEOPLE, 214, 373
THE PEOPLE'S MUSIC, 118
PERE UBU, 518, 562, 622
PERFECTLY FRANK, 651
PERFORMANCE, 622
PERKINS, ANTHONY, 518
PERKINS, PINETOP, 388
PERKINS, WAYNE, 606, 612
PERRONI, MARCO, 241
PERRY, JOE, 14
PERRY, KATY, 536
PERRY, LEE "SCRATCH", 121, 536, 578
PESCI, JOE, 349
PET SHOP BOYS, 90, 159, 250, 522, 538, 711, 743, 762
PET SOUNDS, 106, 684
PETTY, TOM, & THE HEARTBREAKERS, 541, 688, 793
PHANTOM OF THE OPERA, 186
PHELPS, MICHAEL, 800
PHILLIPS, SAM, 459
PHILLIPS, WILLIAM, 264
PHISH, 51
PHOENIX, JOAQUIN, 644
PHOENIX, PAT, 821
PHYSICAL GRAFFITI, 566
PIAF, EDITH, 158, 477

Index

Index

Index

Index

Index

Index

Index

Index

Index

Index